ACCOUNTING

INFORMATION SYSTEMS:

ESSENTIAL CONCEPTS

AND APPLICATIONS

ACCOUNTING TEXTBOOKS FROM WILEY

Arpan and Radebaugh: **International Accounting and Multinational Enterprises, 2nd**

Burch and Grudnitski: **Information Systems: Theory and Practice, 5th**

Cloud, Cook, and Waters: **College Accounting Procedures, 2nd, Chapters 1–12, 1–16, 1–24**

DeCoster, Schafer, and Ziebell: **Management Accounting: A Decision Emphasis, 4th**

Defliese, Jaenicke, Sullivan, and Gnospelius: **Montgomery's Auditing, Revised College Version**

Delaney, Adler, Epstein, and Foran: **GAAP, Interpretation and Application 1989 Edition**

Delaney and Gleim: **CPA Examination Review—Auditing**

Delaney and Gleim: **CPA Examination Review—Business Law**

Delaney and Gleim: **CPA Examination Review—Theory and Practice**

Gleim and Delaney: **CPA Examination Review—Volume I Outlines and Study Guide**

Gleim and Delaney: **CPA Examination Review—Volume II Problems and Solutions**

Guy and Carmichael: **Audit Sampling: An Introduction to Statistical Sampling in Auditing, 2nd**

Haried, Imdieke, and Smith: **Advanced Accounting, 4th**

Helmkamp: **Managerial Accounting**

Helmkamp, Imdieke, and Smith: **Principles of Accounting, 3rd**

Imdieke: **Financial Accounting**

Kam: **Accounting Theory**

Kell, Boynton, and Ziegler: **Modern Auditing, 4th**

Kemp and Phillips: **Advanced Accounting**

Kieso and Weygandt: **Intermediate Accounting, 6th**

Magee: **Advanced Managerial Accounting**

Moriarity and Allen: **Cost Accounting, 2nd**

Moscove and Simkin: **Accounting Information Systems, 3rd**

Newell and Kreuze: **College Accounting, Chapters 1–10, 1–15, 1–27**

Ramanathan: **Management Control in Nonprofit Organizations, Text and Cases**

Robinson, Davis, and Alderman: **Accounting Information Systems, 2nd**

Romney, Cherrington, and Hansen: **Casebook in Accounting Information Systems**

Schroeder, McCullers, and Clark: **Accounting Theory: Text and Readings, 3rd**

Solomon, Vargo, and Walther: **Accounting Principles, 2nd**

Solomon, Vargo, and Walther: **Financial Accounting, 2nd**

Taylor and Glezen: **Auditing: Integrated Concepts and Procedures, 4th**

Taylor, Glezen, and Ehrenreich: **Case Study in Auditing, 4th**

Weygandt, Kieso, and Kell: **Accounting Principles**

Wilkinson: **Accounting and Information Systems, 2nd**

Wilkinson: **Accounting Information Systems: Essential Concepts and Applications**

ACCOUNTING

INFORMATION SYSTEMS:

ESSENTIAL CONCEPTS

AND APPLICATIONS

Joseph W. Wilkinson

Arizona State University

Copyright © 1989, by John Wiley & Sons, Inc.

All rights reserved. Published simultaneously in Canada.

Reproduction or translation of any part of
this work beyond that permitted by Sections
107 and 108 of the 1976 United States Copyright
Act without the permission of the copyright
owner is unlawful. Requests for permission
or further information should be addressed to
the Permissions Department, John Wiley & Sons.

Library of Congress Cataloging-in-Publication Data

Wilkinson, Joseph W.
    Accounting information systems: essential concepts and
applications/Joseph W. Wilkinson.

    Includes index.

    1. Accounting—Data processing. 2. Management information
systems. I. Title.

HF5679.W52 1989   89-30006
657′.028′5—dc19   CIP

Printed in the United States of America

10 9 8 7 6 5 4 3 2 1

To Mark, Tod, and Eric

Preface

This textbook is primarily intended for undergraduate students who are majoring in accounting. Its purpose is to provide, in as concise and straightforward a manner as possible, the essentials of accounting information systems. Although its coverage spans essentially all the topics specified by recent authoritative bodies (e.g., the 1986 American Accounting Association Committee on Contemporary Approaches to Teaching Accounting Information Systems), this textbook is sufficiently brief to allow adequate time for "hands-on" computer assignments and systems design projects.

Several themes are emphasized throughout, notably the following.

1. The key roles of accountants with respect to accounting information systems (i.e., as users, evaluators, and designers).

2. The typical transaction processing systems and cycles employed by an enterprise that culminate in the general ledger, financial statements, and managerial reports.

3. The importance of accounting controls within the accounting information system and its transaction cycles.

4. The step-by-step procedure for analyzing, designing, and implementing a computer-based accounting information system, including numerous and specific design rules and principles.

Certain concepts and facts are reviewed within the various chapters concerning the accounting cycle and computer hardware/software fundamentals. However, such reviews are quite brief, in order to limit the overall size of the textbook. Therefore, a basic presumption is that students using this textbook will have completed courses in (1) elementary financial and managerial accounting, and (2) fundamentals of computer hardware, software, and data processing.

The book is organized in five parts. Part I introduces the basic concepts pertaining to accounting information systems and their environments. It contrasts manual and computer-based systems and surveys the varied internal accounting controls needed in both types of systems. In addition, this introductory part illustrates several forms of documentation that are useful with respect to transaction processing.

Part II examines basic transaction processing systems that are incorporated within the general ledger and financial reporting, revenue, expenditure, and resource management cycles.

Part III describes the data management and information functions of an accounting information system. It also introduces decision support and other user-focused systems, computer networks, and system management issues. It concludes with a survey of computer-based auditing processes.

Part IV traces the phases composing the systems development life cycle, including planning, analysis, design, selection, and implementation.

Part V provides several cases that are suitable for assignment as student system design term projects.

Each chapter contains these learning aids.

1. A brief introductory statement of objectives and a concluding summary.

2. A variety of figures and diagrams that clarify the concepts and techniques.

3. Review questions, assignment problems, and references.

4. A review problem, which is intended to (a) clarify important points in the chapter, and (b) guide students in the preparation of assigned problems. Through several of the chapters the review problems are based on a continuing case (the Campus Bookstore).

Several other features are worth noting.

1. Certain problems scattered throughout the chapters may be assigned for solving on microcomputers.

2. Many of the concepts and techniques are illustrated by means of examples drawn from the real world.

3. A glossary of terms appears at the end of the text.

4. An instructor's manual is available. It contains suggested solutions to all problems, including listings and printouts for those problems suitable for solution on microcomputers. It also contains chapter outlines and an extensive test bank.

A personal note is in order. As you might be aware, I have also written a comprehensive textbook entitled *Accounting and Information Systems,* which is in its second edition. Most of the concepts and techniques covered by the comprehensive version also appear in this essentials textbook, although in more condensed form. However, the overall emphasis has been modified. Thus, in this version I stress the *cycles* approach to transaction processing and analysis. I agree with many other educators that this approach is most relevant to courses in accounting information systems. My coverage of the basic cycles is not new, since several currently available textbooks do likewise. Nevertheless, I present a chain of cycles that appears to be at least as logically consistent as any other presented to date. In addition, I have attempted to provide a reasonably thorough collection of diagrams, flowcharts, documents, reports, and other pictorial aids so that students can easily follow the progression of transactions through both manual and computer-based accounting information systems.

I wish to acknowledge the extremely constructive suggestions of several reviewers: Sue A. Block of the University of California at Santa Barbara, Ronald R. Bottin of the University of Wisconsin at La Crosse, Judith Cassidy of Louisiana State University, Michael Davis and James Hall of Lehigh University, Avi Rushinek of the University of Miami, Arjan T. Sadhwani of the University of Akron, Robert W. Vanasse of California State University at Long Beach, and Christopher Wolfe of Texas A&M University. In addition, Severin Grabski of Michigan State University proposed certain structural changes that have had a profound impact on the entire textbook. Numerous students have responded helpfully during the class testing of the new problems in this version. Finally, I appreciate the continuing support of my Wiley editors, David Anthony, Karen Hawkins, and Lucille Sutton.

Four professional accounting groups have graciously permitted the use of problem materials from past professional examinations: the American Institute of Certified Public Accountants, the Institute of Management Accounting of the National Association of Accountants, the Institute of Internal Auditors, and the Society of Management Accountants of Canada. To all these individuals and organizations, and to others not mentioned (including my family) go my gratitude. It hardly goes without saying that they do not bear responsibility for errors and omissions that may appear within these covers.

Joseph W. Wilkinson
Tempe, Arizona

Contents

PART III   SYSTEM SUPPORT FOR OPERATIONS AND MANAGEMENT   393

PART IV   SYSTEMS DEVELOPMENT LIFE CYCLE   527

15   Systems Analysis and Design   528

16   Systems Justification, Selection, and Implementation   564

PART V   ASSIGNMENT CASES   603

ACCOUNTING

INFORMATION SYSTEMS:

ESSENTIAL CONCEPTS

AND APPLICATIONS

PART I

INTRODUCTION

1

Overview of

Accounting

Information

Systems

THIS CHAPTER'S OBJECTIVES ARE
TO ENABLE YOU TO:

Understand the meanings, purposes, and benefits of an accounting information system.

Describe the major activities performed by an accounting information system.

Identify various examples of accounting information systems and their outputs.

Distinguish among the roles of accountants with respect to accounting information systems.

INTRODUCTION

What is an accounting information system? Why should accounting students study accounting information systems? Who uses the information provided by accounting information systems? How do accountants interact with accounting information systems? What are the key activities that take place within an accounting information system? Questions of this nature may have come to mind when you saw the title of this textbook. Answers to such questions are important to all accountants and prospective accountants. Initial answers are provided in this chapter, and more extensive answers are developed in following chapters.

WHAT IS AN ACCOUNTING INFORMATION SYSTEM?

Before proposing a comprehensive definition of the accounting information system (AIS), we might consider the meanings of each word individually, as well as the relationships between the AIS and other information systems within a business organization or enterprise.

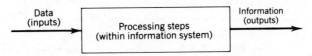

FIGURE 1-1 Information derived from data.

Information

      Information serves as the basis for making decisions and taking actions. Generally consisting of processed data, information is the set of outputs from an AIS or any information system. A financial statement, such as an income statement, is an example of an information output. Other examples include a printed monthly statement for a customer, a video display of a cost analysis for an accounting employee, and an audio response of a checking account balance for a bank depositor.

      Data, on the other hand, are the raw facts and figures and even symbols that together form the inputs to an information system. Figure 1-1 shows the relationship of data to information. Data may arise from a variety of sources. Much data are created by the occurrence of relevant events. For instance, a business enterprise may make sales of merchandise, thus creating sales data. These sales data are then entered into the enterprise's information system for processing. Other data reflect relevant conditions, such as interest rates and the prices of competitors' merchandise.

System

      A **system** is an integrated entity (i.e., a framework) that attempts to achieve a set of objectives. Numerous types of systems exist. Many systems are natural, such as the solar system and the nervous system of an animal. Other systems are man-made, such as a traffic system of a city and the heating system of a building. Most systems are open; they accept inputs and produce outputs. Most are also tangible; they function with physical resources. In addition, all systems have certain characteristics in common, such as boundaries that separate them from their environments. Figure 1-2 shows several characteristics of an open man-made system that employs such physical resources as machines, materials, and supplies.

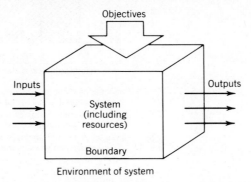

FIGURE 1-2 Basic characteristics of a man-made and open system.

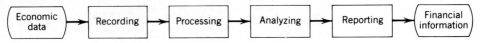

FIGURE 1-3 Steps within the accounting activity.

Accounting

As you have learned from your previous accounting courses, **accounting** has several levels of meaning. First, it is the combined activities of (1) recording economic data, (2) processing and analyzing these data, and (3) presenting the resulting information in financial terms. Figure 1-3 portrays this set of activities. Second, accounting is the "language of business"; it provides the means by which the key affairs of a business enterprise are expressed and summarized. Finally, it may be viewed as the information a business enterprise (i.e., a firm) uses to achieve efficient operations and effective management.

Composite Definition

Based on the preceding description, an **accounting information system** can be defined as an integrated framework within a firm that employs physical resources to transform economic data into financial information for (1) operating and managing the firm's activities, and (2) reporting the firm's achievements to interested parties.

Relationship to Other Information Systems

Although the AIS is an extremely important information system within a firm, it is not the only formal framework for providing information. Another important formal information system is the **management information system (MIS).** An informal information system also exists. Figure 1-4 shows that these three information systems overlap or merge, with respect to both the type of information provided and the users served. The AIS serves both managers and nonmanagerial users (e.g., owners, creditors) with financial information. The MIS

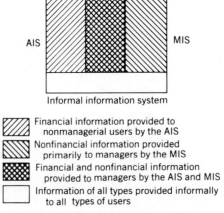

FIGURE 1-4 Overlapping and merging information systems within a firm.

serves only the managers of a firm, but provides nonfinancial as well as financial information. By providing a more complete range of information, the MIS assists marketing, production, finance, and other managers in their controlling and decision-making responsibilities. The informal information system adds information drawn from informal sources (e.g., trade publications, conversations at conventions) to the stock of information provided by the formal systems. Although informal information may be financial (e.g., expected industry profits) or nonfinancial (e.g., expected changes in interest rates), much is qualitative (e.g., perceived customer attitudes).

In essence, however, these overlapping systems comprise only *one* integrated information system. A firm cannot afford to construct and maintain two or more separate information systems. Thus, although this textbook will focus on the AIS, it will nevertheless include such features of the MIS as managerial reports of a nonfinancial nature.

PURPOSES AND BENEFITS OF AN AIS

The two major purposes of an AIS are to provide (1) information for operations and legal requirements, and (2) information for decision making. An AIS that fully achieves both purposes yields benefits of considerable value. The first of these purposes involves the activity of transaction processing, and the second involves the activity of information processing.

Transaction Processing

Transactions are events that are necessary to the functioning of a firm. They enable the firm to conduct its daily operations, maintain up-to-date working files, and reflect financial results and status. **Accounting transactions** are events, such as the billing for goods shipped, that represent exchanges having economic value. Other transactions, such as receiving orders and shipping goods, do not in themselves involve exchanges of value; however, these nonaccounting transactions often pave the way for accounting transactions.

Accounting transactions are processed through the key accounting records by means of a procedure called the **accounting cycle.** Figure 1-5 depicts the accounting cycle, often called the double-entry accounting process.

The accounting cycle is standardized; essentially the same sequence of steps is employed in all firms. It begins with the preparation of a source document that contains the amount of a specific transaction. The transaction is then classified and coded in accordance with a chart of accounts. Next the transaction data are summarized in a journal. The debits and credits in the summarized journal entry are posted to the coded ledger accounts. Periodically the balances of all ledger accounts are summarized in a trial balance in order to verify that all debits equal all credits. Finally, the financial statements are prepared. This same cycle is repeated each accounting period.

Each type of firm requires its own set of accounting transactions. However,

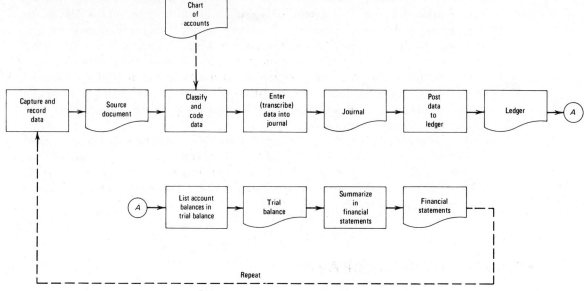

FIGURE 1-5 The accounting cycle.

several basic types of transactions are common to almost all firms. These concern transactions such as

1. Sales of products or services to customers.

2. Purchases of merchandise, materials, services, and fixed assets from suppliers.

3. Receipts of cash from customers and others.

4. Disbursements of cash to suppliers and others.

5. Preparation of payroll and disbursements of cash to employees for services rendered.

Most transactions that occur during an accounting period involve newly arising events. Often they relate to parties external to the firm. Other transactions of a corrective nature, such as the recording of depreciation expense, occur at the end of each accounting period. These transactions, which have the purpose of achieving the proper matching of revenues and expenses during the period, are reflected through adjusting journal entries. Usually a separate adjusted trial balance is prepared after these adjusting journal entries have been posted.

Outputs from transaction processing consist principally of documents and summaries. Documents generated as the products of basic transactions include sales invoices, purchase orders, deposit slips, and checks. These outputs provide operational information to recipients (i.e., users) such as customers, suppliers, banks, and employees. Summaries obtained from transaction processing include the aforementioned trial balances and financial statements plus listings of transactions and income tax returns. Some of these latter outputs also provide assistance in the operations of a firm, whereas others provide stewardship and legal-compliance information to such recipients as stockholders and governmental agencies.

Transaction processing is performed by components, or subsystems, of the AIS known as **transaction processing systems (TPS).** Each type of transaction requires its own TPS, although all merge into a common module that measures the financial health of an entity.

A soundly designed TPS will be easy to use (i.e., user-friendly) and should yield such benefits as

1. Efficient and economical processing of transactions.

2. Timely collection and processing of transactions.

3. Careful checking of input data and accurate processing of transaction data.

4. Thorough security over transaction processing and data storage, as well as over related physical facilities.

5. Prompt adjustments to changes and growth in processing needs.

Information Processing

In contrast to transaction processing, **information processing** provides information for decision making. Outputs from information processing are expressly intended to aid in planning and controlling the operations of a firm. Some of these information outputs, such as financial statements, are obtained as the by-products of transaction processing. However, much of the needed information must be procured from other sources, both internal and external to the firm. Figure 1-6 diagrams the relationships between transaction processing and information processing.

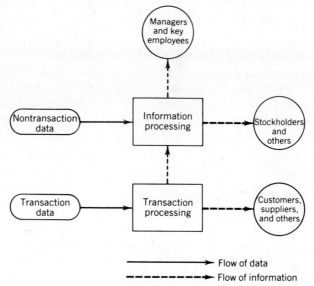

FIGURE 1-6 Relationship of transaction processing to information processing.

The primary users of the outputs from information processing are the various managers of a firm. They have the principal responsibility for making decisions related to planning and controlling the operations. The decisions made will affect strategic (long-range) planning, tactical (short-range) planning, management control, and operational control. Thus, users need a wide variety of planning and control reports ranging from annual budgets to sales analyses.

Other users of the products of information processing include key employees such as accountants and engineers and outside parties such as stockholders and bank creditors. For instance, a cost accountant may need a report concerning the actual costs of producing a new product to aid her in recommending control decisions that the production manager might make. A stockholder needs an annual report to aid him in deciding whether or not to sell his shares of stock.

Information processing is performed by the MIS of a firm, together with the portion of the AIS that overlaps the MIS. The component information processing systems—the subsystems of the MIS—are known by various names. Often they are labeled in accordance with the major business functions that they serve. Thus, a manufacturing firm would include a production information system, a marketing information system, and so on.

A soundly designed system for information processing should provide information that is

1. Relevant to the decision under consideration.

2. Reliable and sufficiently precise.

3. Concise (i.e., avoids overloading the recipient with details).

4. Timely (i.e., received in time to affect the decision).

5. Clearly presented.

ACTIVITIES OF AN AIS

Every AIS performs five major activities: data collection, data processing, data management, data control (plus security), and information generation. Figure 1-7 shows the relationships of these activities to each other, as well as to the sources of data inputs and the users of output information. Each of these activities consists of several types of steps. Moreover, particular sequences of steps that span one or more activities form **procedures.**

Data Collection

The **data collection** activity involves such steps as capturing the transaction data, recording the data onto forms, and validating and editing the data to assure their accuracy and completeness. If the data items are quantitative, they may need to be measured before recording. If the transactions are captured at a point remote to the point where they are to be processed, the data will need to be transmitted.

An example procedure involving a sales transaction should clarify these steps.

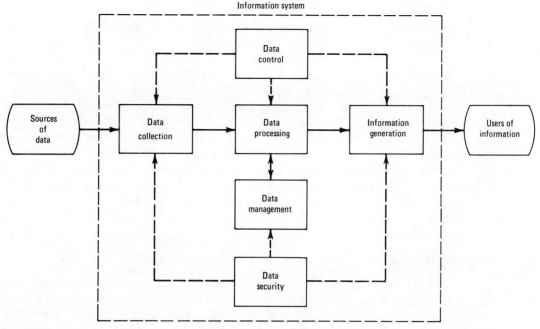

FIGURE 1-7 Activities of an AIS. Adapted with permission from "Report of the Committee on Accounting and Information Systems," in *Committee Reports: Supplement to Vol. XLVI of the Accounting Review* (Evanston, Ill.: American Accounting Association, 1971), p. 290.

The data are captured by a salesperson via a visit with a customer. During the conversation, the salesperson records on a sales order form the pertinent data items, such as customer's name and desired products and quantities. Then the salesperson transmits the order to the home office by telephone. There a clerk validates the name and address of the customer by reference to a file and lists the customer number on the form.

Data Processing

The **data processing** activity involves steps like the following:

- Classifying, or assigning collected data to preestablished categories.
- Transcribing, or copying/reproducing the data onto another document or medium.
- Sorting, or arranging data items according to one or more characteristics.
- Batching, or gathering together groups of transactions of similar nature.
- Merging, or combining two or more batches or files of data.
- Calculating, or performing addition, subtraction, multiplication, and division computations.

- Summarizing, or aggregating quantitative data items.

- Comparing, or examining items from separate batches or files to find those that match or to determine how they differ.

For example, the processing of sales transactions may begin with a clerk classifying the product data by listing product codes alongside the product descriptions. After the goods are shipped, the clerk transcribes the sales data onto a formal sales invoice. Then he or she multiplies the quantities ordered by the unit sales prices to calculate the amount owed by the customer for each product. At the end of each day the clerk batches the invoices and sorts them by customer numbers. Next he or she summarizes the quantities of each product shipped and lists the totals on a sales recap sheet. Finally, the clerk compares today's totals with yesterday's totals and records each increase or decrease in an analysis column.

Data Management

The **data management** activity consists of three steps: storing, updating, and retrieving. Storing involves placing data in repositories called files or data bases. Updating involves the adjusting of stored data to reflect newly occurring events, operations, or decisions. Retrieving involves the accessing and extracting of stored data, either for further processing or for reporting to users.

Data management and data processing are closely related. Batching and sorting, for example, are often performed as a prelude to updating. Data management may therefore be viewed as a subset of data processing, or vice versa.

In the sales transaction example, the clerk stores data concerning new customers by inserting records into the file that contains customer-related data. When the ordered products have been shipped to a customer, the clerk updates the customer's account balance; that is, the clerk adds the total amount on a sales invoice (e.g., $100) to the previous balance in the customer's account (e.g., $900) thereby deriving the current or updated balance owed by the customer (e.g., $1000). At the end of each month, the clerk retrieves all the customer records in order to prepare information that is needed by the customers and managers.

Data Control (Plus Security)

The **data control** (plus security) activity has the objective of safeguarding assets and ensuring the accuracy of data. A variety of techniques may be employed to maintain adequate control and security. One such technique consists of validating input data by checking the transaction data against verified reference records. Other techniques will be discussed later in this chapter and in the chapters that pertain to internal accounting control.

Information Generation

The **information generation** activity includes such information processing steps as interpreting, reporting, and communicating information. In the continuing example, the clerk prepares reports from the retrieved customer records.

He or she prepares monthly statements, which are communicated to the customers via the postal service. Next the clerk prepares an aged accounts receivable report for the credit manager. Then the clerk turns the records over to the accountant, who prepares sales analyses and financial ratio reports. The accountant then writes comments that interpret the substance of these analyses and reports and delivers them to the sales manager.

EXAMPLES OF TRANSACTION PROCESSING AND INFORMATION PROCESSING SYSTEMS

Transaction processing and information processing systems differ appreciably in specific situations. Some principally employ clerical or manual processing, for example, whereas others utilize computer-based processing. To appreciate this divergence, consider several systems found within typical (but hypothetical) business firms and not-for-profit organizations.

A Small Church

The Peaceful Community Church uses simple single-entry transaction processing systems for handling its cash. All collections and disbursements are manually recorded on summary sheets. At the end of each quarter, a statement of cash receipts and disbursements is prepared by hand.

A Small Landscaping Service

Greenthumb Landscapers uses a manual double-entry transaction processing system for handling its sales and accounts receivable. All sales, which are on credit, are recorded on sales tickets. At the end of each month, the sales tickets are posted to individual customer account cards by a mechanized accounting machine. Any payments received during the month are also posted to the account cards in order to reflect the current outstanding balances. Then the account cards are photocopied and mailed as monthly statements to the customers. At the end of each quarter, a local public accountant prepares financial statements on the accrual basis for the firm.

A Local CPA Firm

Cracker and Jack, CPAs, use microcomputer-based TPSs to handle their timekeeping, payroll, and billing activities. All hours worked by the staff are keyed from time sheets into the office microcomputer at the end of each week. A program in the microcomputer then prepares billable time summaries and paychecks. At the end of each month and quarter, other programs prepare bills for clients, accrual-basis financial statements, and various reports.

The CPA firm also uses a microcomputer in decision-making activities. With respect to its internal information processing, the partners interact with the microcomputer in developing the coming year's budget. With respect to consulting engagements, they use the microcomputer to support key decision recommendations to the clients.

A Medium-sized Manufacturer

The Jiffy Manufacturing Company uses a minicomputer-based TPS to maintain its production job costs. Data concerning materials used and labor employed are entered into the minicomputer via terminals at various production floor workstations. These data are processed to yield the material and labor costs for each job in production; then the processing program computes and adds the related costs for overhead. Cost accounting statements are printed at the end of each day.

This same minicomputer is also used as the nucleus of the production information (processing) system. Various control and planning reports are prepared by the system for the production managers. For instance, data concerning actual job costs are compared with standard costs and presented in cost variance reports.

A Regional Airline

On-Time Airlines uses a mainframe computer, which is connected to a network of terminals and microcomputers, as the backbone of its reservations TPS. Reservation requests and cancellations are entered by airline clerks via terminals or microcomputers, which are located in various offices and airports throughout the service area. Small printers also attached to the network issue tickets and boarding passes. Information concerning available seats on all flights is instantly available to the clerks on terminal display screens and to a linking network of travel agents.

This reservations network also serves to link other TPSs. For instance, time records of all airline personnel are entered through the dispersed microcomputers; these records are processed on the mainframe computer to produce the weekly payrolls. Also, maintenance schedules are prepared on the microcomputers located at the various airports; these schedules are forwarded through the network to the mainframe computer, where they are coordinated.

As in the previous example, this network provides by-product information to support various decision-making activities. For instance, summaries of passenger loadings on flights provide information for scheduling upcoming flights and for setting fares. Summaries concerning maintenance activities provide information for making decisions about adding or reducing maintenance personnel.

An Educational Institution

Old Winsockie University has two mainframe computer systems: one for academic uses and one for administrative uses (including transaction processing). In addition, the university has a terminal that is tied to another mainframe computer located many miles from campus. This latter hookup comprises a decision support system, since a budget modeling program and key planning data for the university are stored within the large, distant computer system. The university administrators can access the program and data via the terminal in order to develop proposed operating budgets for the coming year.

ROLES OF ACCOUNTANTS WITH RESPECT TO AN AIS

All students preparing for careers in business can expect to encounter at least one real-world AIS. Many accounting majors are likely to come in contact with a variety of AISs during the spans of their careers. Moreover, these interactions will probably be close and continuous. Thus, accounting majors can benefit greatly from a reasonably extended study of concepts and applications involving the modern-day AIS.

Accountants *use, evaluate,* and *design* an AIS. The exact manner in which accountants interact with an AIS depends on their responsibilities. Six areas of responsibility commonly assumed by accountants are financial accounting, tax accounting, managerial (cost) accounting, accounting management, auditing, and systems development. Accountants in each of these areas (portrayed in Figure 1-8 as interacting with an AIS) deserve further attention.

Financial Accountants

Financial accounting has the major purpose of generating *scorekeeping* information. It provides balance sheets, income statements, funds-flow statements,

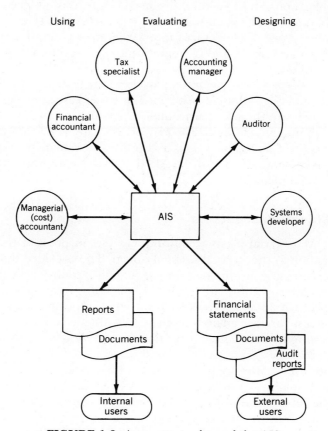

FIGURE 1-8 Accountant roles and the AIS.

and other financial statements to a variety of users. Most users are external to the firm providing the financial statements. External users include owners (e.g., stockholders), prospective owners, lenders (e.g., banks), credit agencies, industry associations, financial analysts, governmental agencies (e.g., the Securities and Exchange Commission), and other interested parties such as university professors. The primary internal users of financial statements are the managers of the firm, who likely receive more details than are provided to external users.

Financial accountants use the AIS to aid in processing the transaction data underlying these financial statements. They also draw from data stored within the AIS to perform interpretive functions such as financial ratio analysis. Likewise, they evaluate the AIS in order to make certain it prepares the financial statements in accordance with generally accepted accounting principles. On occasion, financial accountants may become involved in the design of the AIS. For example, they may recommend that the inventory valuation procedure be changed from the first-in, first-out method to the last-in, first-out method.

Tax Specialists

Tax accounting has the purposes of preparing the returns that reflect tax obligations and of aiding the making of decisions having tax implications. It therefore provides outputs to two types of users: (1) income, property, sales, and other types of tax returns to external taxing authorities, such as the Internal Revenue Service, and (2) reports and analyses to the managers who must make decisions.

Tax specialists may be employees of the firm incurring the taxes, or they may be public accounting consultants. In either case they make use of the firm's AIS to prepare the tax returns and to obtain data for tax planning. Like financial accountants, tax specialists may occasionally need to evaluate the AIS with respect to data that it collects and processes. When tax laws change, they need to recommend revisions to the AIS that enable it to process the information needed for compliance.

Managerial (Cost) Accountants

Managerial (cost) accounting has the purposes of providing financial information to the internal users of a firm. The provided information may be *attention-directing* information for use in aiding control activities. It also may be *decision-making* information for use in aiding planning activities. Much of the information may be processed with the aid of control and decision models, such as cost variance analysis models, cost-volume-profit models, and cash flow forecasting models. The information may be descriptive or predictive in nature.

Managerial accountants use the AIS to develop the information for the various users. They frequently must evaluate and recommend revisions to the AIS, particularly concerning the structures of the decision models and the formats of the reports and analyses. In doing so they are primarily guided by the information needs of the managers. Thus, managerial accountants often work closely with the users, who may range from the production supervisor to the vice president of finance. Although they are frequently challenged to obtain sufficient information for the users, managerial accountants are less constrained than financial accountants; managerial accounting information is not governed by generally accepted accounting principles.

Accounting Managers

Generally the chief accounting manager in a firm is known as the controller. Managers reporting to the controller may include a head financial accountant, a head cost accountant, and a budget manager. These managers guide the activities of the accountants discussed earlier. Thus, they use the AIS to obtain information for controlling the accounting activities, evaluating the performances of the staff accountants, and planning the direction of the firm's accounting function. Even more than their subordinates, accounting managers are responsible for evaluating the usefulness of the AIS and for recommending changes to reports and other components.

Auditors

Auditing has the purposes of evaluating the reliability and integrity of information produced by the AIS, the adequacy of the internal controls used in data and information processing, and the efficiency and effectiveness in using AIS resources. It therefore involves the review of all facets of the AIS.

Auditors fall into two categories: external and internal. External auditors are generally members of public accounting firms or of governmental agencies. They serve as independent reviewers of the AISs of client or regulated firms. Typically they express opinions concerning the adequacy of the internal control structure in an AIS and the fairness of the financial statements produced by the AIS. Auditors from public accounting firms issue their reports to the owners of the firm being audited. Governmental auditors issue their reports to the overseeing agency of the firm being audited. Internal auditors, by contrast, are employees of the firm being audited. They express opinions that focus on the efficiency and effectiveness with which AIS resources are being used. Their reports are issued to the top management of the firm being audited.

While auditors are primarily concerned with evaluation, they must of course make extensive use of the AIS. Also, they may recommend changes to the design of the AIS, particularly with respect to the internal controls.

Systems Developers

Information systems development consists of analyzing, designing, and implementing a new or revised AIS. The users of a newly developed AIS include the accountants listed earlier plus all the other internal and external users.

Systems developers are drawn from a variety of educational majors including computer information systems, computer science, and industrial engineering. Increasing numbers of accounting majors, however, are being attracted to systems development.

Like auditors, systems developers may be subdivided into external and internal categories. Those in the external category are generally described as management consultants or advisory services specialists. Often they are colleagues of external auditors and tax specialists within public accounting firms. Internal systems developers or consultants are employees of the firms whose systems they service.

Systems developers or consultants are continuously involved in designing activities. A good design, however, depends on thorough evaluation, analysis, and use of the AIS and its outputs.

AIMS AND DIRECTIONS OF THE FOLLOWING CHAPTERS

This textbook has the purpose of surveying basic concepts and applications of AIS. It will examine the major activities undertaken by AIS's, with principal attention given to those that incorporate computers. Particular attention is given to the collection, processing, storage, retrieval, control, and auditing of data. Several chapters are also devoted to the basic transaction processing systems in a typical AIS. Finally, the phases that span the development and management of a new or revised AIS are covered.

It is hoped that these coverages will provide you with a better understanding of the modern AIS, as well as the tools to improve any specific AIS's that you might encounter during your career.

SUMMARY

An AIS is the set of resources employed by a firm to transform economic data into financial information for (1) operating and managing its activities; and (2) reporting its achievements to other interested parties. It overlaps with the MIS. The two major purposes of an AIS are to perform (1) transaction processing, and (2) information processing. Transaction processing and information processing differ significantly among business firms and not-for-profit organizations. The AIS performs five major activities: data collection, data processing, data management, data control (including security), and information generation. Each activity involves several steps.

Accountants use, evaluate, and design an AIS. Although individual accountants generally perform all three roles, the degree to which they perform each depends on their areas of responsibility (i.e., whether they are responsible for financial accounting, tax accounting, managerial accounting, auditing, or systems development).

REFERENCES

Bodnar, George H., and Hopwood, William S. *Accounting Information Systems,* 3d ed., Boston: Allyn & Bacon, 1987.

Nash, John F., and Roberts, Martin B. *Accounting Information Systems.* New York: Macmillan, 1984.

"Report of the Committee on Contemporary Approaches to Teaching Accounting Information Systems." Sarasota, Fla.: American Accounting Association, 1986.

Roussey, Robert S. "The CPA in the Information Age: Today and Tomorrow." *The Journal of Accountancy* (Oct. 1986), 94–107.

Wilkinson, Joseph W. *Accounting and Information Systems,* 2d ed., New York: Wiley, 1986.

QUESTIONS

1. What is the meaning of each of the following terms?

Information
Data
System
Accounting
Accounting
  information system
  (AIS)
Management
  information system
  (MIS)
Transaction
Accounting transaction
Accounting cycle
Transaction processing
  system (TPS)

Information
  processing
Procedure
Data collection
Data processing
Data management
Data control
Information
  generation
Financial accounting
Tax accounting
Managerial (cost)
  accounting
Auditing

2. How do the terms *information, system,* and *accounting* clarify the meaning of an AIS?

3. What is the relationship of the AIS to the MIS?

4. What are the basic accounting transactions?

5. What are the benefits from a soundly designed TPS?

6. Contrast the users of transaction processing and of information processing.

7. What are the benefits from a soundly designed system for information processing?

8. Briefly describe several steps often performed within each major activity of an AIS.

9. Discuss the roles of accountants and the extent to which these roles may vary in accordance with assigned responsibilities.

10. Contrast scorekeeping, attention-directing, and decision-making information.

11. Identify several emerging developments affecting the AIS.

12. Why should accountants study the AIS?

13. Has the influence of accountants changed since the advent of computers? If so, in what ways?

REVIEW PROBLEM

Campus Bookstore, First Installment

Statement

The Campus Bookstore occupies two levels in a building adjacent to the campus of a large state university. On the lower level are textbooks and other books; on the upper level are sundry non-book articles and supplies.

Tom Long, who is the sole owner of the bookstore, personally directs all operations. Lois Sutton is in charge of merchandising on the upper level; Don Burgess manages the merchandising activities on the lower level. The remaining personnel consist of one accountant, three bookkeepers, four merchandise order clerks, one inventory manager, one cashier, two stock clerks, four checkout clerks, and one custodian. Temporary personnel are added during peak periods, such as at the beginnings of semesters.

The building occupied by the bookstore is leased. However, the four cash registers, store fixtures, desks and related office furniture, typewriters, desk calculators, dollies, and two small vans are owned.

Merchandise for resale is purchased from over 200 suppliers. Store supplies, ranging from accounting spreadsheets to cleansing powders, are acquired from several other suppliers. Textbooks are bought subject to return privileges, since estimated course sizes do not always materialize. On the other hand, the bookstore buys used textbooks from students at the end of each semester; these used textbooks are then resold to other students or sold to used-book wholesalers.

All merchandise is sold on a cash basis. Funds are also raised by short-term bank loans at the beginning of each semester.

Required

a. Describe the purposes of the bookstore's AIS.

b. Identify key transactions conducted by the bookstore.

c. Identify the varied users of the bookstore's AIS outputs.

d. Identify the resources of its AIS.

e. Identify several useful products (i.e., reports) that might be generated by its AIS.

Solution

a. The two major purposes of the bookstore's AIS are (1) to process transactions in order to provide information for its various operations and to meet legal obligations, and (2) to process information that is useful for decision making.

b. The key transactions processed by the bookstore are (1) cash sales to bookstore customers, (2) purchases from suppliers, (3) returns of purchased textbooks to suppliers, (4) cash disbursements to suppliers and others, (5) payroll payments to employees, and (6) loans from banks. Note that the cash receipts transaction is combined with the sales transaction since sales are not made on credit.

c. The users of the outputs from the AIS include (1) the managers of the bookstore, (2) the employees of the bookstore, (3) the customers (who are primarily students), (4) the suppliers, (5) the banks, (6) the used-book wholesalers, (7) Tom Long (as owner), and (8) governmental agencies who have responsibility with respect to taxes.

d. The resources of the bookstore's AIS consist of the fixed assets, merchandise, supplies, employees, data, and funds from revenues and loans.

e. Among the reports that might be usefully provided to the bookstore's managers by information processing are (1) balance sheet, income statement, and funds-flow statement; (2) reports of actual costs versus budgeted costs for each level; (3) reports of sales and profits for each level and each product line; (4) reports of the status of each merchandise item in stock; and (5) budgets for each level.

PROBLEMS

1-1. Financial statements provide information for more than one purpose and to more than one type of user. Describe the ways that the financial statements of a merchandising corporation are helpful to each of the following types of users:

a. Creditor banks.

b. Securities and Exchange Commission.

c. Stockholders.

d. Managers.

e. Labor unions.

f. Prospective investors.

1-2. For each of the business firms and not-for-profit organizations used as examples in this chapter, list (a) one additional type of transaction processing system; and (b) one example (or additional example) of a helpful managerial report generated by an information processing system.

1-3. As a graduating accounting major, you are currently considering two job offers: one from a Big-Eight public accounting firm and one from a member of the Big-Three automobile manufacturers. It so happens that the automobile manufacturer is a client for all the services offered by the public accounting firm.

a. Assume that you accept the offer of the public accounting firm. (i) Describe the area of responsibility that you personally would be assigned and the interactions that you would likely have with the AIS of your firm and the client firm. *Note:* The choice of the area of responsibility is dependent on your personal desires and qualifications and may differ from the choices of your classmates. (ii) Describe the remaining major areas of responsibility within the public accounting firm and the interactions that individuals in those areas would likely have with the AIS of your firm and the client firm.

b. Assume that you accept the offer of the automobile manufacturer. (i) Describe the area of responsibility that you personally would be assigned and the interactions that you would likely have with the AIS of your firm and with the accountants from the public accounting firm. (ii) Describe the areas of responsibility that other accountants would have within the firm and the interactions they would likely have with the AIS of your firm.

1-4. Describe each of the procedures listed below in terms of the steps and activities performed by an AIS. Underline each verb that represents a step (e.g., record, calculate).

a. A procedure used by a service station to sell gasoline and other products to customers on credit.

b. A procedure used by a department store to obtain and process amounts owed by credit customers.

c. A procedure used by a campus bookstore to purchase merchandise on credit for re-sale.

d. A procedure used by a florist shop to pay bills owed to suppliers.

e. A procedure used by a fast-food establishment to pay its employees.

f. A procedure used by your university to register you for classes and to collect the registration fees.

1-5. The data at the bottom of this page pertain to a batch of 12 business students at a state university who have applied for a scholarship.[1]

Required

a. List the ways by which the students may logically be classified.

b. Calculate the cumulative grade point average (GPA) for each student, and enter into a new column at the right.

c. The student data are currently sorted according to the last four digits of their social security numbers. Re-sort the student data in ascending order three times: first according to cumulative semester hours, then according to last names, and finally according to cumulative GPAs.

---

[1] Some parts of this problem can be solved by using a microcomputer-based data base management software package.

d. Compare John Tigger to the other students. What specific matches do you find?

1-6. Describe the steps that you as an inventory clerk for an appliance dealer would perform for a procedure that involves the following inputs, file, and outputs.

a. The *inputs* are documents that contain the code numbers and quantities of merchandise items received from suppliers and sold to customers. Each individual document refers to *either* a receipt or a sale, although some of the documents may contain the code number and quantity for more than one item of merchandise. About 100 documents are given to you daily in an unsorted batch.

b. The *file* lists the descriptive titles and unit prices for all coded merchandise items.

c. The daily *output* is a report that shows the *dollar amounts* of merchandise received and sold, in terms of both (1) individual merchandise items, *and* (2) totals of merchandise items involved in the day's transactions. The merchandise items are arranged in code number order, and each is identified on the report by its descriptive title.

1-7. Select a small firm in your locality, such as a florist shop, building contractor, delivery service, or bank branch. After visiting the selected firm, prepare a report that contains the following:

Number	Name	Department	Class	Cumulative Semester Hours	Grade Points
0358	Jane Wybert	Accounting	Jr	60	180
0972	George Backus	Economics	Sr	120	396
1358	Tim Spence	Management	So	45	144
2456	Carol Burns	Accounting	Fr	15	60
2867	John Tigger	Marketing	Jr	80	264
3520	Gary Johns	Quantitative Methods	So	30	96
4621	Terry Cummins	General Business	Sr	90	270
5863	Betty White	Management	Sr	100	280
6007	Lisa Manning	Finance	Jr	70	238
6364	Jorge Riche	Marketing	Sr	110	308
7819	Francis Dole	Finance	So	50	190
9215	Dan Long	Accounting	Jr	60	222

a. A brief description of the firm's background and environment, such as the products and services it provides, the industry of which it is a member, its physical facilities and other assets, and its employees.

b. A brief description of the major purposes, characteristics, and resources of its AIS.

c. A listing of its key accounting transactions.

d. A listing of the varied users of its AIS.

e. A brief description of several key reports prepared by the AIS for the managers of the firm.

f. A description of two key procedures in terms of the steps and activities performed by its AIS.

2

Environment and

Components

of an AIS

Describe the environmental settings of an accounting information system and the firm of which it is a part.

Identify the several components comprising a typical accounting information system.

Describe the flows of the basic transactions through the accounting cycle.

INTRODUCTION

An accounting information system (AIS) is an integral part of the firm that it serves. It also interacts with customers and others who reside outside the firm. This chapter first looks at the environments of an AIS and business firm. It then examines the components of the AIS and its accounting cycle. Finally it discusses flows of key accounting transactions in terms of these components.

ENVIRONMENT OF AN AIS

An AIS fits within a framework called a **systems hierarchy.** Figure 2-1 depicts this hierarchy. Above the AIS is its firm, of which the AIS is a part or **subsystem.** In a more remote sense, the AIS is also a subsystem of the firm's environment. On the other hand, the AIS contains such subsystems as the transaction processing systems and information processing systems. It also interacts with two other major subsystems of the firm: the operational system and the organizational structure.[1] These subsystems are highly interdependent.

---

[1] Note that the terms *system* and *subsystem* are interchangeable, depending on the context in which they are used. Thus, the operational system and AIS are subsystems in reference to a firm, but they are also systems in their own right.

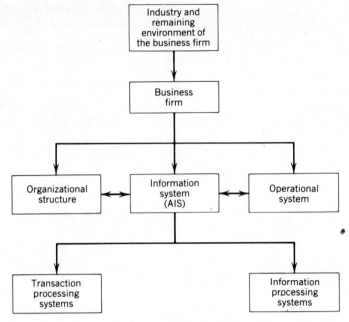

FIGURE 2-1 A hierarchy of systems.

The Business Firm and Beyond

Figure 2-2 displays certain key characteristics that reveal that the typical business firm is itself a system. It has one or more critical **objectives,** such as to maximize profits or to provide service to customers and/or other parties. Within its **boundary** it maintains a variety of highly interdependent subsystems ranging from physical plants and offices to employees and procedures. All such subsystems have numerous common boundaries, or **interfaces,** through which they relate and interact. Three of the most important subsystems, as previously noted, are the AIS, the operational system, and the organizational structure. The stabil-

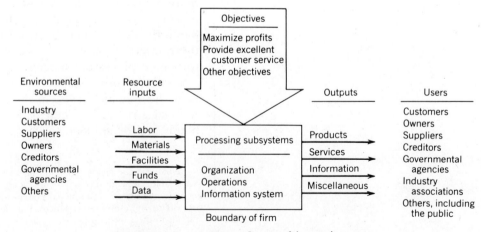

FIGURE 2-2 A business firm and its environment.

ity of such subsystems, as well as of the firm itself, is maintained by a variety of **constraints** and **controls.** In addition to the physical boundary, the constraints include limited resources and available technology. Controls include regulatory processes, such as budgets and quality inspections, which employ feedback to keep the firm "on target" toward its objectives.

Beyond the firm's boundary is an extremely influential **environment.** It provides various opportunities and resources to the firm. For instance, new families may move into the firm's market area and become potential customers. New parts and products may become available from suppliers. New data concerning the economy may be published by a governmental agency. The environment also presents new challenges, as when a new firm in the industry becomes an aggressive competitor. Finally, the environment is the recipient of the primary outputs of the firm. Customers receive products and/or services. Owners receive funds representing profits or returns. All the users listed in Figure 2-2 receive information for use in decision making or in carrying out desired actions. Thus, owners and prospective investors may receive annual reports, while suppliers receive purchase orders.

Although their environments are important to all firms, the relative impacts of the respective sources, resources, and outputs tend to vary widely among individual industries and firms. To a firm in a capital-intensive industry the facilities resource is of paramount concern; to a firm in a labor-intensive industry the labor resource is critical. A bank is very concerned with the funds resource, whereas a grocery chain is equally concerned about the merchandise resource. A highly regulated firm, such as a public utility, must generate a large number of reports to meet its legal obligations; a small photography shop may need only prepare tax returns to meet its legal obligations.

The AIS is significantly shaped by the particular demands of its firm's environment. For instance, the grocery chain must maintain a large number of merchandise inventory records. A steel manufacturer must focus on records concerning facilities (fixed assets) and the production process.

Operational System

The **operational system** is the work system of a firm. It includes such daily operations as running machines and shipping goods. Taken together, these operations comprise the physical process that transforms resources into the products and/or services provided by a firm. Figure 2-3 shows the process within a typical manufacturing firm. The process begins with materials being received from suppliers and ends with the finished goods being shipped to customers. The separate boxes labeled "acquiring materials," "producing finished goods," and so on represent the primary operations. These operations receive assistance from supporting operations, such as production planning and maintenance. They also require suitable amounts of the other four types of resource inputs: labor, facilities, funds, and data.

The AIS has two close relationships to the operational system.

1. As Figure 2-3 suggests, the AIS monitors and records the various actions of the operational system. Consequently, managers can keep abreast of the status of each operation and the accumulated results of all operations.

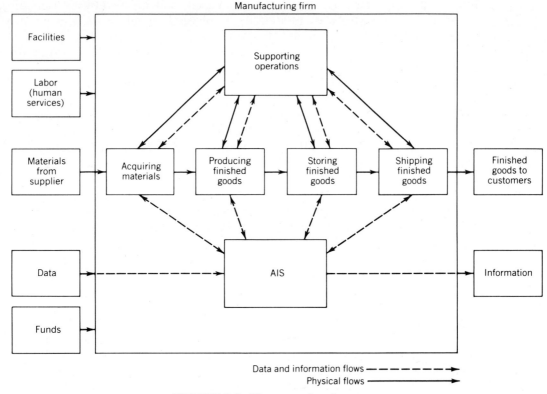

FIGURE 2-3 The operational system.

2. The AIS provides data inputs to the operational system. For example, it provides the purchase orders that trigger the delivery of materials by suppliers.

Organizational Structure

The **organizational structure** or system, another of the major subsystems within a firm, is the means by which the managers direct and coordinate the network of operations. It specifies the responsibilities and delegated authority with respect to each operation and center. In addition, it clarifies the relationships among the various assigned responsibilities.

Figure 2-4 portrays, by means of an **organization chart,** the most commonly adopted type of responsibility structure. This structure is a hierarchical arrangement of managerial levels. (Although only two levels are shown, several additional lower levels would be necessary to complete the organizational structure for a manufacturing firm.) At the top level is the president. Six boxes at the second level are attached to the president's box, thus denoting a span of management of six. That is, the six managers who head the **responsibility centers** labeled "marketing/distribution," "inventory management," and so on report directly to the president. They divide the work of the firm, or segregate the overall responsibilities, into six functional areas.

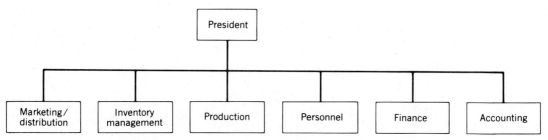

FIGURE 2-4 Key organizational functions of a manufacturing firm.

1. The marketing/distribution function has the objectives of obtaining orders from customers and filling the orders efficiently. The former involves such subfunctions as advertising, sales promotion, and direct selling. The latter generally involves order entry, warehousing, and shipping.

2. The inventory management function has the objective of efficiently managing the materials or merchandise resource. It involves such subfunctions as purchasing, receiving, and storing materials. (The inventory control subfunction is usually under the accounting function.)

3. The production function has the objective of converting raw materials into finished goods, thereby creating form utility. Typical primary subfunctions are parts production and assembly. Supporting subfunctions include engineering design, production planning and control, maintenance, and quality control.

4. The personnel function has the objectives of assuring that the firm's labor (human services) needs are met and that the job-related needs of each employee are likewise met. Among the typical subfunctions are employment, training, employee benefits, compensation, and labor relations.

5. The finance function has the objectives of obtaining funds at the lowest costs and disbursing funds efficiently. It often includes such subfunctions as cash receipts, cash disbursements, and credit checking.

6. The accounting function has the objectives of monitoring physical operations, reporting the financial status and results of operations, providing documents, supporting daily operations, controlling resources, and performing special analyses. Thus, it focuses on the data resource. Figure 2-5 shows a representative organization chart of the accounting function for a manufacturing firm. Note that all the boxes (organizational units) under the cost accounting and general accounting subfunctions are involved in recordkeeping activities. All these recordkeeping units will be examined in later chapters.

The organizations of firms in every industry and of every type are structured according to functions. However, other arrangements are often encountered. Thus, organizations may be structured or segmented according to product lines, geographical territories, or markets served. They may also vary according to the degree of authority that is delegated. Those in which relatively little authority is

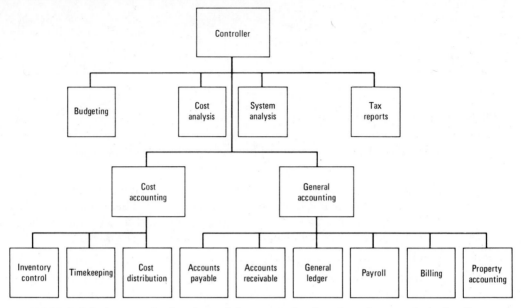

FIGURE 2-5   An organization chart of the accounting function of a manufacturing firm.

delegated to middle and lower managerial levels are known as centralized structures. Those in which considerable authority is delegated to middle and lower managerial levels are known as decentralized structures. Top managers in every firm must decide which alternatives are most suitable to its objectives and circumstances.

The organizational structure is as closely related to the AIS as it is to the operational system.

1. Managers reside in the various responsibility centers; hence, the organizational structure dictates critical flows of information (i.e., managerial reports) generated by the AIS.

2. The transactions processed by the AIS flow through various organizational departments, where personnel perform steps in the procedures. In turn, the processing steps affect the flows of physical resources within the operational system. Figure 2-6 illustrates these relationships for the flow and management of merchandise inventory. It shows that seven organizational departments are involved in processing the documents and records needed to control merchandise inventory, from the point at which new merchandise is found to be needed to the points at which sold merchandise is shipped to customers and suppliers are paid.

3. The informal or social counterpart of the formal organization interacts closely with and overlaps the informal information system (i.e., the "grapevine").

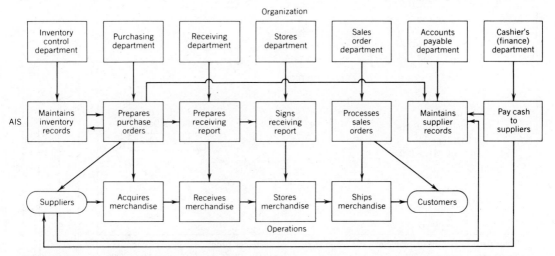

FIGURE 2-6 Relationships among the organizational structure, AIS, and operational system.

COMPONENTS OF AN AIS

In performing its activities an AIS requires specific components or elements. The nature of these components will tend to vary, depending on the degree of automation incorporated into the AIS. In the traditional AIS that employs manual or clerical techniques, the components generally consist of source documents, journals and registers, ledgers, files, reports and other outputs, noncomputerized processing devices and methods, and controls.

Source Documents

Most transactions are recorded on source documents, such as the sales invoice shown in Figure 2-7. **Source documents** serve such important functions as:

1. Depositories of the key facts concerning particular transactions for future reference. These facts are available for preparing reports, for checking during audits, and so forth.

2. Authorizations of transactions. For instance, a purchase order authorizes a supplier to deliver merchandise or materials.

3. Documentations of actions and flows that reflect the accountability of persons or units. For instance, suppliers' invoices are initialed to show that they have been checked for accuracy.

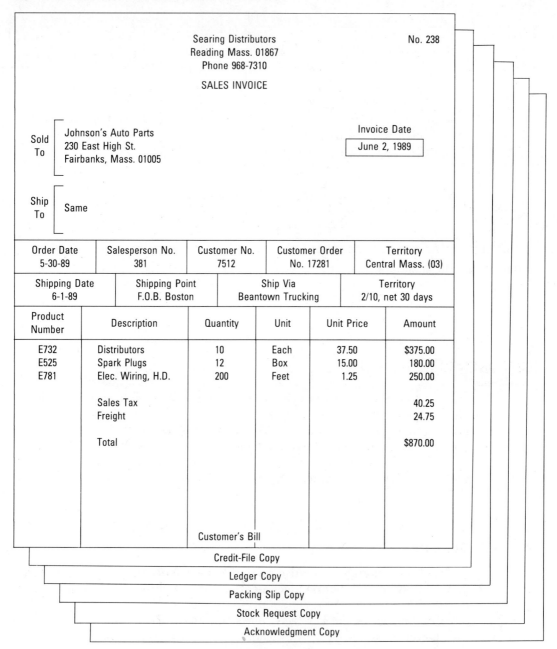

FIGURE 2-7 A sales invoice.

Journals and Registers

A journal is the record of an original entry because it summarizes transaction data. It is an accounting record because it reflects only those transactions that are expressed in financial terms by means of debits and credits. For instance, a journal reflects a loan received from a bank by showing a debit to the Cash account and a credit to the Notes Payable account. As the figure shows, two types of journals are in use in the typical manual system: a general journal and a special journal. A **general journal** has a generalized columnar format that allows any type of accounting transaction to be recorded. A **special journal,** on the other hand, accepts transactions of a particular type. Thus, a sales journal accepts sales transactions only. Special journals are popular because they enable transactions that occur in high volumes to be recorded and posted efficiently. They generally accommodate most of the transaction load of a firm, leaving for the general journal only the relatively unusual transactions and the end-of-period adjustments.

A **register** is a record that may serve as an alternative to a journal or as a chronological log of nonaccounting events. For instance, a check register is a record of cash disbursement transactions; a shipping register is a log of shipments of merchandise to customers.

Ledgers

A ledger is an accounting record that summarizes the status of the accounts in financial terms. Transaction amounts that have been entered into the journals are posted to the appropriate ledger accounts. This posting process updates each affected account by raising or lowering the balance of the account to reflect the transaction amounts.

Two types of ledgers exist: a general ledger and a subsidiary ledger. A **general ledger** contains the summary financial data concerning the status of all the asset, liability, revenue, and expense accounts established by a firm. A **subsidiary ledger** contains the detailed records (grouped items of data) pertaining to a particular account in the general ledger. Two examples are the accounts receivable and accounts payable subsidiary ledgers which hold the records affecting the customers and suppliers, respectively. The sum total of all balances in a subsidiary ledger should equal the balance of the related account in the general ledger. Thus, an account that is supported or detailed by a subsidiary ledger is called a control account.

Files

A **file** is a collection of logically related records within the overall data base of a firm. Four major types of files are the master file, transaction file, reference file, and history file. A **master file** contains the relatively permanent records concerning a firm's entities and activities. All the ledgers just discussed are examples of master files. A **transaction file** contains the relatively temporary records pertaining to specific transactions. A batch of sales invoices represents a transaction file; the sales journal can also be viewed as a type of transaction file. A **reference file** contains data for use in performing steps during transaction processing. Examples are income tax tables and price lists. A **history file** contains data based on past completed transactions. For instance, a file of sales invoices pertaining to completed sales is a history file. In addition to representing an archive of past events, a history file provides the means of making analyses. Thus, data from sales invoices can be summarized to reveal monthly totals and sales trends by products and types of customers.

A **record** within a master or transaction file contains a group of logically related data items. Each data item represents an **attribute** or characteristic pertaining to the entity, activity, or event that is embodied in the record. Consider a record concerning a customer. Typical attributes in this type of record include the customer account number, name, address, credit limit, and balance due. When such attributes appear in a record for a specific customer, they reflect values pertaining to the customer. For example, one particular customer may have an account number of 23456, a name of Jane P. Dunbar, and a balance due of $500.00.

A record employs **fields** in order to exhibit the values of attributes. Each record within a file presents the same format of fields. We can see an instance of these statements in the sales invoice of Figure 2-7, which is a record within a transaction file. The order date field in the invoice contains the value 5-30-89. Although the order date value will likely change from invoice to invoice (i.e., from record to record), its field will retain the same location within the format of the record.

Reports and Other Outputs

A variety of outputs flow from the information generation activity of the typical AIS. Among the most common of these are the balance sheet, income statement, and funds (cash) flow statement. However, numerous reports designed specifically for managers are also generated. Some **managerial reports** reflect the status of operations or resources. Examples are sales summaries and inventory status reports. Others are useful to managers for fulfilling their planning and control responsibilities. Examples of planning reports are budgets and sales forecasts, and an example of a control report is a cost variance analysis.

Outputs also include documents that are utilized in daily operations. An example of an output document is the monthly statement mailed as a bill to a customer of a department store. Many source documents are, in effect, output documents. Not only are they inputs into the accounting cycle process, but they are also the products of prior processing steps. These prior processing steps are detailed in later chapters that examine the various transaction cycles.

Noncomputerized Processing Devices and Methods

Manual processing systems do not, of course, employ computers. However, almost all make use of processing devices that extend beyond humble pencils and pens. The following list includes brief descriptions of the noncomputerized devices that are typically found in manual systems.

- Time clock, which stamps the times that employees begin and complete work shifts or jobs.

- Adding machine, which accumulates columns of figures in journals, prepares batch totals from source documents, and so on.

- Calculator, which verifies extensions of amounts on invoices and performs other computations.

- Sorter, which arranges records, source documents, and reports in desired orders.

- Duplicator, which reproduces source documents and other papers.

- Check writer, which signs checks and "protects" amounts thereon.

- Addressing machine, which prints names and addresses from embossed metal plates onto paychecks, time cards, and so on.

- Accounting machine, which performs calculations, posts to ledgers, and otherwise facilitates the processing steps.

Other familiar devices include typewriters, file drawers, card files, and in-out baskets.

The simplest processing method in manual systems consists of handwritten entries and postings of individual transactions. More sophisticated methods involve the handling of transactions in batches and the use of machine-aided entries and postings. Figure 2-8 shows two fairly popular methods: batch processing and one-write processing.

Batch processing consists of accumulating groups of source documents pertaining to similar transactions and entering them into special journals. Then the source documents are posted to subsidiary ledgers. Totals from the batches of transactions entered into the journals are compared with the totals of amounts

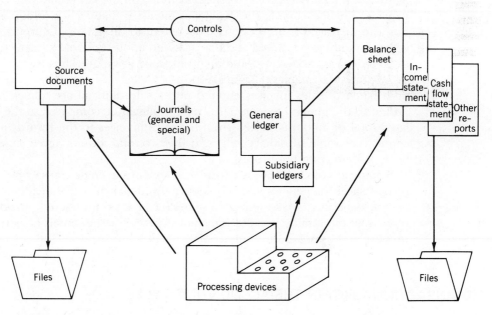

FIGURE 2-8 Alternative processing methods: batch processing and one-write processing.

posted to the ledgers. If they agree, the totals are later posted to the general ledger control accounts and the balances are updated.

One-write processing consists of performing the entering and posting steps simultaneously with the preparation of the source documents. This simultaneous one-write processing occurs because carbons are interleaved between the source document, journal, and ledger. Periodically the general ledger is updated. One-write processing can be performed individually, as when receipts are prepared for cash remitted by customers. It can also be performed in batches, as when paychecks are prepared for employees. Furthermore, it can be performed with the aid of specialized accounting machines.

Controls

Among the variety of controls needed during the processing of transactions are a trial balance, chart of accounts, audit trail, batch total, and journal voucher.

A **trial balance** is a listing of all account balances in the general ledger. It provides a convenient means for verifying that the total of all debit account balances are equal to the total of all credit account balances. While trial balances may be prepared at any time, they are particularly important during the adjusting and closing processes at the ends of accounting periods. Their preparation normally precedes the preparation of the financial statements.

A coded **chart of accounts** is a listing of the general ledger accounts and their codes. It enables transaction data to be classified and coded precisely and concisely. Therefore, it tends to reduce confusion and the likelihood of making recording errors.

An **audit trail** is a set of references included on the key accounting records. It provides linkages among the various elements so that each accounting transaction can be traced from the source document to the financial outputs, and vice versa. In addition to aiding auditors, a sound audit trail enables detected errors to be more easily corrected and inquiries to be more quickly answered.

A **batch total** enables posting errors to be detected. For instance, the amounts on a batch of sales invoices entered into a sales journal are totaled and then posted to the general ledger. This batch total can be compared to the accumulated total of amounts posted from the sales invoices to the records in the accounts receivable subsidiary ledger. If the two totals do not agree, an error has been made during the process.

A **journal voucher (JV)** is a form that contains a single transaction. It therefore replaces the general journal. A journal voucher provides an added measure of control because it is assigned a number (i.e., it is prenumbered). In addition, it reflects accountability because it includes spaces for the initials of persons who prepare and approve the transaction.

TRANSACTIONS WITHIN THE ACCOUNTING CYCLE

To reinforce our understanding of the elements and activities of an AIS, we will trace the flows of the basic transactions through the accounting cycle of a

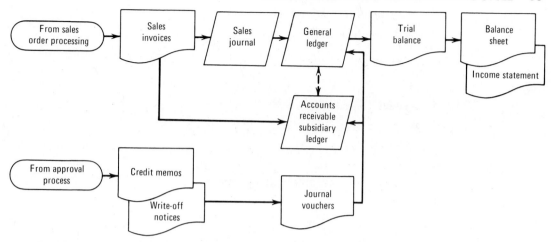

FIGURE 2-9 Diagram showing the flow of sales transactions through the accounting cycle.

typical firm. The generalized view of these flows appeared in Figure 1-5, and the basic transactions were identified as the sales, cash receipts, purchases, cash disbursements, and payroll transactions. As we follow these transaction flows, it is important to remember that only those steps involving accounting records are discussed. Additional processing steps pertaining to each type of transaction are detailed in Chapters 7 through 10.

Sales Transactions

Figure 2-9 diagrams the flow of sales transactions through the accounting cycle. The flow begins with the sales invoices, the source documents that contain amounts affecting ledger accounts. Data from the invoices are (1) entered into a sales journal and (2) posted as debits to individual customer accounts in the accounts receivable subsidiary ledger.[2] Periodically the batch totals in the sales journal are posted to the general ledger as follows:

Dr. Accounts Receivable   XXX

   Cr. Sales   XXX

Adjustments pertaining to accounts receivable are sometimes necessary. Thus, journal vouchers are prepared (or general journal entries are made) to reflect sales returns or allowances or write-offs. After being approved, these vouchers are posted to both the general ledger and the appropriate customers' accounts in the subsidiary ledger. The journal entries would appear as follows:

---

[2] In this and the remaining figures in Chapter 2, documents and journal vouchers are represented by the ☐ symbol and accounting records are represented by the ⬭ symbol.

Dr. Sales Returns and Allowances XXX

    Cr. Accounts Receivable XXX

To adjust customer account balances to reflect returns and allowances on previous sales.

Dr. Bad Debts Expense[3] XXX

    Cr. Accounts Receivable XXX

To write off those customers' account balances that are deemed to be uncollectible.

If the inventory is maintained on a perpetual basis, the following entry would accompany the sales entry.

Dr. Cost of Goods Sold XXX

    Cr. Merchandise (or Finished Goods) Inventory XXX

To record the costs of those goods sold during this date.

At the end of each accounting period, the balances in the accounts receivable subsidiary ledger and sales accounts are listed in the trial balance and then transcribed into the balance sheet and income statement. Periodically the accounts receivable control account balance is compared to the total of the balances in the subsidiary ledger. (Similar steps are performed for each of the transactions; consequently, they will not be repeated.)

Cash Receipts Transactions

Figure 2-10 diagrams the flow of cash receipts transactions through the accounting cycle. The remittance advices (e.g., the top portions or copies of invoices) that accompany customers' checks are the source documents. Amounts appearing on these advices are (1) entered into a cash receipts journal, and (2) posted as credits to the individual customer records in the accounts receivable subsidiary ledger. Periodically the batch totals from the cash receipts journal are posted to the general ledger as follows:

Dr. Cash XXX

    Cr. Accounts Receivable XXX

Cash may be received from sources other than customers. For example, cash receipts may result from loans, payments on notes receivable, and the sales of fixed assets. These miscellaneous cash amounts are entered from special documents into the cash receipts journal or onto journal vouchers. Since they do not involve payments from customers, they are not posted to the subsidiary ledger.

---

[3] This account would be Allowance for Doubtful Accounts if the reserve method for establishing bad debts expense is used.

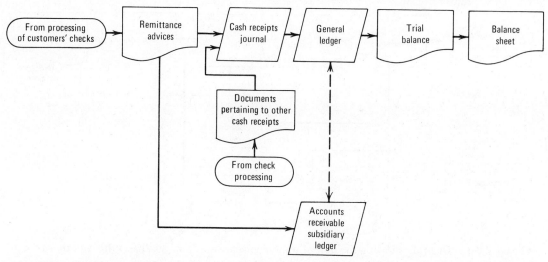

FIGURE 2-10 Diagram showing the flow of cash receipts transactions through the accounting cycle.

An example of a journal entry involving miscellaneous cash amounts is as follows:

Dr. Cash	XXX	
Cr. Notes Payable		XXX
Cr. Fixed Asset (net value)		XXX
Cr. Interest or Dividend Income		XXX

To record cash received from sources other than credit customers.

Purchases Transactions

Figure 2-11 diagrams the flow of purchases transactions through the accounting cycle. Source documents consist of invoices received from the suppliers of ordered merchandise, raw materials, supplies, and services. These suppliers' invoices are (1) entered into a purchases journal or invoice register, and (2) posted as credits to the individual supplier records in an accounts payable subsidiary ledger. Periodically the batch total amounts are posted from the journal to the general ledger. If the periodic inventory method is employed, the posting for merchandise inventory or raw materials is as follows.

Dr. Purchases	XXX	
Cr. Accounts Payable		XXX

If the perpetual inventory method is used, the posting is as follows.

Dr. Merchandise Inventory (or Raw Materials)	XXX	
Cr. Accounts Payable		XXX

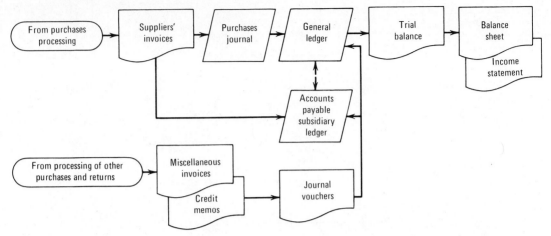

FIGURE 2-11 Diagram showing the flow of transactions arising from purchases through the accounting cycle.

An alternative approach, called the voucher system, is often used instead of the invoice method previously described. In the voucher system or method, the invoices for individual suppliers are grouped on disbursement vouchers. Then they are entered into a voucher register. Otherwise, the procedure is roughly the same as already described.

Obligations for relatively rare purchases, such as for fixed assets, may also be encountered. Likewise, adjustments for purchase returns and allowances must be considered. These miscellaneous transactions are entered from the relevant source documents onto journal vouchers (or in a general journal) and then posted to the ledgers.

Two journal entries that involve adjustments to purchases transactions are as follows.

Dr. Accounts (or Vouchers) Payable	XXX	
Cr. Purchases Returns and Allowances		XXX

To adjust supplier account balances to reflect returns and allowances on previous purchases (assuming that the periodic inventory system is in use).

Dr. Merchandise Inventory, Ending	XXX	
Dr. Cost of Goods Sold	XXX	
Cr. Purchases		XXX
Cr. Merchandise Inventory, Beginning		XXX

To adjust the ending merchandise inventory to its proper amount and to record the cost of goods sold for the accounting period (assuming that the periodic inventory system is in use).

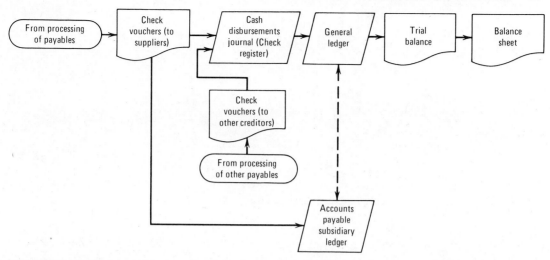

FIGURE 2-12 Diagram showing the flow of cash disbursements transactions through the accounting cycle.

Cash Disbursements Transactions

Figure 2-12 diagrams the flow of cash disbursements transactions through the accounting cycle. Copies of checks, called check vouchers, are the source documents. These check vouchers are (1) entered into a cash disbursements journal or check register, and (2) posted as debits to the individual supplier accounts in the accounts payable subsidiary ledger. Periodically the batch total amounts are posted to the general ledger as follows.

Dr. Accounts Payable   XXX

  Cr. Cash   XXX

Cash may be disbursed to others than suppliers. For instance, cash payments are made to stockholders to distribute dividends and to banks to repay loans. Although check vouchers pertaining to such payments are entered into the journal, they are not normally posted to the subsidiary ledger.

Payroll Transactions

Figure 2-13 diagrams the flow of payroll transactions through the accounting cycle. The source documents are pay records or paycheck vouchers, which in turn are generally based on time cards or time sheets. These documents are used in two phases: labor distribution and paycheck processing. In the labor distribution phase, the pay data are (1) entered on a register called a labor distribution summary, and (2) posted to expense subsidiary ledgers. The totals from the summary are then posted to the general ledger. In the case of a manufacturing firm the debits and credits posted may appear as follows.

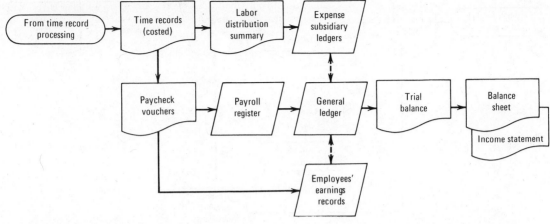

FIGURE 2-13 Diagram showing the flow of payroll transactions through the accounting cycle.

Dr. Work-in-Process	XXX
Dr. Manufacturing Overhead Applied	XXX
Dr. Administrative Expense	XXX
Dr. Selling Expense	XXX
Cr. Payroll Clearing (or Wages and Salaries Payable)	XXX

In the payroll processing phase the paycheck vouchers (i.e., copies of the paychecks) are (1) entered into a payroll register, and (2) posted to the earnings records of the individual employees. Then the totals from the payroll register are posted to the general ledger as follows:

Dr. Payroll Clearing (or Wages and Salaries Payable) XXX	
Cr. Federal Income Taxes Withheld	XXX
Cr. Other Employee Deductions	XXX
Cr. Cash	XXX

Other Accounting Transactions

Most firms also process additional transactions that are inherent in their activities. Manufacturing firms, for instance, encounter events relating to the conversion of raw materials into finished goods. Thus, a manufacturer employing a standard cost system will likely make the following entry to reflect the daily accumulation of costs arising from production events:

Dr. Work-in-Process Inventory XXX	
Cr. Raw Materials Inventory	XXX
Cr. Direct Labor	XXX
Cr. Manufacturing Overhead—Applied	XXX

As production orders are completed, the firm will make the following entry to transfer the total accumulated production costs into the finished goods inventory account.

Dr. Finished Goods Inventory XXX

Cr. Work-in-Process Inventory XXX

SUMMARY

An AIS fits into a systems hierarchy; it is a subsystem of its firm and the environment beyond and it contains such subsystems as transaction processing systems and information processing systems. The firm is a system that contains, in addition to the AIS, such interdependent subsystems as the organization and operational system. It exhibits such other system characteristics as objectives, constraints, controls, inputs, outputs, and process. Its environment provides the resource inputs and receives the outputs. The operational system is the work system and the organizational structure is the means by which the managers coordinate and direct operations. Both are closely related to the AIS.

The components of a traditional manual AIS include source documents, journals and registers, ledgers and files, reports and other outputs, noncomputerized processing devices and methods, and controls. Among the controls are trial balances, coded charts of accounts, audit trails, batch totals, and journal vouchers. All of these are likely to be employed in processing such basic transactions as sales, cash receipts, purchases, cash disbursements, and payroll through the accounting cycle of a manual AIS.

REFERENCES

Lin, W. Thomas, and Harper, William. "A Decision-Oriented Management Accounting Information System." *Cost and Management* (Nov.–Dec. 1981), 32–36.

Page, John, and Hooper, Paul. *Accounting and Information Systems,* 3d ed. Englewood Cliffs, N.J.: Prentice-Hall, 1987.

QUESTIONS

1. What is the meaning of each of the following terms?

Systems hierarchy
Subsystem
Objective
Boundary
Interface
Constraint
Control
Environment
Operational system
Organizational structure
Organization chart
Responsibility center
Source document
General journal
Special journal
Register
General ledger

Subsidiary ledger
File
Master file
Transaction file
Reference file
History file
Record
Attribute
Field
Managerial report
Batch processing
One-write processing
Trial balance
Chart of accounts
Audit trail
Batch total
Journal voucher (JV)

2. What system characteristics does a business firm exhibit?

3. What are several key influences on the AIS from the environment beyond the firm?

4. What are the key relationships between the AIS and the operational system?

5. Briefly describe five organizational functions that are likely to be found within a manufacturing firm.

6. What are the key relationships between the AIS and the organizational structure?

7. What are the functions of a source document?

8. How does a general journal differ from a special journal?

9. Identify the journal in which each of the following transactions would likely be entered, assuming that the firm uses general, sales, purchases, cash receipts, cash disbursements, and payroll journals. (If more than one journal is possible, list both, but place the more likely one first).

a. Credit sale to a customer.
b. Cash sale.
c. Credit purchase of merchandise.
d. Depreciation of a fixed asset.
e. Credit purchase of supplies.
f. Sales return by a customer.
g. Write-off of a bad debt.
h. Payment of employees.
i. Purchase of a delivery truck.
j. Payment of dividends to stockholders.
k. Payment of an invoice from a supplier.
l. Discount on a purchase.

10. How does a general ledger differ from a subsidiary ledger?

11. Describe the differences between a journal and a ledger.

12. Identify six accounts in the general ledger that may suitably be used as control accounts over detailed ledgers maintained by a medium-sized corporation.

13. What are four types of files?

14. What types of outputs are provided by a typical AIS?

15. Contrast batch processing and one-write processing as performed in a manual system.

16. Briefly describe several data controls that are commonly employed in a manual system.

17. Briefly describe the flows of the five basic transactions through the accounting cycle.

18. How does an understanding of a firm and its environment aid in the design of an AIS?

19. Discuss the similarities and differences between the physical processing of materials and the paperwork processing of data.

20. What advantages do students gain when they begin their study of transaction processing systems by focusing on manual rather than computerized examples?

REVIEW PROBLEMS

Campus Bookstore, Second Installment

Statement

The Campus Bookstore (described in the Review Problem at the end of Chapter 1) utilizes an AIS in which the bookkeeper, clerks, cashiers, and managers perform all the activities. In other words, the system is essentially a manual system, although some equipment is used. Sufficient records are maintained to control the cash received, the obligations to suppliers, the levels of merchandise and supplies, and the payments to suppliers and employees.

Required

By reference to the Review Problem in Chapter 1 and the foregoing brief statement,

a. Describe the bookstore in terms of its system characteristics.

b. Briefly describe the operational system of the bookstore.

c. Briefly describe the organizational structure of the bookstore, including the functions that are incorporated.

d. Identify the accounting records that are likely to be used.

e. Discuss the steps involved in processing sales transactions.

Solution

a. The bookstore is a member of a systems hierarchy. Above the firm is its environment, consisting of students and other customers, suppliers, the university campus, the city and other governmental bodies, the bank, and so on. Subsystems within the bookstore include the upper- and lower-level operations, the employees and organizational structure, the AIS, the fixtures and equipment, and so forth. The bookstore has the objectives of earning profits on the sales of merchandise and of providing satisfactory service to all customers. Its inputs consist of the various resources, while its outputs are the merchandise sold and information to outside parties. Finally, it has a number of constraints and controls, such as the physical boundary of the building, the available funds from the owner and sales and bank, the sales seasons that are governed by the university's semesters, the controls over merchandise inventory and repurchases of used textbooks, and so on.

b. The operational system consists of such operations as acquiring merchandise, receiving merchandise, storing merchandise, selling merchandise, returning unsold textbooks, and buying used textbooks from students. These primary operations receive support from such operations as hiring employees, installing fixtures, picking up needed supplies from local firms, cleaning the bookstore, and repairing the various equipment and vans.

c. The organizational structure is a hierarchy with three levels. At the top is the bookstore manager. Reporting to Tom Long are the two merchandise managers, accountant, inventory manager, and cashier. In turn, the merchandise managers direct the salesclerks, checkout clerks, and merchandise order clerks; the accountant directs the three bookkeepers; and the inventory manager directs the stock clerks and custodian. Among the functions around which the personnel are organized are sales, purchasing, accounting, finance, and inventory management. A personnel function is also needed to handle various responsibilities concerning managers and employees.

d. The accounting records that are likely to be used include a general journal, cash receipts journal (which includes all cash sales for new merchandise as well as used textbooks), purchases journal, purchase returns journal (to handle textbook and other merchandise returns), cash disbursements journal, payroll register, general ledger, accounts payable ledger, cash disbursements ledger, employee earnings records, fixed asset records, and inventory ledger or records (for individual merchandise and supply items). It is important to note that the journals and ledgers are unique to this firm, since it has a particular set of circumstances and needs.

e. The steps involved in sales transaction processing are likely to be as follows: First, the salesclerk aids the customer in selecting merchandise. Then, the checkout clerk receives the merchandise from the customer, rings up items on the cash register from price tags, totals the item amounts, adds the sales tax, and informs the customer of the total due. The customer then gives the cashier currency, a check, or a credit card. In the last two cases the cashier then verifies the validity of the check or credit card in some manner. Finally, the checkout clerk bags the merchandise, inserts the cash register receipt, and gives the bag to the customer. At the end of each day the cashier reconciles the cash in the register drawer with amounts listed on a tape locked in the cash register. Then the cashier prepares a bank deposit slip and takes the funds to the bank.

Searing Distributors

Statement

Searing Distributors of Reading, Massachusetts, sells a variety of automotive parts and supplies to automobile repair shops, garages, and supply houses. It currently utilizes a manual AIS that includes such elements as source documents (e.g., sales invoices, purchase orders, employee time cards, checks), journals (e.g., general, sales, cash receipts, purchases, cash disbursements), ledgers (e.g., general, accounts receivable, accounts payable), financial statements (e.g., income statement, balance sheet), and such controls as trial balances and a coded chart of accounts.

Required

Design a set of documents and accounting records and related elements that illustrate each of the categories listed. Include sheets from a general journal, sales journal, cash receipts journal, general ledger, and accounts receivable ledger. The sales journal should provide a single amount column, as well as columns for the date, customer name and account number, and sales invoice number (the audit trail reference). The cash receipts journal should provide two columns for debits (cash and sales discounts) and two columns for credits (accounts receivable and other), together with columns for the date, recipient, and remittance number (the audit trail reference). Illustrative data should be shown in these accounting records, based on the sales invoice document shown in Figure 2-7. Also include a summary chart of accounts, a trial balance, and an income statement.

Solution

		General Journal			Page 75
Date		Account Names and Description	Posting Reference	Debit	Credit
June	16	Note receivable	11	4000.00	
		Land	23		4000.00
		To record the exchange of an unimproved lot for a note from John Broder.			
June	30	Depreciation expense	76	300.00	
		Accumulated depreciation—office equipment and furniture	25C		300.00
		To record depreciation expense for the month.			

EXHIBIT 1 A general journal.

		Sales Journal		Page 32
Date		Customer Name and Account Number	Sales Invoice Number	Amount
June	2	Johnson's Auto Parts #7512	238	870.00
	2	Royal Auto Parts #6158	239	567.50
	2	Automotive Sales #4779	240	1009.00
	2	B & S Auto Supply #5211	241	223.75
	2	Parts Mart #3835	242	818.00
	2	Thomas Motor Exch. #4138	243	1351.25
	2	Fox Auto Service #2816	244	654.50
			Posted 12/50	5494.00

EXHIBIT 2 A sales journal.

		Cash Receipts Journal						Page 41
			Remittance	Other Credits		Accounts Receivable	Sales Discount	Cash
Date		Received from	Number	Acct. No.	Amount	(credit)	(debit)	(debit)
June	2	Fox Auto Service #2816	520			520.00	10.40	509.60
	2	A-1 Auto Parts #1913	521			989.00		989.00
	2	Republic Sales Co. #7008	522			450.00	9.00	441.00
	2	Dividend-West Corp.		86	2000.00			2000.00
	2	Del's Auto Electric #3496	523			1230.00	24.60	1205.40
	2	Flint's Distributors #4653	524			652.00		652.00
	2	Johnson's Auto Parts #7512	525			750.00	15.00	735.00
					2000.00	4591.00	59.00	6532.00
		Posted				12	51	10

EXHIBIT 3 A cash receipts journal.

				General Ledger			
		Account	Accounts Receivable		Account Number	12	

Date 1989		Description	Post. Ref.	Debits	Credits	Balance
June	1	Balance forward				41214.00
	1	Sales	SJ31	4828.00		46042.00
	1	Cash receipts	CR40		5132.00	40910.00
	2	Sales	SJ32	5494.00		46404.00
	2	Cash receipts	CR41		4591.00	41813.00

EXHIBIT 4 A general ledger record.

Name Johnson's Auto Parts				Account Number 7512		
Address 230 East High St.						
Fairbanks, Mass. 01005						

Date		Explanation	Document Number	Debits	Credits	Balance
June	1	Balance forward				750.00
	2	Sale	S238	870.00		1620.00
	2	Payment	R525		750.00	870.00

EXHIBIT 5 A customer's account in an accounts receivable subsidiary ledger.

Searing Distributors
Income Statement
For the Month Ended June 30, 1989

Sales		$96,000
Less: Sales discounts, returns, and allowances		1,900
Net sales		$94,100
Less: Cost of goods sold		38,300
Gross profit on sales		$55,800
Operating expenses		
Selling expenses	$28,600	
Administrative expenses	19,100	
Financial management expenses	1,300	
Total operating expenses		49,000
Net operating income		$ 6,800
Plus: Nonoperating revenues		2,000
Net income		$ 8,800

EXHIBIT 6 An income statement.

Searing Distributors
Trial Balance
June 30, 1989

Account Number	Account Title	Debit	Credit
10	Cash	$ 7,717.00	
11	Notes receivable	4,000.00	
12	Accounts receivable	2,838.00	
13	Merchandise inventory	12,337.00	
14	Supplies inventory	1,260.00	
18	Prepaid insurance	300.00	
20	Investment in long-term securities	3,000.00	
23	Land	1,500.00	
24	Building	90,000.00	
25	Accumulated depreciation—building		$ 22,500.00
26	Office equipment and furniture	18,000.00	
27	Accumulated depreciation—office equipment and furniture		8,400.00
30	Notes payable		2,500.00
31	Accounts payable		6,710.00
33	Taxes payable		4,320.00
40	Long-term notes payable		5,000.00
45	Capital stock		60,000.00
46	Retained earnings		23,650.00
50	Sales of merchandise		96,000.00
51	Sales discounts	1,246.00	
52	Sales returns and allowances	654.00	
55	Purchases	40,020.00	
56	Purchase returns and allowances		1,268.00
57	Freight-in	1,376.00	
61	Sales salaries	22,087.00	
62	Travel expense	3,842.00	
63	Freight-out	2,671.00	
71	Administrative salaries	17,925.00	
72	Utilities expense	200.00	
74	Office supplies expense	75.00	
81	Interest expense	840.00	
82	Bad-debt expense	460.00	
86	Dividend revenue		2,000.00
	Totals	$232,348.00	$232,348.00

EXHIBIT 7 A trial balance.

Account Codes	Major Account Groupings
10–19	Current assets
20–22	Investments
23–29	Fixed assets
30–39	Current liabilities
40–44	Long-term liabilities
45–49	Owners' equity
50–54	Revenues
55–59	Cost of sales
60–69	Selling expenses
70–79	Administrative expenses
80–84	Financial management expenses
85–89	Other revenues and expenses

EXHIBIT 8 A coded chart of accounts, in summary form.

PROBLEMS

2-1. Describe the following types of firms in terms of systems characteristics.

   a. A bank.

   b. A grocery store.

   c. An automobile repair shop.

   d. An electric utility.

   e. A hobby shop.

   f. A university.

   g. A hospital.

2-2. Identify the ways that differences in their environments will lead to differences in the accounting information systems for each of the following pairs of firms.

   a. A retail jeweler versus a passenger airline.

   b. A toy manufacturer versus a public utility.

   c. A drug wholesaler versus a public accounting firm.

2-3. Identify several operations that are primary to each of the following types of firms.

   a. A bank.

   b. A hospital.

   c. A passenger airline.

   d. An electric utility.

   e. An integrated oil company.

   f. A university.

2-4. The Pullen Company is a medium-sized merchandising firm that is owned and managed by Jack Pullen. Reporting to Jack are four managers: Linda Scudder, controller; George Clark, sales manager; Bill Henry, warehouse/distribution manager; and Barbara Rhodes, office manager. Within the accounting department are managers in charge of general accounting, budgets, and systems. Within the sales department are managers in charge of advertising, retail store sales, and direct sales. Within the warehouse/distribution department are managers in charge of purchasing, receiving, shipping, and warehouse operations. Finally, under the office manager are the personnel manager, credit manager, and cashier.

Required

Draw an organization chart for the Pullen Company.

2-5. The Tod Manufacturing Company produces roller bearings in a single plant. The firm is organized functionally, with vice presidents in charge of marketing, production, finance, and administration. Third-level managers include a controller, cashier, chief engineer, purchasing director, sales manager, advertising manager, office manager, production superintendent, production control manager, personnel manager, director of information systems, credit manager, and quality control manager. Reporting to these managers are fourth- and fifth-level managers of accounts receivable, accounts payable, billing, budgets, sales analysis, receiving, timekeeping, finished-goods warehousing, cash receipts, materials storeskeeping, cash disbursements, machining, assembly, cost accounting, financial accounting, general ledger, inventory control, payroll, mailroom, plant maintenance, shipping, sales branches, recruitment, employee services, product design, and plant design.

Required

Draw an organization chart for the Tod Manufacturing Company using sound organizational principles. For instance, group subfunctions having compatible objectives under the same function (e.g., the credit subfunction under the finance function). Do not allow too large a span of management (e.g., more than six managers reporting to a single higher-level manager). Furthermore, do not allow a manager to report to more than one higher-level manager. *Hint:* The organizational functions at the second level in this firm differ somewhat from those in the chapter example, even though both pertain to manufacturing firms. Differences in structures are to be expected in view of differences in circumstances and preferences. However, all the basic responsibilities must be located somewhere within the structure. In order to cope with the differences in this case, it is suggested that the inventory management responsibilities be included within the production function, and the personnel and information systems responsibilities within the administration function.

2-6. List the items of data that should appear on each of the following source documents, assuming that special journals and subsidiary ledgers are incorporated in the accounting cycle.

a. Sales invoice.

b. Remittance advice.

c. Check voucher.

d. Employee paycheck.

2-7. Special journals may be designed in differing formats, as the examples in the second review problem illustrate. Design a purchases journal in two formats. In both designed formats include additional needed columns, such as a column for the supplier's invoice number. Also, mark each amount column as pertaining to a credit or debit account.

a. A format having a single amount column from which totals are posted to the accounts payable and purchases general ledger accounts.

b. A format having amount columns for accounts payable, merchandise purchases, freight-in, supplies, and other debit amounts.

2-8. A check register and cash disbursements journal, though serving essentially the same purpose, generally have somewhat different formats.

a. Design a check register for use in a voucher system that employs disbursement vouchers. Include columns for the amount paid, payee, check number, disbursement voucher number, and date.

b. Design a cash disbursements journal that provides amount columns for cash (credit), accounts payable (debit), other debit amounts, and purchase discounts (credit). Include other needed columns.

2-9. Design a multiple-column sales journal that reflects all sales made by the Easyway Co., which maintains its records manually. The firm makes both credit and cash sales. It needs to record freight, which is prepaid, and a sales tax. Credit sales are to be entered from numbered sales invoices, and daily cash sales are entered in total from a cash register tape. Totals are to be posted to the appropriate general ledger accounts on a daily basis.

2-10. Design a customer's accounts receivable ledger record, post the following data, and reflect the balance after each posting:

Mary Anderson
1385 West Fairway Dr.
Dallas, TX 75262
Credit Limit: $1000

CREDIT SALES: $200 on May 5, posted from sales invoice S558.
$150 on June 16, posted from sales invoice S731.
$180 on August 12, posted from sales invoice S942.

RECEIPTS: $200 on May 13, posted from remittance advice CR318.
$100 on June 25, posted from remittance advice CR487.

The beginning balance on May 1 was zero.

2-11. Design a supplier's accounts payable ledger record, post the following data, and reflect the balance after each posting:

Larry's Supply Mart (No. 37285)
39873 South Plymouth Ave.
Cleveland, OH 44101
Terms: 2/10, n/30

CREDIT PURCHASES: $2000 on October 10, posted from invoice 2191.
$3400 on November 19, posted from invoice 3374.

DEBITS: $2000 on October 19, posted from check CD5832.
$1600 return of goods on November 23, posted from credit memo CM638.

The beginning balance on October 1 was zero.

2-12. Design a raw materials inventory ledger record for a manufacturing firm that maintains a perpetual inventory system. The firm desires to reflect balances both in terms of quantities and dollar amounts for each inventory item. The record should also contain columns that show quantities received from suppliers and issued to production, as well as the unit price of the item in each transaction.

Post data for item number M2389, connecting rod, which has a reorder point of 100 units. On March 1 the quantity on hand is 170 units; the unit price is $10. Issues for the month were as follows: 80 units on requisition I432 dated March 3, 100 units on requisition I476 dated March 14, 90 units on requisition I497 dated March 23, and 150 units on requisition I525 dated March 28. Receipts for the month, all at a unit price of $10, were as follows: 200 units on receiving report RR3462 dated March 10 and 200 units on receiving report RR3503 dated March 27.

2-13. Set up appropriate T accounts for each of the following situations. Show the effects of the given transaction data as they flow through both the general ledger and subsidiary ledgers, and compute the ending balances. Treat each part of the problem independently of the other parts. All beginning account balances are zero, except as follows: $5000 debit balance in the cash account, $200 balance in the account for Susan Pope, and $200 in the accounts receivable control account.

a. Sales of $550 to Paul Murphy, $730 to Sally Dawson, and $390 to Jose Quintero; cash receipts of $200 from Susan Pope (based on a previous sale), $400 from Sally Dawson, and $390 from Jose Quintero; sales return of $250 by Paul Murphy.

b. Purchases of $800 from Plentiful Providers and $660 from Sunny Services; cash disbursements of $660 to Sunny Services; purchase return of $360 to Plentiful Providers.

c. Payroll of $4800 (at gross), representing $1000 paid to Jim Tabor, $1000 to Nancy Omes, $800 to Dave Custer, $800 to Sam Brister, and $1200 to Jane With. Forty percent of each person's gross salary represents deductions. Jim and Nancy are salespersons, Dave and Sam are administrative assistants, and Jane is general manager.

2-14. Design the components of a payroll "one-write" system [i.e., a paycheck, employee earnings record (ledger), and payroll register (journal)]. Place them on the same sheet of paper, from top to bottom, in the order stated. The paycheck should appear the same as any check, except that it contains an earning statement or "stub" attached at the right of the check and separated by a perforation. The check is first to be completed manually by a payroll clerk. Then the clerk will enter data into provided spaces on the earnings statement. By means of carbons, this data will be copied onto the ledger and journal.

Use the following data to determine the needed columns on the forms; then enter these data onto the drawn forms: The Progressive Company pays Pamela V. Bush on check number 1243 for 44 hours worked during the pay period ending on April 14, 1989. The hourly rate is $8.50, with time and a half for all hours over 40. FICA is deducted from gross pay at a rate of 7.1 percent, and federal taxes are withheld at a rate of 14 percent. Other deductions amount to 20 percent of gross pay. (Include columns for employee name, ending date of period, gross pay, the various deductions noted, and net pay. Be sure to align the columns on all three forms.)

2-15. Bellevue Repair Service was organized by Charles Bellevue on August 1, 1988.[4] Following are its account balances, listed in random order, as of August 31. Assume that adjustments have already been made.

Advertising Expense	$ 600
Cash	8,500
Rent Expense	1,000
Service Trucks	28,800
Tax Expense	200
Accounts Receivable	9,600
Insurance Expense	460
Revenue from Repairs	44,000
Salaries and Wages Payable	2,600
Accounts Payable	3,700
C. Bellevue, Capital	55,000
C. Bellevue, Drawing	1,000

---

[4] This problem can be solved by using a microcomputer-based general ledger accounting package. Alternatively, a spreadsheet package can be used to portray the statements.

Accumulated Depreciation—Equipment	400
Accumulated Depreciation—Service Trucks	800
Utilities Expense	700
Miscellaneous Expense	540
Parts and Supplies on Hand	9,900
Prepaid Insurance	1,500
Depreciation Expense	1,200
Parts and Supplies Expense	6,700
Salaries and Wages Expense	11,800
Equipment	24,000

Required

a. Prepare a trial balance from the given account balances.

b. Prepare an income statement for the month of August and a balance sheet as of August 31.

2-16. Contronics Inc. is a large electronics-component manufacturer in San Antonio, Texas. It has grown substantially in the last four years. As the company has expanded its operations, the duties and responsibilities of the accounting department have also increased. The size of the controller's staff has increased, and the department has added more responsibility centers as the department has expanded.

Each responsibility center manager reports directly to William Smart, the company controller. An organization structure in which all subordinates report directly to a single supervisor is referred to as a flat organization. The organization chart presented represents the controllership function of Contronics Inc.

Each manager of a responsibility center supervises a moderate-sized staff and is responsible for undertaking the tasks assigned to the position to accomplish the designated objectives for the individual responsibility center. The managers depend on William Smart for direction in coordinating their separate activities.

Required

a. Identify and explain briefly how a flat organization structure, such as the one em-

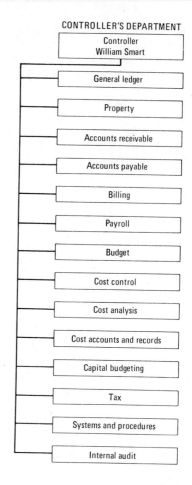

CONTROLLER'S DEPARTMENT

Controller
William Smart

General ledger

Property

Accounts receivable

Accounts payable

Billing

Payroll

Budget

Cost control

Cost analysis

Cost accounts and records

Capital budgeting

Tax

Systems and procedures

Internal audit

ployed by Contronics Inc. in its accounting department, might benefit downward and upward communication between the controller and his subordinates.

b. Identify and explain briefly the downward and upward communication problems that can result from the flat organization structure in Contronics' accounting department.

c. Redraw the organization chart of the controllership function to reflect sound organizational standards; add one or more staff units that should facilitate the communication process of Contronics' controllership function.

(*CMA adapted*)

2-17. Selected Small Firm (A Continuing Case) For the small firm you selected in Chapter 1 (see Problem 1-7), complete the following requirements.

a. A brief description of the firm in terms of its system characteristics.

b. A listing of the primary operations of the firm.

c. An organization chart.

d. A description of the processing of basic transactions through the accounting cycle, including copies of the components employed for one of the transactions and the key financial outputs.

3

Computer

Technology

Recognize the improvements to be gained by processing transactions with computer-based systems.

Identify the functions and components of various computer hardware, particularly processors, input devices, output devices, and storage devices.

Identify the functions and relative advantages of varied computer software, particularly systems software and applications software.

Distinguish between batch processing and online processing of transactions.

Describe current trends in computer hardware, software, and applications.

INTRODUCTION

Computers are essential ingredients in the accounting information system (AIS) of most modern firms. They do no more than manipulate data; nevertheless, computers exert tremendous influence over critically important areas of activity. Their financial impact is also enormous, since AIS costs may amount to as much as 10 percent of sales. This chapter examines the advantages of computer-based transaction processing over the manual processing of transactions. Then it surveys the array of computer hardware and software found in the typical AIS. Computer hardware are the devices, such as processors and terminals and printers, that are readily visible to users. Computer software are the sets of instructions, such as applications programs and operating systems, that guide the processing jobs and direct the hardware devices in computer systems. Finally it contrasts the principal modes of processing transactions in computer-based systems and manual systems, and then considers the trends in applying computers to business problems.

ADVANTAGES OF COMPUTER-BASED PROCESSING

What are the effects on transaction processing and the accounting cycle when one or more computers are installed in an AIS? On one hand, no major activities are added or deleted. The AIS still collects, processes, and stores data. It incorporates controls over the accuracy of data. It generates reports and other information. On the other hand, computerizing an AIS often changes the character of the components. Data may be collected by special devices. Few if any paper accounting records are employed. In some cases even source documents are eliminated. Many if not all of the processing steps are performed automatically. The outputs are neater, more varied in formats, and often more numerous. Additional controls are incorporated that enable the computer itself to check the accuracy of data.

More important than such surface changes, however, are the improvements in performance that computer technology provides:

1. Faster processing of transactions and other data.

2. Greater accuracy in computations and comparisons with data.

3. Lower cost of processing each transaction.

4. More timely preparation of reports and other outputs.

5. More concise storage of data, with greater accessibility when needed.

6. Larger range of choices for entering data and providing outputs.

7. Higher productivity for employees and managers, especially when they effectively use computers to aid in their routine (and also decision-making) responsibilities.

These improvements have caused computers to be utilized by an increasing number of firms for an ever-widening range of applications. Prime candidates for computerization take advantage of several of the improvements. Thus, high-volume accounting transaction processing applications are generally among the first to be computerized. Computerization enables large volumes of transactions to be processed more quickly, accurately, and inexpensively. Applications involving insurance policies, motor vehicle records, and veterans' records have also been computerized at an early stage. Such applications involve huge quantities of data that need to be stored and accessed frequently by clerks and managers, as in strategic planning applications. Other applications that are ideally suited to computerization include those that involve

1. Extensive manipulation and analysis of data, as in sales analysis applications.

2. Continuous monitoring of processes and timely preparation of reports, as in inventory control and quality control applications.

3. Complex and flexible interactions between decision models and data bases and managers, as in strategic planning applications.

Suitable tasks to be performed manually	Suitable tasks to be performed by computer
Processing exceptional and infrequently occurring transactions	Collecting and processing large volumes of routine transactions
Setting objectives and making policies involving considerable judgment	Storing large quantities of data and information
Finding new problems that need solutions	Monitoring and controlling continuous processes
Supervising employees	Answering specific inquiries based on stored data
Fostering social communications (i.e., grapevine)	Preparing complex analyses and extensive reports
Making complex strategic decisions	Helping managers to gather data and understand the relationships concerning all types of decisions

FIGURE 3-1 Suitable tasks to be performed by manual and computer-based information systems.

Figure 3-1 compares the tasks that are more suitably performed manually with those more suitably performed by computers.

COMPUTER HARDWARE

The various mechanisms and devices that collectively compose a computer system are called **computer hardware.** Figure 3-2 lists a variety of hardware that may be found in present-day computer systems. A specific collection of hardware comprising one particular computer system is known as a **hardware configuration.** For instance, a hardware configuration may consist of a mainframe processor, terminal, printer, and magnetic disk.

Our survey in this chapter will span most of the processors, input/output devices, and storage devices/media identified in Figure 3-2. (However, data communications devices are deferred to Chapter 13.) The main purpose of this survey is to review the principal categories of hardware and their functions in order to recall the options available to systems designers and users. It is strongly suggested that you refer to one of the many available textbooks on computer fundamentals for photographs and working details.

Processors

Basic Units The heart of a computer is its **processor,** which consists of a control unit, an arithmetic-logic unit, and a primary storage unit. These basic units, also collectively known as the **central processing unit (CPU),** are linked to each other and to input and output units. Figure 3-3 shows these linkages in terms of flows of data, information, and control.

The **control unit** directs and coordinates the actions of all the other units. It instructs (1), the input unit concerning what data to enter and when, (2) the

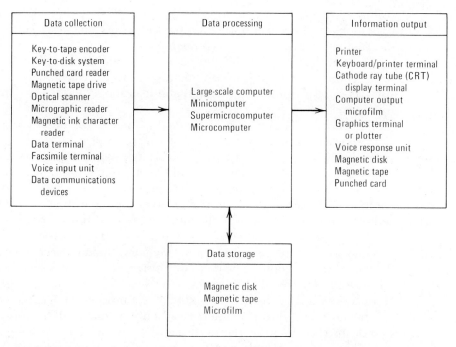

FIGURE 3-2 Hardware and storage media used in modern computer-based information systems.

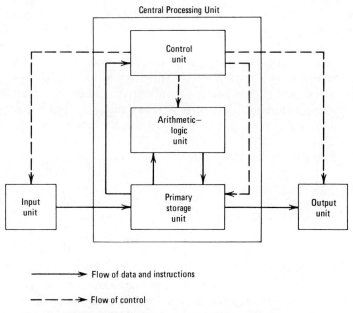

FIGURE 3-3 Major units of a computer.

primary storage unit where to store the data, (3) the arithmetic-logic unit what operations to perform and where to put the results, and (4) the output unit what information to provide on which medium.

The **arithmetic-logic unit** performs all operations specified by the control unit. As the name implies, these operations include calculations (e.g., addition, subtraction, multiplication, division) and logical operations (e.g., comparison of numbers).

The **primary storage unit,** also called main memory, serves as a respository. Data received from input devices, from instructions in computer software, and from arithmetic-logic operations are all brought together (at least temporarily) in this unit. Each item of data is stored at a specific location having a unique address. This unit also provides the required arena in which instructions from computer software are executed. The larger the capacity of the primary storage unit, the more easily it can perform these assigned functions.

Most present-day primary storage units contain two basic types of memory: random access memory and read-only memory. **Random access memory (RAM)** is changeable; it allows new data and instructions to be stored and retrieved. Thus, RAM enables the functions previously described to be performed. The term *random access* refers to the ability of the processor to access any address in the memory in a direct manner. **Read-only memory (ROM)** only allows data and/or instructions to be retrieved (i.e., read from). It is unchangeable; it does not allow new data and/or instructions to be stored. Thus, ROM cannot be altered by users or programmers. Its contents usually consist of **microprograms,** also called microcodes or firmware, that are permanently fixed ("burned" or "hardwired") on a silicon chip by the computer manufacturer. These microprograms can be executed more quickly than instructions that are executed in RAM. They also improve security and reliability, which result from their unchangeable nature.

Various technologies have been tapped in the construction of primary storage during the computer era. Magnetic cores, which are tiny ferrite rings that can be magnetized in two opposite directions, were principally used in earlier decades. Semiconductors, which are on-off circuits mounted on silicon chips, are currently in wide use. They are smaller and have faster access times than magnetic cores, and their costs are competitive. Other technologies will in time replace semiconductors. Two prospects are magnetic bubble and charge-coupled technologies.

Key Processor Measures Processors may be specified by such indicators as

1. Processing speed.
2. Primary storage capacity.
3. Word size.

Processing speed may be measured in either of two ways. It may be measured by the cycle time (i.e., the time required to execute a typical instruction). Cycle time may range from a fraction of a **millisecond** (one-thousandth of a second) for a relatively slow processor to a **nanosecond** (one-billionth of a second) or less for a fast processor. Processing speed may also be measured by the number of instructions processed during a period of time. A widely used measure is **million instructions per second (MIPS).**

Processing speed is affected by such factors as (1) **access time,** which is the time required to retrieve data from primary storage for processing; (2) **execution time,** which is the time required to perform a single computation; and (3) **transfer rate,** which is the speed that data can be moved from one place to another within primary storage, or from a secondary storage medium to primary storage.

Primary storage capacity is the quantity of data that can be stored in the primary storage unit. The basic unit of data is the binary digit, or bit. A **bit** can have a value (state) of either zero or one. Bits in turn are combined in groups of eight to form **bytes,** which are used to represent characters. The primary storage capacity for processors is typically measured and expressed in **kilobytes** (thousands of bytes) or **megabytes** (millions of bytes).

Word size is the number of bits that can be addressed (treated as a unit) by the processor and handled in a single operation. It is typically equal to one or more bytes. Thus, processors may be described as 8-bit processors, 16-bit processors, 32-bit processors, and so forth.

Hierarchy of Sizes Processors may be grouped according to the previously mentioned measures of processing speed, primary storage capacity, and word size. Although a number of groups may be noted, the three most clearly defined categories—in terms of size and power—are

1. Mainframes.

2. Minicomputers.

3. Microcomputers.

Mainframes are the large-scale processors. They often serve as the centers of complex configurations or as the flagships of computer networks. Processors in this category range in processing speeds from a few MIPS to several hundred MIPS. (Cycle times range from about 100 nanoseconds to a few nanoseconds.) Their primary storage capacities may reach a dozen or more megabytes, whereas their word sizes are typically 64 bits or greater.

Minicomputers are the medium scale processors. Although smaller than most mainframes, they can accommodate multiple users and can even control networks of microcomputers. Minicomputers provide processing speeds of several MIPS, primary storage capacities of a dozen megabytes or more, and word sizes of 32 bits.

Microcomputers are the small scale processors, although they are as powerful as the minicomputers and even the mainframes of yesteryear. They are suitable as the sole computers in small firms and as key elements in computer networks of large and medium-sized firms. Microcomputers have been improved so rapidly that any statement concerning them is likely to soon be out of date. Nevertheless, they tend to provide processing speeds of up to one MIPS or more, primary storage capacities of 640 kilobytes or more, and word sizes of 16 or 32 bits. An appendix at the end of this textbook discusses microcomputers in detail.

Processor Enhancements Mainframes and minicomputers typically appear in complex hardware configurations and provide services to a multitude of users. They therefore may require various special features that enhance their performances. Such enhancing features include

1. Overlapping.

2. Multiprogramming.

3. Virtual storage.

4. Parallel processing.

5. Multiprocessing.

6. Time-sharing.

These enhancements are generally achieved through cooperative designs of the processors and their operating systems.

Overlapping enables a computer system to perform processing, input, and output operations simultaneously. This feature improves the computer system's throughput (i.e., the quantity of work processed in a given period of time). Without overlapping, a processor remains idle during much of the time, since it is waiting for data to be entered or for information to be outputted. Overlapping involves the use of devices known as channels, controllers, and buffers, which serve as interfaces between a processor and connected input/output devices.

Multiprogramming enables the processor to execute two or more programs (sets of instructions) concurrently. Each program is allowed to execute instructions for a short time, and then the next program in order takes its turn. This rotation continues for an individual program until it has executed all its instructions. When integrated with the overlapping feature, multiprogramming improves throughput. It also shortens the average turnaround time (the time between the start and finish of execution) for shorter jobs or applications. (Without multiprogramming, a computer system executes each program in the order received; thus, long programs tend to delay the completion of short programs.)

When several programs are being processed in primary storage concurrently, they need to be prevented from interfering with one other. A common approach is to divide primary storage into partitions, thereby providing boundary protection. By means of a technique known as **interleaved storage access,** each partition can be controlled separately. Thus, data may be accessed or retrieved from one partition while data are being entered into another partition.

Virtual storage involves a technique of program swapping that allows users to view primary storage as being virtually unlimited. By means of this feature, programs are divided into segments called **pages.** Pages are stored in secondary storage (such as magnetic disks) and moved into primary storage only when needed for execution. Virtual storage is particularly useful when very lengthy programs are to be processed and when multiprogramming is employed. It allows the processor to be used more efficiently. Figure 3-4 illustrates the technique.

Parallel processing or operation is the simultaneous execution of two or more

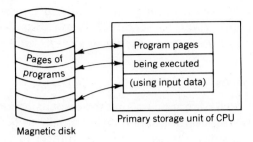

FIGURE 3-4 Virtual storage technique.

programs or program segments within a single processor. This feature represents an improvement over multiprogramming (in which two or more programs are processed in an alternating fashion) and serial processing (in which a single program's instructions are processed one after the other throughout the program). Although only a few large present-day processors can perform parallel processing, this productivity-enhancing feature is expected to become increasingly common.

Multiprocessing, like parallel processing, enables two or more programs or program segments to be processed simultaneously. However, multiprocessing involves the use of two or more processors that share a common primary storage unit. Thus, it is a relatively expensive configuration. On the other hand, multiprocessed processors often provide "built-in backup." If one of the processors fails, the other can take over the processing task. Figure 3-5 shows a multiprocessing system.

Time-sharing involves the concurrent servicing of two or more users, each of whom is directly connected to the processor via an input device. Users are allotted specific intervals of time, called time slices. At the end of each interval, a hardware clock interrupts a user's work so that the next user in order can begin or resume. Because the time slices are very short, each user views the computer system as serving him or her alone. This feature therefore provides relatively fast response times to users, thereby keeping them happy (or at least pacified). As in

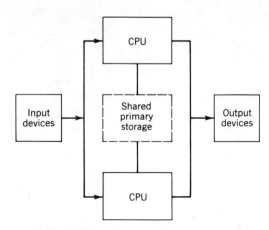

FIGURE 3-5 A multiprocessing system.

the case of virtual storage, time-sharing is typically employed in company with the multiprogramming feature. It is also a very desirable feature of systems that provide commercial computing services to subscriber firms.

Input/Output Devices

A modern computer system can accept data from a wide variety of devices and generate output information on an equally wide variety of devices. When these devices are directly connected to a processor, they are designated as **online** devices. Figure 3-6 portrays typical online input/output devices, together with three types of online storage media. Devices not directly connected to a processor are called **offline** devices. For instance, the key-to-tape encoder listed in Figure 3-2 is an offline input device.

Terminals **Terminals** are online devices widely used for both input and output operations. Terminals enable users to interact directly with the processing sys-

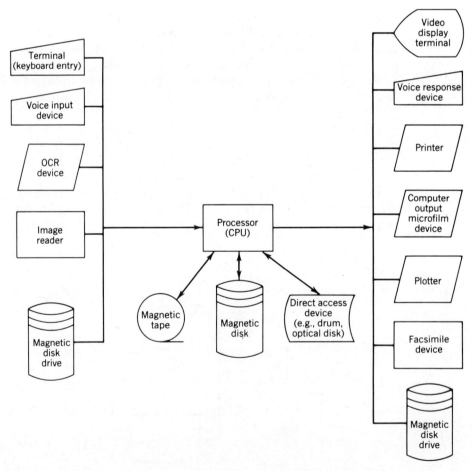

FIGURE 3-6 Online input/output devices and storage media.

tem, in most cases; they also allow data to be entered by a variety of methods and information to be obtained in a variety of modes.

Keyboard/printer terminals, also called teleprinters, have typewriterlike keyboards for entering data, such as numbers and text. Both the entered data and the output information are printed on paper by means of printer mechanisms that are integrated into the terminals. Entering data via a keyboard is a slow process, as is the printing of the outputs. Thus, these terminals are best suited to low-volume users, such as professional employees and managers. Its main advantage is that it provides hard copy outputs (i.e., outputs on a permanent medium, such as paper).

Video display terminals, also known as cathode ray tube (CRT) terminals, employ keyboards of a similar type to those used with keyboard/printer terminals. Instead of printer mechanisms, however, video display terminals incorporate screens that display information in soft copy form. Soft copy displays can be generated much faster than the hard copy printouts provided by keyboard/printer terminals. Another advantage of this type of terminal is that special models allow data to be entered by such alternative methods as (1) a light pen that "writes" on a light-sensitive screen, (2) a fingertip touch that makes selections on a touch-sensitive screen, (3) a pen pad that accepts handwriting via a stylus, and (4) a mouse that gives commands through movements and taps. These alternative methods of data entry render the video display terminal more user-friendly and tolerant of varied forms of data. The greatest drawback of this type of terminal is that a separate printer is needed if hard copy outputs are desired.

Audio input/response terminals, also called voice terminals, allow voice interactions with computer systems. These terminals usually function in conjunction with telephones to accept voice commands. For instance, a bank depositor can orally request the current balance in his or her account, or a retail store clerk can request the credit status of a customer. Voice terminals also usually provide answers to such inquiries orally. At the present time these terminals are limited to relatively brief inquiries and commands. In the future, however, they should be suited to more extensive data entry applications.

Terminals range widely in capabilities and functions, as the aforementioned types suggest. At one end of the spectrum are **intelligent terminals,** which can process and store data to a limited degree. In effect, they can serve as microcomputers as well as terminals. Intelligent terminals are often used in transaction processing systems where they may edit input data and perform tasks such as checking the credit of customers who place sales orders. At the opposite end of the spectrum are **"dumb" terminals** that simply accept data and produce outputs. Most terminals, such as those described in the following paragraphs, fall somewhere between these two extremes.

Computer-readable Devices When feasible, input data should be captured directly onto computer-readable media at the point where the transactions originate. This approach, known as **source data automation (SDA),** captures transaction data at the earliest possible time. It also avoids the need to transcribe data from source documents before processing. Therefore, SDA permits more timely processing while reducing input errors and data entry costs.

Computer-readable devices employed in SDA may be of either the online type or offline type. Online computer-readable devices are in effect highly specialized single function terminals. They include

1. **Data collection terminals,** such as those used at production workstations and in the vehicles of police officers, route salespersons, construction supervisors, and delivery persons. For instance, a data collection terminal at a production workstation will typically be used to collect labor hours worked on production jobs. The data may be entered by alternate methods. Thus, the job number may be keyed in, the number of the employee performing the labor may be entered by inserting the employee's badge into a reader slot in the device, and the time may be entered by pressing a special function lever.

2. **Point-of-sale terminals,** such as those used at checkout counters in retail stores. The method of entering sales data may be keying the item numbers of the merchandise and sales quantities via keyboards on the terminals. More likely, however, the data entry method involves the use of an optical scanner (either a hand-held wand or a fixed device) that "reads" the bar codes or price tags on the merchandise items.

3. **Automated teller machines,** such as those found mounted outside banks.

4. **Reservations terminals,** such as those found in airports and motels.

Offline computer-readable input devices include optical character recognition devices and magnetic ink character recognition devices. (Thus, devices based on optical character recognition can be used in offline as well as online modes.) Both types of offline devices are well suited for the entry of data from large batches of documents.

Optical character recognition (OCR) devices read characters from hard copy documents. The characters may be typed, computer-generated, or even printed by hand. The OCR devices are particularly suited to retail stores, insurance companies, public utilities, and other types of firms that handle numerous documents. For example, they are universally employed to read data from turnaround documents, such as the preprinted portions of bills that retail credit customers return with their payments. Less sophisticated OCR devices, such as those used in grading objective examinations, are able to sense marks entered in pencil. The main drawback to OCR devices is that current models are limited in the types of character fonts they can read and paper they can handle; imperfections in written characters and paper cause documents to be rejected and hence to require reprocessing.

Magnetic ink character recognition (MICR) devices read characters from documents which are encoded with magnetic ink. The MICR devices are universally employed at bank processing centers to read checks into computer systems. These devices have a much lower rejection rate than OCR devices.

Specialized Keying Input Devices Three devices that are designed for continuous keying operations are card punch machines, key-to-tape encoders, and key-to-disk systems. These offline devices key data onto storage media from which the data are later read into a computer system. Thus, they may be described as data preparation devices. They are particularly useful when large volumes of input data are to be prepared for processing.

Card punch machines, also known as keypunches or data recorders, transcribe data from source documents onto punched cards. Then these punched cards are entered into the computer system via card reader devices. Although punched cards were once the prime method of entering data for computer processing, card punch machines are seldom used at the present time. They are relatively inefficient as compared to alternative devices, and punched cards present significant disadvantages in most applications.

Key-to-tape encoders transcribe data onto magnetic tapes. Usually they include CRT screens so that the data entry clerks can visually view the data being transcribed. Key-to-tape encoders may be used as individual units or may be grouped into key-to-tape systems involving several units or stations and small computer processors. Key-to-tape systems partially validate transaction data as they are being keyed in, although the degree of validation varies with the model.

Key-to-disk systems consist of a number of keyboard stations at which data entry clerks prepare data for entry. Although similar to a key-to-tape system, a key-to-disk system may be used to transcribe transaction data onto magnetic tapes or magnetic disks. It also generally includes more stations and performs more validating and editing steps. Transactions containing input data errors are shunted into an error correction procedure. Thus, a key-to-disk system tends to enhance the productivity of the data preparation activity. However, this type of input system tends to be more costly per station employed. Figure 3-7 exhibits the steps performed at one station of a key-to-disk system that records data on magnetic tape (the round symbol). As the figure shows, the system acquires its name from the fact that the data are temporarily stored on a magnetic disk (the cylindrical symbol) while being validated.

Other Input Devices As already noted, key-to-tape and key-to-disk systems transcribe data onto magnetic tapes or magnetic disks. Also, data handled by OCR devices, MICR devices, and card readers are often transcribed onto magnetic tapes or disks, rather than being directly entered into computer systems. (Although such transcriptions are added steps, they can be worthwhile; magnetic tapes and magnetic disks allow the data to be entered into computer systems at much faster speeds.) Thus, magnetic tape drives and magnetic disk drives are frequently needed input devices.

Still another type of input device is the **image reader.** One version of the image reader involves the use of a microfilm recorder, which photographs data from documents onto microfilm. The microfilm form is then either read into a computer system for processing or displayed with the assistance of the computer system. A second version involves a facsimile device, which scans drawings, photographs, or handwritten documents and transmits the images for viewing on output screens.

Printers Printers are output devices that provide hard copy on paper stock. Two categories of printers are available: **impact printers,** which print one line or

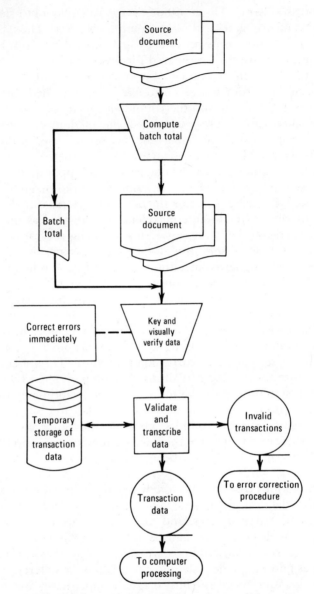

FIGURE 3-7 A station within a key-to-disk system. (*Note:* The symbols used are explained later in this chapter.)

character at a time, and **nonimpact printers,** which may print an entire page at a time. Nonimpact printers—which include such types as thermal, electrostatic, laser xerographic, and ink jet—are gaining in popularity. In addition to performing at high-speeds, they operate quietly and can produce high-quality graphics as well as text and tables.

Computer Output Microfilm Devices Computer output microfilm (COM) devices provide outputs on various microfilm forms. As in the case of the image reader previously described, a COM device produces a microfilm form. Instead of working from hard copy documents, however, the COM device transfers data from the primary storage unit of a processor or from a secondary storage medium, such as magnetic tape. The resulting microfilm form may then be displayed on microfilm readers (viewers) or retrieval terminals. The COM device provides two significant advantages. First, it generates output at an extremely high rate of speed, perhaps exceeding 32,000 lines per minute. Second, the microfilm form is very compact and hence relatively inexpensive to produce and store.

Plotters **Plotters** are devices that convert coded digital data into designs or graphs on paper. Plotters may use either mechanical pens or electrostatics to produce the outputs.

Other Output Devices In addition to printers and COM devices and plotters, information can be outputted from computers via terminals, voice response units, facsimile devices, card punch units, and telecommunications devices. Information can also be transferred onto magnetic tapes or disks, either for storage as a part of the data base or for use in spooling. (**Spooling** means to store information temporarily on a secondary storage medium, and then to print it off-line onto hard copy at a later, convenient time.)

Storage Devices and Media

As a result of its limited capacity, the primary storage unit cannot store most of the data needed by a computer system. Therefore, secondary storage devices are usually attached online to the processor to provide additional storage capacity. Stored on the media controlled by such devices are files of data for use in processing and for preparing reports and answering inquiries. When needed for processing or for outputs, the data are transferred from their secondary storage locations to the primary storage unit.

Among the secondary storage magnetic media employed by current computer systems are magnetic tapes, magnetic disks, magnetic drums, magnetic cards, and data cells. Only the first two media listed are in wide use today.

Magnetic Tapes **Magnetic tapes** are stored on reels or in cartridges. They store data as magnetized bits, which are arrayed along channels or tracks to form bytes (i.e., coded characters). Nine-track tapes are in most common use, although seven-track tapes are also available. One of the tracks provides bit positions for check or **parity bits,** bits that enable the computer system to check the accuracy of the characters stored and transferred.

Tapes can hold huge quantities of data. For instance, a typical reel of tape, measuring ½ in. by 2400 ft., may contain several thousand characters of data per inch of length and perhaps as many as a billion characters of data in total. Tape cartridges may be clustered in mass storage systems to contain over a trillion characters in total.

In addition to their huge storage capacities, magnetic tapes have other advantages:

1. Fast transfer rates, which allow data to be moved within computer systems at speeds of several hundred thousand characters per second to over one million characters per second.

2. Relatively low cost, as compared to magnetic disks.

3. Reliability, with very few errors or losses of data occurring during transfers.

4. Reusability, since data can be erased or written over many times. (However, magnetic tape follows the principle of **nondestructive readout** in which stored data can be "read" into the primary storage unit any number of times without the reading action causing the data on the tape to be erased.)

5. Portability, since magnetic tape reels or cartridges can be easily moved or mailed to other locations.

These advantages cause magnetic tapes to be frequently used in applications involving large volumes of transactions and large numbers of records in master files. For instance, magnetic tape may be suitable for the processing of payroll transactions in many firms. It is also often used to store duplicate files that provide copies or "backups" to active files stored on other media. These backup files may be transported, for reasons of security, to other locations.

The main drawback of a magnetic tape is that it is strictly a sequential medium. That is, a file on a magnetic tape must be scanned from the beginning in order to access, update, add, or delete individual records. A secondary drawback is the need to mount tape reels before processing and to remove them thereafter. This activity is not only time-consuming, but it is also subject to the possibility that undesired tapes will erroneously be mounted.

Magnetic Disks Magnetic disks represent the principal current alternative to magnetic tapes. They are growing in popularity and supplanting magnetic tapes in many applications. Not only do they offer most of the advantages of magnetic tapes, but magnetic disks also provide the highly important additional feature of **direct access.** That is, any record of data stored on a magnetic disk can be accessed directly and transferred immediately to the primary storage unit. This direct access feature is made possible by means of permanent addresses assigned to all locations on a magnetic disk where data may be stored.

Most magnetic disks are assembled into stacks of metal platters, called disk packs. Locations on a disk pack are physically accessed by means of an access mechanism containing read/write heads, which move back and forth while the disk pack rotates at a high speed. Each recording surface is divided into hundreds of concentric tracks. In turn, the corresponding tracks of all the disk recording surfaces of a disk pack form a **cylinder.** Related data are often stored on the tracks comprising a cylinder in order to reduce the access times. Figure 3-8 illustrates these features.

Certain types of disk packs are fixed; others are removable. Fixed disk packs are continuously online; consequently, the inconvenience of removing and mounting is avoided.

Magnetic disks have three drawbacks. They are several times more expensive than magnetic tapes having equal storage capacities. They are less portable than

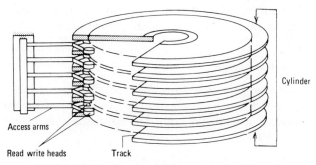

FIGURE 3-8 Features of a magnetic disk pack.

tapes. Finally, data stored on magnetic disks are often lost through **"destructive read-in"**; for instance, data entered to update the balance of an account will cause the previous balance to be wiped out. To avoid the loss of data (e.g., the previous balance), special data backup procedures are needed.

Other Storage Media Nonmagnetic storage media include optical disks, microfilm, and punched cards. **Optical disks,** also called laser disks, are high-density rigid glass substrates that can store large quantities of data (500 million characters or more per disk). Current technology permits optical disks to perform in **WORM** fashion. That is, they can accept data Written only Once, but they allow the written data to be Read Many times. Thus, they are most suited to the storage of archival records and reference data. Microfilm forms, such as microfiche, provide a more traditional substitute for the same type of data. **Microfilm** is very popular because of its low cost, although COM devices can be fairly expensive. Also, microfilm forms are extremely compact and portable. **Punched cards** were popular in earlier decades. However, they are seldom used today except when they can serve as turnaround documents. (A **turnaround document** is an output document that is returned to the system as an input document. For example, bills can be mailed to customers in punched card form, which may be later returned to the billing firm with payments.) Punched cards are quite bulky, can contain relatively little data, and cannot be read by input devices very rapidly.

Hardware Trends

Computer hardware has dramatically improved over the past four decades in the following respects.

- **Size.** An early computer the size of a moving van had less computing power than a present-day microchip the size of half a dime.

- **Speed.** The time required to process a single computation has dropped from 20 milliseconds to 100 nanoseconds.

- **Storage capacity.** The primary storage unit has grown from capacities of a few thousand characters to capacities (for larger computers) of more than 10 million characters.

- **Reliability.** The earliest computers frequently made errors, whereas present-day computers are essentially error-free.

- **Cost.** Processing costs per million instructions have declined from over $1 to less than a cent.

- **Options.** The early computers provided very few choices with regard to processing features, input/output devices, and secondary storage devices and media; present-day computers provide the numerous choices identified in this chapter.

Hardware trends should continue in the same direction for all the aforementioned facets. Even reliability is likely to improve. Diagnostic devices are expected to be incorporated into future computer models; when an element is about to fail, the diagnostic device will signal the user that the element should be replaced.

COMPUTER SOFTWARE

The term **computer software** describes the programs, routines, and sets of instructions that guide the hardware of a computer system in performing its varied operations and functions. As Figure 3-9 shows, specific uses of software are developed by means of computer languages. Software development may be

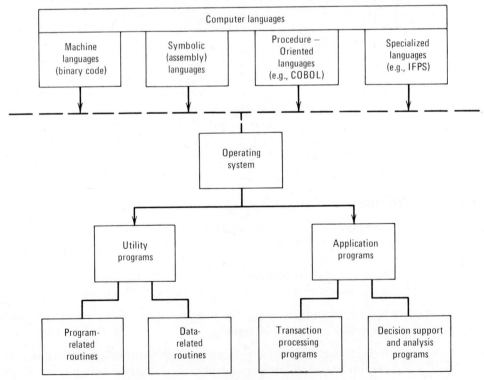

FIGURE 3-9 An overview of computer software.

undertaken by the using firm, in which case it is labeled *customized software.* Alternatively, software may be developed by software firms or computer manufacturers. In this latter case, it is termed *packaged* or *canned software.* Our survey of computer software includes the languages as well as the various types of developed software, whether customized or packaged.

Computer Programming Languages

Like computer processors, computer programming languages have evolved through four generations. The first generation consists solely of machine languages, the second of symbolic languages, the third of procedure-oriented languages, and the fourth of problem-oriented languages. Although languages from all four generations are still being utilized, the first generation was introduced at the advent of computer technology; the fourth generation has come into being during the 1970s and 1980s.

First Generation Each type of computer follows (executes) instructions expressed in a machine language that is unique to it. **Machine languages** employ a binary code composed of zeros and ones. As can be imagined, developing programs in machine language is a slow, tedious, and error-prone task. Thus, human programmers prefer to develop (write) programs in a higher-level language, which is then converted into machine language by special software.

Second Generation The higher-level languages closest to machine language are known as **symbolic** (assembler) **languages.** They utilize mnemonic codes for instructions and even symbolic codes for storage locations. For instance, the instruction to add numbers may be represented by ADD rather than 010, and the location where the total is stored may be named SUM. Since these codes are easier to remember, programs can be written faster and with fewer errors.

Third Generation Still higher-level languages are known as **procedure-oriented languages.** They are also called compiler languages, since compilers are needed to translate programs written in the languages (source programs) into machine-language programs (object programs). Examples of procedure-oriented languages are BASIC, COBOL, FORTRAN, and Pascal. Procedure-oriented languages enable instructions to be expressed by algebraic or Englishlike statements. Thus, they are simpler to learn and easier to use than symbolic languages. COBOL (COmmon Business Oriented Language) is of particular interest to accountants, since it is suited to transaction processing applications, relatively easy to understand, and well documented. However, COBOL, like all procedure-oriented languages, is less efficient and hence slower to execute than symbolic languages.

Fourth Generation Although procedure-oriented languages are still in widespread use, they are being challenged by fourth generation languages and specialized software packages (4GLs). These **problem-oriented languages** are powerful software tools that function at even higher levels than the procedure-oriented languages. In fact, they are designed to be so user-friendly that users having no previous exposure to computers can employ them effectively. For instance, they do not require statements to be arranged procedurally. System-related applications for which the 4GLs are best suited include systems development, financial modeling, spreadsheet analysis, and data base management. Examples of 4GLs are FOCUS, Interactive Financial Planning System (IFPS), Lotus 1-2-3, and dBase IV.[1]

Operating Systems

The software that manages and coordinates the various hardware components and all assorted programs of a computer system is called the **operating system.** Also known as the supervisor or executive, the operating system is a set of component programs usually written in symbolic language. These component programs perform tasks such as (1) regulating the actions of the input/output units and CPU, (2) controlling the movement of data and programs within and between the primary and secondary storage units, (3) scheduling data processing jobs involving the use of utility and application programs, (4) maintaining logs and statistics pertaining to jobs and equipment performance, and (5) communicating with the human operator via a computer console.

Application Programs

The software devoted to specific data and information processing tasks is known as **application software.** For instance, a set of application programs may pertain to sales transactions. One program might verify and edit sales data when entering for processing. A second program may update the accounts receivable and inventory files to reflect the sales data. A third program may print the sales invoices and related reports. Other application programs pertain to information processing activities such as sales forecasting, cash budgeting, and inventory control. Still other application programs broadly aid such activities as word processing and financial analysis. For example, a very popular type of application software is the electronic spreadsheet. In earlier decades many application programs were written by personnel in the firms that were to use the programs. Currently, however, most programs are prepared by commercial firms.

Utility Programs

Utility programs perform routines that are necessary to the functioning of a computer system and the applications that it executes. They are normally written in symbolic languages, since they are expected to operate efficiently on a particular computer system. One category of utility programs is data oriented. Examples include routines that transfer data from one storage medium to another, sort data, and manage data within a data base. In some cases utility routines are incorporated into application programs. Another category of utility programs

---

[1] FOCUS is a registered trademark of Information Builders; IFPS is a registered trademark of Execucom Systems Corporation; LOTUS 1-2-3 is a registered trademark of Lotus Development Corporation; dBase IV is a registered trademark of Ashton-Tate Corporation.

may be described as program oriented. Examples are diagnostic routines, which help programmers to find programming errors, and compilers, which were identified earlier.

Computer Software Trends

Software has become more user-friendly, commercialized, and specialized. As a consequence, users are developing new programs to meet their needs. Programmers are spending less time writing programs from "scratch"; instead, they are often involved in modifying software purchased from sources outside their firms. Users, such as accountants, are able to obtain a variety of software packages that are designed to suit their particular needs. In addition to general ledger and transaction processing packages, these specialized packages include spreadsheet, financial modeling, and audit-assist packages. Most of these packages are compatible with computer processors provided by a variety of hardware manufacturers.

Software has assumed an increasingly important role in the eyes of management and information systems specialists. Thus, the overall cost for software in the typical current computer system is larger than the overall cost for hardware. These comparative costs are the reverse of what they were in the earlier days of the computer age.

COMPUTER-BASED APPLICATIONS

Applications have been mentioned several times in this chapter, most notably with respect to the software that provides the instructions to computer systems. Computer-based applications have changed significantly in certain respects since General Electric pioneered the first large-scale business-oriented application in 1954. For instance, punched cards have been largely replaced by magnetic media. In other respects applications exhibit very similar characteristics to those of 35 years ago. Thus, source documents, printed outputs, and audit trails are features of most current business applications.

An understanding of computer-based business applications begins with transaction processing. Two contrasting approaches are available for processing transactions: batch processing and online processing. This section compares these alternative approaches with one other and with manual-based transaction processing. As in Chapter 2, only those steps that are encompassed by the accounting cycle will be traced.

Computer-based Batch Transaction Processing

Batch processing involves the periodic processing of data in like groups. Transactions are collected and stored temporarily until a sufficiently large batch is accumulated or until a designated time arrives. The time spans between successive processings are called **processing cycles.**

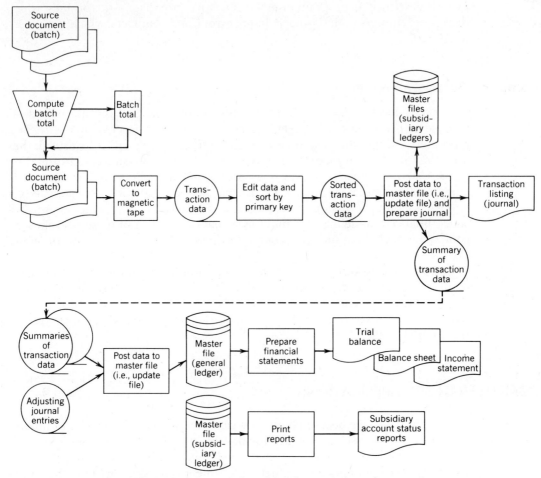

FIGURE 3-10 Computer-based batch processing of transactions.

Sequential Access Batch Processing Application Figure 3-10 diagrams the steps in a typical application of batch processing to a basic type of transaction, such as sales. These steps form several groupings: (1) preparing input data, (2) entering and arranging input data for processing, (3) processing data against records contained in master files and arranged in sequential order, and (4) generating printed outputs.

The four steps are discussed in the following paragraphs. To aid you in relating the diagram (called a system flowchart) to the discussion, Figure 3-11 identifies the meanings of the symbols. Also included are additional symbols that appear in a diagram later in this chapter. A complete collection of system flowcharting symbols is provided in Figure 6-15 in Chapter 6.

Preparation of input data consists of accumulating the source documents into a batch and then computing one or more batch totals of critical data items (e.g., sales amounts). Next the transaction data are transcribed or converted by an offline device. Since the data are shown in the figure as being converted to

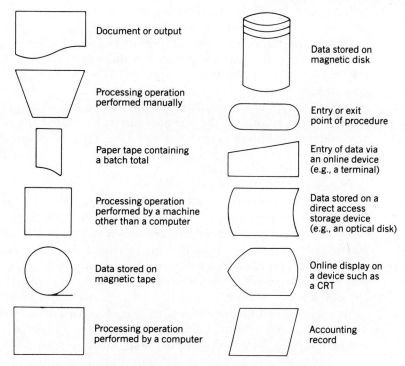

Document or output

Data stored on
magnetic disk

Processing operation
performed manually

Entry or exit
point of procedure

Paper tape containing
a batch total

Entry of data via
an online device
(e.g., a terminal)

Processing operation
performed by a machine
other than a computer

Data stored on a
direct access
storage device
(e.g., an optical disk)

Data stored on
magnetic tape

Online display on
a device such as
a CRT

Processing operation
performed by a computer

Accounting
record

FIGURE 3-11 Selected system flowcharting symbols.

magnetic tape, the device could be a key-to-tape encoder or a key-to-disk system. As noted earlier, the stored data must conform to the physical features of the storage medium. In the case of magnetic tape, the data items converted from each source document, such as customer number and name and sales amount, are collected together and arranged one following the other to form a **record.** In turn, records are formed into **blocks,** and the blocks are accumulated to comprise the transaction file. An **interblock gap (IBG)** at each end of a block separates the block from its neighbors. (The processing program thereby recognizes that the block is the physical unit of data that it is to transfer into primary storage for processing.) At the beginning of the file, the conversion device places a special record, called the **header label,** to identify the file. At the end of the file is placed a **trailer label.** An end-of-file mark is also inserted, since the file may not occupy an entire reel of tape. Figure 3-12 depicts these file features.

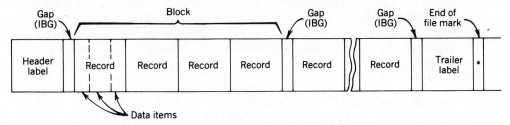

FIGURE 3-12 The composition of a transaction or master file stored on magnetic tape.

Data entry consists of transferring the data from the input medium into the processor via an input device, such as a magnetic tape drive. Upon being entered the transaction data are validated and edited by an edit routine of the application program. Next the data are sorted into the same order as the records in the master file that is to be posted (updated). This sorting step is performed by reference to a sorting key, which is the data item that reflects the sequential order. In the case of sales transactions the **sorting key** is likely to be the customer number, since records in the accounts receivable master file (subsidiary ledger) are arranged according to customer numbers. Often the sorting key is the same as the **primary key,** which is the data item that is designated to identify particular records uniquely within a file.

Processing steps follow these preparatory and data entry steps. A critical step in transaction processing is to update the master files. Within the accounting cycle the two master files of concern are the subsidiary ledger (if any) and the general ledger. These master files are shown in Figure 3-10 as being stored on magnetic disks. Because the records are arranged sequentially, the files are called **sequential access files.** The subsidiary ledger is updated first, since the transaction records have been sorted into the same sequential order. In updating this sequential access master file, the updating routine starts at the first record and reads every record in the file, adjusting each record affected by a transaction. Two by-products of this updating step are a printed journal of transactions and a magnetic tape of the totals posted to the subsidiary ledger. These totals should be compared to the batch totals created at the beginning of this procedure.[2] Periodically the daily totals from the summary tapes are combined with those from other transactions and with adjusting journal entries, sorted by general ledger account numbers, and posted to the general ledger.

A variety of outputs are typically generated, in addition to the transaction journal. Periodically the account balances from the general ledger are arranged to produce trial balances, balance sheets, and income statements. Also, status reports of the subsidiary ledger, such as an accounts receivable aging report, are generated. These outputs are provided as needed by users, whether weekly, monthly, or at the end of each accounting period.

Contrasts with Manual Processing Batch processing with sequential access files is the traditional approach for handling transactions. It is not surprising, therefore, that this computer-based approach has significant similarities to batch processing by manual means. The outputs tend to reflect the same content and printed formats, the processing cycles tend to be identical in length, and most of the steps have the same purposes. Each transaction processing application stands apart from other applications and has its own files and outputs. In other words, it is relatively unintegrated with the remaining transaction processing systems. However, there are significant differences. Processing steps are performed much more rapidly and accurately. The input data and files are stored on magnetic

---

[2] For the sake of simplicity, certain steps are not shown in this flowchart. For instance, this comparison step is omitted, as is the filing of the source documents. Chapter 6 describes the proper manner of showing such steps in a system flowchart.

media and thus not directly readable by humans. The journal is produced as a by-product of the posting step, rather than being a prior step in the processing sequence. In fact, the primary value of a journal in a computer-based system is to provide a visible human-readable link in the audit trail. A final difference is that a computer-based system is normally designed to perform some of the validation (edit) checks customarily performed by human clerks in manual systems. The flowchart of manual processing, shown in Figure 3-13, illustrates these points.

Advantages and Disadvantages of Batch Processing Batch processing with sequential access files provides several advantages. First, it is relatively simple and requires less complex and expensive hardware and software than the online processing approach. Second, because it normally involves sequential processing, the batch processing approach is relatively efficient, especially when large batches are accumulated. Basic accounting transactions give rise to large batches, as we have noted. Third, this approach facilitates the use of such controls as batch totals and thorough audit trails.

The main disadvantage of the batch processing approach is that the records in the master files become out of date, except just following a periodic processing "run." Consequently, most reports from a batch processing application are tied

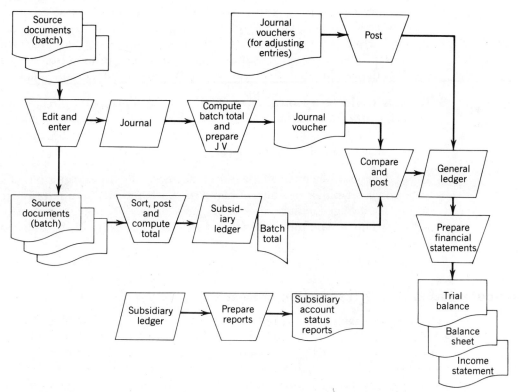

FIGURE 3-13 Batch processing of transactions by a manual system.

to the processing cycles. Another drawback is that errors detected in transaction data cannot easily be corrected at the time of entry; they must be corrected and re-entered, either in a follow-up "run" or during the next processing cycle. A third disadvantage is that the sorting step must be performed before a master file can be updated. Finally, all records in the master file must be read during the updating step, thus increasing the processing time when relatively few records are affected.

Variations in Batch Processing Applications The typical sequential batch processing applications described could be modified as follows.

1. **Different storage media could be used.** Magnetic tapes could be substituted for magnetic disks as storage media for the master files. If this is done, the updated files would be stored on new tape reels. (See Chapter 5.) Alternatively, a magnetic disk could be substituted for a magnetic tape as the storage medium for the transaction file.

2. **Direct access could be used during updating.** Instead of processing the entire file of transactions sequentially against the entire master file, each transaction could be processed randomly against the particular record in the master file that it affects. One advantage of direct processing is that the transaction file does not need to be sorted before updating. Another advantage of direct processing is that individual records can be retrieved at any time, in order to determine their status (e.g., the balance in a customer's account). However, this option is feasible only if the master files are stored on a direct access storage medium, such as magnetic disks. Also, it is less efficient than sequential processing except when the batches are small.

3. **Outputs could be spooled.** Instead of printing the reports directly onto hard copy, the information could be stored temporarily on a magnetic tape or disk. At a later time the reports could be printed offline, thus making more efficient use of the processor.

4. **Input data could be entered via online devices.** The transactions might be entered via terminals, for instance, and then accumulated temporarily on a secondary storage medium, such as magnetic disks, until time for processing a batch. This online input option is discussed more fully in the following paragraphs.

Computer-based Online Transaction Processing

Online processing, also called real-time processing, consists of processing each transaction as soon as captured. Each transaction is therefore entered via an online device and posted immediately and directly to the affected record in one or more master files. For this type of processing to be effective, two conditions must be present: (a) All master files and application programs needed for likely

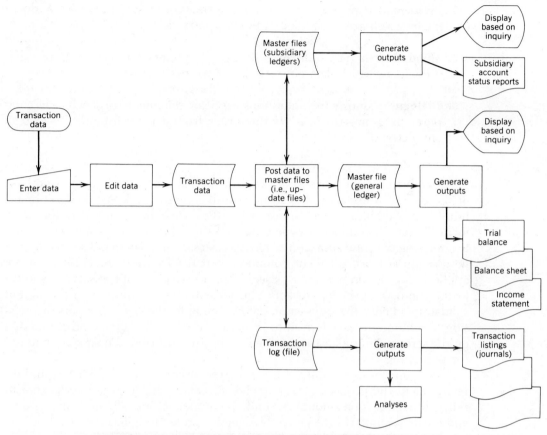

FIGURE 3-14 Computer-based online processing of transactions.

types of transactions are continuously online, usually in secondary storage media, and (b) the available hardware and software enable the human users to interact easily with the computer system.

Online Processing Application Figure 3-14 diagrams the steps involved in the online processing of transactions by a firm. These steps consist of (1) entering the transaction data, (2) processing the transaction data to update the affected master files, and (3) generating outputs.

Data entry involves a device such as a terminal, optical scanner, or voice input unit. The transaction data may be on a source document, such as a sales order. Sometimes, however, the data are acquired without benefit of a source document. For instance, salesclerks may receive sales orders by phone and enter them via the keyboards of terminals. The input device and the data entry software of the application may assist in the entry of data. In the case of a video display terminal, common interactive methods of assistance are

1. **Preformatted screens** (i.e., displayed formats or masks of transaction documents which are to be filled in by data entry clerks).

2. **Menu screens** (i.e., numbered listings of options—such as "1. Enter sales order"—by which data entry clerks are to specify desired actions).

3. **Dialogue prompts** (i.e., questions asked or statements issued by the computer program—such as "Is this order from a new customer?"—to data entry clerks).

An online data entry procedure begins when the computer system is notified of the type of transaction. For instance, a data entry clerk may key the menu number pertaining to a sales order or key the code SO in response to the statement "Enter the transaction type code." (If the data entry terminal is designed for only one type of transaction, such as a cash sale or a merchandise receipt, the notification is automatic.) The computer system software then (1) retrieves the application program needed to process the specified type of transaction, and (2) loads it into the primary storage unit. Next the edit routine of the program validates and edits the transaction data keyed in by the clerk. If errors or omissions are found by the edit routine, it notifies the clerk by some type of message on the screen. After all errors and omissions are corrected, the data are entered for processing.

Processing consists mainly of updating the affected files immediately and directly. First, the proper account in the subsidiary ledger (if any) is posted to reflect the transaction amount. Second, the proper accounts (both debit accounts and credit accounts) in the general ledger are posted to reflect the effects of the transaction. Finally, the transaction data are added to a transaction log, generally just following the most recently posted transaction.

All or most of the outputs provided by a batch processing procedure are likewise generated by an online processing system. Thus, on a periodic basis the system generates trial balances, balance sheets, income statements, and subsidiary account status reports. In addition, transaction listings and source documents can be produced as by-products. Also, online inquiries can be entered by users, such as accountants and managers. The responses to such inquiries are usually displayed on terminal screens. Furthermore, the transactions on the log can be sorted and analyzed as desired.

Contrasts with Computer-based Batch Processing Computer-based online processing is similar to batch processing: Both methods generate the same basic outputs and employ the same data records. There are significant differences, however, between these two computer-based methods. Batch processing generally involves sequential processing of transactions, whereas online processing always employs direct processing. The former method focuses a single application program on a batch of transactions; the latter method often retrieves a separate application program to process each transaction as it is entered. Certain batch processing applications are likely to employ magnetic tape as the storage medium for master files, whereas magnetic tape is principally used in online processing applications to store the backup files. Also, batch processing applications are relatively unintegrated, whereas online processing applications tend to be highly integrated.

Advantages and Disadvantages of Online Processing The major advantage of online processing is better service to users. Since records are updated immediately and are directly accessible, up-to-date information is available in a timely manner. Also, data are accurate and complete, since transactions are checked thoroughly upon capture and detected errors are corrected. Since processing is performed in a direct manner, no sorting or transcribing is necessary. Finally, because online processing applications are integrated, fewer duplicates of files are required and the informational needs of users can be satisfied more fully.

The main disadvantage of the online processing method is that more complex software is needed. Not only must the operating system accommodate varied users and diverse functions, but also the data entry routines in the application programs are expected to provide more user guidance and perform more elaborate checks. Also, the needed hardware, such as terminals and direct-access storage devices, is more expensive than the hardware needed in batch processing. Furthermore, transaction data processed by the online processing method cannot be supported by such controls as batch totals. In addition, complete audit trails are often more difficult to maintain. Finally, the entry of data is slower, since the system must wait for the human clerks to key in the data and respond to error messages.

Variations in Online Processing Applications Fewer variations are allowable in online processing. Transaction data must be entered in an online manner and direct-access storage devices must be employed. The major options concern (1) whether or not to use source documents as the basis for data entry, (2) which type of input device to use, and (3) which method of interactive assistance to provide to users.

Computer Application Trends

After acquiring computer systems, firms normally progress through several stages of applications development. Figure 3-15 identifies three major stages. These stages reflect trends toward greater integration and emphasis on decision-making. First-stage applications focus on narrow unintegrated applications that are transaction oriented. Second-stage applications still focus primarily on transaction processing. However, they are more integrated and provide operational-level decision-making information as a by-product of the processing. Third-stage applications are very integrated and broad, since they cut across the major operational functions of a firm. In addition, they generate a wealth of information for decision making at all managerial levels.

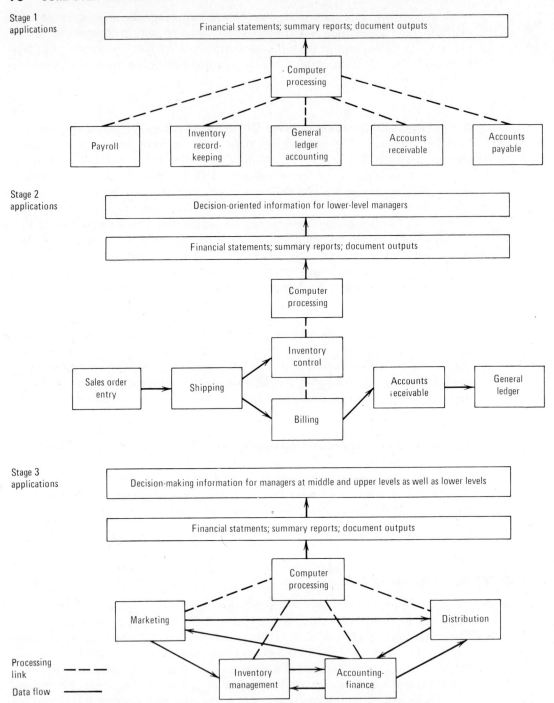

FIGURE 3-15 Three stages of accounting-oriented applications.

SUMMARY

Computers are significantly improving the performance of accounting information systems (AISs) in many firms. Computer hardware includes processors, input/output devices, and storage devices and media. Hardware trends have been dramatic with respect to computer size, speed, storage capacity, reliability, cost, and availability of options. Computer software includes operating systems, application programs, and utility programs. These varied types of computer software are developed by means of machine languages, symbolic languages, procedure-oriented languages, and specialized languages. Over the past decades software has become more "user-friendly," packaged, and specialized. Software also has become more costly relative to hardware.

Computer-based applications have similarities and differences with respect to manual applications. In the area of transaction processing, they involve either of two approaches: batch processing or online processing. Batch processing generally consists of accumulating batches of transactions, computing batch totals, entering the data for processing on magnetic media, sorting the data by sorting keys, posting the transaction data to the sequentially arranged records in master files, and generating printed outputs. This processing approach is similar in most respects to manual processing of transaction data, although the advantages of computers are obtained. Its major drawback is that the records in the master files become out of date between processing cycles.

Online processing consists of entering single transactions, via online input devices; posting the transactions directly to the records in the master files; and generating outputs as needed. This approach has several advantages, including the maintenance of up-to-date records and the ability of users to access this stored information in a timely manner. Its major drawbacks are the added complexity and cost of software and hardware, as well as the lack of controls, such as batch totals.

Trends in computer-based applications have been toward greater integration of transaction processing applications and greater emphasis on generating decision-making information.

REFERENCES

Capron, H. L., and Williams, Brian K. *Computers and Data Processing.* Menlo Park, Calif.: Benjamin/Cummings Publishing, 1982.

Hicks, James O. Jr., and Leininger, Wayne E. *Accounting Information Systems,* 2d ed., St. Paul, Minn.: West Publishing, 1986.

Mandell, Steven L. *Computers and Data Processing Today.* St. Paul, Minn.: West Publishing, 1983.

Withington, Frederic G. "The Golden Age of Packaged Software." *Datamation* (Dec. 1980), 313–314.

QUESTIONS

1. What is the meaning of each of the following terms?

Computer hardware	Interleaved storage
Hardware	access
configuration	Virtual storage
Processor	Page
Central processing	Parallel processing
unit (CPU)	Multiprocessing
Control unit	Time-sharing
Arithmetic-logic unit	Online
Primary storage unit	Offline
Random access	Terminal
memory (RAM)	Keyboard/printer
Read-only memory	terminal
(ROM)	Video display terminal
Microprograms	Audio input/response
Millisecond	terminal
Nanosecond	Intelligent terminal
Million instructions	"Dumb" terminal
per second (MIPS)	Source data
Access time	automation (SDA)
Execution time	Data collection
Transfer rate	terminal
Bit	Point-of-sale terminal
Byte	Automated teller
Kilobyte	machine
Megabyte	Reservations terminal
Word size	Optical character
Mainframe	recognition (OCR)
Minicomputer	device
Microcomputer	Magnetic ink character
Overlapping	recognition (MICR)
Multiprogramming	device
	Card punch machine

Key-to-tape encoder
Key-to-disk system
Image reader
Impact printer
Nonimpact printer
Computer output
  microfilm (COM)
  device
Plotter
Spooling
Magnetic tape
Parity bit
Nondestructive
  readout
Magnetic disk
Direct access
Cylinder
Destructive read-in
Optical disk
WORM
Microfilm
Punched card
Turnaround
  document

Computer software
Machine language
Symbolic language
Procedure-oriented
  language
Problem-oriented
  language
Operating system
Application software
Utility program
Batch processing
Processing cycle
Record
Block
Interblock gap (IBG)
Header label
Trailer label
Sorting key
Primary key
Sequential access file
Online processing
Preformatted screen
Menu screen
Dialogue prompt

2. What are the advantages of computer-based transaction processing?

3. What types of applications are especially suited to the use of computers?

4. Describe the functions of the various units composing a computer processor.

5. In what ways may processor performance be measured?

6. Contrast the three sizes of computers.

7. Describe several types of computer input devices.

8. Describe several types of computer output devices.

9. Contrast magnetic tapes and magnetic disks.

10. Discuss the several trends in computer hardware over the past four decades.

11. Contrast the several levels of computer programming languages.

12. How do operating systems differ from application and utility programs?

13. Discuss the several trends in computer software.

14. Contrast the characteristics of computer-based batch transaction processing and online transaction processing.

15. Contrast the advantages of computer-based batch transaction processing and online transaction processing.

16. Contrast computer-based transaction processing and manual transaction processing.

17. Discuss the three major stages in computer-based applications.

18. What level of understanding should accountants have concerning computer hardware and software?

19. Is the accounting information system of any firm likely to be completely computerized? Why or why not?

20. Should the double-entry method of recording transactions be retained when computers are introduced into the AIS of a firm?

21. An owner of a small firm argues that a computer system for her firm would never pay for itself and that she would lose control over the firm's operations to the computer. Discuss.

22. Discuss the likely effects that a newly installed computer system will have on the scope and complexity of a firm's AIS.

23. Contrast the impacts of computerization on the collection and processing of nontransaction data and transaction data.

24. Suggest applications for which online input, but delayed batch processing, would be suitable in a typical firm.

REVIEW PROBLEM

Campus Bookstore, Third Installment

Statement

The Campus Bookstore (described in the Review Problem as the end of Chapter 1) grows steadily in sales volume as a result of growth in the student body at the adjacent university. To accommodate this growth, the bookstore adds more employees and managers, such as accounting clerks, a cashier, a computer operator, a programmer, and an accounting system manager. It also acquires, on the recommendation of public accountant-consultants, a new minicomputer system. This multiuser computer system consists of a processor (with multiprogramming, overlapping, and virtual storage capabilities), six video display terminals, five point-of-sale terminals (with optical wand-type scanners), one impact printer, one nonimpact printer, four magnetic disk drives, and two magnetic tape drives. The video display terminals are located in purchasing, accounting, and managerial offices, whereas the point-of-sale terminals are located at the checkout stands. Other equipment includes an offline key-to-tape encoder. Accompanying this hardware configuration is an appropriate operating system plus packaged application and utility software.

Required

By reference to this statement (and facts in the previous installments),

a. Draw a hardware configuration diagram of the new computer system.

b. Identify a variety of applications in which the computer system might be utilized.

c. Describe the application of the computer system to the batch processing of cash disbursements transactions. The bookstore does not employ the voucher system of handling suppliers' invoices.

d. Describe the application of the computer system to the online processing of cash sales transactions.

Solution

a. A hardware configuration diagram would appear as shown on the top of page 82.

b. Applications that are suited to the new minicomputer system include: (1) general ledger accounting, (2) cash sales and receipts transaction processing, (3) purchases transaction processing, (4) accounts payable transaction processing, (5) cash disbursements transaction processing, (6) payroll transaction processing, (7) inventory recordkeeping and control, (8) sales analysis and forecasting, (9) cash forecasting and budgeting, (10) operational budgeting, and (11) capital investment analysis.

c. A cash disbursements transaction batch processing system would likely involve these steps: Suppliers' invoices that have been approved for payment would be filed in accordance with the purchase discount period. Each day those invoices reaching the end of the purchase discount period are pulled from the file. Batch totals of this day's invoices are computed on a calculator. For example, separate batch totals might be computed for the net amounts to be paid and the account number of the suppliers being paid, as well as the count of the invoices in the batch being processed. An accounting clerk next keys the pertinent data from each invoice in the batch onto magnetic tape, using the key-to-tape encoder. During this conversion step the encoder edits the data for errors and omissions. Any invoices found to contain errors are returned to the accounts payable clerk for correction. After transcribing all invoices, the clerk compares the batch totals computed by the encoder with the precomputed batch totals. She or he reconciles any differences.

Following these data preparation and entry steps, the bookstore's computer operator mounts the magnetic tape containing the invoice payment data onto an input tape drive. The operator first sorts the transaction data in accordance with the arrangement of the supplier master records (i.e., by supplier account numbers). Then the operator performs a sequential processing check printing and updating step (or "run"). This step consists of (1) printing each check; (2) posting the check amount to the supplier's account, thus reducing the account payable balance; and (3) printing a listing of cash disbursed (i.e., the cash disbursements journal).

Although these are the basic steps in the application, several other steps should be noted. Batch totals are automatically computed by the system during both the sort and update steps. These totals are compared to the precomputed batch totals. Also, at the end of each day the computer operator copies all the data from the magnetic disks, which contain (among other files) the supplier master file, onto magnetic tape. This tape, together with the transaction tape, are stored to provide backup. Furthermore, added reports are likely to be prepared on a periodic basis. For

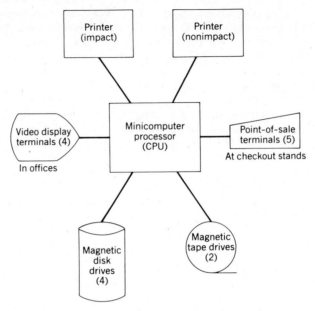

Note: The symbols are based on computer system symbols, as described in Chapter 6. However, any desired symbols (e.g., squares) could be used throughout.

instance, a listing of open accounts payable amounts is printed by the computer system at the end of each month.

d. A cash sales transaction online processing system would likely involve the following steps: As customers present their merchandise at the checkout stands, checkout clerks sweep their scanners across the bar codes on the merchandise packages. The captured coded data are entered via the terminals (to which the scanners are connected) and checked for errors and omissions. Each item of checked data is translated into the description of the merchandise item and its price and then listed on a sales slip. When all merchandise items composing an individual sale have been entered, the clerk presses a key; then the sales tax and total are automatically computed and printed on the sales slip. The remainder of the transaction is handled in the same manner as it was by the former manual system.

The computer system performs several functions that are related to the sales transactions.

(1) In addition to editing the captured data, it retrieves the sales prices from a stored file

on one of the magnetic disks. Based on these sales prices, the system computes the sales amount for each merchandise item and for each sale, as already described. The system also lists the total amount of each cash sale in a cash receipts summary record (similar in purpose to the locked-in tape in the former cash register). This cash receipts summary record, or journal, is printed at the end of each day. It is broken down by point-of-sale terminal station so that a manager can reconcile the cash amounts in the drawers to the totals received for the day.

(2) The computer system posts the quantities of merchandise sold to a merchandise inventory master file, which is stored on one of the online magnetic disks. (When on-hand quantities have been reduced by sales below a critical level, the purchasing department is notified automatically via a reorder report. It then places purchase orders for additional merchandise so that the shelves may be restocked. This procedure is an example of the integrated nature of online processing systems.)

(3) At the end of each day, the computer system posts the total amount of cash sales to the general ledger accounts, which are maintained in a master file on an online magnetic disk, with a debit to Cash on Hand and a credit to Sales. (Also, when the cash is deposited in the bank, the system is instructed by the cashier to post the transaction to the appropriate general ledger accounts.)

PROBLEMS

3-1. Indicate which of the following system-related tasks can best be performed by computers, which by humans, and which by both computers and humans.

a. Setting the objectives of a firm.

b. Making routine decisions concerning inventory control.

c. Processing large volumes of transactions.

d. Making decisions concerning the promotion of managers.

e. Identifying problems needing solutions.

f. Preparing income tax returns.

g. Processing exceptional types of transactions.

h. Answering inquiries concerning the status of customers' orders.

i. Determining the causes of variances that appear in a cost control report.

j. Analyzing stocks and making investment recommendations.

3-2. Explain why each of the following types of organizations was an early user of computer systems, and identify the key hardware components that the current computer systems of these organizations are likely to incorporate.

a. Insurance companies.

b. Airline companies.

c. Governmental intelligence agencies.

d. Hospitals.

e. Engineering research centers.

f. Custom-order manufacturing firms.

3-3. Draw and label a hardware configuration diagram for the following computer systems.

a. A microcomputer, located in the office of a small public accountant, with attached online components consisting of one video display terminal, one printer, and two diskette drives.

b. A minicomputer, located in the main office of a merchandising firm, with online components consisting of one magnetic disk drive, two printers, ten video display terminals, one computer output microfilm device, and two magnetic tape drives.

c. A mainframe computer, located in the main office area of a manufacturing firm, with online components consisting of two magnetic disk drives, three printers (two impact-type, one nonimpact-type), five video display terminals, and four magnetic tape drives. Additional components located elsewhere and connected online to the same computer are six data collection terminals on the production floor, one video display terminal in the warehouse and production office, one printer in the warehouse, and one microcomputer in the executive office.

3-4. Specify the most suitable input or output device for each of the following situations.

a. A public utility needs to employ a specialized means of handling turnaround documents returned by customers with their payments.

b. An insurance company having numerous branches needs to transmit policy data from its regional offices for timely processing by a mainframe computer located at its home office.

c. A bank needs to employ a specialized means of inputting its large volume of checks for processing each day.

d. A grocery store chain desires to capture bar-coded data on grocery and sundry items of merchandise and to transmit these data to a central computer so that each sales transaction can be automatically and immediately completed.

e. A stock exchange desires to provide the latest stock prices to security representatives in brokerage offices who enter requests via special telephones with keyboard attachments.

f. A construction firm desires to process its weekly payroll from time records in which the hours worked have been mark-sensed in pencil.

g. A university desires to employ a specialized means of handling registration forms filled in by students and returned for computer processing.

h. An automobile salvage dealer (one who buys old or wrecked automobiles and salvages key parts) is tired of answering numerous telephone inquiries every day concerning the availability of parts for specified models; instead, the dealer prefers that personalized answers be provided by a computerized system.

i. A large transportation firm having more than 3000 prime and subsidiary accounts desires to post batches of journal vouchers each month to the general ledger, which is maintained on magnetic tape.

j. A wholesaler desires to record its numerous sales of merchandise on media that can be entered quickly in batches for processing by its computer system.

k. An automobile manufacturer desires to receive from its dealers orders that have been directly entered into a computer system and transmitted immediately to the manufacturer's order department at its home office.

l. A steel manufacturer prefers to eliminate the use of time cards for recording attendance times of employees; instead, it plans to assign badges containing employee numbers as bar codes, which would interface with an input device to the computer system.

m. A small business proprietor needs to obtain cash on Saturday to pay for emergency repairs to the company vehicle.

n. A management consultant desires to include high-quality colored graphics in her report to a client firm.

3-5. Assume the availability of these computer-based storage media: magnetic tape, magnetic disk, optical disk, microfilm, primary storage, and punched cards. Indicate which storage medium (or media, if more than one) is preferable for each of the following situations. Briefly state why the selected medium is preferred.

a. A brokerage firm desires to retain records of the complete daily stock quotations as taken from the financial newspapers.

b. A credit card company desires to keep its members' account records readily available so that updates can be made and inquiries can be quickly answered.

c. A private research institute needs to retain files concerning its completed projects; the files are not subject to updating, but they need to be frequently referenced in a timely manner.

d. A bank needs to keep available a series of amortization tables; these tables require relatively little storage space, but they need to be frequently accessed by a computer program that determines interest payments due from debtors.

e. A railway company needs to record transactions pertaining to movements of its freight cars so that it can update the master file (which contains 10,000 records) on a daily basis.

f. A department store needs to record the amounts owed by customers on bills, which are mailed to the customers and returned by them (with payments) for processing.

g. A telephone company desires to retain copies of all checks and drafts that it issues for occasional reference by accounting clerks.

h. A hospital needs to back up all its patient-related records, which are stored on magnetic disk.

3-6. Identify the type of software for each of the following computer-based functions. If a programming language is indicated, specify the level.

a. Coordinating the actions of the hardware components of a computer system.

b. Preparing the payroll.

c. Performing merges of data located in two or more files.

d. Constructing and using financial models for budgeting.

e. Processing the cash receipts from customers.

f. Compiling COBOL programs into machine language.

3-7. Specify likely computer hardware configurations for each of the following situations by means of appropriate diagrams.

a. Batch processing applications in which transaction data are recorded on source documents, transcribed by a key-to-disk system, and entered to update files stored on a medium that requires sequential access processing. Outputs are provided as hard copies.

b. Online processing applications in which transaction data are entered directly through keyboards, edited, and processed to update files stored on a direct access storage device. Outputs are both displayed and provided as hard copies. Contents of the stored files are transferred periodically to a medium that does not permit direct access.

3-8. Teensie University has three students, whose summary records in the student master file include the following data.[3]

Num- ber	Name	Cumulative Semester Hours	Total Grade Points	Cumu- lative GPA
1	John Wills	60	150	2.5
2	Jan Cooper	54	189	3.5
3	Tess Hopper	75	195	2.6

The spring semester just ended, and the summary lines on semester grade slips for the students show the following:

Num- ber	Name	Hours Completed	Grade Points	GPA
2	Jan Cooper	15	45	3.0
1	John Wills	18	51	2.8
3	Tess Hopper	12	30	2.5

A new student, Ronald Reaper, transfers in at this time; he receives credit for 60 semester hours and 180 grade points. He is assigned number 4.

Required

a. Arrange the transaction data in proper order to perform batch processing against the student master file.

b. Prepare the body of a report showing the contents of the *updated* summary records, arranged in the report according to the students' last names. Include the new student's data.

3-9. Three methods of entering and processing transaction data are described in this chapter. These methods are (1) entering and processing data sequentially in batch mode, (2) entering and processing data directly in online mode, and (3) entering data in online mode and processing sequentially in batch mode. Which of these three methods would best suit each of the following applications? Why?

a. Weekly preparation of the payroll by a merchandiser.

b. Reservations of seats on scheduled airline flights.

c. Monthly preparation of statements to department store credit customers.

d. Maintenance of records at a central credit bureau.

e. Production of goods by a manufacturer to fill customers' special orders on tight schedules.

f. Processing of monthly adjusting journal entries by a retailer.

g. Processing and shipment of merchandise by a mail order firm, based on orders selected from a catalog of 400 standard items.

h. Maintenance of patient care records in a hospital.

i. Preparation of monthly customers' bills by a utility.

j. Production of cement by a manufacturer for inventory.

k. Maintenance of policyholder records by an insurance company.

---

[3] This problem can be solved by using a microcomputer-based data base management software package.

l. Processing of customers at checkout counters by a branch of a grocery chain.

m. Daily preparation of checks for suppliers by a contractor.

n. Maintenance of billing records by a professional law firm.

3-10. Auto Barn is an automotive parts retailer with three outlets in a midwestern city. It supplies the outlets from a central warehouse that is adjacent to its office building. The firm sells about 5000 types of parts for cash only. Because it buys in large quantities, it is able to sell the parts at relatively low prices. The firm also takes care to maintain adequate stocks so that the customers can always find the items they want. Thus, its sales volume has been growing rapidly. However, its investment in inventory has been growing even more rapidly. In addition, its costs of performing the necessary paperwork manually have been rising sharply. Consequently, the management is considering the acquisition of a computer system.

Required

a. Identify a variety of applications in which a computer system might be utilized by Auto Barn.

b. Describe two alternative processing methods by which Auto Barn might employ a mainframe computer system to maintain its inventory records and control the level of inventory.

c. Draw hardware configuration diagrams that would be necessary to implement each of the methods described in requirement **b.** Include offline devices, such as key-to-tape encoders, if used in a processing method; however, do not connect them directly to the computer processor.

3-11. The Tangier Company is a construction company in a western state. Currently the firm uses a computer system with a single mainframe computer to help it keep track of construction jobs, to maintain inventory status, to bill customers, and to prepare payrolls. Two key documents employed in the system are time sheets and materials requisitions, which are filled in by the supervisors in charge of the various jobs and turned in to the office at the end of each week.

Appropriate data from these documents are keyed onto magnetic tapes by data entry clerks using key-to-tape encoders. Data from these tapes are then read into the computer system and transaction listings are printed. By reference to these listings, the clerks correct errors in the data on the transaction tapes and, if necessary, generate new magnetic tapes containing corrected data. Then the transaction data from the corrected tapes are sorted and processed to update the master files (on magnetic tapes) containing job records, materials inventory records, customer billing records, and employee time records. During each update run a single type of output, such as a customer bill or inventory report, is printed.

The present computer system has several weaknesses. Separate transaction tapes are prepared daily for updating each master file, since the sorting keys are different and differing data items are needed. (This means that each document must be handled several times.) Correcting the transaction tapes is a time-consuming process; also, certain transactions must be "suspended" for a day until supervisors can be contacted to correct erroneous documents. Moreover, the records containing the current status of jobs, bills, materials inventory, and accumulated labor hours cannot be accessed quickly; instead, an interested user must wait until hard copies of the records are printed during the weekly processing activity.

Required

a. Draw a hardware configuration diagram of the computer system presently employed by the Tangier Company to perform the applications described. Show the minimum number of tape drives and printers required to process the applications. Include offline as well as online devices, but do not show the offline devices connected directly to the computer processor.

b. Draw a hardware configuration diagram of an online processing computer system that will provide improvements over the present system. State how the hardware you include will overcome the listed weaknesses.

3-12. Selected Small Firm (A Continuing Case) For the small firm that you selected in

Chapter 1 (see Problem 1-7), complete the following requirements.

a. If the firm currently uses a computer-based accounting information system, draw a hardware configuration diagram and identify the variety of applications utilizing the system. Also, describe one of the key applications. Suggest additional applications that appear to be feasible.

b. If the firm does not use a computer-based accounting information system, propose a system that appears to be feasible and the applications that it should handle. Also, draw a hardware configuration diagram of the proposed system.

Information

System

Control

Concepts

4

THIS CHAPTER'S OBJECTIVES ARE
TO ENABLE YOU TO:

Understand the nature of control in information systems.

Distinguish among the several types of control systems maintained within an information system.

Describe the exposures to risk that a firm faces with respect to assets and data, including those involving computer crimes.

Identify the impact of computers on the controls needed by firms.

Describe the considerations that affect the feasibility of controls and control systems within firms.

Discuss the forces that are instrumental in the improvement of control systems within firms.

INTRODUCTION

A control and security framework is an integral part of a firm's accounting information system (AIS). Composed of a wide variety of control and security measures, this framework spans all transactions and even embraces the organization and operations and management of the firm. Because these controls and security measures are internal to the firm and are closely interwoven, the framework may be called an **internal control structure.**

If the internal control structure of a firm is strong and sound, all the operations, physical resources, and data will be monitored and kept under control. Information outputs will be trustworthy. On the other hand, a weak and unsound internal control structure can lead to serious repercussions. The information generated by the AIS is likely to be unreliable, untimely, and perhaps unrelated to the firm's objectives. Furthermore, the firm's resources may not be used effectively and may be vulnerable to loss through theft and carelessness.

The control and security framework is of great concern to accountants. Since they are responsible for providing reliable information to management, helping to safeguard assets, and evaluating the fairness of financial statements, accountants need assurance that the framework is strong and adequate.

Because controls and security measures are so important, two chapters are devoted to their study. This chapter sets the stage by surveying the various control systems comprising the internal control structure and examining the ways they are being affected by current risks and developments. In particular it considers the impact of computers on controls and security measures. This chapter takes a broad perspective, since it looks at the effects upon control systems of the humans who use them and the costs these systems require. The next chapter catalogs a wide variety of useful controls and security measures.

NATURE OF CONTROL

The Control Process

Control is essentially a regulatory process. It has the overall purpose of helping an entity (e.g., a firm) to achieve its objectives and plans. In brief, the process consists of (1) measuring and evaluating actual results against planned accomplishments, and (2) taking corrective actions when necessary.

Examined in more detail, the **control process** consists of six elements: (1) a factor being controlled, called the characteristic or performance measure; (2) an operating process that gives rise to the characteristic; (3) a sensor element that detects the actual state of the operating process; (4) a planned accomplishment, or benchmark, against which the actual state of the characteristic is to be compared; (5) a planner who sets the benchmark; and (6) a regulator or control element that compares the actual state of the characteristic against the benchmark and feeds back corrections to the operating process.

Figure 4-1 portrays the control process and illustrates it in terms of a household heating system. The overall purpose of a heating system is to control the temperature, which is the characteristic or performance measure. A home owner begins the process by setting the thermostat reading for the desired temperature

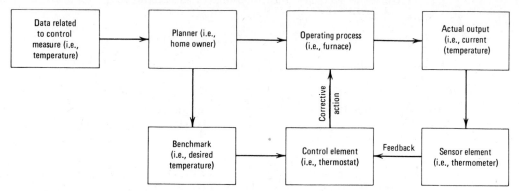

FIGURE 4-1 A feedback control process for a heating system.

(the benchmark). He or she chooses a setting that is determined by personal objectives, such as comfort and economy. Then an automatic process takes over. As the furnace (the operating process) generates heat, the thermostat's thermometer (the sensor element) detects the actual temperature. Next the thermostatic mechanism (the control element) compares the actual temperature (fed to it by the sensor element) with the benchmark temperature. When the actual temperature rises above the preset temperature, the control element notifies the activating mechanism in the thermostat to shut down the furnace. Later, when the actual temperature drops below the preset temperature, the information feedback leads to the furnace being turned on again.

A central feature of the control process is feedback. As the foregoing heating system example shows, **feedback** is an information output that returns ("feeds back") to a control element and then returns to the operating process as an input. Feedback therefore provides the means for deciding when corrective actions (e.g., turning off the furnace) are necessary.

Control processes vary in sophistication. The heating system is an example of a first-order feedback control process or system, if the benchmark is assumed to remain unchanged after being set. By contrast, a second-order feedback control system employs a benchmark that adjusts to meet changing environmental conditions. An example is a flexible budgeting system in which the budget values are adjusted with changing levels of activity. A third-order feedback control system attempts to predict future conditions and results. Based on such predictions, the system anticipates future problems and suggests corrective actions *before* the problems occur. Several third-order feedback control systems, also known as feedforward control systems, are typically used by business firms. One example is a cash planning system. Based on periodic cash forecasts, the treasurer of a firm may anticipate seasonal cash shortages by arranging for bank loans before the shortages actually occur.

Control Objectives

An internal control structure of a firm has four major **control objectives:**

1. To safeguard the assets of the firm.

2. To ensure the accuracy and reliability of the accounting data and information.

3. To promote efficiency in all the firm's operations.

4. To encourage adherence to management's prescribed policies and procedures.[1]

In striving to achieve these objectives, the internal control structure applies such controls as comparisons of actual measures against benchmarks. For in-

---

[1] American Institute of Certified Public Accountants, Committee on Auditing Procedure, *Internal Control—Elements of a Coordinated System and Its Importance to Management and the Independent Public Accountant* (New York: AICPA, 1949).

stance, the actual cash on hand and in the bank should equal the amount reflected in the cash ledger account; the customer number on a remittance advice should correspond to the number of an account in the accounts receivable master file; the date an order is actually shipped should match the scheduled date; the signature on a check should match the name of the person authorized to sign.

Difficulties in Achieving Control Objectives

Control objectives are not easily achieved. Internal control structures face major difficulties. To surmount these difficulties, firms often draw upon the expertise of accountants and auditors in designing the structures.

One difficulty is due to the complexity of modern business conditions. A firm operates within a tangled network that includes its industry, government agencies, technology, and economic systems. Planning and establishing sound benchmarks, such as budget values, can be a confounding task.

Another difficulty is the set of risks to which the structure and its firm is exposed. There are ever-present risks that assets may be lost or stolen, that data may be erroneous or accessed by unauthorized persons, that shipments may be delayed or damaged, and so on. These risks are numerous, and in some cases the exposures are quite substantial.

A third difficulty derives from the human factor, since control objectives are accomplished through people. Managers may establish policies, procedures, and benchmarks that are unclear and unwise. Employees may not follow procedures consistently or may make incorrect comparisons. Both may take unsuitable corrective actions, or may leave necessary actions untaken. These human fallacies and inefficiencies can result in lost revenues and added operating costs.

A fourth difficulty concerns the technology applied to the control structure. The installation of computers, in particular, changes the type of controls and security measures that are needed. Computers also have other effects on the internal control structure.

A final difficulty relates to the costs of controls and security measures. Can a firm afford to install all the controls that may improve the overall effectiveness of the internal control structure, for instance?

COMPONENT INTERNAL CONTROL SYSTEMS

An adequate internal control structure for a firm consists in reality of several component control processes or systems. Although known by various names, we shall label these systems as the operational control system, the management control system, and the accounting control system. Taken together, these component systems employ all three orders of feedback. They also encompass two types of controls: administrative and accounting. Figure 4-2 summarizes key features and relationships of these control systems.[2]

---

[2] The components of the internal control structure are viewed somewhat differently for the purposes of audits pertaining to financial statements. This differing perspective is presented in Chapter 14.

	Name	Objective(s)	Type of controls employed
Internal control structure	Management control system	To encourage compliance with management's policies and procedures	Administrative
	Operational control system	To promote efficiency in operations	Administrative
	Accounting control system	To safeguard assets and ensure the accuracy and reliability of data and information	Accounting

FIGURE 4-2 Three component systems comprising the internal control structure.

Operational Control Systems

Operational control is the process that promotes efficiency in operational tasks. Hence, the operational control system of a firm attempts to achieve the third objective previously listed for the internal control system. Examples of operational control systems are the inventory control system, the credit control system, the production control system, and the cash control system.

Consider the process of controlling inventory within a typical merchandising firm. The performance measure is the level of a merchandise inventory item. For each item handled by the firm, the inventory manager (planner) first sets two benchmarks: reorder point and reorder quantity. These benchmarks are set at levels intended to achieve operational efficiency in inventory management. That is, they are expected to minimize the investment in the inventory item while ensuring that the item will never be out of stock. Periodically the inventory control system compares the actual quantity of the item on hand with the reorder point. When the actual quantity falls to or below the reorder point, the system takes corrective action: It replenishes the inventory stock by purchasing the predetermined reorder quantity. Since this corrective action anticipates and prevents a possible inventory shortage, the inventory control system is an example of a third-order feedback control system.

Management Control Systems

The **management control** process focuses on managerial performance rather than on technical operations. Its purpose is to encourage compliance with the firm's policies and procedures. If the policies and procedures are soundly developed, resources should thereby be acquired and used effectively and efficiently. As the term implies, management control is exercised through the actions of managers. It follows the organizational structure of a firm, since the managers function through responsibility centers.

An example of the management control process can be drawn from the production function of a manufacturing firm. In order to fulfill the responsibility of controlling production-related resources, the production manager (planner) develops policies and production volume and cost targets (benchmarks). These policies and targets are embodied in a production budget for the coming year, as well as in procedures concerning quality inspections and other matters. The budget is broken down by production departments (responsibility centers). Each department head is then evaluated by comparing the actual volumes and costs against the budgeted values. When the variances in volumes and costs are significant, corrective actions may be necessary. For instance, if the volume is below budget, the department head may be assigned more workers, or he or she may be transferred.

All the controls needed to implement both the operational control and management control systems are known as **administrative controls.** As discussed in the next chapter, specific administrative controls include those relating to operational practices, the organizational structure, management policies and procedures, and the processes leading to the authorizing of transactions. Specific administrative controls include (1) preparing adequate documentation such as procedures manuals, job descriptions, and organization charts; (2) logically separating assigned duties and responsibilities; (3) carefully selecting and training employees; and (4) establishing clear rules for authorizing credit, check signing, and other transactions.

Accounting Control Systems

The **accounting control system** of a firm is designed to achieve the first two objectives of the internal control system (i.e., to safeguard the firm's assets and to ensure the accuracy and reliability of the data and information). *Assets* refer to resources, including data and information; **accuracy** means freedom from errors, and **reliability** means consistency in results from processing like data.

In order to achieve these objectives, the accounting control system focuses on a firm's assets and transactions. With respect to the physical assets, it employs both physical security measures and accounting records. Periodically the records of assets are compared to and reconciled with physical inspections of the assets themselves. With respect to transactions, the accounting control system governs their flows—from authorization to delivery of outputs. It employs a series of preventive controls at those points throughout each transaction flow which are subject to significant errors and losses. It also provides comparisons and other means of detecting errors and losses, as well as means of taking corrective actions when certain errors are detected.

Typical **accounting controls** employed by an accounting control system include

1. Locked cash registers and safes.

2. Physical counts of inventory on hand and the reconciliation of these counts with the records concerning inventory.

3. Authorization of sales transactions based on credit approvals.

4. Preparation of well-designed and prenumbered source documents.

5. Preparation and checking of control totals pertaining to batches of transaction documents.

6. Review of deposit slips and bank statements by auditors.

7. Preparation of bank reconciliations.

RISK EXPOSURES

If the controls incorporated into an accounting control system are adequate, they should minimize and counteract various **risks** to which a firm is exposed. In order to design a sound accounting control system, accountants should be aware of these risks and possible degrees of exposure.

Types of Risks

Among the system-related risks that confront the typical firm, other than those resulting from poor decision-making and inefficient operations, are the following:

1. **Unintentional errors.** Errors may appear in input data, such as customer names or numbers. Alternatively, they may appear during processing, as when clerks incorrectly multiply quantities ordered (on customers' orders) times unit prices of the merchandise items. These errors may occur on an occasional basis, or they may occur consistently. For instance, an incorrectly written computer program may cause computational errors to occur each time the program is executed. In any of these situations, the erroneous data damage the accuracy and reliability of a firm's files and outputs. Unintentional errors often occur because employees are inadequately trained or supervised; they may also occur when employees become tired and careless.

2. **Deliberate errors.** Deliberate errors constitute fraud, since they are caused in order to secure unfair or unlawful gain. Deliberate errors, like unintentional errors, may appear in input data or during processing. For instance, a clerk may increase the amount on a check received from a customer or underfoot a column of cash receipts. Either type of error damages the accuracy and reliability of files and/or outputs. However, deliberate errors may also conceal thefts (and hence losses) of assets. For example, a manager may enter a misstatement in a report or financial statement. In addition to affecting the accuracy of the outputs, this error could mislead stockholders and creditors.

3. **Unintentional losses of assets.** Assets may be lost or misplaced by accident. For example, newly received merchandise items may be put into the wrong warehouse bins, with the result that they are not found by pickers when filling orders. Data as well as physical assets may be lost. For instance, the

accounts receivable file stored on a magnetic disk may be wiped out by a sudden power surge.

4. **Thefts of assets.** Assets of a firm may be stolen by outsiders, such as professional thieves who break into a storeroom in the dead of night. Alternatively, assets may be misappropriated through embezzlement or defalcation. That is, they may be taken by employees who have been entrusted with their care. For example, a cashier may pocket currency received by mail, or a production employee may carry home a tool. Employees who embezzle often create deliberate errors in order to hide their thefts.

5. **Breaches of security.** Unauthorized persons may gain access to the data files or other assets of a firm. For instance, a "hacker" may break into a firm's computerized files via a distant terminal, or an employee may peek at a salary report in an unlocked file drawer. Security breaches can be very damaging in certain cases, as when competitors gain access to a firm's confidential marketing plans.

6. **Acts of violence and natural disasters.** Certain violent acts can cause damage to a firm's assets, including data. If sufficiently serious, they can interrupt business operations and even propel firms toward bankruptcy. Examples of such acts are the sabotage of computer facilities and the willful destruction of customer files. Although violent acts are sometimes performed by outsiders, such as terrorists, they are more often performed by disgruntled employees and ex-employees. Also, they may arise from nonhuman sources, such as fires that engulf computer rooms or short-circuits that disable printers.

Degrees of Risk Exposure

In order to combat these risks effectively, the exposure to each type of risk should be assessed. Exposure to risk is affected by such factors as

1. **Frequency.** The more frequent an occurrence, the greater the exposure to risk. A merchandising firm that makes numerous sales is highly exposed to errors in the transaction data. A contractor that bids on custom projects is exposed to calculating errors. A department store with numerous browsing shoppers has a significant exposure to merchandise losses from shoplifting.

2. **Vulnerability.** The more vulnerable an asset, the greater the exposure to risk. Cash is highly vulnerable to theft, since it is easily hidden and fully convertible. A telephone may be highly vulnerable to unauthorized use for long distance calls, especially if it is left untended in a remote office.

3. **Size.** The higher the value of a potential loss, the greater the risk exposure. An accounts receivable file represents a high risk exposure, since it contains essential information concerning amounts owed and other matters that affect credit customers.

When two or more of the foregoing factors act in unison, the exposure to risk is multiplied. Thus, an extremely high exposure occurs in the case of a firm that conducts numerous sales for cash, with each sale involving a sizable amount. As might be imagined, this situation requires more extensive controls than a situation in which the exposure to risk is slight.

Risks Exposures Arising from Computer Crimes

Offenses involving computer-based systems, known as **computer crimes,** constitute an increasingly serious class of risk exposures. Computer crimes pose very high degrees of risk, since all three factors tend to be accentuated. A computer-based system may process hundreds of transactions per hour, with each transaction being subject to error or to fraudulent activity. A computer and its stored data are often vulnerable to damage and unauthorized access. A loss from computer fraud tends to be several times larger than the average fraud loss when manual systems are involved. Individual losses from computer crimes often exceed $1 million. Furthermore, computer crimes are seldom detected or prosecuted.

Computer crimes take various forms. Two forms already listed are unauthorized access of stored data and sabotage of computer facilities. Other forms include

1. Theft of computer hardware and software. The latter, known as "software piracy," is quite prevalent. It involves making illegal copies of programs and software packages, usually from diskettes.

2. Unauthorized use of computer facilities for personal use. This crime may be committed by a hacker, who breaks into a computer system via a remote terminal or microcomputer, or by an employee who runs his or her own programs on the company computer.

3. Fraudulent modification or use of data or programs. In most fraud cases the perpetrator intends to steal assets, such as cash or merchandise. For instance, a purchasing agent may enter unauthorized purchase transactions via a terminal and have merchandise sent to his or her home. A programmer employed by a bank may modify a withdrawal program in a manner that causes withdrawals against his or her personal account to be charged to an inactive account.

The following sampling of reported computer crimes suggests the dimensions of the problem.

1. A self-employed computer expert discovered the daily code that authorized funds to be transferred from a large bank to other banks. One day, five minutes before closing time, he called the wire room, gave the correct authorization code, and transferred $10 million into a bank account opened under his alias.

2. A technician who helped design the computerized ticket system for a major league baseball club stayed around the office one day to show staff workers how to operate the system. Later, club officials discovered that he had also that day printed 7000 tickets, which he illegally sold through ticket brokers.

3. A number of unauthorized persons obtained the password into the files of the largest credit bureau in the country. From home computers they were able thereby to view the credit reports of millions of credit-card users.

4. In a case similar to the preceding one the "414 gang" (a group of young computer hackers) broke into the highly sensitive files of the Los Alamos National Laboratory.

5. Automatic teller machines (ATMs) installed by a large New York bank were the means of an ingenious fraud. Persons posing as bank employees would stop depositors in the middle of ATM transactions and direct them to other ATMs, explaining that the ATMs being used were inoperative. Then these persons would withdraw funds from the abandoned ATMs which had been opened (but not closed) by the depositors.

EFFECTS OF COMPUTERS ON THE ACCOUNTING CONTROL SYSTEM

The accounting control system of a typical firm incorporates numerous controls and security measures. When the firm installs a computer system for the first time, the controls and security measures need to be analyzed. Many of these measures will apply equally well to both manual and computer-based operations and thus should be retained. However, because of the risks of computer crime and other problems, some need to be modified and expanded. Also, certain new controls and security measures should be added. These changes are necessary in spite of the fact that computers process data with extreme accuracy and consistency.

At this point we are not ready to consider specific control details. However, we can weigh the effects of several conditions that arise when computers are introduced. These conditions and their effects on the accounting control system are as follows.

1. **Paper flows are reduced.** Sometimes source documents are not used in computer-based systems, as when sales orders are received via telephones and entered directly through terminals. Also, computers post transactions directly to ledgers, thereby omitting entries into journals. These shortcuts improve processing efficiency but cause a partial loss of the audit trail.

2. **Human judgment is bypassed.** The large volume of transactions normally handled by computer-based systems preclude human clerks from checking for errors. Since computers perform programmed instructions blindly, without judgment, transaction errors may enter the processing and affect the results.

3. **Processing is concentrated.** In manual systems the processing is done by clerks in various departments, thereby providing means for cross-checking the work of one other. In computer-based systems the processing is often concentrated in a mainframe computer. Consequently, there is less opportu-

nity for detecting fraudulent events, such as unauthorized transactions, changes in programmed instructions, and thefts of assets.

4. **Data are stored in invisible, erasable, and compressed form.** Data are invisible and readable only by the computer system. This causes difficulties for human users and auditors of the system and its outputs. Data are erasable, thus leading to possible loss of data. Data are in compressed form, often in centralized data bases. Although specific data items are therefore more accessible to legitimate users, they are also more vulnerable to unauthorized users.

5. **Computer equipment incorporates both powerful capabilities and complexity.** As a result of its processing power, a computer-based system can disseminate errors throughout files and reports more quickly. When linked by communication lines, its data are vulnerable to unauthorized users who may be located many miles away. Because of its complexity, the computer hardware is subject to breakdowns, thus causing interruptions to business operations. Normally being placed in fixed locations, the computer hardware also is subject to natural and man-made disasters such as fires, floods, and vandalism.

Figure 4-3 summarizes these control problems caused by computerization. The two columns on the left side of the figure contrast key characteristics of manual systems with those of computer-based systems. The two columns on the right list the added exposures to risks faced by computer-based systems, as well as the types of controls and security measures needed to offset the risk exposures.

FEASIBILITY CONSIDERATIONS

Building an effective and feasible internal control structure is not a simple task. It involves more than assembling all the controls and security measures that come to mind. Audit, cost, and human factors need to be considered.

A typical AIS undergoes periodic audits. Normally the internal control structure receives particularly close scrutiny during such audits, as will be discussed in Chapter 14. Thus, the internal control structure should be designed to be fully auditable. For instance, certain analyses and reconciliations can be generated on a routine basis for use by the auditors. Generally speaking, auditors should be consulted during the design stage so that all needed controls are considered beforehand. Adding controls after the structure is designed usually tends to be more costly and difficult.

Each control involves a cost. If every conceivable control were included within an internal control structure, the total cost is likely to be exorbitant. Thus, a firm should conduct a cost-benefit analysis in order to justify each control that is to be included. A **cost-benefit analysis** begins with a thorough analysis of the risk exposures. It determines the threats, expressed in dollars, that each risk exposure poses to the firm. Then it compares the benefits, resulting from reduced threats, against the costs of the controls needed to counteract the threats. Controls should not be included if their benefits do not exceed their costs.

Element or activity	Manual system characteristics	Computer-based system		
		Characteristics	Risk exposures	Compensating controls
Data collection	Data recorded on paper source documents	Data sometimes captured without use of source documents	Audit trail may be partially lost	Printed copies of source documents prepared by computer system
	Data reviewed for errors by clerks	Data often not subject to review by clerks	Errors, accidental or deliberate, may be entered for processing	Edit checks performed by computer system
Data processing	Processing steps performed by clerks who possess judgment	Processing steps performed by CPU "blindly" in accordance with program instructions	Errors may cause incorrect results of processing	Outputs reviewed by users of computer system; carefully developed computer processing programs
	Processing steps spread among various clerks in separate departments	Processing steps concentrated within computer CPU	Unauthorized manipulation of data and theft of assets can occur on larger scale	Restricted access to computer facilities; clear procedure for authorizing changes to programs
	Processing requires use of journals and ledgers	Processing does not require use of journals	Audit trail may be partially lost	Printed journals and other analyses
	Processing performed relatively slowly	Processing performed very rapidly	Effects of errors may spread rapidly throughout files	Editing of all data during input and processing steps
Data storage and retrieval	Data stored in file drawers throughout the various departments	Data compressed on magnetic media (e.g., tapes, disks)	Data may be accessed by unauthorized persons or stolen	Security measures at points of access and over data library
	Data stored on hard copies in human-readable form	Data stored in invisible, erasable, computer-readable form	Data are temporarily unusable by humans, and might possibly be lost	Data files printed periodically; backups of files; protection against sudden power losses
	Stored data accessible on a piecemeal basis at various locations	Stored data often readily accessible from various locations via terminals	Data may be accessed by unauthorized persons	Security measures at points of access
Information generation	Outputs generated laboriously and usually in small volumes	Outputs generated quickly and neatly, often in large volumes	Inaccuracies may be buried in impressive-looking outputs that users accept on faith	Reviews by users of outputs, including the checking of amounts
	Outputs usually in hard copy form	Outputs provided in various forms, including soft copy displays and voice responses	Information stored on magnetic media is subject to modification (only hard copy provides permanent record)	Backups of files; periodic printing of stored files onto hard copy records
Transmission of data and information	Usually transmitted via postal service and hand delivery	Often transmitted by communications lines	Data may be accessed or modified or destroyed by unauthorized persons	Security measures over transmission lines; coding of data; verification of transmitted data
Equipment	Relatively simple, inexpensive, and mobile	Relatively complex, expensive, and in fixed locations	Business operations may be intentionally or unintentionally interrupted; data or hardware may be destroyed; operations may be delayed through inefficiencies	Backup of data and power supply and equipment; preventive maintenance of equipment; restrictions on access to computer facilities; documentation of equipment usage and processing procedures

FIGURE 4-3. Control problems caused by computerization.

An internal control structure is only as good as the people who operate it and function within it. A key purpose of the control structure should therefore be to influence the behavior of the employees and others who interact with it. To be effective, it should cause the employees to react favorably (or at least not negatively) toward needed controls. If controls are perceived by affected employees as being punitive or unnecessary, the employees may circumvent the controls. When the controls are vitally needed, their purposes should be carefully explained. For instance, it can be pointed out that controls restricting access to cash are desirable because they remove temptation from honest employees.

FORCES FOR THE IMPROVEMENT OF CONTROLS

During earlier periods many AIS's were deficient with respect to controls and security measures. Often the system was intended primarily to provide the needed day-to-day documents and reports and to satisfy legal obligations. In recent decades, however, various forces have arisen to encourage the improvement of internal control structures. Perhaps the most influential forces have been managements, professional associations, and governmental bodies.

Needs of Management

The managers of most firms have recognized their vital stake in adequate internal control structures. On one hand, they have become aware of the huge losses and damages that can occur to the costly assets entrusted to their care. Newspapers and the other media have publicized the increasing instances of "white collar" crime, as well as overt thefts of merchandise and other portable assets. Managers have noted that the average loss from each crime has also been rising dramatically. On the other hand, they have grown concerned about the accuracy and reliability of the information they receive. Being primary users of information from their AISs, managers appreciate the potential for making poor decisions as a result of inaccurate and incomplete information. Furthermore, with an increasing dependence on computer systems, they have gained a realization of the seriousness of security breaches.

Concerns of Professional Associations

Professional accounting associations, such as the American Institute of Certified Public Accountants (AICPA), the Institute of Internal Auditors (IIA), and the National Association of Accountants (NAA), have studied the need for internal control systems. As a result, these bodies have issued various standards and guidelines pertaining to controls and audits of information systems.

Summaries of several key pronouncements will illustrate the broadness and evolution of these standards and guidelines:

- A professional standard of field work for auditors specifies "a proper study and evaluation of the existing internal controls as a basis for reliance thereon."[3]

- The Statement on Auditing Standards (SAS) No. 3 requires that the computerized portions of an AIS be included in an auditor's study and evaluation of the internal control system.[4]

- A study issued by the AICPA provides lists of control objectives and a step-by-step procedure for analyzing controls in computerized systems.[5]

- A set of standards issued by the IIA pertains to the responsibilities of internal auditors for evaluating controls and otherwise conducting the practice of internal auditing.[6]

- SAS No. 48 amends SAS No. 3 with respect to the effects of computerized systems on accounting controls, as well as the need for specialized auditing skills when evaluating such systems.[7]

- SAS No. 55 supersedes SAS No. 1 in order to restate the need for obtaining a thorough understanding of the internal control structure (formerly called system) before undertaking audits of financial statements.[8]

Acts and Rulings of Governmental Bodies

Investigations by such governmental agencies as the Security and Exchange Commission (SEC) have revealed illegal activities within American firms that were not detected by their internal control structures. As a result, Congress passed the **Foreign Corrupt Practices Act** in 1977. In addition to prohibiting certain types of bribes and hidden ownership, this act requires subject corporations to devise and maintain adequate internal control structures. Managers of corporations who do not comply are liable to large fines and imprisonment. Consequently, many have taken suitable actions to strengthen the internal control structures of their corporations.

The part of the act pertaining to internal control structures echos SAS No. 1. It states that corporations subject to the Securities Exchange Act of 1934 shall

(A) make and keep books, records, and accounts, which, in reasonable detail, accurately and fairly reflect the transactions and dispositions of the assets of the issuer (corporation); and

---

[3] American Institute of Certified Public Accountants, *Statement on Auditing Standards No. 1* (New York: AICPA, 1973).

[4] American Institute of Certified Public Accountants, *Statement on Auditing Standards No. 3* (New York: AICPA, 1974).

[5] American Institute of Certified Public Accountants, *The Auditor's Study and Evaluation of Internal Control in EDP Systems* (New York: AICPA, 1977).

[6] The Institute of Internal Auditors, *Standards for the Professional Practice of Internal Auditing* (Altamonte Springs, Fla.: IIA, 1978).

[7] American Institute of Certified Public Accountants, "The Effects of Computer Processing on the Examination of Financial Statements," *Statement on Auditing Standards No. 48* (New York, 1984).

[8] American Institute of Certified Public Accountants, "Consideration of the Internal Control Structure in a Financial Statement Audit," *Statement on Auditing Standards No. 55* (New York: 1988).

(B) devise and maintain a system of internal accounting control sufficient to provide reasonable assurance that

(i) transactions are executed in accordance with management's general and specific authorization

(ii) transactions are recorded as necessary (I) to permit preparation of financial statements in conformity with generally accepted accounting principles applicable to such statements, and (II) to maintain accountability for assets

(iii) access to assets is permitted only in accordance with management's general or specific authorization

(iv) the recorded accountability for assets is compared with the existing assets at reasonable intervals and appropriate action is taken with respect to any differences.

Subsequent to the Foreign Corrupt Practices Act, the SEC issued rulings pertaining to internal control structures. In time the SEC may issue a ruling that requires auditors to make formal reports concerning their evaluations of the internal control structures of client firms.

SUMMARY

Control is a regulatory process which helps a firm achieve its objectives and plans. The process is implemented within a firm through an internal control structure. Elements in the control process are a characteristic, operating process, sensor, benchmark, planner, and regulator. A central feature is feedback. Control objectives are to safeguard assets, ensure data accuracy and reliability, promote operational efficiency, and encourage adherence to policies and procedures. These objectives are difficult to achieve because of business complexity, risk exposures, human factors, costs, and the presence of computers. Component systems within the internal control structure are the operational control system, the management control system, and the accounting control system. The first promotes operational efficiency, the second encourages compliance with the firm's policies and procedures, and the third safeguards the assets and ensures data accuracy and reliability.

Among the risks that the accounting control system counteracts are unintentional errors, deliberate errors, unintentional losses, thefts of assets, breaches of security, and acts of violence and natural disasters. The degrees of exposure to these risks are affected by such factors as frequency of occurrence, vulnerability of the assets, and size of the potential losses. When computers comprise a part of the accounting control system, the degrees of risk exposure can be very high. Computers reduce the paper flows, bypass human judgment, concentrate processing, store data in invisible and erasable and compressed form, and incorporate powerful capabilities and complexity. Thus, significant changes in controls are necessary.

Building an effective and feasible internal control structure requires that audit, cost, and human factors be considered. Internal control structures are undergoing improvements, partly as a result of such forces as the needs of management, the concerns of professional associations, and the acts and rulings of governmental bodies.

REFERENCES

Alderman, Tom. "Computer Crime." *Journal of Systems Management* (Sept. 1977), 32–35.

Baird, Bryon N., and Michenzi, Alfred R. "Impact of the Foreign Corrupt Practices Act." *The Internal Auditor* (June 1983), 20–22.

Campitelli, Vincent A. "Is Your Computer a Soft Touch?" *Financial Executive* (Feb. 1984), 10–14.

Computer Services Executive Committee. *The Auditor's Study and Evaluation of Internal Controls in EDP Systems.* New York: AICPA, 1977.

Hooper, Paul and Page, John. "Internal Control Problems in Computer Systems." *Journal of Systems Management* (Dec. 1982), 22–27.

Nash, John F. and Roberts, Martin B. *Accounting Information Systems.* New York: MacMillan, 1984.

QUESTIONS

1. What is the meaning of each of the following terms?

Internal control structure

Control process

Feedback

Control objective

Operational control

Management control

Administrative control

Accounting control system

Accuracy

Reliability

Accounting control

Risk

Computer crime

Cost-benefit analysis

Foreign Corrupt Practices Act

2. Why is the internal control structure so important to the proper functioning of the AIS?

3. Describe the elements of the control process.

4. Contrast first-order, second-order, and third-order feedback control systems.

5. What are the four objectives of an internal control structure?

6. Identify several difficulties in achieving these control objectives.

7. Contrast the operational, management, and accounting control systems.

8. Identify several types of AIS-related risks confronting the typical firm.

9. What are three factors that influence the degree of risk exposure?

10. Identify several types of computer crimes.

11. What are several conditions posed by computer-based systems that impact the internal control structure of a firm?

12. Discuss the audit, cost, and human factors that should be considered in designing a feasible internal control structure.

13. Discuss the forces that are influencing the improvement of internal control structures.

14. Discuss the control process for each of the following.

  a. Inventory control.

  b. Quality control.

  c. Budgetary control.

  d. Production cost control.

  e. Credit control.

15. What response would you give a manager who says that his or her firm does not need accounting controls over the assets, since the firm has only one employee.

16. Discuss the costs that a particular accounting control might impose on a firm, including the possible adverse effect on processing efficiency.

17. Provide additional examples of each type of risk listed in the chapter.

18. What are examples of high-risk exposures and low-risk exposures within a typical firm?

19. Which errors, either accidental or deliberate, are most likely to be eliminated or reduced when an AIS is converted from manual processing to computer-based processing?

20. An effective control structure should deter persons from committing fraudulent acts by removing opportunities or by promptly exposing acts where opportunities do exist. However, certain behavioral tendencies may undercut this presumption. Discuss.

REVIEW PROBLEM

Campus Bookstore, Fourth Installment

Statement

The Campus Bookstore (described in the Review Problem at the end of Chapter 1) awaits delivery of its new minicomputer system. Before the system arrives, the manager asks the public accountants-consultants to review the internal control structure of the bookstore. The manager is concerned about the risks to which the bookstore's assets and information are currently exposed, as well as the changes that the minicomputer system will require in needed controls and security measures.

Required

  a. Identify the three component systems comprising the bookstore's internal control structure, and illustrate by means of the cash control system, the budgetary control system, and the general ledger control system.

  b. Discuss the risks to which the assets and information of the bookstore are exposed;

give examples of each type of risk; also, identify high-risk and low-risk exposures.

c. Describe the impacts that the minicomputer system will have on the controls that are currently in place for the manual AIS, assuming that the manual AIS has an adequate internal control structure.

Solutions

a. The first of the component control systems is the operational control system, which promotes efficiency in operational tasks. An important operational task is to maintain an adequate supply of cash to meet operational needs. In order to control cash, the bookstore manager (planner) first sets a minimum bank balance (benchmark) with respect to the level of cash (performance measure). This benchmark is set at a level that is (1) sufficiently high to prevent the bookstore from depleting its funds and entailing bank charges, and (2) sufficiently low to minimize idle cash deposits. Periodically the cash control system compares the actual amount of cash on hand with the minimum balance. When the actual amount on hand falls to or below the minimum balance, the system takes corrective action by borrowing an amount to replenish the account balance. Conversely, when the actual amount on hand rises significantly above the minimum, the system either repays a previous loan or invests the excessive amount. This cash control system, which is operated manually by the bookstore manager or the bookkeeper, may be aided by means of third-order feedback mechanisms such as cash forecasts.

The second component control system is the management control system, which encourages compliance with the bookstore's policies and procedures. An important tool of management control is a budgetary control system. The process begins with policies and revenue and cost benchmarks being set by the bookstore manager (planner). These policies and benchmarks are embodied in annual operating budgets for the three major responsibility areas: the upper-level and lower-level sales areas and the central administrative activities area. During the budget year revenues are accumulated and expenses are incurred. Monthly budget control reports that compare these actual results against the budgeted amounts and computed variances are prepared. The area managers are evaluated on the basis of the feedback provided by these reports. When necessary, corrective actions are taken.

The third component control system is the accounting control system, which has the objectives of safeguarding the bookstore's assets and ensuring the accuracy and reliability of the bookstore's data and information. An important means for providing accounting control is the use of the general ledger system. A key device in this system is the trial balance, which helps to ensure posting accuracy by verifying that total debit account balances equal total credit account balances. Another feature of the system that helps to ensure posting accuracy is the reconciliation of control accounts in the general ledger with the accounts in subsidiary ledgers. A feature that helps to safeguard assets is the reconciliation of physical counts of assets on hand (e.g., inventory) with the balances in general ledger accounts. Other control features include the use of coded accounts and the audit trail.

b. The bookstore is subject to risks with respect to its assets and information. Among these risks are the following.

(1) Unintentional or deliberate errors can be made in recording and processing transactions and related events such as sales, purchases, merchandise receipts, payroll, and cash disbursements. For instance, a clerk might enter an incorrect quantity to order on a purchase order, or might mismultiply the number of hours worked by an employee times the hourly rate of pay.

(2) Deliberate errors can be made in counting assets or in preparing reports or records. For instance, a clerk might deliberately undercount a receipt of merchandise and keep some of the items. A sales manager might inflate the sales amounts on a sales report.

(3) Assets may be stolen by outsiders or by employees. For instance, a customer may shoplift a paperback book or a sweater. A stock clerk may carry merchandise out the back door. (See comments regarding deliberate errors.)

(4) Security may be breached. For instance, a stock clerk may see a budget sheet on the bookkeeper's desk and repeat the key amounts to a friend.

(5) An act of violence may be committed. For instance, a customer may deface textbooks on a shelf.

High-risk exposures faced by the bookstore include theft and damage of merchandise, which is easily available on shelves and racks. Other high-risk exposures are the theft of cash by the cashiers. Low-risk exposures include accidental errors. Although accidental errors may occur fairly frequently, they are not likely to be sizable. Also, breaches of security are likely to be low-risk exposures, since information is not often easily available to unauthorized persons, especially when the system involves manual processing.

c. The minicomputer system should impact the accounting controls currently in place in the following ways.

(1) A variety of new controls will need to be incorporated into the computer programs that process the transactions, since fewer of the errors on source documents are likely to be detected by the clerks and cashiers.

(2) A greater number of analyses and listings of transactions will need to be provided for review by the managers and employees, since most of the files will be stored on computer-readable media and parts of the manual system audit trail will be lost.

(3) Careful procedures will need to be established to ensure that computer programs are not changed without proper authority.

(4) Security measures will need to be introduced to ensure that unauthorized users are not able to access confidential computerized files and data and to modify records concerning assets.

(5) Backup procedures will need to be established to ensure that computerized files and records are not accidentally lost as a result of human errors or equipment breakdowns.

(6) Maintenance procedures will need to be established and disaster prevention devices will need to be installed to prevent breakdowns or damages to the computer equipment.

(7) Procedures manuals and other documentation, as well as adequate training, will be needed to provide the clerks and other employees with the references and knowledge to operate the minicomputer system properly.

(8) Organizational changes will be needed to prevent employees from having opportunities to acquire bookstore assets fraudulently.

(9) Physical restrictions will be needed to prevent unauthorized persons (employees or outsiders) from obtaining access to computer facilities or records.

PROBLEMS

4-1. Jane Huston opens a shoe store and hires two employees. She also asks you, a public accountant, to prepare financial statements for her at the end of each month. You agree, but suggest that she needs an adequate internal control structure to make the venture a success. She replies that she cannot afford more costly outlays and that she does not want to offend the two employees with elaborate precautions.

Required

a. Explain the benefits to Jane of a sound internal control structure.

b. Present the response you would offer to her argument that controls would be too costly.

c. Point out the difficulties in establishing an effective internal control structure in her shoe store.

4-2. The Bronco Manufacturing Company makes wood products to order. Each job order is begun when a customer places a sales order and credit is approved. The order moves through three departments—fashioning, assembly, and finishing—during the production process. Upon completion of a job order the products are shipped and the customer is billed.

Required

Identify and describe each of the following control systems.

a. Credit control system.

b. Production job order time control system.

c. Production job order cost control system.

d. Production department budgetary control system.

e. Sales order transaction control system.

f. Production facilities accountability control system.

4-3. Identify high-risk exposures in each of the following types of organizations.

a. Hospitals.

b. Universities.

c. Atomic-energy generating plants.

d. Credit bureaus.

e. Gold mines.

f. Banks using automatic teller machines.

g. Mail order merchandising firms.

4-4. Jiffy Express is an overnight airfreight delivery service. It guarantees delivery of letters and packages to points throughout the United States by 10 A.M. the day following pickup. The reputation of Jiffy is directly related to the reliability of this service. Thus, it maintains pools of vans for local pickup and delivery as well as a large fleet of planes. Because time is of the essence, Jiffy has installed an online computer-based information system, with terminals located at its offices in all metropolitan centers. In addition to owning its various offices, the firm has its own garages for overnight parking. Moreover, it services both its vans and planes in rented facilities.

Required

Discuss the various high-risk exposures faced by Jiffy, and specify the factors that accentuate the risk in each case.

4-5. Colleges and universities have installed complex networks of computers and microcomputers in recent years. Although the specifics of the networks differ from university to university, they generally serve two major purposes: academic and administrative. They also are subject to a variety of abuses.

Required

Identify at least a dozen abuses and crimes to which a typical university computer network is subject. Assume that a single network, involving one mainframe and numerous microcomputers, serves *both* academic and administrative purposes.

4-6. Hot & Shot, CPAs, have just installed a new minicomputer system. This system includes eight terminals that are directly connected to the minicomputer, as well as an online magnetic disk unit, one magnetic tape cartridge unit, two printers, and one plotter. The firm intends to use the system to perform internal applications, such as billing and budgeting, as well as to prepare tax returns and financial analyses for clients. Each of these applications involves the use of software packages that are to be acquired from an outside software firm. It is anticipated that most of the packages will need to be modified by the single programmer that the firm employs.

Required

Discuss the several control problems that are introduced by the new minicomputer system, assuming that the firm has never used computers before. Illustrate these control problems, where suitable, by reference to the billing and financial analysis applications.

4-7. After undertaking a data security review, a firm adopts plastic cards that are needed for accessing the computer terminals owned by the firm. These cards are then given to those employees whose duties require them to use the terminals. The cost of the cards is $100,000. The probability that unauthorized persons will be able to access the system is thereby reduced from 25 percent to 5 percent. What reasons have likely been used by management to justify the $100,000 investment?

4-8. The Northwestern Division of the PVT Supply Company has the following inventory.

- *Pipe* ($600,000 average balance)—stored in an unfenced, unguarded yard.

- *Valves and Tools* ($300,000 and $100,000 average balances, respectively)—stored in an unguarded warehouse which is attached to the division's sales office.

All personnel have access to the inventory area through the adjoining offices.

The Northwestern Division was opened as a test market area two years ago and has grown rapidly, although it still represents only 5 percent of PVT's total operations. For various reasons (initially, the tentative nature of operations, and then, their rapid growth), the company did not install the same physical controls to safeguard the inventory at its Northwestern Division that it had established at its three other divisions. Such controls are now being considered.

The identified risk is that inventory with a total value of $1 million is not safeguarded. Such an amount is "significant" and a major loss would interrupt the division's business; nevertheless, the asset is not material to PVT's total financial position and results of operations. In the most recent physical inventory, the division determined that it had incurred a 7 percent inventory shrinkage ($70,000) in one year. This is related primarily to certain valves, tools, and smaller diameters of pipe that are readily marketable. Historically, inventory shrinkage at the other divisions has been only one half of 1 percent; therefore, "normal" shrinkage would have been $5000. The division suspects theft, but since it has no proof, it cannot recover under its theft insurance. The annual cost to install the controls at the Northwestern Division that are in place at other PVT divisions is estimated as follows.

Hire a night watchman:

Salary	$12,000
Taxes and fringe benefits @ 20%	2,400

Build a 10-foot high chain-link fence around the pipe yard ($5000 ÷ 10 years = $500 annual cost)   500

Build a special enclosed area (with separate locks) within the warehouse for storing tools and smaller, more expensive valves; assign one of the workers already on the payroll (no incremental cost) exclusive access to the area and responsibility for filling orders for these items. (Cost to build enclosed area: $1000 ÷ 10 years = $100 annual cost)   100

Install separate locks on the warehouse so that access (through the office or from outside) can be limited to authorized personnel ($200 initial cost; annual cost nil)   —

Total $15,000

The proposed controls will not result in any costs of lost sales resulting from a reduction in customer service if (1) the other divisions' abilities to service their customers are not affected by having similar controls and (2) the Northwestern Division believes its experiences will be similar. If this is not the case, the division should consider costs of lost sales in its cost-benefit analysis.

Required

Discuss the desirability of installing the controls and security measures pertaining to the pipe, valves, tools, and warehouse.[9]

4-9. Selected Small Firm (A Continuing Case) For the small firm that you selected in Chapter 1 (see Problem 1-7), complete the following requirements.

a. Describe the operational, management, and accounting control systems.

b. Identify several high-risk exposures.

c. Discuss the control problems that have been introduced by the computer system the firm now owns, or that would be introduced by a proposed new computer system.

---

[9] Courtesy of Arthur Young & Co., CPAs. Adapted with permission from *Evaluating Accounting Controls: A Systematic Approach*. Copyright © 1980 by Arthur Young & Company.

Controls and

Security

Measures

5

THIS CHAPTER'S OBJECTIVES ARE
TO ENABLE YOU TO:

Identify several plans for classifying controls and security measures.

Describe organizational, documentation, and other general controls that pertain to the manual processing portions of accounting information systems.

Describe organizational, documentation, and other general controls that pertain to the computer-based portions of accounting information systems.

Describe security measures that pertain to manual and computer-based accounting information systems.

Describe authorization and transaction controls that pertain to manual and computer-based accounting information systems.

INTRODUCTION

An effective internal control structure consists of numerous and varied controls and security measures. (Hereafter these controls and security measures will simply be called controls.) As Chapter 4 explained, these controls may be grouped according to administrative controls and accounting controls. Also, certain controls may be associated primarily with manual processing, others with computer-based processing, and still others with both. Our first section in this chapter concerns alternative ways of classifying controls. Remaining sections then identify and discuss, within the frameworks of these classification plans, various controls relating to typical accounting information systems (AIS's).

CONTROL CLASSIFICATIONS

In addition to administrative and accounting categories, controls may be classified according to settings, objectives, activism, and system architectures.

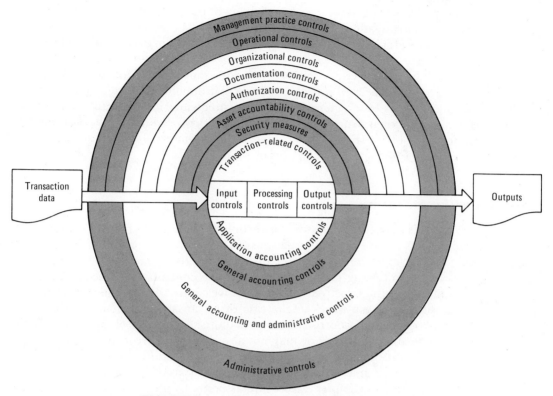

FIGURE 5-1 A framework for classifying controls.

Classification by Settings

The internal control structure incorporates a control environment. This environmental setting consists of those control-related elements within which the transaction flows take place. Included in the control environment are the organizational structure, feedback control systems, management policies and procedures, authorizations, security measures, and so on. As Figure 5-1 shows, they encompass all the administrative controls and those accounting controls known as **general controls.**

The remainder of the internal control structure consists of the transaction-related controls often known as **application accounting controls.**[1] These transaction-related controls may be divided into input, processing, and output controls. For example, each sales transaction is circumscribed by sales input, sales processing, and sales output controls.

Classification by Objectives

The internal control structure reduces significant risk exposures by means of controls. Accounting controls have the broad objectives of safeguarding a firm's

---

[1] Application accounting controls have recently been relabeled the *accounting system* by the AICPA. See American Institute of Certified Public Accountants, *Statement on Auditing Standards No. 55*, "Consideration of the Internal Control Structure in a Financial Statement Audit" (New York: 1988), 6.

assets and ensuring accuracy and reliability of the accounting data and information. In contrast, administrative controls have the broad objectives of promoting operational efficiency and encouraging adherence to management's policies and procedures.

These broad objectives may be subdivided into narrow, focused, and specific subobjectives associated with the control environment and transaction flows. For instance, the asset-safeguarding objective subdivides into objectives concerning the organizational structure, asset accountability procedures, authorizations, and so forth. Controls should be included within an internal control structure only when they fulfill specific objectives or subobjectives.

Classification by Activism

Controls may also be classified according to their active nature. A **preventive control** is a passive control, usually associated with the control environment. It prevents adverse events, such as errors or losses, from occurring. An example is a manual of processing procedures. A **detective control,** which detects errors or irregularities, is more active than a preventive control. It generally causes further processing to be halted, as in the case of a transaction containing a detected error. A **corrective control** is an even more active control, since it aids the correction process. It may or may not also detect the error or irregularity. An example is insurance coverage for theft of assets. Another example is an operational control, such as a predetermined inventory reorder point and quantity.

As described in Chapter 4, costs are associated with each control. Preventive controls generally require the lowest costs, detective controls require somewhat higher costs, and corrective costs are the most expensive.

Classification by System Architectures

Needed controls differ, as we have seen, for manual processing systems and for computer-based processing systems. They also differ for the various computer-based system structures. These systems or architectures include batch processing systems, online processing systems, centralized data base systems, and distributed systems. Our survey of controls in this chapter focuses only on the first two architectures, since we have not examined the others. Controls for centralized and distributed systems are delayed until Chapter 13.

Selected Classification Plan

Several classification plans are therefore available with respect to controls. For the purpose of surveying controls, no single plan is ideal. However, the categories shown in Figure 5-1, roughly corresponding to subobjectives, provide a convenient breakdown for discussion. When controls for a particular category are sufficiently distinctive for manual and computer-based systems, they are discussed separately.

ORGANIZATIONAL CONTROLS

The organization of a firm represents an underlying control framework because it specifies the work relationships of employees and units. A key control objective is to establish **organizational independence,** a clear and logical division of assigned duties and responsibilities. When organizational independence is soundly established, employees and units check on the work of one other. Generally two or more employees or units are involved in each procedure. Thus, errors made by one employee or unit will be detected by another. No single employee is able to commit a fraudulent act and then hide the deed. Fraud under such an arrangement can only be perpetrated by means of collusion. However, **collusion** (a conspiracy among two or more persons to commit fraud) is much less likely to occur than is fraudulent activity by individuals. Most persons who might consider fraud are afraid of being socially rejected if they propose the idea to a co-worker. To avoid the possibility of collusion by related persons, such as father and son, many firms have employment rules that prohibit nepotism.

In addition to divided responsibilities within each procedure, organizational control is based on the diligence of independent reviewers. To be truly effective, these reviewers must stand apart from the procedures themselves. A typical firm has several types of reviewers. The higher-level managers, including the board of directors, represent reviewers who have broad perspectives and responsibilities. Lower-level managers who receive and use the majority of outputs from the AIS represent reviewers with narrower perspectives. Finally, internal and external auditors represent reviewers who are both expert and objective.

Organizational independence is fully achieved only when incompatible duties and responsibilities are separated. Since relevant duties and responsibilities differ for manual and computer-based systems, each type of system should be separately considered.

Manual Systems

Authorizing, recordkeeping, and custodial functions should be organizationally separated. Thus, employees who handle assets, such as cash and inventory, should not authorize transactions involving those assets or keep the records concerning them. Figure 5-2 shows a logical division of duties in handling sales and cash receipts transactions. Not only are numerous units involved in the

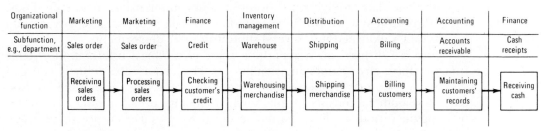

FIGURE 5-2 Organizational independence with respect to the revenue cycle.

procedure, but the previously mentioned functions are separated. The sales order department originates and authorizes sales transactions, whereas the credit department authorizes the credit terms on which the sales are made. Record-keeping is performed by the billing and accounts receivable departments, and custodial duties are handled by the warehouse, shipping, and cash receipts departments. Further examples appear in Chapters 8, 9, and 10.

This control guideline, based on the concept of organizational independence, can be extended as follows: Employees should not be assigned or allowed to perform incompatible duties. Thus, a clerk who is assigned the duty of handling a petty cash fund should not also handle cash received from customers, since the funds might become commingled. Also, an employee who performs key steps in a procedure, such as posting cash receipts, should not perform a check on the procedure, such as preparing a bank reconciliation.

A small firm faces a problem with respect to organizational separation. It generally has too few employees for effective division of duties and responsibilities. This problem can only be overcome by the manager-owner. He or she should closely supervise the employees and personally perform key tasks (e.g., opening the mail, depositing cash, writing and signing checks, signing purchase orders, and reconciling the bank statements).

Computer-based Systems

Organizational independence can also be maintained in computer-based systems, although adjustments are necessary. As with manual systems, the authorizing, custodial, and recordkeeping functions are to be separated. Since the recordkeeping is performed by computers within a data processing function, that function must be organizationally segregated from the custodial and other departments that use information outputs. Furthermore, the custodial departments (which generally remain unchanged when computers are introduced) should be organizationally separate from those user departments that authorize transactions. Examples of such user departments are the purchasing department, the payroll department, and the credit department.

In some cases it may appear that complete separation of these functions is not possible. An instance is when the computer system is programmed to approve or disapprove the credit of customers automatically. However, there is adequate separation in such a case, since the credit department management authorized the credit approval guidelines that were built into the credit program.

Additional organizational adjustments are needed, however, because processing steps and data storage are concentrated in computer-based systems. Thus, the information systems function, including its data processing activity, should be carefully subdivided into several subfunctions or departments.

Figure 5-3 displays an organization chart of a typical information systems function for a firm employing computers. The major separation is between systems development responsibilities and data processing responsibilities. Systems development consists of analyzing, designing, programming, and documenting the various applications and needed data bases. Data processing consists of handling and processing the actual transaction data inflows and outflows. If these functions were organizationally and physically intermingled, an employee

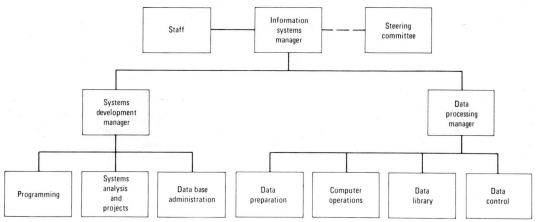

FIGURE 5-3 Organizational independence within the information systems function of a firm using computer-based processing.

(e.g., a programmer) could make unauthorized changes to "live" programs and data bases.

Figure 5-4 displays a suitable division of responsibilities within the data processing function, assuming that transactions are processed in batches. The computer operations activity, which processes data to produce outputs, should be separated from the responsibilities of preparing data, controlling data, and maintaining a data library. Thus, a computer operator should not receive transaction data directly from users, return the printed outputs directly to recipients, nor have access to the data library. Instead, the user departments should provide batches of transactions to the **data control section,** which records the batches in a **control log** and passes them on to the data preparation section. In that section the data are prepared for processing and delivered to the computer operator. The operator obtains files needed in the processing from the **data library** section, signing a log for their use. On completing the processing steps, the operator returns the outputs to the control section and the files to the librarian. The control section then performs certain checks to see that the processing is correct and sends the outputs to the designated recipients (users). It also makes sure that all erroneous transactions are corrected.

In the case of online processing applications, the division of duties is simplified. As Figure 5-5 shows, the user departments enter the transactions via terminals. The transactions are checked by computer programs for accuracy and then processed against online files. Outputs may be printed or displayed on printers, plotters, or terminals located in the departments of the recipients. The data control, data preparation, and data library tasks are performed by the computer system hardware and software, and will be described in a later section.

DOCUMENTATION CONTROLS

Documentation consists of procedures manuals and other means of describing the AIS and its operations. It also should include those aspects of a firm that

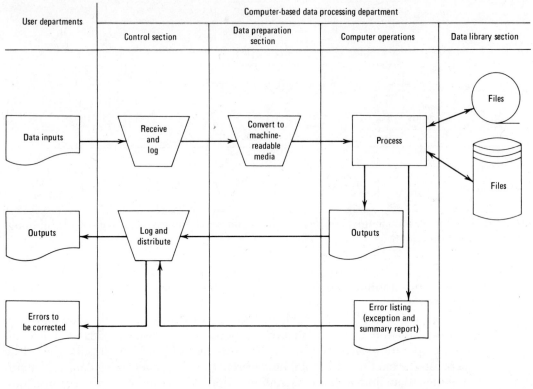

FIGURE 5-4 Flow of batched data within several units of an organization using computer-based processing.

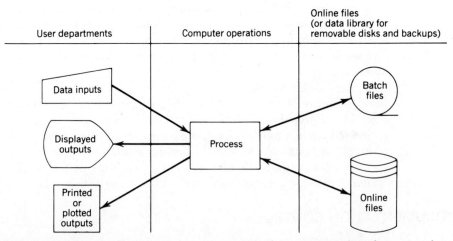

FIGURE 5-5 Simplified organizational separation in a computer-based system using online processing.

impinge on the AIS, such as policy statements and organization charts. Complete, clear, and up-to-date documentation is an important aspect of the internal control structure. It helps employees understand and interpret policies and procedures. Thus, data processing clerks are more likely to perform their AIS-related tasks correctly and consistently. Systems analysts and programmers can redesign transaction processing systems more easily and reliably, especially when the original designers may have left the firm. Auditors are able to examine the internal control structure more quickly and thoroughly.

Manual Systems

Documentation in manual systems should include all the AIS components listed in Chapter 2: source documents, journals, ledgers, reports, document outputs, charts of accounts, audit trail details, processing device manuals, procedural steps, and controls. Numerous examples should be provided, such as typical accounting entries and filled-in source documents. Procedures should be described in alternative ways, such as by narrative descriptions and system flowcharts.

Equally important are those elements that are related to the effective operation of the AIS. Clear policy statements encourage employees to adhere to management's policies. An organization chart and job descriptions inform employees of their roles and responsibilities with respect to data processing.

Computer-based Systems

All of the documentation listed are needed in computer-based systems. Even the most automated system contains some manual processing steps and involves interactions with human users and clerks. However, additional documentation is needed because of the presence of complex hardware and nonvisible programs.

Computer-related documentation concerns the computer system itself and the humans who interface with it. In the former category are the overall system standards, system application documentation, program documentation, and data documentation. In the latter category are operating documentation and user documentation. These types of documentation encompass the following.

1. **System standards** consist of those pertaining to systems development, program testing, computer operations, security, disaster control, and so on.

2. **System application documentation** includes computer system descriptions and flowcharts, input/output descriptions, file descriptions, and control procedures.

3. **Program documentation** includes program flowcharts or other logic diagrams, source program listings, input/output samples, file record layouts, data formats, operating instructions, program change procedures, and error correction procedures.

4. **Data documentation** includes the descriptions of data items stored within the firm's data base, including their relationships. This type of documenta-

tion is of particular importance to online processing and data base–oriented systems.

5. **Operating documentation** includes the operating instructions for the various computer programs, plus the required input/output files, setup procedures, list of programmed halts and related messages and required actions, recovery and restart procedures, estimated run times of programs, distribution of reports, and so forth. Operating documentation, generally organized into computer "run books," is of primary interest to computer operators.

6. **User documentation** includes procedures for entering data on source documents, checks of input data for accuracy and completeness, formats and uses of reports, possible error messages, and correction procedures. User documentation is of primary interest to user department clerks and managers.

ASSET ACCOUNTABILITY CONTROLS

A firm's assets are safeguarded by two means:

1. By permitting access to assets only in accordance with management's authorization.

2. By comparing the recorded accountability for assets with existing assets at reasonable intervals and by taking appropriate action with respect to any differences.[2]

Restricting access to assets is achieved through physical security measures, which are discussed in the next section. Insuring that assets are properly valued in the accounting records requires **asset accountability controls.** Specific controls that aid in providing proper asset accountability include the use of subsidiary ledgers, reconciliations, acknowledgment procedures, logs and registers, and reviews and reassessments.

Subsidiary Ledgers

Subsidiary ledgers can be maintained for such assets as accounts receivable, inventory, fixed assets, and investments. The values reflected in these ledgers are based on postings from transaction documents. As described in Chapter 2, the total of all balances in a particular subsidiary ledger should be equal to the balance in a corresponding control account in the general ledger. Since the postings are performed independently of each other, the use of a subsidiary ledger provides a cross-check on the correctness of the control account, and vice versa.

Reconciliations

A **reconciliation** consists of comparing values computed independently. Thus, a comparison of the balance in a control account with the total of balances

---

[2] American Institute of Certified Public Accountants, *Statement on Auditing Standards No. 1* "Codification of Auditing Standards and Procedures" (New York: AICPA, 1973), 20.

in a corresponding subsidiary ledger is an example of a reconciliation. Reconciliations can also involve comparisons of physical counts with quantities contained in accounting records. For instance, each item of a physical inventory should be counted periodically. These physical counts can then be reconciled with the quantities shown in the accounting records. If differences appear, they may signal the need to adjust the quantities in the accounting records to reflect the physical realities.

Since computer-based systems can compare quantitative values quickly and accurately, they are particularly suited for performing reconciliations. Computer-based systems are less suited for verifying qualitative attributes, such as signatures on checks. However, when discussing security measures we shall note that such personal attributes as thumbprints and spoken words can be translated into patterns that modern computers can authenticate.

Acknowledgment Procedures

In various transactions employees are called upon to acknowledge their accountability for assets. For instance, when merchandise arrives from suppliers, the clerks in the receiving department count the incoming goods, prepare a receiving report, and sign the report. In doing so they acknowledge accountability for the goods. When the merchandise later is moved to the storeroom, the storekeeper recounts the goods and signs for their receipt. Through this **acknowledgment procedure,** he or she accepts the transfer of accountability for the goods.

Logs and Registers

Receipts, movements, and uses of assets can be monitored by means of logs and registers. For example, cash receipts are logged on remittance listings (i.e., registers). Later the amounts recorded on deposit slips are reconciled to the amounts of these remittance listings in order to ensure that all receipts are deposited intact. Files of data on magnetic tapes are noted on logs as they are moved from the data library into the computer room and vice versa. When an employee uses a computer system from a terminal, the access can be recorded on a **console log.** Logs and registers thus help a firm to account for the status and use of its varied assets.

Reviews and Reassessments

Reviews by outside parties provide independent verification of asset balances and hence accountability. For instance, an auditor may verify that the fixed assets reflected in the accounts actually exist and are properly valued. A customer who receives his or her monthly statement will likely verify that the amount owed is correct.

Reassessments are re-evaluations of asset values. For example, accountants make periodic counts of the physical inventory and compare these counts to the inventory records. If necessary, the values in the records may be adjusted downward to reflect losses and breakage and aging.

SECURITY MEASURES

Security measures are necessary to protect the physical and data assets of a firm. The physical assets need protection from loss, damage, and abuse. Data assets also need protection from loss. In addition, the integrity and privacy of data need to be safeguarded. Manual systems employ essentially the same measures to protect both physical and data assets, whereas computer-based systems require distinctive measures for each. Figure 5-6 summarizes security measures that are useful in achieving the aforementioned purposes.

Manual Systems

Most security measures in a manual system prevent or restrict access to assets by unauthorized persons. Restrictive measures include security guards, fenced-in areas, burglar alarms, closed-circuit television monitors, safes, locked cash registers, locked file cabinets, and lockboxes in post offices. Although performed for other purposes, close supervision also serves to protect assets from unauthorized hands. For instance, a mailroom supervisor who closely observes the opening of mail discourages employees from pocketing enclosed currency. Another measure that protects the *value* of assets is adequate insurance coverage. For instance, employees having access to cash and negotiable assets should be bonded. **Fidelity bonds** indemnify a firm in case it suffers loss from defalcations committed by such employees.

Certain security measures protect assets from natural disasters. Sprinkler systems are available to put out fires that may break out in the merchandise warehouse, for instance. Some of these measures overlap with those used to restrict access. A safe or vault, which protects cash and valuable records from theft, is usually constructed to be fireproof as well.

A third type of security measure protects assets from breakdowns and business interruptions. Automobiles, typewriters, calculators, and other fixed assets are protected in this regard by preventive maintenance. When breakdowns occur in spite of such maintenance, a firm can be protected by the availability of backup equipment and business interruption insurance.

Computer-based Systems

All the security measures for manual systems apply equally to computer-based systems, since all firms have the same types of physical assets. Also, all computer-based information systems incorporate some manual operations. In this section, therefore, the focus will be only on those measures that pertain to the computer hardware and software and to computerized data.

Security Measures for Computer Facilities Computer hardware and software need to be protected from the natural environment, from unauthorized access, and from interruption.

1. **Protection from the natural environment.** To provide security with respect to the natural environment, the rooms housing major computer facilities should have

Purpose of security measures	Physical assets in both manual and computer-based systems	Hardware facilities of computer-based systems	Data in computer-based systems
1. Protect from theft or access by unauthorized persons	Security guards Fenced-in areas Burglar alarms Television monitors Safes and vaults Locked cash registers Lockboxes Close supervision Insurance coverage Logs and registers	Security guards Television monitors Locked doors Locked terminals Inaccessible terminals Employee badges Passwords Segregated test terminals	Locked doors, terminals, stacks of blank forms Offline data library Online data and program storage partitions Encoded data Paper shredders Passwords Limited terminal functions Automatic lockouts Callback procedures
2. Protect from natural environment or disasters	Sprinkler systems Fireproof vaults	Air-conditioning Humidity controls Fireproof vaults Halon gas spheres Auxiliary power supplies Insurance coverage Prudent locations Disaster contingency plans	
3. Protect from breakdowns and business interruptions	Preventive maintenance Backup equipment Insurance coverage	Preventive maintenance Backup hardware systems Graceful degradation Insurance coverage	
4. Protect from loss or alteration			Read-only memory Tape file protection rings External file labels Internal file labels Transaction logs Batch control logs Lockouts
5. Detect attempted access or change			Access logs Control logs System and program change logs
6. Reconstruct lost files			Backup procedures Rollback and recovery procedures

FIGURE 5-6 List of selected security measures for physical assets, computer facilities, and data.

a. Air conditioning.

b. Humidity controls.

c. Fireproof construction, including a fireproof vault.

d. Smoke detectors and fire alarm systems together with a fire-inhibiting substance such as halon gas.

e. Uninterruptible auxiliary power supplies.

Other measures may also be employed to protect against natural disasters and their effects. Computer facilities should be constructed on high terrain that minimizes threats of floods. They should not be placed in conspicuous locations that invite possible sabotage or vandalism. They should be covered by adequate insurance against threats of fire, floods, sabotage, and so on.

This array of protective measures can be made more effective by careful planning. A **disaster contingency plan** identifies all potential threats to the computer system, specifies the needed preventive security measures, and outlines the steps to be taken in case each type of disaster actually strikes. It identifies the resources that must be protected and the available resources to minimize the disaster. Furthermore, the plan should assign responsibility for implementation and provide for followup reviews.

2. **Protection from unauthorized access of computer facilities.** Only such personnel as computer operators, librarians, and information systems management should have access to mainframe computer facilities. Other personnel—accountants, clerks, and programmers—should be denied access to the main computer room and to the files and software that do not pertain to their responsibilities. Although these latter personnel may be allowed access to computer terminals and microcomputers, their use should be strictly limited.

In addition to security guards and television monitors, access restrictions may include

a. Locking computer room doors for which keys or magnetic-coded cards are needed to unlock the doors.

b. Locking terminals at the end of each working day.

c. Placing terminals behind counters or locked doors where they are inaccessible to visitors and unauthorized employees.

d. Requiring all personnel to wear color-coded badges.

e. Assigning passwords to those users who have legitimate needs to access terminals. (This measure will be discussed later.)

f. Requiring programmers to use segregated terminals when revising and testing programs.

3. **Protection from interruption.** As in the case of all data processing equipment and assets, computer facilities should be protected from breakdowns. Preventive maintenance is the first line of defense. The second line of defense is to make arrangements for **backup systems.** Thus, a firm might arrange with another firm to share its computer if a breakdown occurs. Alternatively, it may contract for computer usage from a service bureau, or maintain its own duplicate computer facilities. A less expensive approach is to acquire a computer system having the capability of "graceful degradation." That is, it could continue operations in the face of hardware problems, but at lowered efficiency.

Security Measures for Data We have seen that data interact with a computer system in varied ways. Data may move from user departments through a control department into a computer room; data may be entered via terminals located in users' departments. In some cases data may be transmitted from users at remote locations via communications lines. Data may be stored in online data bases or in offline files. When converted into reports data may appear on hard copy outputs. Data in all these circumstances must be adequately secured.

Many of the measures that provide data security are preventive or detective in nature. That is, they prevent data from being accessed or lost or changed, or they detect efforts by persons to access or change data. Other measures are corrective; they enable lost data to be recovered.

1. **Protection from unauthorized access of computerized data.** Access restrictions pertaining to the data within a mainframe computer room include those needed to protect the computer facilities themselves. However, the data need further protection.

   Data not in active use should be isolated in data libraries. Thus, offline files should be stored in a secure data library under the close care of a librarian. (Documentation plus stocks of blank checks and other vital forms should also be kept under lock and key by responsible individuals.) Online data bases, files, and programs should be maintained in separate partitions on the direct access storage media. Programs being tested should also be isolated from the active programs and data.

   To counteract unauthorized tapping of communications lines, data may be encoded during transmission. Since **encryption** is expensive and time consuming, this measure should be employed only on a selective basis.

   To circumvent unauthorized browsing, data records should be destroyed after their need has expired. Computer printouts might be fed to paper shredders. Data on magnetic media should be purged by the operating system, using appropriate erase commands.

   Most access restrictions in modern computer systems focus on terminal access, since hackers and other outside parties as well as unauthorized employees may make attempts. Measures intended to prevent unauthorized access to data via terminals include:

   a. **Identification for authorized users.** Means of identification are passwords, badges, magnetic striped cards, "smart" (computer chip) cards, thumbprints, and voice patterns. Upon receiving the identification data, security software within the computer system performs an authentication step. That is, it compares the entered data against a stored table of authorized codes or patterns. For instance, a **password** is checked against a list of authorized passwords. Often more than one password is used, with the added passwords providing access to specific files, records, fields within records, and programs. For example, an inventory control clerk may have passwords that allow him or her to access the inventory master file and the inventory updating program. Passwords may also specify allowed actions, such as reading data or updating records. A salesclerk, for instance, may be allowed to access the inventory master file but not to update records therein. In this case the file can be said to be "write-protected" from the clerk.

  b. **Limitation on terminal usage.** Particular terminals may be authorized to access data from certain files, to enter specified types of transaction data, to perform certain actions, and so on. For instance, a terminal in the warehouse may allow an employee to access the inventory master file, to enter data concerning movements of inventory items to the shipping department, but only to read (and not update) the on-hand balances of inventory items.

  c. **Automatic lockout.** Special security software may be used to detect and record all attempts to access the computer system via terminals. After a certain number (e.g., three) of unsuccessful attempts, the terminal locks up. This feature should deter hackers and others who may try to guess the assigned passwords.

  d. **Callback procedure.** Under a **callback procedure,** security software breaks the connection after a caller enters the correct password via a terminal. It then dials the authorized phone number of the terminal that apparently has called in. If the reconnection is not made, the entry has likely been made by a hacker from an unauthorized terminal or micro-computer.

2. **Protection from loss or alteration of data.** Security measures that prevent data on computerized media from being lost or altered include

  a. **Read-only memory.** Data stored in **read-only memory (ROM)** cannot be erased or written over. Thus, the data are safe from accidental or unauthorized tampering by programmers, computer operators, or other persons.

  b. **Tape file protection ring.** A **tape file protection ring** prevents data from being accidentally written onto a magnetic tape. Upon mounting a magnetic tape reel containing input data (such as transactions) on a tape drive, the computer operator removes the ring and thereby inhibits write-overs.

  c. **File labels.** Two types of file labels are available: external labels and internal labels. An **external file label** is attached to the exterior of a reel of magnetic tape or a disk pack. It identifies the contents to personnel in the computer facility. An **internal file label** is a record stored on a magnetic tape or disk in computer-readable form. Two internal file labels are the header and trailer labels. The **header label** is the first record in a file and contains identifying data (e.g., file name, file number, and creation date). Before allowing a computer program to use data from the file, the operating system checks the header label to see that the file is the correct one specified by the program. If not, the operating system alerts the operator. The **trailer label,** the last record in a file, contains an end-of-file code and various control totals. These totals are checked by the program to assure that no data are lost during processing.

  d. **Data logs.** Data as well as assets can be monitored by means of logs and registers. A **transaction log** reflects all transactions entered for processing by an online computer system. A batch control log similarly records all batches entering the data control section for processing. Both logs provide key parts of an audit trail.

e. Lockout. A **lockout** is a software feature that is necessary when a computer system employs multiprogramming. It prevents two programs (and hence users) from accessing the same records in a file concurrently. Without the lockout measure data could be written over and lost.

3. **Protection from undetected accesses and changes.** All attempted accesses of stored data and programs in computer-based systems should be monitored; any unwarranted activities should be investigated. Two types of logs facilitate this monitoring process. An **access log,** generally a component of security software, records all attempts to access an online data base. It shows the time, date, password used, type of inquiry, and data accessed. A console log, maintained by the operating system, records the actions of the computer system and the computer operator. It functions during batch as well as online processing activities.

Changes to programs, files, and controls should also be monitored. One suitable means of monitoring is to maintain a system and program change log, usually under the control of a systems development manager.

4. **Reconstruction of lost data.** In spite of sound security measures, data are sometimes lost. Therefore, duplicate copies of documents, files, data bases, programs, and documentation should be kept. If the backup copies are complete, lost master files and even large data bases can be completely and easily reconstructed.

A data backup plan must answer several concerns:

a. How long are the copies to be retained? A useful retention period needs to be established for each file, document, and so on. Someone should be designated to monitor the destruction of data which have reached the end of their retention periods.

b. Where are the backup copies to be stored? For safety from computer room fires and floods, one set of backup copies should be stored at a location that is physically removed from the computer facilities.

c. What backup procedures should be employed? The appropriate procedures depend in large part on the type of storage media used in file processing. The grandfather-father-son procedure is appropriate for magnetic tape files, while the periodic dump procedure is best suited for magnetic disk files.

The grandfather-father-son procedure is shown in Figure 5-7. Assuming that the processing cycle is one day, three generations of master files are created over a three-day period. These three generations consist of the current files, plus two sets of backup files. If the current "son" file is destroyed or damaged, it can be reconstructed by reprocessing the "father" file against the transaction file for today. Even if both the "father" and "son" files are lost, complete reconstruction is possible via the "grandfather."

If the master files are updated several times during a day, more than three generations of backup files will be needed. The imperative of this procedure is to maintain a quantity of backup files sufficient to allow complete reconstruction.

The grandfather-father-son procedure is suitable when new magnetic

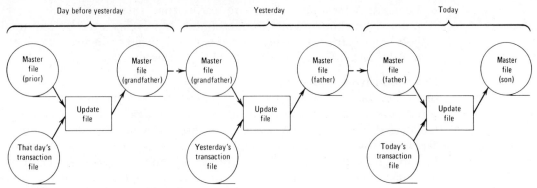

FIGURE 5-7 Grandfather-father-son reconstruction procedure for creating backup magnetic tape files. Reprinted by permission of the publisher from *Management Information Systems*, first edition by Raymond McLeod, Jr. Copyright © 1979 by Science Research Associates, Inc.

tape master files are created. When magnetic disk files are maintained online throughout the day, updated records in the master files are necessarily returned to their same disk addresses. This overlay approach destroys the previous data (i.e., it invokes the "destructive read-in" concept.) Thus, the **periodic dump and reconstruction procedure** shown in Figure 5-8 is required. In this procedure the contents of master files are copied (dumped) periodically from the magnetic disks onto reels of magnetic tape. In addition, activity and transaction logs are accumulated throughout the processing of transactions. The **activity log** contains images or "snapshots" of the items in each file that are changed by a transaction, both before and after the transaction. The transaction file contains numbered copies of each transaction record.

If data are lost during a particular day (e.g., day 2), the data are reconstructed from the dump of the previous day (i.e., day 1). The backup files are first loaded onto the data base. This loading process is called the **rollback phase.** Then during the **recovery phase** the after-change values for each transaction are entered from the activity log and processed against the loaded backup files.

MANAGEMENT PRACTICE AND OPERATIONAL CONTROLS

Two categories of controls that are administrative in nature are management practice and operational controls. Included within these categories are controls pertaining to personnel procedures, computer operating procedures, and systems development procedures.

Personnel Procedures

Employees should be carefully selected and trained to fulfill all positions of responsibility. Each employee's performance should be evaluated periodically.

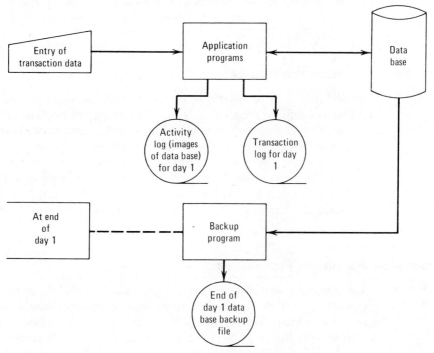

a. Creation of backup during day 1.

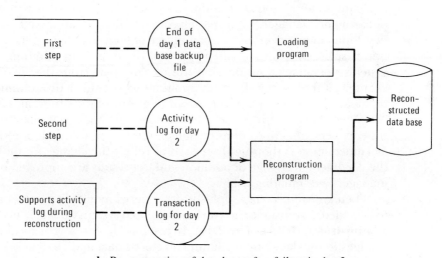

b. Reconstruction of data base after failure in day 2.

FIGURE 5-8 Periodic dump and reconstruction procedure for creating backup magnetic disk files.

Employees having access to cash and other negotiable assets should be bonded. Operational employees such as computer operators should be rotated among jobs and shifts. Also, employees in key positions of trust should be required to take periodic vacations, in order to subject their activities to review by substitutes. Finally, they should be well supervised so that they are encouraged to follow established policies and avoid irregularities. For instance, the manager of data processing and/or shift supervisors should closely observe and review the actions of the computer operators.

Computer Operating Procedures

In addition to close supervision, other sound operating procedures should be employed. Computer operators should be provided procedural manuals concerning all aspects of computer operations, together with run books for relevant applications. Data processing schedules should be prepared in advance and revised as necessary. Frequent control reports should be prepared showing the utilization of computer facilities and the productivity of the operators and other data processing employees. Preventive diagnostic programs should be employed to monitor the hardware and software functions so that problems may be detected.

Systems Development Procedures

Changes and additions to the AIS should be carefully monitored and approved. Even minor changes to application programs should follow the same procedure as major replacements of computer facilities. Otherwise, the personnel involved in the changes could effect undesirable modifications. For instance, a programmer could incorporate into a program a feature that benefits him or her personally or that violates management policy.

Requests for changes or additions should be initiated in writing by a user-department manager. The request should then be approved by the systems development manager (or by a committee of high-level managers if the modification is sufficiently large). After approval the change or addition is assigned to systems personnel, who develop the design apart from the "live" system. For example, if the change affects an application program, a programmer is assigned the task. This programmer uses a working copy of the program, rather than the "live" version currently in use. The new or revised design is next tested jointly by systems personnel (including persons not involved in the design) and the user. Documentation is thoroughly revised to reflect the change or addition. Finally, the documented change or addition and test results are approved by the systems manager and initiating user.

When an AIS becomes sophisticated, special monitoring personnel may need to be added. For instance, a data base-oriented system will likely need a **data base administrator (DBA).** The DBA is responsible for reviewing and approving changes to the data base, including all stored data and all data base software. A security administrator might also be needed when numerous security measures are installed in an online processing and data base–oriented AIS.

AUTHORIZATION CONTROLS

Authorizations serve as a bridge between administrative and accounting controls. They enforce management's policies with respect to the varied transactions flowing into the general ledger system. Because they are granted by persons not involved in the processing, they enhance the concept of organizational independence.

Authorizations may be classified as general or specific. A **general authorization** establishes standard conditions under which transactions are approved and executed. For instance, management sets general criteria by which credit sales are to be approved. A **specific authorization** pertains to a particular event, with the conditions and parties specified. For example, a cashier who has general authorization to sign checks may need specific authorization to sign a $25,000 check that repays a bank loan.

Authorizations are generally reflected on transaction documents. Thus, a customer's order approved by the credit manager authorizes goods to be released from the warehouse and shipped. In manual systems the authorizations are based on a personal review by a responsible individual, such as the credit manager. In computer-based systems the authorizations are often based on instructions built into computer programs. Thus, requisitions authorizing more inventory to be purchased are prepared by an inventory reorder program only when the program determines that the need for inventory meets management's reorder policies.

TRANSACTION CONTROLS

Those controls that pertain directly to the transaction processing systems are called **transaction** or **application controls.** The overall objectives of transaction controls are to provide reasonable assurance that all transactions are properly authorized and accurately recorded, classified, processed, and reported. Thus, transaction controls are generally subdivided into input, processing, and output controls, as Figure 5-9 suggests. **Input controls** consist of well-designed source documents, document registers, account coding, edit checks of input data, and so

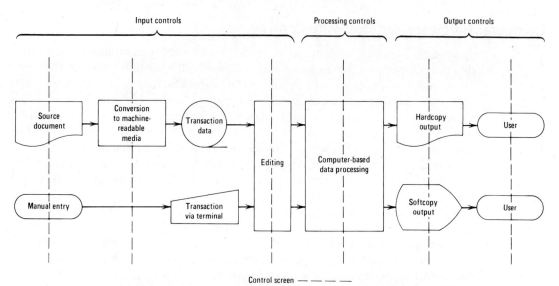

FIGURE 5-9 Subdivisions of transaction (application) controls.

forth. **Processing controls** include batch totals, verifications and cross-checks, and reconciliations. **Output controls** consist of reviews, such as those performed by internal auditors, and include such other controls as **distribution logs** that clearly show to whom reports are to be distributed.

Most transaction controls apply equally to processing systems, regardless of their degree of automation. However, certain controls are applicable only to batch processing systems, and others are applicable only to online processing systems. An example of the former are **batch totals,** which are computed based on data appearing in a batch of transaction documents. Batch totals may be computed for dollars or quantities (called **amount totals**), for identification numbers (called **hash totals**), or for the count of documents in the batch (called **record counts**).

Each system for processing a type of transaction (e.g., the sales transaction processing system) has its own set of control objectives. In order to achieve these objectives, **control points**—points where the exposures to risks (e.g., errors and thefts) are sufficient to require controls—must be identified. At each control point an appropriate control should be incorporated. Since each transaction processing system consequently requires a unique set of controls, we will defer further discussion until we reach the chapters dealing with specific transaction cycles.

OTHER CONTROLS

Certain types of controls have been omitted for various reasons from the categories previously listed. Controls pertaining to data bases and computer networks are deferred until these topics are discussed in Chapters 11 and 13. Computer hardware and software controls are relatively unimportant to system designers, although they do deserve brief mention. Error correction procedures, on the other hand, are transaction-related controls that deserve special attention.

Computer Hardware and Software Controls

Modern computer systems are equipped with a variety of built-in controls that detect malfunctions. Accountants and designers can reasonably assume that they are sound and adequate, unless they are modified by users.

Typical **hardware checks** include the parity check, echo check, read-after-write check, dual read check, and validity check. The parity check, for example, detects the loss of data when they are transferred between components within the computer system. Other safeguards include duplicate circuits and diagnostic test routines. As the term implies, duplicate circuits within the central processing unit (CPU) perform calculations twice and compare results. Diagnostic test routines automatically signal the impending failure of a component.

Software checks include the label check and the read-write check. The former causes the operating system to notify the computer operator automatically of the contents of internal labels on magnetic tapes and disks. The latter automatically halts a program when reading or writing is inhibited or initiates an end-of-file routine when no further processing is possible.

Error-Correction Procedures

Errors should be detected and corrected as early in a procedure as possible. They can be corrected most easily in the input stage. Also, by correcting errors at the point of entry, the data used in processing and stored in files will be accurate. Accuracy is especially critical to online processing systems, since errors are quickly spread throughout such systems. A single error might affect several files and cause a variety of outputs to be distorted. It might even lead to undesirable actions, such as the preparation of an inventory reorder report when inventory quantities on-hand are adequate.

Formalized error-correction procedures are needed. These procedures should ensure that detected errors are corrected and re-entered for processing. However, error-correction procedures differ for batch processing and online processing applications.

Error Correction in Batch Processing Applications Errors in batch processing applications may be detected by such controls as batch totals, **verification of keyed-in data,** and **edit checks** built into the application programs. After the errors are detected, error-correction procedures should involve cooperation between the computer system and clerical personnel.

Error-correction procedures differ somewhat, depending on the means of detection. Assuming that the errors are detected by edit checks, the computer system *flags* the erroneous transactions and suspends their processing. The erroneous transactions, together with explanatory messages, are then entered on a **suspense file.** Hard copy listings of these errors are also printed. Copies of the error listings are returned, by the control section, to the user departments for correction. After the erroneous transactions are corrected, they are re-entered for re-editing and processing. These transactions are automatically removed from the suspense file by the computer system. Any transactions not re-entered for processing after a reasonable interval are investigated by the control section.

Batch control totals are affected by the presence of input errors. Generally they must be adjusted during each computer run in which errors are discovered and transactions are removed for correction. To facilitate the monitoring of batch totals, they are often included on error listings that are printed during the course of each computer run. Error listings containing such data may be labeled as **exception and summary reports.**

Error Correction in Online Processing Applications Almost all errors are detected in online processing applications by means of edit checks. When an error is detected during input operations, the edit program notifies the entering clerk via an error message on the screens of his or her cathode ray tube (CRT). The clerk must immediately correct the error or omission before the program will accept additional data concerning the transaction. The corrected data item and successive items are then edited until all items for the transaction have been accepted. At that point the program may ask the clerk to confirm the transaction by striking a function key. When the clerk does so, the program enters the transaction into the system for processing.

In some cases errors will not be detected until the data appear on outputs, such as listings that show changes to each account balance. When errors are found during reviews of such outputs, the corrections should only be made by authorized persons and approved by the user departments.

SUMMARY

Controls may be classified as administrative and accounting controls; general and application accounting controls; controls that safeguard assets, ensure data accuracy and reliability, promote operational efficiency, and encourage adherence to management's policies and procedures; controls that prevent, detect, and correct errors; and controls for manual systems and for various computer-based system architectures. Drawing from these various classification plans, controls are discussed under the headings of organizational controls, documentation controls, asset accountability controls, security measures, management practice and operational controls, authorization controls, transaction controls, computer hardware and software controls, and error-correction procedures.

Organizational controls center around the concepts of divided responsibilities and independent reviews. Authorizing, recordkeeping, and custodial functions should be organizationally separated. In computer-based systems the separation should pertain to the systems development and data processing functions as well as to user and custodial departments. For batch processing applications the data processing function should have separate computer operations, data control, and data library units. Documentation controls consist of procedures manuals and various records that describe the AIS and its operations. In computer-based systems documentation pertains to system standards, system applications, programs, data, computer operations, and user instructions. Asset accountability controls ensure that assets are properly valued in the records; they include the use of subsidiary ledgers, reconciliations, acknowledgment procedures, logs and registers, and reviews and reassessments.

Security measures protect the physical and data assets. In manual systems they restrict access to the assets, protect the assets from natural disasters, and protect the assets from breakdowns and business interruptions. In computer-based systems they also protect computer hardware and software from the natural environment, from unauthorized access, and from interruption. Furthermore, they protect data from unauthorized access, loss, and alteration; they monitor attempted accesses and changes; and they enable lost data to be reconstructed. Administrative controls include those nonaccounting controls that pertain to sound management practices in such areas as personnel, computer operations, and systems development.

Authorization controls, of both the general and specific varieties, enforce management's policies with respect to the varied transactions that flow into the general ledger. Transaction controls provide reasonable assurance that all transactions are properly authorized and accurately recorded, classified, processed, and reported. They include a wide variety of edit checks and other controls, which are discussed in detail in later transaction cycle chapters. Well-planned error-correction procedures are needed to ensure that detected transaction errors are corrected as early as possible during the handling of transaction data. Finally, computer hardware and software controls are built-in controls that detect malfunctions within the operation of the computer system. Normally they are assumed to be sound and adequate in modern computer systems.

REFERENCES

Auditing Standards Committee, American Institute of Certified Public Accountants. "The Effects of Computer Processing on the Examination of Financial Statements." *Statement on Auditing Standards No. 48.* New York: AICPA, 1984.

Bhaskar, Krish N., Lin, W. Thomas, and Savich, Richard S. "An Integrated Internal Control Framework to Prevent and Detect Computer Frauds." *The EDP Auditor Journal* (Vol. II, 1987), 42–49.

Buss, M. D. J., and Salerno, L. M. "Common Sense and Computer Security." *Harvard Business Review* (Mar.–Apr. 1984), 112–121.

Cerullo, Michael. "Application Controls for Computer-based Systems." *Cost and Management* (June 1982), 18–23.

Davis, Gordon, Schaller, Carol A., and Adams, Donald L. *Auditing and EDP,* 2d ed. New York: AICPA, 1983.

Davis, Keagle, and Perry, William E. *Auditing Computer Applications: A Basic Systematic Approach.* New York: Ronald Press, 1982.

Moscove, Stephen A., and Simkin, Mark G. *Accounting Information Systems: Concepts and Practice for Effective Decision Making,* 3d ed. New York: Wiley, 1987.

Nash, John F., and Roberts, Martin B. *Accounting Information Systems.* New York: Macmillan, 1984.

Porter, W. Thomas, and Perry, William E. *EDP Controls and Auditing,* 5th ed. Boston: Kent Publishing, 1987.

Rushinek, Avi, and Rushinek, Sara F. "Audit Trail Controls in an EDP Information System." *The EDP Auditor Journal* (Vol. II, 1986), 20–30.

Wilson, Glenn T. "Computer Systems and Fraud Prevention." *Journal of Systems Management* (Sept. 1984), 36–39.

QUESTIONS

1. What is the meaning of each of the following terms?

General control
Application
 accounting control
Preventive control
Detective control
Corrective control
Organizational
 independence
Collusion
Data control section
Control log
Data library
Documentation
System standard
System application
 documentation
Program
 documentation
Data documentation
Operating
 documentation
User documentation
Asset accountability
 control
Reconciliation
Acknowledgment
 procedure
Console log
Review
Reassessment
Security measure
Fidelity bond
Disaster contingency
 plan
Backup system
Encryption
Password
Callback procedure
Read-only memory
 (ROM)
Tape file protection
 ring
External file label
Internal file label
Header label
Trailer label
Transaction log
Lockout
Access log
Grandfather-father-son
 procedure
Periodic dump and
 reconstruction
 procedure
Activity log
Rollback phase
Recovery phase
Data base
 administrator (DBA)
General authorization
Specific authorization
Transaction control
Input control
Processing control
Output control
Distribution log
Batch total
Amount total
Hash total
Record count
Control point
Hardware check
Software check
Verification of
 keyed-in data
Edit check
Error-correction
 procedure
Suspense file
Exception and
 summary report

2. In what ways may controls be classified?

3. Contrast preventive, detective, and corrective controls.

4. Which functions should be organizationally separated to provide adequate independence?

5. How may one compensate for the lack of organizational independence in small firms?

6. Describe the modifications that are necessary to achieve adequate organizational independence when a firm acquires a computer system.

7. Identify the various types of documentation needed by a firm having a computer system.

8. By what two key means are the assets of a firm safeguarded?

9. What techniques are available for achieving asset accountability?

10. What are the purposes of security measures when applied in relation to a firm's AIS?

11. Identify a variety of security measures that are suitable to a firm having a manual AIS.

12. Identify security measures that are suitable for protecting computer hardware and software from the natural environment.

13. Identify security measures that are suitable for protecting computer facilities and data from unauthorized access.

14. Identify security measures that are suitable for protecting computer facilities from breakdowns and hence the firm's AIS from interruptions.

15. Identify security measures that are suitable for protecting a firm's data stored on computerized media from loss or alteration.

16. Identify security measures that can detect attempted accesses and changes of computerized data in (a) batch processing systems and (b) online processing systems.

17. Identify security measures that enable lost computerized data to be reconstructed in (a) batch processing systems and (b) online data base systems.

18. Discuss personnel, computer operation, and systems development procedures.

19. Contrast general and specific authorizations.

20. What are the objectives of transaction controls?

21. What types of protection do computer hardware and software controls provide?

22. Describe error correction procedures in (a) batch processing applications and (b) online processing applications.

23. What depth of knowledge should be possessed by accountants concerning (a) computer hardware and software controls, (b) organizational controls, (c) security measures, and (d) transaction controls?

24. When a firm converts from a manual AIS to a computer-based AIS, in what ways does the change help and hinder (a) an accounting employee who is intent on embezzling funds, (b) a competitor who is intent on accessing confidential files, and (c) a disgruntled ex-employee who is intent on disrupting data processing operations?

25. What are the features of online processing systems that create difficulties in establishing a sound control framework?

26. Provide examples of preventive, detective, and corrective controls for (a) batch processing systems and (b) online processing systems.

REVIEW PROBLEM

Campus Bookstore, Fifth Installment
Statement

The Campus Bookstore (described in the Review Problem at the end of Chapter 1) continues to await delivery of its new minicomputer system. As noted in the previous installment, the manager requested a review of the bookstore's internal control structure. After reading the consultant's report, the manager turns his attention to the specific internal accounting controls and security measures that are needed to protect the computer facilities, the store's assets, and the data and information used by the bookstore.

Required

a. Identify the organizational, documentation, asset accountability, and systems development controls that should accompany the bookstore's new minicomputer system.

b. Identify the security measures that should protect the computer facilities, assets, and data of the bookstore.

c. Describe the error-correction procedure to be employed.

Solutions

a. Organizational controls include

(1) Supervision and reviews of reports by the store manager and the managers on the two levels.

(2) Periodic reviews by the bookstore's public accountant.

(3) Adequate organizational separation between the authorizing, recordkeeping, and custodial functions. Consider, for instance, the purchases transaction procedure. A purchase would be authorized by the signature of a merchandise manager on a purchase order. The goods would be re-

ceived and stored under the custody of the inventory manager. The records concerning the receipt and storage of the goods would be maintained by one of the bookkeepers. Similar segregations of functions would be established for the cash receipts, cash disbursements, payroll, and fixed asset transactions.

(4) Careful division of duties within the accounting function, in order to avoid incompatibilities. One sound division would consist of having the first bookkeeper maintain the inventory and purchases and fixed asset records, as well as prepare checks (including paychecks) for signature; having the second bookkeeper maintain the accounts payable records and employee earnings records; having the third bookkeeper maintain the purchase returns, sales returns, and general ledger; and having the accountant reconcile the bank statement and prepare the financial statements. Note that the cashier would handle the received cash, make entries in the cash receipts journal, and prepare the bank deposit slip.

(5) Further organizational separation to accommodate the needs of the new minicomputer system. Thus, if a system analyst-programmer is hired, he or she should be organizationally separate from the actual operations of the computer system. Also, the operators of the minicomputer system (to be hired shortly) should be separated from the various users of the system, such as the merchandise managers, and from a data control clerk (to be hired).

Documentation controls should include all the accounting records involved in the transactions, in addition to policy statements, organization charts, and so on. With the introduction of the minicomputer system, new documentation will be needed, such as system standards, descriptions of all computer-based applications, programs and related flowcharts and so forth, descriptions of all data items, operating instructions for all programs to be run by computer operators, and documentation to aid users in accessing the minicomputer system.

Asset accountability controls include the accounts payable subsidiary ledger plus records concerning the merchandise inventory and fixed assets, periodic physical counts of the merchandise and reconciliations with the records, monthly bank reconciliations, reconciliations of cash received daily with the recorded listings of the receipts, acknowledgment and logging of all receipts and storage of all merchandise and supplies, and periodic reviews of all records pertaining to the various assets of the bookstore.

Systems development controls should include procedures that require all changes and additions to the accounting information system to be initiated in writing by a manager, to be approved by the bookstore manager, to be developed by the systems analyst-programmer (or outside consultant) and tested apart from the "live" system, and to be accepted by the initiating manager.

b. Security measures to protect the cash, inventory, and fixed assets should include locked doors, locked cash registers, burglar alarms, safes, insurance coverage, and sprinkler systems. Measures to protect the minicomputer facilities should include several of these plus air-conditioning, humidity controls, halon gas, a disaster contingency plan, passwords for all authorized users of terminals (including point-of-sale terminals), preventive maintenance, and an arrangement for a backup minicomputer system. Measures to protect the data (in addition to passwords) include limitations on the capability of terminals to access data files, automatic lockouts on all terminals, ROM, internal file labels, transaction logs, console logs, backup copies of all master files, and a reconstruction procedure.

c. Error-correction procedures will be employed for both batch processing and online processing applications. In the former case, an error listing of all detected errors should be obtained by the control clerk after each computer run. It should be logged and then given to the persons who prepared the inputs. They would be expected to correct the errors and resubmit the transactions for processing. In the latter case, edit programs should be employed for all online applications. All transactions should be checked by the edit programs and not accepted until errors and omissions are corrected.

PROBLEMS

5-1. Give an example of an occurrence that each of the following practices is intended to prevent or detect.

a. Assigning one employee to handle the merchandise in the warehouse and another employee to maintain the inventory records.

b. Storing the inventory within a fenced area that is kept locked.

c. Requiring all disbursements (except petty cash transactions) to be made by check.

d. Requiring all returns of sold merchandise to be listed on a special credit memorandum form that is prepared and signed by a manager.

e. Maintaining comprehensive manuals that show detailed steps of all the accounting procedures.

f. Mailing a monthly statement to each customer, showing the details of all transactions and the balance owed.

g. Requiring a clerk who receives ordered merchandise to prepare and sign a form that separately lists all the items and quantities received.

h. Counting the inventory on hand periodically and comparing the count of each item to the inventory records.

i. Listing all the cash remittances received daily by mail and comparing the total to the deposit slip.

j. Depositing all cash received daily intact in the bank.

k. Having auditors examine the financial statements once a year.

5-2. What internal accounting control(s) or security measure(s) would be most effective in preventing or detecting each of the following errors or undesirable practices?

a. A storeroom clerk discovers that a particular part is out of stock, even though the accounting records show that 90 units are on hand.

b. A petty cash custodian removes $100 from the petty cash fund for personal use but replenishes the amount with cash received from customers that day.

c. A general ledger clerk posts a credit to the accounts receivable control account pertaining to a return of merchandise from a customer, but forgets to post the debit to the sales return account.

d. A firm's bank prepares a debit memorandum for an NSF (not sufficient funds) check, but the bank clerk forgets to mail a copy of the memo to the firm.

e. A general ledger clerk forgets to post Wednesday's total cash receipts amounting to $2397.

f. An accounts receivable clerk pockets $100 in currency received by mail from a customer but nevertheless posts the amount of the receipt to the customer's accounts receivable account.

g. A production-line employee walks into the tool room just before quitting time one day, puts a small precision tool in her jacket pocket, and takes it home.

h. A clerk in the personnel department lists a fictitious employee in the personnel records; when the signed paychecks are received from the cashier for distribution, this clerk takes the paycheck for the fictitious employee, cashes the paycheck, and keeps the proceeds.

i. A purchasing manager orders goods from a supplier firm, of which the manager happens to be an owner, that are not needed.

j. A storekeeper takes inventory items home at night; when the shortages become apparent during physical inventory-taking, the storekeeper claims that the receiving department did not deliver the goods to the storeroom.

k. A cashier steals $50 in currency received by mail from a customer; the cashier conceals the theft by preparing a credit memorandum that reduces the balance of the customer's account by $50.

l. A cashier prepares and submits an invoice from a fictitious supplier having the name of his mother, writes a check to the "supplier," and mails the check to his mother's address; the son and mother later split the proceeds.

5-3. What general control(s) or security measure(s) would be appropriate to prevent, detect, or minimize the adverse effects from each of the following occurrences?

a. A fire in an office area spreads to the computer center of a firm. All the computer facilities and many files are destroyed.

b. A computer hardware component malfunctions during a processing run, causing many of the accounts receivable records to be lost. The records must be reconstructed manually from stored transaction documents and past monthly statements.

c. A severe storm causes the computer system to be shut down for several days. As a result confusion reigns, many of the firm's operations are crippled, and employee paychecks are delayed.

d. A five-minute power failure causes the computer system to cease functioning, thereby resulting in the loss of data being transmitted from several terminals.

e. A payroll clerk accesses her salary records from a terminal and increases her salary level.

f. An industrial "spy" taps the communications lines of a high technology firm, acquires confidential product information, and sells it to a competitor.

g. A computer printout of confidential personnel data is sent by mistake to the production manager.

h. A magnetic tape containing yesterday's sales transactions is accidentally moved to the scratch-tape rack and cannot be located.

i. The controller discovers that a newly prepared consolidated financial statement contains several errors, which apparently are due to "bugs" in the computer program that processed and printed the statement.

However, the programmer who developed the consolidation program recently resigned and no one else can understand the logic of the program.

j. A programmer for a local bank modifies the program that computes interest amounts on savings account balances. His modification, known as the "salami fraud," consists of transferring to his account a fraction of a cent from each interest computation (which previously had been rounded in the depositor's favor). This type of programming modification is very difficult to detect.

k. A visitor to the computer center of a nationwide publication carries away a diskette containing a list of subscribers. After using a service bureau to prepare a hard copy printout, she sells the list to direct mail advertisers.

l. A disgruntled computer operator accesses several master files through the main computer console and alters data in their header labels.

m. A programmer for a small firm assists the computer operator during rush periods. One day during the processing of checks he substitutes bogus vouchers and overrides the control in the program designed to prevent the payment of unauthorized vouchers.

n. A warehouse worker accesses the confidential salary file in the data base via a terminal located in the warehouse.

o. An inexperienced computer operator mounts the accounts receivable master file (on a magnetic tape reel) for the daily updating run. However, the operator inadvertently designates the tape drive on which it is mounted as an output drive and erases many of the customers' records.

p. A firm which performs batch processing runs on a regular basis frequently has difficulty in assuring that erroneous transactions are corrected and resubmitted for processing and that batch totals are verified after each processing run.

5-4. The Y Company has three clerical employees who must perform the following functions.

a. Maintain the general ledger.

b. Maintain the accounts payable ledger.

c. Maintain the accounts receivable ledger.

d. Prepare checks for signature.

e. Maintain the cash disbursements journal.

f. Issue credits on returns and allowances.

g. Reconcile the bank account.

h. Handle and deposit cash receipts.

Assuming that the employees are able, the company requests that you assign these functions to the three employees in such a manner as to achieve the highest degree of internal control. It may be assumed that the employees will perform no accounting functions other than the ones listed and that any accounting functions not listed will be performed by persons other than the three employees.

Required

State how you would distribute these functions among the three employees. Assume that with the exception of the nominal jobs of the bank reconciliation and the issuance of credits on returns and allowances, all functions require an equal amount of time.

(CPA adapted)

5-5. Draw a sound organization chart for the information systems function of a moderate-sized firm if it includes the following managers and employees.

Harry Snell, director of information systems.
May Wilks, systems analyst.
Jack Dierks, programmer.
Paul Miller, computer operator.
Bill Parks, data processing manager.
Susan Aspen, data librarian.
Barry Naylor, systems development manager.
Janet Hibbler, data control clerk.
Mary Jackson, data entry clerk.
Dave Johns, systems analyst.
Laura Meyers, data base administrator.
Kirsten Hanes, data entry clerk.
Jarvis Cline, computer operator.

5-6. You have just been assigned to review the documentation pertinent to the computer-based information system of your firm.

Required

a. List three advantages of adequate documentation.

b. Match each of the following elements of documentation with the category in which it is likely to be found. Use every element given but do not use any element more than once.

Categories	*Elements*
A. Systems documentation	**1.** Flowcharts showing the flow of information.
B. Program documentation	**2.** Procedures needed to balance, reconcile, and maintain overall control.
C. Operations documentation	**3.** Contents of data to be stored.
D. Data documentation	**4.** Record layouts.
E. User documentation	**5.** Data relationships.
	6. Logic diagrams and/or decision tables.
	7. Report distribution instructions.
	8. Messages and programmed halts.
	9. Data formats.
	10. Source statement listings.
	11. Instructions to show proper use of each report.
	12. Descriptions of files.
	13. Restart and recovery procedures.
	14. Instructions to ensure the proper completion of all input forms.
	15. List of system controls.

(CIA adapted)

5-7. The Landers Corporation has established the following procedures pertaining to its information systems function.

a. Access to the computer room is limited to the firm's employees.

b. The vault door of the tape library is locked at night and opened each morning by the data processing manager or his assistant. The combination is known only to information systems personnel.

c. The grandfather-father-son retention cycle is used for files, with ancestors stored in the vault.

d. The function has an administrative manager who authorizes the development of applications, approves run schedules, and supervises the work of programmers, analysts, and operators. Another of her responsibilities is to review all program modifications.

e. The programmers and analysts have flexible work requirements and frequently work into the evening or come in at night to "debug" and test programs on the computer.

f. All systems development is initiated by the data processing manager. An informal mechanism exists to assess users' needs and to prioritize application requests. Priorities are determined by the data processing manager according to a long-range master plan initiated last year. The information systems function absorbs all costs of development work.

g. Structured programming (a standardized and efficient method of writing programs) is required when developing all new programs.

h. Each program is assigned to a programmer who is responsible for coding, testing, and documenting that program.

Required

For each of the eight preceding procedures, identify the strengths and/or weaknesses present. For each strength, indicate why it is a strength; for each weakness, suggest a procedure to correct the deficiency.

(CIA adapted)

5-8. Simmons Corporation is a retailing concern with stores and warehouses throughout the United States. The company is in the process of designing a new integrated computer-based information system. In conjunction with the design of the new system, the management of the company is reviewing data processing security to determine what new control features should be incorporated. Two areas of specific concern are (1) confidentiality of company customer records and (2) safekeeping of computer equipment, files, and related facilities.

The new information system will be employed to process all company records, which include sales, purchase, financial, budget, customer, creditor, and personnel information. The stores and warehouses will be linked to the main computer at corporate headquarters by a system of remote terminals. This arrangement will permit data to be communicated directly to corporate headquarters or to any other location from each location throughout the computer network.

At the present time certain reports have restricted distribution, either because not all levels of management need to receive them or because they contain confidential information. The introduction of remote terminals in the new system may provide access to this restricted data by unauthorized personnel. Simmons' top management is concerned that confidential information may become accessible and may be used improperly.

The company is also concerned with potential physical threats to the system, such as sabotage, fire damage, water damage, power failure, and magnetic radiation. Should any of these events occur in the present system and cause a computer shutdown, adequate backup records are available to enable the company to reconstruct necessary information at a reasonable cost on a timely basis. However, with the new system, a computer shutdown would severely limit company activities until the system could become operational again.

Required

a. Identify and briefly explain the problems Simmons Corporation could experience with respect to the confidentiality of information and records in the new system.

b. Recommend measures Simmons Corporation could incorporate into the new system that would ensure the confidentiality of information and records in the new system.

c. Identify safeguards that Simmons Corporation can develop to provide physical security for its (1) computer equipment, (2) files, and (3) computer-related facilities.

(CMA adapted)

5-9. Aidbart Company has recently installed a new online, data base computer system. CRT units are located throughout the company with at least one CRT unit located in each department. James Lanta, vice president of finance, has overall responsibility for the company's management information system, but he relies heavily on Ivan West, director of MIS, for technical assistance and direction.

Lanta was one of the primary supporters of the new system because he knew it would provide labor savings. However, he is concerned about security of the new system. Lanta was walking through the purchasing department recently when he observed an Aidbart buyer using a CRT unit to inquire about the current price for a specific part used by Aidbart. The new system enabled the buyer to have the data regarding the part brought up on the screen as well as each Aidbart product that used the part and the total manufacturing cost of the products using the part. The buyer told Lanta that, in addition to inquiring about the part, he could also change the cost of parts.

Lanta scheduled a meeting with West to review his concerns regarding the new system. Lanta stated, "Ivan, I am concerned about the type and amount of data that can be accessed through the CRTs. How can we protect ourselves against unauthorized access to data in our computer file? Also, what happens if we have a natural disaster such as a fire, a passive threat such as a power outage, or some active threat resulting in malicious damage—could we continue to operate? We need to show management that we are on top of these things. Would you please outline the procedures we now have, or need to have, to protect ourselves."

West responded by saying, "Jim, there are areas of vulnerability in the design and implementation of any EDP system. Some of these are more prevalent in online systems such as ours—especially with respect to privacy, integrity, and confidentiality of data. The four major points of vulnerability with which we should be concerned are the hardware, the software, the people, and the network."

Required

a. For each of the four major points of vulnerability identified by Ivan West,

  (1) Give one potential threat or risk to the system.

  (2) Identify the action(s) to be taken to protect the system from that threat or risk.

b. Ivan West knows that he must develop a contingency plan for Aidbart Company's new system in order to be prepared for a natural disaster, passive threat, or active threat to the system.

  (1) Discuss why Aidbart should have a contingency plan.

  (2) Outline and briefly describe the major components of a contingency plan that could be implemented in the case of a natural disaster, passive threat, or active threat to the system.

(CMA adapted)

5-10. Gosse Hotels utilizes an online computer system to maintain room reservations. Operators key data concerning each reservation into online terminals. Included in each entry are the name of the person making the reservation, the code of the hotel for which the reservation is being made, the reservation dates, the expected time of arrival, and special requests (e.g., a roll-away bed). The system then updates the room master file and creates a new record for the traveler. All files are maintained on magnetic disks.

Required

Describe specific general controls and security measures needed to provide an adequate control framework for this system.

5-11. Recently the Central Savings and Loan Association installed an online computer system. Each teller in the association's main office and seven branch offices has an online terminal. Customers' mortgage payments and savings account deposits and withdrawals are recorded in the accounts by the computer from data input by the teller at the time of the transaction. The teller keys the proper account by account number and enters the information via the terminal keyboard to record the transaction. The accounting department at the main office also has terminals. The computer is housed at the main office.

In addition to servicing its own mortgage loans, the association acts as a mortgage servicing agency for three life insurance companies. In this latter activity the association maintains mortgage records and serves as the collection and escrow agent for the mortgagees (the insurance companies), who pay a fee to the association for these services.

Required

List specific general controls and security measures needed to provide an adequate control framework for this system.

(CPA adapted)

5-12. Contrast the controls and security measures needed in the following three situations.

a. A fast-food restaurant that has installed a microcomputer together with several terminals located at the order counter to compute amounts of sales and change from payments as well as to accumulate sales totals by food items.

b. A local grocery chain that has installed a centralized medium-sized computer, which is linked to point-of-sale terminals located at the checkout counters of several stores throughout a metropolitan area.

c. A statewide bank that has installed a centralized large-sized computer, which is linked to visual display terminals located at the teller windows of its several dozen branches and to automated teller terminals located in stores, airports, and so forth.

5-13. Selected Small Firm (A Continuing Case) For the small firm that you selected in Chapter 1 (see Problem 1-7), complete the following requirements.

a. List all general accounting controls and security measures currently employed.

b. Note any observed weaknesses in the general accounting controls and security measures.

6

THIS CHAPTER'S OBJECTIVES ARE
TO ENABLE YOU TO:

Describe the purposes and types of documentation that are used to portray transaction processing systems and related accounting controls.

Prepare documentation pertaining to inputs, outputs, files, and procedures for typical transaction processing systems.

Discuss the steps involved in constructing flowcharts relating to manual transaction processing systems, computer-based batch transaction processing systems, and computer-based online transaction processing systems.

Documentation

of Transaction

Processing

Systems

INTRODUCTION

Documentation is difficult to ignore in a textbook concerning accounting information systems (AISs). As early as Chapter 2, we discussed and illustrated such examples of documentation as source documents, accounting journals and ledgers, and charts of accounts. In Chapter 5 we included documentation among the major categories of controls. In fact, we noted that documentation spans all system applications, programs, data, operations, and outputs for users.

This chapter focuses on documentation related to transaction processing systems and cycles, especially of the computer-based variety. Included in our survey are those documentation techniques that are particularly useful and popular for describing inputs, outputs, files, and procedures. The system flowchart receives intensive attention. An understanding of such techniques should be very helpful when studying the several following chapters on transaction cycles.

OVERVIEW OF DOCUMENTATION

Purposes

As discussed in Chapter 5, the central purpose of documentation is to communicate knowledge. Documentation concerning transaction processing systems informs users, system designers, and evaluators of all relevant elements and components. Thus, effective forms of documentation should enable

1. Users such as shipping clerks, cost accountants, and computer operators to perform prescribed procedures reliably, efficiently, and consistently. The documentation should also aid in the training of newly employed users.

2. Designers such as systems analysts, industrial engineers, accountants, and programmers to visualize more clearly the elements and flows being designed or redesigned. As a result, the newly designed or redesigned transaction processing systems should be better constructed.

3. Evaluators such as internal auditors, external auditors, and accounting managers to spot deficiencies in current transaction processing systems. In some cases the evaluators may prepare their own documentation of the current systems in order to see the deficiencies more clearly. In other cases they may locate deficiencies by comparing existing documentation of current systems against observed lapses in the actual functioning of the current systems.

Types of System-related Documentation

A wide variety of documentation techniques is necessary to describe fully a transaction processing system. Figure 6-1 lists most of those included in this textbook. At the center are the documentation techniques pertaining to the procedures, such as flowcharts, data flow diagrams, questionnaires, worksheets, and various structured techniques. Documentation techniques related to the storage of data include layouts of records within files, descriptions of data (often within dictionaries), data structure diagrams, and entity-relationship models. Documentation related to inputs and outputs include formats of documents, forms, and reports; CRT screens for entering and displaying data; and coding formats.

Most of these techniques are described in this chapter. The descriptions will generally include examples and guidelines for their construction. Remaining types of documentation, such as data structure diagrams and coding formats, are covered in later chapters.

INPUTS

Data are typically entered into transaction processing systems by means of hard copy forms and/or CRT (soft copy) screens. Thus, input documentation consists principally of the hard copy or soft copy formats that are designed to contain the transaction data.

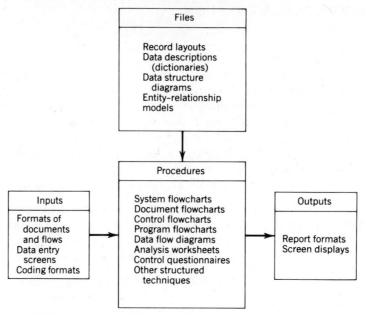

FIGURE 6-1 Types of documentation for transaction processing systems.

Hard Copy Documents and Other Forms

A firm needs a variety of hard copy documents, whether it processes its transactions manually or by means of a computer-based AIS. These documents, called source documents, were briefly discussed in Chapter 2. Other forms, such as accounting journals and ledgers, are closely related. Well-designed documents and forms are necessary if transaction processing systems are to function smoothly. Thus, their design should be based on careful analysis. Figure 6-2 portrays a typical source document and a related **form analysis sheet.**

Figure 6-3 provides a list of questions to be asked when designing a form. If prepared in accordance with this list, a form should

1. Exhibit a clear purpose.

2. Be easy for the preparing employee to fill in.

3. Minimize the number of data entry errors.

4. Enable the data to be easily absorbed by users or entered into the system for processing.

5. Minimize the combined costs of printing, preparing, and using.

Soft Copy Screens

Transactions increasingly are being entered via online video display (CRT) terminals. In many cases the transactions are keyed onto CRT screens from hard copy documents. However, in other cases they are entered without reference to

The HIJ Company

Sales Order   No. 2653

Date Received 3-16-89	Customer's Order Number 1738-6	Salesperson K. Brown

Sold to   Handy Warehousing Co.
718 South Desert
Phoenix, Arizona 85208

Ship to   Handy Warehouse No. 5
6100 No. College Drive
Tempe, Arizona 85282

F.O.B. Destination	Routing Via Western Rail Lines	Terms Net 30 Days

Product number	Quantity ordered	Unit of measure	Description	Unit price
26-B	10	50 gal. dr.	Cleaning Solvent	76.50
75-A	5	Unit	Steel Brush	8.75
106-D	50	Yard	Heavy Duty Hosing	5.07

Form No.   HIJ162

Form Analysis Sheet

Title: Sales order   Form Number HIJ162

Purpose: To record on a company form the receipt of an order, so that shipment of the order can be assured.

Point of origin: Sales order department when customer's order received

Source of data: Customer's order by letter, telegram, or call; salesperson's order slip.

Method of preparing: Typed

Average lines of data: 11   Frequency of use: Daily

Annual quantity used: 2500   Peak weekly volume: 130

Size of form: $6\frac{1}{2}'' \times 8\frac{1}{2}''$ Cost of preparing 100 forms: $145.00

Disposition—   Original: Sales order department
Copy 1 : Shipping department
Copy 2 : Billing department
Copy 3 : Acknowledgement to customer
Other copies: None

Other forms using data: Sales invoice, shipping order

Transcription onto machine-readable media: Magnetic tape
Files affected: Inventory, customer, open orders, various reference files
Volume of errors per week: 20   Approval signatures required: None
Data added after form originated: Back order number, if any; unit costs; freight cost
Use of form for internal checking and control: Initialed by clerks who review for completeness and who enter in register; compared with shipping report.
Remarks: No spaces for priority, delivery date scheduled, unit costs, special instructions

FIGURE 6-2 A sales order document and related form analysis sheet.

What is the purpose of the form?

What is the source of the information?

Who are the users of the form?

Has a title been established?

Has an identification number been assigned for control purposes?

Are the information items adequate to meet the purpose, with all unnecessary items omitted?

Are clear but brief instructions provided, when necessary, for use by the preparer?

Is a space provided for the date?

Is related information grouped together?

Is there a logical flow of the information items (e.g., from left to right and from top to bottom) to minimize backtracking?

Is the quantity of information to be entered kept at a minimum by such devices as check boxes and preprinted descriptions?

Is adequate space provided for entering needed information?

Are key information items stressed by heavy type or distinctive color?

Are the margins adequate?

Is standard-size paper ($8\frac{1}{2}'' \times 11''$) used?

Is the vertical spacing appropriate for the machines used to enter the items?

Are such technical features as perforations, scoring, type size, and paper weight suited to the intended use?

Are adequate copies prepared for distribution and filing, and are they prebound in multicopy sets?

Are copies color-coded to reduce mistakes in distribution?

FIGURE 6-3 A checklist for forms design.

source documents. In all cases the terminal screens should assist users in their entry. Figure 6-4 displays a **preformatted screen;** its purpose is to aid tellers of savings institutions in keying journal entries that are to be processed by an online system. It provides labels and boxes for entering the data, even though the data are to be entered directly from a hard copy deposit slip.

Certain of the principles of forms design apply to screen design. Thus, a **data entry screen** should have a clear purpose and a logical arrangement. On the other hand, screens have distinctive characteristics that should be recognized. Because of the fatigue factor, the number of items to be entered should be minimized. The computer system should be programmed to enter standard data

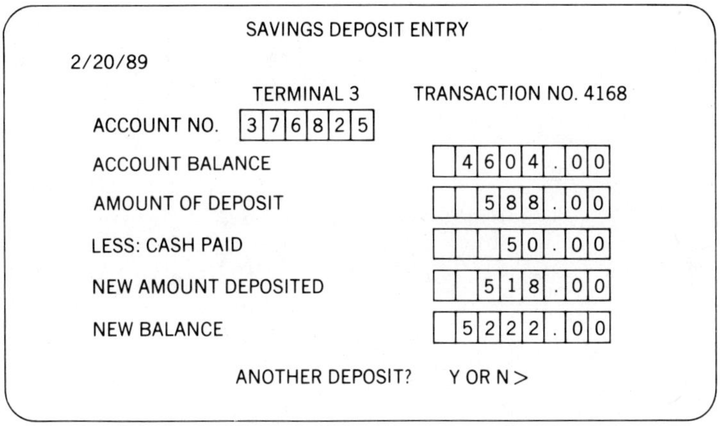

SAVINGS DEPOSIT ENTRY

2/20/89

TERMINAL 3   TRANSACTION NO. 4168

ACCOUNT NO. 3 7 6 8 2 5

ACCOUNT BALANCE 4 6 0 4 . 0 0

AMOUNT OF DEPOSIT 5 8 8 . 0 0

LESS: CASH PAID 5 0 . 0 0

NEW AMOUNT DEPOSITED 5 1 8 . 0 0

NEW BALANCE 5 2 2 2 . 0 0

ANOTHER DEPOSIT? Y OR N >

FIGURE 6-4 A preformatted screen for entering data pertaining to one cash deposit transaction. Note that the date, terminal number, transaction number, and prior account balance are entered automatically by the computer system after the account number is entered manually. In addition, the net amount deposited and the new account balance are computed automatically after the amount of deposit and cash paid amount are entered manually.

(e.g., the date) and to perform needed computations (e.g., compute totals). It can be designed to respond with ("to echo") clarifying data (e.g., customer names) upon the entry of codes (e.g., customer numbers). Also, clear instructions should guide the data entry person in completing the transactions. Note, for instance, the instructions appearing at the bottom of the screen in Figure 6-4.

Data entry screens should fit into a broad framework of screens. Other input screens within this framework are menu screens that present listings of numbered options. Also included in this framework are various types of screens for presenting output information. All screens should present consistent formats in order to avoid confusing the users.

OUTPUTS

Most outputs from computer-based systems appear as hard copies or as soft copy screen displays. The formats of these outputs represent another key type of systems documentation.

Hard Copy Documents and Reports

In terms of volume, the dominant type of output for a typical firm is the document produced during transaction processing. Examples of output transaction documents are sales invoices, purchase orders, and checks. Generally speaking, the checklist in Figure 6-3 applies as fully to the design of output documents as to input source documents. Figure 6-5 presents a monthly statement that reflects several features of sound design.

Every firm needs a variety of reports in order to meet its responsibilities.

Arvin ArvinAir Division
Arvin Industries, Inc.
500 South 15th Street
Phoenix, Arizona 85034

STATEMENT

TO:

ACCOUNT NUMBER   STATEMENT DATE

INVOICE DATE	INVOICE NO.	CUSTOMER NO.	CUSTOMER LOCATION	TERMS	LINE CODE	DUE DATE	AGE CODE	DAYS OVERDUE	INVOICE AMOUNT

AMOUNT CURRENTLY DUE WITHIN NEXT 30 DAYS	AMOUNTS OVERDUE (AGED IN DAYS)				TOTAL AMOUNT DUE
CODE A	1 - 30 DAYS OVERDUE CODE B	31 - 60 DAYS OVERDUE CODE C	61 - 90 DAYS OVERDUE CODE D	90 + DAYS OVERDUE CODE E	CURRENT AND OVERDUE ITEMS

TO ASSIST YOU IN YOUR CASH PLANNING, THE FOLLOWING IS AN AGING OF FUTURE DUE AMOUNTS

DUE IN 31 - 60 DAYS	DUE IN 61 - 90 DAYS	DUE IN 91 - 120 DAYS	DUE IN OVER 120 DAYS	TOTAL FUTURE DUE CODE F	ACCOUNT BALANCE

LINE CODE:

INV = INVOICE
C/B = CHARGE BACK
C/M = CREDIT MEMO
LPC = LATE PAYMENT CHARGE
OAP = ON ACCOUNT PAYMENT
U/D = UNRESOLVED DEDUCTION

PLEASE REMIT TO:

CUSTOMER COPY

FIGURE 6-5 A monthly statement. Courtesy of Arvin Industries.

Certain of these reports are provided to users who are external to the firm. **Stewardship reports** are intended to disclose the custodianship of the resources entrusted to management. They are prepared for the eyes of stockholders, prospective investors, creditors, and others. **Legal compliance reports** are intended to fulfill requirements specified by laws. Examples are Form 10-K reports filed with the Securities and Exchange Commission and income tax returns filed with the Internal Revenue Service.

Other reports are prepared for internal users, such as managers throughout the organization. These managerial reports enable managers to direct and control the firm's operations and to make key planning decisions. **Operational reports** reflect past events and/or current status. Most operational reports, such as sales summaries and inventory status reports, are largely based on transactions. **Control reports** aid managers in controlling the acquisition of resources needed in operations and their ongoing use. These reports also are often based on data from transactions. However, they must include benchmarks that provide means of comparison. Examples of control reports are (1) production control reports that compare actual costs with standard costs, and (2) inventory control reports that compare actual quantities on hand with established reorder point quantities. **Planning reports** aid managers in making decisions concerning the firm's future need for resources. These reports are least dependent on transaction data. Examples are (1) budgets, and (2) analyses of alternative choices (e.g., an analysis of alternative products newly developed for marketing).

An effective report exhibits several attributes. It serves at least one clear purpose, such as aiding managerial control or planning. It is issued in a timely manner in order to allow the user to take effective action. Needless to say, it meets a high standard of accuracy. Finally, it presents the information in a format that is clearly understandable and optimally useful to the recipient.

An example of a **report format** appears in Figure 6-6. Upon analyzing this specific piece of documentation, we find that it is reasonably effective in communicating information. That is, it has several attributes:

1. **Dominant purpose.** Assuming that the sales manager of Maxy Sales Corporation is the recipient, the report is intended primarily to provide control over sales activities. The control purpose is emphasized because two bases of comparison are provided: (a) variances of actual sales from budgeted sales, and (b) differences in sales performances among the various sales offices and product lines.

2. **Appropriate scope and discrimination.** The report spans all regional sales offices and product lines of the firm, and thus it corresponds to the sales

	Maxy Sales Corp. Sales Report (Thousands of Dollars) July 1989									
	Product line									
	A			**B**			**Total**			
Regional Sales Office	**Budget**	**Variance Over (Under) Budget**	**Percent Variance**	**Budget**	**Variance Over (Under) Budget**	**Percent Variance**	**Budget**	**Variance Over (Under) Budget**	**Percent Variance**
Western:									
sales	$6,000	($500)	(8.3)	$10,000	$400	4.0	$16,000	($100)	(0.6)
contribution	2,000	(167)	(8.3)	1,000	40	4.0	3,000	(127)	(4.2)
Eastern:									
sales	$9,000	($200)	(2.2)	$14,000	($100)	(0.7)	$23,000	($300)	(1.3)
contribution	3,000	(67)	(2.2)	1,400	(10)	(0.7)	4,400	(77)	(1.8)
Northern:									
sales	$7,500	$100	1.3	$12,000	$600	5.0	$19,500	$700	0.8
contribution	2,500	33	1.3	1,200	60	5.0	3,700	93	2.5
Total:									
sales	$22,500	($600)	(2.7)	$36,000	$900	2.5	$58,500	$300	0.5
contribution	7,500	(201)	(2.7)	3,600	90	2.5	11,100	(111)	(1.0)

FIGURE 6-6 A managerial report format.

manager's scope of responsibility. Since it breaks down the sales and contributions (profits) to the levels of individual sales offices and product lines, the report provides enough detail for the manager to make the indicated comparisons.

3. **Conciseness.** Because the report appears on a single sheet, it does not overload the busy sales manager with too much information. If the manager desires more details, such as actual sales, he or she can compute them from given information or ask for more reports.

4. **Understandability.** Although the report appears crowded, its information is neatly arranged within a tabular format. Also, a clear heading is provided. However, more clarity can be attained by means of a graphical presentation. Graphs are being increasingly employed as reporting formats.

5. **Consistency.** This report can fit into a reporting system. For instance, detailed sales reports can be provided to the managers of the respective sales offices. If so, each detailed sales report (which has the scope of an individual sales office) should have a format that corresponds to the report shown in Figure 6-6.

Screen Displays

In computer-based systems CRT screens are increasingly being employed to display outputs. These outputs may take the forms of responses to specific online inquiries. Alternatively, they may be elaborate ad hoc reports that are constructed with the help of report generation software. Both types of outputs are called **screen displays.**

Screen displays should be designed in a manner that enables the user to locate needed information quickly and easily. An effective screen display arranges the information items logically and meaningfully for the user. Figure 6-7 shows a screen display that meets this standard. Key descriptions appear at the top of the display. Details are balanced throughout and organized into columnized groupings. Labels are expressed in bold letters. Where necessary for clarity, words are written out; however, some words are abbreviated for conciseness.

FILES

A file is a collection of related records. A record contains a group of fields, with each field being reserved for a specific data item. In turn, data items are composed of characters such as letters, numbers, and special symbols. Two types of documentation related to files are record layouts and data dictionaries.

Record Layouts

A file **record layout** shows the respective fields comprising the record, plus the size, sequence, and data item pertaining to each field. Figure 6-8a depicts a record layout, on magnetic tape or disk, for a stockholder master file; Figure 6-8b

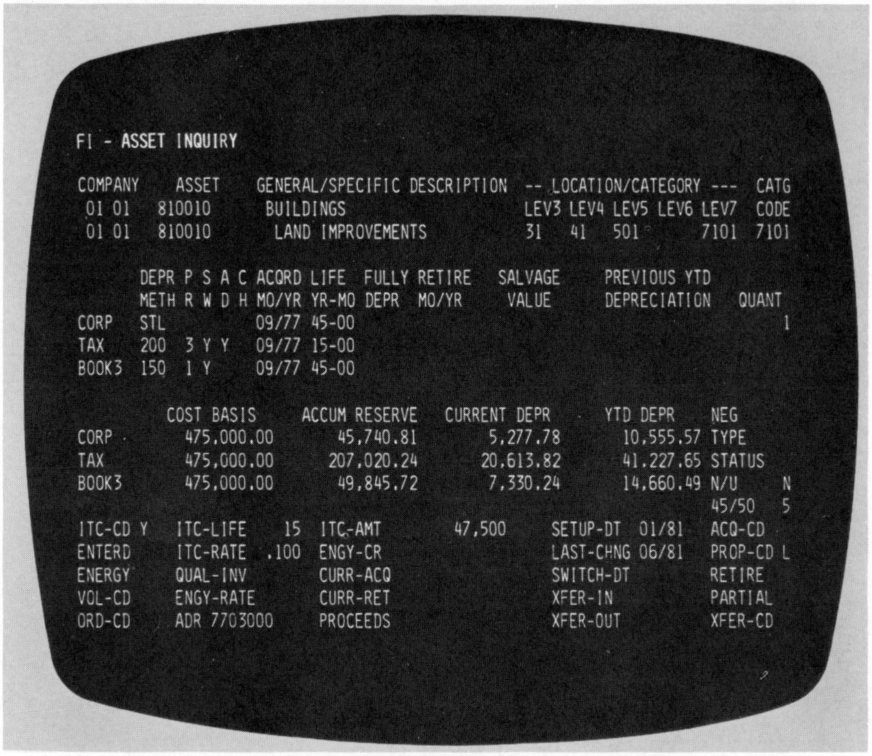

FIGURE 6-7 A screen display that shows a response to a fixed asset inquiry. Courtesy of Data Design Associates.

shows an alternative form of a record layout for a customer master file. Still other forms may be employed.

Data Dictionaries

Although record layouts are useful in documenting the files of a data base, they are not sufficient. A record has additional features that must be described. As Figure 6-9 suggests, each data item (called an attribute in the context of a record) has a degree of permanency, mode, and key type. For instance, the attribute labeled "customer number" is relatively permanent, numeric in mode, and the primary key that uniquely identifies the accounts receivable record. Any of these features could be added to the record layout, of course. For instance, the mode is sufficiently important that it is often included.

A type of documentation that focuses on each data item within a record and file is known as a **data dictionary.** Figure 6-10 portrays a segment of a data dictionary for a manufacturing firm. As the example shows, the relevant characteristics pertaining to a data item should be included. Since one column reflects the records in which each particular data item appears, the data dictionary also provides a cross-reference to record layouts. Furthermore, in our discussion of integrated data bases (in Chapter 11) we shall see that data dictionaries specify established relationships among all the data items within a data base.

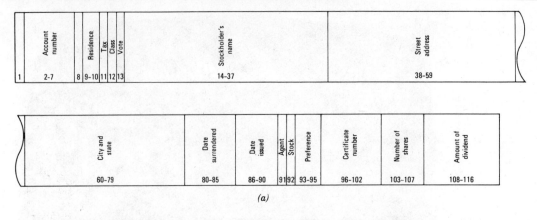

Account number	Residence	Tax Class	Vote	Stockholder's name		Street address
2-7	8	9-10	11 12 13	14-37		38-59

City and state	Date surrendered	Date issued	Agent Stock	Preference	Certificate number	Number of shares	Amount of dividend
60-79	80-85	86-90	91 92	93-95	96-102	103-107	108-116

(a)

CUST.NO.	CUSTOMER NAME	STREET ADDRESS	CITY	ST.	ZIP
1 1 5 8	C. JAMES	1 1 3 MAIN ST.	PORTLAND	OR	9 7 1 3 2

CREDIT	BEG. BAL.	TR.	DATE	DOC.	AMOUNT	CUR. BAL.
1 0 0 0 0	0 . 0 0	CRS	8 1 4 8 6	2 3 8 5	1 5 0 . 0 0	1 5 0 . 0 0

(b)

FIGURE 6-8 Record layouts. (*a*) A record layout for a stockholder master file. (*b*) A record layout for a customer master file.

Occurrence or value:	23861	Eric Peters	1550.00
Attribute:	Customer number	Customer name	Account balance
Degree of permanency:	Fixed	Fixed	Variable
Data mode:	Numeric	Alphabetic	Alphanumeric
Record key type:	Primary	Secondary	Secondary

FIGURE 6-9 Added features of an accounts receivable record.

	Precise Manufacturing Co.
	Data Dictionary
Item code	Item name	Item description	Field length	Mode of data item	Records in which found	Source	Number of appearances	Outputs in which used
01	Customer order number	The code on the customer order that identifies the order	5	Numeric	Open order, sales history, back-order record	Customer order	500-600 daily	Sales invoices, back orders, production orders, shipment records
02	Customer number	The code assigned to identify a customer	6	Numeric	Customer, open order record	Customer number list	10,500-12,000	Sales analysis by customer, list of outstanding orders, aging report, sales invoice
03	Customer name	The first name, middle initial and last name of a customer	25	Alphabetic	Customer record	Initial customer order	10,500-12,000	New business report, credit flash report, sales invoice, back order, shipment record
04	Credit limit	The maximum dollar amount that a customer may incur in outstanding credit sales	5	Numeric	Customer record	Credit record	10,500-12,000	Credit flash report
52	Sales this month by salesperson	The dollar sales made by each salesperson in the current month	8	Numeric	Sales history record	Sales orders	200	Sales analysis by salesperson
53	Scheduled delivery date	The date that a customer order is scheduled for delivery to customer	8	Alphanumeric	Open order, back order, production order record	Sales order acknowledgment or production order	500-600 daily	Unfilled orders on hand, delayed orders, delayed invoices

FIGURE 6-10 A data dictionary.

PROCEDURES

Flowcharts

Flowcharts are diagrams that pictorially portray the sequential flows of data and/or operations. No documentation technique is utilized more widely to depict transaction processing procedures. Various types of flowcharts are currently used. As Figure 6-11 indicates, they range from the very broad to the very detailed. An overview diagram subdivides an area of concern, such as a transaction cycle, into several functions. Each function, such as a transaction processing system or major subsystem, is next pictured by means of a system flowchart. The processing steps within a system flowchart may then be detailed by means of program flowcharts, assuming that the procedure is computerized. In fact, two

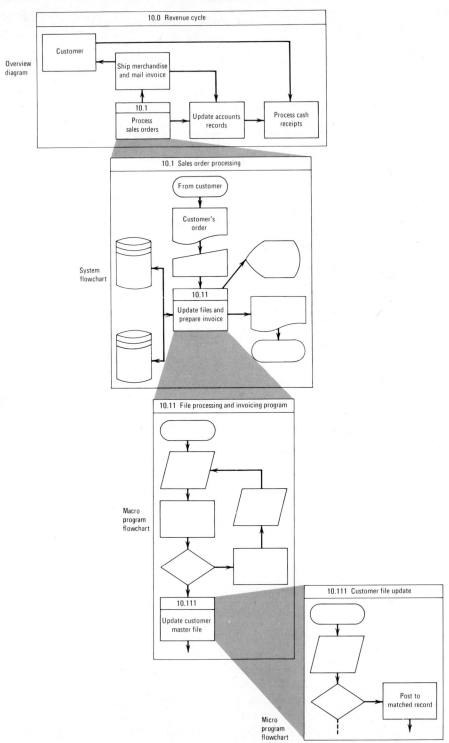

FIGURE 6-11 A flowchart hierarchy.

levels of program flowcharts may be prepared if needed. A macroprogram flow-chart contains the programming instructions for a major step, such as posting a transaction to all affected files and printing output documents. A microprogram flowchart in turn contains more detailed programming instructions for a portion of a macroflowchart, such as updating a particular master file.

Of greatest interest to accountants are system flowcharts. **System flowcharts** highlight relationships among the elements within transaction processing systems. That is, they provide answers to such questions as

1. What inputs are received, and from whom?

2. What outputs are generated, in what form do they appear, and to whom are they sent?

3. What is the next step in the processing sequence?

4. What files and accounting records are affected?

5. Which accounting and organizational controls are employed (assuming that they can be pictorially portrayed)?

System flowcharts can be adapted to emphasize one or more aspects of trans-action processing systems. A process flowchart emphasizes the procedural steps. A **document flowchart** emphasizes the inputs and outputs and their flows through organizational units. Figure 6-12 presents a simplified form of a docu-ment flowchart. A **computer system flowchart** emphasizes the computer-based portions of transaction processing systems, including computer runs or steps and accesses of online files. A **control-oriented flowchart** emphasizes the control points within a transaction processing system, especially as they relate to the accounting documents and records. Figure 6-13 displays the basic structure of a control-oriented flowcharting approach called SEADOC.

Data Flow Diagrams

A **data flow diagram** documents the logical flows of data through a transaction processing system. Since data flows are emphasized, it is similar to a system flowchart. However, the two documentation techniques differ significantly. A system flowchart specifies the physical aspects of a procedure, such as processing by computer and storage of data on magnetic disks. In contrast, a data flow diagram merely specifies essential data sources, data destinations, processing steps, and data stores. Thus, it is a purely logical model. An example of a data flow diagram appears in Figure 6-14. Symbols in the figure have the following meanings: (1) lines with arrowheads are data flows, (2) circles are processing steps, (3) rectangles are entities (persons or organizations) that represent sources or destinations of data, and (4) open-ended rectangles are stores of data (e.g., files).

Structured Diagrams

A data flow diagram is a member of a class of documentation techniques known as structured diagrams. Other diagrams that may be described as struc-

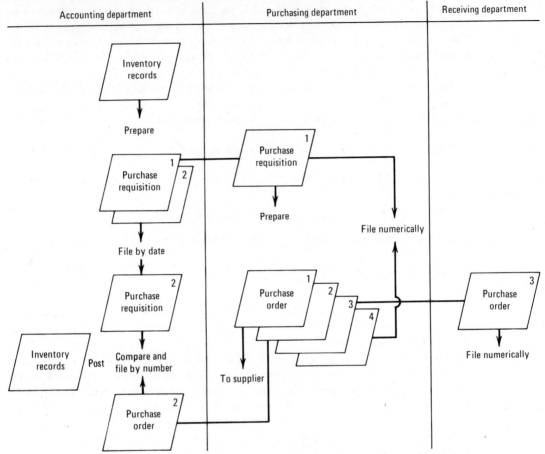

FIGURE 6-12 A document flowchart involving a purchases procedure.

tured include hierarchical diagrams and analysis worksheets. These diagrams will be illustrated in later chapters.

CONSTRUCTION OF SYSTEM FLOWCHARTS

Since system flowcharts are widely used, accountants should develop skill in their construction. Thus, the remainder of this chapter is devoted to sound flowcharting practices. Our discussion will cover system flowcharts for both manual and computer-based information systems. However, to avoid confusion we will emphasize only the more commonly encountered variations.

Flowcharting Symbols

The building blocks for a system flowchart are a set of symbols, most of which are generally accepted by accountants and analysts. Figure 6-15 displays the set of symbols to be used in this textbook. These symbols may be grouped as input/output symbols, processing symbols, storage symbols, flow symbols, and

Illustration of the Four Zones and Their Contents
(Note that this is not a completed SEADOC flowchart; it is intended only to
illustrate the appropriate location of the flowchart symbols.)

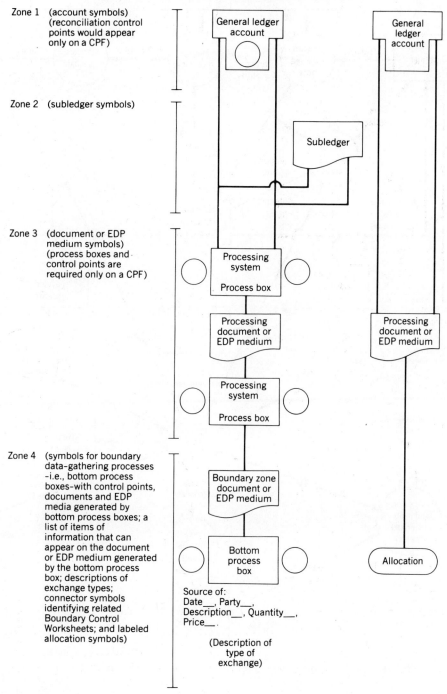

Zone 1   (account symbols)
         (reconciliation control
         points would appear
         only on a CPF)

Zone 2   (subledger symbols)

Zone 3   (document or EDP
         medium symbols)
         (process boxes and
         control points are
         required only on a CPF)

Zone 4   (symbols for boundary
         data-gathering processes
         -i.e., bottom process
         boxes-with control points,
         documents and EDP
         media generated by
         bottom process boxes; a
         list of items of
         information that can
         appear on the document
         or EDP medium generated
         by the bottom process
         box; descriptions of
         exchange types;
         connector symbols
         identifying related
         Boundary Control
         Worksheets; and labeled
         allocation symbols)

FIGURE 6-13 The structure of a control-oriented flowchart. Adapted with permission from Peat, Marwick, Mitchell & Co., *PMI SEADOC Guide,* 1985.

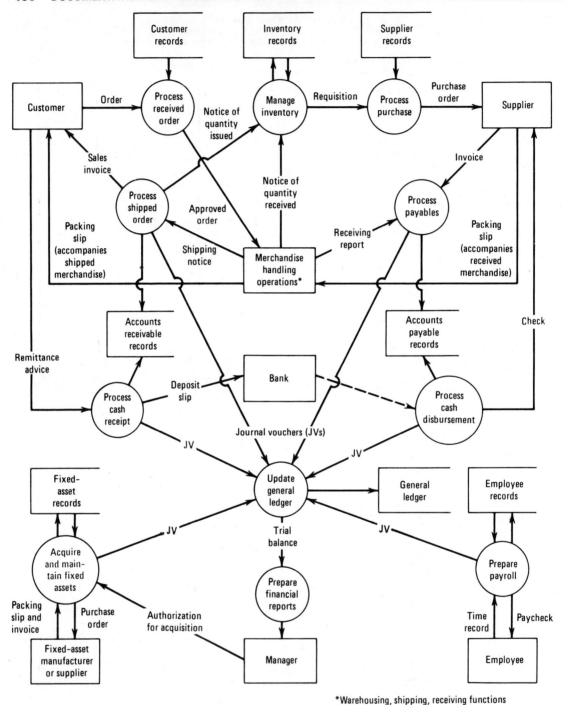

FIGURE 6-14 An overview data flow diagram of basic transaction processing systems.

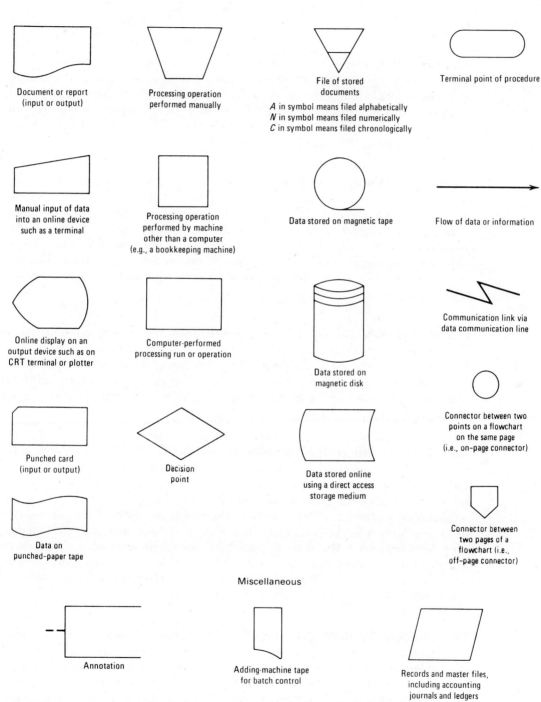

Input/output	Processing	Storage	Flow

Document or report (input or output)

Processing operation performed manually

File of stored documents

A in symbol means filed alphabetically
N in symbol means filed numerically
C in symbol means filed chronologically

Terminal point of procedure

Manual input of data into an online device such as a terminal

Processing operation performed by machine other than a computer (e.g., a bookkeeping machine)

Data stored on magnetic tape

Flow of data or information

Online display on an output device such as on CRT terminal or plotter

Computer-performed processing run or operation

Data stored on magnetic disk

Communication link via data communication line

Punched card (input or output)

Decision point

Data stored online using a direct access storage medium

Connector between two points on a flowchart on the same page (i.e., on-page connector)

Data on punched-paper tape

Connector between two pages of a flowchart (i.e., off-page connector)

Miscellaneous

Annotation

Adding-machine tape for batch control

Records and master files, including accounting journals and ledgers

FIGURE 6-15 A set of symbols for system flowcharting. Based on American National Standards Institute, *Standard Flowchart Symbols and Their Use in Information Processing (X3.5)*. New York: ANSI, 1971, and other sources.

miscellaneous symbols. All the symbols in the figure can be drawn with the assistance of a flowcharting template, which is available at most university bookstores.

Input/Output Symbols The top symbol in the first column represents data on source documents or information on output documents or reports. The second and third symbols reflect the entry of data by keyboards or other online means and the display of information on CRT screens or other online devices. The last two symbols in the column, involving punched cards and punched paper tape, are seldom used in modern-day systems.

Processing Symbols Symbols are available to indicate the processing of data by clerks, noncomputerized machines, and computers. The decision symbol is used to indicate when alternative processing paths exist. For instance, in a flowchart showing sales transaction processing, a decision symbol may be placed at the point just after a credit check. If an ordering customer's credit is found to be satisfactory, one path may lead to continued processing of the order. Alternatively, if the credit is not satisfactory, another path might lead to the writing of a rejection letter.

Storage Symbols The top symbol is used to show documents and/or records being stored in an offline storage device, such as a file cabinet or hold basket. Remaining symbols are available to show data being stored on computerized media. The bottom symbol pertains to any online storage device, including a magnetic disk. However, it may be employed to indicate that data are being stored on a temporary basis.

Data and Information Flow Symbols The five symbols in the last column provide direction throughout a flowchart. The oval terminal symbol marks a beginning or ending point within the flowchart being examined, such as the receipt of an order from a customer. Often a beginning or ending point is also a link to an adjoining procedure. The flow line shows the flow of data or information, usually in written form. The communication link symbol (the one that looks like a lightning bolt) represents the flow of data from one physical location to another. Finally, two connector symbols are available to provide further linkages. The on-page connector is used within a single page of a flowchart, whereas the off-page connector links two pages of a multipage flowchart.

Miscellaneous Symbols The annotation symbol can be connected to any symbol within a flowchart; its purpose is to provide space for a note concerning the procedure. For instance, it could indicate how often a particular processing step takes place, or who performs it. The remaining two symbols are useful in flowcharts portraying transaction processing through the accounting cycle. In fact, the parallelogram—representing accounting records—could be viewed as an offline storage medium.

Example of a Document System Flowchart for a Manual Procedure

The following narrative describes the purchasing procedure for the Easybuy Company: A clerk in the accounting department periodically reviews the inventory records in order to determine which items need to be reordered. When she notes that the quantity on hand for a particular item has fallen below a pre-established reorder point, the clerk prepares a prenumbered purchase requisition in two copies. The original is sent to the purchasing department, where a buyer (1) decides on a suitable supplier by reference to a supplier file, and (2) prepares a prenumbered purchase order in four copies. The original copy of the purchase order is signed by the purchasing manager and mailed to the designated supplier. The second copy is returned to the inventory clerk in the accounting department, who pulls the matching requisition copy from a temporary file (where it had been filed chronologically), posts the ordered quantities to the inventory records, and files the purchase requisition and order together. The third copy is forwarded to the receiving department, where it is filed numerically to await the receipt of the ordered goods. The fourth copy is filed numerically, together with the original copy of the purchase requisition, in an open purchase order file. When the invoice from the supplier arrives, this last copy will be entered into the accounts payable procedure.

Several features of this procedure should be noted. It involves manual processing of transactions, it moves among three departments, and it generates documents having several copies. To present all these features in a clear manner, a system flowchart blends characteristics of a document flowchart with those of a process flowchart. In the next several paragraphs we will see how this can be done.

We begin by sectioning a sheet of paper into three columns, which we label as "Accounting department," "Purchasing department," and "Receiving department." Next we select those symbols from Figure 6-15 that pertain to manual processing. These symbols are then combined in strict accordance with the sequence of the narrative. For convenience we subdivide our work into four key steps or functions:

1. **Preparation of the purchase requisition.** As this segment shows, the flowcharted procedure begins in the accounting department with a terminal symbol. This symbol is connected by a flow line to a clerical or manual processing symbol. Inserted inside this second symbol is a notation that briefly states the actions taken by the inventory clerk. In order to explain the basis on which the clerk prepares the document labeled "Purchase requisition," an annotation symbol is also attached to the manual processing symbol. Another flow line connects an accounting record symbol, labeled "Inventory records," to the manual processing symbol. This connection *from* the inventory records *to* the manual processing symbol denotes that inventory data are used during the preparation of the purchase requisition. A flow line *from* the manual processing *to* the document symbol indicates that a purchase requisition, in two copies, is an output from the processing step. Note that when multiple copies of a form are prepared, they are numbered and shown in an offset manner.

Accounting department

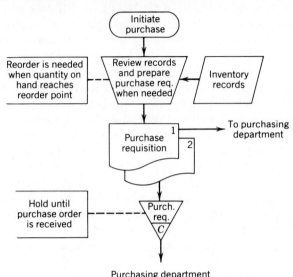

Purchasing department

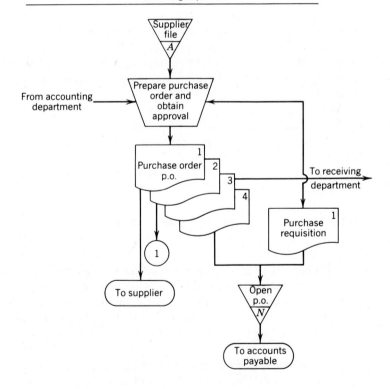

The final function of this flowchart segment is to show the disposition of the two copies of the purchase requisition. A flow line pointing to the right directs copy 1 to the purchasing department, and a downward flow line indicates that copy 2 is filed in a folder. The letter *C* in the file symbol means that copy 2 is arranged chronologically (by date) within the file.

2. **Preparation of a purchase order.** The activity in the second segment also centers on a manual processing symbol. Two flow lines lead *to* this processing symbol, one from the first copy of the purchase requisition and the other from the supplier file. Based on data from these two sources, a buyer in the purchasing department prepares a purchase order in four copies. Again, a flow line pointing from the processing symbol to the document symbol(s) designates the latter as being an output. Another "output" flowing from the processing symbol is copy 1 of the purchase requisition. Since it entered the processing symbol, as noted by the flow line from the accounting department, it must also leave the processing symbol. As the segment shows, it is then deposited in the open purchase order file. (An important rule of flowcharting is to show the final disposition of every copy.)

The remainder of this flowchart segment depicts the disposition of the four purchase order copies. Copy 1 is mailed to the supplier. Since this mailing ends our treatment of copy 1 (as far as the flowchart is concerned), we indicate this final disposition by means of a terminal symbol. (Alternatively, we could have added a column on the flowchart labeled "Supplier" and shown the flow of copy 1 to that column.) Copy 2 terminates with an on-page connector labeled "1." The next segment will continue the disposition of copy 2. Copy 3 is directed to the receiving department. Copy 4 is filed together with copy 1 of the purchase requisition. The terminal symbol below the file indicates that the filed copies will be used in the accounts payable procedure (shown on a separate flowchart).

One additional flowcharting convention is illustrated in this segment. When flow lines cross, a "jumper" (‿⌒‿) denotes the crossover.

3. **Updating of the inventory records.** This flowchart segment, like the first segment, is located organizationally in the accounting department. Two inputs, copy 2 of the purchase requisition and copy 2 of the purchase order, enter into the processing. The former is pulled from the file folder, whereas the latter arrives from the purchasing department. (Note that the on-page connector in effect links to the on-page connector shown in the previous segment.)

Processing is performed by the inventory clerk. He matches the documents, accesses the proper inventory records, posts the ordered quantities, and then replaces the posted inventory records within the inventory file. A bidirectional flow line (i.e., one with arrowheads on both ends) symbolically represents these accessing, posting, and replacing actions. As the last step in this segment, the two documents leave the processing symbol and flow into a file. Note that when two or more documents move together, a single flow line is sufficient.

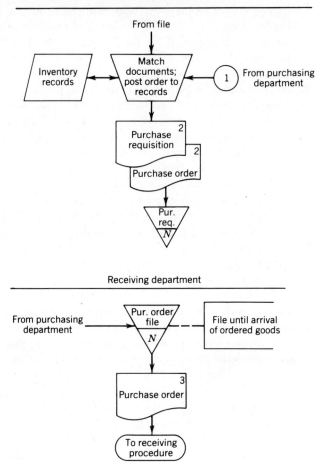

4. Filing of the receiving department's copy of the purchase order. In this brief segment copy 3 of the purchase order is placed temporarily into a file maintained in the receiving department. Upon the arrival of the ordered inventory goods, the copy is withdrawn (pulled) and entered into the receiving procedure. Since the receiving procedure is shown on a different flowchart, a terminal symbol is employed to denote the interface with that procedure.

Figure 6-16 combines the four segments just described into a document system flowchart of the purchases procedure. A variation of this flowchart, which omits the columns for organizational units, appears in Figure 6-17.

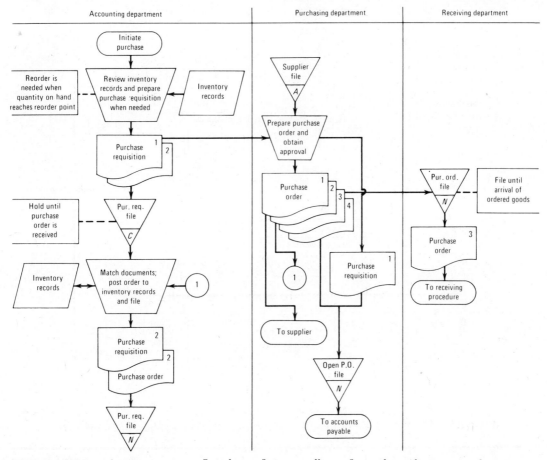

FIGURE 6-16 A document system flowchart of a manually performed purchases procedure.

Example of a System Flowchart for Computer-based Batch Transaction Processing

A system flowchart of a computer-based procedure uses special symbols that pertain to computer processing, input/output devices, and storage media. It also employs most of the symbols needed for a manual procedure, since certain steps are likely to be performed manually in the typical computer-based system.

In this section we examine a flowchart that portrays batch processing, and in the next section we consider a flowchart for online processing. Both computer-based examples portray essentially the procedure previously discussed. Our discussions focus on the computerized features.

Figure 6-18 shows a system flowchart of a computer-based batch processing

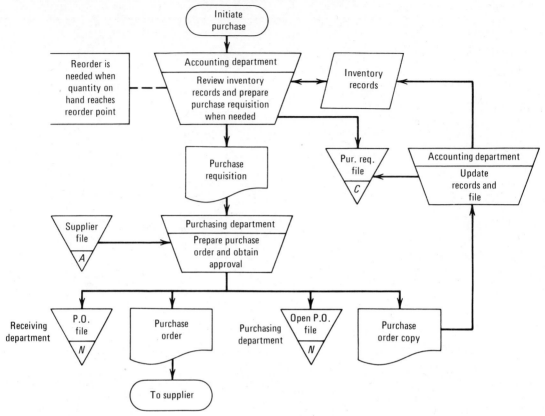

FIGURE 6-17 A variation of the document system flowchart shown in Figure 6-16.

system. For convenience the computer processing steps (called *runs* in a batch-oriented procedure) are numbered. Each computer run, represented by a rectangle symbol, directly involves the use of a computer.

Run 1. The first run consists of extracting data from the inventory master file (on magnetic tape) concerning those inventory items whose on-hand quantities have fallen below their reorder points. Such items are listed on an inventory reorder list, which in effect replaces the purchase requisitions. This list is forwarded to the purchasing department, perhaps after being reviewed and approved by an accounting manager. In the purchasing department one or more buyers select suitable suppliers and enter the necessary data on drafts of purchase orders. Then these drafts or forms are sent to the data processing department, where clerks key the data onto magnetic tape and verify the keyed data.

Run 2. The second run consists of editing the keyed and verified purchase order data. The editing process is performed by means of programmed checks built into an edit program. (As mentioned in Chapter 5, any detected errors are listed on an exception and summary report. This report is not shown in Figure 6-18 in order to reduce its complexity. However, exception and summary

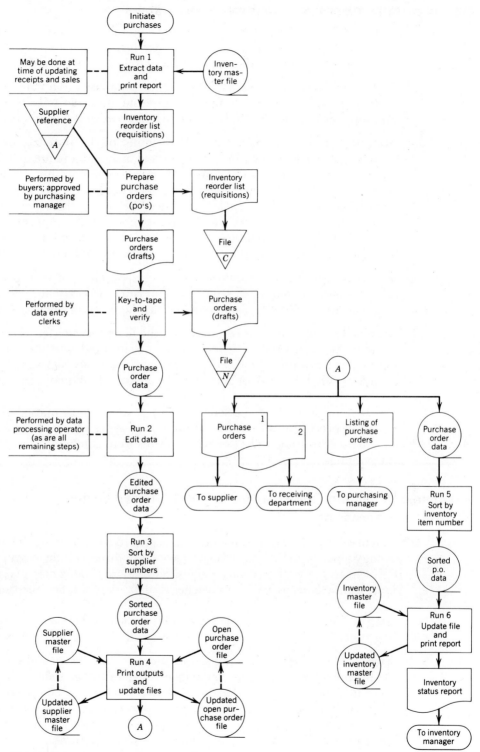

FIGURE 6-18 A system flowchart of a computer-based purchases procedure involving batch processing.

reports will be included in all subsequent flowcharts of batch processing systems. Also not shown in this flowchart are batch control totals, which would customarily be computed on data in the purchase order drafts.)

Run 3. The next run consists of sorting the purchase order data into supplier number sequence. This sorting run is necessary in order to be able to update the supplier master file, which is also arranged in supplier number sequence.

Run 4. The fourth run involves the printing of the purchase orders. Each purchase order is printed in two copies and assigned a sequential number by the computer program. The third and fourth copies are not needed, since a "copy" is stored on magnetic tape in the open purchase order file. In addition, the supplier master file is updated to reflect the orders; that is, the number and date of each purchase order is added to the record of the appropriate supplier. Finally, a listing of purchase orders is printed in order to inform the purchasing manager that the purchase orders have been completed.

Run 5. The next run consists of resorting the purchase order transaction tape into inventory item number sequence. This run is necessary in order to arrange the transactions into the same sequence as the inventory master file.

Run 6. The final run involves updating the inventory master file. That is, the quantity of each ordered inventory item is inserted into the record of the appropriate inventory item. Then an inventory status report is printed in order to inform the inventory or accounting manager of all quantities on order.

As we have seen, a batch-oriented system flowchart is composed of a series of connected processing runs. Most of the typical types of runs have appeared in our example. In some cases two types of runs were combined (e.g., the updates and printings in runs 4 and 6).

Example of a System Flowchart for Computer-based Online Transaction Processing

Figure 6-19 depicts the same purchases procedure, assuming that online processing is performed. This flowchart contains three rectangle symbols which represent computer processing actions. Since these actions may pertain to individual transactions as well as to batches of data, they will be called steps.

Step 1. This initial processing action corresponds to run 1 in the batch processing system, except that the data are extracted from an online file.

Step 2. The second processing action illustrates data entry and editing. Based on the inventory reorder list and data extracted from an online supplier reference file, the purchasing department buyers enter the data needed for purchase orders. The entered data are edited by an online purchase program. All errors detected by the program and displayed on the terminal screen are corrected by the buyers. Then the data are stored on a transaction file.

Step 3. The final step occurs immediately after the previous step. It involves both the updating of files and the preparation of reports. The supplier master

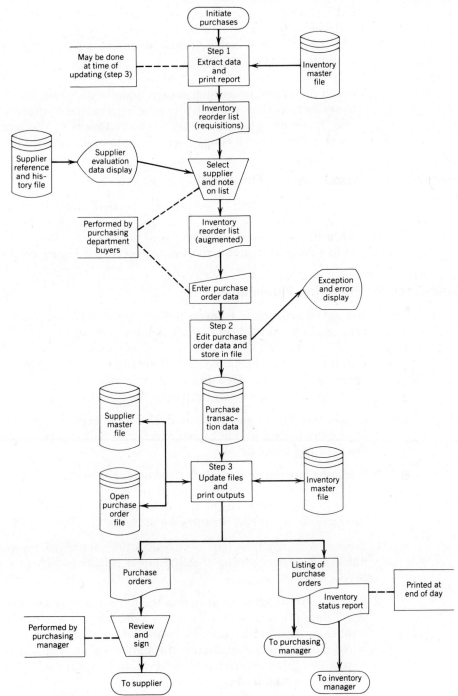

FIGURE 6-19 A system flowchart of a computer-based purchases procedure involving online processing.

file and inventory master file are updated to reflect the items that are being ordered; the open purchase order file receives a copy of each purchase order. Outputs from this step include purchase orders, a listing of purchase orders, and an inventory status report.

Although the online processing system updates the same files and generates the same reports as does the batch processing system, it involves fewer steps. Thus, the flowchart is simpler in appearance. However, the underlying programs used in online processing systems tend to be more complex.

Example of a Hybrid System Flowchart

In both computer system flowcharts (Figures 6-18 and 6-19), the departments performing the processing steps were indicated by annotations. An alternative approach is to use column headings (as in Figures 6-12 and 6-16). Figure 6-20 presents in columnar form an abbreviated version of Figure 6-19.

Guidelines for Preparing Flowcharts

Good flowcharts result from sound practices consistently followed. Sound practices can be grounded on such guidelines as these:

1. Carefully read the narrative description of the procedure to be flowcharted. Determine from the facts the *usual* or *normal* steps in the procedure, and focus on these steps when preparing the flowchart.

2. Choose the size of paper to be used. Use either regular size (8½ in. by 11 in.) or an extra-large size. Then gather such materials as pencils, an eraser, and a flowcharting template.

3. Select the flowcharting symbols to be used. Generally the symbols should be drawn from those listed in Figure 6-15. Although other symbols are available and may appear on the template you purchase, the variety of symbols used should be limited for the sake of clarity.

4. Prepare a rough flowchart sketch as a first draft. Attempting to draw a finished flowchart during the first effort usually results in a poorer final product.

5. Review your sketch to be sure that the following have been accomplished.
   a. All steps are clearly presented in a sequence or a series of sequences. No obvious gaps in the procedure should be present.
   b. Symbols are used consistently throughout. Thus, the symbol for manual processing (an inverted trapezoid) should appear each time a clerk is to perform a step in the procedure.
   c. The dispositions of all documents and reports are shown. In fact, the final "resting place" of every copy of every prepared document should be specified. Typical dispositions include placing documents in files, sending documents to outside parties such as customers, forwarding documents to connecting procedures (such as a general ledger procedure), and dis-

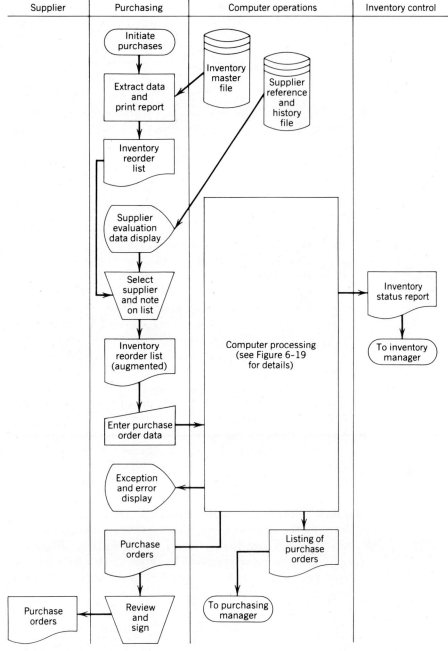

FIGURE 6-20 A computer system flowchart similar to Figure 6-19, but in columnar form.

tributing reports to managers. If the disposition consists of destroying a document, this action may be represented in the following manner.

d. The "sandwich" rule is consistently applied. This rule states that a processing symbol should be sandwiched between an input symbol and an output symbol in the following manner.

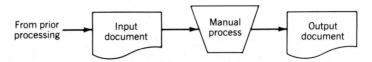

e. The flows generally begin in the upper left-hand corner of the sheet and move from left to right and from top to bottom.

f. All symbols contain brief but specific labels written inside the symbols. For instance, "Sales Invoice" might appear inside a document symbol. (Do not simply write "Document" inside a document symbol, since the shape of the symbol indicates its nature.) When it is necessary to use lengthy labels, draw the symbols sufficiently large to contain the labels completely. (The size of a symbol may vary without affecting its meaning.)

g. Multiple copies of documents are numbered in the upper right-hand corners, and these numbers remain with the copies during their flows through the procedure.

h. Added comments are included within annotation symbols and attached to appropriate symbols, such as the processing symbols to which the comments relate.

i. Persons and departments performing processes or steps are specified by the use of either column headings or annotations.

j. Ample connections (cross-references) are provided. The symbols used in forming the connections depend on the situation. Thus, if two sheets are needed to contain the flowchart, the flows between pages are formed by off-page connector symbols. In those cases where the procedure being flowcharted links to an adjoining procedure, the connection can be formed by a terminal symbol as follows.

k. Exceptional occurrences, such as back-orders, are clearly noted. They may appear as (1) comments within annotation symbols, (2) separate flowcharts, with references to the main flowchart, or (3) decision branches. The last alternative may be illustrated as shown at the top of the next page.

l. Special presentation techniques are adopted when their use increases both the content and clarity of the procedure. An apt illustration of this rule is the portrayal of batch control totals in computer-based batch pro-

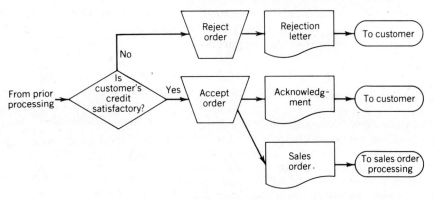

cessing systems. As described earlier, batch control totals are generally computed from key data in each batch of transactions prior to processing runs. Then during each processing run the totals are recomputed and compared to the precomputed totals. These run-to-run comparisons may be performed at the direction of the computer processing programs, and the results may be shown on printed exception and summary reports. If the results show differences in the totals, the differences must be located before processing can continue. This batch control procedure may be diagrammed as follows, where the dashed lines indicate the run-to-run comparisons with the precomputed totals.

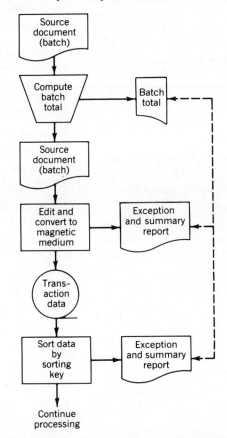

6. Complete the flowchart in final form. A finished flowchart should be neatly drawn and uncrowded. Normally it also should contain a title, date, and the name(s) of the preparers.

SUMMARY

Documentation communicates knowledge concerning transaction processing systems to users, system designers, and system evaluators. Pertinent documentation techniques include formats of documents, forms, CRT screens, and reports; screen displays; record layouts; data dictionaries; and flowcharts, data flow diagrams, and structured diagrams.

Documentation is most effective when the various elements are well designed and fully illustrated. Thus, forms should exhibit clear purposes, be handily prepared, and be easily usable. Each report should exhibit a clear purpose, have an appropriate scope and adequate discrimination, be concise, be understandable, and fit into a reporting system. A flowchart should employ a consistent set of symbols, clearly portray a sequence of steps in a procedure, show connections to other flowcharts, show the final dispositions of all documents and reports, and incorporate adequate labels and added comments. It should focus on the normal flows, although it may recognize any exceptional occurrences.

REFERENCES

Bower, James B., Schlosser, Robert E., and Newman, Maurice S. *Computer-Oriented Accounting Information Systems.* Cincinnati: South-Western, 1985.

Cushing, Barry E. and Romney, Marshall B. *Accounting Systems and Business Organizations*, 4th ed. Reading, Mass.: Addison-Wesley, 1987.

Kneer, Dan C. "Systems Procedures and Controls." *Journal of Systems Management* (Sept. 1983), 28–33.

Lauderman, Max. "Document Flowcharts for Internal Control." *Journal of Systems Management* (Mar. 1980), 22–30.

Li, David H. "Control Flowcharting for Internal Control." *The Internal Auditor* (Aug. 1983), 28–30.

Litecky, Charles R. and Rittenberg, Larry E. "Systems Flowcharting: Principles for Uniform Practice." *EDP Auditor* (Dec. 1979), 17–29.

PMI SEADOC Guide. New York: Peat, Marwick, Mitchell & Co., 1985.

Weil, Joseph J. "System Flowcharting Techniques for the Internal Auditor." *The Internal Auditor* (Apr. 1977), 52–58.

QUESTIONS

1. What is the meaning of each of the following terms?

Form analysis sheet	Record layout
Preformatted screen	Data dictionary
Data entry screen	Flowchart
Stewardship report	System flowchart
Legal compliance report	Document flowchart
Operational report	Computer system flowchart
Control report	Control-oriented flowchart
Planning report	Data flow diagram
Report format	
Screen display	

2. Which individuals need documentation of transaction processing systems?

3. How are those individuals benefited by effective documentation?

4. List the various types of documentation applied to transaction processing systems.

5. What are the attributes of a well-designed form?

6. What questions should be asked when designing a form?

7. What additional concerns apply to the design of a screen for the entry of transaction data?

8. What types of reports are needed by the typical firm?

9. What are the attributes of an effective report?

10. What are several features that may be employed to enhance the usefulness of a CRT screen display?

11. What are the components of a typical record layout?

12. What characteristics pertaining to data items should appear in a data dictionary?

13. Describe the several levels of flowcharts.

14. What elements are highlighted in a system flowchart?

15. How does a data flow diagram differ from a system flowchart?

16. Identify the various symbols that may be used in system flowcharts.

17. Contrast the features of system flowcharts prepared for (a) a computer-based batch transaction processing system, and (b) a computer-based online transaction processing system.

18. List several guidelines for preparing system flowcharts.

19. What are the costs of documentation?

20. Is it beneficial to prepare more than one type of flowchart or diagram of the same transaction processing system?

REVIEW PROBLEM

Campus Bookstore, Sixth Installment

Statement

The Campus Bookstore (described in the review problem at the end of Chapter 1) accepts delivery of its new minicomputer system. While awaiting delivery, the accounting system manager had designed, with the aid of consultants from the public accounting firm, those applications identified earlier. (See the lists of applications in the review problem at the end of Chapter 3.) Now the accounting system manager engages the consultants to prepare adequate documentation of the designed applications.

Required

  a. Identify typical parties that should benefit from the prepared documentation.

  b. Describe the array of documentation that the consultants might prepare with respect to the transaction processing systems.

Solution

a. Beneficiaries of the documentation include those persons who will operate the new system, such as the computer operator, bookkeepers, order clerks, accounting clerks, cashier, and so on. These users of the system need the documentation to aid them in performing the prescribed procedures. Also, the accounting system manager and programmer will use the documentation when the transaction processing systems need to be revised or redesigned. Finally, the public accountants who audit the financial records will use the documentation as an aid for evaluating the adequacy of the transaction processing systems and related controls.

b. The transaction processing systems to be installed on the new minicomputer system include general ledger accounting, cash sales and receipts, purchases and inventory record-keeping, accounts payable and cash disbursements, and payroll. Documentation for such transaction processing systems might suitably consist of (1) computer system flowcharts of all the aforementioned systems, including their relationships to the general ledger and the financial statements; (2) formats of all source documents, including cash sales slips, purchase orders, checks, and time cards; (3) preformatted screens for entering transaction data relating to the receipt of ordered merchandise and any other online applications (except cash sales, which are entered via scanners); (4) formats of all reports and summaries, such as sales analyses and cash receipts summaries; (5) screen displays of all information to be available via online terminals, such as displays of inventory quantities on hand and supplier status; and (6) record layouts pertaining to all stored files, such as the inventory master file, supplier master file, and receiving report file. Other types of documentation will be needed if and when the system is modified to incorporate data structures other than files.

PROBLEMS

6-1. Design a suitable format of a form for entering the courses that you request to take next semester at your university or college. The form should show all necessary information concerning you and the courses, including your name, your ID number, your major department, the course numbers and descriptions, the times of the courses, and the room locations of the courses. Space should be provided your adviser's signature.

6-2. Design a suitable format of a form to be used by a manufacturing firm. The purpose of the form is to account for tools checked out to production employees, as well as to enable production planners to compute average times of usage. Each tool is identified by a brief description and a number, such as "socket wrench, no. 3" (of ten available for checking out). In addition to this data concerning the tool, the form should contain the employee number and department, dates, and times. It also should be prenumbered.

6-3. Design a suitable format of a form to be used by a depositor of Thrift Savings and Loan. The form should accommodate either a deposit or withdrawal of funds from a savings account. When filled in, it is given to the teller together with the depositor's passbook. The form should allow checks or currency to be deposited and allow cash to be returned to the depositor from the total of deposited checks if desired.

6-4. Refer to Problem 6-3. Assume that Thrift Savings and Loan employs an online depositor transaction processing system with video display terminals. Design a suitable preformatted data entry screen to aid the tellers in entering deposit and withdrawal transactions. Provide for the "echo" of the depositor's name and current account balance on the screen upon the entry of the depositor's account number.

6-5. The Good Shepherd Hospital employs an online patient transaction processing system, including video display terminals. Design a preformatted data entry screen to aid the receptionist in admitting a patient to the emergency room. Data to be entered include the patient's name, address, age, medical insurance plan; the means by which the patient was delivered to the hospital; the code for the suspected type of injury or illness; the attending physician; the time of arrival; and so on. Allow space for the description of the injury or illness to be "echoed" upon the entry of the code.

6-6. A recently employed systems analyst of the Newhall Company prepared the following sales invoice. The invoice has been designed for computer preparation from data provided on shipping notices. It is to be printed in three copies, with the original and one copy to be sent to the customer and the other copy to be placed into a customer file (arranged alphabetically in file folders). The accounts receivable master file, on magnetic tape, is to be updated during the invoicing run.

The sales invoices currently in use are prepared manually. About 3000 sales invoices are prepared annually, although as many as 800 are

Newhall Company New Haven, Connecticut				
Amount due:		Date:		
Ship to:		Salesperson:		
Sold to:		Ship via:		
Product number	Quantity sold	Unit price	Amount	Description
Total				
Terms:		Freight charge:		Sales tax:

Notes: **1.** Actual size is 7″ × 10″.
2. All copies are white.
3. Weight of paper: 20-pound bond.

prepared during the busiest week. Roughly 2 percent of the sales invoices this year have been found to contain errors; with the use of the computer, the firm expects to reduce the errors by 75 percent. The cost of preparing each invoice, now averaging $3, is expected to be cut in half. Three separate products are shipped on a typical order.

Required

As a forms consultant, you have been asked to examine the newly designed sales invoice and the related processing prior to its adoption. Prepare a form analysis sheet, including remarks pertaining to possible weaknesses and needed improvements.

6-7. Valpaige Co. of Omaha is an industrial machinery and equipment manufacturer with several production departments. The company employs automated and heavy equipment in its production departments. Consequently, Valpaige has a large repair and maintenance (R & M) department for servicing this equipment.

The operating efficiency of the R & M department has deteriorated over the past two years. Further, repair and maintenance costs seem to be climbing more rapidly than other department costs. The assistant controller has reviewed the operations of the R & M department and has concluded that the administrative procedures used since the early days of the department are outmoded due in part to the growth of the company. The two major causes for the deterioration, in the opinion of the assistant controller, are an antiquated scheduling system for repair and maintenance work and the actual cost system to distribute the R & M department's costs to the production departments. The actual costs of the R & M department are allocated monthly to the production departments on the basis of the number of service calls made during each month.

The assistant controller has proposed that a formal work order system be implemented for the R & M department. The production departments would submit a service request to the R & M department for the repairs and/or maintenance to be completed, including a suggested time for having the work done. The supervisor of the R & M department would prepare a cost esti-

mate on the service request for the work required (labor and materials) and indicate a suggested time for completing the work on the service request. The R & M supervisor would return the request to the production department which initiated the request. Once the production department okays the work by returning a copy of the service request, the R & M supervisor would prepare a repair and maintenance work order and schedule the job. This work order provides the repair worker with the details of the work to be done and is used to record maintenance hours worked and the materials and supplies used.

Producing departments would be changed for actual labor hours worked at a predetermined standard rate for the type of work required. The parts and supplies used would be charged to the production departments at cost.

The assistant controller believes that only two documents would be required in this new system—a repair maintenance service request initiated by the production departments and the repair maintenance work order initiated by the R & M department.

Required

a. For the repair maintenance work order document:

    (1) Identify the data items which would be important to the R & M department and the production departments which should be incorporated into the work order.

    (2) Indicate how many copies of the work order would be required and explain how each copy would be distributed.

b. Prepare a document system flowchart to show how the repair maintenance service request and the repair maintenance work order should be coordinated and used among the departments of Valpaige Co. to request and complete the repair and maintenance work, to provide the basis for charging the production departments for the cost of the completed work, and to evaluate the performance of the R & M department. Provide explanations to the flowchart as appropriate.

(CMA adapted)

6-8. Design formats of reports that will provide needed information to enable the responsible managers to achieve the following purposes.

a. Review the activity and status of each merchandise item.

b. Project the expected requirements for cash during the four quarters of the coming year.

6-9. The Arguay Corporation of St. Petersburg, Florida, prepares a weekly comprehensive inventory control report, such as the example shown below. The report was developed by the firm's data processing department from a sketch prepared by the plant manager. The report is sent regularly to the production manager, purchasing manager, and cost accounting manager.

Required

Based upon the displayed segment of the inventory control report and the circumstances previously described, discuss why the report is not an effective communication vehicle.

(CMA adapted)

6-10. The National Association of Trade Stores is located in Columbus, Ohio. Each month the department heads receive a financial report of the performance of their departments for the previous month. The report is generally distributed around the 16th or 17th of the month. Although the association is a not-for-profit trade and educational association, it does attempt to generate revenues from a variety of activities to supplement the member dues. The association has several income-producing departments: research, education, publications, and promotion consulting services. As a general rule, each department is expected to be self-supporting, and the department head is responsible for both the generation of revenue and the control of costs for the department.

As an example of the monthly department report, the March 1989 report of the education department is presented on the next page, with the comments of the accounting department noted at the bottom of the report.

The annual revenue target, which becomes the revenue budget, is established by the execu-

---

Arguay Company
Comprehensive Inventory Control Report
Week Ended August 5, 1989

Part Number	Quantity			Standard Cost per Unit	Total Actual Costs	Variance
	Inventory on Hand	Used	Purchased			
. . .						
53 Series						
. . .	. . .	. . .	. . .	. . .	. . .	. . .
5397	175	8,433	8,556	$1.0325	$9,033	$ (199)
5398	215	9,717	9,810	.0786	765	6
. . .	. . .	. . .	. . .	. . .	. . .	. . .
Total 53 Series	12,387	647,305	649,077	.6438	423,068	(5,192)
54 Series						
. . .	. . .	. . .	. . .	. . .	. . .	. . .
5401	1,191	15,448	16,352	.3597	5,723	159
5402	1,723	37,236	35,897	.5500	19,815	(72)
. . .	. . .	. . .	. . .	. . .	. . .	. . .
Total 54 Series	42,786	1,437,233	1,435,865	.7490	1,074,173	1,290
Total Inventory	708,113	10,797,828	10,872,560	1.4350	15,657,100	(54,976)

Note: The series of dots (i.e., . . .) represent other data omitted from the report to simplify presentation.

tive director and the association's board of directors. The annual and monthly expense budgets are then developed at the beginning of the year by the department heads for all costs except rent, utilities, and janitorial services; equipment depreciation; and allocated general administration. The amounts for these accounts are supplied by the accounting department. The monthly budget figures for revenues are also determined by the department heads at the beginning of the year. The monthly budget amounts for revenues and expenses are not revised during the year.

For example, the following changes in operations have taken place but the monthly budgets have not been revised: (1) a new home-study course was introduced in February, one month earlier than scheduled; (2) a number of the week-long courses were postponed in February and March and rescheduled for April and May; and (3) the related promotion effort—heavy direct-

mail advertising in the two months prior to a course offering—was likewise rescheduled.

Required

Identify and briefly discuss the good and bad features of the monthly report presented for the education department as a means of communication in terms of

a. Its format for presenting data concerning the operating performance of the education department.

b. Its content in providing useful information to the department head for managing the education department.

Include in your discussion the changes you would recommend to improve the report as a communication device.

(CMA adapted)

National Association of Trade Stores
Education Department
Report for the Month of March 1989

	Budget			Actual			Variance		Variance as a % of Budget	
	Person Days or Units	$	%	Person Days or Units	$	%	Person Days or Units	$	Person Days or Units	%
Revenue										
Week-long courses	1500	$225,000	71.4%	1250	$187,500	66.4%	(250)	$(37,500)	(16.6)%	(16.6)%
One-day seminars	50	15,000	4.8	17	5,100	1.8	(33)	(9,900)	(66.0)	(66.0)
Home-study courses	1000	75,000	23.8	1100	89,700	31.8	100	14,700	10.0	19.6
		$315,000	100.0%		$282,300	100.0%		$(32,700)		(10.4)%
Expenses										
Salaries		$174,000	55.2%		$167,000	59.1%		$7,000		4.0%
Course material		35,500	11.3		34,670	12.3		830		2.3
Supplies, tele. & tele.		4,000	1.3		4,200	1.5		(200)		(5.0)
Rent, utilities & janitorial serv.		7,000	2.2		7,000	2.5		—		—
Equipment depreciation		700	.2		700	.2		—		—
Allocated gen. admin.		5,000	1.6		5,000	1.8		—		—
Temporary office help		5,000	1.6		3,750	1.3		1,250		25.0
Contract employees		15,000	4.8		18,500	6.6		(3,500)		(23.3)
Travel		12,000	3.8		11,500	4.1		500		4.2
Dues & meetings		500	.2		500	.2		—		—
Promotion & postage		32,000	10.1		36,500	12.9		(4,500)		(14.1)
Total expenses		$290,700	92.3%		$289,320	102.5%		$1,380		0.5%
Contribution to the Association		$24,300	7.7%		$(7,020)	(2.5)%		$(31,320)		(128.9)%

Note: The department did not make its budget this month. There was a major short-fall in the week-long course revenues. Although salaries were lower than budget, this saving was entirely consumed by overexpenditure in contract employees and promotion. Further effort is needed to increase revenues and to hold down expenses.

6-11. Draw record layouts and enter the indicated values for the accounts payable, finished-goods inventory, and employee payroll earnings records below. Assume fields of suitable sizes.

a. Morris Winston, a supplier whose address is 20 Tern Street, Boise, Idaho 83702, and whose number is 735, is due on May 18 an amount of $568.27 for a purchase initiated by purchase order number 2381, dated April 19. His invoice number is 723, dated April 28.

b. A quantity of 50 camshafts, product 76A, is on hand in the warehouse (bin location L81B) on September 30. During the month of September, 30 were received from production and 15 were issued. The unit cost of product 76A is $75.25.

c. George Briscoe, employee number 93565 in department 56, is salaried (code 1) and thus does not earn overtime premium. As of March 15 he had earned gross pay of $2000, with deductions of $700. He was employed in 1971 (code 71) and was born in 1929 (code 29). His occupational code is 536.

6-12. Design a record layout for a student master file. Include at least 10 data items, beginning with the student identification number. Do not include transcripts. Arrange the data items within the record, specifying field lengths and modes for the respective items. (Modes may be numeric, alphabetic, or alphanumeric.)

6-13. The Lockspar National Bank maintains separate master files pertaining to checking accounts, savings accounts, and installment loans. Design record layouts for each of these files. Each type of record should begin with a customer account number and end with the current balance. Include additional data items that are needed to maintain the accounts, specifying the field length and mode for each item. (Modes may be numeric, alphabetic, or alphanumeric.) Assume that each file is maintained independently of the others; thus, if a particular customer appears in all three of the files, he or she would be assigned three separate account numbers.

6-14. J. B. Means, a retail chain based in Buffalo, uses the following fixed-length master records to retain data concerning its charge customers:

Data Item	Field Size (Characters)
Account number	10
Customer name	35
Customer address	40
Customer ZIP code	5
Credit limit	10
Account balance, beginning of month	10
Account balance, current	10

These records are maintained in a sequential file on magnetic tape. Each day the account balances are updated from sales and cash receipts transaction tapes; any customer whose balance exceeds the credit limit is listed on a credit notification report. At the end of each month the daily transaction tapes are merged and re-sorted; then they are used, together with the master records, to print the monthly statements to customers.

Required

a. Identify the likely primary key and at least three secondary keys in the foregoing master record.

b. Describe, with the aid of a computer system flowchart, the steps required to produce a report that lists customers, arranged alphabetically within ZIP codes; also, draw the report format.

c. Draw a monthly statement for a customer and enter sample data.

d. Draw a record layout for the master record. Key each data item in the master record to the printed item in the monthly statement. For instance, enter a circled *A* under the account number field in the record layout, and also a circled *A* next to the assumed value for the account number (e.g., 01234567) in the statement.

e. Draw a record layout for the transaction record, beginning with a transaction code field. Include in the record layout at least those data items that are to reflect the monthly account activity in the customer's monthly statement. Key each data item from the record layout to a like item in the monthly statement.

6-15. Draw segments of system flowcharts that depict each of the activities described.

a. Manually prepares invoices in five copies, by reference to a customer's order and pricing file.

b. Manually sorts purchase orders by assigned numbers and then files.

c. Manually compares the purchase order and receiving report with the pertinent supplier's invoice, marks the invoice approved, and files all documents together in chronological order in an open-to-pay file.

d. Manually posts a batch of check vouchers to the accounts payable subsidiary ledger, resorts the batch by suppliers' names, and files in suppliers' folders.

e. Processes by computer a batch of sorted sales transactions (on magnetic tape) to update a customer master file (on magnetic tape).

f. Processes by computer a batch of cash receipts transactions (on magnetic tape) to update a customer master file (on magnetic disk).

g. Processes by computer in order to extract data from an employee earnings file and an employee personal history file (both on magnetic disks) onto a report file (on magnetic disk), and then to print a personnel report from the extracted data.

h. Converts sales data from a batch of OCR documents to magnetic tape by means of a computer run.

i. Enters data concerning shipments from documents by means of CRT terminals, with the data being checked upon entry by an edit program, and stores the edited data on an online magnetic disk file.

j. Enters data from a batch of checks into a computer system by means of an MICR device and stores the data on an online magnetic disk.

k. Enters data from a diskette onto a magnetic disk that is online to a large computer system.

l. Merges a sales transaction file and cash receipts transaction file, both sorted by customer account numbers and stored on separate magnetic tapes; sequentially updates the accounts receivable master file, stored on a magnetic disk; and concurrently prints an accounts receivable aging report.

6-16. The SEADOC flowchart shown in Figure 6-13 is characterized as a type of control-oriented flowchart. Contrast the features of this type of flowchart with the type of system flowchart appearing in Figure 6-16. Describe the ways that the SEADOC flowchart aids in the evaluation of accounting controls relating to such transaction processing systems as purchases and cash disbursements.

6-17. Academy State University maintains an online computer system for the registration of its students. Each student brings a completed and approved course request sheet to an online registration site. There a registration clerk enters the student's identification number, plus the schedule line numbers (e.g., 12369) that identify the particular sections of courses being requested by the student. The course request data are edited upon entry and then stored in an online course request file (on a magnetic disk). On course assignment day the computer operator processes the course request data to produce confirmed course schedule listings. (In preparing these listings the computer program refers to a course schedule file that contains descriptive data concerning the courses, to a class status file that shows the number of vacancies remaining in each course section, and to the student file that contains descriptive data—name, address, and so on—concerning students. It also increases the count by one in each course section to which the student is added.) The course schedule listings are then mailed to the students' addresses.

Required

Prepare a computer system flowchart of the registration procedure described.

6-18. The Mobile Insurance Co. of Birmingham, Alabama, issues automobile insurance policies. Currently the firm has about 20,000 policies in force. Transactions affecting these policies are processed on a relatively small card-oriented computer system with magnetic tape storage.

Policy processing involves several steps. Transaction data pertaining to billing, payments, renewals, new policyholders, canceled policy-holders, and changes in status are first recorded on standardized source documents. These documents are forwarded by the initiating departments to the input preparation section, where the data therein are keypunched and key verified. The punched cards containing transaction data are edited in a computer run and then sorted by policyholder number. Then they are processed against the policyholder master file in order to update the records. During this updating run a transaction listing (journal) is prepared. Also, data are extracted from the policy-holder records concerning those policyholders who are due to pay premiums or to renew policies. A tape containing this extracted data is then processed to print premium notices and renewal notices.

Required

a. Draw a computer system flowchart of the policy processing procedure described.

b. Draw computer system flowcharts that re-flect the following changes made in the aforementioned procedure.

(1) Eliminate the use of punched cards; instead, key the data from the source documents directly onto magnetic tape.

(2) Eliminate the use of punched cards; instead, key the data from the source documents directly onto magnetic tape. Also, substitute magnetic disks as the storage medium for the policyholder master file.

(3) Eliminate the use of punched cards; instead, enter the transaction data individually via video display terminals (located in the initiating departments) directly into the computer system. Also, substitute magnetic disks as the storage medium for the policyholder master file, and have the computer system update the affected record directly as soon as the data are entered and edited.

Note: In the batch processing procedures described, use batch totals plus run-to-run comparisons if specified by your instructor.

PART II

TRANSACTION

PROCESSING

SYSTEMS AND

CYCLES

General

Ledger and

Financial

Reporting

System

7

Describe the purposes and functions of the general ledger and financial reporting system.

Identify the data sources, inputs, data flows, interrelationships, files, financial outputs, and accounting controls pertaining to the general ledger system.

Describe the classification and coding approaches that underlie the general ledger and other transaction processing systems.

Contrast the general ledger systems for merchandising, manufacturing, and service-oriented organizations.

INTRODUCTION

Transaction processing systems are of major concern to accountants. Thus, they should form a central core within the study of accounting information systems (AISs). Our focus on transaction processing systems spans Chapters 7 through 10. We begin in this chapter with the general ledger and financial reporting system, since it provides an integrating perspective of the remaining transaction processing systems.

PURPOSES AND FUNCTIONS

The general ledger system has the key purpose of providing information for an array of financial reports concerning an accounting entity (e.g., a business firm or a governmental agency). A sound general ledger system (1) records all accounting transactions promptly and accurately, (2) posts these transactions to the proper accounts, (3) maintains an equality of debit and credit balances among the accounts,

(4) accommodates needed adjusting journal entries, and (5) generates reliable and timely financial reports pertaining to each accounting period.

In order to achieve these purposes or objectives, a general ledger system performs several functions. The manner in which these functions are performed depends in part on the extent and type of computerization employed. However, all general ledger systems must perform the following.

1. **Collect transaction data.** Transactions arise from a variety of sources, such as sales and purchases. The more numerous types of transactions are grouped by component transaction processing systems. These component systems then interface with and feed their summarized data to the general ledger system. Other transactions are recorded individually, generally on specially designed forms and journal vouchers.

2. **Process transaction inflows.** Collected transaction data undergo several processing steps before coming to rest in the general ledger. First, they are checked to see that debit amounts equal credit amounts, that eligible account names are used, and so on. Also, individual transactions may be verified to see that they are in conformity with generally accepted accounting principles. Then the transactions are posted to the general ledger accounts. If the posting is performed sequentially, the transactions are sorted beforehand. Proof listings of the posted transactions may be prepared.

3. **Store transaction data.** The general ledger (as well as each subsidiary ledger) reflects account balances. Thus, the general ledger represents a master file within a firm's data base. If the balances in the accounts of the general ledger "master file" are to be kept current, they must be updated through the posting of transaction data.

   In addition to updating the general ledger accounts, the system generally accumulates the details of the transactions into transaction files for backup and ready reference. Linkages between these transactions and the postings to the general ledger are provided by an audit trail. The audit trail in turn is enhanced by journals and journal listings, which include cross-references between the transactions and their postings.

4. **Maintain accounting controls.** Since the general ledger system is an integral part of the AIS, it incorporates certain accounting controls. As we are well aware, the structure of the general ledger itself provides a fundamental control. That is, the total of the credit account balances must constantly equal the total of the debit account balances. Checks of this equality are made periodically by means of trial balances. Other controls range from checks or edits of the transaction data as they are entered into the system to reviews of the financial reports by managers and other recipients. Organizational independence represents yet another type of essential control.

5. **Generate financial reports.** The most familiar financial reports generated by the general ledger system are the income statement and balance sheet. However, a wide variety of other beneficial reports may be prepared. Some of these reports aid in the verification of the general ledger accounts them-

selves. Other reports, such as financially oriented operating budgets, aid managers with regard to planning and control responsibilities.

6. **Classify and code transaction data and accounts.** Underlying the maintenance of the general ledger system are adequate classification and coding systems. Classification is necessary when assigning the various accounts within the general ledger. Coding is desirable for identifying accounts, transactions, files, and other elements that impinge on the general ledger.

Each of these functions will be explored more thoroughly in the following sections. We then conclude the chapter by contrasting the differences exhibited by the general ledger systems of varying types of organizations.

TRANSACTION-ORIENTED RELATIONSHIPS AND CYCLES

Before examining the various functions, we might consider an overview of transaction processing. As Figure 7-1 portrays, the various component **transaction processing systems** of a typical firm form several distinct though highly interrelated groupings. For instance, the sales transaction processing system involves the processing of sales orders as well as the preparation of bills (invoices) and sales analyses. It also interrelates, however, with cash receipts through the accounts receivable records and with purchases through the inventory records. Of particular interest is the general ledger system and its financial reporting activity. Not only does it interrelate with the sales transaction processing system

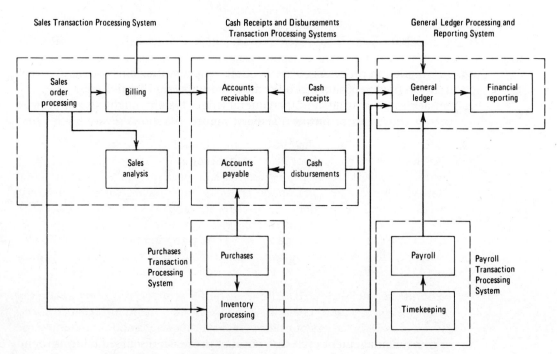

FIGURE 7-1 Relationships among transaction processing systems.

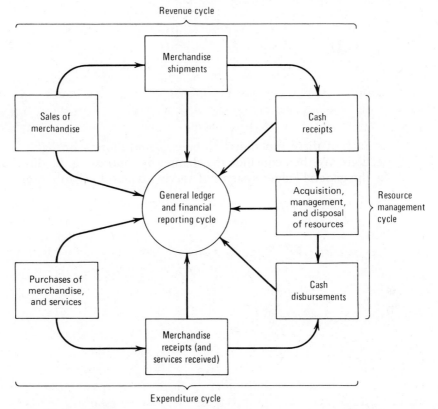

FIGURE 7-2 Transaction-oriented cycles for a merchandising firm.

(through the billing activity), but it also interrelates with *all* the remaining component transaction processing systems. Consequently, the general ledger system serves as the final repository of all transaction data entering the AIS.

Transaction processing, and the general ledger system, might also be viewed in terms of the cycles of business activity. Figure 7-2 shows several cycles that pertain to a merchandising firm. Although the particular set of business activity cycles varies somewhat with the type of organization, those shown in the figure will illustrate the cycle concept and the place of the general ledger system.

1. The **revenue cycle** includes events pertaining to the sale of merchandise and the receipts of cash in payment thereof.

2. The **expenditure cycle** includes events pertaining to the acquisition of merchandise and services and the disbursements of cash in payment thereof.

3. The **resource management cycle** includes events pertaining to the acquisition, management, and disposal of such resources as investments and fixed assets. (Since the labor of employees is both a service and a resource, the payroll system may fit either within this cycle or the expenditure cycle.) The resource management cycle also encompasses cash disbursed to acquire the resources and cash received upon their disposal.

4. The **general ledger and financial reporting cycle** (i.e., system) accepts all the financial transactions deriving from the first three cycles, including adjustment-type transactions, and generates financial reports on a cyclical basis.

Figure 7-2 clearly shows the general ledger and financial reporting cycle (system) to be pivotal. Regardless of the type of organization and the consequent array of bordering cycles, the general ledger and financial reporting cycle remains at the center of the transaction-oriented process and the AIS. (Figure 6-14 also portrays the central position of the general ledger and its relationship to the transaction processing systems that comprise the first three cycles.)

Three following chapters in this part are organized around the revenue, expenditure, and resource management cycles. Therefore, no further details concerning them need be noted at this point.

Certain types of organizations require additional transaction-oriented cycles. For instance, banks generally require demand deposit and installment loan cycles. A particularly important cycle is the product conversion cycle of manufacturing firms. It is therefore included in a later chapter.

DATA SOURCES AND INPUTS

Sources

The general ledger system receives inputs from a wide variety of sources. Figure 7-3 emphasizes this variety. It shows the source documents of the various component transaction processing systems being entered into special journals. Summary totals from these entries are posted to the general ledger, as well as to any subsidiary ledgers that are maintained. Most transactions that affect the general ledger arise from such sources.

Other sources of general ledger inputs are financial transactions that traditionally have been entered into the general journal. Included in this group are

1. Nonroutine transactions that occur during the accounting period, such as a transaction that records the exchange of a fixed asset for capital stock.

2. End-of-period adjusting transactions that (a) are recurring, such as the depreciation of fixed assets and the expiration of insurance, and (b) are nonrecurring, such as a change of inventory valuation methods.

3. Reversing transactions that are entered at the beginning of accounting periods, such as an entry that reverses the accrual of payroll expense at the end of the previous period.

Forms of Input

Manual Systems The primary source document to the general ledger system is the general ledger **journal voucher,** which has generally replaced the general journal sheet. A journal voucher is typically prepared for each nonroutine, ad-

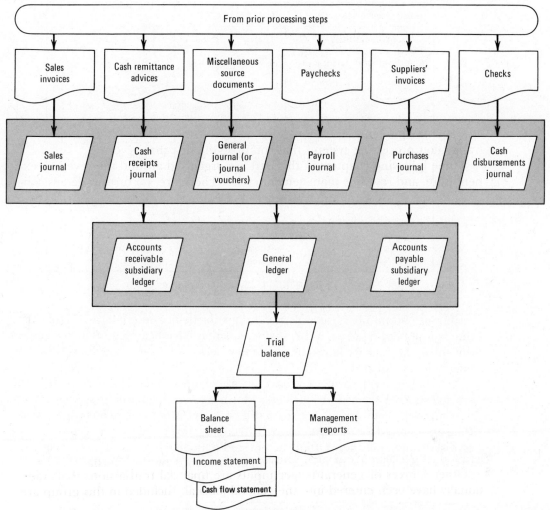

FIGURE 7-3 Sources of inputs and their flows through the general ledger system.

justing, and reversing transaction. Figure 7-4 illustrates a manually prepared journal voucher that reflects a standard adjusting transaction. A journal voucher is also often prepared to summarize the results of a batch of routine transactions that have been manually entered into special journals. For instance, after today's checks have been written and entered into the check register, a clerk may prepare a journal voucher that reflects the total of the cash disbursements.

Computer-based Systems Although the journal voucher remains the primary input to the general ledger in computer-based systems, its form will likely vary from that employed in manual systems. Three variations worth noting are the individual journal entry form, the batch entry form, and the online screen.

The journal voucher for entering individual transactions may be similar in appearance to Figure 7-4. It likely contains columns for entering account de-

Journal Voucher No. 688		Date 12/31/88			
Account titles	Codes	Debit		Credit	
Amortization of patent costs	88	15,000.00	√		
Patents	29			15,000.00	√

To amortize the costs of patents held by the firm, by 1/17 of the original costs, during 1988

Written by: Sylvia Brown	Approval: Ted Johnson	Auditor: John Eweb

FIGURE 7-4 A journal voucher.

scriptions and numbers, as well as columns for debit and credit amounts. After the data pertaining to an individual transaction have been manually written on this form, the data are keyed by data entry clerks onto transaction files stored on magnetic tape or disk.

The batch entry form may have an appearance that closely resembles the journal voucher form. The batch entry form is used to replace the special journal in computer-based systems, or to record the entry of miscellaneous transactions. Data are entered manually onto the batch entry form and then keyed onto tape or disk transaction files. Often the entered data are then listed on a hard copy printout in order to provide a permanent record of the journal. Figure 7-5

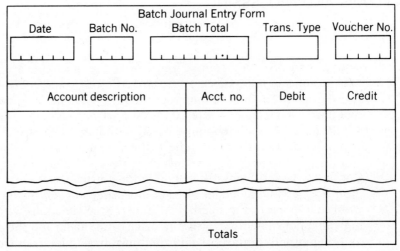

FIGURE 7-5 A batch entry journal voucher.

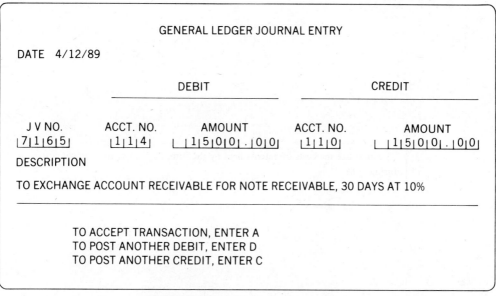

FIGURE 7-6 A journal entry screen.

depicts a batch entry journal voucher. Note that it includes details concerning the batch itself so that the system can verify the completeness of the entered data.

A data entry screen can be used to record transactions when the general ledger system employs online files. Transactions are entered interactively with the aid of a CRT screen that is preformatted to exhibit a journal voucher. Either individual transactions or batches of transactions may be entered in this manner. Figure 7-6 exhibits a preformatted journal voucher screen for an individual transaction.

DATA FLOWS AND PROCESSING

In the traditional manual system, transaction data flow into journals (both special and general), then are posted to subsidiary ledgers, and finally are posted to the general ledger.

In computer-based systems, the transaction data are entered from the forms previously described and temporarily stored on either magnetic tapes or magnetic disks. Periodically the individual transactions are processed to update the master files, known as subsidiary ledgers, and their summarized amounts are processed to update the general ledger. If the transaction data are stored on magnetic tapes, the summary data are extracted, sorted by account numbers, and then processed sequentially against the general ledger accounts. If the transaction data are stored on magnetic disks, they will likely be processed directly to the general ledger accounts.

Figure 7-7 shows a system flowchart of the latter situation. During the accounting period transaction data are drawn from sales, cash receipts, purchases, cash disbursements, payroll, fixed asset, and other types of events. Computer

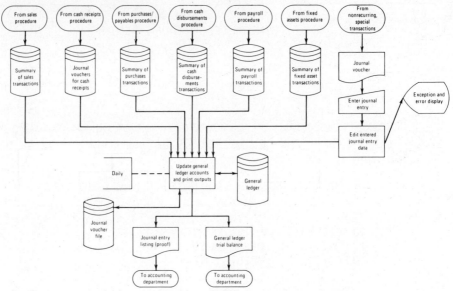

FIGURE 7-7 A computer-based general ledger processing procedure.

programs incorporated into the component transaction processing systems perform steps such as summarizing the transaction amounts and generating prenumbered journal vouchers. Since the general ledger is online, these processing programs may also post the summary amounts to the general ledger accounts. In fact, the general ledger postings can be done concurrently with, and as a byproduct of, the updating of the various subsidiary ledgers (master files).

As nonrecurring special transactions arise, they are entered by accountants via CRT terminals from manually prepared journal vouchers. Each day the general ledger system generates a journal entry listing and a trial balance, in order that the accountants can verify the correctness and accuracy of the processing.

At the end of each accounting period the journal entries for adjusting transactions must be recorded and processed. Figure 7-8 portrays the processing of **standard** and **nonrecurring adjusting journal entries,** assuming an accounting period of one month. Standard (recurring) adjusting journal entries are stored in an online file from month to month. Nonrecurring adjusting journal entries are entered via a CRT terminal from a manually prepared journal voucher coding form. The two types of adjusting journal entries are merged and next sorted into general ledger account number sequence. Then the general ledger accounts are updated and the printed outputs are generated.

DATA BASE

The data base pertaining to the general ledger and financial reporting system contains a variety of master, transaction, and history files. In addition to financial data concerning past events and current status, the data base often contains budgeted data that relates to planned future operations and status.

Although their exact contents and composition will vary from firm to firm, the following set of files is representative (see page 192).

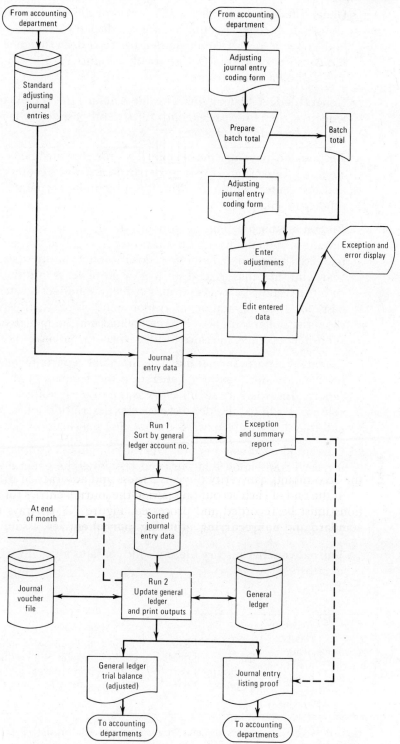

FIGURE 7-8 A month-end general ledger processing procedure.

- **General ledger master file.** Each record of this file contains data concerning one general ledger account. Figure 7-9 displays a suggested layout of a general ledger record. Taken together, the records in the **general ledger master file** constitute the complete chart of accounts for the firm and the current status of all account balances.

- **General ledger history file.** This file contains the actual balances of general ledger accounts for each month for several past years. It is used to provide financial trend information.

- **Responsibility center master file.** This file contains the actual revenues and costs for the various divisions, departments, work centers, and other profit and cost centers within the firm. It is used in the preparation of responsibility reports for managers.

- **Budget master file.** This file contains the budgeted values of assets, liabilities, revenues, and expenses for the various responsibility centers of the firm. The budgeted values may be broken down on a monthly basis for the following year, and they may extend for five or more years into the future. Together with the responsibility center master file, the **budget master file** provides the basis for the preparation of responsibility reports. (Responsibility reports show the dollar variances between actual and budgeted values for each responsibility center, measured with respect to the most recent month.)

- **Financial reports format file.** The **financial reports format file** contains the information necessary for generating the formats of the various financial reports. Included are such factors as the headings of each report, all needed column headings, all side labels (such as descriptions of accounts and subtotal and total lines), and spacing and totaling instructions.

- **Current journal voucher file.** This file contains all significant details concerning each transaction that has been posted to the general ledger during the current month. Included for each voucher would be the journal voucher number, the date of the transaction, accounts debited and credited and the corresponding amounts, and description of the transaction. In effect this file is a summary of all journals for the current month.

- **Journal voucher history file.** This file contains journal vouchers for previous months.

Account number	Account description	Account classification (asset, liability, revenue, expense)	Account balance, beginning of year	Total debits, year-to-date	Total credits, year-to-date	Total debits, current month	Total credits, current month	Current account balance	Dr. or Cr.

Note: Lengths of fields and modes of data items are omitted for simplicity, although they are necessary for complete documentation.

FIGURE 7-9 A record layout for the general ledger master file.

In addition to these files, a firm will need detailed transaction files that support the journal voucher file. Various detailed transaction files are discussed in the chapters that deal with component transaction processing systems. Also, certain firms need various reference files. One example of a needed reference file is a cost allocation file that contains factors for allocating incurred costs (e.g., administrative costs) to responsibility centers, to products, and to other segments within the firm. Those firms that employ the data base approach need files that contain "pointers," which link together the data in two or more files. (The data base approach is discussed in Chapter 11.)

ACCOUNTING CONTROLS

The general ledger system is expected to provide reliable financial reports for a variety of users. In order to achieve this purpose, it must perform an independent check on the component transaction processing systems and carefully monitor the array of nonroutine transactions that it accepts.

Risk Exposures

Among risk exposures that exist in the maintenance of the general ledger are the following.

1. Journal entries may be improperly prepared.
2. Journal entries may be left unposted.
3. Total debit balances and total credit balances in the accounts in the general ledger may become out of balance.
4. Control account balances in the general ledger may become out of balance with the totals of balances in subsidiary ledgers.
5. Unauthorized persons may gain access to data in the general ledger.
6. The audit trail that links the general ledger with source documents may become obscured.
7. Data pertaining to the general ledger and source documents may be lost or destroyed.

An adequate set of general controls and transaction (application) controls is necessary to counteract these risk exposures and to realize the primary purpose of the general ledger system.

General Controls

Suitable general controls are as follows.

1. Organizationally, the function of posting journal vouchers to the general ledger should be separated from the functions of preparing and approving

journal vouchers and from the function of preparing the trial balances of the general ledger.

2. Documentation should consist of at least a fully descriptive chart of accounts, plus a manual of general ledger procedures.

3. Operating practices should be clearly established, including period-end schedules and the preparation of control reports. Figure 7-10 presents an example of a general journal listing, which serves as a proof for verifying that posted journal entries are in balance and as an audit trail aid. Figure 7-11 shows a screen display which summarizes the status of the various journals, indicating those needing corrections, those that have been posted, and so on.

4. Security should be maintained (in the case of online systems) by such techniques as (a) requiring clerks to enter passwords before accessing the general ledger file, (b) employing special terminals for the sole entry of journal voucher data, (c) generating audit reports (access logs) that monitor entries, and (d) dumping the general ledger onto magnetic tape backups.

```
Northcreek Industries                          Time 15:52:00  Date  4/30/88  Page   1  37402
Journal - GJ001  Batch -   1      General Journal           Posting date   4/30/88


         Reference  Reference                      Account
            date     number   Description          number     Debit       Credit

          4/05/88    JV4-01   Deposits              1010    3,556.52
          4/05/88    JV4-01   Deposits              1110                  3,056.52
          4/05/88    JV4-01   Deposits              1140                    123.00
          4/05/88    JV4-01   Deposits              1130                    377.00
          4/05/88    JV4-02   Travel advances       1010   10,000.00
          4/05/88    JV4-02   Travel advances       1560                 10,000.00
          4/12/88    JV4-03   City power            6110    1,675.42
          4/12/88    JV4-03   City water            6120       30.00
          4/17/88    JV4-04   Central loan          2030    1,200.00
          4/17/88    JV4-04   Central loan          1010                  1,200.00
          4/21/88    JV4-05   Trash collection      6260       47.25
          4/21/88    JV4-05   Security service      6270      237.00
          4/21/88    JV4-05   Utility bills         1010                  1,989.67
          4/30/88    JV4-06   FET Transfer to bank  1010                  3,250.00
          4/30/88    JV4-06   FET Transfer to bank  2150    3,250.00
          4/30/88    JV4-07   Dep land improve      1720                    318.54
          4/30/88    JV4-07   Dep land improve      6020      318.54
          4/30/88    JV4-08   Dep buildings         1730                  1,500.00
          4/30/88    JV4-08   Dep buildings         6030    1,500.00
          4/30/88    JV4-09   Dep machinery & equip 1750                    309.39
          4/30/88    JV4-09   Dep machinery & equip 6050      309.39
          4/30/88    JV4-10   Dep auto & truck      1760                    153.23
          4/30/88    JV4-10   Dep auto & truck      6060      153.23
          4/30/88    JV4-11   Dep office equip      1740      150.00
          4/30/88    JV4-11   Dep office equip      6040                    150.00
                                                            ----------  ----------
                                                            22,427.35   22,427.35
```

FIGURE 7-10 A general ledger listing. Courtesy of International Business Machines Corporation.

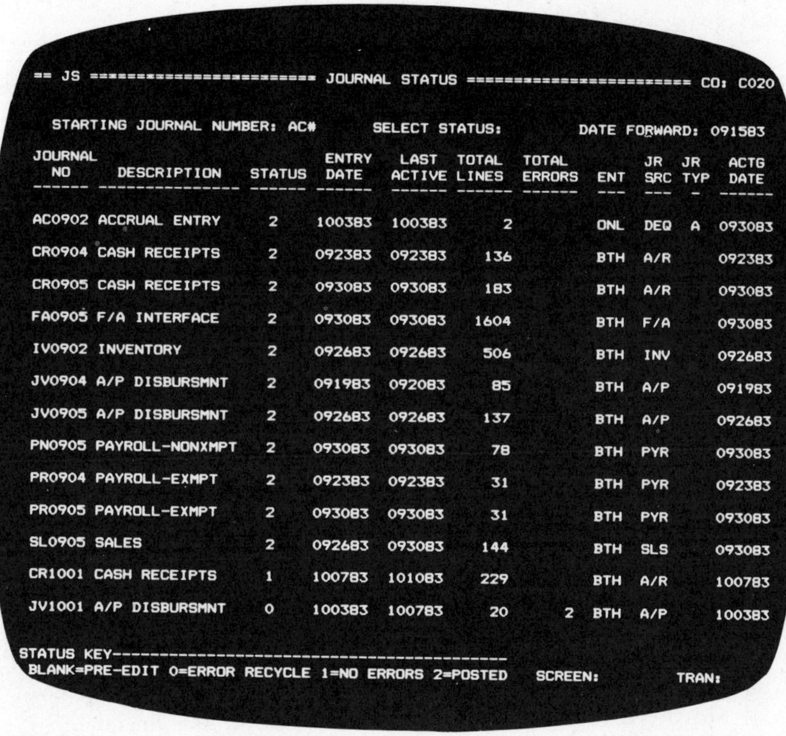

```
== JS ======================== JOURNAL STATUS ======================== CO: C020

   STARTING JOURNAL NUMBER: AC#        SELECT STATUS:          DATE FORWARD: 091583

JOURNAL                          ENTRY   LAST  TOTAL  TOTAL           JR  JR   ACTG
NO       DESCRIPTION     STATUS  DATE   ACTIVE LINES  ERRORS   ENT   SRC TYP  DATE
------   ------------    ------  ------ ------ ------ ------   ---   --- ---  ------
AC0902 ACCRUAL ENTRY       2     100383 100383   2             ONL   DEQ  A   093083

CR0904 CASH RECEIPTS       2     092383 092383   136           BTH   A/R      092383

CR0905 CASH RECEIPTS       2     093083 093083   183           BTH   A/R      093083

FA0905 F/A INTERFACE       2     093083 093083   1604          BTH   F/A      093083

IV0902 INVENTORY           2     092683 092683   506           BTH   INV      092683

JV0904 A/P DISBURSMNT      2     091983 092083   85            BTH   A/P      091983

JV0905 A/P DISBURSMNT      2     092683 092683   137           BTH   A/P      092683

PN0905 PAYROLL-NONXMPT     2     093083 093083   78            BTH   PYR      093083

PR0904 PAYROLL-EXMPT       2     092383 092383   31            BTH   PYR      092383

PR0905 PAYROLL-EXMPT       2     093083 093083   31            BTH   PYR      093083

SL0905 SALES               2     092683 093083   144           BTH   SLS      093083

CR1001 CASH RECEIPTS       1     100783 101083   229           BTH   A/R      100783

JV1001 A/P DISBURSMNT      0     100383 100783   20       2    BTH   A/P      100383

STATUS KEY----------------------------------------------------
 BLANK=PRE-EDIT  0=ERROR RECYCLE  1=NO ERRORS  2=POSTED   SCREEN:        TRAN:
```

FIGURE 7-11 A journal status screen display. Courtesy of Data Design Associates.

Transaction Controls

The following controls and control procedures relating directly to general ledger accounts and processing are generally adequate.

1. Prenumbered journal vouchers are prepared in the appropriate accounting or finance departments. For instance, a journal voucher that reflects the declaration of a dividend may be prepared in the treasurer's office. These prepared journal vouchers are then approved by the responsible department managers.

2. The data in journal vouchers, such as the account numbers, are checked for accuracy.
   a. In the case of manual systems, general ledger clerks perform the checks, referring if necessary to the chart of accounts and procedures manuals.
   b. In the case of computer-based systems, the checks are mainly performed by computer edit programs. Figure 7-12 lists several suitable programmed edit checks pertaining to transaction data.

3. Detected errors in journal entries are corrected before the data are used in posting to the general ledger.

4. Approved journal vouchers are posted by specially designated persons who are not involved in their preparation or approval.

Type of edit check	Typical transaction data items checked	Assurance provided
1. Validity check	General ledger account numbers; transaction codes	The entered numbers and codes are checked against lists of valid numbers and codes stored within the computer system.
2. Field check	Transaction amounts	The amount fields in the input records are checked to see if they contain the proper mode of characters for amounts (i.e., numeric characters). If other modes are found, such as alphabetic characters or blanks, an error is indicated.
3. Limit check	Transaction amounts	The entered amounts are checked against pre-established limits that represent reasonable maximums to be expected. (A separate limit is set for each account.)
4. Zero-balance check	Transaction amounts	The entered debit amounts are netted against the entered credit amounts, and the resulting net amount is compared to zero. (A nonzero net amount indicates that the debits and credits are unequal.)
5. Completeness check[a]	All entered data items	The entered transaction is checked to see that all required data items have been entered.
6. Echo check[a]	General ledger account numbers and titles	After the account numbers pertaining to the transaction are entered at a terminal, the system retrieves and "echoes" back the account titles; the person who has made the entry can visually verify from reading the titles that the correct account numbers were entered.

Note: When entered data do not match or otherwise meet the expected conditions or limits, alerting messages are displayed by the edit program on the CRT screen.

[a] Applicable only to online processing systems.

FIGURE 7-12 Programmed edit checks that validate journal entry data.

a. In the case of manual systems, the journal vouchers are posted by general ledger clerks directly to the general ledger sheets.

b. In the case of batch computer-based systems, the journal vouchers are keyed by data entry clerks onto a magnetic medium; then the batches of entries are sorted by general ledger account numbers and posted during computer runs to the accounts. Figure 7-13 lists various checks that should be made during the posting run.

Type of edit check	Typical transaction data items checked	Assurance provided
1. Internal label check[a]	Name of file	The internal header label of the file to be updated (posted to) is checked before processing begins to ascertain that the correct general ledger master file has been accessed for processing.
2. Sequence check	General ledger account numbers	The transaction file, which has been sorted so that the amounts in the various journal vouchers are ordered according to account numbers, is checked to see that no transaction item is out of sequence.
3. Redundancy matching check[b]	General ledger account numbers and titles	Each transaction debit and credit is checked to see that its account number matches the account number in the general ledger record it is to update. Then the account titles in the transaction record and master file record are also matched, thus providing double protection against updating the wrong file record.
4. Relationship check[b]	Transaction amounts and account numbers	The balance of each general ledger account is checked, after the transaction has been posted, to see that the balance has a normal relationship to the account. If an account balance that normally exhibits a debit balance (e.g., accounts receivable) appears as a credit, the relationship will be flagged by the check.
5. Posting check[b]	Transaction amounts	The after-posting balance in each updated account is compared to the before-posting balance to see that the difference equals the transaction amount.
6. Batch control total checks	Transaction amounts	The amounts posted are totaled and compared to the precomputed amount total of the batch being processed; also, the total number of transaction items processed is compared to the precomputed count of the transaction.

[a] Although these are not true edit checks, they are programmed, and they help to assure that updated data will be accurate.

[b] These checks are also applicable to the posting step in online computer-based systems.

FIGURE 7-13 Programmed edit checks that validate batched data during posting (updating) runs.

    c. In the case of online computer-based systems, the journal vouchers are entered directly into the system with the aid of preformatted CRT screens; then the entries are posted directly to the accounts by the computer system.

5. The equality of debits and credits for each posted journal entry is verified.

6. Adequate cross-references are included to provide a clear audit trail. For instance, the journal voucher number and general ledger numbers are shown in printed listings of the general journal (see Figure 7-10), and the source page number of the general journal or journal voucher number is shown in each posting to the general ledger.

7. Journal vouchers are filed by number, and periodically the file is checked to see that the sequence of numbers is complete.

8. Standard adjusting journal entries (including accruals and reversing entries) are maintained on preprinted sheets (or on magnetic media) in order to enhance posting at the end of each accounting period.

9. Trial balances of general ledger accounts are prepared periodically, and differences between total debits and credits are fully investigated.

10. General ledger control account balances are reconciled periodically to totals of balances in subsidiary ledger accounts.

11. Special period-end reports are printed for review by accountants and managers before the financial statements are prepared. Figure 7-14 shows a general ledger change report that reflects beginning and ending account balances, as well as various control totals.

12. Periodic reviews of journal entries and financial reports are performed by managers, and when feasible, general ledger procedures are reviewed by internal auditors.

FINANCIAL REPORTS

The financial reports generated by the general ledger system may be classified as general ledger analyses, financial statements, and managerial reports. A wide variety of examples are found in each category.

General Ledger Analyses

Most **general ledger analyses** are prepared to aid accountants in verifying the accuracy of postings. Two examples already presented are the general ledger proof listing and the change report. Other general ledger analyses

1. List by account number all transactions posted during an accounting period.

2. Show allocations of expenses to various cost centers.

GENERAL LEDGER

CLIENT 00125					PAGE 14		DECEMBER 31, 19xx
MO DAY YR	ACCT.	DESCRIPTION	REFERENCE	DEBITS	CREDITS	NET CHANGE	NEW BALANCE
11-30-xx	5130	ACCOUNTING & LEGAL	BALANCE	4750.00			
12-05-xx	5130	DEC. RETAINER	10131	450.00			
				450.00		450.00	5200.00
11-30-xx	5140	SALARIES	BALANCE	20769.83			
12-20-xx	5140	DEC. PAYROLL	12332	1885.12			
				1885.12		1885.12	22654.95
11-30-xx	5150	INSURANCE	BALANCE	1125.00			
12-15-xx	5150	ALLTOWN INSURANCE	652	105.10			
				105.10		105.10	1230.10
11-30-xx	5160	OFFICE RENT	BALANCE	3323.33			
12-15-xx	5160	CORRECT NOVEMBER ERROR	J12		23.33		
12-31-xx	5160	DEC. RENT	0012	300.00			
				300.00	23.33	276.67	3600.00
11-30-xx	5170	OFFICE SUPPLIES	BALANCE	895.26			
12-02-xx	5170	K & C FORMS	6736	33.75			
12-17-xx	5170	JACKS STATIONERY	J211A	51.25			
				85.00		85.00	980.26

***************************** CONTROL TOTALS *****************************

	REFERENCE	DEBITS	CREDITS
PRIOR PERIOD BALANCE TOTALS	523,721.12	523,721.12	.00
CURRENT PERIOD TRANSACTIONS	33,968.22	33,968.22	.00
TRIAL BALANCE TOTALS	557,689.34	557,689.34	.00
TRANSACTION COUNT CURRENT PERIOD		453	

FIGURE 7-14 A general ledger change report. Copyright © 1979 by American Institute of Certified Public Accountants, Inc.

3. Compare account balances for the current period with those for the same period last year, and compare year-to-date account balances for this year with those for last year.

Financial Statements

The most visible financial statements are the balance sheet, the income statement, and the funds (cash) flow statement. These statements, which are based directly on the general ledger, are provided to various parties outside the firm. In addition to stockholders or other owners, the financial statements are made available to government agencies, creditors, prospective owners, and financial analysts. Often the financial statements are accompanied by additional information that is useful to the recipients. For instance, they may be accompanied by comparative statements for previous years, by ratio analyses, and by detailed schedules. In special cases they may be altered to suit reporting requirements. An example is the income tax return.

Managerial Reports

The greatest number of reports based on the general ledger are prepared for the use of the firm's managers. Most of these managerial reports are derivatives of the financial statements. However, the financial statements for managers tend to be much more detailed than those provided to outside parties. For instance, analyses based on individual general ledger accounts are often prepared. Examples are analyses of sales, broken down by products or sales territories or markets; analyses of cash, broken down by types of receipts and expenditures; analyses of receivables, broken down by customers and ages of amounts due.

Many of the financial statements prepared for managers involve budgetary amounts. A firm's budget reflects the expected future results of operations and financial status. Thus, the budgetary values represent a critical gage against which the actual results can be measured. Figure 7-15 shows financial reports for managers that compare budget amounts and actual amounts. One of the reports is a comparative balance sheet; the other is a comparative income statement for the United Industries Company. An interesting computation in the income statement is the budget variance, both for the current month and for the year to date.

Two sets of financial reports are based on comparisons of budget and actual amounts for various centers and segment within the firm. These financial reports are incorporated into the responsibility and profitability reporting systems. They enable managers to exercise more precise control over cost centers, profit centers, products, sales territories, and so on. Figure 7-16 presents screen displays of data drawn from the files that underlie such reporting systems. In Chapter 12 we will explore more fully the responsibility and profitability reporting systems and the entire budgetary process.

CLASSIFICATION AND CODING

The general ledger is built on a foundation called the chart of accounts. A **chart of accounts** is a coded listing of all the classified accounts pertaining to a

FIGURE 7-15 Comparative financial statements. Courtesy of Data Design Associates.

Balance Sheet:

UNITED INDUSTRIES COMPANY CO2O GLRO100 REQ 8				BALANCE SHEET CORPORATION	AS OF 12/31/88 RUN DATE 01/04/89		PAGE 21:35:49
BEGINNING OF YEAR	PCT CHG	PRIOR MONTH	PCT CHG		CURRENT BALANCE	CURRENT BUDGET	PRIOR YR BALANCE
				ASSETS: CURRENT ASSETS:			
1,044,500	46.4	1,028,899	48.6	CASH	1,529,480	598,000	1,044,500
922,000	-15.7	841,020	-7.6	ACCOUNTS RECEIVABLE	776,580	0	922,000
-117,582	-10.2	-104,122	1.3	ALLOW DOUBTFUL ACCT	-105,542	-2,500	-117,582
908,000	36.2	732,820	68.8	NOTES RECEIVABLE	1,237,180	200,000	908,000
62,100	16.8	58,940	23.1	INTEREST RECEIVABLE	72,580	5,000	62,100
972,000	73.3	1,026,207	64.2	INVENTORY	1,685,259	210,000	972,000
19,645	131.4	28,158	61.4	OFFICE SUPPLIES	45,462	5,000	19,645
113,450	137.6	168,482	60.0	PREPAID INSURANCE	269,578	25,000	113,450
				TOTAL--			
3,924,113	40.4	3,780,404	45.7	CURRENT ASSETS	5,510,577	1,040,500	3,924,113
				FIXED ASSETS:			
8,346,400	72.7	8,368,314	72.3	MACHINERY	14,419,310	2,015,000	8,346,400
-6,513,500	71.0	-6,541,080	70.2	ACC DEPR - MACH	-11,138,600	-1,583,600	-6,513,500
1,560,000	100.0	1,560,000	100.0	BUILDINGS	3,120,000	0	1,560,000
-50,000	220.0	-80,000	100.0	ACC DEPR - BLDGS	-160,000	0	-50,000
891,000	85.5	899,550	83.8	OFFICE EQUIP	1,653,433	250,000	891,000
-256,390	21.6	-273,430	14.1	ACC DEPR - OFF EQUIP	-311,990	-10,000	-256,390
1,175,000	100.0	1,175,000	100.0	LAND	2,350,000	0	1,175,000
				TOTAL--			
5,152,510	92.7	5,108,354	94.4	FIXED ASSETS	9,932,153	671,400	5,152,510
				TOTAL--			
9,076,623	70.1	8,888,758	73.7	ASSETS	15,442,730	1,711,900	9,076,623

LIABILITIES:

857,800
0
1,358,800
164,200
0
153,200
2,534,000
463,900
1,500,000
1,963,900
4,497,900
1,010,000
2,000,000
0
3,010,000
1,568,723
9,076,623

Income Statement:

UNITED INDUSTRIES COMPANY CO2O GLRO120 REQ 9					INCOME STATEMENT CORPORATION		AS OF 12/31/88 RUN DATE 01/04/89		PAGE 21:35:49
CURRENT MONTH						YEAR-TO-DATE			
ACTUAL AMOUNT	BUDGET AMOUNT	BUDGET VARIANCE	PCT VAR			ACTUAL AMOUNT	BUDGET AMOUNT	BUDGET VARIANCE	PCT VAR
					INCOME SALES INCOME:				
1,931,600	1,500,000	431,600	22.3		SALES	2,624,650	1,500,000	1,124,650	42.8
-26,860	-22,500	-4,360	16.2		SALES RETURNS & ALL	-34,630	-22,500	-12,130	35.0
					TOTAL--				
1,904,740	1,477,500	427,240	22.4		SALES INCOME	2,590,020	1,477,500	1,112,520	42.9
					OTHER INCOME:				
315,968	300,000	15,968	5.0		INTEREST INCOME	345,994	300,000	45,994	13.2
0	0	0	0.0		DIVIDEND INCOME	0	0	0	0.0
0	0	0	0.0		CURRENCY GAIN/LOSS	1,367	0	1,367	100.0
36,360	30,000	6,360	17.4		MISC INCOME	48,680	30,000	18,680	38.3
					TOTAL--				
352,328	330,000	22,328	6.3		OTHER INCOME	396,041	330,000	66,041	16.6
					TOTAL--				
2,257,068	1,807,500	449,568	19.9		INCOME	2,986,061	1,807,500	1,178,561	39.4
					EXPENSE: COST OF GOODS SOLD:				
-29,052	0	-29,052	100.0		CHANGE IN INVENTORY	-83,081	0	-83,081	100.0
544,160	300,000	244,160	44.8		PURCHASES	974,980	300,000	674,980	69.2
0	0	0	0.0		PURCHASES-I/C	0	0	0	0.0
12,592	15,000	-2,408	-19.1		PURCH RETURNS & ALL	8,126	15,000	-6,874	-84.5
0	0	0	0.0		PURCH RET-I/C	0	0	0	0.0
22,360	15,000	7,360	32.9		FREIGHT	35,780	15,000	20,780	58.0
					TOTAL--				
550,060	330,000	220,060	40.0		COST OF GOODS SOLD	935,805	330,000	605,805	64.7
					OPERATING EXPENSES:				
99,760	75,000	24,760	24.8		DEPR - MACH	146,130	75,000	71,130	48.6
110,000	80,000	30,000	27.2		DEPR - BLDGS	140,000	80,000	60,000	42.8
39,908	37,500	2,408	6.0		INSURANCE	44,474	37,500	6,974	15.6
24,496	15,000	9,496	38.7		MISC OPERATING EXP	42,138	15,000	27,138	64.4
					TOTAL--				
274,164	207,500	66,664	24.3		OPERATING EXPENSES	372,742	207,500	165,242	44.3
					GENRAL EXPENSES:				
789,980	685,500	104,480	13.2		RENT EXPENSE	942,530	685,500	257,030	27.2
581,556	557,000	24,556	4.2		ADMIN SALARIES	614,443	557,000	57,443	9.3
274,736	274,000	736	0.2		OFFICE SUPPLIES	272,178	274,000	-1,822	-0.6
106,000	101,000	5,000	4.7		INCOME TAXES	111,000	101,000	10,000	9.0
23,316	22,500	816	3.5		STATE & LOCAL TAXES	27,968	22,500	5,468	19.5
22,500	22,500	0	0.0		BAD DEBT EXPENSE	22,500	22,500	0	0.0
295,908	284,500	11,408	3.8		INTEREST EXPENSE	309,474	284,500	24,974	8.0
20,960	13,600	7,360	35.1		DEPR - OFF EQUIP	34,480	13,600	20,880	60.5
11,400	10,000	1,400	12.2		DATA PROC EXPENSE	12,800	10,000	2,800	21.8
106,720	92,000	14,720	13.7		MKTG EXPENSE	133,160	92,000	41,160	30.9
477,172	475,500	1,672	0.3		MISC EXPENSE	480,416	475,500	4,916	1.0
-3,666,400	-265,000	-3,401,400	92.7		SUSPENSE	-3,655,260	-265,000	-3,390,260	92.7
					TOTAL--				
-956,152	2,273,100	-3,229,252	337.7		GENERAL EXPENSES	-694,311	2,273,100	-2,967,411	427.3
					TOTAL--				
-131,928	2,810,600	-2,942,528	2230.4		EXPENSE	614,236	2,810,600	-2,196,364	-357.5

firm. In fact, it represents perhaps the most fully developed application within a firm of classification and coding techniques. Thus, this is an apt point at which to pause and consider these subjects. We will discover their overall importance to the AIS and illustrate their roles through typical charts of accounts.

Benefits

Classification and coding are related but different concepts. **Classification** is the act of grouping into classes or categories. Within the AIS transaction, data

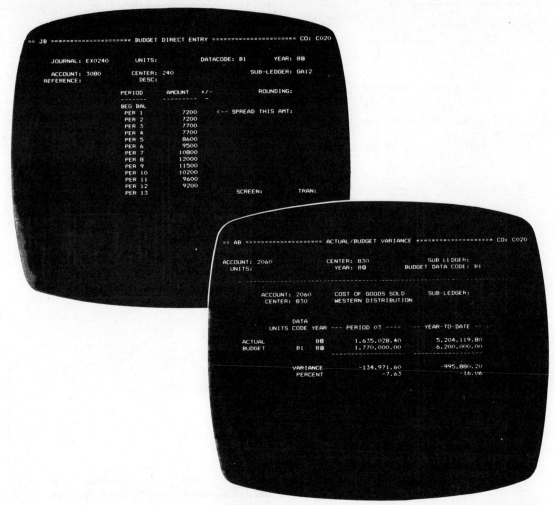

FIGURE 7-16 Screen displays containing budget and actual general ledger data for responsibility centers. Copyright © 1987 by Data Design Associates.

may be grouped in various ways. Sales data may be classified according to the products sold, the dates the products were sold, and the salespersons making the sales. **Coding** is the assigning of symbols in accordance with a classification plan. For instance, the code CS might be assigned to identify a credit sales transaction, and the code 1234 to identify the product being sold.

Classification plans relating to the AIS enable data to be suitably organized so that information derived from the data is meaningful to users. Consider the example involving sales. Because sales data are classified into several categories, a variety of sales reports may be prepared. These reports can aid the sales manager in analyzing the results of the sales activity. For instance, he or she might compare the sales for each product against the sales of that product for last week to see if the sales have improved.

Codes enable data within an AIS to be used more efficiently and effectively. Consider the code 2-8761, which represents the customer whose name is Smith Supply House. Because this code is more concise than the name it represents, the code can be recorded and posted more quickly. It also occupies less space in computer storage. Because the code is unique, it cannot be confused with another code (as the Smith Supply House might be confused with another customer of the same name). Finally, the code can incorporate meaning. In our example the first digit specifies the type of customer (here, the 2 means a retail firm).

Basic Coding Schemes

Codes can assume a variety of forms. Familiar examples are bar codes (found on merchandise items), color codes (found on copies of multicopy forms), and ciphers (used in confidential messages). However, the most useful codes to business firms are based on alphabetic, numeric, and alphanumeric characters. Four schemes that use these characters are mnemonic, sequence, block, and group codes.

Mnemonic Codes Mnemonic codes provide visible clues concerning the objects they represent. For instance, AZ is a code for Arizona, and WSW-G7814 represents a white sidewall tire of a specific size. Thus, a mnemonic code is easy to remember.

Sequence Codes The simplest of the coding schemes, the **sequence code,** consists of assigning numbers in consecutive order. In business applications, sequence codes are used mainly to identify source documents. For instance, if the last prepared sales invoice is numbered 102, the next sales invoice will be assigned the number 103. Sequence codes aid employees in searching for particular documents. Also, they help account for all items in a document file, since gaps in the sequence signal missing documents.

Block Codes Sequence codes have disadvantages, however. New items must be assigned the next number in the sequence. Also, the codes have no inherent significance. Consequently, other coding schemes are needed for certain applications.

Block codes reserve blocks of numbers within a sequence for objects (i.e., entities or events) having common features. A particular code within a block therefore has limited meaning to the user of the code. Within a business setting, block codes are often applied to

1. Customers, who are blocked by region or territory.

2. Employees, who are blocked by department.

3. Products, which are blocked by product line.

4. Accounts, which are blocked by major type.

Although each block is reserved for an array of individual codes, it is not necessary to assign every possible number within the block. In fact, one advantage of a block code is that unassigned numbers are usually available to be assigned to new objects (e.g., products) as they are added to the firm's scope of activity.

Group Codes A **group code** refines a block code by providing precise and extensive meaning within the code structure. In effect, a group code contains two or more subcodes, each of which reveals a facet pertaining to the object being coded. Each subcode is assigned a specific location, called a field, within the code format.

Raw materials stored for use by a metal products manufacturer may be assigned a group code having the format

$$ABBCCC$$

where A is the field for the type of material, BB is the field for the storage bin location, and CCC is the field for the size of material. A particular item of raw material could be coded 573201 (or 5-73-201 for ease of reading), where 5 specifies a steel rod, 73 specifies the seventh row in the warehouse and third shelf from the bottom, and 201 specifies 20 ft. by 1 sq. in.

Group codes are extremely versatile. They may be a combination of block and sequence codes. They may be expressed as hierarchical structures, ranging from broad to increasingly detailed classifications. Group codes also facilitate the preparation of a variety of analyses and reports.

Applications to Charts of Accounts

A chart of accounts is built around the major financial categories of assets, equities, revenues, and expenses. Usually the accounts in these categories are block coded.

Account Code	Account Categories
100–199	Current assets
200–299	Noncurrent assets
300–399	Liabilities
400–499	Owners' equity
500–599	Revenues
600–699	Cost of sales
700–799	Operating expenses
800–899	Nonoperating expenses

Individual accounts are next established within each block. The particular accounts, and the degree of detail they represent, are based on various sets of needs. These needs in turn derive from the financial statements and reports required by users both inside and outside the subject firm.

Coding of the individual accounts must conform to the coded block. Thus, a noncurrent asset account code will fall between 200 and 299. If additional meaning is to be provided, the individual account code may be a group code of the hierarchical type. The first digit would represent the major category (e.g., noncurrent assets), the second digit would represent an intermediate classification within the major category (e.g., fixed assets), and the last digit would represent the minor classification (e.g., the type of fixed assets). For example, the account code 212 may refer to the type of fixed assets known as machinery.

Additional facets can be linked to the general ledger account codes. Possibly useful additions are codes for subsidiary ledgers, organizational units, locations, and products. A group code format encompassing two of these facets might appear as

$$AAA\text{-}BBBB\text{-}CC$$

where AAA is the general ledger account number, BBBB is the subsidiary ledger account number, and CC is the responsibility center number. A sales transaction coded according to this format could involve a debit to combined account 121-5634-00 and a credit to combined account 820-1738-08. The 121 and 820 refer to the general ledger accounts entitled Accounts Receivable and Sales. The 5634 refers to the customer account against which the credit sale is charged, and the 1738 refers to the salesperson whose account is credited in the commissions payable ledger. The 08 refers to the sales region (responsibility center) where the sale is made. Finally, the 00 indicates that the Accounts Receivable account is general in nature and thus is not related to a particular responsibility center.

Design of a Sound Code

A sound code exhibits the following attributes.

1. It uniquely identifies an object.

2. It is as concise and simple as possible. Therefore, if a combination group code is desirable, its subcodes should be divided by hyphens or periods to aid the users.

3. It allows for expected growth so that it will not need to be changed in the foreseeable future. Thus, a growing firm with nine product lines should allow two digits (assuming a numeric code) for the product line code.

4. It is standardized throughout all functions and levels within the firm so that reporting systems can be well integrated.

DIFFERENCES AMONG VARIOUS TYPES OF ORGANIZATIONS

Organizations as well as data may be classified. Separately identifiable types of organizations include

1. Business firms, such as wholesalers and retailers, that merchandise products.

2. Business firms, ranging from professional firms and custodial service firms to universities and hospitals, that market services.

3. Business firms, ranging from automobile manufacturers to electric utilities, that manufacture and distribute products.

4. Not-for-profit organizations, ranging from government agencies to churches.

Each type of organization displays distinctive accounts in its general ledger system as well as unique features in its operating procedures. The wholesalers and retailers focus on merchandise inventory and the activities related thereto. The service firms, in contrast, de-emphasize inventories and focus on the performance and pricing of services. Manufacturers must look to raw materials and work-in-process inventories as well as to finished goods. They also must distinguish between direct labor and indirect labor used in production, and decide how to allocate overhead costs to the manufactured products. Not-for-profit organizations focus much more on costs than revenues; in fact, they may receive allocations of funds rather than revenues. In addition, these varied types of organizations must devote attention to their types of ownership, which may range from stockholders to individual proprietors.

Although examples in this chapter have centered on merchandising firms, examples will be drawn from manufacturing and the other types of firms in later chapters.

SUMMARY

General ledger systems are involved in collecting transaction data, classifying and coding transaction data, processing transaction inflows, storing transaction data, maintaining accounting controls, and generating financial reports. The general ledger system is also called the general ledger and financial reporting cycle, which is at the center of such transaction-oriented cycles as the revenue cycle, the expenditure cycle, and the resource management cycle.

The general ledger system receives inputs from the various transaction processing systems (cycles), from nonroutine transactions, from adjusting transactions, and from reversing transactions. The inputs are normally on general ledger journal vouchers, which in the case of computer-based systems may be transferred to batch entry forms or to data entry screens. The entered data, in journal entry form, are then posted to the general ledger to update the accounts during the accounting period. At the end of each accounting period, standard and nonrecurring adjusting journal entries are posted. The exact methods of processing vary, depending on whether the processing is performed by manual or computer-based systems. The data base includes such files as the general ledger master file, general ledger history file, responsibility center master file, budget master file, financial reports format file, current journal voucher file, and journal voucher history file.

A variety of general and transaction controls are needed to offset a number of risks to which the general ledger is exposed. These controls include adequate documentation, organization segregation, data security, carefully designed and prepared journal vouchers, and periodic trial balances.

Financial reports typically generated by the general ledger system include analyses of general ledger accounts, financial statements, and such managerial reports as sales analyses and responsibility reports. Many of the managerial reports involve comparisons between budget amounts and actual amounts.

The chart of accounts is a coded listing of all the classified accounts of a firm. Sound classification and coding techniques can make a chart of accounts more meaningful to users. Often it embodies such coding schemes as block coding and group coding, and its general ledger account codes are linked to codes relating to organizational units and subsidiary ledger accounts. Charts of accounts vary among different types of organizations, such as merchandising firms, manufacturing firms, and not-for-profit organizations.

REFERENCES

General Ledger Financial Control System. Sunnyvale, Calif.: Data Design Associates, 1984.

A Guide for Studying and Evaluating Internal Accounting Controls. Chicago: Arthur Andersen & Co., 1978.

Guidelines to Assess Computerized General Ledger and Financial Reporting Systems for Use in CPA Firms. New York: American Institute of Certified Public Accountants, Inc., 1979.

Hicks, James O. and Leininger, Wayne E. *Accounting Information Systems,* 2d ed. St. Paul, Minn.: West Publishing Co., 1986.

Wilkinson, Joseph W. *Accounting and Information Systems,* 2d ed. New York: Wiley, 1986.

QUESTIONS

1. What is the meaning of each of the following terms?

Transaction processing system
Revenue cycle
Expenditure cycle
Resource management cycle
General ledger and financial reporting cycle
Journal voucher
Standard adjusting journal entry
Nonrecurring adjusting journal entry
General ledger master file
Budget master file
Financial reports format file
General ledger analysis
Chart of accounts
Classification
Coding
Mnemonic code
Sequence code
Block code
Group code

2. What are the typical functions of a general ledger system?

3. Identify four transaction-oriented business activity cycles in a merchandising firm.

4. What are several sources of inputs to the general ledger system?

5. How are the forms of input likely to differ between manual and computer-based general ledger systems?

6. Describe the processing of transactions in an online computer-based general ledger system.

7. How are processing steps likely to differ in a computer-based general ledger system between (a) transaction data entered during an accounting period and (b) transaction data entered at the end of an accounting period?

8. What is the sorting key when the general ledger is to be updated sequentially?

9. Identify the various types of files that might be found in a general ledger data base.

10. What are the risks to which the general ledger maintenance activity is exposed?

11. What general controls are needed to counteract the risks to which the general ledger is exposed?

12. What transaction (application) controls are needed to counteract the risks to which general ledger processing is exposed?

13. How may the financial reports generated by the general ledger system be classified?

14. What are the benefits of classification plans? Of coding schemes?

15. Contrast the three basic schemes of coding by the use of numbers.

16. Describe the applications of block and group codes to charts of accounts.

17. What additional facets may logically be linked to general ledger account codes?

18. What are the attributes of a sound code?

19. Identify several types of organizations.

20. Contrast the general ledger accounts needed by a merchandising firm with those needed by a manufacturing firm.

21. What are the advantages of having a general ledger that is continuously online?

22. Describe the differences in general ledger accounts needed by a not-for-profit organization and a merchandising firm.

REVIEW PROBLEM

Campus Bookstore, Seventh Installment

Statement

The Campus Bookstore (described in the review problem at the end of Chapter 1) has just received documentation, prepared by consultants, for its newly designed computer-based transaction processing systems. The accounting system manager begins his review of the documentation with the general ledger system. As stated in the review problem to Chapter 6, this documentation ranges from source documents to system flowcharts and reports. One item of particular importance to the general ledger system—a coded chart of accounts—is incomplete, since the accounting system manager is most knowledgeable concerning needed accounts.

To aid in completing the chart of accounts, the accounting system manager scribbles these notes of relevant facts about the bookstore: The major product lines are textbooks, other books, and sundry items. Payments are generally made to the over 200 suppliers within 10 days, in order to receive 2 percent discounts. Utilities (heat, water, electricity, telephone) are paid within 30 days. All managers and employees are paid on the first and fifteenth of each month, with deductions made for federal and state income taxes, social security tax, federal and state unemployment taxes, the pension plan, medical insurance, and various miscellaneous items. Paychecks are written on a special bank account after funds are transferred from the regular checking account. Each of the four cash registers is provided with a change fund. Payments for returns of sale items are made from a cash register. The accounting period is one month, and financial reports are prepared at each month-end. (Other notes are omitted, since they appeared in earlier review problem statements.)

Required

a. Present the chart of accounts that the accounting systems manager is likely to prepare. Include a suitable code.

b. Develop an account code format for the accounts payable subsidiary ledger.

c. Provide illustrative journal entries for a routine transaction, a nonroutine transaction, a standard (recurring) adjusting transaction, and a nonrecurring adjusting transaction that would be posted to the general ledger.

d. Briefly describe the entry and processing of the transactions, including the affected online file(s).

e. Identify several controls that are to be maintained over data entry and processing relative to the general ledger.

f. Design the format of a report that shows gross profits on sales, broken down according to product lines.

g. Briefly describe how the chart of accounts would need to be expanded to enable the preparation of responsibility reports for the upper and lower levels of the bookstore.

Solution

a. The chart of accounts that follows is based on the following assumptions.

(1) Sales and gross margins are to be computed for the three product lines. However, no responsibility reports for the upper and lower levels of the bookstore are presently required.

(2) The periodic method of recording purchases and inventory is employed. If the perpetual method were assumed to be employed, the Purchases and Purchase Returns and Allowances accounts would not be included. (In reality, the perpetual method is likely to be used in a computer-based system, with the purchases and returns data being maintained apart from the chart of accounts.)

(3) The net method is employed with respect

to purchase discounts, and hence a Purchase Discounts Lost account is shown. If the gross method is assumed to be employed, Purchase Discount accounts for the three product lines would be needed.

(4) The coding scheme employs three-digit blocks for the major areas (e.g., assets). Within these blocks the middle digit has meaning, and thus the individual accounts can be viewed as being group coded. For instance, within the asset block (in which the first digit is a 1), a middle digit of 0 means a cash account.

Assets (100–199)

101 Cash on Hand
102 Cash in Bank—General
103 Cash in Bank—Payroll
104 Change Fund
110 Inventory—Textbooks
111 Inventory—Other Books
112 Inventory—Sundries
113 Supplies
120 Prepaid Expenses
130 Leasehold Improvements
131 Allowance for Amortization—Leasehold Improvements
132 Furniture and Fixtures
133 Allowance for Depreciation—Furniture and Fixtures
134 Noncomputerized Office Equipment
135 Allowance for Depreciation—Noncomputerized Office Equipment
136 Computer Hardware and Software
137 Allowance for Depreciation—Computer Hardware and Software
138 Motorized Vehicles
139 Allowance for Depreciation—Motorized Vehicles
140 Other Assets

Liabilities and Capital (200–299)

201 Notes Payable—Bank
210 Accounts Payable
220 Sales Taxes Payable
221 Employee Income Taxes Payable
222 FICA Taxes Payable
223 Federal Unemployment Taxes Payable
224 State Unemployment Taxes Payable
225 Pension Expense Payable
226 Medical Insurance Withholdings Payable
227 Other Withholdings Payable
230 Salaries and Wages Payable
240 Lease Payable
250 Accrued Expenses Payable
260 Accrued Interest Payable
270 Tom Long, Capital
271 Tom Long, Drawing

Revenues (300–399)

310 Sales—Textbooks
311 Sales—Other Books
312 Sales—Sundries
320 Sales Returns and Allowances—Textbooks
321 Sales Returns and Allowances—Other Books
322 Sales Returns and Allowances—Sundries

Cost of Sales (400–499)

410 Cost of Sales—Textbooks
411 Cost of Sales—Other Books
412 Cost of Sales—Sundries
420 Purchases—Textbooks
421 Purchases—Other Books
422 Purchases—Sundries
430 Purchase Returns and Allowances—Textbooks
431 Purchase Returns and Allowances—Other Books
432 Purchase Returns and Allowances—Sundries
440 Freight In—Textbooks
441 Freight In—Other Books
442 Freight In—Sundries

Expenses (500–599)

500 Expenses—Control
510 Salaries and Wages—Clerical and Sales
511 Salaries—Professional
512 Salaries—Managerial
513 Employee Welfare Expense
520 Advertising
530 Rent Expense
540 Heating Expense
541 Water Expense
542 Electricity Expense
543 Telephone Expense
550 Repairs and Maintenance Expense

551 Janitorial Supplies
552 Office Supplies
553 Insurance Expense
554 Legal and Accounting Expense
555 Donations
556 Tax Expense
560 Amortization of Leasehold Improvements
561 Depreciation of Furniture and Fixtures
562 Depreciation of Noncomputerized Office Equipment
563 Depreciation of Computer Hardware and Software
564 Depreciation of Motorized Vehicles
570 Interest Expense
580 Purchase Discounts Lost
590 Miscellaneous Expenses

b. An account code format for the accounts payable subsidiary ledger would also be an identification code for suppliers. Since the bookstore has over 200 suppliers, a sequential numeric code must contain at least three digits in order to be a unique identifier. However, a meaningful code may need more digits. Among the facets that could be incorporated into a supplier code are (1) the year in which the first purchase from the supplier was made, and (2) the product line(s) provided by the supplier. Using these two facets, plus a sequential code, the format might be ABCCC, where A is the last digit of the year of first purchase, B represents the product line(s) provided, and CCC is the next sequential number assigned. An example code would be 74165, where 7 refers to 1987, and 4 stands for the provision of textbooks and other books.

c. Illustrative journal entries are as follows.

(1) Routine transaction:

Sales Returns and Allowances	XXX	
Cash		XXX

To record returns and allowances on cash sales for (date).

(2) Nonroutine transaction:

Cash	XXX	
Notes Payable—Bank		XXX

To record the receipt of cash in exchange for a _____-day, _____ percent note payable to the _____ Bank.

(3) Standard (recurring) adjusting transaction:

Amortization of Leasehold Improvements	XXX	
Allowance for Amortization—Leasehold Improvements		XXX

To record amortization of leasehold improvements for one month at _____ percent.

(4) Nonrecurring adjusting transaction:

Miscellaneous Expenses	XXX	
Inventory—Sundries		XXX

To record the write-down of inventory damaged by floodwaters and not covered by insurance.

d. These types of transactions are entered and processed in various ways, since the bookstore employs both batch and online transaction processing systems. In the case of routine transactions processed by batch processing systems, such as daily cash disbursements, the daily summary journal entries are entered individually via video display terminals, edited, and then posted to the general ledger accounts by a general ledger update program. The same approach is followed with respect to nonroutine transactions. In the case of routine transactions processed by online processing systems, such as daily cash sales, the summary journal entries are posted automatically by online programs. (See the solution to the review problem in Chapter 3 for a more detailed discussion.) In the case of standard recurring adjusting transactions, the related journal entries are stored on a magnetic disk and posted by means of a special end-of-period program. Finally, the nonrecurring adjusting transactions are processed in the same manner as nonroutine transactions.

The principal file is the general ledger master file, which is maintained as an online file. However, the bookstore also stores all of the transactions affecting the general ledger on a journal voucher file, maintained on magnetic disk, with each entry having a number assigned in sequence as the transaction is posted. At the present time the bookstore does not maintain other related files, such as a budget master file.

e. The general ledger controls for the bookstore are expected to include those described in this chapter that pertain to computer-based systems.

f. The format of the specified report is as follows.

Campus Bookstore Gross Profits on Sales by Product Lines For the Month Ended _____			
	Textbooks	Other Books	Sundries
Sales	$........	$........	$........
Less: Sales Returns and Allowances	....	....	....
Net Sales	$........	$........	$........
Cost of Sales: Beginning Inventory	$........	$........	$........
Purchases, Net	....	....	....
Goods Available	$........	$........	$........
Less: Ending Inventory	....	....	....
Cost of Sales	$........	$........	$........
Gross Profit on Sales	$........	$........	$........

g. Both the upper and lower levels of the bookstore represent responsibility centers, since they are headed by individual managers. Responsibility reports for these managers should show the revenues and expenses that are directly assignable to their centers. The revenues can be easily assigned on the basis of the chart of accounts that has been designed in a. The manager of the upper level is responsible for the revenues from the sundries line, while the manager of the lower level is responsible for the revenues from all book sales. Expenses, however, cannot be collected and assigned by use of the chart of accounts alone. For instance, all salaries and wages for sales and clerical personnel are charged to a single account. In order to assign expenses directly to each center, it is necessary to expand the chart of accounts. A simple means of expansion is to add a digit for the responsibility cen-

ter (e.g., 1 for the upper level) when coding an expense. (Not all expenses should be so coded, however. When preparing responsibility reports no joint expenses, such as the salary paid to Tom Long, should be allocated to individual centers.)

PROBLEMS

7-1. Describe transaction-oriented cycle(s) that are unique or special for each of the following types of organizations.

a. Manufacturing firm.

b. Bank.

c. Hospital.

d. University.

e. Municipality.

f. Electric utility.

g. Insurance company.

h. Architectural firm.

i. Brokerage firm.

7-2. Merchandise Unlimited, Inc., records on numbered journal vouchers those daily and end-of-period transactions that affect the general ledger. Each journal voucher is entered by Joan Campbell and approved by Martin Turner. Selected general ledger account codes are as follows: Cash in Bank, 101; Accounts Receivable, 120; Prepaid Rent, 163; Capital Stock, 280; Rent Expense, 547.

Required

Draw journal voucher forms and enter the data to show how each of the following selected transactions would appear after being recorded by Joan Campbell. (Assigned journal voucher numbers appear in parentheses.)

a. Payments received from credit customers on October 12 and deposited in the bank total $12,435.20   (569).

b. Additional capital stock issued and sold at par value for $10,000 on October 27   (598). (The full amount in cash is received the same day from several large acquirers.)

c. One month's prepaid rent of $2400 expired on October 31 (617).

7-3. Your firm employs an online general ledger system. When you sign on to the system, the following menu appears on the video display screen. Draw the appearance of the screen after you press the number 1, and then enter this transaction on August 15, 1989: A dividend of $5.00 per share is declared on the capital stock, payable on September 15 to stockholders of record on August 31. (Outstanding shares of capital stock total 10,000; account codes for Dividends Payable and Retained Earnings are 2780 and 2900, respectively.)

GENERAL LEDGER MAIN MENU

1. INPUT OF JOURNAL ENTRY

2. CORRECTION OF PREVIOUS JOURNAL ENTRY

3. CHANGE OF PERMANENT DATA IN ACCOUNT RECORD

4. INQUIRY INTO ACCOUNT RECORD

5. MONTH-END STANDARD ADJUSTING JOURNAL ENTRIES

6. MONTH-END CLOSING ENTRIES

7. FINANCIAL STATEMENT PREPARATION

8. GENERAL LEDGER LISTING PROOF REPORTS

9. MANAGERIAL REPORTS MENU

ENTER DESIRED NUMBER >

7-4. The Deckman Company is a wholesale distributor of beers and wines. It sells on credit to retail establishments such as grocery chains. Merchandise is obtained by credit purchases from bottlers and wineries. Other transactions involve cash receipts and disbursements, payroll, inventories, and fixed assets. Some of the transactions, such as those involving cash and payroll, are processed in batches. Other transactions are processed by the online approach. All master files are maintained on magnetic disks. The firm has several video display terminals for entering data and obtaining output displays.

Required

Describe a suitable system for entering and processing the various types of journal entries that affect the general ledger. Identify in your description all files that would be useful in storing data relating to journal entries and the general ledger.

7-5. Refer to the Review Problem. Design a record layout for the general ledger to be used by the Campus Bookstore. Include assumed data for the Cash in Bank—General and the Accounts Payable accounts, and enter onto copies of the record layout. Also, design the record layout for the journal voucher transaction file to be stored on magnetic tape. *Note:* Use Figure 7-9 as a guide in preparing the record layout, but make at least one significant modification.

7-6. Design a five-digit group code for fixed assets. The code should be of the hierarchical type and based on the ledger accounts codes. Thus, the first digit should designate the broad category of assets, with the remaining digits specifying increasingly narrow categories. Illustrate your code format by coding drill presses owned by a firm, assuming that the firm employs three types of drill presses.

7-7. Refer to the Review Problem on page 208. A transaction code has been selected with the following format: AAA-B-CCCCC, where AAA is the general ledger account to be debited or credited, B is the responsibility center (1 means upper level, 2 means lower level), and CCCCC is the subsidiary ledger account number. For the purposes of this problem, assume that the only subsidiary ledger is accounts payable, and that only suppliers of merchandise are maintained in the ledger. Assign codes to both the debit and credit portions of the following transactions, using the above format and the chart of accounts provided in the solution to the Review Problem. When a part of the coding format is not applicable, assign zeros in place of significant digits.

a. A valid and correct invoice is received from supplier number 52179 relating to the purchase of 10 dozen university-inscribed sweatshirts.

b. A check is prepared and mailed to supplier number 64231 relating to the purchase of 200 textbooks for an accounting course.

c. A valid and correct bill is received from the bookstore's accountants for general auditing services, and a check is duly prepared and mailed.

d. A valid and correct bill is received from the electric utility, and a check is duly prepared and mailed. Separate meters are employed to measure usage on each level so that amounts can be fairly allocated.

7-8. Joel Mutt and Anne Jeffers are combining their individual public accounting practices into a two-person partnership. One of the first requirements is to establish a new chart of accounts. Their firm will provide audit, tax, and management consulting services. Each service area is to be headed by a separate manager, who is responsible for the profits of the area. In addition, the firm will have an office manager, who will have responsibilities for secretarial services, the internal AIS, insurance, payroll, and so on.

The assets to be owned by the firm include furniture and fixtures, office equipment, microcomputers, short-term investments, receivables from clients, supplies, office building, and land. Liabilities include notes payable to the bank, accounts payable, the various payroll withholdings, and other customary accruals. The major expense is for salaries to the professional accountants and other staff, as well as bonuses to managers and partners. However, travel and entertainment expenses are significant, as are telephone and other utilities expenses, taxes, and insurance. Other expenses typical of a service enterprise are also incurred.

Required

Design a coded chart of accounts that will facilitate the preparation of a monthly balance sheet and income statement. Add a set of organizational codes that will enable the preparation of responsibility reports for the three major service areas and the office management activity. The responsibility reports will be profit-oriented for the service areas and cost-oriented for the office

management activity. Expenses that are jointly incurred for the benefit of all areas are not to be included in the responsibility reports.

7-9. Refer to the Review Problem. Assume that each of the following error situations are independent.

a. The credit portion of a nonroutine transaction is inadvertently omitted when the transaction is entered for processing.

b. The debit amount of a nonroutine transaction contains an inadvertent transposition upon entry of the transaction.

c. A nonroutine transaction is entered twice inadvertently.

d. The cashier forgot to enter the accrual of the interest on the note payable last month.

e. A nonexistent number of an accounts payable account is entered during the posting of cash disbursements, and hence the accounts payable ledger is out of balance with the general ledger account.

f. A nonexistent number of a general ledger account is entered during the entry of a nonroutine transaction, and hence the debits do not equal the credits in the general ledger.

g. A nonrecurring adjusting entry is prepared and entered by the cashier to conceal the theft of cash.

Required

Describe one or more transaction controls that should have prevented or detected each of these error situations during the period that the Campus Bookstore used a manual accounting system.

7-10. Refer to Problem 7-9. Describe one or more transaction controls that should prevent or detect each of the error situations when the Campus Bookstore uses its new computer-based accounting system.

7-11. The Brassila Corporation performs all its transaction processing on computers by the batch approach. Its sales, purchases/payables, cash receipts and disbursements, payroll, and fixed assets transactions are gathered into batches, batch totaled, and then transcribed onto magnetic tapes from the source documents. Then, as the individual transactions are processed daily or weekly to update the subsidiary ledgers, the summary data (i.e., total amounts affecting the various general ledger accounts) are transferred or extracted onto account distribution tapes. These account distribution tapes are merged daily with each other and with a daily tape containing entries for all nonroutine transactions originally recorded that day on journal vouchers. The resulting tape is sorted according to general ledger account numbers and then processed to update the accounts in the general ledger. Batch totals of the account distribution tapes are not computed.

At the end of each month a tape containing all adjusting journal entries is processed to update the general ledger, just after the last day's tapes are processed. Then the firm performs computer processing runs that (1) close all temporary accounts and produce a magnetic tape containing all financial statement data pertaining to actual and budget values for the month, and (2) print balance sheets and income statements that compare actual and budget values. The subsidiary ledgers, general ledger, and budget are maintained as separate files on magnetic disks throughout the month.

Required

Prepare a system flowchart that reflects the daily and monthly processing of the general ledger.

7-12. Refer to the review problem. Design a monthly report that shows the profits for the upper and lower levels of the Campus Bookstore. The following are joint expenses that cannot be reasonably allocated to separate outfit centers: salaries of managers, advertising, heating, water, repairs and maintenance, janitorial supplies, insurance, legal and accounting expenses, donations, taxes, interest, amortization of leasehold improvements, depreciation of motorized vehicles, purchase discounts lost, and miscellaneous.

7-13. The budget and actual values pertaining to the January 1989 income statement for Hargreaves, Ltd., are as follows.[1]

---

[1] This problem can be solved by using a microcomputer-based spreadsheet software package.

	Budget	Actual
Sales	$10,000	$9,000
Cost of Goods Sold	6,500	5,600
Gross Profit on Sales	$ 3,500	$3,400
Selling Expenses	$ 500	$ 450
Administrative Expenses	1,400	950
Total Expenses	$ 1,900	$1,400
Net Income before Taxes	$ 1,600	$2,000
Estimated Income Taxes	240	300
Net Income	$ 1,360	$1,700

Required

Prepare a report for management in good form that reveals the performance of the firm during January.

7-14. The Mountainair Public Service Company of Fort Collins, Colorado, serves approximately 195,000 gas and electric customers throughout a portion of the state. The firm's operations and maintenance activities are divided into five districts, each headed by a manager. Within each district are from 7 to 20 offices, each headed by a supervisor.

As a public utility, Mountainair employs the uniform chart of accounts prescribed by the Federal Power Commission. Thus, codes in the 100s pertain to assets, in the 200s to liabilities, in the 400s to revenues, in the 500s and 600s to operating expenses associated with electricity, in the 700s and 800s to operating expenses associated with gas, and in the 900s to selling and administrative expenses.

However, the controller of Mountainair feels that the coding system might usefully be expanded. For instance, she would like a coding system that would enable the preparation of the following reports.

Balance sheet.
Income statement, by types of revenues.
Responsibility report for each supervisor, showing the types of expenses charged to his or her office, broken down by those that are controllable by the supervisor and those that are noncontrollable overhead.
Responsibility report for each district manager,

showing the totals of expenses incurred by each supervisor within his or her district. Operating statement showing expenses by district and by office.

Required

a. Design and illustrate a coding system that will enable the preparation of these reports while retaining the coding prescribed by the Federal Power Commission.

b. Design a customer code that will be useful to the firm in analyzing sales. Note that some customers are residential, others are commercial, and still others fall into special categories such as public street lighting and school lighting; some use gas only, some use electricity only, and some use both.

7-15. Pitman Auto Sales and Service has just been established as a sole proprietorship in Blacksburg, Virginia. It plans to sell three lines of cars: Econs, Meds, and Quals. In addition to new-car sales, it has set up service, parts, and used-car sales departments, with a manager in charge of each department. The firm owns its buildings, land, furnishings, and service equipment. Some of the expenses that it expects to incur are salaries for salespersons and mechanics and for the office force (including managers), utilities, advertising, supplies, taxes, gas and oil, insurance, telephone, and various administrative items. Since it will not handle financing of sales contracts, its receivables will be due from financing agencies. Its inventories of cars and parts, as well as its suppliers, will likely be rather numerous.

Required

Design a coded chart of accounts, together with a group coding format that extends the chart of accounts to include subsidiary ledgers and organizational units. In addition to providing control over inventories and suppliers' accounts, the group code should enable the following reports to be prepared.

a. A balance sheet and income statement for the firm.

b. A report that reflects gross profits on sales related to each line of new cars, used cars, parts, and service.

c. An expense report that shows total expenses, plus a breakdown of the direct expenses chargeable to each department.

7-16. Ollie Mace has recently been appointed controller of a family-owned manufacturing enterprise. The firm, S. Dilley & Co., was founded by Mr. Dilley about 20 years ago and is 78 percent owned by Mr. Dilley. Located in Indianapolis, Indiana, it has served the major automotive companies as a parts supplier. The firm's major operating divisions are heat treating, extruding, small-parts stamping, and specialized machining. Last year, sales from the several divisions ranged from $150,000 to over $3,000,000. The divisions are physically and managerially independent, except for Mr. Dilley's constant surveillance. The accounting system for each division has evolved according to the division's own needs and to the abilities of individual accountants or bookkeepers. Mr. Mace is the first controller in the firm's history to have responsibility for overall financial management. Mr. Dilley expects to retire within six years and has hired Mr. Mace to improve the firm's financial system.

A new chart of accounts, as it appears to Mr. Mace, is essential to getting started on other critical financial problems. The present account codes used by divisions are not standard. They also do not reflect organizational responsibility or product groups.

Mr. Mace sees a need to divide asset accounts into five major categories: current assets, plant and equipment, and so on. Within each of these categories, he sees a need for no more than 10 control accounts. Based on his observations to date, 100 subsidiary accounts are more than adequate for each control account.

Each division now handles five or less product groups, such as the radiator group. The maximum number of cost centers Mr. Mace foresees within any product group is six, including operating and nonoperating groups. He views general divisional costs as a nonrevenue-producing product group. Altogether, Mr. Mace estimates that about 44 natural expense accounts, such as for tools and advertising, plus about 12 cost of sales accounts (including variance accounts) would be adequate.

Mr. Mace is planning to implement the new chart of accounts in an environment that at present includes manual records systems and one division using a computer-based system. Mr. Mace expects that in the near future most accounting and reporting for all units will be automated. Therefore, the chart of accounts should facilitate the processing of transactions manually or by computer. Efforts should be made, he believes, to restrict the length of the code for economy in processing and convenience in use. (To achieve this condensation, the same code fields should be used to contain data pertaining to assets, expenses, equities, and revenues. Thus, each coded transaction should incorporate a separate code field which specifies the type of account.)

Required

a. Design the structure of a chart of accounts coding system that will meet Mr. Mace's requirements. Your answer should begin with a layout of the code format. You should explain the type of code you have chosen and the reason for the size of your code fields. Explain your code as it would apply to asset and expense accounts.

b. Use your chart of accounts coding system to illustrate the code needed for the following data.

(1) In the small-parts stamping division, $100 was spent on cleaning supplies by supervisor Bill Shaw in the polishing department of the door-lever group. Code the expense item using the code you have developed.

(2) A new motorized sweeper has been purchased for the maintenance department of the extruding division for $3450. Code this asset item using the code you have developed.

(CMA adapted)

7-17. Selected Small Firm (A Continuing Case) For the small firm that you selected in Chapter 1 (see Problem 1-7), complete the following requirements.

a. Prepare a detailed chart of accounts.

b. Describe the journal voucher, processing steps, files, and reports and analyses provided by the general ledger system.

c. List all transaction controls currently being employed in the general ledger system.

d. Note any observed weaknesses in transaction controls for the general ledger system.

8

The Revenue

Cycle

THIS CHAPTER'S OBJECTIVES ARE
TO ENABLE YOU TO DO THE FOLLOWING
WITH RESPECT TO THE REVENUE CYCLE:

Describe its purposes, functions, and relationships to the pertinent organizational units.

Identify its data sources and forms of input.

Identify the files composing its data base.

Describe the steps and approaches employed in processing its transaction data flows.

List needed accounting transaction controls.

Describe a variety of operational and managerial reports and other outputs that may be generated.

INTRODUCTION

Most organizations depend on revenues for their continued existence. Certain of these revenue-oriented organizations generate revenues through the sales of products, others generate revenues through the provision of services, and still others generate revenues through both product sales and services. The functions related to the generation of revenues compose the revenue cycle. As noted in the previous chapter, the **revenue cycle** is one of the principal transaction-oriented cycles that interfaces with and provides key inputs to the general ledger and financial reporting system.

OVERVIEW OF THE REVENUE CYCLE

Purposes

The revenue cycle's major purpose is to facilitate the exchange of products or services with customers for cash. Typical objectives within this broad purpose are to (1) verify that the customers are worthy of credit, (2) ship the products or perform the services by agreed-on dates, (3) bill for products or services in a timely and accurate manner, (4) record and classify cash receipts promptly and accurately, (5) post sales and cash receipts to proper customers' accounts in the accounts receivable ledger, (6) safeguard products and cash until shipped or deposited, and (7) prepare all needed documents and managerial reports related to the product sales or services.

Functions

In the case of product sales, the functions of the revenue cycle generally include obtaining the order from the customer, checking the customer's credit, entering and processing the sales order, assembling the goods for shipment, shipping the goods, billing the customer, receiving and depositing the cash payment, maintaining the receivables record, posting transactions to the general ledger, and preparing the needed financial reports and other outputs. In the case of services, the functions of assembling and shipping goods are replaced by the function of performing the ordered services. In the case of cash sales, the function of maintaining the receivables records is unnecessary. These groups of functions are pictured in Figure 8-1. Each function pertaining to a credit sale of a product is explained in the following discussion.

Obtain Order from Customer Orders from customers may be obtained in various ways. A customer may mail or wire a purchase order. Alternatively, the customer might phone in an order or might enter the merchandising firm's store and buy one or more items from a salesperson. Or, the salesperson (an employee or an independent broker) may travel to the customer's premises and obtain the order directly. Regardless of the means of receiving the order, it is customarily expressed in writing on some form (e.g., the customer's purchase order or the salesperson's order blank). The final step in obtaining an order is to determine that it is valid. For instance, a sales order clerk may verify that the customer is a reputable firm.

Check Credit When the order pertains to a sale on credit, more checking is necessary. Most credit sales, including credit card sales for more than $50, are

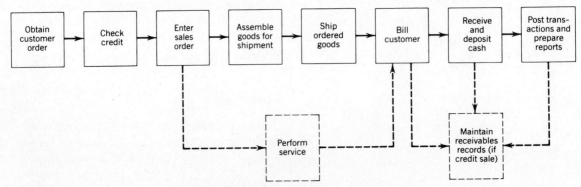

FIGURE 8-1 Typical functions of a revenue cycle.

subject to credit checks. If an order is received from a repeat credit customer, the firm will normally have credit information concerning the customer in its data base. The information will be summarized in the form of a credit rating (e.g., excellent, good, poor) or a credit limit (e.g., a cumulative $5000 of automatic credit). If an order is from a new customer, or if the customer applies for a credit card, the firm may refer to a credit bureau to ascertain the applicant's credit worthiness. Criteria of credit worthiness include the prospective customer's financial status, previous payment record, and future earnings prospects. In the case of a customer (new or old) who has a special situation, the credit manager will typically be expected to make a judgment.

Enter Sales Order Orders that have been approved for credit are next entered into the sales processing procedure. Entry of a sales order usually consists first of preparing a formal sales entry document (unless the salesperson's form is to be used instead). This formal sales entry document may be prepared manually or may be prepared automatically in the case of a computer-based system.

Three types of document preparation procedures may be employed: prebilling, incomplete prebilling, and separate order and billing. In the **prebilling procedure** the sales invoice (bill) is completely filled in, including prices and extensions and total, as soon as the order is approved. This procedure reduces the paperwork but is only feasible if all data are known, including the availability of ordered quantities. In the **incomplete prebilling procedure,** a sales order invoice is prepared at the time the order is approved. This document shows quantities but not price extensions, freight charges, and so on. After the order has been shipped, the sales order–invoice is completed and becomes the sales invoice. In the **separate sales order and invoice procedure,** the invoice is prepared as a separate document only after the goods have been shipped. The sales order is used only as a shipping order. Although this procedure involves more paperwork, it is necessary when ordered goods are often out of stock or frequent back ordering occurs. Regardless of the procedure used, a copy is generally sent to the customer to acknowledge the order and to confirm the shipping date. Other copies are used to initiate processing steps and to store data concerning the transaction.

Assemble Goods for Shipment Goods that are ordered must physically be moved to the shipping dock. Often this function involves picking the goods from a warehouse, using a picking ticket or a copy of the sales order, and moving the goods to the shipping dock. In the cases of expensive goods or special made-to-order goods, it may consist of acquiring the goods from suppliers or of producing the goods within the firm's manufacturing facilities. Also, any step affecting the firm's inventory of goods for sale must be noted in appropriate records.

Ship Ordered Goods Unless the customer is to pick up the ordered goods at the shipping dock, the goods must be physically distributed to the customer. Before being distributed, the goods are generally packaged with a packing slip enclosed. The goods are then shipped by means of the firm's own delivery vehicles, by parcel service, by the U.S. Postal Service, or by an independent common carrier. In the last case, the carrier is selected (often in accordance with the customer's instructions), the packages are weighed and labeled, the charges are established, and the shipping documents are prepared. The shipping documents must include a bill of lading and often involve a shipping report or order. The freight charges are paid to the carrier either by the selling firm or customer, depending on the f.o.b. designation.

Bill Customer The preparation of the invoice has already been discussed under the entry of the order. Billing is not complete, however, until the bill is presented for payment. The terms stated on the invoice specify the due date of the payment; often the terms allow a cash discount for payment by an earlier date. An alternative type of billing occurs when a retail merchandising firm accepts credit cards serviced by an independent financing firm. In that case the retail firm forwards the merchant's copy of the sales slip to the financing firm and immediately receives cash in return. The financing firm then bills the customer via a monthly statement.

At this point most of the functions involving the sale itself have been completed. The data flow diagram in Figure 8-2 portrays these sales-related functions, as well as the interfacing functions of posting the transaction to the subsidiary and general ledgers.

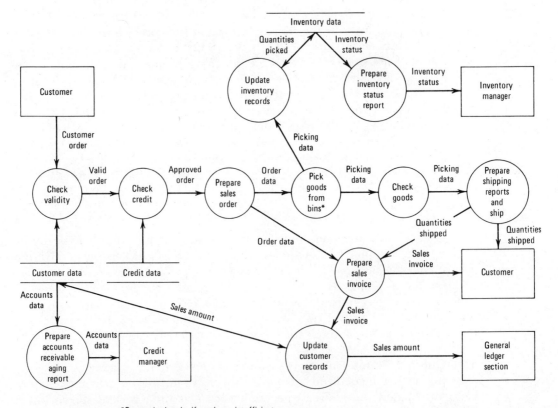

*Prepare back order if goods are insufficient
to fill order.

FIGURE 8-2 A data flow diagram of the functions related to credit sales transactions.

Receive and Deposit Cash Payment Cash remitted by customers may be received through the mail or over the counter. Each cash payment is recorded immediately upon receipt. Preferably all remitted amounts are listed on a deposit slip during the same day and delivered intact to the firm's bank. An alternative means of receiving cash is through a lockbox collection system. Under this type of system, customers mail cash remittances to a post office box; the bank opens the box daily, deposits the remittances to the creditor firm's account, and prepares a detailed listing for the firm.

Maintain Accounts Receivable A separate accounts receivable record is maintained for each active credit customer. Each billed sale amount is debited to the account, and each cash remittance is credited to the account. An outstanding balance appears in the account as long as all sales have not been paid in full. Either of two methods may be employed in adjusting the balance to reflect payments made by customers. The **balance forward method** applies a payment against the outstanding balance, rather than against a specific invoice. The **open invoice method** matches each payment with a specific invoice. The monthly statement, usually mailed to customers, merges all invoice amounts of previous months and simply shows a "balance forward" in the case of the former method; it continues to show all invoices as "open" in the case of the latter method. Thus, disputed invoices are more easily isolated under the open invoice method, whereas the balance forward method enables the processing to be simplified.

Post Transactions to the General Ledger Summarized sales and cash receipts transactions are posted to the general ledger. This function represents the interface between the revenue cycle and the general ledger system or cycle, which was discussed in Chapter 7.

Prepare Needed Financial Reports and Other Outputs A variety of outputs are generated as by-products of the revenue cycle functions. One example already mentioned is the monthly statement for customers. Summaries of sales and cash receipts, akin to journal listings, are also needed. Financial reports ranging from the accounts receivable aging schedule to sales analyses are typically viewed as necessary. If an online computer-based system is employed, displays of individual accounts and other specific information are also available.

Other Related Functions Additional functions of interest involve salespersons' commissions, product costing, sales returns and allowances, collection procedures, miscellaneous cash receipts, and back orders. Salespersons' commissions are noted in Chapter 10 in the sections involving payrolls; product costing is discussed with production procedures in the same chapter. The remaining functions are briefly scanned in the following discussion, and their relationships (except for back orders) to the revenue cycle are shown in Figure 8-3.

Sales returns arise when unsatisfied customers send back all or part of the ordered goods. Sales allowances are adjustments in prices granted to customers as compensation for damaged goods, shortages, or similar deficiencies. In either case credit memoranda are prepared to formalize the agreements reached. The credit memoranda are then signed by an authorized person, such as the credit

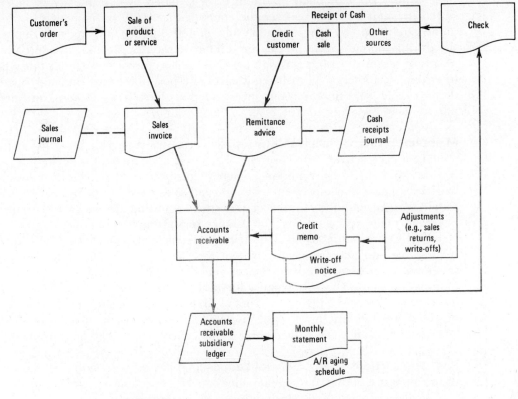

FIGURE 8-3 Relationships within the revenue cycle.

manager, on the basis of supporting documents. One copy of each credit memorandum is mailed to the customer, another copy is used to post the amount of the return or allowance as a credit to the customer's accounts receivable record, and a third copy is filed. Periodically a journal voucher is prepared to summarize accumulated sales and allowances; it is then posted to the general ledger.

Most customers pay their outstanding balances, or make installment payments, upon receiving statements. Collection procedures are unfortunately necessary, however, in the case of slow-paying customers. Generally these procedures begin with second notices of balances due. Then delinquency notices are likely to be sent. If payments are still not received, the firm may hire a collection agency, factor the receivables with a financing agency, or eventually write off the balance. The last action involves the preparation of a write-off notice.

Miscellaneous cash receipts include amounts received from sales of fixed assets, income from investments, and bank loans. These receipts are generally recorded in the cash receipts journal or other daily cash summary. They are further discussed in Chapter 10.

Back orders are necessary when insufficient quantities of inventory are on hand to fill all orders. Back ordering involves the preparation of a back-order form, which shows the customer for whom the order was placed, the order number, the quantity needed, and the data requested. This form is sent to the selected supplier, and the data are posted to inventory records. When the back-ordered items arrive, they are immediately shipped to the customer, and the notation is removed from the inventory records. A new sales invoice is also prepared for the back-ordered items and mailed to the customer.

Relationships to the Organization

The revenue cycle functions are typically achieved under the direction of the marketing/distribution and finance/accounting organizational functions (units) of the firm, as Figure 8-4 illustrates. Thus, the revenue cycle involves the interaction of the marketing information system and the accounting information system. Moreover, the results attained and information generated by the revenue cycle further the objectives of the marketing/distribution and finance/accounting functions.

Marketing/Distribution Marketing management has the objectives of (1) satisfying the needs of customers, and (2) generating sufficient revenue to cover costs and expenses, replace assets, and provide an adequate return on investment.

As Figure 8-4 shows, the top marketing manager is a vice president in many firms, with responsibilities relating to market research, product development and planning, sales, promotion and advertising, customer service, and shipping and transportation. Market research focuses on the markets for the firm's products or services. It studies the customers and potential customers, including their attitudes, preferences, and spending power. Product (or service) development and planning focuses on the product lines (or services), including styling, packaging, and performance. It also plans for the introduction of new products (or services). Sales concentrates on the selling effort, usually through a sales force. It is interested in sales forecasts, current sales performance (including profitability), and expenses incurred in selling activities. It also enters sales orders for processing. The promotion and advertising unit deals with such activities as dealer incentive programs, trade shows, and advertising campaigns. Customer service handles customer servicing needs after the sale of the product (or the performance of the service). It may deal with complaints, user training, and maintenance.

The shipping and transportation unit is the distribution arm of the marketing function. In some firms it may be under the direct sales organization, in other firms it may constitute a separate organizational function, and in service-oriented firms it is nonexistent. Its major concern is to assure that ordered goods are delivered to customers promptly, in good condition, and in accordance with customer specifications.

Finance/Accounting The objectives of financial and accounting management relate broadly to funds, data, information, planning, and control over resources. With respect to the revenue cycle, the objectives are limited to cash planning and control, data pertaining to sales and customers' accounts, inventory control, and information pertaining to cash and sales and customers. For instance, with respect to cash planning and control, the objectives are to maintain an optimal level of cash (not too low nor too high) and to safeguard cash from loss or theft.

The top financial manager in many firms is the vice president of finance. Two managers often report directly to this top manager: a treasurer and a controller.

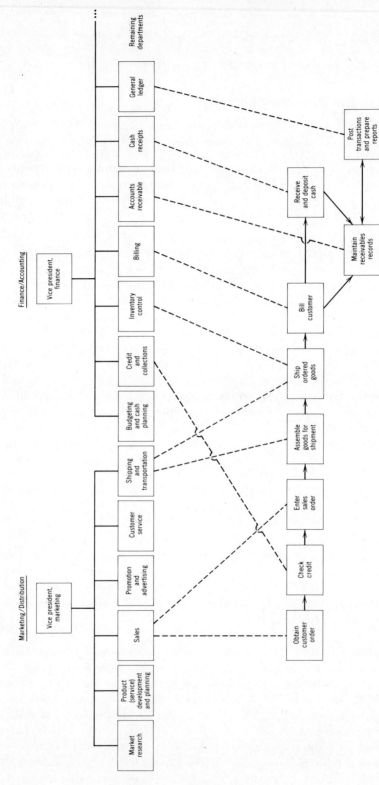

FIGURE 8-4 Relationships of organizational units to revenue cycle functions.

The treasurer has such responsibilities in the finance area as budgeting and cash planning, credit and collections, and cash receipts. The controller has such responsibilities in the accounting area as billing, inventory control, accounts receivable, and general ledger. (Both the treasurer and controller have other responsibilities that are irrelevant to the revenue cycle.) The budgeting and cash planning unit develops short-range and long-range budgets and cash forecasts. The credit and collections unit develops credit and collection policies and administers the policies with respect to individual customers. Cash receipts, an arm of the cashier, deposits cash received and maintains the related records. Billing prepares the sales invoices. Inventory control maintains the records pertaining to inventory balances. Accounts receivable maintains the accounts of individual customers. General ledger, of course, maintains the ledger of all balance sheet and income statement accounts, from which the financial reports are prepared.

DATA SOURCES AND INPUTS

Sources

Data used in the revenue cycle are mainly based on inputs from customers. Customers initiate both the sales and cash receipts transactions. In the case of product sales, other sources include the salespersons, customer reference and credit records, inventory records, finished goods warehouse, suppliers (and/or the firm's production function), shipping department, and common carrier. In some cases a financing agency or bank may also be a source of data.

Forms of Input

Manual Systems The revenue cycle source documents typically found in firms that employ manual processing and make product sales include the

1. **Customer order.** Often the **customer order** is the customer's purchase order and thus not a document prepared by the selling firm. However, it may be a form prepared by the salesperson, as shown in Figure 8-5.

2. **Sales order.** Figure 8-6 presents a **sales order.** Although similar to the customer order in Figure 8-5, it has significant differences. First, it is a more formal, multicopy form. (Note the words *Salesman's Copy* at the top right.) Second, it is prenumbered for more effective control. Third, it contains price and extension columns so that it can be completed as an invoice. Finally, it has a space for the customer's purchase order number. Incidentally, the sales order is sometimes called the shipping order, since it provides authorization for the shipping action.

3. **Order acknowledgment.** Usually the **order acknowledgment** is a copy of the sales order, although it may be a separate form. (In some cases the customer also requires that the selling firm return a signed acknowledgment that has been prepared by the customer.)

PRODUCTS / PARTS

Sold To:*
No. ☐☐ – ☐☐☐☐

CUSTOMER ORDER

Ship To:*
No. ☐☐ – ☐☐☐☐

Order No:* └┴┴┴┴┘

Date:* └┴┴┴┴┴┘

Sold-To:
Name: └┴┴┴┴┴┴┴┴┴┴┴┴┴┴┴┴┴┘ / └┴┴┴┴┴┴┴┴┴┴┴┴┴┴┴┴┴┘

Address: └┴┴┴┴┴┴┴┴┴┴┴┴┴┴┴┴┴┴┘ / └┴┴┴┴┴┴┴┴┴┴┴┴┴┴┴┴┴┘ Zip: └┴┴┴┴┘

Ship-To:
Name: └┴┴┴┴┴┴┴┴┴┴┴┴┴┴┴┴┴┘ / └┴┴┴┴┴┴┴┴┴┴┴┴┴┴┴┴┴┘

Address: └┴┴┴┴┴┴┴┴┴┴┴┴┴┴┴┴┴┘ / └┴┴┴┴┴┴┴┴┴┴┴┴┴┴┴┴┴┘ Zip: └┴┴┴┴┘

Sman: (Products) └┴┴┘ Terms: └┴┴┴┴┴┴┘ B/O# └┴┴┴┘

Page Qn:* └┴┴┴┘ Ship From: (Products) └┴┘ Cust Date: └┴┴┴┴┘

PO# └┴┴┴┴┴┴┴┘ How to Ship:: Date:* └┴┴┴┴┘

: └┴┴┴┴┴┴┴┴┴┘ / └┴┴┴┴┴┴┴┴┴┴┴┴┴┘

Item #	Charge Description		Override		Special Instructions
	Quan.*	Model/Part No.*	Price	Disc	
1					
2					
3					
4					
5					
6					
7					
8					
9					
10					
11					
12					
13					
14					

Note: *Denotes Required Entries!

Special Price Approval _____

Order Taken By _____

Computer Form No. T-100

PC-3-76026

FIGURE 8-5 A customer order. Courtesy of Arvin Industries.

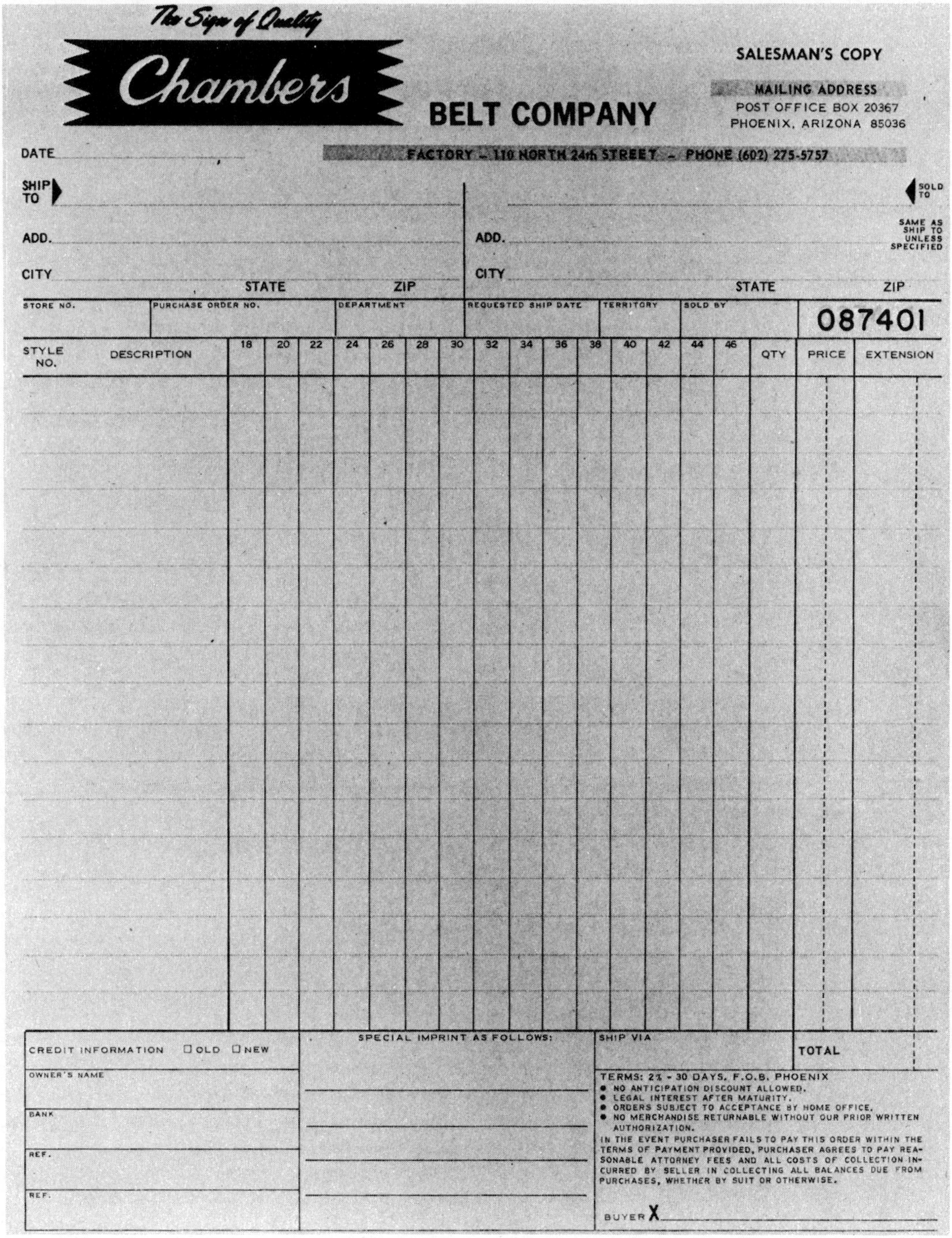

The Sign of Quality

Chambers

BELT COMPANY

SALESMAN'S COPY

MAILING ADDRESS
POST OFFICE BOX 20367
PHOENIX, ARIZONA 85036

FACTORY – 110 NORTH 24th STREET – PHONE (602) 275-5757

DATE_____

SHIP TO ▶_____   SOLD TO ◀

ADD._____   ADD._____

CITY_____ STATE_____ ZIP_____   CITY_____ STATE_____ ZIP_____

SAME AS SHIP TO UNLESS SPECIFIED

STORE NO.	PURCHASE ORDER NO.	DEPARTMENT	REQUESTED SHIP DATE	TERRITORY	SOLD BY	087401

STYLE NO.	DESCRIPTION	18	20	22	24	26	28	30	32	34	36	38	40	42	44	46	QTY	PRICE	EXTENSION

CREDIT INFORMATION ☐ OLD ☐ NEW

OWNER'S NAME_____

BANK_____

REF._____

REF._____

SPECIAL IMPRINT AS FOLLOWS:

SHIP VIA_____

TOTAL_____

TERMS: 2% – 30 DAYS, F.O.B. PHOENIX
• NO ANTICIPATION DISCOUNT ALLOWED.
• LEGAL INTEREST AFTER MATURITY.
• ORDERS SUBJECT TO ACCEPTANCE BY HOME OFFICE.
• NO MERCHANDISE RETURNABLE WITHOUT OUR PRIOR WRITTEN AUTHORIZATION.
IN THE EVENT PURCHASER FAILS TO PAY THIS ORDER WITHIN THE TERMS OF PAYMENT PROVIDED, PURCHASER AGREES TO PAY REASONABLE ATTORNEY FEES AND ALL COSTS OF COLLECTION INCURRED BY SELLER IN COLLECTING ALL BALANCES DUE FROM PURCHASES, WHETHER BY SUIT OR OTHERWISE.

BUYER X_____

FIGURE 8-6 A sales order.

4. **Picking list.** In some cases a copy of the sales order is sent to the warehouse for use in picking the ordered goods from the bins. Alternatively, a separate **picking list** document may be prepared. The ordered product data are arranged in such a list in accordance with the bin locations in the warehouse. Thus, the picking can be done more efficiently.

5. **Packing list or slip.** The **packing list** is enclosed with the goods when they are packaged. It is generally a copy of the sales order, or it may be the picking list.

6. **Bill of lading.** Figure 8-7 displays a straight **bill of lading,** which is relatively uniform from firm to firm. It is intended for the agents of the common carrier that is to transport the products, informing them that goods are legally on board the carrier, that the freight has been paid or billed, and that the consignee is authorized to receive the goods at the destination. In addition to the carrier, the shipping department and the customer receive copies. Another copy may serve as the freight bill (invoice) and may be forwarded to the traffic department (if any) of the customer or seller, depending on who is paying.

7. **Shipping notice (report, order).** Often a copy of the sales order, when duly noted by the shipping manager, serves as proof that the goods were shipped. However, a separate **shipping notice** may be prepared by the shipping department (perhaps as one copy within the bill of lading set). This notice is forwarded to the billing department for use in completing the invoice.

8. **Sales invoice.** The **sales invoice** serves as the key sales input to the accounting cycle, since it contains the total amount of the transaction. An example of a multiple-copy sales invoice appears in Figure 2-7 in Chapter 2.

9. **Remittance advice.** The **remittance advice** is a counterpart to the sales invoice, since it contains the amount of the cash receipt from the customer. An example of a cash remittance is shown in Figure 8-8. The example can be described as a turnaround document, since it represents a portion of the sales invoice that is returned by the customer with the cash. (If the customer does not return a cash remittance, the firm must prepare one for use as the posting medium.)

10. **Deposit slip.** Deposits of cash in the bank must be accompanied by **deposit slips.** Figure 8-9 shows a deposit slip that contains imprints of both the firm name and the bank name. Coding at the bottom of the slip refers to the account number and bank code.

11. **Back order.** The back-order form is prepared when insufficient quantities are in inventory to satisfy sales orders. It should be prenumbered and contain data concerning the customer for whom the **back order** is being placed, the original sales order number, the quantity needed, and the date requested. If the original order is partially filled and the remaining quantities are back ordered, the back-order number and relevant data should be

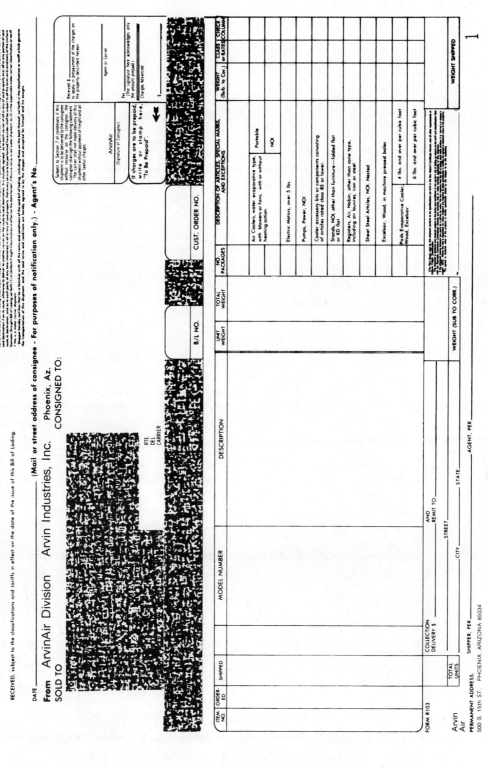

FIGURE 8-7 A bill of lading. Courtesy of Arvin Industries.

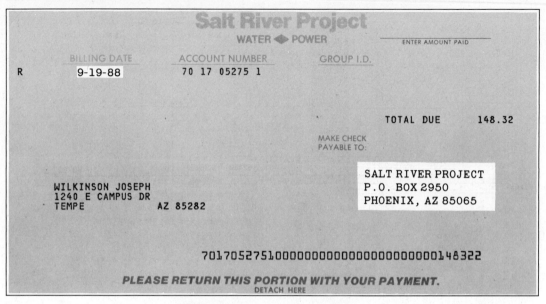

FIGURE 8-8 A remittance advice.

entered on the sales invoice. Figure 8-10 depicts a sales invoice showing that back-order number 3128 has been placed with the Universal Supply Company. This back-order data most likely has also been posted to the inventory records. When the back-ordered items are received from the supplier, they will be immediately shipped to the customer, and the notation will be removed from the inventory records. A new sales invoice will also be prepared for the back-ordered items and mailed to the customer.

12. **Credit memo.** Before shipped goods can be accepted back or before allowances can be granted, a **credit memo** must be prepared and approved. Figure 8-11 shows a credit memo containing the number 12542. A credit memo should only be approved on the basis of clear evidence, usually

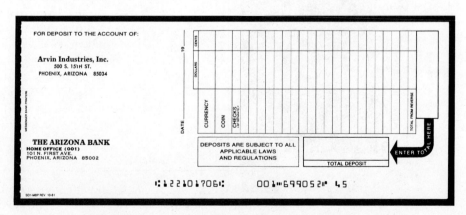

FIGURE 8-9 A deposit slip. Courtesy of Arvin Industries.

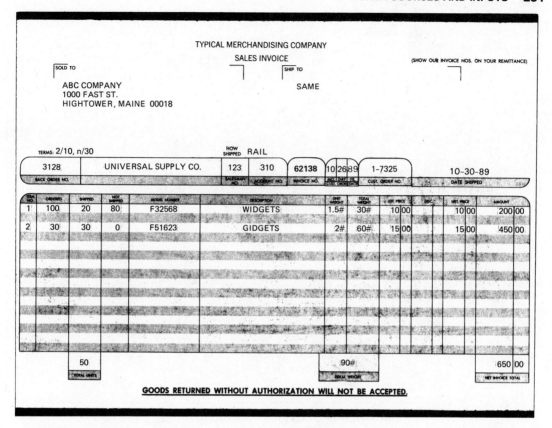

FIGURE 8-10 A sales invoice showing back-ordered items. Courtesy of Arvin Industries.

consisting of a complaint letter from the affected customer as well as a receiving report (or sales return notice) from the receiving department.

13. **Other documents.** A new customer *credit application* is useful when customers apply for credit. It should include all the data pertaining to the applicant's current financial condition and earning level. A *salesperson call report* may be used to describe each call upon a prospective customer and to indicate the result of the call. A *delinquent notice* may be sent to customers who are past due on their credit account balances. A *write-off notice or form* is a document prepared by the credit manager when an account is deemed to be uncollectible. As described in Chapter 7, a *journal voucher* is prepared as the basis for each posting to accounts in the general ledger. For instance, a journal voucher will be prepared to reflect one or more account write-offs. Finally, in the case of retail firms that make cash sales, receipted *sales tickets* or *cash register receipts* are used to reflect cash received.

Computer-based Systems All of the aforementioned hard copy documents may also be used in computer-based systems. In some cases, however, they may be generated automatically upon the entry of data via terminals or microcom-

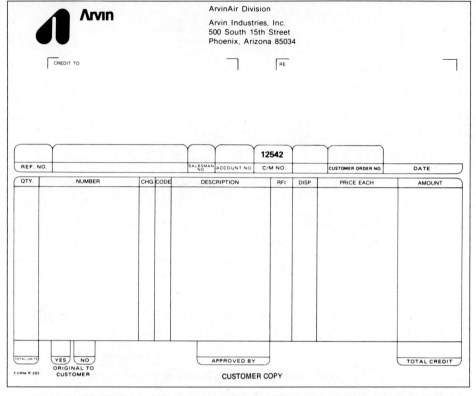

FIGURE 8-11 A credit memo. Courtesy of Arvin Industries.

puters. Also, some of the source documents may be designed to speed the entry of data into the computer system with fewer errors. The customer order in Figure 8-5 and the sales order in Figure 8-12 are examples of user-friendly forms.

Preformatted screens may be used to enter data concerning sales orders, sales returns, and cash receipts transactions. These screens, like simplified entry forms, may be designed to handle individual transactions or batches of transactions.

Figure 8-13 displays the online entry of a batch of cash receipts. Note that the blank columns will be filled in when command key number 1 is pressed. The data for these columns, which are stored in the open sales invoice and customer files, will be retrieved by the computer entry program. This program will also compute the total of all payment amounts entered and place the result in the box labeled "Entered Total"; in addition, when the batch has been fully entered, the program will automatically compare the entered total and previously computed control total and display the difference. (Although the screen and described procedure are simplified, they illustrate the essentials of an online cash receipts entry.)

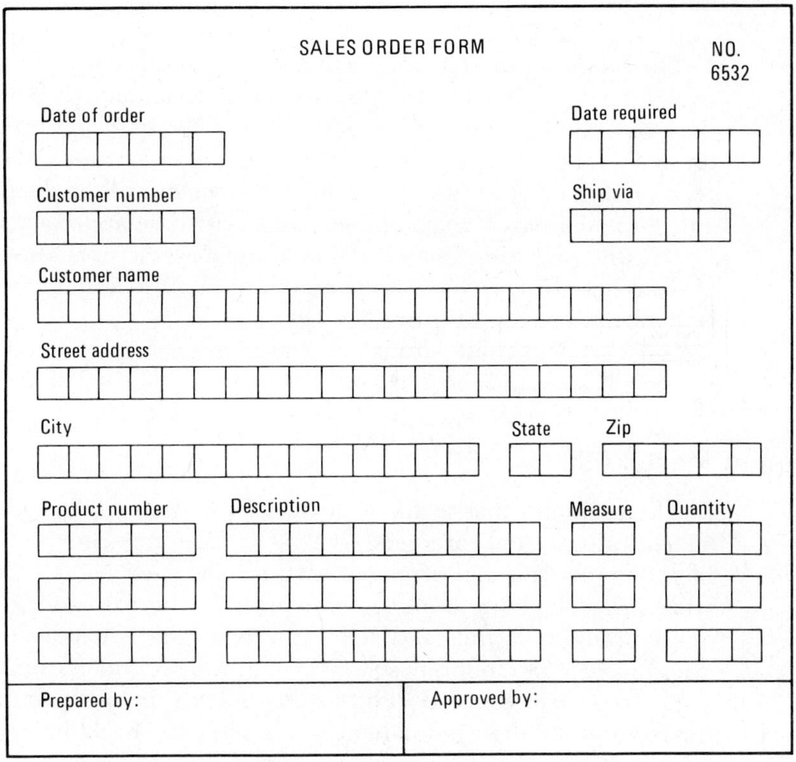

SALES ORDER FORM

NO.
6532

Date of order

Date required

Customer number

Ship via

Customer name

Street address

City

State

Zip

Product number

Description

Measure

Quantity

Prepared by:

Approved by:

FIGURE 8-12 A source document for manually recorded data.

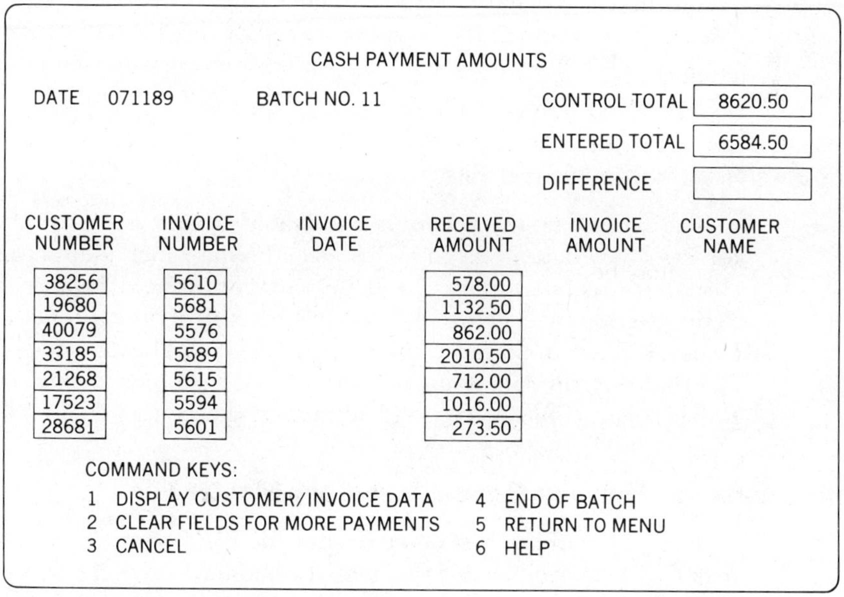

CASH PAYMENT AMOUNTS

DATE 071189

BATCH NO. 11

CONTROL TOTAL 8620.50

ENTERED TOTAL 6584.50

DIFFERENCE

CUSTOMER NUMBER	INVOICE NUMBER	INVOICE DATE	RECEIVED AMOUNT	INVOICE AMOUNT	CUSTOMER NAME
38256	5610		578.00		
19680	5681		1132.50		
40079	5576		862.00		
33185	5589		2010.50		
21268	5615		712.00		
17523	5594		1016.00		
28681	5601		273.50		

COMMAND KEYS:

1 DISPLAY CUSTOMER/INVOICE DATA
2 CLEAR FIELDS FOR MORE PAYMENTS
3 CANCEL
4 END OF BATCH
5 RETURN TO MENU
6 HELP

FIGURE 8-13 Online entry of cash receipts.

DATA BASE

The following master, transaction, history, and reference files are representative of the revenue cycle data base for a firm that makes product sales. Of course, the exact number and content of the files will vary from firm to firm, depending on such factors as types of customers and markets, variety of desired managerial reports, degree of computerization, and structure of the data base. For instance, a firm that employs the computer-based data base approach, discussed in Chapter 11, will use a different set of files and data structures. Also, some of the listed files, such as the merchandise inventory master file, will not be needed if the firm is involved solely in offering services.

Our survey of these files is necessarily brief. A more complete description of the data base would include a data dictionary such as that shown in Figure 6-10.

Customer Master File

The **customer master file** is needed only when credit sales are made. Generally, its primary and sorting key will be the customer number. Each record of this file contains data concerning the customer, such as the shipping and billing addresses, telephone number, past payment performance, credit rating, trade discount allowed, and sales activity. These data items are useful in preparing sales invoices and monthly statements, as well as in determining the credit limit.

An important concern with this file, as with the other master files, is keeping the records and their permanent data up to date. Each time a customer moves to a new address, for instance, the change must be quickly reflected in the record. Whenever a new customer is granted credit, another record must be added to the file. When a customer's credit account becomes inactive, for whatever reason, the record must be deleted. These changes can be made during the processing of sales orders, although they complicate the processing. Alternatively, they may be made at other times. An advantage of on-line computer-based files is the convenience they afford in making such changes at any time.

Accounts Receivable Master File

The records in the **accounts receivable master file** also relate to credit customers. Two data items are essential, the customer identification (usually the customer account number) and the current account balance. Remaining data items are optional. Figure 8-14 arrays several suggested data items in a record layout. If desired, however, the added items could be moved to the customer file. Alternatively, all data items pertaining to a customer, including all transactions for this year, could be consolidated into the accounts receivable file.

Merchandise (or Finished Goods) Inventory Master File

The merchandise **inventory master file** is relevant to the revenue cycle for a firm that sells products. If the firm also manufactures the products sold, the file includes the words *finished goods* rather than *merchandise*. Data items that might appear in a record layout include the product (inventory item) number, descrip-

Customer account number	Customer name	Credit limit	Balance, beginning of year	Year-to-date payments	Current account balance

Note: Although the lengths of fields and modes of data items are necessary for complete documentation, they have been omitted for the sake of simplicity.

FIGURE 8-14 A layout of an accounts receivable record.

tion, warehouse location code, unit of measure code, reorder point, reorder quantity, unit cost, quantity on order, date of last purchase, and quantity on hand. If inventory is maintained on the perpetual basis, the current balance will also be included. The primary and sorting key is usually the product or inventory item number.

Open Sales Order File

The open sales order file consists of copies of sales orders pertaining to sales that have not yet been shipped and billed. In both manual and computer-based systems the printed copies contain data items such as those shown in Figures 8-5 and 8-6. In computer-based systems a record of each order is also stored on magnetic media, with the primary and sorting key usually being the sales order number. The record layout should allow for such repeating line items as product number and quantity ordered. Customer names and product descriptions, however, may be omitted in the case of computer-based systems; these data will be drawn from the customer and merchandise inventory files when preparing the sales invoices.

Open Sales Invoice Transaction File

In a manual system the open sales invoice transaction file consists of a copy of each current sales invoice, such as the one shown in Figure 8-10. In a computer-based system a printed copy may or may not be filed. The record stored on magnetic media likely omits customer names and product data, since the data are available in other files. The primary (and sorting) key is usually the sales invoice number. Each record remains open until payment is received from the customer (or until the end of the period if the balance forward method is used). Records in this file provide the details of the sales transactions posted to the accounts receivable records; by being maintained in a separate file, they enable the size of the accounts receivable records to be reduced.

Cash Receipts Transaction File

In a manual system the cash receipts transaction file likely consists of a copy of each current remittance advice. In a computer-based system the record layout on magnetic media may contain the customer's account number, sales invoice number against which the payment is being applied, date of payment, and amount of payment. It also includes a code to identify the record as a cash receipt transaction, and it may be assigned a transaction number.

Other Transaction Files

In addition to the basic sales and cash receipts files, the revenue cycle data base will normally include a shipping report file, credit memo file, and back-order (or production order) file. Each of the records in these files would contain roughly the data shown in the documents discussed earlier.

Shipping and Price Data Reference File

The shipping and price data reference file (which may be split into two files) contains freight rates, common carrier routes and schedules, current prices of all products, trade discounts, and so on. (Another reference file often used in manual systems is a credit file, which is used to check and approve the credit of customers.)

Sales History File

The sales history file contains summary data from sales orders and invoices. In a computer-based system the records pertaining to sales orders and invoices are

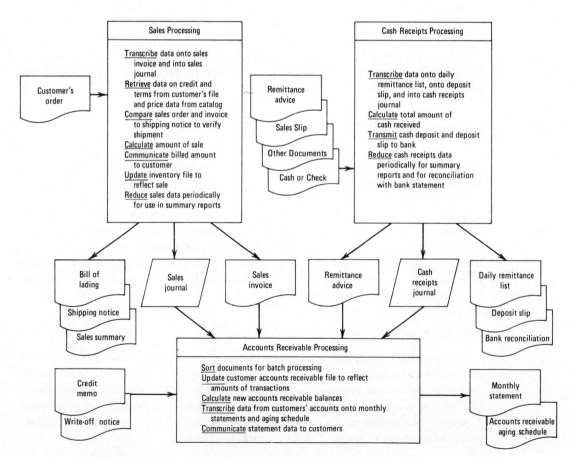

FIGURE 8-15 Processing steps and related documents for the revenue cycle.

transferred to this file when they are removed from the open files. These records are retained in the history file for a reasonable period. For instance, a firm may decide to maintain a history file for the past five years. Records older than five years would be purged from the file. (However, the firm that employs computer-based processing may retain printed copies of sales orders and invoices for a longer period.) Data from this file are used to prepare sales forecasts and analyses.

DATA FLOWS AND PROCESSING

Within the revenue cycle the data flows and processing steps can be divided into three major subsets: processing of sales transactions, processing of cash receipts transactions, and maintenance of the accounts receivable ledger. Figure 8-15 depicts these subsets of processing steps, together with related documents and reports. Each processing subset can be portrayed in more detail, showing specific transaction data and the processes that convert these data into outputs with the aid of a data base. Figure 8-16 portrays these detailed activities for sales

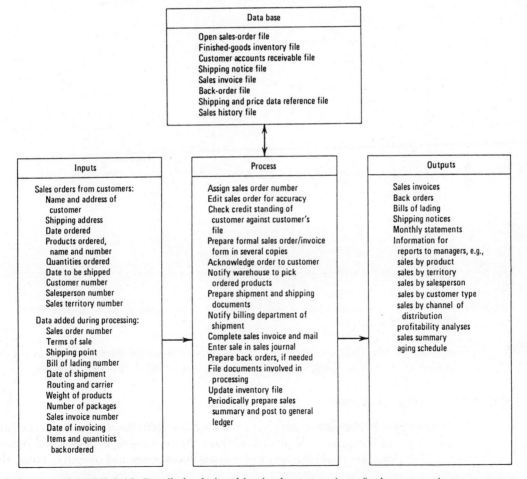

FIGURE 8-16 Detailed relationships in the processing of sales transactions.

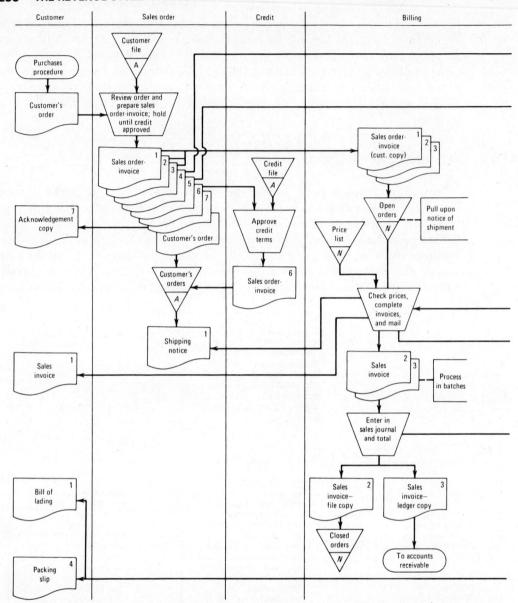

FIGURE 8-17 System flowchart of a manual credit sales transaction processing procedure, with an emphasis on document flows.

transaction data. These diagrams should provide useful springboards as we examine several flowcharts of processing systems in the following sections.

Manual Processing Systems

Credit Sales Procedure Figure 8-17 presents a system flowchart of a procedure involving the credit sales of products. Since the processing is performed manually, the emphasis is on the flows of source documents and outputs. Thus, the

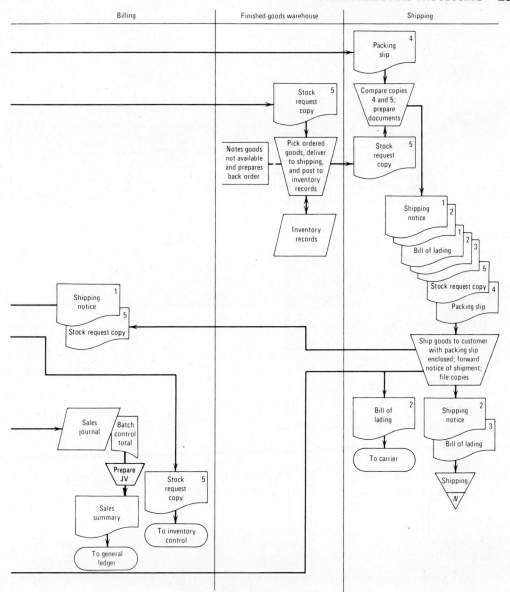

FIGURE 8-17 *(Continued)*.

flowchart provides a good introduction to processing within the revenue cycle. An understanding of these document flows will enable you to grasp more easily the processing steps performed by computer-based systems.

The credit sales procedure begins with the receipt of the customer's purchase order in the sales order department. After verifying that the order is valid and accurate, a clerk prepares the sales order–invoice by reference to the customer master file. A copy is sent to the credit department for credit check and approval. If approval is provided, the customer is sent an acknowledgment. Also, the order is entered for processing, with copies distributed to the billing department (to

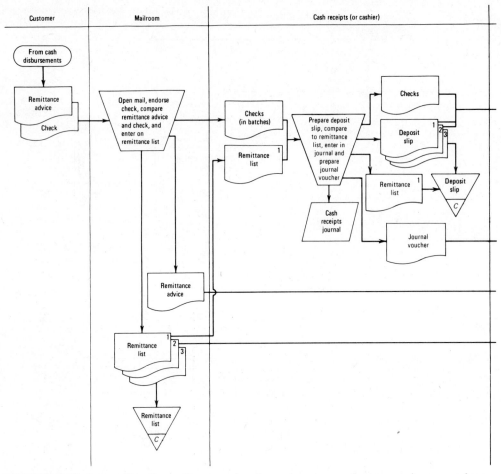

FIGURE 8-18 System flowchart of a manual cash receipts transaction processing procedure, with an emphasis on document flows.

await notice of shipment), to the warehouse (for picking), to the shipping department (as prior notification), and to the customer order file.

In the warehouse a picker is given the stock request copy (or a picking slip); he
or she assembles the ordered goods. Then the goods, together with the stock
request copy, are forwarded to the shipping department. There a shipping clerk
pulls the packing slip copy from the file, checks the goods against the copies, and
prepares the shipping-related documents. The goods are packed for shipment,
with the packing slip enclosed. The goods are shipped and the documents are
distributed as shown.

Upon notification of shipment, a billing clerk completes the sales order–
invoice set. Other clerks in the department enter the invoice amount in the
journal, accumulate sufficient invoices to form a batch, and compute batch totals.
A journal voucher is prepared for use in posting to the general ledger. Each sales
invoice is mailed to the appropriate customer, with copies distributed to the

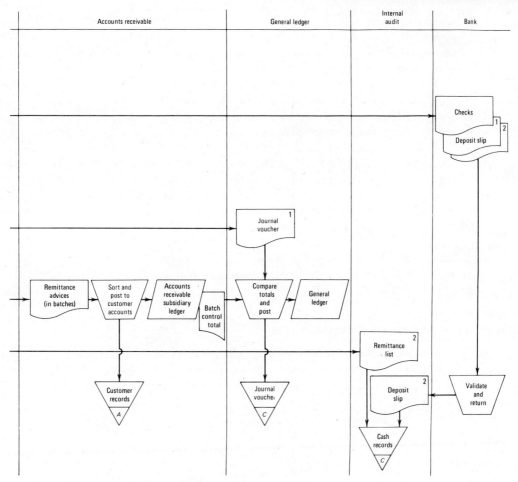

FIGURE 8-18 *(Continued).*

accounts receivable department and filed. Also, a copy of the sales invoice may be sent to the inventory control department, in order to reflect the reduction in the quantity of inventory (products) on hand.

Cash Receipts Procedure Figure 8-18 shows a flowchart of a procedure involving the receipts of cash related to credit sales. This particular procedure begins with receipts of mailed cash and remittance advices from customers. A mailroom clerk compares the checks with the remittance advices (and prepares advices when none are received). Then the clerk endorses the checks "For Deposit Only," enters their amounts on a remittance list, and computes a total of the batch received. One copy of the list is sent to the cashier with the checks, the second copy is sent to the internal audit department (if any) for later review, and the third copy is filed.

The cashier prepares a deposit slip in triplicate by listing all checks from customers (plus cash received from other sources that day). Then the cashier compares the total with that shown on the remittance list and delivers the deposit intact to the bank. A cash receipts clerk enters the total receipts in the cash receipts journal and prepares a journal voucher, which is sent to the general ledger department for posting.

The internal audit department receives a copy of each deposit slip, stamped and initialed by a bank teller and delivered direct by the bank. This deposit slip is compared to the remittance list, as well as to the deposit slip in the cashier's office and to the general ledger posting.

Accounts Receivable Procedure Figure 8-19 illustrates the procedure of posting sales and cash receipts transactions to the ledgers. (For greater clarity the figure appears as a simplified diagram rather than as a flowchart.) Sales invoices and remittance advices are the posting media. The posted amounts of sales and cash receipts are totaled, and then each total is compared with the journal voucher entry to which it corresponds. Any differences are located and corrected. When the posted batch total and the precomputed batch total (as shown on the journal voucher) are in agreement, the accounts in the general ledger are posted.

Computer-based Processing Systems

When computer-based systems are used, sales and cash receipts transactions may be processed by the batch method, by the online method, or by a combination of the batch and online methods. In the batch method the transaction data

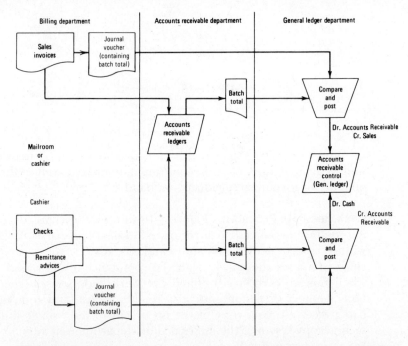

FIGURE 8-19 Diagram showing the processing of transactions affecting accounts receivable.

are keyed onto magnetic tape or disk, sorted according to customer account numbers, and posted sequentially to the accounts receivable master file. In the online method the transaction data are entered via a terminal and posted individually to the master file. In the combined method the transaction data are entered via a terminal; however, they are gathered into a batch before being processed, either sequentially or directly, to the master file. The combined method is popular since it aids data entry and editing while retaining batch total controls.

Credit Sales Procedure Figure 8-20 presents a system flowchart of the online/batch sales processing procedure. The flowchart logically divides into three segments: order entry (segment *a*), shipping (segment *b*), and billing (segment *c*).

Each customer's order when received is entered by means of a terminal in the sales order department. The edit program validates the accuracy of the data, performs the credit check, and verifies that adequate merchandise is on hand to fill the order. (If insufficient quantities of goods are available, the sales order

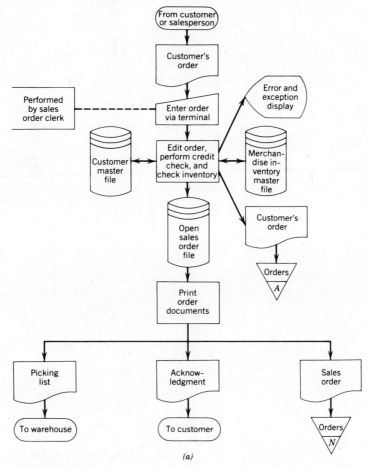

FIGURE 8-20 System flowchart of an online/batch computer-based credit sales transaction processing procedure.

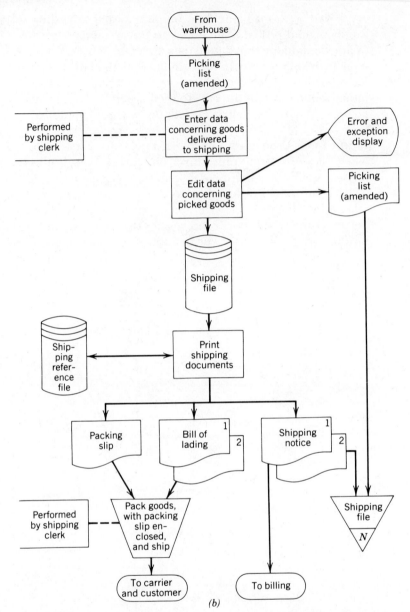

FIGURE 8-20 *(continued)* (*a*) Order entry procedure. (*b*) Shipping procedure. (*c*) Billing procedure.

clerk may specify to the computer system that a back order is to be prepared.) If
the order is accepted, it is placed in the open order file. When the order is ready
to be filled (which may be immediately), the order entry program prints the
acknowledgment to the customer, a picking list, and a backup file copy.

After the ordered goods have been picked in the warehouse, the picking list is
initialed by the picker and amended to show any changes (e.g., items out of stock,

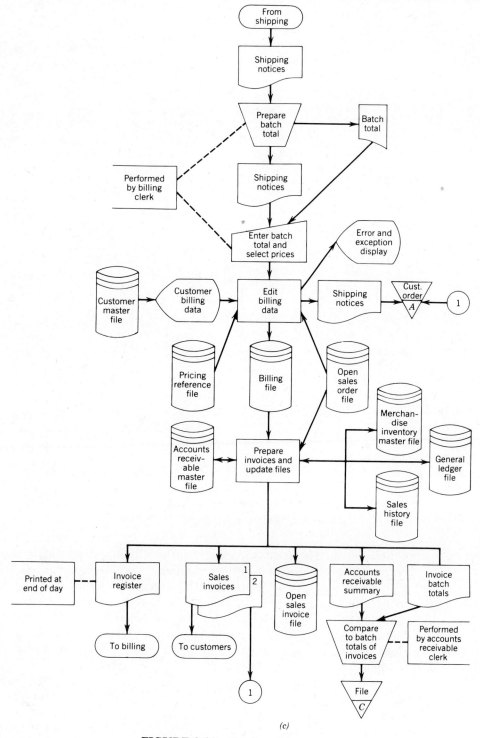

(c)

FIGURE 8-20 *(Continued)*.

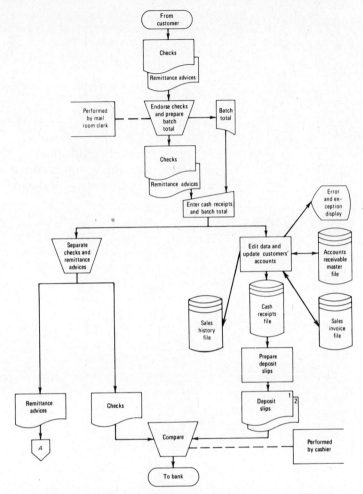

FIGURE 8-21 System flowchart of an online computer-based cash receipts transaction processing procedure.

substitutions). The goods are moved to the shipping department, where a clerk counts the goods and enters the quantities ready for shipment from the picking slip. A shipping program prepares the necessary documents for the shipment. When the goods are packed, they are delivered to the carrier for shipment. A shipping notice concerning the shipment (which is, in effect, a copy of the bill of lading) is generated on the billing department's printer. It shows not only quantities shipped, but also the shipping routes, freight charges, and other needed shipping data.

Upon receiving the shipping notices for the day, a billing clerk prepares and enters the batch total of quantities shipped. The clerk also converts each order to a completed invoice by viewing the order on the terminal screen, specifying product prices, and activating the invoice preparation program. After all invoices have been completed, (1) the invoices are printed, (2) each customer's account is debited, (3) the inventory records are reduced by the quantities shipped, (4) the

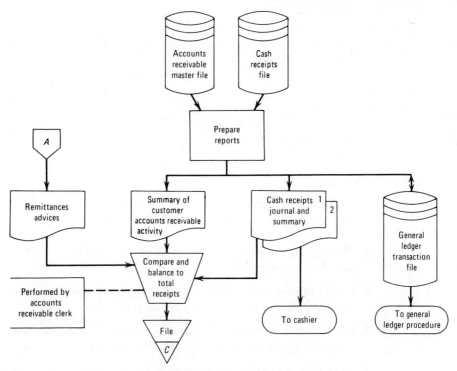

FIGURE 8-21 *(Continued).*

sales order is closed to the sales history file, (5) a new record is created in the sales invoice file, (6) a sales invoice register and summary of accounts receivable are printed, and (7) the total amounts affecting the sales and accounts receivable accounts are posted to the general ledger accounts. Finally, the accounts receivable clerk verifies that the postings to the accounts receivable ledger agree with the batch total.

Cash Receipts Procedure Figure 8-21 presents a system flowchart of the online cash receipts procedure. It is divided into two segments: (1) entry and deposit and (2) end-of-day processing.

As checks and remittances are received, one mailroom clerk endorses the checks and prepares a batch total. Another clerk enters the batch total and the data (amount, customer number, and sales invoice number) for each payment. If the indicated sales invoice pertaining to an amount is unpaid, and if the customer number is correct, the amount is accepted. If the total of all the individual amounts entered (as computed by the edit program) is equal to the precomputed batch total, the batch is accepted. Then the accounts receivable records for the remitting customers are credited, the affected sales invoices are marked "paid," and the sales invoices are closed to the sales history file. As a last step, the mail clerk sends the remittance advices to the accounts receivable department and the checks to the cashier. The cashier compares the checks to deposit slips prepared by a print program; if they agree the checks are delivered to the bank.

At the end of the day an accounts receivable clerk compares the advices against summary reports, in order to verify the correctness of the processing. If the open invoice method is employed, the clerk will match the cash payments directly against previous sales amounts in the customers' accounts. A summary journal entry, reflecting the total of receipts for the day, is transferred to the general ledger transaction file. That evening it is posted to the general ledger accounts.

ACCOUNTING CONTROLS

Risk Exposures

Among the risk exposures that exist in the processing of sales and cash receipts are the following.

1. Orders may be accepted from customers who prove unwilling or unable to pay their account balances.

2. Unintentional errors may be committed in shipments, in preparing sales invoices, and in posting to accounts receivable.

3. Orders from customers, shipping documents, accounts receivable records, and cash remittances may be accidentally lost.

4. Sales returns from customers may be excessive, or they may be fictitious, with unauthorized persons pocketing the proceeds.

5. Customers' accounts may be fraudulently written off, with subsequent collections being illegally pocketed.

6. Goods in the warehouse or on the shipping dock may be stolen.

7. Back orders may be misplaced and never filled.

8. Cash receipts, especially currency, may be abstracted by mail clerks, cashiers, accounts receivable clerks, and others.

9. Payments from customers may be lapped when posting to accounts receivable records. **Lapping** is a type of embezzlement that involves the theft of cash and its concealment by a succession of delayed postings to customers' accounts. A clerk who undertakes lapping first cashes a check from a customer and keeps the cash. Since the check cannot be recorded, the customer's account is in error. To cover his or her tracks, the clerk credits the customer's account upon receiving a check for an equal or larger amount from another customer. Then the clerk credits the second customer's account with the proceeds from the check of still another customer. This falsifying process continues indefinitely, unless the clerk decides to return the embezzled funds.

10. Accounts receivable, customer, merchandise inventory, and other records may be accessed by unauthorized persons.

11. Cash, merchandise inventory, and records may be damaged or destroyed by violence, fire, and other man-made or natural disasters.

Examples of Risk Exposures

Losses have been sustained by firms from all these types of risk exposures. In many cases the losses have been quite severe, as the following examples involving fraud indicate.[1]

- Customer service representatives of a large public utility, together with an outside confederate, used computer error correction codes to erase customer receivable accounts from files on magnetic tapes maintained by the utility. In return they received kickbacks from the affected customers. The total established losses amounted to $25,000, although the probable losses were much greater.

- A vice president of computer systems with a brokerage house misappropriated $277,000 of the firm's funds by making illegal debits to the interest earned account.

- A director of a publishing subsidiary altered computer programs so that false sales were added to the revenue account and certain expenses were not recorded; the effect was to inflate the operating results by at least $11.5 million.

- An employee of a savings bank perpetrated a lapping fraud that involved unrecorded transactions, altered transactions, and unauthorized transfers with respect to customers' accounts; the loss to the bank amounted to $1.4 million.

An adequate set of general controls and transaction (application) controls is necessary to counteract the listed risk exposures and to realize the objectives of the revenue cycle.

General Controls

General controls that particularly concern the revenue cycle include the following.

1. Within the organization the units that have custodial functions (warehouse, shipping department, cashier) are separate from those units that keep the records (billing department, accounts receivable department, inventory control department, data processing department). Also, the sales order and credit departments, whose managers authorize credit sales transactions as well as account adjustments and write-offs, are separate from all these units.

2. Complete and up-to-date documentation are available concerning the revenue cycle, including copies of the documents, flowcharts, record layouts, and reports illustrated in this chapter. In addition, details pertaining to sales and cash receipts edit and processing programs are organized into separate books or "packages" that are directed respectively to programmers, computer operators, and system users.

---

[1] These fraud cases are based on Brandt Allen, "The Biggest Computer Frauds: Lessons for CPAs," *The Journal of Accountancy* (May 1977), 52–63.

3. Operating practices relating to processing schedules, preparation of control summaries and reports, and other matters are clearly established.

4. Security is maintained (in the case of online systems) by such techniques as (a) requiring clerks to enter assigned passwords before accessing accounts receivable and other customer-related files, (b) employing terminals with restricted functions for the entry of sales and cash receipts transactions, (c) generating audit reports (access logs) that monitor accesses of system files, and (d) dumping the accounts receivable and merchandise inventory master files onto magnetic tape backups. Security measures for manual and computer-based systems include the use of physically restricted warehouses (for protecting goods) and safes (for holding cash receipts). Also, a lockbox collection system may be considered where feasible.

Transaction Controls

Control points within the revenue cycle include (1) the receipt of the sales order, (2) the credit check, (3) the shipping of ordered goods, (4) the billing for goods shipped, (5) the postings of each transaction to ledgers, (6) the receipt of goods by the customer, (7) the receipt of cash, and (8) the deposit of cash in the bank.

The following controls and control procedures are applicable to revenue cycle transactions and customer accounts.

1. Documents relating to sales, shipping, and cash receipts are prenumbered and well designed.

2. Data on sales orders and remittance advices are validated (and key-verified if suitable) as the data are prepared and entered for processing. In the case of computer-based systems, validation is performed by means of such edit checks as listed in Figure 8-22 (see pages 252 and 253).

3. Errors detected during data entry or processing are corrected as soon as possible by means of an established error-correction procedure.

4. Multiple-copy sales orders (and/or invoices) are issued on the basis of valid authorizations, usually including customers' orders and credit approvals.

5. Ordered goods are transferred from the finished goods warehouse and shipped only on the basis of written authorizations, such as picking lists or stock request copies.

6. Customers are billed only upon notification by the shipping department of the quantities shipped.

7. Sales returns and allowances and write-offs of accounts are subject to prior approvals by the credit manager and one other manager.

8. All data items on sales invoices, including computations, are verified by a billing clerk other than the preparer or by a computer program.

9. After preparation sales invoices are compared against shipping notices and

open sales orders in order to assure that the quantities ordered and billed agree with the orders shipped and back ordered.

10. All cash receipts are deposited intact with a minimum of delay, thus eliminating the possibility of cash receipts being used to pay employees or to reimburse petty cash funds.

11. If processing is performed in batches, control totals are precomputed from sales invoices (or shipping notices) and remittance advices; these batch control totals are compared with totals computed during postings to the accounts receivable ledger and during all other processing runs. In the case of cash receipts, the total of remittance advices is also compared with the total on deposit slips.

12. Accounts in the accounts receivable subsidiary ledger are periodically reconciled with the accounts receivable control account in the general ledger.

13. Monthly statements are prepared and mailed to all credit customers. Since a customer will likely complain if overcharged, this practice provides control over accidental and fraudulent acts.

14. Copies of all documents pertaining to sales and cash receipts transactions are filed by number, and the sequence of numbers in each file is periodically checked to see if gaps exist. If transactions are not supported by preprinted documents, as is often the case in online computer-based systems, numbers are assigned to the documents, and they are stored in a transaction file.

15. In the case of computer-based systems, transaction listings and account summaries are printed periodically in order to provide an adequate audit trail.

16. All bank accounts are reconciled monthly by someone who is not involved in revenue cycle processing activities, and new bank accounts are authorized by the proper managers.

17. Employees who handle cash are required to be bonded and are subject to close supervision.

REPORTS AND OTHER OUTPUTS

Outputs generated by the revenue cycle include both financial reports and nonfinancial reports, sales-related and cash-related reports, daily and weekly and monthly reports, hard copy and soft copy reports. All these reports may be arbitrarily classified as operational listings and reports, inquiry screens, and managerial reports.

Operational Listings and Reports

The **monthly statement** is a listing of all outstanding sales invoices for a customer. It is based on information in the customer, accounts receivable, sales

Type of edit check	Typical transaction data being checked		Assurance provided
	Sales	Cash receipts	
1. Validity check	Customer account numbers, product numbers, transaction codes	Customer account numbers, transaction codes	The entered numbers and codes are checked against lists of valid numbers and codes that are stored within the computer system.
2. Self-checking digit	Customer account numbers	Customer account numbers	Each customer account number (e.g., 34578) contains a check digit (e.g., 8), whose value is based on an established mathematical algorithm involving the other digits of the number (e.g., 3, 4, 5, 7). When a customer account number is entered as a part of a sales or cash receipts transaction, the same computation is performed on the digits (e.g., 3, 4, 5, 7). If the value computed at this time (e.g., 2) differs from the attached digit (e.g., 8), the difference signals an input error (e.g., a transposition of 4 and 5) in entering the customer account number.
3. Field check	Customer account numbers, quantities ordered, unit prices	Customer account numbers, amounts	The fields in the input records that are designated to contain the data items (listed at the left) are checked to see if they contain the proper mode of characters (i.e., numeric characters). If other modes are found (such as alphabetic characters or blanks), an error is indicated.
4. Limit check	Quantities ordered	Amounts received	The entered quantities and amounts are checked against preestablished limits that represent reasonable maximums to be expected. (Separate limits are set for each product and class of customer.)
5. Range check	Unit prices	None	Each entered unit price is checked to see that it is within a pre-established range (either higher or lower than an expected value). To find the pre-established range, the edit program must first check the entered product number corresponding to the unit price and then look in a stored table of unit prices arranged by product numbers.

Check			Description
6. Relationship check	Product numbers	Amounts received	When two or more products are involved in a sales transaction, their numbers are checked to a stored table of reasonable combinations of products that appear on the same order; if the entered products do not appear in one of the combinations, the sales transaction is flagged by the edit program. When a payment amount is entered in a cash receipts transaction, together with the number of the sales invoice to which the amount applies, the amount in the sales invoice file is retrieved and compared with the entered amount. If a difference appears, the transaction is flagged.
7. Sign check	Product on-hand balances	Customer account balances	After the ordered quantities of products for a sales transaction are entered and posted to the inventory master file (thereby reducing the on-hand balances of the affected products), the remaining on-hand balances are checked. If any of the balances is preceded by a negative sign, the transaction is flagged. After the amount of a cash receipts transaction is entered and posted to the account in the accounts receivable ledger (thereby reducing the account balance of the customer), the remaining balance is checked. If the balance is preceded by a negative sign (indicating a credit balance), the transaction is flagged.
8. Completeness check[a]	All entered data items	All entered data items	The entered transactions are checked to see that all required data items have been entered.
9. Echo check[a]	Customer account numbers and names, product numbers and descriptions	Customer account numbers and names	After the account numbers for customers relating to a sales or cash receipts transaction (and also the product numbers in the sales transaction) have been entered at a terminal, the edit program retrieves and "echoes" back the related customer names (and product descriptions in the case of sales transactions). The person who entered the data can visually verify from reading the names (or descriptions) on the screen that the correct numbers were entered.

[a] Applicable only to online processing systems.

FIGURE 8-22 Programmed edit checks that are useful in validating transaction data entered into the revenue cycle.

Arvin   ArvinAir Division
Arvin Industries, Inc.
500 South 15th Street
Phoenix, Arizona 85034

STATEMENT

TO:

ACCOUNT NUMBER   STATEMENT DATE

INVOICE DATE	INVOICE NO.	CUSTOMER NO.	CUSTOMER LOCATION	TERMS	LINE CODE	DUE DATE	AGE CODE	DAYS OVERDUE	INVOICE AMOUNT

AMOUNT CURRENTLY DUE WITHIN NEXT 30 DAYS	AMOUNTS OVERDUE (AGED IN DAYS)				TOTAL AMOUNT DUE
CODE A	1 - 30 DAYS OVERDUE CODE B	31 - 60 DAYS OVERDUE CODE C	61 - 90 DAYS OVERDUE CODE D	90 + DAYS OVERDUE CODE E	CURRENT AND OVERDUE ITEMS

TO ASSIST YOU IN YOUR CASH PLANNING, THE FOLLOWING IS AN AGING OF FUTURE DUE AMOUNTS

DUE IN 31 - 60 DAYS	DUE IN 61 - 90 DAYS	DUE IN 91 - 120 DAYS	DUE IN OVER 120 DAYS	TOTAL FUTURE DUE CODE F	ACCOUNT BALANCE

LINE CODE: PLEASE REMIT TO:

INV = INVOICE
C/B = CHARGE BACK
C/M = CREDIT MEMO
LPC = LATE PAYMENT CHARGE
OAP = ON ACCOUNT PAYMENT
U/D = UNRESOLVED DEDUCTION   CUSTOMER COPY

FIGURE 8-23 A monthly statement. Courtesy of Arvin Industries.

invoice, and cash receipts files. Figure 8-23 shows a monthly statement, including the total amount due. As added information, this particular version also provides an aging of overdue amounts.

The **open orders report** lists those sales orders that are not completely shipped and billed. It may be arranged chronologically, by sales order numbers, or by customers. Figure 8-24 presents an open orders report by customer. Note that it also indicates back orders. This report thus provides operational control, since it helps to expedite the processing of sales orders. Related operational control reports include the *unbilled shipments report,* the *late shipments report,* and the *back order status report.*

Various registers and journals help to maintain the audit trail. The *sales invoice register* is a listing of all sales invoices, arranged by sales invoice numbers. It is, in effect, the sales journal. The *shipping register* is a listing of all shipments, arranged by shipping date. The *cash receipts journal* is a listing of amounts received, arranged chronologically. Figure 8-25 shows a cash receipts journal which includes a summary of debits and credits distributed to accounts.

4/25/89

OPEN ORDERS BY CUSTOMER
REPRESENTATIVE MERCHANDISING COMPANY

ORDER NO	ITEM NO		W/H LOC'N	ITEM CLASS	VENDOR NO	ORDERED QTY	ORDERED U/M	UNIT PRICE	U/M	SOURCE SHIPMT	BACK ORDER
CUSTOMER-11111800		BOYER PLUMBING SUPPLY									
25137	7762000000000-1	ALUMINUM PAINT	L-147	07	1630VE	3	CS		CS	0	—
25137	8210000000000-1	RADIAL PIPE CUTTER 1-3	P-112	08	4155RR	2	EA		EA	0	—
25137	8960000000000-1	C12 L D CHAIN WRENCH 4CP	P-116	08	4115RR	1	EA	7.100	EA	0	—
CUSTOMER-11610000		FIELDS APPLIANCES									
80349	3325000000000-1	REFRIGERATOR – 20.7 S/S COPPER	A-120	03	2010AB	1	EA		EA	0	—
80349	3341000000000-1	REFRIGERATOR – 19 S/S GOLD	A-140	03	2010AB	2	EA		EA	0	—
80349	7890000000000-1	LATEX SEMI-GLOSS WHITE	L-169	07	9060LE	2	CS		CS	0	—
80349	7890000000000-1	LATEX SEMI-GLOSS WHITE	L-169	07	9060LE	3	GAL			0	—
CUSTOMER-11750000		FRIED & JONES SUPPLY CORP.									
25111	1111000000000-1	TWO-LIGHT WALL MOUNT	R-119	01	6000AR	10	EA		EA	0	—
25111	5681000000000-1	EVAPORATIVE COOLER	Q-190	05	7710JW	6	EA		EA	0	—
25111	6664000000000-1	BATHTUB FAUCET	F-100	06	7370UN	12	EA		EA	0	—
25111	8210000000000-1	RADIAL PIPE CUTTER 1-3	P-112	08	4155RR	6	EA		EA	0	—
CUSTOMER-11800010		WESTERNWIDE *STORE 1*									
77999	5789000000000-4	AIR FILTER 12 × 14 × 1	033	05	2250SS	32	EA	.900	EA	0	B
CUSTOMER-12780000		HEARN MANUFACTURERS									
5	9120000000000-1	6 OZ COLD CUPS	X-380	09	7960BL	17	CS	6.900	CS	0	B
CUSTOMER-17640000		MADSEN CORPORATION									
75968	9502000000000-1	ROBOT – 3FT	D-181	10	1180AB	27	EA	19.270	EA	0	B
CUSTOMER-21000000		QUINN & ASSOCIATES									
9	7797000000000-1	CALUMET 750	L-160	07	1630VE	19	CS	88.960	CS	0	B
CUSTOMER-25000020		UNIVERSITY CONTRACTORS – APTOS									
80348	6836000000000-1	SINK – LAV	F-124			1	EA	42.500	EA	0	B
CUSTOMER-28000000		XAVIER HARDWARE & PAINT									
77996	2249000000000-1	U-BOLT FOOT MOUNT	M-115	02	6400IC	1	DZ	14.950	DZ	0	B

FIGURE 8-24 An open orders status report. Courtesy of International Business Machines Corporation.

Representative Merchandising Company   1
Journal - CJ001   Batch - 1   Cash receipts journal   Time 17:35:18   Date   5/31/89   Page 1   35441
                                                                                                             Posting date 5/31/89

Date	Customer number	Customer name	Ref number	Inv number	1110 Accts rec CR	1010 Cash DR	8130 Cash disc DR	1150 Adjustment DR	General Ledger amount DR	number
5/31/89		Vending machine				15.60			(15.60)	8040
5/31/89		Pay phone				20.80			(20.80)	8040
5/31/89	10400	Anderson Inc.			100.00			100.00		
5/31/89	10700	Andrus Inc.	ck123		150.00	150.00				
5/31/89	10700	Andrus Inc.	adj90		(7.48)			(7.48)		
5/31/89	10800	Angeroth Incorporated			110.76	110.76				
5/31/89	11810	Westernwide *Store 1*		UN	66.76	66.76				
5/31/89	11810	Westernwide *Store 1*		20915	325.99	325.99				

Representative Merchandising Company   1
Journal - CJ001   Batch - 1   Cash receipts journal summary   Time 17:36:55   Date   5/31/89   Page 1   35442
                                                                                                             Posting date 5/31/89

Account number	Debits	Credits
8040	.00	36.40
1010	6,917.67	.00
1110	.00	6,976.62
1150	92.52	.00
8130	2.83	.00
Totals	7,013.02	7,013.02

FIGURE 8-25 A cash receipts journal and summary. Courtesy of International Business Machines Corporation.

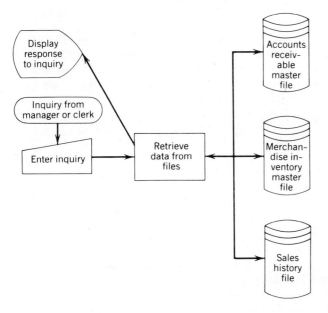

FIGURE 8-26 Response to an inquiry of online files in the revenue data base.

The **accounts receivable aging schedule** is based on the same files as the monthly statement. However, it contains data concerning the status of the open balances of all active credit customers. Since it arrays the overdue amounts by time periods, it flags those accounts that are urgently in need of collection. Thus, it provides operational control over the collection of open accounts and aids the credit manager in making collection and write-off decisions.

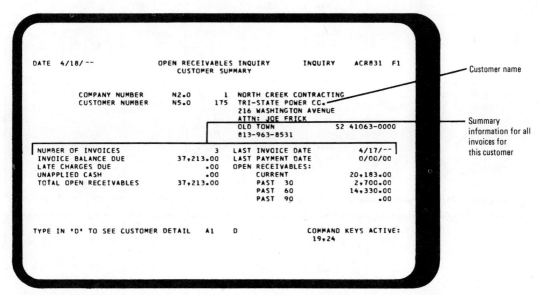

FIGURE 8-27 An inquiry screen relating to an open receivable. Courtesy of International Business Machines Corporation.

Inquiry Screens

If the revenue cycle data base is stored in online files, a variety of inquiries can be made interactively. Figure 8-26 shows a response from the system to an inquiry by a manager or clerk of key files in the data base. Figure 8-27 presents a screen display output concerning the status of a customer's account receivable. Note that aging information is included as well as the current balance. Other inquiries might concern (1) the on-hand quantity of a particular product, (2) the dates that certain orders are expected to be shipped, and (3) the detail of a single cash remittance or a batch of remittances.

Managerial Reports

The revenue cycle data base can provide a wealth of information to aid managers in making decisions. One example already listed is the accounts receivable

Eastern Manufacturing Co.
Analysis of Sales by Salesperson, Product, and Territory
For the Month of August 1989
Central Massachusetts Territory (03)

Salesperson Name	No.	Product Line	Current Month Quota ($)	Current Month Actual ($)	Current Month Variance ($) Over (Under)	Year-to-date Quota ($)	Year-to-date Actual ($)	Year-to-date Variance ($) Over (Under)
Comden, K. J.	325	A	4,000	5,000	1,000	32,000	34,600	2,600
		B	3,000	2,500	(500)	24,000	24,300	300
		C	1,000	800	(200)	8,000	7,100	(900)
		D	6,000	7,400	1,400	48,000	50,700	2,700
		E	10,000	12,100	2,100	80,000	83,200	3,200
		F	8,000	8,400	400	64,000	62,800	(1,200)
		G	2,000	1,700	(300)	16,000	15,300	(700)
		All	34,000	37,900	3,900	272,000	278,000	6,000
George, M. P.	381	A	5,000	4,800	(200)	40,000	39,200	(800)
		B	4,000	4,100	100	32,000	31,800	(200)
		C	1,000	900	(100)	8,000	6,900	(1,100)
		D	7,000	6,200	(800)	56,000	54,800	(1,200)
		E	12,000	11,800	(200)	96,000	96,500	500
		F	9,500	9,900	400	76,000	78,100	2,100
		G	2,500	3,200	700	20,000	25,300	5,300
		All	41,000	40,900	(100)	328,000	332,600	4,600
Totals		A	50,000	53,300	3,300	400,000	410,700	10,700
		B	35,000	34,700	(300)	280,000	281,500	1,500
		C	10,000	8,900	(1,100)	80,000	77,700	(2,300)
		D	65,000	69,100	4,100	520,000	528,100	8,100
		E	108,000	111,800	3,800	864,000	891,000	27,000
		F	86,000	84,700	(1,300)	688,000	679,300	(8,700)
		G	23,000	24,000	1,000	184,000	183,900	(100)
		All	377,000	386,500	9,500	3,016,000	3,052,200	36,200

FIGURE 8-28 A sales analysis report.

aging schedule, which is useful for decision-making as well as operational control. Several other useful reports and analyses are worth noting.

Performance reports reflect results in terms of such key measures as average dollar value per order, percentage of orders shipped on time, and the average number of days between the order date and shipping date.

Sales analyses reflect the relative effectiveness of individual salespersons, sales regions, product lines, customers, and markets. Figure 8-28 shows a sales analysis that compares the actual sales for three of these factors against established quotas.

Cash flow statements provide the basis for developing cash forecasts and budgets. Hence, they aid the process of managing the cash resource.

SUMMARY

The revenue cycle facilitates the exchange of products or services with customers for cash. Functions of the revenue cycle (for product sales) are to obtain the order from the customer, check the customer's credit, enter the sales order, assemble goods for shipment, ship the ordered goods, bill the customer, receive and deposit the cash payment, maintain accounts receivable records, post transactions to the general ledger, and prepare needed financial reports and other outputs. Related functions involve back orders and sales returns. These functions are achieved under the direction of the marketing/distribution and finance/accounting organizational units.

Most of the data used in the cycle arise from customers. Documents typically employed are the customer order, sales order, picking list, packing list, bill of lading, shipping notice, sales invoice, remittance advice, deposit slip, back-order form, and credit memo. Preformatted screens may be used in online computer-based systems to enter sales and cash receipts data. The data base includes such files as the customer master, accounts receivable master, merchandise inventory master, open sales order, open sales invoice, cash receipts transaction, shipping and price data reference, and sales history files. Data processing consists of processing sales transactions, processing cash receipts transactions, and maintaining accounts receivable records. Processing may feasibly be performed by manual systems, batch computer-based systems, and online computer-based systems.

A variety of exposures exist in the processing of sales and cash receipts transactions. Risks resulting from these exposures can be counteracted by means of adequate general and transaction controls.

Among the outputs generated by the revenue cycle are the customer's monthly statement, open orders report, sales invoice register, accounts receivable aging schedule, customer inquiry screen, performance report, sales analyses, and cash flow statement.

REFERENCES

Eliason, Alan I. *Business Information Processing: Technology, Applications, Management.* Palo Alto, Calif.: Science Research Associates, Inc., 1980.

A Guide for Studying and Evaluating Internal Accounting Controls. Chicago: Arthur Andersen & Co., 1978.

Introducing Accounts Receivable, 2d ed. Atlanta: IBM, 1982.

Nash, John F., and Roberts, Martin B. *Accounting Information Systems.* New York: Macmillan, 1984.

Page, John, and Hooper, Paul. *Accounting Information Systems,* 3d ed. Englewood Cliffs, N.J.: Prentice-Hall, 1987.

QUESTIONS

1. What is the meaning of each of the following terms?

Revenue cycle	Incomplete prebilling procedure
Prebilling procedure	

Separate sales order
and invoice
procedure
Balance forward
method
Open invoice method
Customer order
Sales order
Order
acknowledgment
Picking list
Packing list
Bill of lading
Shipping notice

Sales invoice
Remittance advice
Deposit slip
Back order
Credit memo
Customer master file
Accounts receivable
master file
Inventory master file
Lapping
Monthly statement
Open orders report
Accounts receivable
aging schedule

2. What are several subpurposes or objectives of the revenue cycle?

3. What are the major functions of the revenue cycle?

4. Contrast the three alternative procedures for billing customers.

5. Describe the back-ordering procedure.

6. Describe the relationships of the marketing and distribution organizational functions to the revenue cycle.

7. Describe the relationships of the finance and accounting organizational functions to the revenue cycle.

8. What are the sources of data used in the revenue cycle?

9. Identify the various documents used in the revenue cycle.

10. Identify the accounting entries needed to reflect the transactions within the revenue cycle.

11. Identify the various files used in the revenue cycle.

12. Describe the credit sales procedure when processing is performed manually.

13. Describe the cash receipts procedure when processing is performed manually.

14. Describe the accounts receivable procedure when processing is performed manually.

15. Describe the revenue cycle procedure when processing is performed by a computer-based system involving a combination of the batch and online methods.

16. What are the risk exposures that exist in the processing within the revenue cycle?

17. Identify various general and transaction controls that concern the revenue cycle.

18. Identify various reports and other outputs that may be generated from information provided by the revenue cycle.

19. In what ways does the revenue cycle procedure differ when performed by computer-based systems (a) using the batch processing approach, and (b) using the online processing approach?

20. What are sources of information for marketing managers other than from revenue cycle processing?

21. In what ways does a cash sale differ from a credit sale, especially with regard to documents, files, procedure, and outputs?

22. Describe several programmed edit checks, such as the redundancy matching check, that can be applied by the posting programs used in processing sales and cash receipts transactions.

23. Why should a bank reconciliation be prepared periodically?

24. Which transaction controls, that are needed in a revenue cycle procedure involving an online computer-based system, are not suitable when a batch computer-based system is employed, and vice versa?

REVIEW PROBLEM

Millsap Stationers

Statement

Millsap sells stationery products on credit to department stores, bookstores, greeting card stores, and other retailers. It receives orders from these customers by mail. After validating the orders, checking and approving their credit status, and issuing formal sales orders, the firm ships the ordered merchandise. The shipping clerk amends the shipping notice copies of the sales orders to reflect appropriate data concerning the shipments. Then the shipping department batches these shipping notice copies of the sales orders at the end of each day and arranges them in sales-order number sequence.

The figure on page 261 presents a system

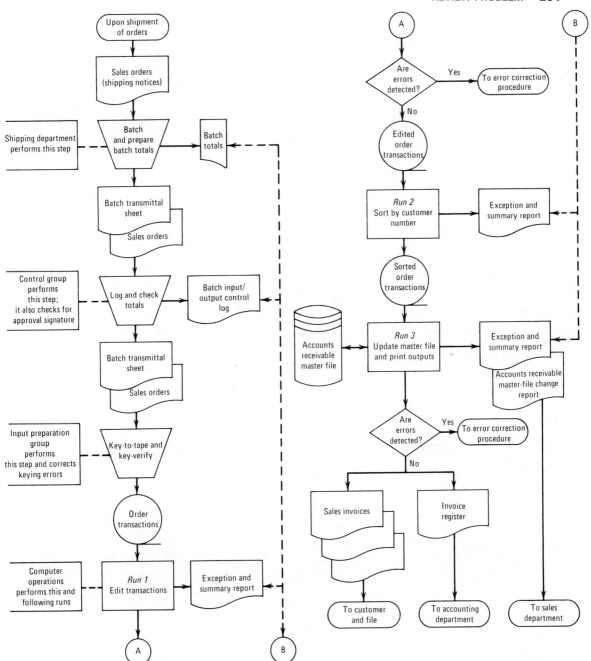

EXHIBIT 1 System flowchart of computer-based batch processing of sales transactions, with an emphasis on controls.

flowchart that diagrams the manner in which the batched copies of sales orders are processed by the firm's computer-based system. (However, to simplify the procedure, the updating of the mer-

chandise inventory master file is omitted.) The diagram on page 262 presents the procedure for correcting errors detected during the entry and processing of the sales orders.

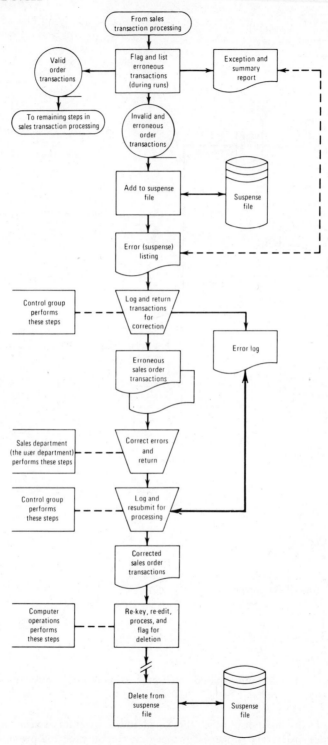

Required

a. Identify key data items that appear on the shipping notice copies of the sales orders being entered into processing.

b. Identify and describe the transaction controls and pertinent general controls reflected by the two flowcharts. Also, add descriptions of controls that do not explicitly appear in the flowcharts but that are needed in the batch processing approach being shown.

c. Briefly discuss the changes that would be needed to the flowchart in order to reflect the updating of the merchandise inventory master file.

Solution

a. Key data items that should appear on each amended sales order are the sales order number, date of order, customer account number, customer name, shipping address, billing address, terms, customer purchase order number, shipping date, salesperson number (if any), method of shipping and carrier, back-order data (if any), product numbers, quantities of each product shipped, unit price of each product, and the initials of the shipping clerk.

b. The accounting controls involved in the computer-based batch processing system are as follows.

(1) Three batch control totals are computed in the shipping department: an amount total of the quantities ordered, a hash total of the customer account numbers, and a record count of the number of shipping notices. These totals are entered on a prenumbered batch transmittal sheet and forwarded to the control section or group. It logs the batch data on an input/output control log and verifies that the count of the batch is correct. (The dashed line between the batch total and the batch input/output control log reflects this verification.)

(2) Data entry clerks in the data preparation section or group key the data from the documents onto magnetic tape, thereby creating an order transaction file. Each keyed transaction is key-verified, and errors are corrected. The clerks also record the batch control totals within a trailer label on the tape so that they may be checked at a later point in the processing.

(3) The computer operator mounts the tape containing the transaction file; then he or she removes the tape file protection ring, thereby preventing the tape from being written on and the data destroyed.

(4) If the accounts receivable master file is stored on a magnetic tape or removable magnetic disk, the computer operator obtains the medium from the data library by signing the library log and mounts the master file. (If the file is online, this step is not necessary.)

(5) The computer operator begins run 1 by opening the run manual, which contains detailed operating instructions. As the first step, he or she performs internal label checks (i.e., verifies that the correct master file and transaction header labels are displayed on the console log).

(6) During run 1 the edit program performs a variety of programmed checks on the data pertaining to each transaction. Among the checks applied are the validity, field, limit, range, relationship, sign, and self-checking digit checks. (See Figure 8-22 for the types of data items checked and descriptions of the checks.)

(7) Errors or exceptional conditions detected by these edit checks are listed on an exception and summary report and entered into the error-correction procedure (which will be discussed later).

(8) During the edit run the program accumulates transaction totals and counts and then compares the values for the entire batch against the precomputed batch control totals. Any differences are listed on the exception and summary report, and these are investigated by the control group.

(9) Before run 2 begins, the computer operator removes the tape file protection ring from the newly created tape of edited transactions and performs an internal label check on the tape. Also, the operator removes the exception and summary report and gives it to the control group for investigation.

(10) Before run 3 begins, the computer operator performs the same actions as earlier with respect to the files.

(11) During run 3 the updating and invoicing program performs checks to see that the transactions are in correct customer account number sequence and that each transaction is posted to the correct master file record. It assigns sequential numbers to the sales invoices. It updates the data in the header and trailer labels. It reflects any differences in batch totals on the exception and summary report and also includes data for the summary journal entry that is to be posted to the general ledger.

(12) Reports that aid the audit trail and provide the basis for review are printed. Included are the invoice register and the accounts receivable master file change report.

(13) The various outputs from run 3 are logged and distributed by the control group to the appropriate recipients.

The error-correction procedure shown in the flowchart on page 262 ensures that all detected errors are properly handled.

(1) All detected errors are listed on an exception and summary report during the run.

(2) All transactions containing errors are transferred to a suspense file, which is monitored by the control group so that erroneous transactions are not mislaid.

(3) All detected errors are corrected by user departments, which are most knowledgeable concerning the transactions.

(4) All corrected transactions are re-edited in order to verify that all errors are corrected and that no new errors have been introduced.

(5) The batch control totals are adjusted to reflect the amounts involved in all suspended transactions.

c. In this batch processing procedure the updating of the merchandise inventory master file will likely take place before the accounts receivable master file is updated. Thus, the edited order transaction file (after run 1) would first be sorted by product numbers. Then the merchandise inventory master file can be sequentially updated.

It should be noted, however, that many orders will likely involve more than one product. Consequently, steps in addition to those listed are necessary. Before sorting by product numbers, the data composing the headings of the orders (e.g., customer account number and addresses) must be transferred to a file that is separate from the file contining the product line order data (e.g., product number and quantity ordered). Even before this is done, each product in an order must be coded with the sales order number, since it will be detached from the order heading. Then, after the updating run is completed, the heading and product data for each order must be reassembled via a merge run.

PROBLEMS

8-1. The Flip Shopper sells a variety of merchandise for cash only at a single location. Four cash registers are used for checking out customers. Describe the cash sales procedure—including documents, processing steps, controls, and reports—if this merchandiser does not employ computers. Identify the likely changes if point-of-sale terminals are installed in place of the cash registers. Assume that the terminals are, in effect, stand-alone microcomputers.

8-2. The Overlord Company has just employed a new credit manager. Because the firm has an outstanding total of $3 million in accounts receivable (when last year's sales were $12 million), the credit manager realizes that her most urgent task is to reduce the level of accounts receivable. Credit customers are billed at the end of each month, based on individual accounts receivable records. The credit manager has been assured by the president that a new computer-based system is to be installed within the coming year.

Required

   a. List the types of transactions that affect the accounts receivable balance.

   b. Describe at least two reports that can aid the credit manager in controlling outstanding accounts receivable.

   c. Discuss the relative advantages of processing the various daily transactions that affect the accounts receivable records by a computer-based system that (1) uses the batch processing method, and (2) that uses the on-line processing method.

8-3. Sapphire Department Stores, Inc., has eight locations in a major eastern city. Sales are made on credit to customers who have applied and received credit cards from Sapphire. All other sales are made for cash. Deliveries of purchased merchandise are made upon request, whether the sale is for cash or on credit. Merchandise may be returned by customers, with refunds being made in the case of cash sales and credits against account balances being provided in the case of credit sales. Credit customers are billed once a month, based on the accounts receivable records. Overdue balances are automatically assessed interest charges.

Required

   a. List the data items needed to record and process cash sales, credit sales, payments on account, and sales returns transactions.

   b. List the files needed to store these data items.

   c. Describe the reports that would be useful to the firm's management in analyzing the sales and cash receipts transactions and the activities related to the credit customers' accounts.

8-4. Antler and Horn, Consultants, bill their clients for services rendered. The invoices, which itemize the hours worked by the various classes of consultants in the firm, are sent at the end of each month. One invoice sent on September 30, 1989, to the Mover Construction Company showed the following billable hours: 4 hours for a partner, 10 hours for a manager, 85 hours for a senior staff consultant, and 230 hours for staff consultants. Hourly rates charged by the firm are $250 for partners, $180 for managers, $150 for senior staff consultants, and $90 for staff consultants. All taxes are included within the billing rates. Design and complete the invoice to be sent to the Mover Construction Company, whose offices are located at 50 Lark Lane, Prescott, Arizona 86301. The consultants are located at 1000 Woolshire Blvd., Los Angeles, California 90028.

8-5. At the end of each month the Egress Corporation of Andover, Massachusetts 01810 prepares monthly statements for its credit customers, plus an accounts receivable aging schedule. The files on which these reports are based are the accounts receivable master file, the customer master file, the sales invoice file, and the cash receipts file. (The firm does not maintain a sales history file, but it does retain all sales and cash receipts data in related files for one year.) The files are all maintained on magnetic disk and can be accessed as needed during the end-of-month printing runs.

Required

   a. Design the monthly statement, assuming that it is not intended to be used as a turn-around document.

   b. Design the accounts receivable aging schedule, including such columns as customer account number and name, current balance, amount of the receivable balance that is not overdue, and amounts that are 31–60 days old, 61–90 days old, and over 90 days old. Terms are net 30 days.

   c. Draw suggested record layouts (omitting field sizes and modes of data items) for the listed files. Be sure that all the information in the two outputs can be derived from one of the files or can be computed or generated by the computer system. (For instance, the date may be computer-generated.)

8-6. Computers Unlimited carries two makes of microcomputers, Speedos and Whizbangs, plus software and hardware accessories. Its retail stores are located in three sales districts, and it sells to individuals and to businesses. Since sales growth has been rather erratic in recent years, the sales manager desires a variety of monthly sales analyses. Based on these analyses, he believes that he can better determine where to emphasize sales efforts.

Required

Design for Computers Unlimited formats of sales analyses that show the following.

a. Sales of the four product lines (the two makes of microcomputers, the software, and the accessories).

b. Sales of the two classes of customers, individuals and businesses.

c. Sales of the three sales districts (I, II, and III).

d. Sales of the four product lines within the three districts.

e. Sales of the two classes of customers within the three districts, which in turn are within the four product lines.

8-7. What error or fraudulent activity might occur if each of the following procedures is allowed?

a. The person who maintains the accounts receivable records also receives the cash payments from customers.

b. The person who approves the write-offs of uncollectible accounts also carries the cash receipts to the bank.

c. The sales invoices are not prenumbered (or if prenumbered, are not filed in a sequential file that is periodically checked for gaps in the numbers).

d. The accounts receivable ledger is not periodically reconciled to the control account in the general ledger.

e. Incompleted sales order–invoice copies are filed in the billing department but are not accounted for on a periodic basis.

f. After billing is completed the shipping notices are not marked in some manner, stapled to copies of the invoices, or filed.

8-8. What internal accounting control(s) would be most effective in preventing or detecting each of the following errors or fraudulent practices?

a. The amount of $380 is posted from a sales invoice to a customer's accounts receivable record as $308.

b. A customer is billed for all 100 units ordered, even though only 80 units are shipped because there is an insufficient quantity on hand to fill the order.

c. A customer is not billed for ordered merchandise shipped.

d. A general ledger clerk posts a debit to sales returns but does not post the credit to the accounts receivable control account.

e. A shipment never reaches a customer, even though it leaves the shipping dock via a common carrier.

f. Goods are shipped to a customer who is delinquent in paying for past sales.

g. Goods are taken from the finished goods warehouse and knowingly shipped by the shipping clerk to a person who did not place an order.

h. A sale that is billed to a customer is not posted to the accounts receivable record.

i. Goods are never returned to the firm, in spite of the fact that a credit memo is issued and approved.

j. A cash receipt is stolen by the cashier.

k. A computer-prepared sales analysis is mistakenly sent to the personnel manager rather than the sales manager.

l. A computer operator mounts the magnetic tape containing the cash disbursements for the day, rather than the cash receipts, and incorrectly updates the accounts receivable master file.

m. A payment from a customer in the amount of $100.10 and properly listed on a remittance advice is keyed by a data entry clerk onto the transaction tape as $101.00.

n. A sales order clerk accidentally omits the quantity of one of the ordered products when entering sales data via a terminal.

o. A sales order is coded with an incorrect and nonexistent customer number. The error is not detected until the file updating run, when no master is located to match the erroneous number.

p. A sales order clerk accidentally keys the letter *o* instead of a 0 as a part of the quantity 30.

q. A sales order clerk accidentally enters the quantity 2000 when entering an order on her terminal for motorcycles from a small dealer.

8-9. Fast Burger is a chain of fast food establishments. List the control objectives to be achieved during cash sales transactions, as well as the internal accounting controls and security measures needed to achieve the objectives.

(CIA adapted)

8-10. The Jason Department Store of Ann Arbor, Michigan, sells a wide variety of merchandise for cash or credit. It mails account statements to credit customers monthly. Customers then return their payments, including in the envelopes the detached portions of the statements, which serve as remittance advices for the cash receipts procedure. These remittance advices are processed against the accounts receivable master file. Daily lists of cash receipts are prepared. At the end of each month aging schedules are printed in addition to the statements. Jason is considering the conversion of its cash receipts procedure to computer-based processing.

Required

a. Prepare a system flowchart of a proposed computer-based cash receipts procedure, assuming that the firm adopts the batch processing method and stores both master and transaction files on magnetic tape.

b. List the transaction controls that are suitable to a computer-based system that processes Jason's cash receipts by the batch method.

8-11. Jersey Wholesalers, Inc., of Athens, Georgia, performs sales order, shipping, and billing procedures as shown in the document system flowchart on page 268. All documents used in the procedures are prenumbered. There are numerous partial shipments on customers' orders, since quantities on hand are frequently not sufficient to fill orders completely; however, goods not shipped in such cases are *not* automatically back-ordered.

Required

List the control weaknesses in the flowcharted procedures and recommend improvements.

(CIA adapted)

8-12. A cash sale procedure in a small department store involves several steps. First, the sales clerk prepares a prenumbered sales slip as a triplicate set. The original and second copy, together with the payment, are presented to the cashier by the salesclerk. The cashier validates the original copy and gives it to the customer. The third copy of the sales slip is retained in the sales book; when the sales book has been depleted of sales slip sets, it is filed in the sales office.

At the end of each day the cashier prepares a sales summary, counts the cash, and prepares a deposit slip in duplicate. He or she next takes the cash to the bank, where one copy of the deposit slip is retained and the other is validated to reflect the amount deposited. Then the cashier turns over the validated deposit slip, second copies of the sales slips, and the sales summary to the firm's accountant. The accountant compares these documents and accounts for all numbered sales slips. Then he or she gives the sales summary to the general ledger clerk, who posts the sales totals to the appropriate accounts and files the sales summary chronologically. The accountant files the sales slips numerically and the deposit slip chronologically.

Required

Prepare a document system flowchart of the procedure described.

8-13. The Robinson Company is a small paint manufacturer in Lincoln, Nebraska. Its customer billings and collections are attended to by a receptionist, an accounts receivable clerk, and a cashier who also serves as a secretary. The company's paint products are sold to wholesalers and retail stores.

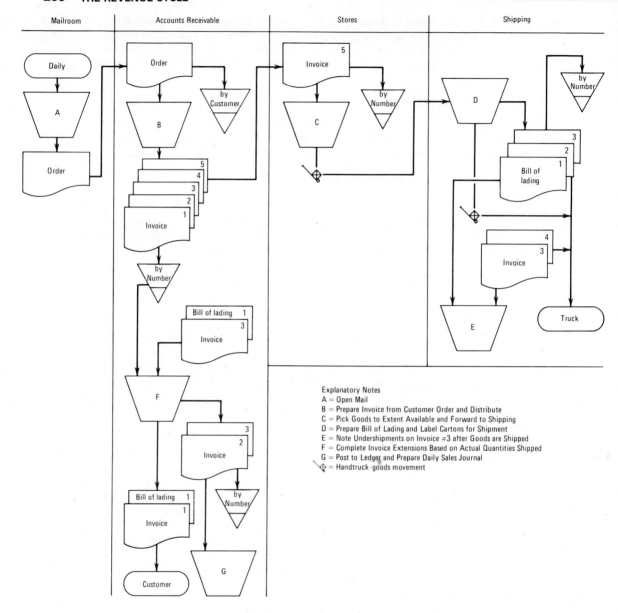

Explanatory Notes
A = Open Mail
B = Prepare Invoice from Customer Order and Distribute
C = Pick Goods to Extent Available and Forward to Shipping
D = Prepare Bill of Lading and Label Cartons for Shipment
E = Note Undershipments on Invoice #3 after Goods are Shipped
F = Complete Invoice Extensions Based on Actual Quantities Shipped
G = Post to Ledger and Prepare Daily Sales Journal
⊕ = Handtruck-goods movement

The following describes the procedure pertaining to customer billings and collections.

The mail is opened by the receptionist, who gives the customers' purchase orders to the accounts receivable clerk; 15 to 20 orders are received each day. Under instructions to expedite the shipment of orders, the accounts receivable clerk at once prepares a five-copy sales invoice form, which is distributed as follows.

Copy 1, the customer billing copy, is filed alphabetically by the accounts receivable clerk until notice of shipment is received.

Copy 2, the accounts receivable department copy, is held with copy 1 for ultimate posting of the accounts receivable records.

Copies 3 and 4 are sent to the shipping department.

Copy 5 is sent to the storeroom as authority for

release of the goods; it then accompanies the goods to the shipping department.

After the ordered paint has been moved from the storeroom to the shipping department, the shipping department prepares bills of lading (in three copies) and labels the cartons. Sales invoice copy 4 is inserted in a carton as a packing slip. After the trucker has picked up the shipment and its bill of lading copy, the customer's copy of the bill of lading and copy 3 (on which any undershipments are noted) are returned to the accounts receivable clerk. The company does not back order in the event of undershipments; customers are expected to reorder the merchandise. The Robinson Company's copy of the bill of lading is filed by the shipping department in numerical order, together with copy 5.

When copy 3 and the customer's copy of the bill of lading are received by the accounts receivable clerk, copies 1 and 2 are completed by numbering them and inserting quantities shipped, unit prices, extensions, discounts, and totals. The accounts receivable clerk then mails copy 1 and the original of the bill of lading to the customer. Copies 2 and 3 are stapled together.

The individual accounts receivable ledger cards are posted by the accounts receivable clerk by a bookkeeping machine procedure whereby the sales register is prepared as a carbon copy of the postings. Postings are made from copy 2, which is then filed, along with staple-attached copy 3, in numerical order. Every month the general ledger clerk summarizes the sales register for posting to the general ledger accounts.

Since the Robinson Company is short of cash, the deposit of receipts is also expedited. The receptionist turns over all mail receipts and related correspondence to the accounts receivable clerk, who examines the checks and determines that the accompanying vouchers or correspondence contains enough detail to permit posting of the accounts. The accounts receivable clerk then endorses the checks and gives them to the cashier, who prepares the daily deposit. The cashier then carries the deposit to the bank and files the duplicate deposit slip. No currency is received in the mail and no paint is sold over the counter at the factory.

The accounts receivable clerk uses the vouchers or correspondence that accompanied the checks to post the accounts receivable ledger cards. The bookkeeping machine prepares a cash receipts register as a carbon copy of the postings. Each month, the general ledger clerk summarizes the cash receipts register for posting to the general ledger accounts. The accounts receivable clerk also corresponds with customers about unauthorized deductions for discounts, freight or advertising allowances, returns, and so on, and prepares the appropriate credit memos. Disputed items of large amount are turned over to the sales manager for settlement. Each month, the accounts receivable clerk prepares a trial balance of the open accounts receivable and compares the resultant total with the general ledger control account for accounts receivable.

Required

a. Prepare a document system flowchart, using appropriate symbols. Ignore returns, and so on.

b. List the control weaknesses in Robinson's procedure and recommend improvements.
(CPA adapted)

8-14. Until recently, Consolidated Solar Products of Houston employed a batch processing system for recording the receipt of customer payments. The following narrative and the flowchart presented on page 270 describe the procedures involved in this system.

The customer's payment and the remittance advice (a punched card) are received in the treasurer's office. An accounts receivable clerk in the treasurer's office keypunches the cash receipt into the remittance advice and forwards the card to the EDP department. The cash receipt is added to a control tape listing and then filed for deposit later in the day. When the deposit slips are received from EDP later in the day (approximately 2:30 P.M. each day), the cash receipts are removed from the file and deposited with the original deposit slip. The second copy of the deposit slip and the control tape are compared for accuracy before the deposit is made and then filed together.

In the EDP department, the remittance advices received from the treasurer's office are held until 2:00 P.M. daily. At that time the customer payments are processed to update the records on magnetic tape and to prepare a deposit slip in triplicate. During the update process, data are

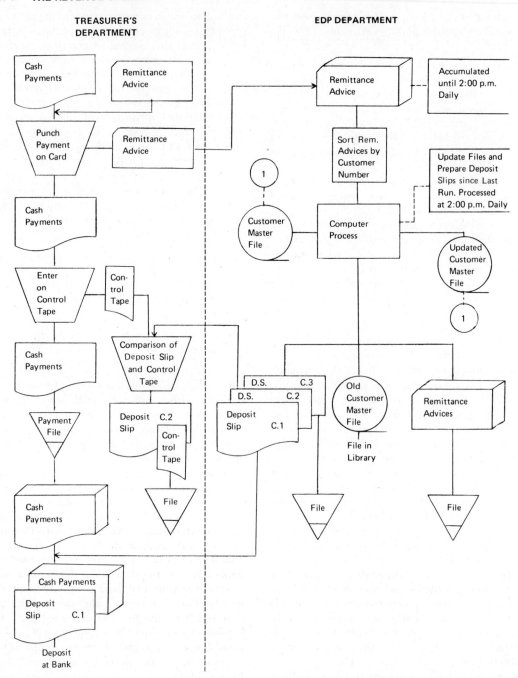

read, nondestructively, from the master accounts receivable tape, processed, and then recorded on a new master tape. The original and second copy of the deposit slip are forwarded to the treasurer's office. The old master tape (former accounts receivable file), the remittance advices (in customer number order), and the third copy of the deposit slip are stored and filed in a secure place. The updated accounts receivable master tape is maintained in the system for processing the next day.

The firm has revised and redesigned its computer system so that it has online capabilities. The new cash receipts procedures, described below, are designed to take advantage of the new system.

The customer's payment and remittance advice are received in the treasurer's office, as before. A CRT terminal is located in the treasurer's office to enter the cash receipts. An operator keys in the customer's number and payment from the remittance advice and check. The cash receipt is entered into the system once the operator has confirmed that the proper account and amount are displayed on the screen. The payment is then processed online against the accounts receivable file maintained on magnetic disk. The cash receipts are filed for deposit later in the day. The remittance advices are filed in the order they are processed; these punched cards will be kept until the next working day and then destroyed. The computer prints out a deposit slip in duplicate at 2:00 P.M. for all cash receipts since the last deposit. The deposit slips are forwarded to the treasurer's office. The cash receipts are removed from the file and deposited with the original deposit slip; the duplicate deposit slip is filed for further reference. At the close of business hours (5:00 P.M.) each day, the EDP department prepares a record of the current day's cash receipts activity on a magnetic tape. This tape is then stored in a secure place in the event of a systems malfunction; after 10 working days the tape is released for further use.

Required

Prepare a computer system flowchart of the firm's new online cash receipts procedure.

(CMA adapted)

8-15. O'Brien Corporation is a medium-sized, privately owned industrial instrument manufacturer supplying precision equipment manufacturers in the midwest. The corporation is 10 years old and operates a centralized AIS. The administrative offices are located in a downtown St. Louis building, and the production, shipping, and receiving departments are housed in a renovated warehouse a few blocks away. The shipping and receiving areas share one end of the warehouse.

O'Brien Corporation has grown rapidly. Sales have increased by 25 percent each year for the last three years, and the company is now shipping approximately $80,000 of its products each week. James Fox, O'Brien's controller, purchased and installed a computer last year to process the payroll and inventory. Fox plans to fully integrate the AIS within the next five years.

The marketing department consists of four salespersons. Upon obtaining an order, usually over the telephone, a salesperson manually prepares a prenumbered, two-part sales order. One copy of the order is filed by date and the second copy is sent to the shipping department. All sales are on credit, f.o.b. (free on board) destination. Because of the recent increase in sales, the four salespersons have not had time to check credit histories. As a result, 15 percent of credit sales are either late collections or uncollectible.

The shipping department receives the sales orders and packages the goods from the warehouse, noting any items that are out of stock. The terminal in the shipping department is used to update the perpetual inventory record of each item as it is removed from the shelf. The packages are placed near the loading dock door in alphabetic order by customer name. The sales order is signed by a shipping clerk indicating that the order is filled and ready to send. The sales order is forwarded to the billing department where a two-part sales invoice is prepared. The sales invoice is only prepared upon receipt of the sales order from the shipping department so that the customer is billed just for the items that were sent, not for back orders. Billing sends the customer's copy of the invoice back to the shipping department. The customer's copy of the invoice serves as a billing copy, and shipping inserts it into a special envelope on the package in order to save postage. The carrier of the customer's choice is then contacted to pick up the goods. In the past, goods were shipped within two working days of the receipt of the customer's order; however, shipping dates now average six working days after receipt of the order. One reason is that there are two new shipping clerks who are still undergoing training. Because the two shipping clerks have fallen behind, the two clerks in the receiving department, who are experienced, have been assisting the shipping clerks.

The receiving department is located adjacent to the shipping dock, and merchandise is received daily by many different carriers. The clerks share the computer terminal with the shipping department. The date, vendor, and number

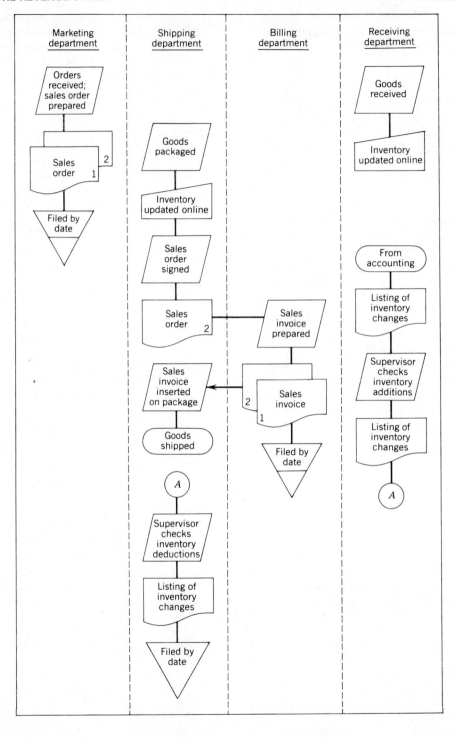

of items received are entered upon receipt in order to keep the perpetual inventory records current.

Hard copy of the changes in inventory (additions and shipments) is printed once a month. The receiving supervisor makes sure the additions are reasonable and forwards the printout to the shipping supervisor, who is responsible for checking the reasonableness of the deductions from inventory (shipments). The inventory printout is stored in the shipping department by date. A complete inventory list is only printed once a year when the physical inventory is taken.

The diagram on page 272 presents the document flows employed by O'Brien Corporation.

Required

O'Brien Corporation's marketing, shipping, billing, and receiving information system has some weaknesses. For each weakness in the system

a. Identify the weakness and describe the potential problem(s) caused by the weakness.

b. Recommend controls or changes in the system to correct the weakness.

Use the following format in preparing your answer.

Weaknesses and   *Recommendation(s) to*
Potential Problem(s)   *Correct Weaknesses*

(CMA adapted)

8-16. Bingo Hotels of Reno, Nevada, utilizes an online computer system to maintain room reservations. Operators key data concerning each reservation into online terminals. Included in each entry are the name of the person making the reservation, the code of the hotel for which the reservation is being made, the reservation dates, the expected time of arrival, and special requests (e.g., a roll-away bed). The system then updates the room master file and creates a new record for the traveler. All files are maintained on magnetic disks.

Required

Describe specific transaction controls and security measures needed to provide an adequate control framework for this system. With respect to programmed edit checks, list both the specific checks (e.g., field check) and the input data items that they are designed to check or test.

8-17. VBR Company of Lubbock, Texas, has recently installed a new computer system that has online, real-time capability. The system uses CRT terminals for data entry and inquiry. A new cash receipts and accounts receivable file maintenance system has been designed and implemented for use with this new equipment. All programs have been written and tested, and the new system is being run in parallel with the old system. After two weeks of parallel operation, no differences have been observed between the two systems other than keying errors on the old system.

Al Brand, data processing manager, is enthusiastic about the new equipment and system. He reveals that the system was designed, coded, compiled, debugged, and tested by programmers utilizing an online CRT terminal installed specifically for around-the-clock use by the programming staff; he has claimed that this access to the computer saved one-third in programming elapsed time. All files, including accounts receivable, are online at all times as the firm moves toward a full data base mode. All programs, new and old, are available at all times for recall into primary storage for scheduled operating use or for program maintenance. Program documentation and actual tests confirm that data entry edits in the new system include all conventional data error and validity checks appropriate to the system.

Inquiries have confirmed that the new system conforms precisely to the flowchart, part of which appears on page 274. A turnaround copy of the invoice is used as a remittance advice (R/A) by 99 percent of the customers; if the R/A is missing, the cashier applies the payment to a selected invoice. Sales terms are net 60 days, but payment patterns are sporadic. Statements are not mailed to customers. Late payments are commonplace and are not vigorously pursued. VBR does not have a bad-debt program, because bad-debt losses average only 0.5 percent of sales.

Before authorizing the termination of the old system, Cal Darden, controller, has requested a review of the internal control features that have been designed for the new system. Security against unauthorized access and fraudulent actions, assurance of the integrity of the files, and

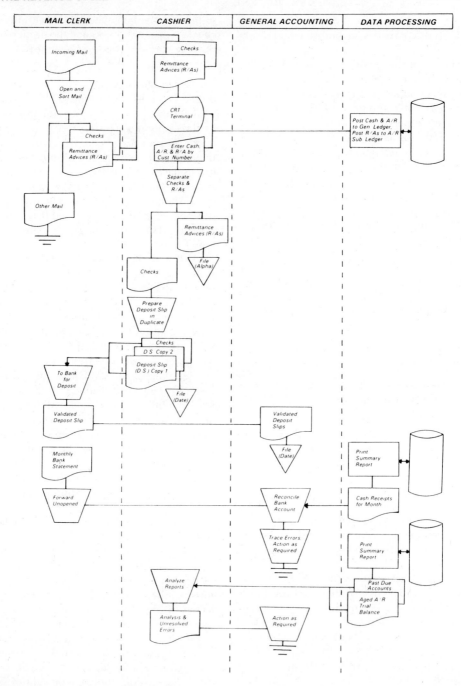

protection of the firm's assets should be provided by the internal controls.

Required

a. Describe how fraud by lapping of accounts receivable could be committed in the new

system, and discuss how it could be prevented.

b. Based on the description of VBR Company's new system and the flowchart that has been presented:

(1) Describe any other defects that exist in the system.

(2) Suggest how each identified defect could be corrected.

(CMA adapted)

8-18. Thistle Co. of Berkeley, California, manufactures and sells 10 major product lines. About 25 items, on the average, are in each product line. All sales are made on credit, and orders are received by mail or telephone. The firm's transaction processing systems are computer based, with all active files maintained on magnetic disks.

All orders received during regular working hours are entered immediately by sales order clerks via video display terminals. Orders are first edited by an edit program. A second program (a) checks for credit acceptability by reference to the accounts receivable file, and (b) checks for product availability by reference to the finished-goods inventory file. Outputs from this program for accepted orders are shipping notices and packing slips plus a sales order transaction file on magnetic disk. (If on-hand quantities are short of the ordered quantities, back-order cards are prepared. These cards are sent to the production planning department to initiate production of needed quantities.) The shipping notices and packing slips are sent to the warehouse.

After the products are shipped, with packing slips enclosed, the shipping notices are initialed (to verify shipments) and forwarded to the billing department. Billing clerks enter the data from the shipping notices via video display terminals. The shipping transaction data—consisting of the customer number, product number, and quantities shipped—are edited and stored temporarily.

At 7 P.M. that evening the shipping transaction data for the day are processed as a batch by a series of runs under the guidance of processing programs. First, batch totals are computed and printed on an exception and summary report. Next the data are sorted by customer numbers. Then the transactions are processed to update the records in the accounts receivable file. Sales invoices are generated during this update run; the originals are mailed to customers and copies are stored in an online sales invoice file. Batch totals are verified on an exception and summary report. Next, the same data are re-sorted by product number and processed sequentially to update the records in the finished-goods inventory file. A listing of products shipped and on back order is also generated during this second update run for the sales manager. Batch totals are again verified, and a copy of the exception and summary report is sent to the general ledger clerk.

Inquiries concerning the quantities of products on hand and on back order, as well as of the customers' current account balances, are frequently entered via their video display terminals by sales order clerks and accounting clerks.

At the end of each month a sales summary and analysis is prepared for the sales manager. Also, monthly statements are prepared and mailed to customers. Furthermore, an aging analysis of accounts receivable is prepared for the credit manager.

Each record in the accounts receivable master file contains the customer's account number, customer's name and address, credit rating, invoice numbers and dates and amounts of all sales, remittance numbers and dates and amounts of all payments, and account balance.

Each record in the finished-goods inventory master file contains the product number, description, reorder point, units on back order, selling price, and units on hand.

Required

Prepare a computer system flowchart consisting of the following segments:

a. The online entry and initial processing of sales orders.

b. The online entry and nightly batch processing of shipping data.

c. Online inquiries.

d. The monthly preparation of reports and statements from the master files.

Hint: The flowchart segments described as **a** and **b** may be prepared in columnar fashion akin to document flowcharts.

8-19. Value Clothing is a large Atlanta distributor of all types of clothing acquired from buyouts, overstocks and factory seconds. All sales are on account with terms of net 30 days from date of monthly statement. The number of delinquent accounts and uncollectible accounts have increased significantly during the last 12 months. Management has determined that the information generated from the present accounts receivable system is inadequate and untimely. In addition, customers frequently complain of errors in their accounts.

The current accounts receivable system has not been changed since Value Clothing started its operations. A new computer was acquired 18 months ago, but no attempt has been made to revise the accounts receivable application, because other applications were considered more important. The work schedule in the systems department has slackened slightly, enabling the staff to design a new accounts receivable system. Top management has requested that the new system satisfy the following objectives.

a. Produce current and timely reports regarding customers which would provide useful information to

   (1) Aid in controlling bad debts.

   (2) Notify the sales department of customer accounts that are delinquent (accounts which should lose charge privileges).

   (3) Notify the sales department of customers whose accounts are considered uncollectible (accounts which should be closed and written off).

b. Produce timely notices to customers regarding

   (1) Amounts owed to Value Clothing.

   (2) A change of status of their accounts (loss of charge privileges, account closed).

c. Incorporate the necessary procedures and controls to minimize the chance for errors in customers' accounts.

Input data for the system would be taken from four source documents—credit applications, sales invoices, cash payment remittances, and credit memoranda. The accounts receivable master file will be maintained on a machine-readable file by customer account number. The preliminary design of the new accounts receivable system has been completed by the systems department. A brief description of the proposed reports and other outputs generated by the system follows.

a. Accounts receivable register. A daily alphabetical listing of all customers' accounts which shows the balance as of the last statement, activity since the last statement, and account balance.

b. Customer statements. Monthly statements for each customer showing activity since the last statement and account balance; the top portion of the statement is returned with the payment and serves as the cash payment remittance.

c. Aging schedule, all customers. A monthly schedule of all customers with outstanding balances displaying the total amount owed with the total classified into age groups: 0–30 days, 30–60 days, 60–90 days, over 90 days; the schedule includes totals and percentages for each age category.

d. Aging schedule, past due customers. A schedule prepared monthly which includes only those customers whose accounts are past due (i.e., over 30 days outstanding) classified by age. The credit manager uses this schedule to decide which customers will receive delinquent notices, receive temporary suspension of charge privileges, or have their accounts closed.

e. Activity reports. Monthly reports which show

   (1) Customers who have not purchased any merchandise for 90 days.

   (2) Customers whose account balances exceed their credit limits.

   (3) Customers whose accounts are delinquent yet who have current sales on account.

f. Delinquency and write-off register. A monthly alphabetical listing of customers' accounts which are

   (1) Delinquent.

   (2) Closed.

These listings show name, account number, and balance. Related notices are prepared and sent to these customers.

g. Summary journal entries. Entries are prepared monthly to record write-offs to the accounts receivable file.

Required

a. Identify the data that should be captured and stored in the computer-based file records for each customer.

b. Review the proposed reports to be generated by the new accounts receivable system.

  (1) Discuss whether the proposed reports should be adequate to satisfy the objectives enumerated.

  (2) Recommend changes, if any, that should be made in the proposed reporting structure generated by the new accounts receivable system.

(CMA adapted)

8-20. The Sunshine Housewares Company of Evansville, Indiana, is organized on a divisional basis, with each division having profit responsibility. The kitchenwares division has three product lines: utensils, ceramic cookwares, and cutlery. Each product line has a separate markup percentage. The division's 80 salespersons sell the three product lines to department stores, hardware stores, and other retail outlets. Groups of 10 salespersons are assigned to each of eight branch offices. At the end of each day the salespersons submit to their branch offices call reports that show, for each call, the type of outlet visited, the time involved, and the result of the call. At the end of each week they submit a report of expenses based on mileage traveled, telephone calls made, and meals and lodging purchased.

Required

a. Design a salesperson's call report.

b. Design a weekly report for a branch manager that will enable him or her to evaluate the performances of all salespersons within the branch and the levels of expenses incurred. Each salesperson is assigned a weekly quota in terms of sales amounts and contributions to profits. Each branch office has an expense budget that includes office salaries, supplies, and miscellaneous expenses in addition to the expense budgets for the salespersons.

c. Design a monthly report for the general sales manager that will enable her to evaluate the performances of all branch offices, in terms of sales, contributions to profits, and expenses incurred. The general sales office incurs the same type of expenses as the branches.

d. Design for the marketing vice president a monthly report that will enable him to evaluate the performances of all major subordinate units. In addition to the sales manager for the kitchenwares division, other managers reporting to the marketing vice president are the sales manager for the patio division, the sales manager for the general housewares division, an advertising manager, and a manager of marketing planning. The vice president's office incurs the expenses noted in **b**, plus office equipment expense.

e. Design a code by which to classify costs incurred by salespersons and organizational units within the marketing function.

9

The

Expenditure

Cycle

Describe its purposes, functions, and relationships to the pertinent organizational units.

Identify its data sources, accounting entries, and forms of input.

Identify the files composing its data base.

Describe the steps and approaches employed in processing its transaction data flows.

List needed accounting transaction controls.

Describe a variety of operational and managerial reports and other outputs that may be generated.

INTRODUCTION

Every organization makes expenditures for goods and services. Goods may consist of merchandise, raw materials, parts, subassemblies, supplies, and fixed assets. Services may include those provided by outside parties, such as telephone and legal services, as well as the services provided by the organization's employees. Conceptually all these goods and services may be encompassed by the **expenditure cycle.**

Most of these goods and services also represent resources to the organization. For instance, merchandise and raw materials and supplies are materials resources, fixed assets are facilities resources, and hours worked by employees are human services resources. All such resources also fall within the resource management cycle, an activity cycle that is closely related to the expenditure cycle. Because the procedures involving goods and services vary significantly, even within the same firm, we will split their coverage into two chapters. This chapter focuses on the goods involved in the materials resource, plus outside services, whereas the next chapter examines such resources as facilities and employee services.

OVERVIEW OF THE EXPENDITURE CYCLE

Purposes

The expenditure cycle's major purpose is to facilitate the exchange of cash with suppliers for needed goods and services. Typical objectives within this broad purpose are (1) to ensure that all goods and services are ordered as needed, (2) to receive all ordered goods and verify that they are in good condition, (3) to safeguard goods until needed, (4) to determine that invoices pertaining to goods and services are valid and correct, (5) to record and classify the expenditures promptly and accurately, (6) to post obligations and cash disbursements to proper suppliers' accounts in the accounts payable ledger, (7) to ensure that all cash disbursements are related to authorized expenditures, (8) to record and classify cash disbursements promptly and accurately, and (9) to prepare all needed documents and managerial reports related to the acquired goods and services.

Functions

In the case of purchased goods (i.e., merchandise, supplies, or raw materials), the functions of the expenditure cycle consist of recognizing the need for the goods, placing the order, receiving and storing the goods, ascertaining the validity of the payment obligation, preparing the cash disbursement, maintaining the accounts payable, posting transactions to the general ledger, and preparing needed financial reports and other outputs. In the case of services, the functions of receiving and storing the goods are replaced by the function of accepting the ordered services. In the case of direct payments by cash (as is done through a petty cash fund), the function of maintaining the payables records is unnecessary. These groups of functions are pictured in Figure 9-1. Each of these functions pertaining to the purchase of goods or services is explained in the following discussions.

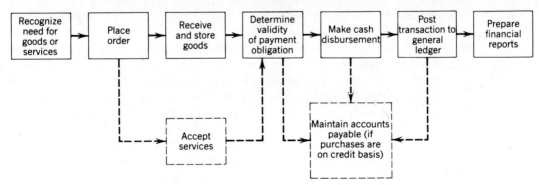

FIGURE 9-1 Typical functions of an expenditure cycle.

Recognize Need for Goods or Services The need for goods is often triggered by inventory records, which show the on-hand quantity or balance of each inventory item (whether merchandise, supply, or raw material). These records are routinely checked by an inventory clerk or a computer program. When the current balance of an item is seen to have fallen below a pre-established reorder point, the time for reordering has arrived.

Other means of recognizing needs are also employed by most firms. A back-order request from the sales procedure signals the need to place an order for a specific customer. A long-term procurement contract may specify that orders be initiated at regular intervals.

Services may be acquired on a continuing basis, as in the case of utilities; on a regular but noncontinuing basis, as with once-a-year audit service; or on an ad hoc basis, as in the case of a systems consulting service. The need for a service is generally initiated by the manager of a department, division, or other organizational unit of the firm. In some cases the need is brought to the attention of such managers by agents who represent the service, such as the salesperson of an office cleaning service.

Place Order for Goods or Services When a need is recognized, a legally binding order must be placed with a supplier. Generally the order is not placed by the person or unit that recognizes the need, although exceptions do occur. For instance, a vice president may sign an agreement with a management consultant concerning an organizational redesign project. Nevertheless, most orders for goods and services are placed through a central purchasing department.

The principal tasks in placing an order are to select the supplier (also called the vendor) and to establish the specifications, such as the expected unit price and the quality level of ordered goods. These tasks may be simple, as when the needed items are listed in the catalog of a previously approved supplier who quotes reasonable prices. Complications, however, often arise.

One complication concerns large purchases in which the needed goods are not routinely available and for which there are no established prices. Competitive bids must normally be obtained in such cases. The bidding procedure, which should be set by management policy, usually involves sending a **request for proposal (RFP)** to each of several prospective suppliers. Upon receiving the bids or proposals from those suppliers who respond, the purchasing manager evaluates them by means of a rating procedure. If one of the bids is preferable, it is accepted and the order is placed; if necessary a contract is also signed.

Receive and Store Goods or Accept Services When incoming goods arrive at the receiving dock, they are accepted only if they can be matched to order documents. Next they are unloaded, counted, inspected for damage, and checked to see that all goods conform exactly to specifications in the order. Then they are moved, in accordance with proper controls, to an inventory storeroom or warehouse. (The storeroom as well as the shipping dock should be physically and organizationally separate from the receiving dock.)

Services are accepted, often over an extended period of time. Where the quality or duration of service is a factor, a written acceptance or evaluation should be provided by the recipient.

Ascertain Validity of Payment Obligation Invoices received from suppliers (vendors) are listed in a register or log upon receipt. Each invoice is checked against documents that show that the goods or services were duly (1) ordered, and (2) received. This checking, called **vouching,** includes such steps as (1) tracing data items to the supporting documents, (2) recalculating extensions and totals, and (3) ascertaining the discount period, if any. All questionable items and adjustments are settled with the supplier. The various charges on an invoice are distributed to the proper inventory or expense accounts. Then each vouched invoice is approved for payment and filed.

Prepare the Cash Disbursement Most goods and services are acquired under credit arrangements. (Payments under cash arrangements are discussed later.) If cash discounts are allowed by the suppliers, the acquiring firm should generally pay before the end of the discount period; otherwise the cash discounts will be lost. Goods and services not subject to discounts should be paid before the due dates stated on the invoices. If goods and services are provided under contracts calling for progress payments, the conditions specifying the payment times should be carefully monitored.

Checks are prepared on the basis of approved invoices. Then they are given to the person(s) designated by management policy to sign checks. Often these persons are the cashier and/or treasurer. The signer reviews the documents that support each check, signs the check if it is a proper disbursement, and mails the check promptly.

Maintain Accounts Payable A firm must keep track of amounts owed to suppliers of goods and services. Two opposing approaches are currently in use.

In the first approach a separate record is maintained for each supplier with which the firm has a credit arrangement. The file containing these records is generally called the supplier or vendor file, although it is, in effect, the accounts payable subsidiary ledger. Each approved invoice is credited to a supplier's account, and each cash disbursement check is debited to the account. Traditionally the invoices from suppliers have been entered into a purchases journal or invoice register and have been posted directly to the ledger. A variation of this approach is to prepare a disbursement or payment voucher for one or more invoices, to enter it in a voucher register, and to post from the voucher to the ledger.

In the ledgerless approach no formal accounts payable records are maintained during the period. Instead, the unpaid invoices or vouchers are filed and paid when due. At the end of each accounting period all remaining unpaid invoices or vouchers are totaled, and the total amount is posted to the general ledger accounts. A supplier file is kept, but it only contains copies of both the paid and unpaid invoices (or vouchers).

Post Transactions to the General Ledger Summarized payables and cash disbursements transactions are posted to the general ledger. This function represents the interface between the expenditure cycle and the general ledger system or cycle, as discussed in Chapter 7.

Prepare Needed Financial Reports and Other Outputs A variety of outputs are generated as by-products of the expenditure cycle functions. Summaries of purchases and disbursements, akin to journal listings, are needed. Useful financial reports include evaluations of suppliers and summaries of open payables. If an online computer-based system is employed, displays of individual supplier accounts and other specific information are also available.

Other Related Functions Additional functions of interest include payroll disbursements, expense distribution, purchase returns and allowances, miscellaneous cash disbursements, and petty cash disbursements. Payroll disbursements (together with the distribution of employee labor expenses) are discussed in Chapter 10.

Purchase returns and allowances represent adjustments to the expenditure cycle, as Figure 9-2 shows. Needed adjustments usually are discovered when the goods are received and inspected or when the invoice is being vouched. Perhaps the supplier sends goods that were not ordered, the goods were damaged en route, or the invoice contains an overcharge. The person who discovers the needed adjustment should notify the purchasing department. A buyer or purchasing manager prepares a prenumbered debit memorandum and forwards it to the accounts payable department. There a clerk pulls the original disburse-

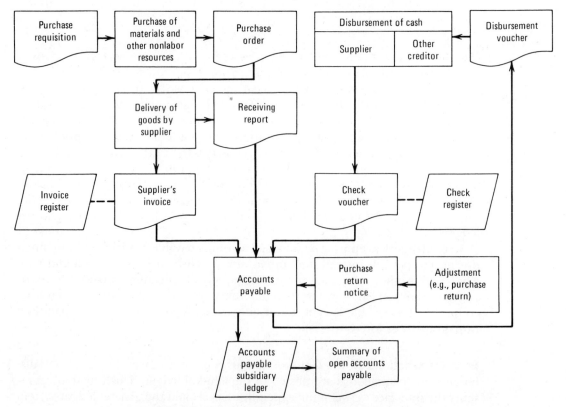

FIGURE 9-2 Relationships within the expenditure cycle.

ment voucher (if prepared), the invoice(s), and supporting documents. After comparing these documents, the clerk prepares a journal voucher to reflect the transaction. Other clerks (or the computer system) post the adjustment to the accounts payable ledger and general ledger.

In the case of a return, copies of the debit memorandum are also sent to the storeroom (or receiving department) and shipping department. The goods being returned are then released to the shipping department, which counts the goods, notes the count on the debit memorandum, and ships. The shipping department then forwards the debit memorandum to the accounts payable department, which performs the steps described.

Miscellaneous cash disbursements include amounts paid to acquire fixed assets, to acquire investments or the firm's stock, and to discharge bank loans and mortgages. These disbursements are generally recorded in the cash disbursements journal or check register. They are further discussed in Chapter 10.

Petty cash disbursements consist of payments of currency for expenses involving small amounts. In effect a petty cash disbursement is a type of miscellaneous disbursement. In order to maintain effective control over these amounts, an **imprest system** is normally used. It begins with the establishment of a petty cash fund at some level (e.g., $500). The fund remains fixed in the general ledger at the established level. However, the currency itself, which is locked in a cash box or drawer, fluctuates in amount during use. One person, who has no other responsibilities related to cash, is assigned to administer the fund. This petty cash custodian prepares in ink a petty cash voucher for each disbursement from the fund, which the payee signs before receiving currency. At all times the total amount of the paid vouchers plus the cash remaining in the box or drawer should equal the established amount of the fund. When the remaining currency reaches a low point, the accounts payable department is requested to prepare a disbursement voucher. The petty cash vouchers are attached to this voucher, together with a prepared check. The authorized check signer reviews the vouchers and signs the check. Then the custodian cashes the check and replenishes the fund. The replenishment check is listed in the check register.

Relationships to the Organization

The expenditure cycle functions are typically achieved under the direction of the logistics management and finance/accounting organizational functions (units) of the firm. Figure 9-3 illustrates these relationships.

The expenditure cycle therefore involves the interaction of the logistics information system and the accounting information system (AIS). Moreover, the results attained and information generated by the expenditure cycle further the objectives of these organizational functions.

Logistics **Logistics management** has the objectives of (1) procuring needed goods, (2) receiving and storing procured goods, (3) converting procured goods into salable products, and (4) disposing of products. In the illustrative organization shown in Figure 9-3, the top logistics manager has been assigned the responsibilities for purchasing, receiving, storing, and producing goods. The responsi-

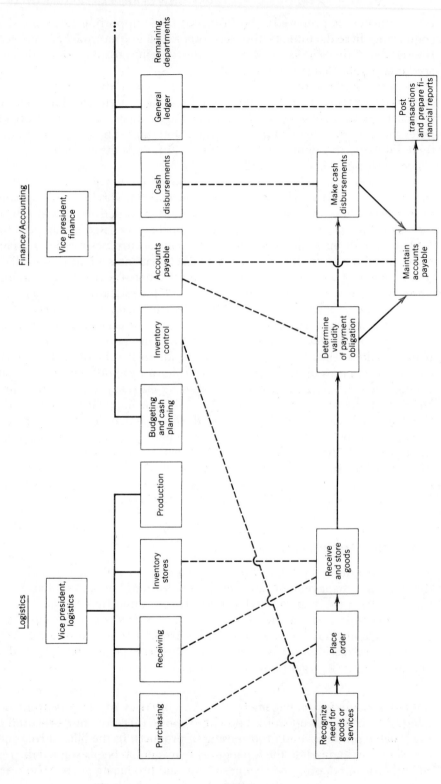

FIGURE 9-3 Relationships of organizational units to expenditure cycle functions.

bility for disposing of the goods, however, is not included. As we noted in Chapter 8, it is more often assigned to the marketing/distribution function.

Purchasing focuses primarily on selecting the most suitable suppliers or vendors from whom to order goods and services. It makes the selections on the basis of such factors as the unit prices charged for the goods or services, the quality of the goods or services offered, the terms and promised delivery dates, and the reliability of the supplier. As discussed earlier, it also uses competitive bids when necessary. Together with inventory control, purchasing also ascertains the quantity of goods to acquire. The optimal order quantity is determined by a formula that includes such factors as the expected demand for the good, the carrying cost, and the ordering cost. However, this formula is normally applied only to the high-cost or high-volume goods. Order quantities for low-cost or low-volume goods are more likely to be determined on a rough basis that seeks to avoid stockouts. In some cases a good buying opportunity or a price break determines the quantities to order.

Receiving has the responsibilities of accepting only those goods that were ordered, verifying their quantities and condition, and moving the goods to the storeroom. Storing has the responsibilities of safeguarding the goods from theft and loss and deterioration, and of assembling them promptly when proper requisitions or requests are presented. Production's responsibilities are discussed in Chapter 10.

Finance/Accounting The objectives of financial and accounting management relate broadly to funds, data, information, planning, and control over resources. With respect to the expenditure cycle, the objectives are limited to cash planning and control, to data pertaining to purchases and suppliers' accounts, to inventory control, and to information pertaining to cash and purchases and suppliers.

As described in Chapter 8, the top financial managers are often the vice president of finance, the treasurer, and the controller. The treasurer's responsibilities include cash disbursements; the controller's responsibilities include accounts payable. Cash disbursements, an arm of the cashier, prepares checks for disbursement and maintains the related records. Accounts payable maintains the records of individual suppliers and approves their invoices for payment.

DATA SOURCES AND INPUTS

Sources

Data used in the expenditure cycle are mainly based on inputs from the inventory records and from suppliers. The inventory records are the primary source of most purchase transactions, whereas supplier invoices are the source of payable/disbursement transactions. Other sources are department heads, buyers, supplier history files, receiving and stores departments, and (in the case of manufacturing firms) the production departments. If payroll disbursements are included within the expenditure cycle, such sources as the personnel and payroll records would be added.

Forms of Input

Manual Systems The expenditure cycle source documents typically found in firms that employ manual processing include the

1. **Purchase requisition.** The initiating form in the expenditure cycle is the **purchase requisition.** It provides authorization for the purchasing department to place an order for goods or services. Figure 9-4 shows a prenumbered requisition for goods. Key items of data that it conveys are the quantities and identifications of the goods to be purchased, plus the date needed, the name of the requester and department, and the approver's name or initials. Optional data include the suggested supplier (vendor), suggested unit prices, and shipping instructions. The shaded items in Figure 9-4 are filled in by the purchasing department on the confirmation copy and returned to the requester.

2. **Purchase order.** Figure 9-5 presents a prenumbered **purchase order.** It is a formal document that is signed by an authorized buyer or purchasing manager. If the supplier agrees to all stated terms and conditions on the order, it is binding upon the issuing firm. In addition to the signature area at the bottom of the form, a typical purchase order has two sections: a heading and a body. The heading contains the supplier's name and address, shipping

Purchase Requisition

Requisition Number 11359

Vendor	Requisition Date	Date Wanted*
	Ordered By	Approved By
Contact Person / Phone No.	Date Ordered	P.O. Number
Ship To	Terms	F.O.B.
	Ship Via	Shipping Date
	☐ Confirming ☐ Non Confirming	☐ Sales/Use Tax ☐ Tax Exempt

Mark for (stencil 1 each package)

Item #	Quantity	Description	Price/Unit	Account Number: Div.	Cost Ctr	Acct	Sub Acct	Extended Cost: $	¢

Requesting Department Name

Purpose or Use

MER Number

*ASAP is not a date

PC3-7635 Rev. 4/82

FIGURE 9-4 A purchase requisition. Courtesy of Arvin Industries.

Arvin

ArvinAir Division

Arvin Industries, Inc.
500 South 15th Street
Phoenix, Arizona 85034

PURCHASE ORDER

Vendor

Ship To (If Different Than Address Above)

Purchase Order No.
7653

Order Date	Vendor No.	Terms	F.O.B.		Ship Via	Sales Tax	Confirmed To

Requisitioned By   Approved By

Item	Quantity	Our Part Number	Description	Unit Price	U/M	Delivery Date

This order is not binding upon buyer
unless accepted under the terms and conditions on the reverse side. Acknowledgement copy should be executed and
returned promptly.

1. Submit all invoices in duplicate to the Accounts Payable
   Department at the above address.
2. Attach evidence of delivery or shipment, such as bills of
   lading, freight receipts or delivery receipts to original
   copy of invoice.
3. Forward packing slips in each shipment, and identify
   container with packing slip.
4. Show P.O. Number, Arvin part number and quantity on all
   packing slips.
5. Stencil P.O. Number, Arvin part number and quantity on all
   boxes and cartons.
6. Show purchase order item numbers on your invoice.

**SUBMIT ALL INVOICES TO ACCOUNTS
PAYABLE DEPARTMENT.**

Direct All Inquiries
To Buyer

Not Valid Unless
Signed By Authorized
Buyer

VENDOR ORIGINAL   R 848

FIGURE 9-5 A purchase order. Courtesy of Arvin Industries.

instructions, and reference items. The body contains one or more line items, with each line item pertaining to a single item of merchandise or material being ordered. Although unit prices for the various line items are included, cost extensions are not normally provided because the unit prices are tentative.

A purchase order is usually prepared as a multiple copy form. Copies typically are sent to the supplier, to receiving, to accounts payable, and to inventory control.

3. **Receiving report.** A prenumbered document prepared by a clerk in the receiving department is called a **receiving report** (or record, memorandum, or ticket). Figure 9-6 shows an example. This document provides proof that the listed quantities of goods have been received and indicates their condition. It is used to reflect the receipt of any goods, such as goods on consign-

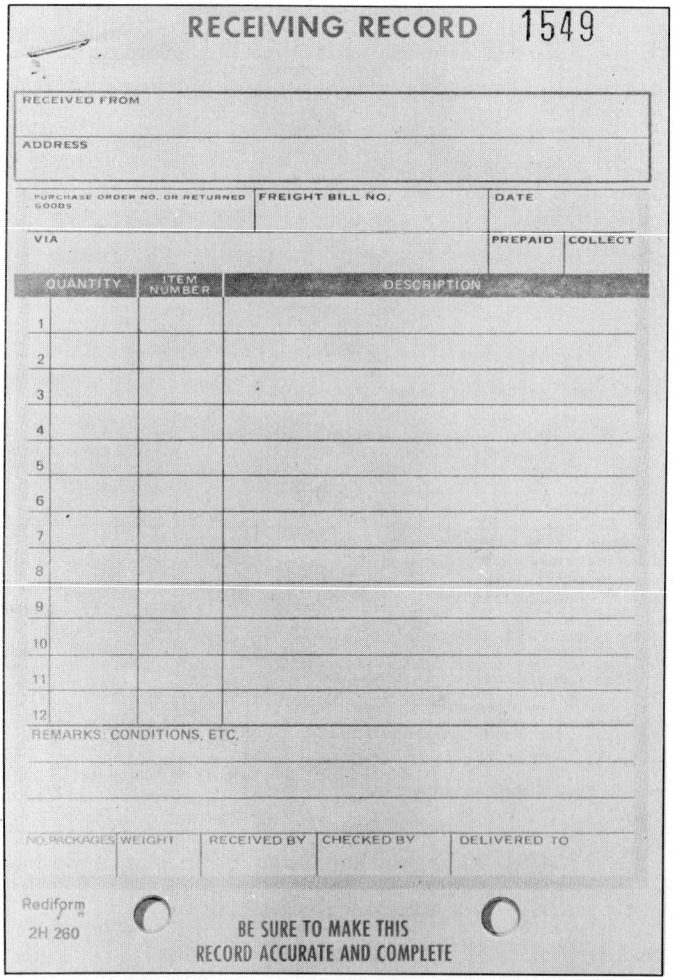
RECEIVING RECORD 1549

RECEIVED FROM

ADDRESS

PURCHASE ORDER NO. OR RETURNED GOODS | FREIGHT BILL NO. | DATE

VIA | PREPAID | COLLECT

QUANTITY	ITEM NUMBER	DESCRIPTION
1		
2		
3		
4		
5		
6		
7		
8		
9		
10		
11		
12		

REMARKS: CONDITIONS, ETC.

NO. PACKAGES	WEIGHT	RECEIVED BY	CHECKED BY	DELIVERED TO

Rediform 2H 260

BE SURE TO MAKE THIS RECORD ACCURATE AND COMPLETE

FIGURE 9-6 A receiving record or report.

ment or goods returned by a dissatisfied customer. However, most receipts of goods—and receiving reports—relate to issued purchase orders. A copy of the receiving report usually accompanies the goods to the storeroom and then is forwarded to accounts payable.

4. **Supplier's (vendor's) invoice.** To the buying firm, a **supplier's invoice** is a response to a previously issued purchase order. To the supplier, it is a sales invoice akin to the document discussed in Chapter 8. For an example, see Figure 8-10.

5. **Disbursement or payment voucher.** The **disbursement voucher** is prepared when the widely popular **voucher system** is used. As Figure 9-7 illustrates, a voucher is generated when one or more invoices are received from a supplier. It is entered in a **voucher register,** which serves as a journal. Then the voucher may be used as the medium for posting to the accounts payable ledger, if one is maintained. Totals from the voucher register are posted to the general ledger. As the columns in the voucher register indicate, miscellaneous disbursements as well as disbursements to suppliers may be encompassed within the voucher system.

   Vouchers may assume a wide variety of forms, since they must fit the needs of different types of organizations. Figure 9-8 shows a voucher (called a payment request) that is used by a book publisher. Forms that itemize claims for expenses incurred also represent a type of voucher.

   A disbursement voucher offers several advantages. It allows several invoices to be accumulated, thereby reducing the number of checks to be written. Because it is prenumbered, the voucher provides numerical control over the payables. Finally, it provides a convenient means for grouping the vouching documents (i.e., the invoices, purchase orders, and receiving reports) together into a package and reflecting the approval for payment.

6. **Check voucher.** A disbursement check is the final document in the expenditure cycle. Usually the check has an attachment, which in effect is a copy or abbreviated version of the voucher. Figure 9-9 shows a check with attached voucher. (In some systems the **check voucher** is prepared in lieu of the disbursement voucher.)

   The check is signed by an authorized signer. In some cases, as when the amounts are large, it may be countersigned. Then it is entered in a cash disbursements journal or **check register.**

7. **Other documents.** A *new supplier (vendor) form* is useful in the selection of new suppliers. It contains such data as prices or rates, types of goods or services provided, experience, credit standing, and references. A *request for proposal (or for quotation)* is a form used during a competitive bidding procedure. It lists the various goods or services needed and provides columns into which the bidding suppliers are to enter their proposed prices, terms, and so on. A *bill of lading* generally accompanies received goods. (See page 229 for details.) A **debit memorandum** is prepared when a purchase return or allowance is granted. Finally, a *journal voucher* is prepared as the basis for each posting to the general ledger. For instance, a journal voucher is prepared from the debit memorandum.

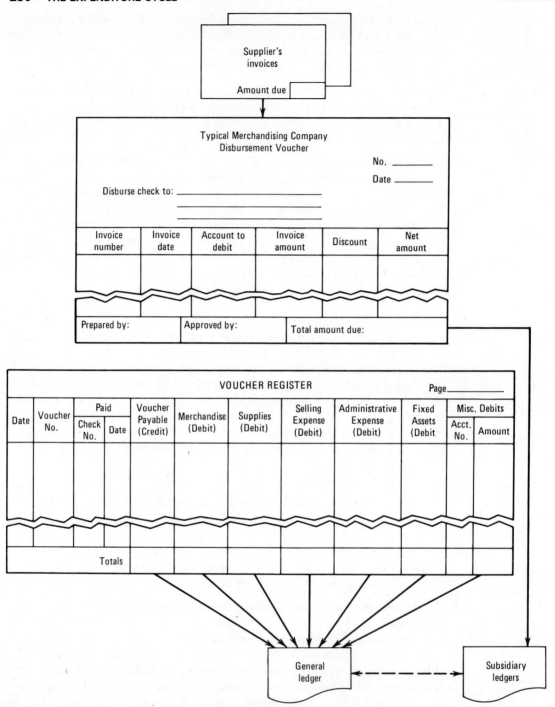

FIGURE 9-7 A disbursement voucher, together with key accounting records, used in the voucher system

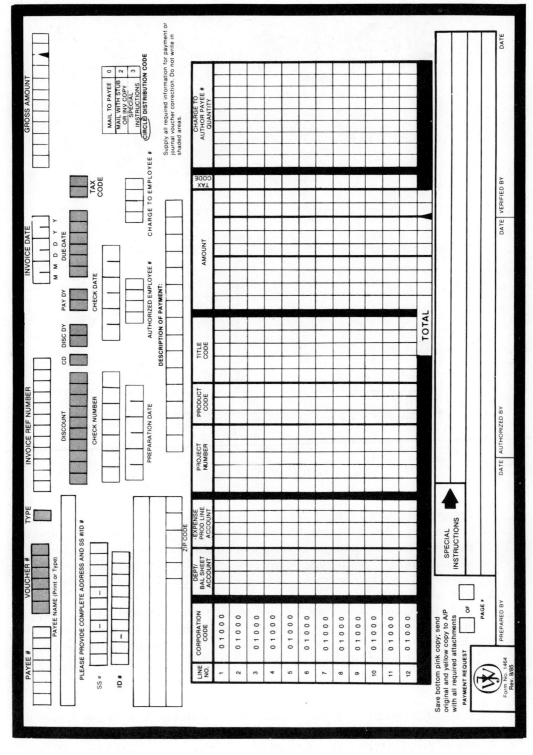

FIGURE 9-8 A voucher or payment request used in a publishing organization. Courtesy of John Wiley & Sons, Inc.

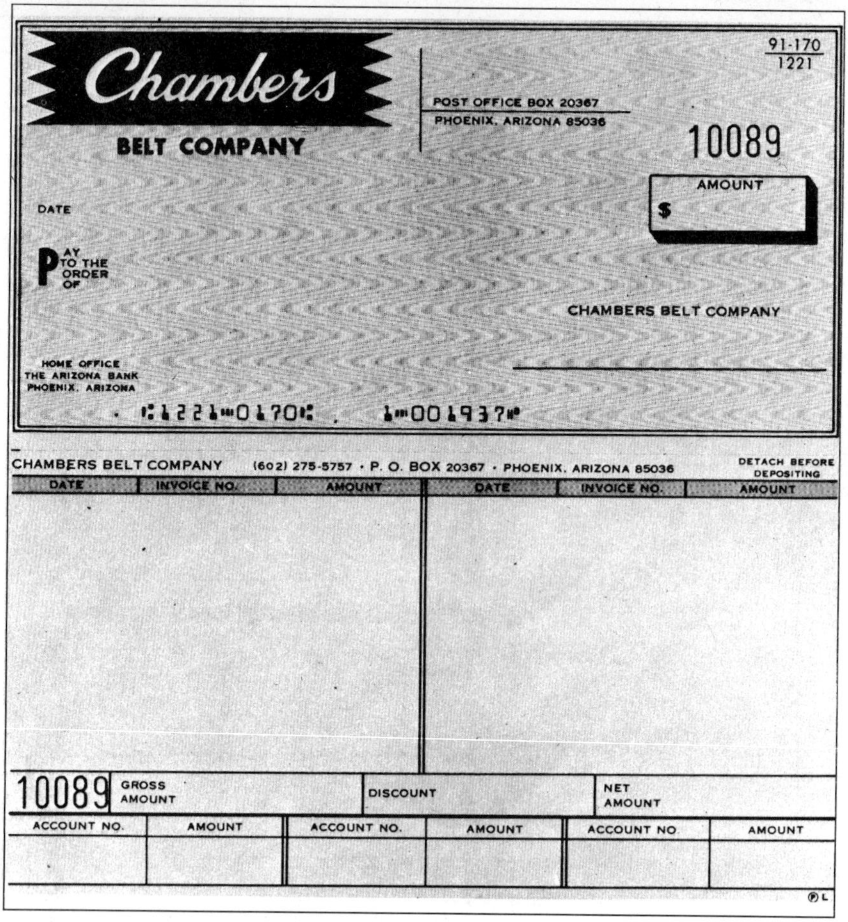

Chambers
BELT COMPANY

POST OFFICE BOX 20367
PHOENIX, ARIZONA 85036

91-170
1221

10089

AMOUNT
$

DATE

PAY TO THE ORDER OF

CHAMBERS BELT COMPANY

HOME OFFICE
THE ARIZONA BANK
PHOENIX, ARIZONA

⑆1221⑈0170⑆ ⑈0019 37⑈

CHAMBERS BELT COMPANY (602) 275-5757 · P. O. BOX 20367 · PHOENIX, ARIZONA 85036 DETACH BEFORE DEPOSITING

DATE	INVOICE NO.	AMOUNT	DATE	INVOICE NO.	AMOUNT

10089 GROSS AMOUNT	DISCOUNT	NET AMOUNT

ACCOUNT NO.	AMOUNT	ACCOUNT NO.	AMOUNT	ACCOUNT NO.	AMOUNT

FIGURE 9-9 A check with attached voucher.

Computer-based Systems All of the hard copy documents listed for manual systems may also be used in computer-based systems. In some cases, however, they may be generated automatically upon the entry of data via terminals or microcomputers. Also, some of the source documents, such as that shown in Figure 9-8, may be designed to aid the entry of data into the computer system with fewer errors.

Preformatted screens may be used to enter data concerning purchases, payables, purchase returns, and cash disbursement transactions. These screens, like simplified entry forms, may be designed to handle individual transactions or batches of transactions.

DATA BASE

The following master, transaction, history, and reference files are representative of the expenditure cycle data base for a firm that purchases merchandise for resale. Of course, the exact number and content of the files will vary from firm to firm, depending on such factors as types of suppliers and sources of services, variety of desired managerial reports, degree of computerization, and structure of the data base. For instance, a firm that employs the computer-based data base approach, discussed in Chapter 11, will use a different set of files and data structures.

Our survey of the data base is necessarily brief. A more complete description would include a data dictionary, such as the one shown in Figure 6-10, and additional record layouts.

Supplier (Vendor) Master File

The **supplier master file** is vital to the expenditure cycle, since it specifies where the checks for suppliers are to be mailed. In many firms it also serves as the accounts payable subsidiary ledger by showing the amount currently owed to each supplier. Figure 9-10 presents a layout of the data items that may usefully appear in a supplier file. Generally the primary and sorting key of the file is the supplier number.

An important concern with this file, as with the inventory master file, is keeping the records and their permanent data up to date. When a supplier obtains a new mailing address, for instance, this change must be quickly reflected in the record. When a new supplier is added to the approved supplier list, a new record should appear in the file; when a supplier is dropped, the corresponding record should be deleted also. These changes can be made during the processing of payables, or they may be made at other times as they arise.

Accounts Payable Master File

The records in the **accounts payable master file** also relate to suppliers. Two data items are essential: the supplier identification (usually the supplier account number) and the current account balance. If this file is used, the account balance data item would be removed from the supplier master file. A separate accounts payable master file is useful, since records containing fewer fields can be processed faster during file update runs.

Merchandise Inventory Master File

The merchandise inventory master file is essentially the same as the file discussed in Chapter 8. If the firm is a manufacturer, the file will be called the raw materials inventory master file. Some firms also maintain a separate file of supplies.

Supplier account number	Supplier name	Mailing address	Phone number	Credit terms	Year-to-date purchases, in total	Year-to-date payments, in total	Current account balance

Note: Although the lengths of fields and modes of data items are necessary for complete documentation, they have been omitted for the sake of simplicity.

FIGURE 9-10 A layout of a supplier (vendor) record.

Open Purchase Order File

The open purchase order file consists of copies of issued purchase orders pertaining to purchases that have not yet been approved for payment. In both manual and computer-based systems the printed copies contain such data items as are shown in Figure 9-5. In computer-based systems a record of each order is also stored on magnetic media, with the primary and sorting key usually being the purchase order number. The record layout should allow for such repeating line items as item number, quantity ordered, and expected unit price. Other items such as supplier names and item descriptions may be omitted, however, since they can be drawn from the supplier and inventory master files when preparing the vouchers and checks.

Open Voucher File

In a manual system the open voucher file consists of copies of the disbursement vouchers. (If vouchers are not prepared, the file would be replaced by an open invoice file.) Thus, the primary and sorting key is normally the voucher number. Most of the data items pertain to the supplier's invoice, although cross-references to the purchase order, requisition, and receiving report may also appear. In a computer-based system only a few key items may be stored on magnetic media, since the hard copies of the invoice and supporting documents are kept in an accessible file. A record in this file is closed when the payment is made.

Check Disbursements Transaction File

In a manual system the check disbursements transaction file consists of a copy of each current check voucher, arranged in check number order. In a computer-based system the record layout on magnetic media may contain the supplier's account number, related purchase order number(s), date of payment, and amount of payment. It also includes a code to identify the record as a cash disbursement transaction.

Other Transaction Files

In addition to the basic purchase and cash disbursement files, the expenditure cycle data base will likely include a purchase requisition file, a receiving report file, and a debit memo file.

Supplier Reference and History File

The supplier reference and history file contains summary data pertaining to each active supplier. Included are evaluations based on the relevant factors noted earlier, as well as a history of the past purchases. Data from this file are used to select suppliers with which to place orders and to analyze purchasing trends.

DATA FLOWS AND PROCESSING

Within the expenditure cycle the data flows and processing steps can be divided into three major subsets: processing of purchases transactions, establishment of accounts payable, and processing of cash disbursements. Each of these subsets can be examined through system flowcharts for manual and computer-based processing procedures.

Manual Processing Systems

Purchases Procedure Figure 9-11 presents a system flowchart of a procedure involving the purchases of goods on credit. Since the processing is performed manually, the emphasis is on the flows of source documents and outputs. Thus, this flowchart provides a good introduction to processing within the expenditure cycle. However, it is quite detailed and therefore imposing. A simpler version of purchasing steps was offered in Figure 6-16 as an illustration of the flowcharting technique. A review of that flowchart before reading the following paragraphs might be beneficial.

The first step in the procedure for purchasing goods takes place in the inventory control department. There an accounting clerk determines that goods are needed and prepares a purchase requisition. Upon approval of the requisition, perhaps by the inventory manager, copies are sent to the purchasing department and receiving department.

In the purchasing department a buyer is assigned by the purchasing manager to handle the requisition. If the goods or circumstances are nonroutine, competitive bids are obtained. If the needed goods are routine (or after bids have been evaluated), the buyer selects the most suitable supplier and prepares a purchase order. When signed by an authorized person, such as the purchasing manager, two copies of the purchase order are mailed to the supplier. Other copies are forwarded to the inventory control, receiving, and accounts payable departments. The copy sent to inventory control (which actually may be an amended copy of the requisition) is used to post ordered quantities to the inventory records. The copy for the receiving department (which has the quantities blanked out or "blind") is used later to verify the authenticity of the received goods. The copy sent to accounts payable is to provide prior notification that an invoice is soon to be received. Also, the last copy is filed in the open purchase order file to await the arrival of the invoice.

When the ordered goods arrive at the receiving dock, the blind copy of the purchase order is matched to the packing slip (and the bill of lading, if one is received). Next the receiving clerk inspects the goods for damage and counts the quantities received. Then he or she prepares a receiving report upon which the findings are recorded. The original copy of this report accompanies the goods to stores, where the storeskeeper or warehouse worker signs the copy (to acknowledge receipt) and forwards it to accounts payable. Other copies of the receiving report are sent to the purchasing department (to update the open purchase order) and to the inventory control department (to update the inventory records).

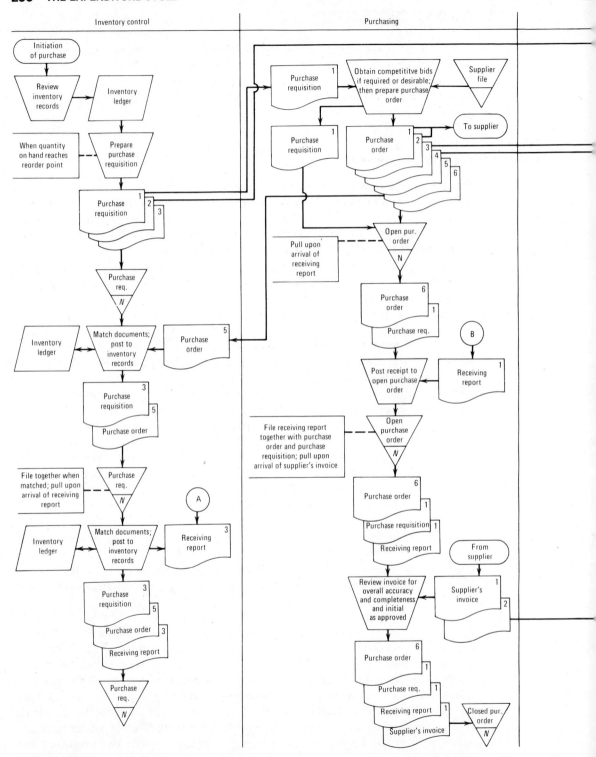

FIGURE 9-11 System flowchart of a manual purchases transaction processing procedure, with an emphasis on document flows.

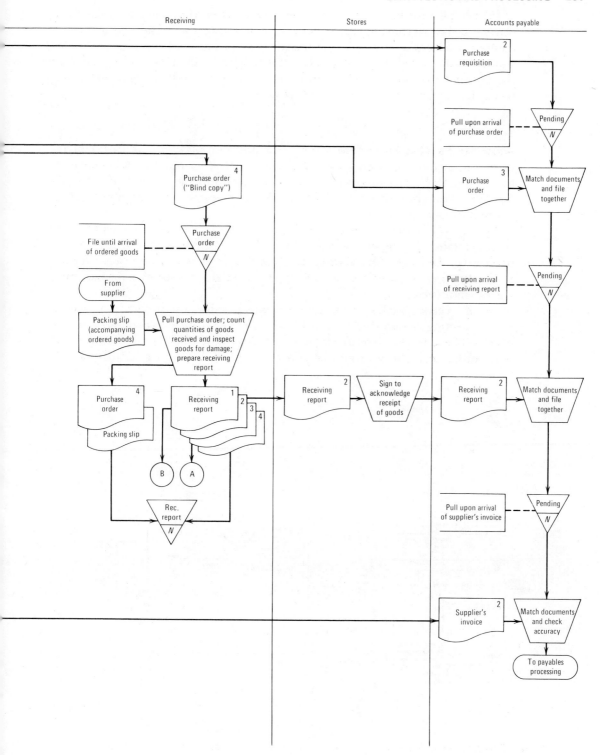

FIGURE 9-11 *(Continued).*

When the supplier's invoice arrives shortly after the ordered goods, it is routed to the purchasing department for comparisons with the relevant documents pertaining to the order. If found to be proper and complete, it is forwarded to the accounts payable department and combined with other copies of the relevant documents. (Many firms bypass the purchasing department and route the invoice directly to accounts payable.)

Accounts Payable Procedure Whether or not the purchasing department reviews the invoice, a careful vouching by the accounts payable department is highly desirable. Since accounts payable is an accounting department not directly involved in purchasing and receiving goods, its review serves as an independent verification of these activities.

Figure 9-12 illustrates the processing of invoices that leads to payables. Invoices pertaining to services as well as to purchases of goods are included in this processing. However, the former are first routed to the using departments, where they are approved for payment by the managers responsible for incurring the expenditures.

Upon receiving each invoice in the accounts payable department, a clerk pulls the supporting documents from a file and performs various comparisons and checks. These verifications are intended to determine that (1) the purchase has been authorized, (2) the goods or services listed in the invoice have been duly

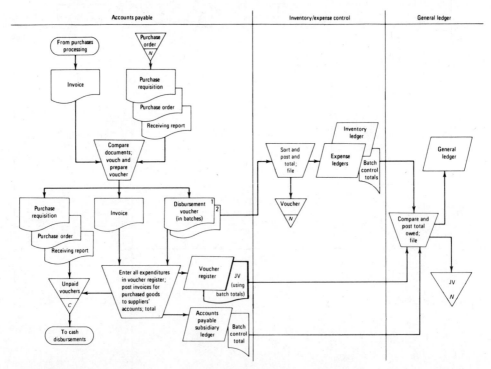

FIGURE 9-12 System flowchart of a manual payable processing procedure, with an emphasis on document flows.

ordered, (3) the goods or services have been received in full, (4) the unit prices are in conformity with the purchase order, or are satisfactory to the purchasing department, (5) the terms and other specifications are in agreement with the purchase order, and (6) all computations are correct. After finishing, the clerk initials an audit box (either stamped on the invoice or on another document such as a voucher) to acknowledge that the verifications have been performed. Any differences must be settled before the invoice can be approved for payment. For instance, if only part of the order is received, the purchase order should be so marked and returned to the file.

When the voucher system is used, as described earlier, a disbursement voucher is prepared on the basis of one or more approved suppliers' invoices. Then the voucher is entered in a voucher register. Batch control totals are computed from the columns in the voucher register, including the total amount of payables, the total merchandise cost, the total selling expense, and so on. A journal voucher is prepared from these totals.

A clerk posts the vouchers to the suppliers' accounts in the accounts payable subsidiary ledger. Batch totals are computed of the posted credits. Also, copies of the vouchers are forwarded to accounting departments that maintain the ledgers relating to the various expenditures (labeled in the flowchart as inventory/expense control). Clerks in these departments post debits to inventory, supplies, fixed assets, selling expense, and administrative expense ledgers. Batch totals are computed from the posted debits. Then the batch totals of the posted debits and credits are compared to the journal voucher previously prepared. If all amounts agree, the entry is posted to the accounts in the general ledger.

Finally, the originals of the vouchers, together with the supporting documents, are placed in a tickler file. (A **tickler file** is a file drawer in which documents awaiting processing are arranged by due dates.) There the unpaid vouchers are ready for use in cash disbursements processing.

Cash Disbursements Procedure Figure 9-13 shows a flowchart of a procedure involving the disbursements of cash related to purchases on credit. This particular procedure begins with the unpaid voucher file in the accounts payable department. Each day (or at specified periods) a clerk extracts the unpaid vouchers due to be paid that day. After computing the total amount to be paid and posting the amounts of the vouchers to the appropriate suppliers' accounts, the clerk forwards the vouchers and supporting documents to the cash disbursements department.

A cash disbursements clerk inspects each voucher for completeness and authenticity and then prepares a prenumbered check. When done, the clerk submits the checks to an authorized check signer (e.g., the cashier). This person reviews the supporting documents, signs each check that is properly supported, and routes the checks directly to the mailroom. From the mailroom the checks are delivered to the post office.

Checks are entered in a check register, and the total of the paid amounts is computed. A journal voucher is prepared based on this total and sent to the general ledger department. If the amount in the journal voucher agrees with the total debits posted to the accounts payable ledger, the entry is posted to the accounts in the general ledger.

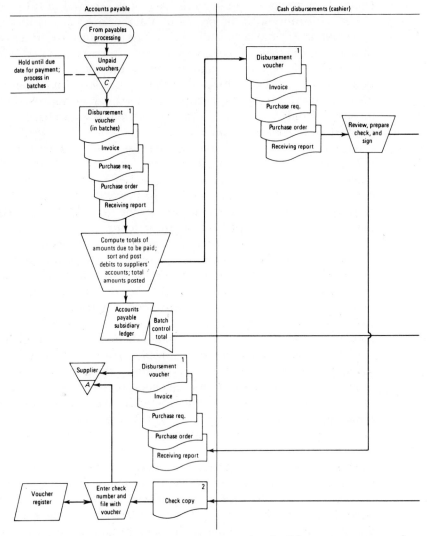

FIGURE 9-13 System flowchart of a manual cash disbursements transaction processing procedure, with an emphasis on document flows.

The cash disbursements clerk stamps all supporting documents as paid and staples them to the disbursement and check vouchers. Then these voucher packages are returned to the accounts payable department, where the number of each check and date are entered in the voucher register. Finally, the voucher packages are filed alphabetically by supplier (or in a closed payables file).

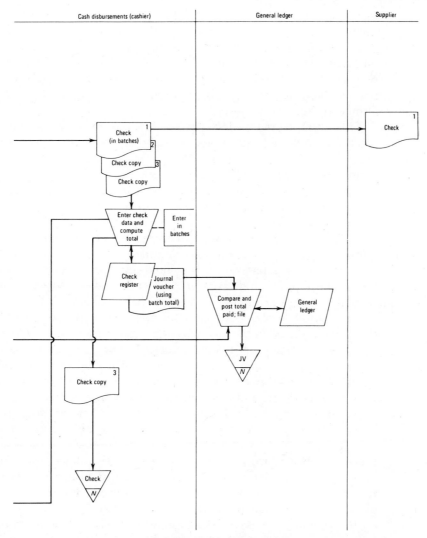

FIGURE 9-13 *(Continued).*

Computer-based Processing Systems

When computer-based systems are used, purchases and cash disbursements transactions may be processed by the batch method, by the online method, or by a combination of the batch and online methods. In our examples the online method is used for purchases, the combined method for payables, and the batch method for cash disbursements.

Purchases Procedure Several system flowcharts were presented in Chapter 6 to illustrate the flowcharting technique. Our discussion of the purchases procedure will be based on Figure 6-19, which shows the online method of processing. (You may also find Figure 6-18, which shows the contrasting batch method, useful to review.)

In the first step the inventory records are checked to find those items whose on-hand quantities have been drawn below their reorder points. This step may be performed when batches of sales transactions are being processed to update the inventory master file. If back orders are prepared and processed, they could also be an input to this step.

The output from this first step is an inventory reorder list, which is, in effect, a batch of purchase requisitions. After being approved by an inventory control manager, the list is sent to the purchasing department. Buyers are assigned the various items on the list. By making inquiries of an online supplier reference file, which contains evaluation data, the buyers select suitable suppliers and enter their relevant data (e.g., names and numbers) on the list. Then they enter the data needed to prepare purchase orders into their video display terminals. Upon being validated by an edit program (in step 2), the purchase order data are stored temporarily in a purchase transaction file.

In step 3 a purchase order is printed, using data from the transaction file as well as the supplier and inventory master files. Also, the computer system automatically assigns a number to the purchase order and dates it. A copy of the purchase order is placed in the online open purchase order file and a notation of the order is placed in the appropriate record(s) of the inventory master file. The purchasing manager, or other authorized signer, reviews the purchase order. If he or she approves and signs the order, it is mailed to the supplier. If revisions are necessary, the buyer retrieves the purchase transaction data via the terminal, makes the changes, and prints a revised purchase order.

At the end of the day a listing of the day's purchase orders is printed. Other reports, such as an inventory status report, may also be generated.

Receiving Procedure Figure 9-14 shows a system flowchart of an online receiving procedure. A clerk in the receiving department first counts and inspects the received goods. Then he or she keys the count and inventory item numbers into a departmental terminal, together with the related purchase order number listed on the packing slip. A receiving program checks the entered data against the online open purchase order file. Any differences between the ordered quantities and the counted quantities are displayed on the terminal screen. Also, if a matching purchase order number is not found in the online file, an alerting message is displayed.

Assuming that the goods are accepted, the program prints a prenumbered receiving report. A copy of this report accompanies the goods to the stores department to be signed and forwarded to the accounts payable department. The receiving program also (1) updates the inventory master file, increasing the on-hand quantity and eliminating the quantity on order, (2) notes the quantity received in the open purchase order file, and (3) notes the date of receipt in the supplier history file. If a back order is involved, the back-order record is flagged.

Inventory Maintenance Procedure Figure 9-15 presents a system flowchart that pertains to the maintenance of the inventory records. It draws together the processing activities that affect the inventory master file (namely purchase order-

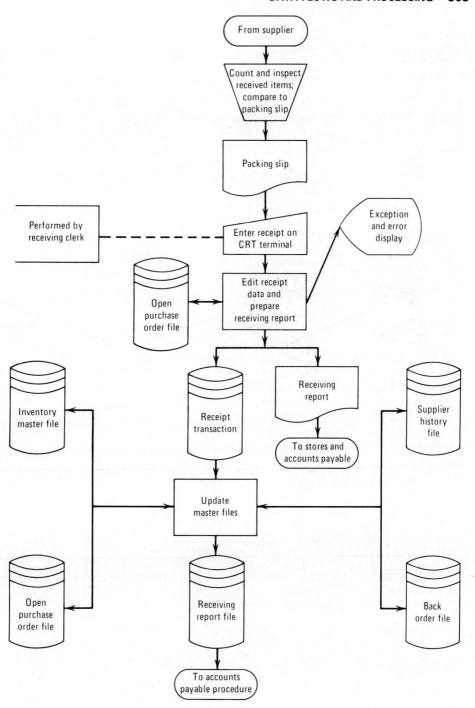

FIGURE 9-14 System flowchart of an online computer-based receiving procedure.

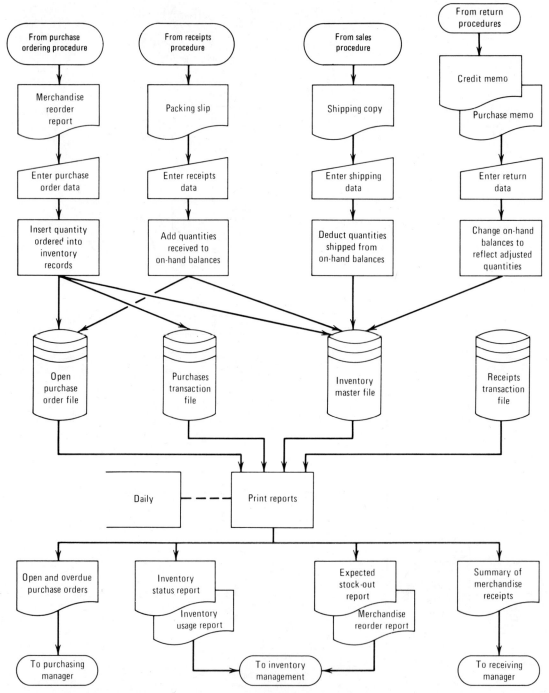

FIGURE 9-15 System flowchart of an online computer-based inventory procedure.

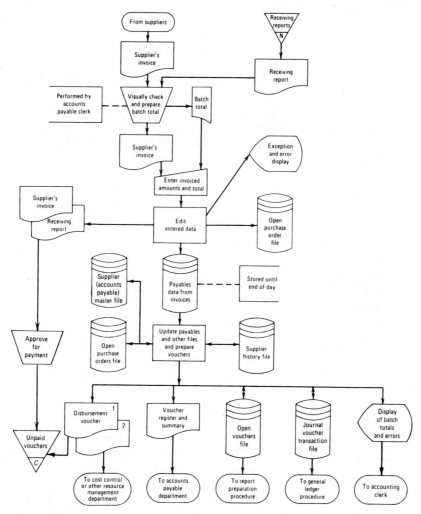

FIGURE 9-16 System flowchart of an online/batch computer-based payables procedure.

ing), receipts of ordered goods, shipping of goods to customers, and returns of goods. The flowchart also emphasizes the variety of reports that can be provided from several files that are related to inventory processing.

Payables Procedure Figure 9-16 portrays a system flowchart of a combined online/batch payables procedure. As invoices are received from suppliers, an accounts receivable clerk performs a visual check for completeness, pulls the related receiving reports, and then computes a batch control total based on the invoice amounts. He or she enters into a terminal the batch total, plus key data items from each invoice. An edit program validates the entered data, checks the quantities against those in the open purchase order file, recomputes the batch totals, and displays any differences. Then the batched transaction data are stored until a designated processing time (e.g., at the end of the day).

When the processing time arrives, an accounts payable posting program updates each record in the supplier master file (i.e., the accounts payable subsidiary ledger) which is affected by an invoice. No sorting is necessary, since the program accesses and retrieves each supplier record directly from its location in the file. Then the program adds the amount of the invoice to the balance in the account. If all the quantities pertaining to the related purchase order have been received, it also closes the purchase order and transfers its record to the supplier history file.

A variety of outputs are generated during this posting of the supplier master file. Prenumbered disbursement vouchers are printed, with one copy being filed together with the supporting documents in an unpaid vouchers file. A voucher register is printed to provide a key part of the audit trail. Summaries of the vouchers are added to the online open vouchers file. The debits from the summary vouchers are accumulated by account number; the totals are then compiled by the program into a sequentially numbered journal voucher and added to the

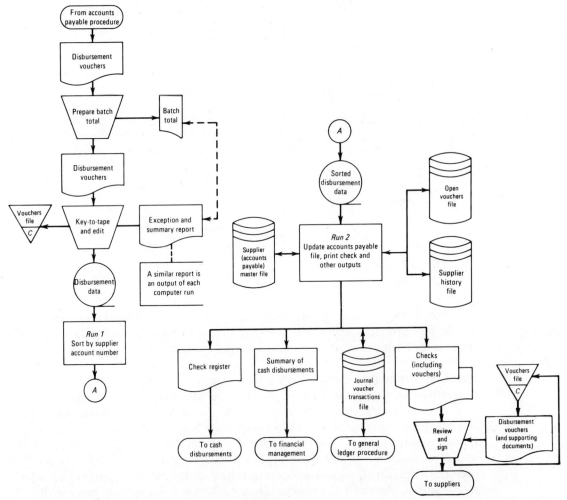

FIGURE 9-17 System flowchart of a batch computer-based cash disbursements procedure.

journal voucher transaction file (or posted immediately to the accounts in the general ledger.) A total of the invoice amounts is also computed by the program and displayed on a terminal in the accounts payable department. A clerk verifies that this total agrees with the precomputed batch total.

Cash Disbursements Procedure Figure 9-17 shows a system flowchart of a batch cash disbursements procedure. Our illustrated procedure begins with the approved disbursement vouchers that have been printed during the payables procedure and filed with the supporting documents. This procedure has been selected because it has been widely used and it provides a contrast to the online procedures already discussed. Also, it facilitates the prior computation of batch control totals and the review of documents by the check signer. However, we should recognize that the alternative online procedure offers significant benefits. For instance, it can use as transaction data the open vouchers stored in an online file, thereby omitting the need to key data from the vouchers. The vouchers in that file would be sorted by due date at the end of each day, and the vouchers due to be paid on the next payment date would be extracted.

The batch procedure shown in the flowchart can be described as follows. Each payment date the vouchers due to be paid are pulled from the unpaid vouchers file. As in all batch processing procedures, the first step is to compute one or more batch control totals. Then the data needed for preparing checks are keyed from the vouchers onto magnetic tape. The data are edited, either during the keying or during a separate edit run. Next the data are sorted by supplier account numbers. Finally, in run 2 the voucher amounts are posted to the accounts payable ledger. The program also prints the checks and a check register, as well as a summary of disbursements. It removes the paid vouchers from the open vouchers file (if one is maintained online) and adds the data concerning disbursements to the supplier history file. Finally, it accumulates the amounts disbursed and prepares a sequentially numbered journal voucher, which it adds to the journal voucher transaction file.

The person authorized to sign the checks reviews the checks and supporting documents. After signing he or she forwards the checks to the mailroom. Alternatively, the checks may be signed automatically by the program, using a signature plate, in run 2. If this is done, the checks are later reviewed to see that they pertain to authorized obligations.

ACCOUNTING CONTROLS

Risk Exposures

Among the risk exposures that exist in the processing of purchases and cash disbursements are the following.

1. Goods may be ordered that are not needed, or more goods may be ordered than are needed.

2. Goods may be received that are not ordered.

3. Goods may be ordered but not received, or received in larger or smaller quantities than ordered.

4. Buyers may favor suppliers with whom they have personal or financial interests, even though other suppliers may provide better goods or services.

5. Suppliers may inadvertently or intentionally charge higher prices or bill for larger quantities than ordered or received.

6. Goods may be damaged en route to the buying firm.

7. Suppliers may make errors in computing bills or may not provide services or the quality levels that are promised.

8. Balances in suppliers' accounts payable may be incorrect as a result of erroneous postings, omitted postings, improper debits for returns and allowances, and so on.

9. Amounts charged to purchases and expenses may be incorrect because of improperly assigned debits, erroneous postings to accounts, and so on.

10. Purchase discounts may be lost because of late payments.

11. Invoices from suppliers may be paid more than once.

12. Disbursements may be made to improper or fictitious parties, or they may be for incorrect amounts.

13. Disbursements may be made for goods or services not received.

14. Checks may be fraudulently altered and/or cashed by employees.

15. Checks may be kited. **Kiting** is a type of embezzlement that involves covering cash shortages by transferring checks among bank accounts. The transfers take place near the end of a month so that float—that is, delay—causes the checks to not be recorded until the following month.

16. Supplier records may be accessed by unauthorized persons.

17. Cash, inventory, and records may be damaged or destroyed by violence, fire, and other man-made or natural disasters.

Examples of Risk Exposures

Actual losses sustained by firms include the following.[1]

• A clerk in a department store defrauded his employer of $120,000 by issuing unauthorized vouchers that were paid to a fictitious supplier firm (in reality a friend's address).

• A partner in a brokerage house who was in charge of the computer system transferred a total of $81,000 to his account by means of adjusting entries that increased the expense accounts of the firm.

---

[1] These fraud cases are based on Brandt Allen, "The Biggest Computer Frauds: Lessons for CPAs," *The Journal of Accountancy* (May 1977), 52–63.

- A claims reviewer who was employed by an insurance company prepared false claims totaling $128,000 that were payable to friends and were automatically paid by the computer system.

- An organized crime ring, operating through an assistant branch manager, used a check kiting scheme that involved a transfer of $900,000 between accounts in two banks; the same amount was withdrawn from both accounts before discovery, since the insider had the opportunity to alter records allowing immediate withdrawal.

An adequate set of general and transaction (application) controls is necessary to counteract such risk exposures and to realize the objectives of the expenditure cycle.

General Controls

General controls that particularly concern the expenditure cycle include the following.

1. Within the organization the units that have custodial functions (the stores department or warehouse, receiving department, cashier) are separate from those units that keep the records (the accounts payable department, inventory control department, expense control departments, and data processing department). Also, the purchasing department, whose manager authorizes purchase orders and debit memoranda, is separate from all the listed units.

2. Complete and up-to-date documentation is available concerning the expenditure cycle, including copies of the documents, flowcharts, record layouts, and reports illustrated in this chapter. In addition, details pertaining to purchases and cash disbursements edit and processing programs are organized into separate books or "packages" that are directed respectively to programmers, computer operators, and system users.

3. Operating practices relating to processing schedules, reports, changes in programs, and other matters are clearly established.

4. Security is maintained (in the case of online systems) by such techniques as (a) requiring clerks to enter assigned passwords before accessing supplier and inventory files, (b) employing terminals with restricted functions for the entry of purchases and cash disbursement transactions, (c) generating audit reports (access logs) that monitor accesses of system files, and (d) dumping the supplier and inventory files onto magnetic tape backups. Security measures for manual and computer-based systems include the use of physically restricted stores areas (for protecting goods) and safes (for holding stocks of blank checks and signature plates).

Transaction Controls

Control points within the expenditure cycle include (1) the determined need for goods or services, (2) the preparation of the purchase order, (3) the receipt of

| Type of edit check | Typical transaction data being checked | | Assurance provided |
	Purchases	Cash disbursements	
1. Validity check	Supplier account numbers, inventory item numbers, transaction codes	Supplier account numbers, transaction codes	The entered numbers and codes are checked against lists of valid numbers and codes that are stored within the computer system.
2. Self-checking digit	Supplier account numbers	Supplier account numbers	Each supplier account number contains a check digit that enables errors in its entry to be detected. (See Figure 8-22 for further details.)
3. Field check	Supplier account numbers, quantities ordered, unit prices	Supplier account numbers, amounts paid	The fields in the input records that are designated to contain the data items (listed at the left) are checked to see if they contain the proper mode of characters (i.e., numeric characters). If other modes are detected, an error is indicated.
4. Limit check	Quantities ordered	Amounts paid	The entered quantities and amounts are checked against pre-established limits that represent reasonable maximums to be expected. (Separate limits are set for each product.)
5. Range check	Unit prices	None	Each entered unit price is checked to see that it is within a pre-established range (either higher or lower than an expected value).
6. Relationship check	Quantities received	Amounts paid	The quantity of goods received is compared to the quantity ordered, as shown in the open purchase orders file; if the quantities do not agree, the receipt is flagged by the edit program. When an amount of a cash payment is entered as a cash disbursement transaction, together with the number of the voucher or invoice to which the amount applies, the amount in the open vouchers (or invoices) file is retrieved and compared with the entered amount. If a difference appears, the transaction is flagged.

| Type of edit check | Typical transaction data being checked | | Assurance provided |
	Purchases	Cash disbursements	
7. Sign check	None	Supplier account balances	After the amount of a cash disbursement transaction is entered and posted to the supplier's account in the accounts payable ledger (thereby reducing the account balance of the supplier), the remaining balance is checked. If the balance is preceded by a negative sign (indicating a debit balance), the transaction is flagged.
8. Completeness check[a]	All entered data items	All entered data items	The entered transactions are checked to see that all required data items have been entered.
9. Echo check[a]	Supplier account numbers and names, inventory item numbers and descriptions	Supplier account numbers and names	After the account numbers for suppliers relating to a purchase or cash disbursements transaction (and also the product numbers in the purchase transaction) have been entered at a terminal, the edit program retrieves and "echoes back" the related supplier names (and product descriptions in the case of purchase transactions).

[a] Applicable only to online processing systems.

FIGURE 9-18 Programmed edit checks that are useful in validating transaction data entered into the expenditure cycle.

goods or services, (4) the movement of goods into storage, (5) the receipt and approval of the supplier's invoice, and (6) the disbursement of cash.

The following controls and control procedures are applicable to expenditure cycle transactions and supplier accounts.

1. Documents relating to purchases, receiving of goods, payables, and cash disbursements are prenumbered and well designed.

2. Data on purchase orders and receiving reports and invoices are validated (and key-verified if suitable) as the data are prepared and entered for processing. In the case of computer-based systems, validation is performed by means of such edit checks as listed in Figure 9-18.

3. Errors detected during data entry or processing are corrected as soon as possible by means of an established error correction procedure.

4. Multiple-copy purchase requisitions, purchase orders, disbursement vouchers, checks, and debit memoranda are issued on the basis of valid authorizations.

5. Purchasing policies are established that require competitive bidding for large and/or nonroutine purchases and that prohibit conflicts of interest, such as financial interests by buyers in current or potential suppliers.

6. Verifications are performed to ensure that all requisitioned goods and services are ordered, all ordered goods and services are received, all received goods are transferred to stores, and all goods and services are recorded as obligations and paid before due dates.

7. All open transactions, such as partial deliveries and rejected goods, are monitored, and all transactions missing one or more supporting documents are investigated.

8. Purchase returns and allowances are subject to prior approval by the purchasing manager.

9. All suppliers' invoices are matched to corresponding purchase orders and receiving reports (in the case of goods), and all data items on the invoices, including computations, are verified by an accounts payable clerk or a computer program.

10. Account balances in the accounts payable subsidiary ledger, the inventory master file, and the expense ledgers (if any) are periodically reconciled with the control accounts in the general ledger.

11. All inventories on hand are verified by physical counts at least once every year under proper supervision, reconciled with the quantities shown in the inventory records, and adjusted when necessary to reflect the actual quantities on hand.

12. Receiving and payables cutoff policies are clearly established so that inventory and accounts payable are fairly valued at the end of each accounting period.

13. Budgetary control is established over purchases, with periodic reviews of actual purchase costs and key factors such as inventory turnover rates.

14. Evidence supporting the validity of expenditures and the correctness of amounts is reviewed prior to the signing of checks.

15. Discount periods relating to payments are monitored to ensure that all purchase discounts are taken.

16. If processing is performed in batches, control totals are precomputed on amounts in received suppliers' invoices and in vouchers due for payments; these batch totals are compared with totals computed during postings to the accounts payable ledger, as well as during each processing run in the case of computer-based processing.

17. Check protectors are used to protect the amounts on checks against alteration before the checks are presented to be signed.

18. Checks over a specified amount are countersigned by a second person.

19. Balances in monthly statements from suppliers are compared with balances appearing in the suppliers' accounts.

20. Copies of all documents pertaining to purchases and cash disbursement transactions are filed by number, and the sequence of numbers in each file is periodically checked to see if gaps exist. If transactions are not supported by preprinted documents, as is often the case in online computer-based systems, numbers are assigned to the documents, and they are stored in a transaction file.

21. In the case of computer-based systems, transaction listings and account summaries are printed periodically in order to provide an adequate audit trail.

22. All bank accounts are reconciled monthly by someone who is not involved in expenditure cycle processing activities, and new bank accounts are authorized by the proper managers.

23. Employees who handle cash are required to be bonded and are subject to close supervision.

24. An imprest system is used for disbursing currency from petty cash funds, with the funds being subject to surprise counts by internal auditors or a manager.

REPORTS AND OTHER OUTPUTS

Outputs generated by the expenditure cycle include both financial and nonfinancial reports, purchases-related and cash-related reports, daily and weekly and monthly reports, and hard copy and soft copy reports. All these reports may be arbitrarily classified as operational listings and reports, inquiry screens, and managerial reports.

Operational Listings and Reports

Various registers and journals help to maintain the audit trail. The *invoice or voucher register* is a listing of invoices received from suppliers or a listing of the vouchers prepared from the invoices. The *check register* is a listing of all checks written. It may alternatively be called the cash disbursements journal. Each day's listing is accompanied by a summary of the gross amount of payables reduced, the discounts taken, and the net amount paid. A related **cash requirements report,** such as the one shown in Figure 9-19, lists the payments to be made on a particular upcoming day.

The **open purchase orders report** is based on one of the key open document files. It shows all purchases for which the related invoices have not yet been approved for payment. The open vouchers or **open payables report** is related to the open purchase orders report; it lists all approved invoices or vouchers that are currently unpaid. It may be arranged by invoice or voucher number, by

REPRESENTATIVE MERCHANDISING COMPANY 1 — Accounts Payable — Time 15:00:06 Date 4/30/86 Page 1 3948

Batch - 6 Session 1 — Cash requirements report — Expected payment date 4/30/86

Line number	Vendor name		Invoice number	Due date	Balance due	Payment amount	Discount taken	Net amount	Hold	Comments
1	Able Manufacturing Co.		000123	3/03/86	100.00	100.00	.00	100.00		
2			000789	2/28/86	600.00	600.00	.00	600.00		
3			004560	3/31/86	500.00	500.00	.00	500.00		
4			123457	4/30/86	100.50	100.50	10.00	90.50		
	Vendor A1011	Total			1,300.50	1,300.50	10.00	1,290.50		
7	Butler Supply Co.		112	4/30/86	1,567.98	1,567.98	235.20	1,332.78		
5			156710	4/15/86	400.00	400.00	.00	400.00		
	Vendor B2893	Total			1,967.98	1,967.98	235.20	1,732.78		
9	Bishop Brothers		2034	5/05/86	750.00	750.00	37.50	712.50		
	Vendor B4056	Total			750.00	750.00	37.50	712.50		
8	Sanford Stationery Store		10	4/30/86	12.00–	12.00–	.00	12.00–		
	Vendor S3123	Total			12.00–	12.00–	.00	12.00–	Debit memo	
6	Doral, Inc.		32	4/30/86	7,200.00	7,200.00	800.00	6,400.00		
	Vendor 0	Total			7,200.00	.00	800.00		Exceeds maximum check amt	
	Total debit memo amount				12.00–	12.00–	.00	12.00–		
	Total check amount				11,218.48	11,218.48	1,082.70	10,135.78		

Cash required	10,125.78
Number of checks	4
Number of debit memos	1
Summary totals check	1
Total number of checks	6

FIGURE 9-19 A cash requirements report. Courtesy of International Business Machines Corporation.

Toddlers', Inc.
Inventory Status Report
for October 1986

Item Description	Item Number	Quantity Received	Quantity Shipped	Ending Quantity on Hand
Rubbers	2861	375	205	815
Diapers	3765	2100	1280	8646
Sleepers	5617	—	120	424
Cribs	7311	72	98	338

FIGURE 9-20 An inventory status report.

inventory and expense account number, or by due date. Those invoices or vouchers that are past their due dates may be highlighted.

Other operational reports may focus on inventory and receiving activities. The **inventory status report** contains quantities received, shipped, and on-hand for the respective items of inventory. Figure 9-20 shows a brief inventory status report for a retail infant goods store. This type of report is based on sales as well as purchases transactions and reflects the balances in the inventory master file. The *receiving register or summary* lists all incoming shipments from suppliers, including those that are rejected. It also contains comments based on the inspection of received goods. The **overdue deliveries report** pinpoints those purchase transactions whose requested delivery dates have passed without shipments having arrived from suppliers.

Inquiry Screens

If the expenditure cycle data base is stored in online files, a variety of inquiries can be made interactively. Figure 9-21 presents a screen display output that is based on the open payables file. The display shows the summary of total payables due, broken down by due dates. Figure 9-22 shows a screen display of the recent invoices and corresponding vouchers for a particular vendor (supplier). Other inquiries might concern (1) the status of an individual purchase order, (2) the current on-hand balance and other details pertaining to an inventory item, (3) a summary of open purchase orders, and (4) the detail of a single cash disbursement or a batch of disbursements.

Managerial Reports

The expenditure cycle data base contains considerable information that can aid managers in making decisions. Some of these reports, such as the cash flow statement and the inventory status report, overlap with the revenue cycle. We can identify others, however, that focus on expenditures.

Purchase analyses show the levels of purchasing activity for each supplier and inventory item and buyer. Thus, they aid in evaluating performances. A more detailed evaluation of suppliers is provided by the supplier or **vendor performance record,** such as the one appearing in Figure 9-23.

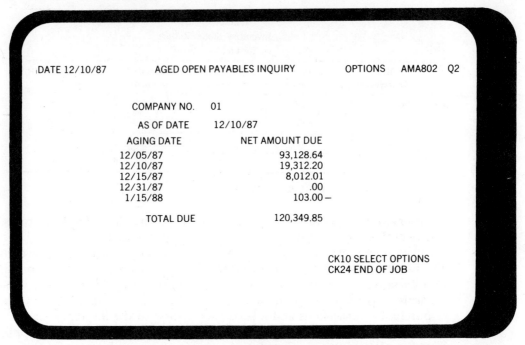

```
ıDATE 12/10/87          AGED OPEN PAYABLES INQUIRY          OPTIONS    AMA802   Q2


                  COMPANY NO.     01

                   AS OF DATE      12/10/87

                  AGING DATE            NET AMOUNT DUE
                  12/05/87                 93,128.64
                  12/10/87                 19,312.20
                  12/15/87                  8,012.01
                  12/31/87                       .00
                   1/15/88                    103.00 −

                  TOTAL DUE              120,349.85



                                           CK10 SELECT OPTIONS
                                           CK24 END OF JOB
```

FIGURE 9-21 A screen display based on an inquiry concerning the current status of total payables. Courtesy of International Business Machines Corporation.

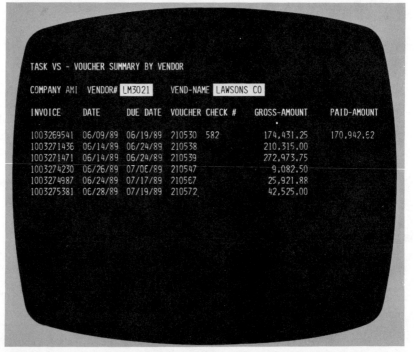

```
TASK VS - VOUCHER SUMMARY BY VENDOR

COMPANY AMI   VENDOR# LM3021    VEND-NAME LAWSONS CO

INVOICE      DATE      DUE DATE  VOUCHER CHECK #   GROSS-AMOUNT    PAID-AMOUNT

1003269541  06/09/89  06/19/89   210530   582       174,431.25     170,942.62
1003271436  06/14/89  06/24/89   210538             210,315.00
1003271471  06/14/89  06/24/89   210539             272,973.75
1003274230  06/26/89  07/06/89   210547               9,082.50
1003274987  06/24/89  07/17/89   210567              25,921.88
1003275381  06/28/89  07/19/89   210572              42,525.00
```

FIGURE 9-22 A screen display based on an inquiry concerning the recent history of an individual vendor (supplier). Courtesy of Data Design Associates.

REPRESENTATIVE MERCHANDISING COMPANY   VENDOR PERFORMANCE REPORT   REPORT DATE 06/30/89   PAGE 1

COMPANY AMI   REPORT APR62-1   RUN DATE   06/30/89

| ------ VENDOR ------ | | | ------- SHIPMENTS ------- | | | ----- AVERAGE ----- | | --- PRICE --- -- VARIANCE -- | | VENDOR RATINGS |
NUMBER	NAME		TOTAL	PCT LATE	DEFECTIVE	DAYS LATE	PCT DEFECTS	AMOUNT	PCT	
AT3022	ANDREWS CO	THIS PERIOD	60	.9	11	3.5	5.0	7,364	8.0	IMPORTANCE MEDIUM
		THIS YEAR	222							QUALITY.... AVERAGE
		LAST YEAR								SERVICE.... GOOD
LM3021	LAWSONS CO	THIS PERIOD	30	50.0		3.4		118,245-	6.0-	IMPORTANCE HIGH
		THIS YEAR	97	12.1	4	4.6	.2	113,920-	3.0-	QUALITY.... GOOD
		LAST YEAR	130	3.0	13	8.5	3.0	8,500		SERVICE.... GOOD
RM3023	RIVERTON	THIS PERIOD	11	70.0	1	4.6		6	1.0	IMPORTANCE MEDIUM
		THIS YEAR	22	41.7	2	4.2	.1	436		QUALITY.... AVERAGE
		LAST YEAR								SERVICE.... AVERAGE
TF1028	TRIANGLE	THIS PERIOD	12							IMPORTANCE HIGH
		THIS YEAR	79							QUALITY.... GOOD
		LAST YEAR	242							SERVICE.... GOOD
VI3024	VOLMER IND	THIS PERIOD	2							IMPORTANCE HIGH
		THIS YEAR	12	5.0		.5	1.0			QUALITY.... GOOD
		LAST YEAR								SERVICE.... EXCELLENT

FIGURE 9-23   A supplier (vendor) performance evaluation report. Courtesy of Data Design Associates.

SUMMARY

The expenditure cycle facilitates the exchange of cash with suppliers for needed goods and services. Functions of the cycle (in the case of goods) are to recognize the need, place the order, receive and store the goods, ascertain the validity of the payment obligation, prepare the cash disbursement, maintain the accounts payable, post transactions to the general ledger, and prepare needed financial reports and other outputs. Related functions include purchase returns and allowances and petty cash disbursements. These functions are achieved under the direction of the

Element	Purchases	Accounts Payable Component	Cash Disbursements
Source documents	Purchase requisition Purchase order Receiving report	Supplier's invoice Disbursement voucher	Check voucher
Processing steps	Determine needs and requisition merchandise Prepare purchase order and mail to supplier Receive merchandise Transfer merchandise to storeroom	Receive and vouch supplier's invoice Prepare disbursement voucher Enter transaction in purchases journal Post obligation to accounts payable ledger Transmit for posting to general ledger	Prepare check voucher Enter transaction in check register Mail check Post payment to accounts payable ledger Transmit for posting to general ledger
Files	Supplier file Inventory file Purchase requisition file Purchase order file Receiving report file	Accounts payable (A/P) ledger General ledger Disbursement voucher file	Supplier (A/P) ledger General ledger Check file
Outputs	Open purchase order report Purchase analysis by product, supplier, etc.	Accounts payable aging summary Open and unpaid suppliers' invoices report	Cash disbursement summary Cash requirements statement
Selective transaction controls	Approval of purchase order Prenumbered purchase requisitions, orders, etc. Verification of received merchandise	Prenumbered disbursement vouchers Verification of billed prices, quantities, terms, accuracy Authorization of payment Batch totals of invoice amounts Reconciliation of A/P control account with A/P ledger	Prenumbered checks Signing of checks by authorized managers Reconciliation of cash balance with bank statement

FIGURE 9-24 Analysis worksheet for expenditure cycle. Based on a technique described by Dan C. Kneer in "System Procedures and Controls," *Journal of Systems Management*, Sept. 1983, 28–32.

logistics management and finance/accounting organizational units.

Most of the data used in the cycle arise from suppliers and inventory records. Documents typically employed are the purchase requisition, purchase order, receiving report, supplier's (vendor's) invoice, disbursement voucher, and check voucher. Preformatted screens may be used in online systems to enter purchases and cash disbursements data. The data base includes such files as the supplier (vendor) master, accounts payable master, merchandise inventory master, open purchase order, open voucher, cash disbursements transaction, and supplier reference and history files. Data processing consists of processing purchases transactions, maintaining accounts payable records, and processing cash disbursements transactions. Processing may feasibly be performed by manual systems, batch computer-based systems, and online computer-based systems.

A variety of exposures exist in the processing of purchases and cash disbursements transactions. Risks resulting from these exposures can be counteracted by means of adequate general and transaction controls.

Among the outputs generated by the expenditure cycle are the voucher register, check register, cash requirements report, open purchase orders report, open vouchers or payables report, inventory status report, receiving summary, overdue deliveries report, supplier inquiry screens, inventory item inquiry screens, purchase analyses, supplier performance report, and cash flow statement. Figure 9-24 summarizes many of these system components.

REFERENCES

Accounts Payable and Purchase Control System. Sunnyvale, Calif.: Data Design Associates, 1982.

A Guide for Studying and Evaluating Internal Accounting Controls. Chicago: Arthur Andersen & Co., 1978.

MSA Inventory and Purchasing System. Atlanta, Ga.: Management Science America, Inc., 1983.

Nash, John F., and Roberts, Martin B. *Accounting Information Systems,* New York: Macmillan, 1984.

Robinson, Leonard A.; Davis, James R.; and Alderman, C. Wayne. *Accounting Information Systems: A Cycle Approach,* 2d ed. New York: Harper & Row, 1986.

QUESTIONS

1. What is the meaning of each of the following terms?

Expenditure cycle
Request for proposal (RFP)
Vouching
Imprest system
Logistics management
Purchase requisition
Purchase order
Receiving report
Supplier's invoice
Disbursement voucher
Voucher system
Voucher register
Check voucher
Check register
Debit memorandum
Supplier master file
Accounts payable master file
Tickler file
Kiting
Cash requirements report
Open purchase orders report
Open payables report
Inventory status report
Overdue deliveries report
Purchase analysis
Vendor performance record

2. What are several subpurposes or objectives of the expenditure cycle?

3. What are the major functions of the expenditure cycle?

4. In what ways may the need for goods or services be established?

5. Describe the competitive bidding procedure.

6. How is the validity of a supplier's invoice established?

7. Describe the procedure for handling purchase returns.

8. Describe the imprest basis for handling petty cash disbursements.

9. Describe the relationships of the logistics management organizational function to the expenditure cycle.

10. Describe the relationships of the finance and accounting organizational functions to the expenditure cycle.

11. What are the sources of data used in the expenditure cycle?

12. Identify the various documents used in the expenditure cycle.

13. Identify the accounting entries needed to reflect the transactions within the expenditure cycle.

14. Identify the various files used in the expenditure cycle.

15. Describe the purchases of goods and services when processing is performed manually.

16. Describe the payables procedure when processing is performed manually and accounts payable are maintained.

17. Describe the cash disbursements procedure when processing is performed manually and payments are made by check.

18. Describe the expenditure cycle procedure when processing is performed by a computer-based system involving a mixture of the online and batch methods.

19. What are the risk exposures that exist in the processing within the expenditure cycle.

20. Identify various general and transaction controls that concern the expenditure cycle.

21. Identify various reports and other outputs that may be generated from information provided by the expenditure cycle.

22. In what ways does the expenditure cycle procedure differ when performed by computer-based systems using (a) the batch method, and (b) the online method?

23. What are sources of information for logistics managers, other than from expenditure cycle processing?

24. Describe several programmed edit checks, such as the redundancy matching check, that can be applied by the posting programs used in processing payables and cash disbursements transactions.

25. In what ways is the purchases activity related to the inventory management activity?

26. What are the ethical considerations that a purchasing department buyer faces?

27. How does information developed during the expenditure cycle aid the preparation of the cash forecast?

28. How do logistics activities in merchandising firms differ from logistics activities in manufacturing firms?

REVIEW PROBLEM

Hartshorn Manufacturing Company

Statement

The Hartshorn Manufacturing Company of Wichita, Kansas, recently engaged a public accountant to review its various transaction processing procedures. During her review of the expenditure transaction cycle, the public accountant made the following notes.

A production supervisor initiates a purchase by calling the purchasing department on the phone and stating his or her request. A buyer then prepares a letter concerning the requested materials, mails the letter to a supplier, and files his or her copy in the supplier's file folder. As the materials arrive, they are laid in any convenient area until the storeskeeper has an opportunity to store them in their bins or until the production supervisor carts them direct to the production line. When the supplier's invoice reaches the accounting department, an accounting clerk enters the invoice in the purchase journal. Near the end of each month the clerk prepares an unnumbered check for the amount of the invoice, has the treasurer sign the check, and mails the check to the supplier. Then the same clerk enters the amount of the check in the check register, posts the amount to the subsidiary ledger account sheet for the supplier, and files the check copy by supplier's name. Just before the trial balance is prepared, the same clerk totals the various special journals and posts the totals to the general ledger. When the work load is too heavy for this single clerk to perform, another clerk is assigned to handle those invoices from suppliers whose names begin with letters in the range from N to Z. No one at any time counts the materials on hand, compares documents involved in a particular transaction, or reconciles accounting ledgers. When asked why such checks are not made, the accounting clerk replies that there is not enough time in a day and that the more urgent tasks have to be done.

Required

Analyze weaknesses in the accounting controls and suggest improvements.

Solution

Control Weakness	Suggested Improvements
1. Verbal request for materials made by production supervisor.	**1.** Prepare a written request on a purchase requisition form; send the requisition to the purchasing department, with a copy to the accounts payable department; assign the preparation of the purchase requisition to the storeskeeper or to an inventory control clerk, who likely would have a better knowledge of inventory needs than the supervisor.
2. Letter prepared by buyer, with copy filed in supplier's folder.	**2.** Prepare a formal prenumbered purchase order, which is to be signed by the purchasing manager and sent to the supplier; send copies of the purchase order to a newly organized receiving department and to the accounting department as prior notification; also send a copy to the person who requested the order as verification and file a copy by number in the purchasing department. (*Note:* The copy to the receiving department should be blind. Also, consider requesting bids from suppliers before deciding on the supplier with whom to place the order.)
3. Arriving materials accepted without use of formal receiving procedures.	**3.** Require arriving materials to be formally accepted by a receiving department, organizationally separate from the stores department, which should perform the following steps. **a.** Verify that the materials were ordered by referring to its copy of the purchase order. **b.** Count the materials and note their condition. **c.** Prepare and sign a prenumbered receiving report, listing the quantities counted and the condition of the materials. **d.** Forward the materials with a copy of the receiving report to the storeskeeper, who should count the materials, sign the receiving report to acknowledge receipt, and then send the receiving report to the accounting department. **e.** Send other copies of the receiving report to (1) an inventory control clerk for entry in inventory records, and (2) the purchasing department for verification; also file a copy by number.
4. Materials laid in any convenient area accessible to the production supervisor.	**4.** Store materials promptly as received in a stores area that is physically restricted to authorized stores personnel; issue materials to the production supervisor on a prenumbered materials issue slip, which he or she should sign to acknowledge receipt.
5. Supplier's invoice adequately verified and approved for payment.	**5.** Perform the following steps. **a.** Compare quantities shown to quantities listed on the receiving report. **b.** Compare unit prices shown to acceptable prices listed on the purchase order. **c.** Check the accuracy of the extensions and the totals. **d.** Initial and date the invoice, in a box stamped on its face, to indicate the completion of these actions. **e.** Prepare a disbursement voucher, attach supporting documents, and file by due date.

Control Weakness	Suggested Improvements
6. Cash disbursement not adequately controlled.	**6.** Prepare a prenumbered check and protect the amount; then forward the check to the treasurer, who should review the supporting documents, sign the check, and mail direct from his or her office (instead of returning to the accounting clerk for mailing); stamp "Paid" on all supporting documents and file by check number.
7. Inadequate separation of responsibilities in the accounting department.	**7.** Assign the responsibility for posting to the general ledger to another clerk in the accounting department so that the work of the accounting clerk will be independently verified.
8. Tardy posting and lack of reconciliations.	**8.** Post daily from the journals to the general ledger and check the accuracy of posting by means of batch control totals; reconcile the accounts payable control account with the subsidiary ledger accounts on a frequent basis; count the materials on hand once or twice a year, and reconcile with the perpetual inventory records maintained by an inventory control clerk.
9. Inappropriate assignment of duties during peak periods.	**9.** Assign a second clerk to particular tasks, such as making entries in the check register, filing copies of checks prepared for all suppliers, and totaling special journals. *Note:* This allocation of tasks is preferable to the assignment of a block of suppliers' invoices to the second clerk, since it enables one clerk to verify the work of the other.

PROBLEMS

9-1. North Enterprises, Inc., has been experiencing increased difficulties in the accounts payable area. Numerous payments have been late, causing the loss of a significant amount in purchase discounts. A small minority of suppliers have been overcharging, either by raising their unit prices or by shipping larger quantities than appear on the purchase orders. In some cases it has been found that the same invoices have been paid two or three times. More errors than seem reasonable have appeared in the suppliers' accounts payable accounts. Many checks have been prepared for signing each day. In fact, often three or more checks are prepared for the same supplier during a day. These difficulties have led the accounts payable manager to press for a new computer-based system that will process accounts payable.

Required

a. List the types of transactions that affect the accounts payable balances.

b. Describe several reports that can aid the manager in accessing the extent of the difficulties and the success in overcoming them.

c. Describe one or more ways of correcting each of the difficulties raised, other than by installing a new computer system.

d. Assuming that a computer-based system is approved for installation, weigh the relative advantages between (1) a system that uses the batch processing method, (2) a system that uses the online processing method, and (3) a system that uses online data entry but batch processing.

9-2. The city of Rockrib is a southern city of 100,000 people. It has a centralized purchasing department, a receiving department, an accounts payable department, and a cashier's office, among other departments. Routine, widely used supplies are ordered on the basis of reorder reports, which are prepared daily by an inventory search program within the city's computer system. Nonroutine supplies and services are ordered upon request by the various operating departments, such as the water department. Most of these nonroutine supplies and services are obtained after competitive bidding. Unacceptable receipts of supplies are returned to suppliers, with requests for refunds. Invoices from suppliers are approved via a voucher system. Checks are prepared on the computer system and mailed to suppliers within the discount periods. Balances owed and paid to suppliers are maintained in records on magnetic media.

Required

a. List the data items needed to record and process purchases on credit, purchase returns, and cash disbursements transactions.

b. List the files needed to store the listed data items.

c. Describe reports that would be useful to city managers in analyzing the purchases and cash disbursements transactions and the activities related to the suppliers' accounts.

9-3. Two recent graduates of Midwest University have decided to start their own firm, which will sell microcomputer supplies at discount prices. Since one is a graduate in general business, he undertakes the task of designing needed forms. He begins with the purchase requisition and purchase order forms. Since he believes the forms should be as simple as possible, he limits the data on each form. Each form begins with the name of the document. Then on the purchase requisition the heading contains space for the "Supplier Name and Address," the body contains columns headed "Description" and "Dollar Amount," and the bottom of the dollar amount column is labeled "Total." On the purchase order the heading contains the firm's address, "Supplier Name and Address," "Shipping Address," "Discount Terms," "Ship Via," and "Freight Terms"; the body contains columns headed "Description" and "Dollar Amount"; and the bottom contains "Purchase Conditions."

Required

Specify data items that should be added to and deleted from each designed form, and the reasons for their addition or deletion. Indicate the number of copies each form should have, the disposition of each copy, and any differences that should appear between copies of the same form.

9-4. Wooster Company is a beauty/barber supplies and equipment distributorship servicing a five-state area. Management has generally been pleased with the firm's operations to date. However, the present purchasing system has evolved through use rather than formal design. It may be described as follows: Whenever the quantity of an item is low, the inventory supervisor phones the purchasing department and provides the description and quantity of each item to be ordered. The purchasing department then prepares a purchase order in duplicate. The original is sent to the supplier, and a copy is filed in the purchasing department numerically. When the ordered items arrive, an inventory clerk (under the supervisor) checks off each item on the packing slip that accompanies the shipment. The packing slip is then forwarded to the accounts payable department. When the invoice arrives from the supplier, the packing slip is compared with the invoice by an accounts payable clerk. After any differences between the two documents have been reconciled, a check is drawn for the appropriate amount and is mailed to the supplier together with a copy of the invoice. The packing slip is attached to the invoice and is filed alphabetically in the paid invoice file.

Required

a. Identify all documents that are needed to fulfill the requirements of an adequate expenditure cycle, and the number of copies each form should have.

b. List each copy of the identified documents and trace its route through the various departments involved in the expenditure cycle, including its final disposition. Add new departments if they are desirable.

(CMA adapted)

9-5. Mason Pharmaceuticals is a large manufacturer of drugs and other medical products. It receives numerous deliveries of raw materials and supplies at its central receiving dock. As each delivery arrives, a receiving clerk checks, via the receiving department's online terminal, to ascertain that a related purchase order is on file. Then the clerk counts and inspects the received goods and lists the received items (and their condition) on a receiving form. Next the clerk transfers this receiving data to the computer system via the terminal. In doing so the clerk is aided by a preformatted receiving form that appears on the screen of the terminal. If the entered data corresponds to the ordered data in the open purchase orders file, the transaction is accepted. This entry updates the inventory master file, makes a notation in the open purchase orders file, and creates a prenumbered formal receiving report.

Required

a. Draw a preformatted screen format that shows all the data items to be entered by the receiving clerk which will aid him or her in the data entry process. Also, include in the screen format those items that would be automatically entered by the computer program, either to identify the transaction or to aid in reducing input errors. Denote these system-generated items by a star (*).

b. Identify the programmed edit checks that should be incorporated into the data entry program, plus all security measures that should pertain to the use and protection of this receiving department terminal. Specify the data items that each identified programmed edit check is designed to check or test.

9-6. The Arrington Wholesaling Co. of Little Rock, Arkansas, services a number of retailers with several thousand grocery and sundry items. In turn it acquires merchandise from a wide range of suppliers across the country. Although it uses a computer-based system for billing, purchasing, and payroll processing, it has just recently turned to the application of cash disbursements.

Mary Brenner, a systems analyst, has been assigned the task of developing the processing procedure for cash disbursements. She begins by ascertaining the desired outputs from the procedure, as well as the file record layout and input document format. They are as follows.

Outputs

a. A check, which contains the check number, date, payee, accounts debited, invoice numbers, gross amount, discount, and net amount.

b. A cash disbursements journal, which contains the date, check numbers, supplier numbers, supplier names, debits to accounts payable, credits to cash, and purchase discounts.

Master File

Accounts payable, which contains in each record the supplier number, supplier name and address, invoice numbers, voucher number, date payment due, invoice amounts, discount, and account balance.[2]

Input

A disbursement voucher, which contains the voucher number, date, supplier number and name, account to be debited, invoice numbers and dates, invoice accounts, discounts, and net amounts.

Required

a. Indicate the source (i.e., the input document or master file) from which each item in the outputs is derived. If the item is produced by the computer system, state "System-generated."

b. Prepare a computer system flowchart to reflect the batch processing of cash disbursements. Assume that the master file is stored on a removable magnetic disk pack.

c. Draw the outputs and the input, with all the data items being included within suitable formats.

d. List the accounting transaction controls that are suitable to a computer-based system which processes cash disbursements by the batch method.

9-7. Regal Supply, Ltd., of Windsor, Ontario, maintains the following records pertaining to its

---

[2] This record layout reflects the assumption that only one voucher is unpaid at any time.

vendors (suppliers) and outstanding (unpaid) accounts payable transactions. The general ledger account number refers to the type of expense incurred through the vendor: for example, purchases of new merchandise, purchases of used merchandise, or purchases of supplies, utility service, insurance service, and custodial service.

Accounts Payable Transaction Record

Data Item	Field Size
Vendor number	7
General ledger account number	4
Invoice number	7
Voucher number	7
Invoice date	6
Due data	6
Invoice amount	10
Discount	5
Net amounts	10

Vendor Master Record

Data Item	Field Size
Vendor number	7
Vendor name	21
Street number	6
Street name	15
City	15
Province/state	15
Country	6
Postal/ZIP Code	9

Required

a. Draw record layouts for both records. Include the modes of data items.

b. Design a report listing the outstanding payables according to account numbers. Reported data concerning each payable should include the vendor name, city, province/state, invoice number, due date, and net amount due.

c. Key each item in the report to a field in one of the record layouts drawn in **a**. For instance, enter a circled A under the account number column in the report, and also a circled A under the general ledger account number field in the transaction record.

d. Describe, with the aid of a system flowchart, the preparation of the report. Assume that

the transaction records are on magnetic tape and the master records on magnetic disk.

(SMAC adapted)

9-8. Bargains, Inc., a retail firm of Evansville, Indiana, purchases merchandise for resale. A wide variety of merchandise items are acquired from about 200 suppliers. The firm employs an online processing system, with terminals located in the purchasing and receiving departments (among others) to handle its purchases procedure.

Purchase orders are prepared by buyers, who select suitable suppliers from whom to order needed merchandise specified on purchase requisition sheets received from the inventory control department. (To aid the selection process, they make online inquiries via their terminals and obtain displays of suppliers' records on their CRT screens.) A buyer next enters the necessary data into his or her terminal relating to each purchase, including the transaction code, the number of the selected supplier, the numbers of the merchandise items being ordered and corresponding order quantities and expected unit prices, the expected data of arrival of the merchandise, the terms, the method of shipment, shipper, the code of the warehouse to which the merchandise is to be shipped, and the buyer's number. The computer system then generates a printed purchase order, which contains this data plus a computer-assigned order number, the order date, the supplier name and address, the merchandise descriptions, the units of measure, the shipping address, and so on. (The computer system also posts the number of the purchase order and ordered quantities, plus the expected date of arrival, to all pertinent records of the merchandise inventory master file.) After review, the purchasing manager signs and mails each purchase order.

When ordered merchandise arrives at the receiving dock, it is counted by a receiving clerk and entered on a simplified receiving report containing fields for the date, supplier number, related purchase order number, the merchandise item numbers and corresponding quantities, a space for comments concerning the condition of the received merchandise, and a box for the initials of the receiving clerk. After completing the form, the clerk keys the receiving data into his or her terminal. The computer system then posts the receipt of the quantities to the pertinent records of the merchandise inventory master file. It also posts the date of receipt to the pertinent record in the open purchase order file. Then it generates a printed copy of a prenumbered receiving report, containing the entered data plus the supplier's name and address and the merchandise descriptions. (It also adds a copy of this receiving report to a file stored on magnetic disk.)

Required

a. Prepare a formatted screen for inputting the purchase order data and enter assumed sample data.

b. Draw the simplified receiving report form used by receiving clerks and enter assumed sample data.

c. Prepare record layouts for the following files, using assumed lengths for the various fields.

　(1) Open purchase order file.

　(2) Supplier master file.

　(3) Merchandise inventory master file.

　(4) Receiving report file.

d. Place circled POs by those data items within the foregoing record layouts that provide the sources of data for the printed purchase order (PO) (other than those provided by the screen).

e. Place circled RRs by those data items in the foregoing record layouts that provide the sources of data for the printed receiving report (RR) (other than those provided by the input form).

9-9. What error or fraudulent activity might occur if each of the following procedures is allowed?

a. The buyer in the purchasing department owns part interest in a supplier who provides merchandise of the type used by this firm.

b. The person who maintains the accounts payable records also prepares and signs checks to suppliers.

c. Suppliers' invoices are not compared to pur-

chase orders or receiving reports prior to payment.

d. Purchasing, receiving, and stores functions are combined into a single organizational unit.

e. Purchasing and accounts payable are combined into a single organizational unit.

f. The purchase orders are not prenumbered (or if prenumbered, are not filed in a sequential file that is periodically checked for gaps in the numbers).

g. The accounts payable ledger is not periodically reconciled to the control account in the general ledger.

h. After checks are written, the suppliers' invoices are not marked in some manner, stapled to the supporting documents, and filed.

i. The bank statement is reconciled by the person who signs the checks or by the accounts payable clerk.

9-10. What internal accounting control(s) would be most effective in preventing or detecting the following errors or fraudulent practices?

a. A supplier sends an invoice showing an amount computed on the basis of $10 per unit. However, the buyer in the purchasing department had listed the expected unit price as $7.

b. A supplier sends an invoice in the amount of $150. However, the goods were never ordered.

c. A supplier sends an invoice showing a quantity of 120 units shipped. However, only 100 units were actually received.

d. The cashier signs two checks, on successive days, to pay the same invoice from a supplier.

e. A firm's bank prepares a debit memorandum for an NSF (not sufficient funds) check, but the bank clerk forgets to mail a copy of the memo to the firm.

f. A cashier prepares and submits an invoice from a fictitious supplier having the name of his neighbor, writes a check to the "supplier," and mails the check to his neighbor's address; the neighbor then cashes the check and splits the proceeds with the cashier.

g. A cashier prepares and signs a check that is not supported by an invoice. She cashes the check and conceals this theft by overfooting the columns of the check register.

h. A petty cash custodian removes $80 from the petty cash fund to pay personal debts.

i. A truck driver who delivers goods to an electronics firm extracts for his use several small but expensive items from each delivery. Upon receiving one of these deliveries, a receiving clerk signs a bill of lading that shows the number of items leaving the shipping dock and returns a copy to the driver.

j. A storeskeeper takes inventory items home at night; when the shortages become apparent, she claims that the receiving department did not deliver the goods to the storeroom.

k. A purchasing department buyer orders unnecessary goods from a supplier firm, of which she happens to be an officer.

l. A receiving clerk posts the receipt of goods, via a terminal, to an incorrect inventory record.

m. During an inventory updating run, a receipt transaction is accidentally posted as an issue transaction, thereby reducing the on-hand balance in the computerized record to a negative quantity.

n. A buyer accidentally omits the unit price of one of the ordered products when keying the data for a purchase into a terminal.

o. A purchase order is coded with an incorrect and nonexistent supplier number. The error is not detected until the file updating run, when no master record is located to match the number.

p. Two supplier invoices are lost in transmitting the invoices to the data preparation room.

q. A check is written in the amount of $1000, whereas the disbursement voucher shows the amount to be paid as $100.

r. An error in an inventory transaction is referred by the data control group to the receiving department for correction. A week later the stores department complains that the weekly inventory status report is suspicious with respect to the inventory item in question. However, the data processing department cannot determine if the error has been corrected and reprocessed.

s. Errors in posting and pilferage have led to a large difference for a particular item between the on-hand quantity shown in the inventory record and the actual physical quantity.

t. A posting error to the accounts payable control account has resulted in a large overstatement of the account.

9-11. The following data pertain to vouchers that have been transmitted from the accounts payable department to the data processing department on May 18, where the data have been keyed onto a magnetic tape file. The vouchers represented by the data are to be used in preparing disbursement checks on this date.

Voucher Number	Supplier Number	Invoice Date	Discount Percentage	Amount
6673	532	042089	0.00	540.00
6674	321	042089	0.00	892.00
6675	285	042089	0.00	1,276.00
6676	502	042089	0.00	773.00
6678	477	042089	0.00	2,343.50
6679	331	042089	0.00	390.00
6682	492	042089	0.00	3,109.00
6723	294	050989	2.00	582.50
6726	439	050989	2.00	1,500.00
6728	588	050989	3.00	668.00
6730	447	050989	1.50	800.00

Required

  a. The list of data comprises a batch, for which control totals were precomputed in the accounts payable department. Identify all the suitable batch control totals that might have been computed for this batch, and compute their values based on the listed data.

  b. Explain why gaps appear in the document numbers.

  c. Various edit checks may be applied to the batched data during processing runs. For instance, the sequence of voucher numbers could be checked. If voucher number 6730 appeared ahead of 6728, an error would be listed on the exception and summary report. Identify five additional edit checks that may reasonably be applied, and illustrate each by means of the listed data.

9-12. The Old Missou Manufacturing Company is located in Columbia, Missouri. It has had many difficulties in materials control. Recently a raw materials inventory shortage was discovered. The resulting investigation revealed the following facts: Stock ledger cards are maintained in the storeroom and indicate the reorder point for each item. When the reorder point is reached, or when a special production order is received, the stock ledger clerk calls the purchasing agent and instructs him to order the item or items required. The purchasing agent prepares the purchase order in two copies, sending the original to the supplier and retaining the duplicate as the firm's record. All incoming materials are delivered direct to the storeroom. A receiving report is prepared; it is the basis for posting to stock ledger cards. Invoices are received by the purchasing agent, who verifies price, terms, and extensions. He sends them to the stock ledger clerk, who verifies the receipt of the materials against stock ledger card postings. If the materials have been received, the invoice is sent to the cash disbursements section for payment. The stock ledger clerk verifies the balances shown by stock ledger cards with materials actually on hand as filler work. There has been little time recently to check ledger cards, since two clerks have been sick. No annual physical inventory is taken.

Required

  List the control weaknesses in Old Missou's procedures and recommended improvements.

9-13. Babbington-Bowles is a Toronto advertising agency. It employs 625 salespersons whose responsibilities require them to travel and entertain extensively. Salespersons, who earn both salaries and commissions, receive paychecks at the end of each month. Formerly, the paycheck for each salesperson included reimbursement for expenses. These expense reimbursements were based on expense reports submitted by the salespersons, approved by supervisors, and computer-processed in batches.

  Although this procedure was satisfactory to the firm, it displeased the salespersons. They were forced to wait a month (sometimes two) for the reimbursement, which often amounted to several thousand dollars. Thus, they requested permission to submit expense reports with receipts directly to the accounting department, and to receive reimbursement very promptly thereafter.

  To provide this service, the accounting department would need a video display terminal and small online printer. The accounting clerk would enter the salesperson's name into the terminal, together with the requested expense amounts and account numbers to which the amounts would be charged. An online program would process the data and, if valid, print a check on presigned blank-check stock kept in the printer.

Required

  Identify the general and transaction controls that are needed for this proposed expense reimbursement procedure. With respect to programmed edit checks, list both the specific checks (e.g., field check) and the input data items that they are designed to check or test.

(SMAC adapted)

9-14. Masters Merchandising, Inc., acquires and sells a wide variety of housewares. Purchasing, shipping, and inventory management are therefore critical functions. The firm recently analyzed the activities related to these functions. It found that at least six parties are involved: the inventory control clerks, suppliers, customers, purchasing manager, shipping clerks, and inventory manager. Three data stores contain data regarding inventory, suppliers, and purchase orders. Activities include preparing requisitions, receiving reports, purchase orders, inventory aging reports, inventory status reports, supplier evaluation reports, and shipping records; determining quantities to order; determining quantities received and moved to storage; shipping merchandise; mailing purchase orders; updating inventory records to show reductions, quantities ordered, and receipts; determining suppliers from which to order; and matching receipts with orders.

Required

Prepare a data flow diagram that portrays the logical flows of data through the described activities.

9-15. ConSport Corporation of Chattanooga, Tennessee, is a regional wholesaler of sporting goods. The document system flowchart on page 330 and the following description present ConSport's cash disbursements system.

a. The accounts payable department approves for payment all invoices (I) for the purchase of inventory. Invoices are matched with the purchase requisitions (PR), purchase orders (PO), and receiving reports (RR). The accounts payable clerks focus on vendor (supplier) name and skim the documents when they are combined.

b. When all the documents for an invoice are assembled, a two-copy disbursement voucher (DV) is prepared, and the transaction is recorded in the voucher register (VR). The disbursement voucher and supporting documents are then filed alphabetically by supplier.

c. A two-copy journal voucher (JV) that summarizes each day's entries in the voucher register is prepared daily. The first copy is sent to the general ledger department, and the second copy is filed in the accounts payable department by date.

d. The vendor file is searched daily for the disbursement vouchers of invoices that are due to be paid. Both copies of disbursement vouchers that are due to be paid are sent to the treasury department along with the supporting documents. The cashier prepares a check for each supplier, signs the check, and records it in the check register (CR). Copy 1 of the disbursement voucher is attached to the check copy and filed in check number

order in the treasury department. Copy 2 and the supporting documents are returned to the accounts payable department and filed alphabetically by supplier.

e. A two-copy journal voucher that summarizes each day's checks is prepared. Copy 1 is sent to the general ledger department and copy 2 is filed in the treasury department by date.

f. The cashier receives the monthly bank statement with canceled checks and prepares the bank reconciliation (BR). If an adjustment is required as a consequence of the bank reconciliation, a two-copy journal voucher is prepared. Copy 1 is sent to the general ledger department. Copy 2 is attached to copy 1 of the bank reconciliation and filed by month in the treasury department. Copy 2 of the bank reconciliation is sent to the internal audit department.

Required

ConSport Corporation's cash disbursements system has some weaknesses. Review the cash disbursements system and for each weakness in the system

a. Identify where the weakness exists by using the reference number that appears to the left of each symbol in the flowchart.

b. Describe the nature of the weakness.

c. Make a recommendation to correct the weakness.

Use the following format in preparing your answer:

Reference Number	Nature of Weakness	Recommendation to Correct Weakness

(CMA adapted)

9-16. GoodLumber Company of Greensboro, North Carolina, is a large regional dealer of building materials that requires an elaborate system of internal controls. The flowchart of the purchasing activities is presented on page 331.

The activities in the purchasing department start with the receipt of an approved copy of the purchase requisition (PR) from the budget department. After reviewing the purchase requisition, a prenumbered purchase order (PO) is is-

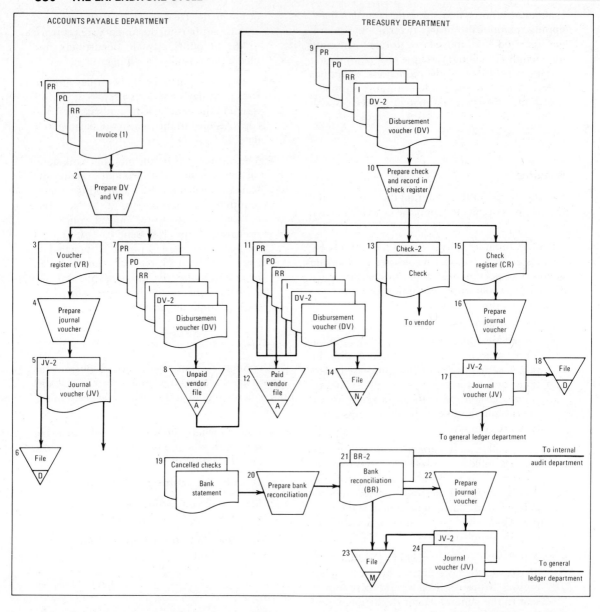

sued in multiple copies. Two copies are sent to a vendor (supplier), one is retained in the purchasing department, and the remainder are distributed to various other departments. The second copy of the purchase order is to be returned by the supplier to confirm the receipt of the order; this copy is filed according to PO number in the PO file.

A receiving report (RR) is completed in the receiving department when shipments of materials arrive from suppliers. A copy of the receiv-

ing report is sent to the purchasing department and attached to the purchase order and purchase requisition in the supplier's file.

The accounts payable department normally receives two copies of a supplier's invoice. These two copies are forwarded to the purchasing department for review with various documents related to the order. Purchasing will either institute authorization procedures for the payment of the invoice or recommend exception procedures.

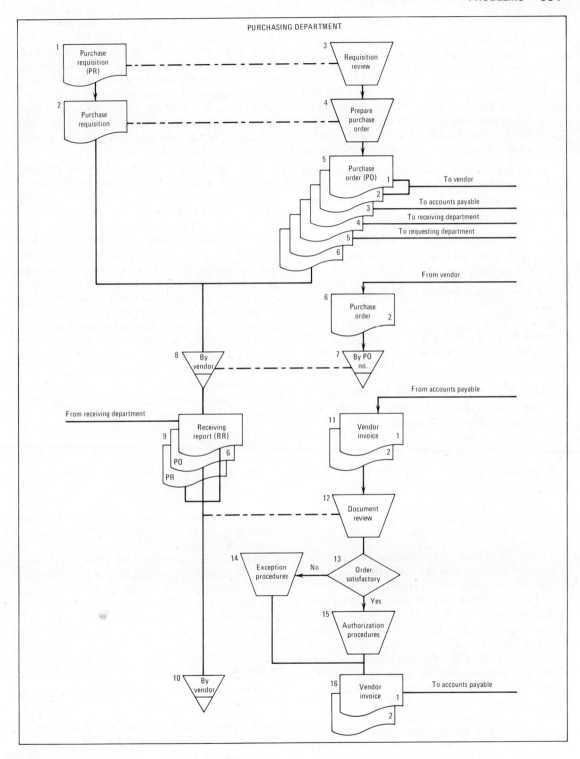

Required

a. A primary purpose for preparing a flow-chart is to identify system control points. Explain what a control point is.

b. Control points are not specifically identified in the flowchart presented for the purchasing department of GoodLumber Company. Review the flowchart and identify where control points exist. For each control point,

  (1) Identify where the control point exists in the flowchart. Use the reference number that appears to the left of each symbol.

  (2) Describe the nature of the control activity required for each control point.

  (3) Explain the purpose of or justification for each control activity.

Use the following format in preparing your answer:

Reference Number	Control Activity	Purpose or Justification

(CMA adapted)

9-17. The diagram on page 333 illustrates a manual system for processing purchases and cash disbursements transactions.

Required

Indicate what each of the letters *A* through *L* represent. Do not discuss adequacies or inadequacies in the system of internal control.

(CPA adapted)

9-18. The Roster Distributing Company of Logan, Utah, employs the following purchasing and cash disbursements procedures.

The purchasing department prepares a four-part purchase order from a verbal request by the plant superintendent or by one of the supervisors. Copies 1 and 2 are sent to the supplier. Copy 4 is sent to the receiving department for use as a receiving report. Copy 3 is filed as a control and followup copy for open orders.

Goods received are noted on the copy being used as the receiving report. This copy is then sent to the purchasing department, where it is filed with copy 3 of the purchase order and held until the supplier's invoice is received. (No perpetual inventory records are maintained.)

When the supplier's invoice is received, purchase order copies 3 and 4 are pulled from the file and checked against the invoice. The clerical accuracy (including prices) is checked and the invoice is assigned a number and recorded in the invoice register. The code for the account(s) to be debited is written on the invoice. Copy 3 of the purchase order is filed numerically. The invoice and copy 4 of the purchase order are sent to the accounts payable clerk.

The accounts payable clerk files the invoice and copy 4 of the purchase order by due date. When the invoices are due, the clerk pulls the invoices and purchase orders and prepares checks and check copies; on the check copies she notes the account distribution. From the checks, the clerk prepares an adding machine tape of the cash amounts. She then forwards the invoices, purchase orders, checks, check copies, and tape to a clerk in the general accounting department.

The general accounting clerk posts by hand the check copy amounts to the cash disbursements book. The tape forwarded from the accounts payable clerk is compared with the totals in the cash disbursements book; if they agree, the tape is discarded. The clerk then forwards the invoices, purchase orders, checks, and check copies to the treasurer for his signature.

The treasurer reviews the support, signs the checks, and returns all items to the general accounting clerk.

The general accounting clerk "protects" the checks with a protector device, mails the checks to the vendors, files the check copies by number, stamps the invoices "Paid," and forwards the invoices and attached receiving reports to the purchasing department.

The firm's books are not on an accrual basis. The invoice register is used only as a control device. Accounts payable are set up at month's end by a journal entry. The amounts are determined by running a tape of the invoices listed as unpaid in the invoice register.

Required

a. Prepare a document system flowchart, using appropriate symbols.

b. List the control weaknesses in Roster's procedures and recommend improvements.

9-19. The Alberta Company is a large research institute located in Calgary, Alberta. It

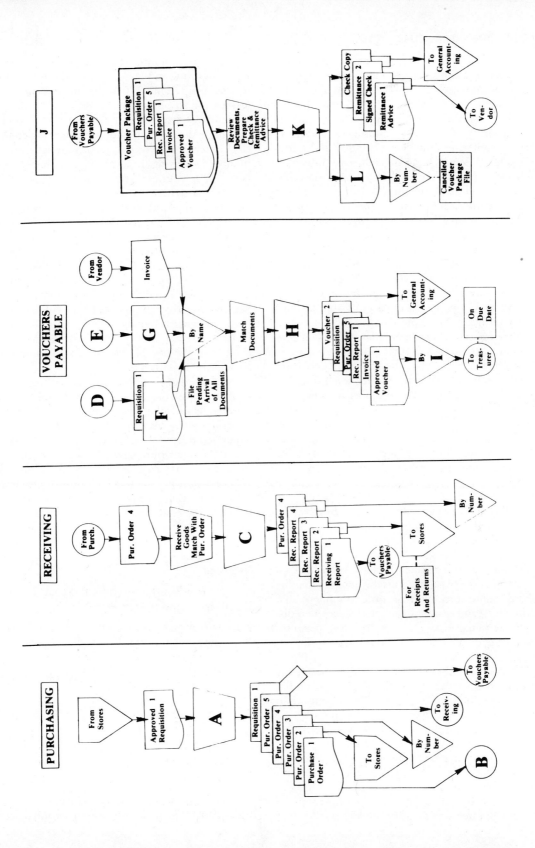

employs a mainframe computer for transaction processing and research support. Magnetic disks provide all secondary storage, and online terminals are located in all the departments.

The institute allows managers in the various departments to acquire supplies, furniture, equipment, and other items needed and budgeted for. The purchases procedure begins with a requisition prepared by a department manager. Included on the purchase requisition are the description of each item to be purchased, the account number to be charged for the purchase, and the signature of the manager. Upon receipt of the requisition, a buyer in the purchasing department inserts the name and number of a suitable supplier and the estimated price of the item.

The buyer then enters the data from the requisition into the computer system via a video display terminal. First, the data are edited via an online program. Then a purchases program generates a prenumbered purchase order on a small impact printer in the purchasing department, with a copy of the purchase order being stored in an open purchase order file on magnetic disk. After the purchase order is signed by the purchasing manager, copies are distributed as follows: copy 1 to the supplier, copy 2 to accounts payable, copy 3 to receiving, and copy 4 to the requisitioner. However, if the amount of the purchase order exceeds the budget, as indicated by a message on the CRT screen, the buyer puts the purchase order in a hold file and notifies the requisitioner by preparing a hold notice.

When the ordered items arrive at the receiving dock, a receiving clerk pulls the purchase order (on which the quantities have been blanked out) from the file and counts the goods. Then the clerk enters the purchase order number, item numbers, and quantities counted via a video display terminal in the area. A receiving program edits the data, verifies that a purchase order exists, and updates the open purchase order file. It also updates either (1) the fixed-asset master file or (2) the expense control file, depending on the nature of the items received. The program then produces a prenumbered receiving report on a small printer in the receiving area, as well as a copy of the receiving report on a receiving report file (stored on a magnetic disk). The receiving clerk signs the receiving report and sends it, together with the items, to the requisitioning department. He refiles the purchase order copy by number, after stamping it completed.

The requisitioning department receives the items, signs the receiving report, and forwards it to accounts payable. When the supplier's invoice arrives, the payables clerk pulls the purchase order and receiving report from the file (where they have been filed by supplier name). Then the clerk enters the invoice number, purchase order number, receiving report number, item numbers, and quantities invoiced into a video display terminal. A payables program compares the data on the three documents and displays any differences. The clerk approves the invoice for payment if no differences appear (or puts it into a hold basket if differences must be reconciled) and enters the amount to be paid via the terminals. She files the documents by supplier name. The payables program (1) groups all payment data into an accounts payable file, (2) updates the open purchase order file by removing the completed purchase order, and (3) deducts the amount of the payable from the remaining balance in the department's budget.

At the end of each week the checks pertaining to all approved invoices are printed from the accounts payable file; data from the supplier file are also used in this run. A listing of the checks is generated during this run. In addition, a weekly report of open purchase orders is printed, arranged by order date. Finally, summary journal vouchers showing the total amounts of new payables and disbursements for the week are printed; these are sent to the general ledger clerk.

Required

Prepare a computer system flowchart consisting of the following segments.

a. The preparation of purchase requisitions and purchase orders, including the editing of requisition data.

b. The processing of receipts of ordered goods.

c. The processing of invoices and recording of accounts payable.

d. The preparation of checks and weekly reports.

(SMAC adapted)

9-20. The Wedge Manufacturing Co. of Cleveland, Ohio, processes purchases and inventory transactions as follows: The request for purchases begins in the plant operations department. That department prepares a two-part prenumbered inventory materials request, which indicates the description and quantity of inventory items and the date they are needed. The request must be approved by the plant manager. One copy of the request is forwarded to the manager of the purchasing department and the other copy is filed temporarily by inventory item name in the plant operations department.

On receiving its copy of the inventory materials request, the purchasing department prepares a six-part prenumbered purchase order. The distribution of the purchase order is as follows.

Original—supplier.
Second copy—plant operations department.
Third copy—receiving department.
Fourth copy—accounts payable department.
Fifth copy—filed temporarily with the inventory materials request by supplier name.
Sixth copy—filed by number for two years.

The plant operations department matches its copy of the purchase order to the inventory materials request, then files and retains for two years the two documents together according to the inventory materials request number.

The receiving department temporarily files its copy (the receiver copy) of the purchase order by supplier name until inventory materials are delivered. The receiving clerk indicates on the receiver the quantity of items received and the date. The clerk then photocopies the receiver and sends the original to the accounts payable department. The photocopy is sent to the purchasing department.

The purchasing department matches its supplier file copy of the purchase order with the receiver returned from the receiving department. When all items ordered are received, the purchase order, receiver, and the initial inventory materials request are filed by supplier name for two years.

The accounts payable department matches the receiver with its copy of the purchase order and files the documents by supplier name.

When a supplier's invoice is received, an accounts payable clerk compares the invoice and the related purchase order and receiver for description of material, quantities, and price. The

three documents are then stapled together with a prenumbered two-part voucher ticket. The clerical accuracy of the invoice is verified and account distribution is assigned and indicated on the face of the voucher ticket. The voucher ticket also indicates the supplier name and number and the invoice number and date. This set of documents, called the voucher package, is filed by supplier name for seven years.

Before filing, however, the original copy of the voucher ticket is detached from the package and forwarded to another clerk in the accounts payable department, who verifies the clerical accuracy of the voucher ticket. Voucher tickets are accumulated and batched using a batch ticket, which indicates the date, the number of voucher tickets, and the total amount of invoices. From the batch ticket an adding machine tape is prepared of the daily total amount of invoices. The batch ticket and the related batch of voucher tickets are sent to the data processing (DP) department for processing.

On receiving the batch ticket and the voucher tickets, the DP department compares the documents for number of vouchers and the total amount of invoices. At this point, the batch ticket is assigned a number, and the batch is entered in the batch log (batch input control sheet). The voucher tickets are keyed to tape and forwarded for processing within the computer operations room. The voucher tickets are held in the DP department until all edit errors are corrected, then they are forwarded to the accounts payable department. The batch ticket is filed and retained in the DP department by batch number for two years.

Computer operations performs a report processing run that produces a daily voucher register, together with an error report. The accounts payable master file and the general ledger are the two disk files used in processing. The voucher tickets and error records from previous runs, on magnetic tape, serve as input.

The daily voucher register is returned to the same person in the DP department who prepared the batches for input. This person reviews the error report, accounts for the batches and control totals, and corrects errors. No approval is required for error corrections, which are processed the next day.

The accounts payable department receives the daily voucher register, together with the voucher tickets. The tickets and register are compared to ensure that each voucher ticket sequence number is in the daily voucher register. The voucher tickets are destroyed. The adding machine tape of the daily total amount of invoices on the batch ticket is compared to the total of the daily voucher register. The adding machine tape and the daily voucher register are filed separately by date and retained in the department for three years.

Required

  a. Prepare a document system flowchart that incorporates the manual and computer-based system operations described.

  b. Identify any weaknesses in controls, indicate the possible errors or discrepancies that might occur because of such weaknesses, and recommend improvements.

  c. Describe several transaction controls that would be suitable to this processing system and that have not already been noted.

10

The Resource

Management

Cycles

THIS CHAPTER'S OBJECTIVES ARE TO ENABLE YOU TO DO THE FOLLOWING WITH RESPECT TO THE RESOURCE MANAGEMENT CYCLES:

Identify the purposes and functions of several cycles involved in the management of resources.

Describe key relationships and components involved in the management of the employee services resource.

Describe relationships and components involved in the management of the facilities resource.

Describe key relationships and components involved in the management and conversion of the raw materials resource.

Review briefly the key relationships involved in the management of the cash resource.

INTRODUCTION

Every organization uses resources that may be categorized as materials, human and technical services, facilities, cash, and data. Each type of resource must be managed. **Resource management** gives rise to inputs, events or transactions, processing steps, and data flows. To provide means of reference, these dynamic facets are recorded, filed, and presented in reports and other outputs. To assure their reliability, controls and security measures are established and maintained.

Thus, the process of managing resources necessarily creates the same types of transaction-oriented activity cycles as discussed in the two previous chapters. In this chapter we survey several cycles related to the basic resources. These cycles are portrayed in Figure 10-1. The employee services and facilities management cycles are truly expenditure cycles. However, they pertain to employee services and facilities rather than materials and outside services. Although they could have been logically included in Chapter 9, they

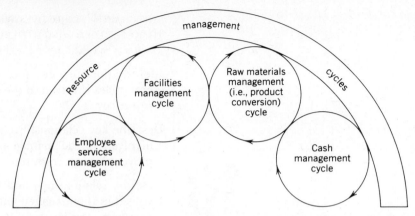

FIGURE 10-1 Several cycles within the resource management umbrella.

also fit within the resource management cycles. A third cycle pertains to raw materials, but it focuses on their conversion into finished goods, rather than on their acquisition and disposal. A fourth cycle, pertaining to the management of the cash resource, is briefly treated because of the earlier treatments of cash receipts and disbursements. The management of the fifth resource, data, is deferred until Chapter 11.

EMPLOYEE SERVICES MANAGEMENT CYCLE

Services performed by employees represent the major component of the human services resource employed by organizations. In traditional management textbooks employee services have traditionally been called the labor or manpower resource. In certain organizations, such as service-oriented firms and governmental agencies, this resource consumes the greatest portion of the recurring expenditures. Employee services in such organizations may be encompassed within the expenditure cycle. In other organizations, such as manufacturing firms, this resource is a key cost in the conversion of raw materials into finished goods. Employee services in such organizations may be considered as a part of the product conversion cycle. In order to accommodate all types of organizations, however, we have placed employee services within the resource management cycles.

Purposes

The major purpose of the **employee services management cycle** is to facilitate the exchange of cash with employees for needed services. (Because this cycle centers on payments to employees, it is also known as the payroll cycle.) Key objectives within the broad purpose of this cycle are to ensure that the status, pay rates or salaries, and pay deductions of employees are authorized; that payments are made for actual services rendered; and that employee-related costs are promptly and accurately recorded, classified, summarized, distributed, and reported.

Functions

Functions related to employees including hiring, training, transferring, terminating, classifying, adjusting pay levels, establishing safety measures, preparing payrolls, maintaining employee benefits programs, and reporting to governmental agencies. Although all of these are important concerns within the field of personnel administration, the employee services management cycle focuses primarily on the payroll expenditures. Therefore, a more relevant listing of functions for our use consists of establishing pay status, measuring the services rendered, preparing paychecks, issuing and distributing paychecks, distributing labor costs, and preparing required reports and statements.

Establish Pay Status Before an employee can be paid, his or her status should be clearly stated in writing. Status is a multifaceted concept. It first implies that the employee has successfully completed the hiring process, which usually consists of filling out a detailed application form and undergoing interviews. When the applicant is hired, the data from the application form becomes a part of the employee's personnel data record.

Status also involves classification and type of remuneration. An employee may be classified as an accounting clerk, a salesperson, a production worker, a manager, and so forth. Production, other operational employees (e.g., truck drivers), and many clerks are paid according to hourly rates; professional and managerial employees and certain clerks are generally paid monthly salaries; and salespersons are often paid on a commission basis. Certain classifications are eligible for overtime rates and shift differentials; others are exempt from such premiums.

In addition, pay status is affected by the types of and number of deductions that are to be offset against gross pay amounts. Certain deductions are required, such as the deduction for social security. Other deductions are voluntary, such as payments on U.S. savings bonds.

Measure the Services Rendered The means by which employee services are measured vary according to the type of remuneration. Those employees on hourly wages are expected to record their times on the job rather precisely; each time they enter and leave the job locations they enter the times on time cards. Salaried employees prepare attendance records of some sort (e.g., time sheets), showing attendance and absences during the various days composing the pay period. Commission employees prepare vouchers that reflect the amounts of sales made during the period on which commissions are to be computed. Each type of service-related document serves as the legal basis for payment when approved by the employee's supervisor.

Prepare Paychecks Employees are normally paid by checks, since they provide relative safety and written records of the amounts due. In some cases, however, hourly employees may be paid by currency.

Issue and Distribute Paychecks Employees must be paid, by law, on an established schedule. The schedule may be weekly, biweekly, semimonthly, or monthly. After being signed, paychecks may be distributed to the employees at their job sites or at a designated place. If currency is paid, the employees may be expected to obtain the amount at the cashier's window and to sign a receipt. Salaried employees, including managers, are generally encouraged to have the firm deposit their checks directly into bank accounts.

In many firms the paychecks are written on a special payroll-imprest bank account.[1] When this is the case, the firm first prepares a disbursement voucher. Next a check is drawn on the firm's regular bank account and given to the person who signs checks. He or she signs the check and delivers it to the bank for deposit in the special account. Then the paychecks are signed and distributed.

Distribute Labor Costs Those employees whose payroll costs are to be absorbed into the values of products or services must also maintain another record. This record is the job-time ticket, which will be described later.

Prepare Required Reports and Statements Numerous reports and statements related to payrolls must be prepared. Many of these are carefully specified by a maze of federal and state regulations, since various amounts from paychecks are destined for governmental and private funds. For instance, the Federal Insurance Contributions Act (FICA) specifies the manner of computing and reporting employer and employee contributions for old age, survivors', disability, and hospital insurance benefits. State and federal unemployment compensation laws specify the manner of computing and reporting contributions by employers for unemployment benefits. The correct amounts must be withheld from the employees' paychecks and deposited, together with the employer's portions, in designated financial institutions. Then, at the end of each quarter and year certain reports and statements must be generated concerning these withholdings.

Relationships to the Organization

These payroll functions are typically achieved under the direction of the personnel and finance/accounting organizational functions (units) of the firm. The employee services management cycle therefore involves the interaction of the personnel information system and the accounting information system (AIS). In addition, every department or other organizational unit is involved, since the employees are located throughout the organization.

Personnel Personnel management has the primary objective of planning, controlling, and coordinating the employees—the internally employed human resource—within an organization. Among the various functions it performs is the establishment of the employees' pay status. This function is most relevant to the payment for services rendered. The personnel department performs this function by preparing and distributing the necessary paperwork concerning personnel actions.

Finance/Accounting The objectives of financial and accounting management relate broadly to funds, data, information, planning, and control over resources.

---

[1] An imprest bank account is a fund that is periodically replenished with the amount of cash needed for a particular purpose, such as funding payrolls on specific dates.

Organizational units within this function and involved in the management of employee services include timekeeping, payroll, accounts payable, cash disbursements, cost distribution, and general ledger. Timekeeping maintains control over the time and attendance records of hourly employees. Payroll prepares paychecks, maintains the payroll records, and prepares required reports and statements. Accounts payable, in the context of this cycle, approves the disbursement voucher pertaining to employee services. After the cashier signs the paychecks, cash disbursements records and distributes the checks. Cost distribution maintains the records reflecting detailed costs of the products. General ledger maintains control over all asset, equity, expense, and income accounts. Note that the timekeeping and cost distribution units are more typically found in manufacturing firms than in other types of organizations.

Data Sources and Inputs

Data used in this cycle are mainly based on inputs from the time records and from documents provided by the personnel department. Other sources are the payroll files and the departments in which jobs are performed requiring direct labor.

Source documents typically used in the management of employee services include the following.

1. **Personnel action form.** A **personnel action form** serves to notify interested parties of actions concerning employees. These actions may pertain to the notice of hiring, a change of status, an evaluation of job performance, and so on. Figure 10-2 shows a personnel action form that notifies the payroll department of a situation or change affecting the status of an employee's pay. Another category of personnel actions concerns deductions. Some of these forms are issued by the firm and some by government agencies. An example of the latter is the W-4 Form, Employee Withholding Allowance Certificate, which is provided by the Internal Revenue Service.

2. **Time and/or attendance form.** A time card or clock card records the actual hours spent by hourly employees at their work locations. This card, in effect a **time and/or attendance form,** contains an employee's name and number, plus the dates of the applicable pay period. Each time the employee enters or leaves, he or she "punches" the card in the time clock. At the bottom of the card is a space for the supervisor's signature. Other attendance forms, as noted earlier, include a time sheet for use by salaried employees.

3. **Job-time ticket.** In contrast to the time card, which focuses on attendance at the work site, the **job-time ticket** focuses on specific jobs or work orders. Each time an hourly employee, such as a production worker, begins and ends work on the job, he or she records the time on the card. As in the case of the time card, the means of entering the times may be a time clock or terminal. Figure 10-3 pictures a job-time ticket (called here a labor ticket). Note that spaces are provided for entering the productivity in terms of pieces completed during the elapsed periods.

PERSONNEL FORM 1174

Distribution:
White, Green, Canary: Personnel
Pink: Originator

PERSONNEL — PAYROLL ACTION NOTIFICATION

Name_____

Effective Date_____ Organization Unit No. _____ Employee Number _____

Address *(Change Only)* _____

Enroll or transfer only — Overtime Exempt ☐   Overtime Non-Exempt ☐

ACTION TO BE TAKEN — CHECK APPLICABLE BOX(ES)

☐ Enroll   ☐ Termination   ☐ Vacation (Specify dates & pay request below)

☐ Transfer   ☐ Leave of Absence   ☐ Other (Explain)

☐ Rate Change   ☐ Cross Charge

Present Status:

Job Title _____ Salary_____

Dept. & Div. _____ Job Class_____

New Status:

Job Title _____ Salary_____

Dept. & Div. _____ Job Class_____

If salary increase, give following information:

Amount of increase as % of present salary_____ .

Midpoint of salary range for job class_____ .

Date of last increase_____ ; amount of last increase_____ .

(Guidelines per Sec. -0500 must be observed.)

Date of last appraisal _____ summary evaluation_____ .

(Within 6 mos. of requested increase.)

Explanation: _____
_____
_____
_____

Originated by _____ Transmittal date_____

Management Approval_____ Personnel Approval_____

PAYROLL USE ONLY

Pay Period_____ Permanent

Follow Up Yes _____ No _____   _____ hrs. $ _____

Action PR# _____ Temporary

Action Type_____   _____ hrs. $ _____

REMARKS:

FIGURE 10-2 A document relating to personnel actions. Courtesy of John Wiley & Sons, Inc.

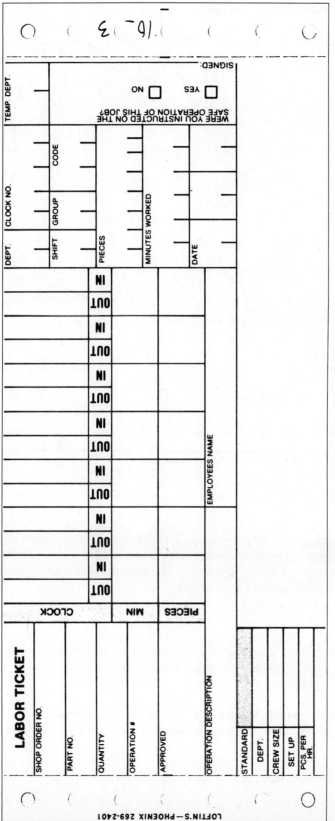

FIGURE 10-3 A job-time (labor) ticket.

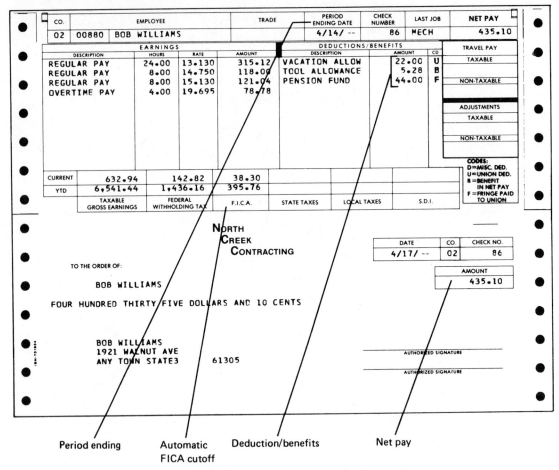

CO.	EMPLOYEE		TRADE	PERIOD ENDING DATE	CHECK NUMBER	LAST JOB	NET PAY
02	00880	BOB WILLIAMS		4/14/ --	86	MECH	435.10

EARNINGS				DEDUCTIONS/BENEFITS			TRAVEL PAY
DESCRIPTION	HOURS	RATE	AMOUNT	DESCRIPTION	AMOUNT	CD	TAXABLE
REGULAR PAY	24.00	13.130	315.12	VACATION ALLOW	22.00	U	
REGULAR PAY	8.00	14.750	118.00	TOOL ALLOWANCE	5.28	B	
REGULAR PAY	8.00	15.130	121.04	PENSION FUND	44.00	F	NON-TAXABLE
OVERTIME PAY	4.00	19.695	78.78				

ADJUSTMENTS
TAXABLE
NON-TAXABLE

CODES:
D=MISC. DED.
U=UNION DED.
B=BENEFIT
IN NET PAY
F=FRINGE PAID
TO UNION

CURRENT	632.94	142.82	38.30			
YTD	6,541.44	1,436.16	395.76			
TAXABLE GROSS EARNINGS	FEDERAL WITHHOLDING TAX	F.I.C.A.	STATE TAXES	LOCAL TAXES	S.D.I.	

NORTH
CREEK
CONTRACTING

DATE	CO.	CHECK NO.
4/17/ --	02	86

TO THE ORDER OF:

BOB WILLIAMS

AMOUNT
435.10

FOUR HUNDRED THIRTY FIVE DOLLARS AND 10 CENTS

BOB WILLIAMS
1921 WALNUT AVE
ANY TOWN STATE3   61305

AUTHORIZED SIGNATURE

AUTHORIZED SIGNATURE

Period ending   Automatic   Deduction/benefits   Net pay
FICA cutoff

FIGURE 10-4 A paycheck and voucher stub. Courtesy of International Business Machines Corporation.

4. **Paycheck.** A **paycheck,** with voucher stub, is the final document in the employee services management cycle. Figure 10-4 presents a typical paycheck prepared by computer. The stub shows all necessary details, including overtime pay and deductions.

Data Base

Among the files needed in managing employee services are the employee payroll master, personnel reference and history, time record transaction, paycheck transaction, and compensation reference files.

Employee Payroll Master File The **employee payroll master file** contains the earnings records of the employees. It is updated to show the amounts received from paychecks at the end of each pay period. Figure 10-5 displays a record layout of the variety of data items that might appear in this file. Generally the primary and sorting key is the employee number.

Employee number	Employee name	Social security number	Department or center code	Pay classification	Pay rate or salary	Overtime rate	Marital status	Number of exemptions

Deduction code	Deduction rate or amount per pay period	Year-to-date withheld	Year-to-date gross pay	Year-to-date net pay	Quarter-to-date gross pay	Quarter-to-date net pay

Repeat for each deduction

Note: Although the lengths of fields and modes of data items are necessary for complete documentation, they have been omitted for the sake of simplicity.

FIGURE 10-5 A layout of an employee payroll record.

An important concern with this file is keeping the records and their permanent data up to date. When an employee marries and obtains a new last name, for instance, this change should appear quickly in her record. When a new employee is hired, a record must be established before the end of the pay period. On the other hand, when an employee is terminated, the record should not be discarded until after the end of the year. Certain year-end reports require data concerning all employees who were active during any part of the year.

Personnel Reference and History File The personnel reference and history file is the main source of personnel data in the firm. It compliments the payroll master because it contains a variety of nonfinancial data as well as financial data concerning each employee. For instance, it might contain the employee's address, skills, job title, work experience, educational history, performance evaluations, and even family status.

This file may be consolidated and maintained in the personnel department. Alternatively, it may be split into several reference files, which may be located in the payroll and/or data processing departments as well as the personnel department.

A related file is a *skills file,* which provides an inventory of skills required by the firm and the employees who currently possess each skill. This type of file would enable a firm to locate qualified candidates when an opening or new need arises, as well as to aid in establishing a sound salary structure.

Time Record Transaction File The time record transaction file consists of copies of all the time cards or sheets for a particular pay period. In computer-based systems they are likely to be stored on magnetic media for use in processing the payroll.

Paycheck Transaction File In a manual system the paycheck transaction file consists of a copy of each current paycheck, arranged in check number order. In a computer-based system the record layout on magnetic media may appear similar to a record in the check disbursements transaction file.

Compensation Reference File The compensation reference file is, in effect, a table of pay rates and salary levels for the various job descriptions within the firm.

Data Flows and Processing

Both manual and computer-based processing systems are described in this section. The former emphasizes the flows of source documents and outputs, whereas the latter focuses on the processing runs.

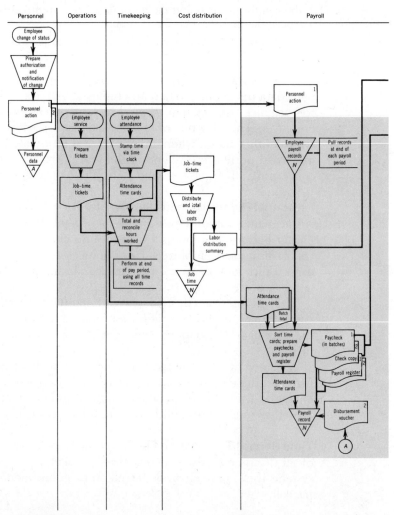

FIGURE 10-6 System flowchart of a manual employee payroll transaction processing procedure, with an emphasis on document flows.

Manual Processing System Figure 10-6 presents a system flowchart of a procedure involving the payment of hourly operations-type employees (e.g., production employees) who also work directly on specific jobs. The discussion of this procedure parallels the functions of the cycle listed earlier.

1. **Establish pay status.** This initial step takes place in the personnel department, where all of the personnel actions and changes are prepared and then transmitted to the payroll department.

2. **Measure the services rendered.** The time records are prepared in the operational (e.g., production) departments and timekeeping areas. Time cards are maintained in racks near the entrance to the work site. Employees clock in and clock out under the eye of a timekeeper. The job-time tickets are

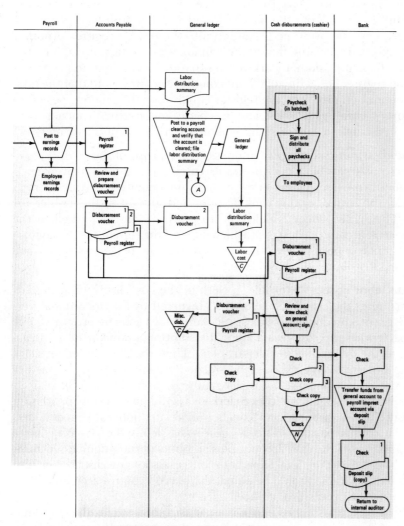

FIGURE 10-6 (*Continued*).

available right at the work site. Employees punch the tickets on a clock (or mark them manually) under the eye of their supervisor.

At the end of each day, the job-time tickets are collected and approved by the employees' supervisor. Then the supervisor forwards the tickets to the timekeeper. At the end of the pay period the timekeeper compares the total hours shown on the job-time tickets, for each employee, with the total hours shown on his or her attendance time cards. If the two sets of total hours are approximately equal (allowing for breaks, lunch, etc.), the time records are said to be reconciled. Then the timekeeper sends the attendance time cards to the payroll department (together with the total of hours worked) and the job-time tickets to the cost distribution department.

3. **Prepare the paychecks.** In the payroll department a clerk prepares a paycheck and voucher stub for each employee, based on data from the time card and from the employee's payroll reference file. Next the clerk enters the relevant information from the paycheck and voucher stub (i.e., gross pay, deductions, net pay, overtime premium) into the payroll register. Another clerk then posts the information to the employee's earnings record (i.e., the payroll master). Still another clerk verifies that the hours used in preparing the payroll register equal the total hours on the time cards, and that the total payroll amount entered into the register equals the total amount posted to all employees' earnings records. The paychecks and attached voucher stubs are sent, in a batch, to the cash disbursements department (or cashier).

4. **Issue and distribute paychecks.** Upon receiving a copy of the payroll register, an accounts payable clerk verifies its correctness and then prepares a disbursement voucher. A clerk in the cash disbursements department draws a check on the firm's regular bank account and gives it to the cashier for signing. The signed check is delivered to the bank and deposited in the special payroll account. Then the cashier signs all the paychecks. A paymaster (a designated person not otherwise involved in personnel or payroll procedures) distributes the paychecks.

5. **Distribute labor costs.** Meanwhile, a clerk in the cost distribution department distributes the employee labor costs incurred by the operational personnel (e.g., production employees) on the various jobs in progress. The clerk next reports the costs, via a **labor distribution summary** or a journal voucher, to the general ledger department. Then the general ledger clerk debits the amounts to the various labor-related accounts (e.g., direct factory labor) and credits a payroll control account (e.g., accrued payroll).

Subsequently, the general ledger clerk clears the payroll control account by reference to the disbursement voucher (or related journal voucher) prepared by accounts payable. That is, he or she debits the payroll control account and credits the cash account plus accounts pertaining to deductions being withheld. Since the total from both sources (labor cost distribution and disbursement voucher) should be equal, the payroll control account will be cleared to zero if processing has been correct.

Note that this clearing procedure is a partial substitute for the computation of formal batch totals in the timekeeping department. When attendance time records are not accompanied by time records related to jobs, it is desirable to compute batch totals at the point where the time records are assembled.

   6. Prepare required reports and statements. The only report shown in the flowchart is the payroll register. Other reports are discussed later.

Computer-based Processing System Although the online method may be used in computer-based processing, the batch method is better suited to the payroll procedure. Since all the records in the employee payroll master file are affected, sequentially accessing and updating the records is the more efficient alternative. Figure 10-7 therefore shows a system flowchart in which the batch method is applied to prepare paychecks.

   The flowchart begins with the attendance time cards being gathered in a batch by the timekeeper and transmitted to the payroll department. In the system described, the employees do not prepare job-time tickets. Therefore, to enhance control the timekeeper (or a payroll clerk) computes batch totals based on the time records. One total is based on the hours worked, a second total (of the hash variety) is based on the employee numbers, and a third total is based on a count of the time cards.

   The batch of time cards, prefaced by a batch transmittal sheet, is forwarded to the data processing department. There the time data are keyed onto magnetic tape and edited. In the first computer processing run the data are sorted by employee numbers. In run 2 the time data are processed to produce paychecks (and voucher stubs). The program also updates the employee payroll master file and prints the payroll register. The paychecks and a copy of the register are sent to the cashier, where the paychecks are signed and distributed. (The transfer of funds from the regular account may be included if desired.) The program in run 2 also adds a journal voucher concerning the payroll transaction to the general ledger transaction file.

   The flowchart also portrays the online maintenance of employee pay status data. Clerks in the personnel department enter all personnel actions via departmental terminals. Since the employee payroll master file is stored on a magnetic disk, the actions (e.g., a change in pay rate) can be entered into the affected employee records promptly by direct access. Thus, all actions can be effected during the pay period and before the payroll processing begins.

Accounting Controls

Risk Exposures Among the risk exposures that exist in the management of employee services are the following.

   1. Unqualified or larcenous persons may be hired.

   2. Time records may be incorrect or incomplete.

   3. Incorrect payments may be made to employees.

   4. Payments may be made to fictitious employees or terminated employees, and the paychecks may be cashed by dishonest persons.

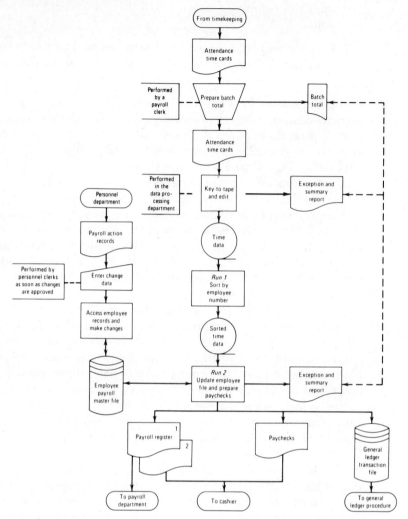

FIGURE 10-7 System flowchart of a batch computer-based employee payroll transaction processing procedure.

5. Labor expenses or payroll liabilities may be incorrectly stated.

6. Government regulations and laws may be violated, especially those pertaining to reporting requirements.

General Controls Among the general controls needed to counteract the listed risk exposures are the following.

1. Within the organization the persons and units that have custodial functions (the cashier, paymaster) are separated from those units that keep time records (timekeeping) and that prepare the payroll documents (payroll department). Also, the persons and units that authorize and approve (i.e., the personnel department that authorizes personnel actions and the departmental supervisors who approve time records) are separated from all other units.

2. Complete and up-to-date documentation is available concerning the management of employee services.

3. Operating practices relating to processing schedules, reports, changes in programs, and other matters are clearly established.

4. Security is maintained (in the case of online systems) by such techniques as (a) requiring clerks to enter assigned passwords before accessing employee payroll files, (b) employing terminals with restricted functions for the entry of personnel actions, (c) generating audit reports (access logs) that monitor accesses of system files, and (d) dumping the employee files onto magnetic tape backups. Physical security measures include the use of safes for holding stocks of blank paychecks and signature plates.

Transaction Controls Control points within the cycle involving employee payrolls include (1) the establishment of pay status for each employee, (2) the recording of time-related services, (3) the conversion of time into payments due, and (4) the disbursement of cash.

The following controls and control procedures are applicable to employee services transactions and employee records.

1. Documents relating to payables and cash disbursements are prenumbered and well designed. Also, time cards and job-time tickets where applicable are preprinted with the employees' names and numbers.

2. Data on time records are validated (and key-verified if suitable) as the data are prepared and entered for processing. In the case of computer-based systems, validation is performed by means of edit checks such as (a) validity checks on employee numbers, (b) limit checks on hours worked, (c) field checks on key identification and amount data, and (d) relationship checks on employee numbers and related departments to which employees are assigned.

3. Errors detected during data entry or processing are corrected as soon as possible by means of an established error-correction procedure. A part of this procedure may involve the printing of suitable exception and summary reports during edit runs. An example of such a report appears in Figure 10-8. In the case of the payroll application, processing of paychecks may be delayed until all transaction data errors and discrepancies have been corrected.

4. Personnel actions, such as new hires and pay rate changes, and paychecks are issued promptly on the basis of valid authorizations.

5. Time cards and job-time tickets where applicable are approved by the employees' supervisors.

6. Where job-time tickets are used, the hours that they reflect for each employee are reconciled with the hours shown on the attendance time cards.

NORTHCREEK IND.　　CO. 01　　　　　LABOR EXCEPTION REPORT　　　　　　　　　DATE 11/14/89　TIME 09.13.42　PAGE　1 AND30

FOREMAN – MK　　　　　　　　　　　　　　　　　　　　　　　　　　　　　　　　OPER DAN　　　BATCH　6

RECORD NUMBER	CODE MX	AC	DESCRIPTION	BADGE	DAY	DATE	–SHIFT– WORK PAID	TIME	ORDER NO.	OPER SEQ.	WORK CTR	DEPT	1st KEY ENTRY	2nd KEY ENTRY	3rd KEY ENTRY
DAN HANVILLE				EMP NO - 00210											
1	01	01	TIME/ATT	10012	2	11/14/89	01 1	8:07							
2	01	01	TIME/ATT	10012	2	11/14/89	01 1	11:56							
3	01	01	TIME/ATT	10012	2	11/14/89	01 1	12:30							
4	01	01	TIME/ATT	10012	2	11/14/89	01 1	16:33							
5	38	10	PROD-ON	10012	2	11/14/89	01 1	8:10	M000390	0010	ML025	DP20			
6	11	15	PROD-OFF	10012	2	11/14/89	01 1	13:42	M000390	0010	ML025	DP20	00000004	00000000	00000001
			TRAN QTY 0004			SCRAP QTY 0000	COMP CODE 1								
7	11	15	PROD-OFF	10012	2	11/14/89	01 1	13:42	M000390	0030	OR045	DP20	00000000	00000000	00000001
7 ****			E AM-6317 ON RECORD MISSING												
8	12	15	PROD-OFF	10012	2	11/14/89	01 1	16:33	M000390	0030	DR045	DP20	00000002	00000000	00000000
8 ***			E AM-6317 ON RECORD MISSING												
CAROL HARRIS				EMP NO - 00220											
9	01	01	TIME/ATT	10063	2	11/14/89	01 1	7:55							
10	01	01	TIME/ATT	10063	2	11/14/89	01 1	11:58							
11	01	01	TIME/ATT	10063	2	11/14/89	01 1	12:29							
12	28	14	INDIR-ON/OFF	10063	2	11/14/89	01 1	7:55	M000390	0010	ML025	DP20			
13	28	14	INDIR-ON/OFF	10063	2	11/14/89	01 1	16:27	M000390	0010	ML025	DP20			
			E AM-6271 T/A RECORD MISSING												

　　　NORTHCREEK IND. CO. 01　　　　　LABOR EXCEPTION REPORT　　　　　　　DATE 11/14/89　TIME 09.13.42　PAGE　2 AMD30

　　　FOREMAN – MK　　　　　　　　　　　　　　　　　　　　　　　　　　　　　　OPER DAN　　　BATCH 6

RECORD COUNTS:

A – TOTAL TIME RECORDS _ _ _ _ _ _ _ = 43

B – TIME RECORDS MARKED AS ERRORS _ _ _ _ _ = 13

C – RECORDS MARKED FOR DELETION _ _ _ _ _ = 0

RECORDS ACCEPTED (A–B–C) _ _ _ _ _ _ _ = 30

FIGURE 10-8 An example of an exception and summary (edit) report for the payroll application. Reprinted courtesy of International Business Machines Corporation.

7. Batch control totals are precomputed on hours worked, as reflected by time cards, and on net pay amounts, as shown in the payroll register; these batch totals are compared with totals computed during paycheck preparation and during postings to the employee payroll master file, respectively. Also, the total gross pay for all employees is compared with the footings of net pay plus all deductions.

8. Paychecks are drawn on a separate payroll-imprest bank account.

9. Voided paychecks are retained in order to account for all paycheck numbers.

10. Unclaimed paychecks are traced back to the time records and employee payroll master file to verify that they belong to actual current employees.

11. In the case of computer-based systems, a preliminary payroll register is reviewed before the paychecks are printed in order to determine that all errors have been corrected. Also, payroll account summaries are printed periodically to enhance the audit trail.

12. All controls pertaining to cash disbursements also apply to the issuance of paychecks. See transaction controls numbered 14, 17, 18, 20, 22, and 23 in Chapter 9.

Reports and Other Outputs

Operational Listings, Statements, and Reports One of the most used outputs is the **payroll register.** It essentially lists the key payment data concerning each employee for a single pay period, ranging from gross pay to net pay. A related output is the *deduction register,* which provides a detailed breakdown of the deductions for each employee. The cumulative **earnings register** shows amounts earned year-to-date, and possibly quarter-to-date, for each employee and the totals for all employees. Figure 10-9 provides an excerpt from an earnings register. Required governmental reports include those pertaining to withholdings of social security and federal income taxes, plus a variety of others. Some are due at the end of each quarter; others are due at the end of each year.

Inquiry Screens Most inquiries concern employees, so online systems usually enable personnel clerks and others to view the data in an individual employee's payroll or personnel data record. Other inquiries may relate to departmental payrolls or to cumulative earnings.

```
Northcreek Industries            1              Payroll            Time 20:23:03  Date  4/08/8X  Page 2 41503
Journal — PR002 Batch —          1       YTD and QTD earnings register         Period ending  4/03/8X

Emp                     Home         Gross       Gross     Sick  Tips  Tips not                            Weeks
number   Employee name  dept         earnings    taxable   pay   taxed taxed          FIT    FICA  EIC    worked

71500  Thomas C. Ryan
                        DADM   YTD    4,500.00    4,500.00  .00   .00   .00        784.50  299.25  .00      16
                               QTD      562.50      562.50  .00   .00   .00        107.39   37.41  .00       2

75000  Russ A. Stinehour
                        DADM   YTD   13,800.00   13,800.00  .00   .00   .00      4,303.28  917.70  .00      16
                               QTD    1,725.00    1,725.00  .00   .00   .00        511.66  114.71  .00       2

76000  Vince J. Tavormina
                        DOFC   YTD    2,254.00    2,254.00  .00   .00   .00        234.80  149.89  .00      15
                               QTD      304.00      304.00  .00   .00   .00         68.01   20.22  .00       2

         TOTAL YTD           84,472.77             520.98              .00                 5,582.81
                                      84,472.77                 .00           18,847.16            .00
         TOTAL QTD           10,844.60              63.28              .00                   716.97
                                      10,844.60                 .00            2,551.13            .00
         TOTAL pay period     9,764.60              63.28              .00                   645.14
                                       9,764.60                .00            2,443.60            .00
```

FIGURE 10-9 A cumulative earnings register. Courtesy of International Business Machines Corporation.

Managerial Reports Various analyses are of interest to managers, such as those pertaining to absenteeism, overtime pay, sales commissions, and indirect labor costs. Other reports that are often helpful include (1) surveys of average pay rates per occupational category, comparing rates to those of similar firms, and (2) personnel strength reports, showing levels of staffing and changes during the past month.

FACILITIES MANAGEMENT CYCLE

The facilities resource concerns the fixed assets also known as property, plant, and equipment. Within the wide range of fixed assets are buildings, machines, furniture, fixtures, vehicles, and other items requiring capital expenditures. Because they have lives of longer than one year, fixed assets are subject to depreciation. Another feature of fixed assets is that their dollar value is often a relatively large portion of the total asset value of a firm. Because of these distinctions, we have separated the acquisition of fixed assets from the expenditure cycle discussed in Chapter 9.

Purposes

The major purposes of the **facilities management cycle** are to facilitate the acquisition, economic life, and disposal of needed fixed assets. Typical objectives within this broad purpose are (1) to ensure that all acquisitions are properly approved and recorded and exchanged for cash or equivalents, (2) to safeguard the fixed assets in assigned locations, (3) to reflect depreciation expense properly and consistently in accordance with an acceptable depreciation method, and (4) to ensure that all disposals are properly approved and recorded.

Functions

The three major functions of the facilities management cycle consist of acquiring the fixed assets, maintaining the fixed assets during their economic lives, and disposing of the fixed assets.

Acquire Fixed Assets The capital expenditure process begins when a manager within an organizational unit perceives a need for an additional fixed asset or a need to replace an asset. For instance, a shipping manager may learn from his or her drivers that certain delivery trucks need replacement. This need should be substantiated through formal capital investment analyses. As we recall from managerial accounting, this type of analysis requires that expected benefits and costs be gathered for the economic lives of the new fixed assets, as well as such factors as the expected disposal or salvage values of the assets. Furthermore, these benefits and costs must be discounted to the present time by a factor (i.e., desired rate of return or opportunity cost of capital) that management specifies.

The manager places a formal request for the needed fixed assets. Higher-level management must approve such a request. The larger the amount involved, generally the higher the request must go for approval. Upon receiving approval, the request then follows a procedure similar to the acquisition of merchandise. That is, a copy of the request is sent to the purchasing department (or in the case of highly technical equipment, the engineering department, if any). Bids are requested, a supplier is selected, and a purchase order is prepared. When the fixed asset arrives, a receiving report is completed and the asset is delivered to the requesting organizational unit. Upon receipt of the supplier's invoice, a disbursement voucher is prepared (if the voucher system is in effect). On the due date a check is written and mailed.

If a firm constructs its own fixed assets, the procedure is closely related to the product conversion procedure. That procedure is discussed in the next main section of this chapter.

Maintain Fixed Assets Fixed assets usually represent valuable property. In order to safeguard and maintain each acquired fixed asset, all relevant details are generally recorded. Included are all acquisition costs, the estimated salvage value, the estimated economic life, and the location. If the fixed asset is transferred to a new location, this move is recorded. If costs are incurred during the life of the asset that increase its value or extend its economic life, these costs are added to the asset's current value.

A fixed asset diminishes in value during use or the passage of time. An allocated portion of the asset's cost, called depreciation expense, must be removed at periodic intervals. The amount of the depreciation expense is determined in part by the method of depreciation that is selected for the asset and in part by the estimated economic life of the asset. These depreciation amounts are included in the record of the individual fixed asset as well as in adjustments to general ledger accounts.

Dispose of Fixed Assets When their economic lives have come to an end, fixed assets are either sold, retired, or exchanged for replacement assets. These disposals, like acquisitions, require the approval of management. They also lead to the removal of asset values from the general ledger accounts.

Relationships to the Organization

The facilities management cycle functions are mainly achieved under the direction of the finance/accounting organizational function (unit) of the firm. The key departments involved are budgeting, accounts payable, cash disbursements, property accounting, and general ledger. The budgeting department develops capital expenditure budgets and coordinates these budgets with the short-range and cash budgets. The accounts payable department approves the suppliers' invoices pertaining to fixed assets for payment. The cash disbursements department, an arm of the cashier, prepares checks for disbursement to suppliers of fixed assets. The property accounting department establishes and maintains the records concerning fixed assets. The general ledger department maintains control over all asset, equity, expense, and income accounts.

Other units of the organization are involved to a degree. Higher-level managers, from various organizational functions (e.g., production) in addition to the

ARVIN INDUSTRIES, INC.

786
CIP Number

Division

CAPITAL INVESTMENT PROPOSAL (CIP)

Plant/Office   Project Title   Date

CAPITAL ASSET NAME	PLANT/DEPT.	ACCOUNT NO.	AMOUNT
1			
2			
3			
4			
5			
		Total	

PROJECT PURPOSE AND DESCRIPTION (Alternative 1 on Capital Investment Analysis Form)

DESCRIBE ANOTHER ALTERNATIVE REVIEWED (Alternative 2 on Capital Investment Analysis Form)

INVESTMENT CATEGORY	OTHER INFORMATION
☐ Replacement	Included in budget? Yes ☐ No ☐
☐ Expansion	Has the Corporate Insurance Department been informed?
☐ Cost Reduction/Productivity*	Yes ☐ No ☐ N/A ☐ (Refer to para 1.12 in exhibit B)
☐ Compliance (OSHA, etc.)	Is surplus equipment available from other divisions?
☐ Rebuilding	Yes ☐ No ☐ If Yes, provide further details.
☐ New Product*	For Cost Reduction/Productivity or New Product CIP:
☐ Energy Conservation	Alternative 1: IRR% _____ NPV $ _____
☐ Other _____	Discounted Payback Years _____
_____	Alternative 2: IRR% _____ NPV $ _____
	Discounted Payback Years _____
*Complete Capital Inv. Analysis Form	

INVESTMENT REVIEW AND APPROVAL

Division	Signature	Date	Group	Signature	Date
Originator _____		_____	Controller _____		_____
Dept. Mgr. _____		_____	Vice Pres. _____		_____
Plant Mgr. _____		_____	**Corporate**	**Signature**	**Date**
President _____		_____	Off. of Pres. _____		_____

ID-9099

FIGURE 10-10 A request for fixed-asset acquisition. Courtesy of Arvin Industries.

finance/accounting function, approve the acquisition and disposal of fixed assets. As in the case of the expenditure cycle, the purchasing and receiving departments are responsible for ordering and receiving the fixed assets.

Data Sources and Inputs

Data used in this cycle are mainly based on inputs from the managers in departments needing new fixed assets. Other sources are the fixed asset records maintained by accounting departments.

Source documents typically used in the management of facilities include the

1. **Capital investment proposal.** The initiating form is the **capital investment proposal,** also called the property expenditure request. Figure 10-10 displays a copy of this form. As the form indicates, it is accompanied by a capital investment analysis form, which lists all future cost and benefit flows that are expected to accrue from the asset investment, with the net cash flows being discounted to present values. The proposal package, including both forms, is forwarded for approval to higher-level managers, such as the controller and vice president and president. Upon approval a copy of the proposal is sent to the purchasing department, where it serves as a requisition.

2. **Fixed assets change form.** The **fixed assets change form** is used as the basis for (a) transferring fixed assets from one department to another or for (b) retiring, selling, or trading-in fixed assets. It lists the asset's net book value and the amount to be received (if retired). It also provides spaces for justifying the disposal and for the approval signatures of higher-level managers.

3. **Other source documents.** Since expenditures are involved, additional documents include the request for quotation, purchase order, bill of lading, receiving report, supplier's invoice, disbursement voucher, check voucher, and journal voucher. See Chapter 9 for descriptions of these documents.

Data Base

The distinctive files needed in managing facilities are the fixed assets master file and the fixed assets transaction file. Other files are those used in all expenditure transactions, such as the supplier master file, open purchase order, open voucher, and check disbursement files. See Chapter 9 for details of these files.

Fixed Assets Master File The **fixed assets master file** is the subsidiary ledger that supports the fixed asset control accounts in the general ledger. Figure 10-11 portrays the layout of the contents of a typical record for a fixed asset. Included is the fixed asset number, a unique identifier that generally serves as the primary and sorting key. The asset type code identifies the major classification of fixed assets (e.g., buildings, equipment) to which the individual asset belongs. The location code refers to the department or physical site to which the asset is assigned.

Fixed asset number	Description	Asset type code	Location code	Supplier number	Date acquired	Estimated economic life

Estimated salvage value	Depreciation method	Depreciation annual rate	Cost basis	Accumulated depreciation

Note: Although the lengths of fields and modes of data items are necessary for complete documentation, they have been omitted for the sake of simplicity.

FIGURE 10-11 A layout of a fixed assets record.

An important concern is keeping the records and their permanent data up to date. When an asset is relocated, for instance, the location code should be promptly changed. When a new fixed asset is approved and acquired, a new record should appear in the file.

Fixed Assets Transaction File The fixed assets transaction file contains transactions pertaining to new acquisitions, sales of currently held fixed assets, retirements, major additions to asset costs or to economic lives, and transfers between locations. It is needed if fixed asset transactions are accumulated for a period of time (e.g., a week) and then processed in a batch. If the transactions are posted to the records as they arise, the file will likely not exist in a physical sense.

Transactions that allocate depreciation expense for each fixed asset are not included in this file. Instead, they are included in the adjusting journal entries at the end of each accounting period.

Data Flows and Processing

Both manual and computer-based processing systems are described. The former emphasizes the flows of source documents; the latter focuses on the processing of the master file.

Manual Processing System Figure 10-12 (on pages 360 and 361) presents a simplified document system flowchart of the procedure for processing fixed assets transactions. The upper portion of the flowchart pertains to acquisition transactions, whereas the lower portion concerns disposal transactions. Depreciation transactions are included at the lower right.

To begin an acquisition, a manager in a user department prepares a request. Together with a capital investment analysis, this form is forwarded to higher-level management. After the request is reviewed and approved, it is distributed to the purchasing and accounts payable departments. Then the regular expenditure procedure is followed. Finally, the property accounting department prepares a record for the new fixed asset and the general ledger accounts are posted.

The disposal procedure likewise begins with a request. After the request is approved, the fixed asset is shipped for disposal. Based on a copy of the approved request form, a property accounting clerk posts and removes the appropriate record from the fixed asset file. Then the clerk prepares a journal voucher that reflects the final depreciation expense, actual salvage value (if any), and the gain or loss on the disposal.

With regard to depreciation, a property accounting clerk prepares a journal voucher at the end of each accounting period. (Alternatively, depreciation entries may be pre-established when the fixed asset is acquired and entered in the file of standard adjusting entries.) Then the clerk posts the amounts to the fixed asset record and sends the journal voucher to the general ledger department for posting.

Computer-based Processing System Figure 10-13 (on page 362) shows a system flowchart of a procedure involving fixed assets transactions. The online method has been selected for discussion because the number of fixed asset transactions is relatively small in many firms and the records can be kept up to date. However, the batch method is suitable for firms that have numerous acquisitions.

The flowchart begins at the point when the approved request forms have been received by the property accounting department, as shown in Figure 10-12. A clerk uses the department terminal to enter data from each transaction document when received. The entered data are first validated by edit checks. Then the data are immediately posted by an updating program to the appropriate record in the fixed asset master file. If the transaction affects general ledger accounts, the program also prepares a journal voucher and stores it on the general ledger transaction file. At the end of the accounting period (e.g., month) a print program generates useful reports. It also prepares journal vouchers that reflect depreciation entries.

Accounting Controls

Risk Exposures Among the risk exposures that exist in the processing of fixed assets are the following.

1. Fixed assets may be improperly acquired or retired.

2. Fixed assets may be stolen or lost.

3. Fixed assets that have been ordered may be incorrectly billed.

4. Balances in fixed asset accounts may be incorrect.

General Controls Among the general controls needed to counteract risks resulting from listed exposures are the following.

1. Within the organization the managers who approve requests relating to fixed assets are separated from the users of the fixed assets and from all units involved in the processing of expenditures and disposals. Otherwise the organizational segregation described for the expenditure cycle pertains.

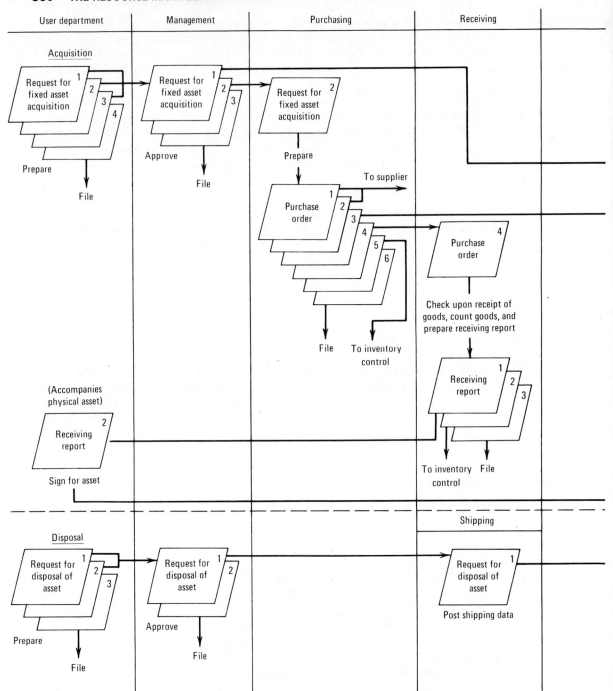

FIGURE 10-12 System flowchart of a manual fixed assets processing procedure, with an emphasis on document flows.

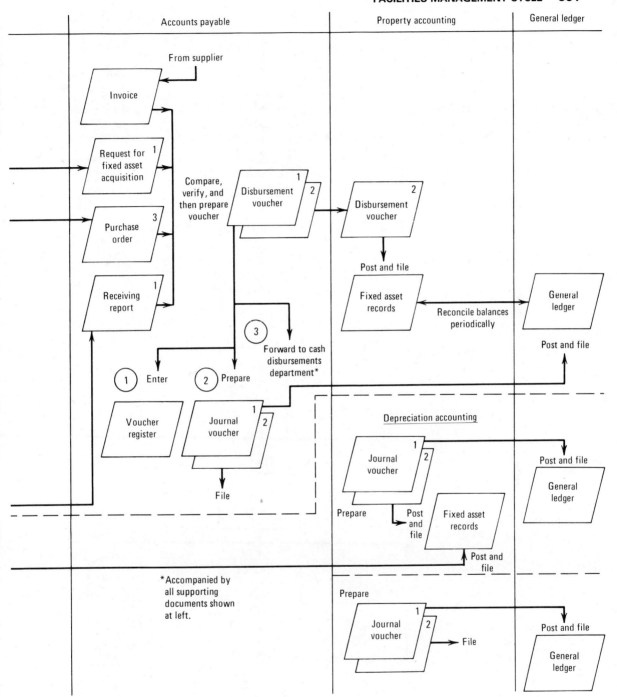

FIGURE 10-12 (*Continued*).

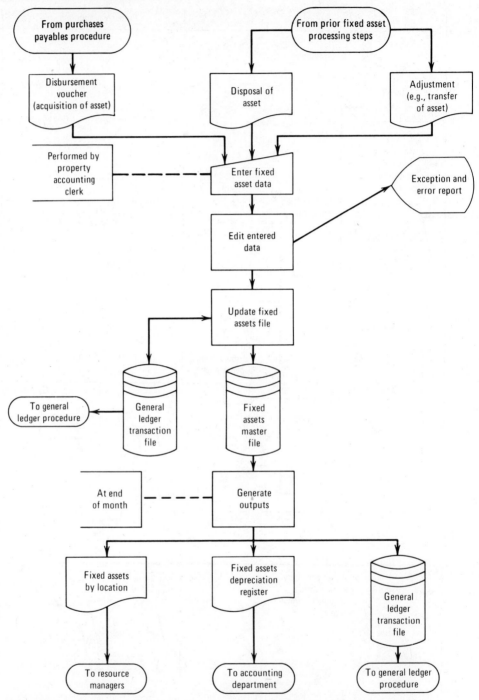

FIGURE 10-13 System flowchart of an online computer-based fixed assets transaction processing procedure.

2. Complete and up-to-date documentation is available concerning fixed assets transactions.

3. Operating practices relating to processing schedules, reports, changes in programs, and other matters are clearly established.

4. Security is maintained (in the case of online systems) by such techniques as (a) requiring clerks to enter assigned passwords before accessing fixed assets files, (b) employing terminals with restricted functions for the entry of fixed assets transactions, (c) generating audit reports (access logs) that monitor accesses of system files, and (d) dumping the fixed assets files onto magnetic tape backups.

Transaction Controls Control points within the facilities management cycle include (1) the approval of requests, (2) the purchase order, (3) the receipt (or shipment) of fixed assets, (4) the movement of new assets to an assigned location, (5) the receipt and approval of the supplier's invoice, (6) the disbursement of cash, and (7) the preparation of a fixed asset record.

The following controls and control procedures are applicable to fixed assets transactions.

1. Documents relating to requests for fixed assets acquisitions and disposals are prenumbered and well designed. Also, they are approved by higher-level managers responsible for such approvals before being issued.

2. Fixed assets acquisitions are required to follow the same purchasing, receiving, payables, and cash disbursements procedures employed for merchandise, raw materials, and supplies.

3. A unique identification number is assigned to each fixed asset, and a tag bearing this number is affixed to the asset.

4. Detailed and up-to-date fixed assets records are maintained.

5. Balances in the fixed assets subsidiary ledger (master file) are reconciled at least monthly with the balances of the fixed assets control accounts in the general ledger.

Reports and Other Outputs

Operational Listings and Reports The **fixed assets register** is a listing of all fixed assets, arranged by fixed asset numbers, and showing book and/or tax values of the assets. The *fixed assets acquisition listing* shows all assets acquired during an accounting period, including capitalized values and estimated salvage values. The *assets retirement register* shows all assets disposed of during the accounting period. The *fixed assets depreciation expense report* lists depreciation expenses for every fixed asset for the current accounting period, plus related costs and accumulated depreciation amounts. Figure 10-14 provides an example of this report. Certain reports are needed to fulfill information requirements of the Securities and Exchange Commission, the Internal Revenue Service, and local property tax authorities. An example is a summary of all acquisitions, transfers, and retirements during a year.

CORP 01   CO. 01   FEDERAL IMPORTS   FIXED ASSETS PROPERTY LISTING   FARO5-2   5 PERIODS AS OF 2 QTR 8-   PAGE   3

ASSET NO.	DIST	STOR	DEPT	ACCT	R ACORD C INSTL	COST BASIS	ACCUM RESERVE	CURRENT DEPR	YTD DEPR	NET BOOK	EXPN RESV	OLDN
BUILDINGS					05/66	165,531.29	141,531.29	.00	.00	24,000.00	910100	BLDG 4
850011 BUILDINGS	31	41	503		06/59 06/59	73,020.00 73,020.00	25,108.75 31,303.87	473.75 458.43	568.50 550.11	47,911.25 41,716.13	710100 910100	BLDG W3
850012 BUILDINGS	31	41	503		11/70 11/70	83,321.88 83,321.88	13,319.47 19,711.37	520.29 671.00	624.35 805.20	70,002.41 63,610.51	710100 910100	BLDG 12
CATG 7101												

						---COST BASIS---	-ACCUM RESERVE--	--CURRENT DEPR--	----YTD DEPR----	----NET BOOK----		
CATG 7101				CORP TAX		1,261,873.17 1,261,873.17	185,333.31 585,490.37	11,008.22 31,392.45	13,209.88 37,670.93	1,076,539.86 676,382.80		
810014 AIR COND	31	41	501	7201	11/78 11/78	30,000.00 30,000.00	8,000.03 12,720.00	1,250.01 1,600.01	1,500.01 1,920.00	21,999.97 17,280.00	720100 920100	
810015 AIR COND	31	41	501	7201	11/78 11/78	2,000.00 2,000.00	533.33 848.00	83.33 106.67	100.00 128.00	1,466.67 1,152.00	720100 920100	
810020 AIR COND	31	41	501	7201	11/78 11/78	-57.00 -57.00	-15.20 -35.29	-2.37 -2.02	-2.85 -2.42	-41.80 -21.71	720100 920100	
CATG 7201												

						---COST BASIS---	-ACCUM RESERVE--	--CURRENT DEPR--	----YTD DEPR----	----NET BOOK----		
CATG 7201				CORP TAX		31,943.00 31,943.00	8,518.16 13,532.71	1,330.97 1,704.65	1,597.16 2,045.58	23,424.84 18,410.29		
800016 LAND	31	41	501	7800	06/72 06/72	80,000.00 80,000.00	.00 .00	.00 .00	.00 .00	80,000.00 80,000.00	780000 980000	HQL
810016 LAND	31	41	501	7800	06/72 06/72	.00 .00	.00 .00	.00 .00	.00 .00	.00 .00	780000 980000	HQL
CATG 7800												

						---COST BASIS---	-ACCUM RESERVE--	--CURRENT DEPR--	----YTD DEPR----	----NET BOOK----		
CATG 7800				CORP TAX		80,000.00 80,000.00	.00 .00	.00 .00	.00 .00	80,000.00 80,000.00		
CO. 01				CORP TAX		1,507,941.17 1,507,941.17	213,390.34 620,186.45	21,259.45 42,620.65	24,217.58 50,035.19	1,294,550.83 887,754.72		
CORP 01				CORP TAX		1,507,941.17 1,507,941.17	213,390.34 620,186.45	21,259.45 42,620.65	24,217.58 50,035.19	1,294,550.83 887,754.72		

FIGURE 10-14 A fixed assets depreciation expense report. Courtesy of Data Design Associates.

Inquiry Screens Most inquiries concern individual fixed assets. A screen displaying this type of inquiry appeared in Figure 6-7. Other inquiries may relate to specific fixed assets transactions or capital budgeting data.

Managerial Reports Various analyses are of interest to managers, such as those showing fixed assets reported by location or by department. Other reports show maintenance schedules and costs and projected depreciation expenses.

RAW MATERIALS MANAGEMENT (PRODUCT CONVERSION) CYCLE

The management and conversion of raw materials constitute a cycle primarily within manufacturing and construction firms, although a similar cycle may be found within health care and certain other service-oriented organizations. Because this cycle is relatively specialized, as well as quite complex, our survey will be very limited. We will focus only on production activities, where the products or finished goods are manufactured in a single plant on the basis of job orders. Although some of the orders concern batches of standard products that are to go into finished goods inventory, many of the orders are for customized products.

Purposes

The major purpose of the **raw materials management or product conversion cycle** is to facilitate the conversion of raw materials (and parts) into products or finished goods. Key objectives within this broad purpose are to ensure that adequate raw materials and other resources are available, that orders are completed in a timely and cost-efficient manner, that the finished goods are shipped on schedule, and that the costs for each order are accumulated. In order to achieve such objectives, a mind-boggling set of decisions must be made. These decisions range from forecasting sales to selecting maintenance schedules for machines.

Functions

The functions related to these objectives are (1) entering and readying customers' orders, (2) planning and initiating the process to fill orders, (3) moving orders through the production process, (4) completing the production process and shipping orders, and (5) costing the orders. Each of these functions is discussed more fully later with the aid of system flowcharts.

Relationships to the Organization

The functions listed are typically achieved under the direction of the logistics management and finance/accounting organizational functions (units) of the firm. Figure 10-15 depicts many of the involved organizational departments within these two major organizational units. The figure also indicates the basic flows of data and information among these units.

Logistics Logistics management within a manufacturing firm encompasses more activities than in a merchandising firm. All the units and flows shown within the dashed box in Figure 10-15 can be viewed as closely related to the logistics function. (The sales order entry and shipping units, however, may alternatively be grouped under the market/distribution function.)

Since we have described the roles of several logistics units in Chapter 9, we will consider only the remaining units in this section. **Engineering design** determines the specifications by which the products are to be manufactured. **Production planning** determines the quantities of products to be manufactured, the production schedule, and the resources to use; **production control** dispatches an order into the production process, monitors the order, and takes corrective actions when necessary. **Materials requirements planning (MRP)** assures that the proper quantities of materials, parts, and subassemblies will be available to manufacture the scheduled orders. The MRP procedure consists of "exploding" the materials requirements by multiplying the quantity of products scheduled by the number of materials and parts required per unit. It then leads to the requisitioning of needed materials and parts from the storeroom and requesting the purchasing department to order any additional materials and parts not in house. [The ultimate MRP process is the **just-in-time (JIT) system,** which virtually

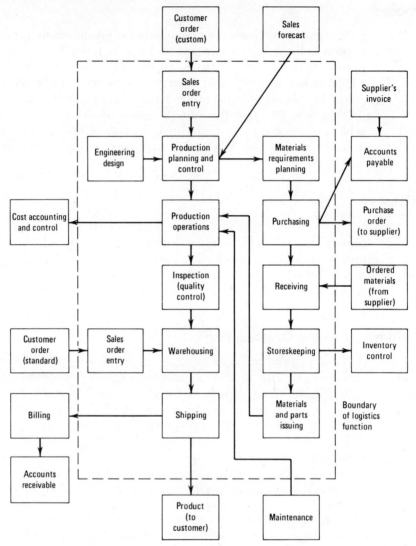

FIGURE 10-15 Organizational units that direct the functions involved in the product conversion cycle and the filling of customers' orders.

eliminates materials and parts inventories by precisely timing their receipts to coincide with production schedules.] Upon the issuance of materials and parts into the production process, line production departments actually perform the work in progress. Then inspection ensures that the products meet established quality standards.

Finance/Accounting The objectives and most of the units of the finance/accounting function have been discussed in earlier chapters. The cost accounting and control unit, however, appears for the first time. It accumulates material, labor, and overhead costs incurred in the production process and prepares cost variance reports. This unit also develops labor and material cost standards and assigns values to work-in-process inventory.

Data Sources and Inputs

Data used in the product conversion cycle are based on a variety of inputs from documents generated by customers and logistics departments. Other sources are the various finance and accounting files pertaining to raw materials purchases, receivables, and payables.

Source documents typically used in the product conversion cycle (other than those already discussed) include the

1. **Bill of material.** The **bill of material** specifies the quantities of materials and parts to be used in a particular product.

2. **Operations list.** An **operations list,** also known as a routing form, specifies the sequence of operations to be performed in fashioning and assembling the materials and parts required for a particular product. In effect, it is a "recipe" or guide for the production employees. The list may include the work centers at which the operations are to take place, as well as machine requirements and standard time allowances.

3. **Production order.** The document identifying a specific job that is to flow through the production process is known as a **production order** or work order. It incorporates key data from the initiating customer order (or from a sales forecast, in the case of standard products), from the relevant operations list, and from the production schedule.

4. **Material issue slip.** The **material issue slip,** also known as a materials requisition form, directs the storeskeeper to issue materials or parts to designated work centers or persons. Figure 10-16 shows an example prepared by hand. (In the case of computer-based systems, the issue slips would be printed.) The costs seen on the example are entered later by the inventory control department.

5. **Move ticket.** A **move ticket,** also called a traveler, authorizes the physical movement of a production order from one work center to the next one listed on the order. It records the quantities of items received; it also shows the date received, thereby enabling progress to be tracked. Figure 10-17 presents an example of a move ticket.

6. **Other source documents.** Among the other source documents used are the sales order, purchase requisition, purchase order, receiving report, labor job-time ticket, and the documents involved in payables and disbursements.

Data Base

The product conversion cycle data base consists of several files, including the work-in-process master, open production order, product structure, and production data reference files. This data base closely interfaces with the data bases that support the revenue cycle and expenditure cycle. As we recall, the key files in the

Material Issue Slip   No. 704

Issued to _Work Center A_   Date _10/20/89_

Charged to production order number ___8333___

Material or part number	Description	Quantity issued	Unit cost	Total cost
18568	Casting for rotor shaft	5	500.00	2500.00

Authorized by _D. W. Munro_

Received by _T. J. Boswell_

Costed by _P. G. Johnson_

FIGURE 10-16 A material issue slip.

revenue cycle are the customer master, accounts receivable master, finished goods inventory master, open sales order, and related transaction files. The key files in the expenditure cycle are the supplier master, raw materials inventory, open purchase order, and related transaction files.

Each of the key files supporting product conversion are briefly discussed. Other files are identified.

Move Ticket

Move to _____ Work Center B _____

Operations _____ G200 _____

_____ G300 _____

Production order no. _____ 8333 _____

Start date of order _____ 10/23/89 _____

Date received _____ 10/25/89 _____

Quantity received _____ 5 _____

Received By _R. E. Green_

Posted By _LeRoy Gainer_

FIGURE 10-17 A move ticket.

Production Order Cost Sheet

Product_____ Generator PG21 _____   Production Order No. 8333

Quantity_____ 5 _____

Date Started_____ 10/21/86 _____

Date Finished_____

Material costs			Labor costs				Overhead costs		
Date	Issue number	Amount	Date	Work center	Operation	Amount	Date	Applied level	Amount
10/20/86	704	2500.00	10/21/86	A	G100	35.00	10/21/86	3.5 hrs.	70.00
Total material cost			Total labor cost				Total overhead cost		

FIGURE 10-18 A work-in-process ledger sheet.

Work-in-Process Master File Each record in the **work-in-process master file** summarizes the costs incurred—for raw materials (including parts), direct labor, and overhead—with respect to a current (open) production order. An example of a record for a manual system appears in Figure 10-18. Although the example is labeled "production order cost sheet," the label "work-in-process ledger sheet" is used by some firms. All the records in this file comprise a subsidiary ledger supporting the work-in-process inventory account in the general ledger.

Production order number	Sales order number	Finished goods item (product) number	Date started in production	Scheduled completion date	Operation number*	Work center number*	Machine number*

Starting date[a]	Date completed and moved[a]	Quantity completed[a]	Inspection evaluation[a]

[a] Repeated for each operation; times and quantities are actual for those operations completed and estimated for those operations not yet completed.

Note: Although the lengths of fields and modes of data items are necessary for complete documentation, they have been omitted for the sake of simplicity.

FIGURE 10-19 A layout of an open production order record.

Open Production Order File Like the work-in-process master file, the focus of this file is the individual production order. Thus, the two files are closely related. For instance, both use the production number as the primary and sorting key. However, the open production order file does not contain costs. Instead it shows the current status of each production order in the production process. Figure 10-19 portrays a layout of a record to be stored on magnetic tape or disk.

Product Structure Reference File The product structure reference file replaces the collected bills of materials in a computer-based system, thereby saving considerable storage space. It consists of a series of multilevel product trees, which in effect codify the relationships between products and their constituent materials and parts. When processed with the raw materials inventory file, this file enables bills of materials to be generated.

Production Data Reference File Although the exact content of this file may vary widely from firm to firm, possible data include the production schedule, operations lists, and standard costs.

Other Files Additional files that are useful to the product conversion cycle include a *machine loading file,* which shows the status of each machine, and a production history file, which contains copies of all completed production orders.

Data Flows and Processing

Figure 10-20 presents a flowchart that emphasizes the flows of source and output documents among organizational units. In effect it connects the pertinent documents to the units portrayed in Figure 10-15.

Our description of data flows and processing will be in accordance with the listed functions. The focus will be upon online computer-based information systems, since they offer benefits to product conversion, such as

1. Better integration of the highly interdependent activities.

2. Improved production efficiency and use of resources resulting from better scheduling of orders.

3. Easier entry of data via preformatted terminal screens.

4. Better control over orders because of up-to-date files and timely reports.

Enter Customer Orders Upon receipt of an order from a customer for custom products, a sales order clerk enters the data into a terminal, where the transaction is placed in the open sales order file. If the order is approved by a credit checking program, a copy of the order is sent to engineering design.

Plan and Initiate the Production Process Figure 10-21 shows a system flowchart of production planning that is aided by an online computer-based system. One input into the planning process is a set of specifications for the customer's special order, as prepared by engineering design. These specifications are added

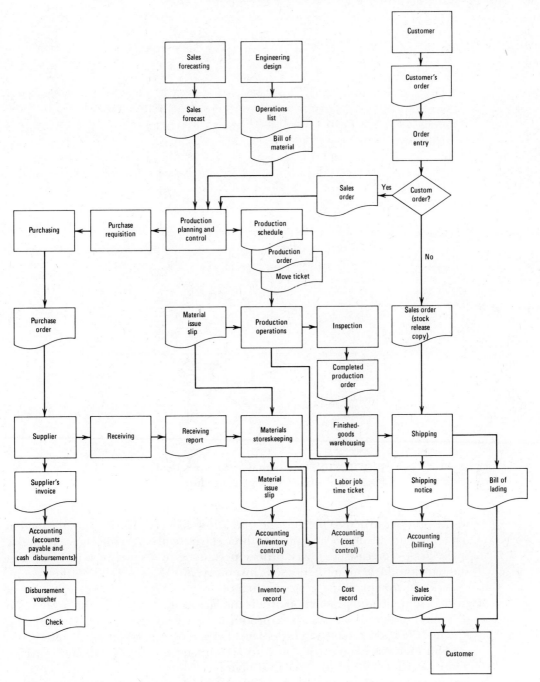

FIGURE 10-20 Flows of documents among the organizational units involved in product conversion and logistics.

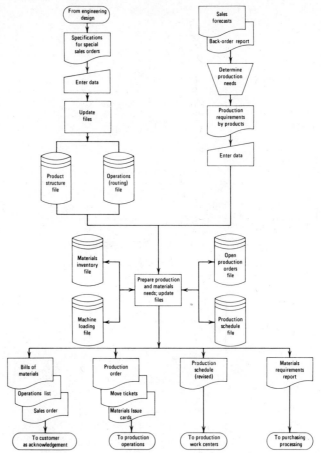

FIGURE 10-21 System flowchart of an online computer-based production planning procedure.

to the product structure file and the operations file. (For clarity, the production data reference file has been split into three separate files.) At the end of each day revised sales forecasts and back orders, pertaining to needed replenishments of standard products in finished-goods inventory, are also entered into the system.

A production planning program then performs several complex steps. First, it prints prenumbered production orders that are needed to initiate the production of custom-ordered and standard products, based on the listed inputs. It also updates the open production orders file. Second, the program prints move tickets and material issue cards (slips) to accompany the new production orders. Third, it prints bills of material and operations lists for each product (custom-ordered and standard) shown on the new production orders so that they may be reviewed by customers and used by production planning personnel. Fourth, the program prints a revised production schedule, showing start dates for the new orders, and updates the schedule in the file. Fifth, it prints a materials requirements report showing the materials and parts needed to fill the production orders and to replenish materials inventories. It then updates the materials file to

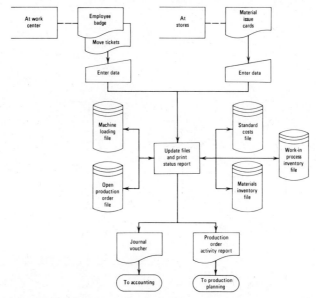

FIGURE 10-22 System flowchart of an online computer based production operations procedure.

reserve materials in the current inventory. Finally, it updates the machine loading file to assign machines as needed for the new orders.

Move Orders through Production Operations Figure 10-22 shows the system flowchart pertaining to production operations. When a new production order is scheduled to start into production, raw materials and parts are issued by the storeskeeper. They are delivered to the first work center and accompanied by the first move ticket. Employees and machines are assigned in accordance with data in the production order. As each employee begins work on the order, he or she enters the employee number (from the badge) and order number (from the move ticket). When the employee finishes the operation involving the order, he or she repeats the entry.

Based on these variously entered inputs, the production operations program performs several steps. First, it updates the materials inventory file to reflect the issued materials and parts. Second, it updates the open production order file to show that the operation at the work center is completed. In addition, the program prints a production order activity report to show the current status of all open production orders. Third, it updates the machine loading file to show that the machine is free for the next scheduled operation. Fourth, the program updates the work-in-process file to show the addition of labor, materials, and overhead. These costs are computed by reference to the standard unit costs and overhead rates in the standard costs file. Finally, it prints a journal voucher that shows the added costs so that they can be later charged to the work-in-process inventory account in the general ledger. (Alternatively, the program could directly charge the general ledger account, if it is maintained in an online file.)

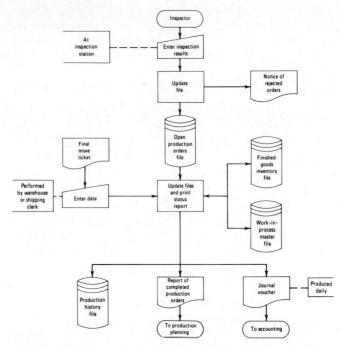

FIGURE 10-23 System flowchart on an online computer-based procedure for completing production operations.

Complete the Production Process Figure 10-23 shows the system flowchart relating to the completion of production operations. As work is completed on a production order, the finished goods are inspected; the results are entered into a terminal to update the production order. Those orders that pass inspection are transferred either to the warehouse or to the shipping department, where data from the final move ticket are entered. This notification causes the production order to be closed, transferred to the history file, and listed in a report. It also causes the work-in-process record for the order to be totaled and then transferred to the finished goods inventory as a new record. Finally, the program prints a journal voucher that transfers incurred costs for the day's completed orders to finished goods inventory.

Cost the Production Orders The costs relating to production orders have been mentioned in discussing both the work-in-process file and production operations. Cost accounting is such an important aspect of production conversion, however, that it deserves separate attention.

The overall cost of a product consists of three elements: direct materials costs, direct labor costs, and overhead costs. Throughout production operations these cost are attached to the product via a production (job) order or via a process. When the focus is on the order, as in our assumed situation, the cost accumulation activity is labeled a job order cost accounting system.

Each cost element is based on a separate input. Direct materials costs are derived from the materials issues slips (requisitions), direct labor costs are obtained from the job-time tickets, and overhead costs are based on predetermined rates. If a standard cost system is employed, the unit prices for materials, the hourly rate of labor, and the overhead rate are carefully established by engineering methods and applied consistently throughout a reasonable period (e.g., a year).

Accounting Controls

Risk Exposures Among the risk exposures that exist in the management and conversion of raw materials are the following.

1. Incorrect costs may be charged to production orders.
2. Recorded quantities of work in process and finished goods may be inaccurate.
3. Excessive quantities of finished goods may be produced.
4. Excessive or inadequate quantities of raw materials may be ordered or issued into production.
5. Raw materials or finished goods may be stolen or lost.
6. Production orders may be lost or delayed during production operations.

General Controls Among the general controls needed to counteract risks resulting in the listed exposures are the following.

1. Within the organization the production operations are separated from the custodial functions (receiving, materials storeskeeping, finished goods warehousing), and both are separated from the recording functions (production planning, inventory control, cost accounting and control).
2. Complete and up-to-date documentation is available concerning production planning and operations.
3. Operating practices relating to processing schedules, reports, changes in programs, and other matters are clearly established.
4. Security is maintained (in the case of online systems) by such techniques as (a) requiring clerks to enter assigned passwords before accessing production-related files, (b) employing terminals with restricted functions, (c) generating audit reports (access logs) that monitor accesses of system files, and (d) dumping the production files onto magnetic tape backup. Physical security measures include locked enclosures for materials and finished goods.

Transaction Controls Control points within the product conversion cycle include (1) the scheduling of the production order, (2) the recording of issued materials and time-related services, (3) the monitoring of progress through production operations, and (4) the transfer of completed production orders.

The following controls and control procedures are applicable to product conversion transactions and product records.

1. Authorization is required to issue materials and orders into production.

2. Documents relating to production are prenumbered and well designed.

3. Documents (i.e., move tickets) accompany materials for orders through the various operations, and progress is posted to the production orders.

4. Input data are validated by edit programs containing a variety of edit checks.

5. Transfer of responsibility takes place at every step through the production process and into the warehouse or shipping area.

6. Balances in work-in-process records are reconciled periodically with the balance in the general ledger control account.

7. Physical inventories of materials, parts, and finished goods are taken periodically under proper supervision; the results are reconciled with the balances in the inventory records.

Reports and Other Outputs

Operational Listings and Reports In addition to the materials requirements reports, production orders activity report, and completed production orders report already discussed, operational listings include the **raw materials status report** and the **finished goods status report.**

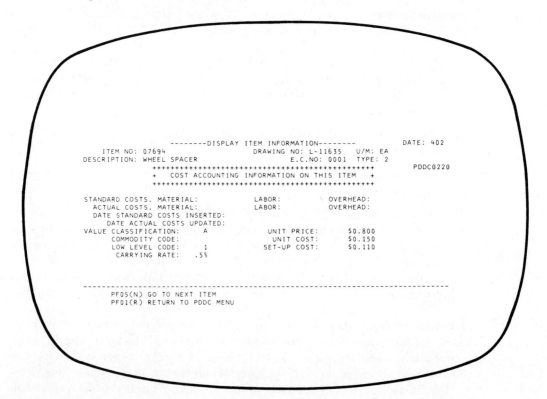

FIGURE 10-24 An inquiry screen that shows cost information relating to materials. Courtesy of International Business Machines Corporation.

Inquiry Screens Inquiries may involve individual production orders, machine loadings at work centers, and specific materials and parts. Figure 10-24 shows a screen in response to an inquiry concerning the cost of a part.

Managerial Reports Among the production-oriented reports of interest to managers are those concerning (1) equipment utilization; (2) efficiency of production employees; (3) variances of actual production order costs from budgeted costs; (4) production orders behind schedule; (5) percentages of scrap, rework, and rejects; and (6) work center performance. Figure 10-25 shows an example of this last type of report.

CASH MANAGEMENT CYCLE

Because cash is the most liquid asset, the management of cash requires considerable planning and control. We have already examined cash-related concerns in our surveys of the revenue and expenditure cycles. At this point we will briefly focus on cash as a resource.

The *purposes* of the **cash management cycle** are (1) to ensure that adequate, but not excessive, quantities of funds are available to meet all legitimate needs, and (2) to safeguard cash from theft and loss. Among the *functions* are (1) acquiring needed cash from likely sources at the lowest feasible cost, and (2) disbursing cash to meet all obligations when due, while avoiding unnecessary costs such as those from lost purchase discounts. Cash may be acquired mainly from customers, sales of fixed assets, loans from banks, issues of bonds, and sales of stock. Cash may be disbursed for purchases of goods and services, acquisitions of fixed assets and investments, repurchases of stock, and repayments of loans and bond issues.

Planning for cash can best be done through the use of cash budgets and forecasts. Financial modeling techniques, including "what ifs," provide added analytical power.

Control over cash may be applied by a variety of techniques and procedures.

WORK CENTER PERFORMANCE SUMMARY

SHOP DATE 615

MACH GROUP	NO. MCHS.	CAP. HRS.	LOAD HRS.	ACTUAL HRS.	% UTILIZ.	% EFFEC.	TOT. IDLE HRS.	IDLE HOURS BY REASON CODE						
								1	2	3	4	5	6	7
0810	2	800	812	782	977	1038	18			15	3			
1930	1	400	338	398	995	849	12							2

IDLE TIME REASON CODES

1. No Operator	5. Other (See Cards for Detail)
2. No Work	6. Set Up
3. Machine Breakdown	7. Re Set
4. Tool Trouble	

FIGURE 10-25 A managerial report concerning work center performances. Courtesy of International Business Machines Corporation.

Those that relate most directly to cash management include the following.

1. Requiring that all cash receipts, from whatever sources, flow through a single cash receipts journal and be deposited intact.

2. Requiring that all cash disbursements be approved and issued through check vouchers (except for petty cash).

3. Requiring that bank statements for all accounts be reconciled monthly by a person not otherwise involved in cash transactions. The bank reconciliation should include complete verification of all deposits and disbursements.

4. Providing all sound security measures, including adequate organizational independence.

SUMMARY

Four important resource management cycles involve employee services, facilities, materials, and cash. Functions within the employee services management cycle include establishing pay status, measuring the services rendered, preparing paychecks, issuing and distributing paychecks, distributing labor costs, and preparing required reports and statements. This cycle involves the personnel, timekeeping, payroll, accounts payable, cash disbursements, cost distribution, and general ledger units. Key inputs are the personnel action form, time record, job-time ticket, and paycheck. The data base includes the employee payroll master and personnel reference and history files. Outputs include the payroll and other registers, plus analyses of labor cost components.

The facilities management cycle includes the functions of acquiring fixed assets, maintaining the fixed assets, and disposing of fixed assets. This cycle involves such organizational units as budgeting, accounts payable, cash disbursements, property accounting, and general ledger. Key inputs are the capital investment proposal and fixed asset change form. The data base includes the fixed assets master and transaction files. Outputs include the fixed assets register; fixed assets acquisition, retirement, and depreciation expense registers; fixed assets by location reports; and inquiry screens concerning individual fixed assets.

The raw materials management or product conversion cycle includes the functions of entering customers' orders, planning and initiating the production process, moving orders through production, completing the production process, and costing the orders. This cycle focuses on such organizational units as engineering design, production planning and control, production operations, materials resource planning (MRP), and cost accounting and control. Key inputs include the bill of materials, operations list, production order, material issue slip, and move ticket. The data base includes the work-in-process master, open production order, and product structure reference files. Outputs include inventory status reports, inquiry screens concerning production orders, and various reports of production performance.

The cash management cycle is concerned with maintaining an adequate level of cash and safeguarding the cash. Achieving these purposes involves the cash receipts and disbursement functions and supporting system components that are integral parts of the revenue and expenditure cycles.

REFERENCES

Cushing, Barry E., and Romney, Marshall B. *Accounting Information Systems and Business Organizations,* 4th ed. Reading, Mass.: Addison-Wesley, 1987.

Gand, Harvey, and Cook, Milt E. "Choosing an MRP System," *Datamation* (Jan. 1985), 84–98.

Guide to Accounting Controls: Production Costs and Inventories. New York: Price Waterhouse & Co., 1979.

Horngren, Charles T., and Sundem, Gary. *Cost Accounting: A Managerial Emphasis,* 7th ed. Englewood Cliffs, N.J.: Prentice-Hall, 1987.

MSA Manufacturing System. Atlanta, Ga.: Management Science America, Inc., 1982.

MSA Payroll Accounting System. Atlanta, Ga.: Management Science America, Inc., 1986.

QUESTIONS

1. What is the meaning of each of the following terms?

Resource management
Employee services management cycle
Personnel action form
Time and/or attendance form
Job-time ticket
Paycheck
Employee payroll master file
Labor distribution summary
Payroll register
Earnings register
Facilities management cycle
Capital investment proposal
Fixed assets change form
Fixed assets master file
Fixed assets register
Raw materials management or

product conversion cycle
Engineering design
Production planning and production control
Materials requirements planning (MRP)
Just-in-time (JIT) system
Bill of material
Operations list
Production order
Material issue slip
Move ticket
Work-in-process master file
Raw materials status report
Finished goods status report
Cash management cycle

2. What are the purpose and related objectives of the employee services management (payroll) cycle?

3. Identify the functions that pertain to payroll expenditures.

4. Which organizational units are involved in paying employees?

5. Identify the source documents used in the management of employee services.

6. Which files are related to employees and the payroll?

7. Describe the steps in a typical manual payroll procedure.

8. Describe the payroll procedure when a batch-oriented computer-based system is used.

9. What risk exposures exist in the management of employee services?

10. What are several general and transaction controls that can counteract the exposures to risks within the cycle involving employee payrolls?

11. Identify several control points within the cycle involving employee payrolls.

12. What is the impact of governmental requirements on reports related to employee payrolls?

13. What are several listings and reports that may be generated from payroll transactions, other than required reports?

14. What are the purposes and related objectives of the facilities management cycle?

15. Identify the major functions that pertain to the facilities management cycle.

16. Which organizational units are involved in transactions pertaining to facilities (fixed assets)?

17. What source documents are used in the management of facilities?

18. Identify the major files that relate to fixed assets.

19. Describe the procedures for fixed assets transactions when a manual system is employed.

20. How is the processing of fixed assets transactions changed when an online computer-based system is used?

21. What risk exposures exist in facilities management?

22. Identify several general and transaction controls that can counteract the exposures to risks within the facilities management cycle.

23. Identify several listings and reports that may be generated from fixed assets transactions.

24. What are the purpose and related objectives of the product conversion cycle?

25. Identify the major functions that pertain to the product conversion cycle.

26. Describe the logistics management organization within a manufacturing firm, and identify the incorporated units.

27. What source documents are used in the production process?

28. What files are employed in the production process?

29. Describe the data entry and processing steps within the product conversion cycle, assuming the presence of an online computer-based system.

30. Discuss the costing of production orders and the related journal entries.

31. What risk exposures exist in the management and conversion of raw materials into finished goods?

32. Identify several general and transaction controls that can counteract the exposures to risk in the management and conversion of raw materials.

33. Identify several reports that are useful to management in controlling the production process.

34. Discuss the purposes and functions of the cash management cycle.

35. Why might the acquisition of a computer system for use in processing payroll transactions result in much extra work on the part of the payroll clerks?

36. Describe several programmed edit checks, such as the redundancy matching check, that can be applied by the posting programs used in processing payrolls.

37. Contrast a computer-based processing system in a manufacturing firm using job order costing with a system in another manufacturer who uses process costing.

38. Discuss emerging developments in production systems, including computer-aided design

(CAD), computer-aided manufacturing (CAM), just-in-time (JIT) inventory procedures, and robotics.

39. Discuss the emerging development known as human resource accounting (HRA).

40. Discuss the emerging developments in financial modeling, especially as they relate to capital investment analysis.

REVIEW PROBLEM[2]

Olympia Manufacturing Company
Statement

The Olympia Manufacturing Company of Seattle, Washington, produces consumer goods by the job order approach. It pays all production employees on the basis of hourly rates, with time and a half for overtime hours. The five organizational units actively involved in the payroll and labor cost determination procedures are timekeeping, factory operating departments, payroll audit and control, data preparation, and computer operations. The basic data collection and processing steps, together with their locations, are as follows.

A (Timekeeping). Employee time (clock) cards are prepared.

B (Factory operating departments). Job-time tickets are prepared and forwarded.

C (Timekeeping). Employee time cards and job-time tickets are compared and forwarded.

D (Payroll audit and control). Preceding source documents are reviewed and forwarded.

E (Data preparation). Preceding source documents are converted to magnetic tape and forwarded.

---

[2] Adapted from the November 1972 CPA examination, with permission of the American Institute of Certified Public Accountants.

F (Computer operations). Data on magnetic tape are edited, sorted, and then processed against the employee payroll master file (on magnetic disk) to produce paychecks, a payroll hour summary, a payroll register, and a labor cost distribution sheet.

Required

a. List the possible errors or discrepancies that might occur at the data collection or processing step.

b. For each possible error or discrepancy, cite the corresponding control or security measure that should be in effect. (Assume that personnel procedures related to hiring, promotion, termination, and pay rate authorization are adequate.)

c. Describe changes in the preceding procedure that would enable a computer-based system to be employed more fully in the data entry and processing steps.

Solution

For requirements **a** and **b**:

Step	Possible Errors or Discrepancies	Controls or Security Measures
A	1. Time improperly reported by employees.	1. Independent timekeeping function; requirement that employees punch time clock; periodic checks of employees on duty.
	2. Payroll padded by timekeeper.	2. Paychecks distributed by payroll function, not timekeeping function.
	3. Employees work unauthorized overtime hours.	3. Overtime authorized by supervisor.
B	4. Employees loaf on duty.	4. Hours worked on each job recorded on time clock on factory floor; job-time tickets approved by supervisor.
	5. Overtime work not charged at premium rate.	5. Hours worked at premium rate marked by timekeeping.
C	6. Total hours on job-time tickets and employee time cards not in balance.	6. Hours checked by timekeeper and differences reconciled.
D	7. Job-time ticket or employer time cards lost in transit from timekeeping to payroll audit and control.	7. Batch control totals computed by timekeeping separately for job-time tickets and employee time cards; totals agreed; batch transmittal sheet prepared to accompany documents.
E	8. Job-time tickets or employee time cards lost in transit from payroll audit and control to data preparation.	8. Batch control totals logged on batch input control log by control group that is independent of computer operations; totals recomputed during keying operation and compared to predetermined totals.
	9. Data incorrectly transcribed from documents onto magnetic tape.	9. Keyed data on tape verified; also, batch control totals compared (in step 8).
F	10. Employee number incorrectly recorded or keyed.	10. Self-checking digits used on employee number and verified by programmed check.
	11. Errors in recording or keying time data, in sorting time records, etc.	11. Various programmed checks written into payroll processing program.

Step	Possible Errors or Discrepancies	Controls or Security Measures
	12. Employee time records lost in transit from data preparation to computer operations.	12. Batch control totals computed during processing and printed on exception and summary report; these totals compared to totals logged in batch input control log.
	13. Wrong master file disk mounted for processing.	13. Internal header label check employed at beginning of run.
	14. Employee payroll master file misplaced.	14. File signed out of the data library only when needed for processing, and then returned to library afterwards.
	15. Detected errors not corrected and documents re-entered for processing.	15. Logging of errors performed by payroll audit and control, and error-correction procedure carefully followed.
	16. Outputs lost or diverted in transit to intended destinations.	16. Outputs routed in accordance with distribution log maintained by payroll audit and control; payroll register personally delivered to payroll representative, paychecks to treasurer or cashier or paymaster, and summary totals to the general ledger section.

For requirement **c**.

Function Affected	Data Collection and Processing Steps Subject to Computerization
Data preparation	Instead of recording time data on job-time tickets and employee time cards and later converting this data to magnetic tape, the data could be captured via online terminals located in timekeeping and the factory operating departments.
Timekeeping	If data are captured online, the computer system could be programmed to zero-balance total hours on job-time tickets with total hours on employee time cards; differences could be printed out on the exception and summary report for investigation by timekeeping and supervisors. The computer system could also be programmed to compute the batch control totals that are to be used for later comparisons.
Payroll audit and control	If data are captured online, the computer system could be programmed to perform prompt validity checks of employee numbers.
Computer operations	Regardless of the manner in which the data are captured, the computer system could be programmed to compare the computed batch control totals against predetermined batch control totals and to print any differences for investigation.

PROBLEMS

10-1. The Hardmon Manufacturing Company produces metal products for industrial customers. Although some of the products are standard items (e.g., pistons), many are made in response to special orders. The firm therefore maintains a number of work centers, each with a particular type of machine or assembling equipment. It puts each order into the production process via a production order and accumulates the related costs on a work-in-process record. Standard unit costs are applied to material quantities and direct labor hours, while standard work center overhead rates are applied on the basis of machine hours. When special orders are completed, they are delivered directly to the shipping area. Completed standard items are delivered to the finished goods warehouse.

Required

a. Identify the types of accounting transactions related to (1) the conversion of raw materials into finished goods, (2) the payment of production employees, both direct and indirect, and (3) the management of factory machines and equipment.

b. Assuming that a computer-system is approved for installation, describe the type of system (i.e., batch, online, mixed) that appears to be preferable for each of the following: (1) monitoring the production process, (2) preparing employee payrolls, and (3) managing machines and equipment. List the reasons for your choice in each situation.

10-2. Boone and Bower, CPAs, is a public accounting firm in the northeast. It has two offices and approximately 50 employees. The firm has been very progressive in its use of microcomputers. Recently it acquired a software package that manages the time records of its clerical and professional employees and that also prepares the payroll and related reports. Now the firm is also considering a software package to manage its various fixed assets, such as furniture, office machines, fixed and portable microcomputers, and fixtures.

Required

a. List the data items that are likely to be needed by the time-management–payroll package in order to generate the outputs.

b. List the data items that are likely to be needed by the fixed assets package in order to manage the fixed assets and prepare outputs.

c. List the files needed by both of the packages.

d. Describe several listings and reports that can be provided by each of the packages and would likely be useful to the partners and office manager. (Do not include reports that are required by governmental agencies.)

10-3. Custom Woodcrafters is a small firm that manufactures custom-made pieces of home and office furniture. Its employees consist of 30 craftspersons, 7 master craftspersons, 1 scheduler, plus several clerks. The owner is the sole manager. No salespersons are needed, since the quality of its products attracts more orders for the firm than it can handle. Each order is assigned to a master craftsperson, who designs the product and guides it through the production process, and approves the final result. At least two craftspersons are assigned by the scheduler to work on each order, depending on the complexity, requested date, and so on. After the product is completed, the price is determined by accumulating all related costs and then adding a percentage markup.

Required

a. List the data items that are needed in order to plan, manufacture, and monitor the progress of an order.

b. List the data items that are needed in order to price an order.

c. List the files that would store the data items listed.

d. Describe reports that would be useful to the scheduler and master craftspersons in performing their duties.

10-4. Design each of the following source documents.

a. An attendance time card, which is used to clock in and out of the plant by the same employees who use the card shown in Figure 10-3 to clock in and out of jobs. The time card should provide four spaces for clocking each day for six days. Enter data for Jacob Keeley, no. 45982, week ending 9/9/89. On September 4 his times are 7:52A, 12:01P, 12:58P, and 5:03P.

b. A bill of materials, which has a heading section and body section. In the heading is the product name and number, effective date, and signature of the authorizing person. In the body are the material or part numbers, descriptions, and quantities needed. Enter the following data for Generator PG21, which was authorized by Paul Jenks on January 4, 1989.

18568	Casting for rotor shaft	1
32151	Salient poles	4
33592	Field windings	4
44276	Slip rings	2
98105	Ventilating fan	1

10-5. Refer to Problem 10-4**b**. Prepare a materials requirements report that is based on production order no. 8333, which involves the production of five units of Generator PG21. The report was prepared on 10/19/89 and is to be used by the production planning department in preparing materials issues slips. *Hint:* See Figures 10-16, 10-17, and 10-18.

10-6. The Shriver Computer Services Company of Pullman, Washington, uses an online processing system to keep its fixed assets records up to date and available for inquiry. It employs preformatted screens for the entry, modification, and retrieval of data pertaining to fixed assets. In order to access the preformatted screens, a user first specifies the following master menu. When this menu screen is displayed on the user's CRT terminal, the user enters the desired number. The computer software then presents the requested screen or asks for additional information (e.g., the number of the desired asset). For instance, if the user needs to adjust the depreciation amount of an asset, he or she enters the number 1; the software then asks the number of the asset to be adjusted.

```
FIXED ASSETS MASTER MENU

1. ASSET DATA ENTRY

2. ASSET ACQUISITION ENTRY

3. ASSET DISPOSAL ENTRY

4. ASSET ACCOUNT STATUS INQUIRY

5. INDIVIDUAL ASSET STATUS INQUIRY

6. REPORT DISPLAY

7. DEMAND REPORT GENERATION

ENTER DESIRED NUMBER > _____
```

Assume that the user enters the number 2. A screen would appear that provides spaces for entering data concerning the acquisition of a fixed asset. Among the data items provided in the preformatted screen are date of purchase, manufacturer from whom purchased, class of asset, general ledger account number, assigned property number, description of asset, location of asset within the firm, method of depreciation, esti-

mated life, cost basis, and estimated salvage value.[3]

Required

Design a preformatted screen that arranges these items in a structured manner, and simulate the action of the data entry clerk by entering sample values for the items. Include in the screen format those items that would be automatically entered by the computer program, either to identify the transaction or to aid in reducing input errors. Denote these system-generated items by a star (*).

10-7. Draw the layout for a record of a work-in-process master file stored on magnetic disk. The file belongs to a manufacturing firm that accumulates costs by production orders. Enter data based on the following for production order no. 3569, started on February 16, 1989: direct materials issued, 40 units at $13 per unit; direct labor, 12 hours at $6.50 per hour and 20 hours at $8.30 per hour; and overhead, applied on the basis of $7.00 per direct-labor hour. Assume values for other data items that you include in the record layout. Ignore the lengths of the data fields.

10-8. Deake Corporation is a medium-sized, diversified manufacturing company located in Norman, Oklahoma. Frank Richards has been promoted recently to manager of the property accounting section. Richards has had difficulty in responding to some of the requests from individuals in other departments of Deake for information about the company's fixed assets. Some of the requests and problems Richards has had to cope with are as follows.

a. The controller has requested schedules of individual fixed assets to support the balances in the general ledger. Richards has furnished the necessary information, but he has always been late. The manner in which the records are organized makes it difficult to obtain information easily.

b. The maintenance manager wished to verify the existence of a punch press which he thinks was repaired twice. He has asked

---

[3] This problem can be solved by using a microcomputer-based data base management software package.

Richards to confirm the asset number and location of the press.

c. The insurance department wants data on the cost and book values of assets to include in its review of current insurance coverage.

d. The tax department has requested data that can be used to determine when Deake should switch depreciation methods for tax purposes.

e. The company's internal auditors have spent a significant amount of time in the property accounting section recently, attempting to confirm the annual depreciation expense.

The property account records that are at Richards' disposal consist of a set of manual books. These records show the date the asset was acquired, the account number to which the asset applies, the dollar amount capitalized, and the estimated useful life of the asset for depreciation purposes.

After many frustrations Richards has realized that his records are inadequate and he cannot supply the data easily when they are requested. He has decided that he should discuss his problems with the controller, Jim Castle.

Richards: Jim, something has got to give. My people are working overtime and can't keep up. You worked in property accounting before you became controller. You know I can't tell the tax, insurance, and maintenance people everything they need to know from my records. Also, that internal auditing team is living in my area and that slows down the work pace. The requests of these people are reasonable, and we should be able to answer these questions and provide the needed data. I think we need an automated property-accounting system. I would like to talk to the information systems people to see if they can help me.

Castle: Frank, I think you have a good idea, but be sure you are personally involved in the design of any system so that you get all the information you need.

Required

a. Identify and justify several major attributes Deake Corporation's computer-based property-accounting system should possess in or-

der to provide the data necessary to respond to requests of information from company personnel.

b. Identify the data that should be included in the record for each asset included in the property account.

(CMA adapted)

10-9. Design formats for two reports that are to provide needed information to enable the responsible managers to achieve these stated purposes.

a. The first report should allow the evaluation of cost levels incurred in production. Costs relate to direct materials, direct labor, and overhead for the production orders that have been completed this month. The evaluation should consist of comparing the actual (or applied) costs for these three elements against budgeted costs and the computation of variances. No specific production numbers or cost values need to be entered.

b. The second report should allow the daily evaluation of the use of materials in production operations in order to control waste caused by the carelessness and inefficiency of employees. The report should pinpoint individual employees, by name, as well as specific materials and operations. Enter into the format the following identifying data: employees May Banks, Jerry Kimble, Robert Lambert, Judy Pierpoint, and Sandy Tempo; materials Delta and Omega; operations I, II, III, and IV. It is not necessary to enter numerical values for the actual quantities of materials used or for any comparisons.

10-10. The Brown Printing Company of Fairfax, Virginia, accounts for the services it performs on a job-cost basis. Most jobs require a week or less to complete and involve two or more of Brown's five operating departments. Actual costs are accumulated by job. To ensure timely billing, however, the firm prepares sales invoices based on cost estimates.

Recently, several printing jobs have incurred losses. To avoid future losses, management has decided to focus on cost control at the department level. Since labor is a major cost element, one proposal is to develop a departmental labor cost report. This report is to be issued by the payroll department as one of the biweekly payroll outputs. The report is to be sent to an accounting clerk for comparison with the labor cost estimates of each department. If the actual total department labor cost in a payroll period is not significantly more than the estimated amount, the accounting clerk is to send the report to the department supervisor. However, if the accounting clerk concludes that a significant variance exists, the report will be sent to the assistant controller. She will investigate the cause, if time is available, and will recommend corrective action to the production manager.

Required

List the features of the proposed report and related procedure that represent sound management control principles, as well as those that appear to be unsound. *Hint:* Refer to the control reporting sections of a managerial or cost accounting textbook.

(CIA adapted)

10-11. Royal Payne Cleaners performs janitorial and cleaning services for office buildings and business firms in a large metropolitan area. The firm uses small computers to process its various accounting transactions and to manage its cash. With respect to cash management, the treasurer develops a cash requirements projection at the end of each month for the following month. He refuses to look more than one month ahead, since he believes that the economic and monetary uncertainties are too great. Based on the month-ahead projection, he adjusts the cash balance. If it appears to be too low, he borrows from the firm's bank at the prime rate. If the balance seems to be too high, he invests in short term certificates of deposit (CDs). (These investments safeguard the principal amount, although they do impose a penalty for early withdrawal.)

With regard to sales, the firm bills all credit customers at the end of each month. Most customers receive services on a continuing basis. However, a significant minority of sales each month are to customers who need services only sporadically. For instance, a customer will call five months after the previous service and ask for a cleaning "overhaul." This may occur early in the month. Terms of sale are net 45 days.

Payments on credit sales are received in the forms of checks and currency. These cash receipts are first sent to the receivables clerk, who posts the amounts to the accounts on her small accounting computer. Then she sends the cash receipts to the cashier, who makes out the deposit slip and enters the total in the cash receipts journal. She withholds about $200 each day for small expenditures. Occasionally cash amounts are received from the sale of fixed assets or from additional investments by the owner; these special receipts are deposited directly by the owner in a bank account in the owner's name. In most cases he informs the cashier orally of the amounts.

Invoices from suppliers are approved for payment. Most specify terms of 2/10, net 30 days. Since supplies are acquired in large quantities from only a few suppliers, the number of invoices received per week is considered too few for efficient check processing. Hence, checks are written on a biweekly basis for all invoices that have been approved during the period. The cashier signs most checks, although the owner signs all checks that pertain to relatively unusual and large transactions (e.g., the acquisition of a new panel truck).

Required

List the weaknesses in Royal Payne Cleaner's cash management system. Provide a recommended improvement for each listed weakness.

10-12. What error or fraudulent activity might occur if each of the following procedures is allowed?

a. Personnel and payroll are combined into the same organizational unit.

b. Departmental supervisors distribute paychecks to their employees.

c. The same person who prepares paychecks also signs the paychecks.

d. The fixed assets ledger is not periodically reconciled to the control accounts in the general ledger.

e. The work-in-process ledger is not periodically reconciled to the control account in the general ledger.

f. The paychecks are not prenumbered (or if prenumbered, copies are not filed in a sequential file that is periodically checked for gaps in the numbers).

g. Voided paychecks are destroyed.

h. Production supervisors do not observe factory employees clocking in and out on production jobs.

i. Scrapped materials are not maintained in a separate inventory and are not reported as they are generated during production.

j. Fixed assets do not have attached tags or labels showing their assigned numbers.

k. Fixed assets retirements are not reported.

10-13. What internal accounting control(s) would be most effective in preventing or detecting each of the following errors or fraudulent practices?

a. A payroll clerk computes 40 hours times $6 per hour to equal $250 gross pay.

b. An employee spends four hours in working on job order 782; however, he erroneously enters five hours on the labor job-time ticket.

c. A supervisor does not notify the personnel department when one of her employees quits; the supervisor turns in phony time cards for the employee each week and then keeps the paychecks for the employee when given the paychecks for distribution.

d. An engineering technician employed by a firm removes a complex testing machine from the premises and then reports to the property accounting department that it has been scrapped.

e. As production orders are received, the production supervisor requisitions the materials that he believes are needed for completing the job. Often he overestimates the materials needed; the excess materials are then taken home by production employees.

f. A production planning clerk accesses the confidential salary file via an online terminal in the department.

g. The number of hours worked by a production employee is incorrectly entered into an online terminal as 84 hours; it should appear as 48 hours.

h. The manager of a production work center questions the direct materials cost and asks to see the materials requisitions. Personnel from the production planning department search for hours to find the requested documents.

i. Ten time cards are accidentally lost in transmitting the time cards to the payroll department.

j. A personnel clerk accidentally omits a deduction code when entering a personnel action change for an employee into an online terminal.

k. A data entry clerk accidentally keys the letter l for the number 1 when entering time-card data onto a magnetic tape.

l. A computer-prepared fixed assets analysis is mistakenly sent to the storeskeeper rather than to the property accounting manager.

m. A payroll clerk increases the pay rate for a friend from $7 per hour to $9 per hour, and then uses this higher rate to compute the friend's pay amount.

n. A cost distribution clerk makes an arithmetic error in calculating the total costs allocated to all production jobs.

o. A computer operator enters a correction to a transaction via the console terminal and accidentally erases part of the employee payroll master file stored on magnetic tape.

p. A programmer obtains the employee payroll master file and increases her salary in her record.

q. A department manager has a large fireproof vault installed in the department, even though company policy is to maintain a centralized vault for use by all departments.

r. An employee is assigned a microcomputer for use in her job; however, she keeps it at home for personal use.

s. One fixed asset account in the general ledger reflects a considerable overstatement of asset value, since two posting errors were made earlier this year.

t. A production employee keys an incorrect job number when entering his job hours, and the hours are posted to the wrong production order.

u. In entering data into an online terminal for a new production order, a production planning clerk keys a number for a product that is obsolete.

v. A property accounting clerk accumulates depreciation on a machine in an amount that exceeds the cost of the machine.

10-14. Tempo Retailers of Durham, New Hampshire, processes its payroll by means of a small computer system. The following table presents sorted transaction data pertaining to the first several employees for a recent pay period.

Employee Number	Employee Name	Department Number	Hours Worked
13251	Smith, John	1	40
13620	Black, Charles	1	40
13543	Adams, Steve	1	48
13658	Br6wn, Rodney	1	40
13752	Jones, Paul	2	42
24313	Krause, Ken	2	44
25001	Tingey, Sharon	2	84

The first digit of the employee number indicates the employee's department, and the last digit is a nonzero self-checking digit.

Required

Assuming that the data represent the entire group of employees to be paid:

a. Compute three types of batch control totals.

b. Identify errors in the data and the specific type of programmed check that should detect each error.

10-15. Refer to the Review Problem for this chapter.

Required

a. Prepare a system flowchart that portrays both the manual and computer-based payroll procedure described in the problem. Use a columnar flowchart similar to the manual flowcharts, with columns labeled "Factory operating departments," "Timekeeping," "Payroll audit and control," "Data preparation," "Computer operations," and "Data library." Do not show the computer-based preparation of the labor cost distribution sheet, however.

b. Identify the programmed edit checks that should be used in step F (substep 11), assuming that the key-to-tape device used in step E cannot perform edit checks. Indicate the data items that each edit check is intended to test.

10-16. The Superior Co. of Huntington, West Virginia, manufactures automobile parts for sales to the major auto makers in the United States. Based on a recent review of the procedures concerning machinery and equipment, the firm's internal auditors noted the following findings in a memorandum.

a. Requests for purchases of machinery and equipment are normally initiated by the supervisor who needs the asset. This supervisor discusses the proposed acquisition with the plant manager. A purchase requisition is submitted to the purchasing department when the plant manager is satisfied that the request is reasonable and when he or she determines that the balance in the plant's share of the total corporate budget for capital acquisitions is adequate to cover the acquisition cost.

b. Upon receiving a purchase requisition for machinery or equipment, the purchasing department manager looks through the records for an appropriate supplier. A formal purchase order is then completed and mailed. When the machine or equipment is received, it is immediately sent to the requesting department for installation. This allows the economic benefits from the acquisition to be realized at the earliest possible date.

c. The property, plant, and equipment ledger control accounts are supported by lapsing schedules organized by year of acquisition. These lapsing schedules are used to compute depreciation as a unit for all assets of a given type that are acquired in the same year. Standard rates, depreciation methods, and salvage values are used for each major type of fixed asset. These rates, methods, and salvage values were set 10 years ago, during the firm's initial year of operation.

d. When machinery or equipment is retired, the plant manager notifies the accounting department so that the appropriate entries may be made in the accounting records.

e. There has been no reconciliation, since the firm began operations, between the accounting records and the machinery and equipment physically on hand.

Required

Identify the internal control weaknesses in the fixed assets procedure described, and recommend improvements.

(CMA adapted)

10-17. The narrative description and document flowchart on page 390 pertain to the payroll procedure of Croyden, Inc., of Fullerton, California.

The internal control structure with respect to the personnel department is well functioning and is not included in the accompanying flowchart.

At the beginning of each workweek payroll clerk no. 1 reviews the payroll department files to determine the employment status of factory employees and then prepares time cards and distributes them as each individual arrives at work. This payroll clerk, who is also responsible for custody of the signature stamp machine, verifies the identity of each payee before delivering signed checks to the supervisor.

At the end of each workweek the supervisor distributes payroll checks for the preceding workweek. Concurrent with this activity, the supervisor reviews the current week's employee time cards, notes the regular and overtime hours worked on a summary form, and initials the aforementioned time cards. The supervisor then delivers all time cards and unclaimed payroll checks to payroll clerk no. 2.

Required

a. Based on the narrative and accompanying flowchart, describe the weaknesses in the structure of internal control.

b. Based on the narrative and accompanying flowchart, what inquiries should be made with respect to clarifying the existence of possible additional weaknesses in the structure of internal control?

Note: Do not discuss the internal control structure of the personnel department.

(CPA adapted)

10-18. The Vane Corporation of Miami, Florida, is a manufacturing concern that has been in business for the past 18 years. During this period the company has grown from a very small, family-owned operation to a medium-sized manufacturing concern with several departments. Despite this growth a substantial number of the procedures employed by Vane Corporation have been in effect since the business was started. Just recently, Vane Corporation has computerized its payroll function.

The payroll function operates in the following manner. Each worker picks up a weekly time card on Monday morning and writes in his or her name and identification number. These blank cards are kept near the factory entrance. The workers write on their cards their daily arrival and departure times. On the following Monday the factory supervisors collect the completed time cards for the previous week and send them to data processing.

In data processing the time cards are used to prepare the weekly time file. This file is processed with the master payroll file, which is maintained on magnetic tape according to worker identification number. The checks are written by the computer on the regular checking account and imprinted with the treasurer's signature. After the payroll file is updated and the checks are prepared, the checks are sent to the factory supervisors, who distribute them to the workers or hold them for absent workers to pick up later.

The supervisors notify data processing of new employees and terminations. Any changes in hourly pay rate or any other changes affecting payroll usually are communicated to data processing by the supervisors.

The workers also complete a job-time ticket for each individual job they work on each day. The job-time tickets are collected daily and sent to cost accounting, where they are used to prepare a cost distribution analysis.

Further analysis of the payroll function reveals the following information.

a. A worker's gross wages never exceed $600 per week.

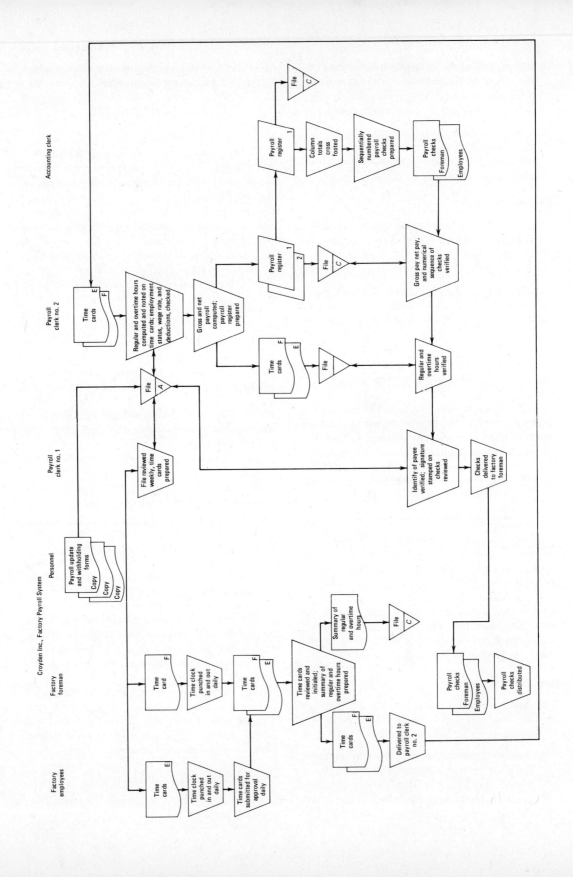

Croyden Inc., Factory Payroll System

b. Raises never exceed $1.50 per hour for the factory workers.

c. No more than 20 hours of overtime is allowed each week.

d. The factory employs 150 workers in 10 departments.

The payroll function has not been operating smoothly for some time, but even more problems have surfaced since the payroll was computerized. The supervisors have indicated that they would like a weekly report indicating worker tardiness, absenteeism, and idle time so that they can determine the amount of productive time lost and the reason for the lost time. The following errors and inconsistencies have been encountered the past few pay periods.

a. A worker's paycheck was not processed properly because he had transposed two numbers in his identification number when he filled out his time card.

b. A worker was issued a check for $5,531.80 when she should have received $553.18.

c. One worker's paycheck was not written, and this error was not detected until the paychecks for that department were distributed by the supervisor.

d. Part of the master payroll file was destroyed when the tape reel was inadvertently mounted on the wrong tape drive and used as a scratch tape. Data processing attempted to re-establish the destroyed portion from original source documents and other records.

e. One worker received a paycheck for an amount considerably larger than he should have. Further investigation revealed that "84" had been keyed instead of "48" for hours worked.

f. Several records on the master payroll were skipped and not included on the updated master payroll file. This was not detected for several pay periods.

g. In processing nonroutine changes a computer operator included a pay rate increase for one of her friends in the factory. This was discovered by chance by another employee.

Required

Identify the control weaknesses in the payroll procedure and in the computer processing as it is now conducted by the Vane Corporation. Recommend the changes necessary to correct the system.

(CMA adapted)

10-19. The Prescott Manufacturing Company employs an online processing system to track its production orders. Each production order is first issued by the production planning department after a clerk enters data from a customer's order. In addition to three copies of the production order, which is automatically prenumbered and dated, the issuing program generates a move ticket for the initial work center and a materials requisition. The production data file (containing the schedule, machine loadings, bill of materials, and product structures), open production order file, work-in-process master file, and requisition file are accessed by this program.

The second step is to deliver a copy of the production order, move ticket, and requisition (the "package") to the initial work center. (The other copies of the order are filed numerically and sent to the sales order department). Materials are delivered to the work center by the storeskeeper, who has received a copy of the requisition on his printer. The same program that generates the requisition for him reduces balances in the raw materials inventory master file to reflect their issuance. When materials are received, they are compared with the requisition already received.

Before and after the operation is performed at the initial work center, the involved employee enters the production order number and employee number into the work center terminal. The quantity completed is also entered upon completion. The computer system automatically records the start and completion times and dates. The program generates a move ticket for the next work center and enters the costs in a general ledger transaction file. The work-in-process is moved to the next center, together with the production order package. The files accessed by this program are the production order file, employee payroll file, work-in-process file, production data file, and general ledger file.

At the final work center, the employee who performs the last operation enters the same data.

The program recognizes, after accessing the production order file, that the order is completed. Then the program totals the work-in-process record, transfers it to the finished goods inventory file, and enters the journal entry into the general ledger transaction file. It also removes the production order from the open file and transfers it to a completed order file, and enters time data into the employee payroll file. The production order package is returned to the production planning department.

At the end of each day, a program posts the production transactions to the general ledger file and prints a summary of all completed production orders.

Required

a. Prepare a series of five system flowcharts that show the major steps described. Assume that one operation is performed at each work center.

b. List programmed checks that should be performed by each program listed and the data on which the checks are performed.

10-20. Industrial Builders of Austin, Texas, is a general building contractor specializing in shopping centers, office complexes, factories, hotels, and other large buildings. When the firm learns of a proposed project, it assigns an estimator to review the plans and prepare a bid quotation. Included within the quotation are estimates for materials, labor, subcontracted work, and such overhead items as building permits and supervision. The estimator draws on his or her experience, plus generally accepted cost guidelines and figures from the subcontractors, in developing these estimates. A profit margin then is added to the total estimated cost to arrive at the contract bid price.

If the contract is awarded to Industrial Builders, the project is assigned to a project manager. He or she has the responsibility for keeping costs within the total estimated cost and for meeting a scheduled deadline.

Unfortunately, most of the projects incur cost and time overruns. These overruns appear to be the cause of the firm's declining profitability during the past several years. The project manager blames these problems on the estimators and schedulers, saying that the estimated costs and scheduled deadlines are unrealistic. The estimators concede that cost estimates often tend to be low, since the inflation rate has been rather severe in recent years. However, they contend that the project managers are careless about watching costs and time schedules.

Required

a. Describe the source needed by Industrial Builders in recording the costs of projects.

b. Design formats for reports that will aid the firm in (1) developing values for estimates, (2) compiling the total estimated costs, and (3) controlling project costs and schedules.

PART III

SYSTEM

SUPPORT FOR

OPERATIONS AND

MANAGEMENT

Computer-based

Data

Management

Describe the objectives and functions of data management.

Identify key methods by which files may be structured and measured.

Contrast the file-oriented and data base approaches.

Describe three logical data models.

Describe the relationships and functions of data base management software.

Discuss the effect of the data base on needed accounting controls.

INTRODUCTION

Data can be viewed as a resource. Even though this resource does not appear as a valued asset on the balance sheet of a firm, it nevertheless is extremely valuable to the firm. When relevant data are lost or inaccessible or uncollected, the firm can suffer severe economic consequences. Managing data is therefore a vital activity of an accounting information system (AIS).

As we have seen, data involved in transaction processing are generally stored in data files. In manual systems these files serve as the main repository of data—the **data base**—from which reports can be prepared and inquiries answered. When the AIS is computerized, data management becomes more complex. Files are likely to be linked, for instance, and data may be grouped into structures other than files.

Accountants are deeply involved in data management. On the input side, they devise and control the transactional data flows. On the output side, they design reports and other means of providing needed information to users. To meet these responsibilities accountants should clearly understand file concepts and organization methods. They should also be aware of alternative approaches to managing data.

OBJECTIVES

Of what does sound data management consist? Perhaps the foremost objective is that the collected data bases contain *sufficient* data to meet the purposes of the AIS (i.e., to handle transactions and to provide users with information for decision-making). All these needed data should be safe from loss and unauthorized access. Furthermore, the data should be readily *accessible* to all qualified users on a timely basis. The data should be *up to date* and *accurate* so that users can rely on the resulting information. Still another objective is *efficiency* in handling the data, both in terms of time and storage space. Finally, all the functions involved in managing data should be achieved in as *economical* a manner as possible.

FUNCTIONS

These objectives point to the existence of three primary data management functions: (1) creating a stored base of data, (2) maintaining the stored data within the data base, and (3) retrieving needed data from the data base. Figure 11-1 portrays these three functions and the various steps they encompass. The functions and steps are discussed in the following paragraphs.

Create a Data Base

The initial function is to create the means whereby data may be stored and managed. Three of the steps necessary in creating a data base are defining the logical and physical structures, coding data items, and implementing the data management mechanism.

Define Logical and Physical Structures The **logical data structure** is the organization of the stored data from the viewpoint of the user. For instance, the logical record structure of an accounts receivable master file, one file comprising the revenue cycle data base, was defined in Figure 8-14. It consists of a sequence of fields, each of which is to contain the value of a data item. Knowledge of this structured set of data items, plus related sets in other files comprising the data base, is important to the accounts receivable clerk and other users of the revenue cycle data base. This information is also vital to the computer programs that are to process the sales and cash receipts transactions.

The **physical storage structure** refers to the way the data are tangibly stored and arranged on such physical media as magnetic disks, magnetic tapes, optical disks, and microfilm. For example, the accounts receivable master file might be stored on a magnetic disk at storage addresses along numbered track 067.

The physical structure is the responsibility of the data base administrator. However, the accountant should be aware of the physical media being selected,

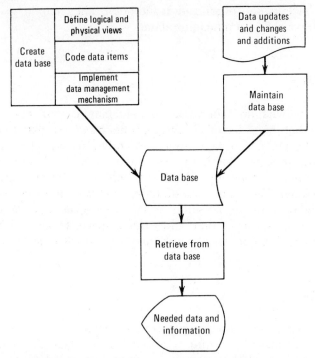

FIGURE 11-1 Functions of data management.

since the media affect such objectives as accessibility and data currency (up-to-dateness). For example, magnetic disks enhance both of these objectives by allowing records to be directly accessed. Also, the physical grouping of data can affect certain objectives. For instance, several logical records can be blocked on a magnetic tape or disk, as shown in Figure 3-12. This blocking action forms larger physical records (i.e., contiguous data between two gaps). Since a program instruction such as READ DATA causes an entire physical record or block to be handled by the computer system, larger physical records lead to faster and hence more efficient processing.

Code Data Items In order to store data in an organized manner, unique coded identifiers are needed. As we have noted, each record should have a **primary key,** the coded data item by which the records in the file are most likely to be sequenced. Records are also likely to have **secondary keys,** attributes which represent logical, alternative ways of sequencing the file. For instance, the customer account number in the accounts receivable master file is usually the primary key, whereas the customer's last name and ZIP Code may be secondary keys. When attributes are coded (as in the case of ZIP Codes), they are more easily applied as secondary keys.

Implement Data Management Mechanism In a computer-based system, a means or method is needed by which to access and manipulate requested data within the physical structures of a data base. This capability can be achieved through a software package called a data base management system (discussed later in the chapter).

Maintain the Data Base

Once created, a data base must be kept up to date. Updating the master files is therefore a central purpose of data processing. We have seen a variety of examples involving sequential processing and online processing, the two approaches to file updating.

Complete data base maintenance consists of more than the updating of balances in master files. It includes (1) changes to the relatively permanent data in master files, (2) additions of records for new entities (e.g., new customers), and (3) deletions of records for discontinued entities.

Retrieve Data from the Data Base

Data must be retrieved in order to be used. When magnetic tape is the physical storage medium, the only feasible method of retrieving data is the **sequential search method,** which consists of searching from the beginning of the tape for the desired record(s). When magnetic disk is the storage medium, several faster search methods are available. These alternative search methods are made possible by the presence of permanent disk addresses.

When the records in a file are arranged sequentially on a disk, either the binary search method or the index method may be employed. The **binary search method** consists of checking the value of the key at the midpoint of the file, determining in which half the desired record resides, then checking the midpoint of that half, and so on until the record is located. The **index search method** consists of preparing an index or directory, in which the key (usually primary) of each record is cross-referenced to its address on the magnetic disk.

Two other search methods do not require the records to be arranged sequentially. One method consists of inserting values within the records that "point" to other records that are logically related. Another method consists of performing computations that provide the storage location of the record. Each of these search methods is illustrated later.

FILE STRUCTURES AND MEASURES

Several types of files are used in computer-based accounting information systems. For instance, programs for processing transactions are kept in files, as are narrative textual reports. Our major concern, however, is with data files.

Data files, as we have seen, consist of a number of records. These records have identical sequences of data items. They may be fixed in length, or they may vary in length. Although fixed length records are easier to accommodate in programs, variable length records can provide considerable savings in required storage space. For instance, variable length records are suitable for employee personal history records, since employees vary widely in work experience and education.

The physical structure of records within files is related to the methods by which they are organized and accessed. Records may be organized in some specified sequence or randomly (i.e., in no specified sequence). Records may be accessed by any of the search methods already listed. Three resulting file structures are known as sequential files, indexed sequential files, and random files; two file-related structures are inverted files and linked lists. Less commonly encountered structures, such as direct and virtual storage files, are not discussed.

Sequential Files

The records in a **sequential file** are organized sequentially, usually in ascending order, according to the primary key. An example is a master file whose primary key values begin 102, 126, 127, 138. . . . Each record immediately follows the preceding record within a block. At the end of each block an interblock gap appears. Thus, sequential organization makes very efficient use of storage space.

A sequential file is normally accessed sequentially. Each record is scanned, beginning with the first record of the file. During this scanning process the key value of each record is compared with the value of the desired record. When the two values match, the desired record has been located. Then it can be updated or retrieved. On the average, one half of the records in a sequential file must be scanned to locate a single record. Thus, this access method is relatively inefficient for individual records. On the other hand, when a large number of records are to be located, the sequential access method is relatively efficient. Consequently, this method is suited to the processing of a sizable batch of transactions against a master file.

Since the physical characteristics of magnetic tape dictate sequential organization and access methods, sequential files have typically been employed with magnetic tape. This medium is still in use, especially for transaction files and very large master files, because it is relatively inexpensive. Increasingly, though, sequentially organized files are being stored on magnetic disks. In addition to providing efficient storage and batch processing, such files enable individual records to be retrieved by the binary search method.

Indexed Sequential Files

When an index is added to a sequential file, the file becomes an **indexed sequential file** (often called an ISAM file). Besides providing the advantages of the sequential file, this type of file structure enables individual records to be retrieved more quickly than by sequential or binary search methods. Thus, an ISAM accounts receivable file can be used to process batches of sales and payments transactions efficiently or to generate periodic aging schedules based on all the records in the file; between such processings, individual customer records can be accessed quickly in order to answer inquiries or make changes to permanent data.

Figure 11-2 shows portions of an index and the file to which it relates. In the left column of the index are values for the primary keys of records within a sequentially organized file. To reduce the size of the index, only key values for the first record in each block are listed. Cross-referenced to each listed key value

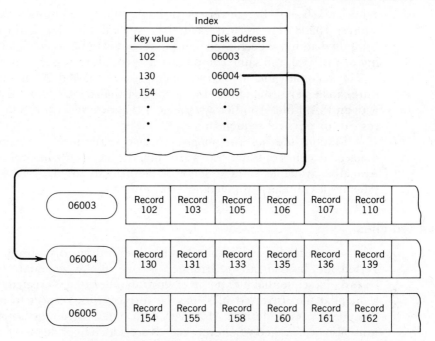

FIGURE 11-2 A portion of an indexed sequential file.

is the disk address (where the first three digits are the track number and the last two digits are the record surface number). When a user makes an inquiry concerning a desired record, the computer data base software searches the index for the specified key. If the desired record has a key value of 136, the search program selects the second block (since 136 is between 130 and 154). The software "looks" in the index for the disk address (06004) at which the desired block is stored. Then the block (called a **bucket**) is searched sequentially until the record with the key value of 136 is located.

An ISAM file is stored on a direct access medium such as a magnetic disk. The sequentially organized records must be retained in the same locations, in order that the index values remain valid. Thus, adding new records is not easy. In cases when the key values fall somewhere within the file, pointers must be used to link the new records to their proper places. When such linked records become numerous, the file must be reorganized and the index revised.

Random Files

When the records of a file are stored throughout a direct access storage medium in no apparent order, the file is described as having a random organization. Individual records in such files are usually accessed directly by means of a randomizing procedure. Hence, such files may be described as direct access or **random files.**

The randomizing procedure, often called a **hashing scheme,** transforms the primary key of a record into a randomized number. This number, in turn, is converted into the storage address of the record. For instance, the primary key value of 136 may be converted, through various computations, into the disk address 10208. The record having the key value of 136 is then stored at the computed address. Each time that the record is to be accessed, either for updating or retrieval, the same computational procedure is performed.

The major advantage of a random file is access speed. A computational procedure can be performed faster by a computer than a table look-up procedure used with an ISAM file. Another advantage is that new records can be added without regard for physical sequencing.

A random file has two major drawbacks. Because its records are not sequenced, batches of transactions affecting the file cannot be processed efficiently. Also, the available storage space is inefficiently used, since known hashing schemes leave many storage addresses unfilled.

Inverted Files

A sequential file is typically arranged according to its primary key. An **inverted file,** by contrast, is arranged by one of the secondary keys within the record of a sequential file. It is in essence an index that is created *in addition to* the sequential file. Inverted files may be formed with respect to as many of the secondary keys as desired. However, each index consumes storage space. Each must also be changed whenever records are added to or deleted from the sequential file that it supports.

Figure 11-3 shows, in the top part, several records of a sequential file. The customer number is the primary key; customer name, credit limit, and current

Disk address	Customer number	Customer name	Credit limit (000$)	Current balance ($)
1000	100	Waters, John	2	715.00
1100	101	Jacobs, Paul	4	3010.00
1200	104	Adams, Steve	3	0.00
1300	106	Trimble, Shirley	2	1497.50
1400	107	Baker, Trevor	4	50.00
1500	110	Early, Kristin	3	882.75
1600	112	Malcolm, Doris	2	100.00

Credit limit	Disk addresses
2	1000, 1300, 1600
3	1200, 1500
4	1100, 1400

FIGURE 11-3 Records in an accounts receivable master file and an inverted file based on the credit limit secondary key.

balance may be used as secondary keys. Of these data items, the credit limit attribute has been inverted in the lower part of the figure. That is, the values assigned to credit limits, ranging from $2000 through $4000, have been listed in order and cross-referenced to the disk addresses at which the records are located. If a user makes a request for those customers having a credit limit of $2000, the data base software can scan the inverted file, retrieve the records located at disk addresses 1000 and 1300 and 1600, and display the names of the customers for the requester. Because the inverted file is smaller than the sequential file and best arranged to handle the request, the response time will be much faster.

The prime benefit of inverted files is therefore to enhance the retrieval of data. They are particularly useful for **multiple-key inquiries.** Consider, for instance, the availability of inverted files formed with respect to these three attributes from an employee file: skill code, employee location, and years of experience. It would then be possible to quickly answer inquiries such as: Which employees having two or more years of experience as a cost accountant are located in the firm's Denver plant?

Linked Lists

A **linked list** is a collection of logically related data. It is formed by means of pointers that are embedded within the records of a file. Thus, a linked list is a structure that is attached, in effect, to an existing file structure.

A **pointer** employed in a linked list is a data item whose value typically consists of the storage address where associated data are located. In contrast to other data items in a record, it provides *direction* rather than *content*. Figure 11-4 illustrates pointers by means of the accounts receivable master file shown in Figure 11-3. A right-most field has been added to each record. In the pointer field for the first record has been added the value of 1300. This value refers to the disk address of a record containing related data. In our example the related data is the credit limit, which is the same level ($2000) as in the first record. The 1600 in the pointer field of this latter record in turn points to the next record containing the same credit limit of $2000.

Linked lists enable desired data to be accessed and retrieved more rapidly. Several variations are employed. One variation involves the linking of attributes,

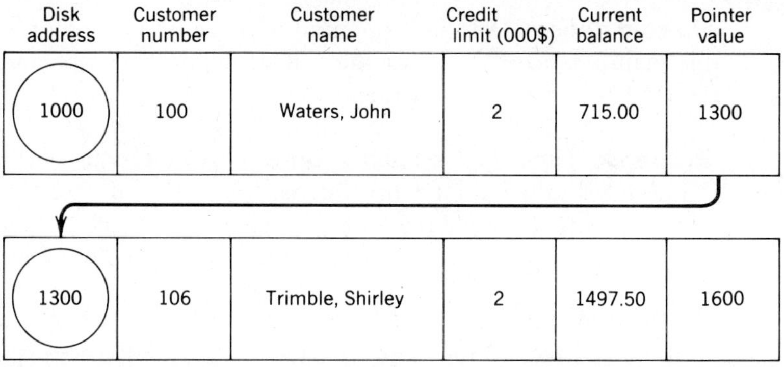

Disk address	Customer number	Customer name	Credit limit (000$)	Current balance	Pointer value
1000	100	Waters, John	2	715.00	1300
1300	106	Trimble, Shirley	2	1497.50	1600

FIGURE 11-4 Pointers within accounts receivable master file records.

such as credit limits, to form **attribute lists** or chains. In our example, which illustrates this variation, three chains are formed because three different credit limits are available. (As you have very likely deduced, attribute lists and inverted files represent alternative means of achieving the same data associations.) Other uses of linked lists are (1) to enable reports to be prepared without the need for re-sorting an entire file, and (2) to enable records in one file to be linked to related records in a separate file.

When used extensively, pointers can create linked lists that are quite complex and sophisticated. For instance, pointers can point backwards to preceding records in a list; they can form **ring lists** by connecting the last record in a list to the first.

File-related Measures

As we have noted, each type of file structure offers certain relative advantages. Several measures—such as size, activity, volatility, up-to-dateness, and response time—can aid a system designer in choosing among the structures.

File Size Files range in size from a few short records to millions of large records. Certain files of insurance companies and the Internal Revenue Service, for instance, fit at the upper end. Magnetic tape has generally been selected for very large files, since it is relatively inexpensive. This choice has in turn dictated the use of sequential files. Since retrieval has become increasingly important, however, direct access storage media are often being selected even for large files. In such cases ISAM files provide the best balance between storage efficiency and retrieval speeds.

Activity Ratio The busyness of a file is measured by the **activity ratio,** the number of records affected during a file maintenance run divided by the total number of records in the file. If 1000 records of a 10,000 record master file are affected during an update run, for instance, the activity ratio is 10 percent. The higher the activity ratio, the greater the benefit gained from sequential processing. Hence, a sequential or ISAM file should be considered when the activity ratio is 10 percent or higher. Conversely, a low activity ratio suggests the choice of a random file.

Up-to-dateness Data in sequential files are up to date only just following each file maintenance run. If currency of stored data is important, either random or ISAM files should be considered.

Response Time The **response time** is the interval that elapses between the request for information and the receipt of the information. If the acceptable response time is only a few seconds, a random file is likely to be most appropriate. Alternatively, inverted files or linked lists may be added to sequential files.

File Volatility Volatility refers to the frequency with which records are added and deleted from a file over a period of time. The records in the guest file of a motel are very volatile, for instance. A random file is likely to be preferable to a sequential file, since accessibility is more important than processing efficiency.

Also, in a random file the problem of positioning new records within the file does not arise.

Conclusions A random file is most suitable when up-to-dateness and fast response times are important, the activity ratio is low, the volatility is high, and the file is limited in size. A sequential file is most suitable under an opposite set of conditions. An ISAM file is a good choice when processing efficiency and accessibility are both important. An inverted file or linked list can reduce response times when sequential files (on direct access storage media) are employed.

DATA BASE APPROACH

Two alternative approaches for managing a firm's data are available. These contrasting approaches are pictured in Figure 11-5. The **file-oriented approach** focuses on individual applications, such as transaction processing applications. Each application maintains its own set of files. The **data base approach** focuses on the integrated store of data needed by a variety of applications. In this approach data are arranged in structures called **data sets.** Although data sets include files, they also encompass many varied arrangements of data. Each application that requires data from these data sets accesses them with the aid of software known as a data base management system (DBMS).

Shortcomings of the File-oriented Approach

The file-oriented approach is currently used by many firms, since it is the means originally employed by computerized accounting systems. Moreover, it serves the needs of individual applications and their users quite efficiently. From the perspective of a firm's broader information needs, however, this approach has several shortcomings, which are noted in the following discussions.

Data Redundancy Since each application maintains its own files, those files that are needed by more than one application must be duplicated. For instance, separate versions of the inventory master file are used in processing sales transactions and purchases transactions. Also, the same data items often appear in more than one file. Thus, the numbers of inventory items (and perhaps their descriptions) are likely to be repeated in the inventory master file, the open purchase order file, and the supplier file. Data redundancy is costly in storage space.

Data Inconsistency As a consequence of data redundancies, the names of data items and their values are likely to be inconsistent. For example, the inventory item number may be assigned the name ITEM in one application program and ITNO in another. The quantities of an inventory item shown as being on-hand may differ between inventory files used in two applications, since the files are updated at different points in time.

Inaccessibility of Data Reports based on the primary key of one or more files in a single application can be easily accommodated. Thus, listings of the status of inventory items and monthly customer statements are routinely prepared. How-

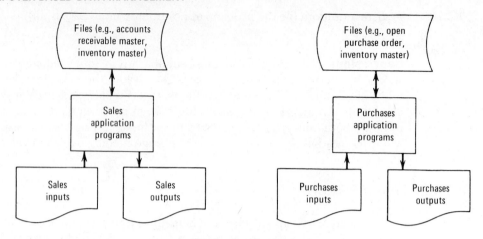

a. The file-oriented approach

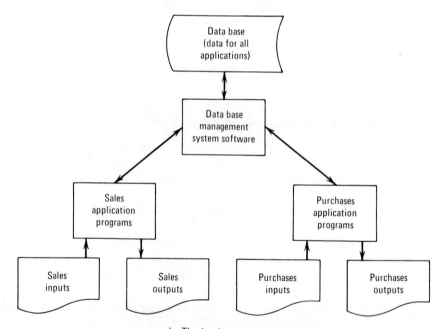

b. The data base approach

FIGURE 11-5 The two approaches to computer-based data management.

ever, data are less accessible for other information needs. Special reports based on secondary keys cannot be easily or quickly prepared. If special or ad hoc reports are to be based on data from more than one application, the data are even less accessible. For instance, if management requests a sales forecast or a budgetary control report, a new application (with its own files) is likely to be needed.

Dependence of Application Programs Each application program refers directly to the physical locations and characteristics of records and data items within the stored files. Because of this close dependence between the program and data, modifying programs is often costly and time-consuming.

Features of the Data Base Approach

Data Independence As Figure 11-6 illustrates, **data independence** refers to the independence of the data base from the various application programs. It is achieved by inserting a data base management system between the data base and the application programs. As a result, the application programs do not need to include the details of the data they use or be "aware" of the physical details of storage.

Data Standardization Every data item is standardized; each has only a single name, meaning, and format. Thus, stored data are compatible with every application program that accesses the data base.

One-time Data Entry Individual values of data items, such as the amount of a sales transaction, are entered into the data base only once from a single source. Thus, inconsistencies in input data cannot occur.

Shared Data Ownership All data are shared, or "owned in common" by users. No organizational unit, such as the marketing function, has the right to prevent legitimate uses of the data. Therefore, informational reporting can freely draw on data from more than one function.

Data Security Shared data ownership does not mean free access to all. Data are protected from unauthorized users by various specialized security measures, which will be discussed later.

Data Integration A variety of associations are formed among data sets and items having logical relationships. These associations aid users in obtaining desired data from the data base. The logical view, or "blueprint," of all these associations among the data sets comprising a data base is called a **schema**. A **subschema** is the portion of the schema—a partial view—that is of interest to a particular user. Thus, a schema is like the map of your city, and the subschema is the portion of the map that includes your neighborhood and other points of interest to you.

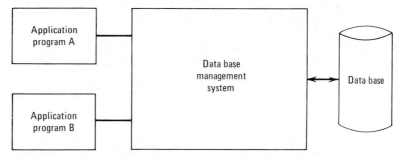

FIGURE 11-6 The data-independence feature of the data base approach.

Benefits of the Data Base Approach

The data base approach overcomes most of the shortcomings of the file-oriented approach. Redundancies in stored data are reduced through the integration of data sets. Redundant collection of data is also reduced because of the one-time entry of each transaction. Inconsistencies are eliminated, since all data sets affected by transaction data are updated simultaneously. Increased flexibility is provided through data independence and standardization, thereby enabling application program changes to be made more quickly and inexpensively. Finally, accessibility to the data is improved, due both to data sharing and extensive data relationships. Thus, diverse qualified users (e.g., managers, accountants, clerks) can obtain needed information more quickly and easily. Figure 11-7 ties these benefits to the features of the data base approach.

Drawbacks of the Data Base Approach

As might be expected, the data base approach exacts some penalties. The required computer hardware and software are quite costly (although the costs are decreasing). For instance, the hardware must include direct access storage devices and generally requires a powerful processor with a large primary storage unit and online terminals. Qualified technical personnel are scarce and command high salaries. Often current information systems employees must be extensively retrained. Because of its radical differences from the file-oriented approach, the data base approach generally creates severe difficulties during its development and implementation. Finally, because of its integrated nature and central role within an information system, the data base causes data to be highly vulnerable. A breakdown in hardware can have a much greater adverse effect on operations.

Feature(s)	Benefit(s) provided	Result achieved
Data independence Data standardization	Increased flexibility	Application programs can be changed faster and less expensively.
One-time data entry Data integration	Reduced redundancy; eliminated inconsistencies	Storage space is conserved, and data are totally consistent.
Data integration Shared data ownership	Increased accessibility	Needed information can be obtained faster and more easily.
Data security	Increased protection of data	Unauthorized persons are prevented from accessing stored data.

FIGURE 11-7 Correlation of data base features with the benefits they provide and the positive results the benefits achieve.

LOGICAL DATA MODELS

One of the most powerful aspects of the data base approach is the association of related data items. Three types of data-related structures may be formed by means of currently available data base management systems. These data-related structures—generally called **logical data models**—are the tree model, network model, and relational model. These models or structures are in addition to the flat file structures described earlier, which consist of identical records containing related sequences of data items. (The set of accounts receivable records in Figure 11-3 is an example of a flat file.)

Each of the logical data models is described in detail. The underlying physical storage structures will not be considered, other than to note that they usually involve pointers, indexes, inverted files, and/or linked lists.

Tree Model

The **tree,** or **hierarchical, model** expresses relationships between a **parent** node and related but subordinate data nodes, which are called its **children.** At the top of the structure is the **root node.** Extending downward from the root node at lower levels are the branches and nodes that give the structure its name.

The simplest form of a tree structure is the **set.** Figure 11-8 shows a set consisting of a customer record (the parent and root node) and a sales invoice record (the child and single subordinate node). In effect, this structure links records in the customer master file (arranged by customer account numbers) with records in the sales invoice transaction file (arranged by sales invoice numbers). By means of this structure, specific customer records are linked, by pointers in the customer records, to the specific sales invoices that are associated with the customers. For instance, the record for customer number 1016 may be linked to sales invoice records numbered 357 and 403. Because this linkage has been established, a user (e.g., an accounts receivable clerk) may quickly locate the sales made to a particular customer.

Tree structures may extend downward for several levels. Figure 11-9 portrays, by means of a data structure diagram, a structure having three levels. It is an expansion of the set just discussed. Inserted at the second level is a transaction type record, which contains the code for transaction type (e.g., S for a sale), the document number, date, and amount of the transaction. At the third level are the detailed records relating to sales, sales returns, and cash receipts transactions.

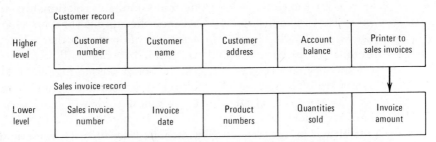

FIGURE 11-8 A set of two data records.

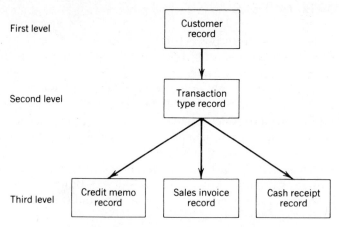

First level

Second level

Third level

FIGURE 11-9 A three-level tree structure.

These changes provide two benefits. First, more information needs can be quickly satisfied. For instance, with the inclusion of cash receipts and sales returns amounts, the customers' monthly statements can now be easily prepared. Second, more flexibility has been added, since the key data for each transaction now appears in a separate node.

The primary benefit of a tree structure is that it enables the prompt retrieval of data concerning a particular type of entity. It reflects a **one-to-many relationship,** since each particular parent will often have more than one child; on the other hand, each child has only one parent. Examples of entities that often serve as parents in tree structures are bank depositors, inventory items, and job orders.

Network Model

The **network model,** also called a plex structure, expresses more extensive relationships than the tree model. It allows more than one root node; it also requires at least one child (subordinate node) to have multiple parents. In effect, it provides a more realistic modeling of the multitude of relationships encountered by the typical business firm.

As Figure 11-10 illustrates, two degrees of intricacy are reflected by network structures. A simple structure, such as the one shown in Figure 11-10a, includes more than one parent; however, all relationships between a parent and child are on a one-to-many basis. A complex structure, such as the one shown in Figure 11-10b, must include at least one **many-to-many relationship.** In the example, this type of relationship exists between the supplier and merchandise inventory records, as denoted by the two-way flow of arrows. If that relationship were not present, the structure—though expanded—would still be of the simple type.

Many-to-many relationships can be better seen in Figure 11-11. Students and classes are both parents and children. Each student generally takes more than one class (i.e., *many* classes) during a semester; likewise, each class contains more than one student (i.e., *many* students). By means of the two-way structure, it is possible for users to obtain (1) class schedules for each student, and (2) student listings for each class.

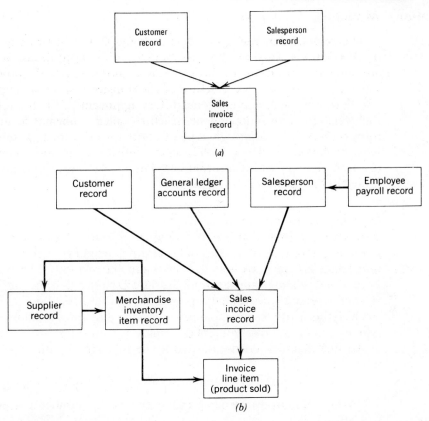

FIGURE 11-10 Examples of network structures. (*a*) A simple structure. (*b*) A complex structure.

A typical network structure creates more relationships than a tree structure. Hence, it enables a wider variety of information requests to be satisfied. Also, because each parent represents a point of entry into the structure, it is more flexible. Nevertheless, its added complexity causes the network structure to be used less often than the alternative structures.

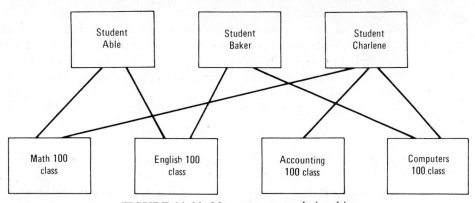

FIGURE 11-11 Many-to-many relationships.

Relational Model

The **relational model** views data as being stored in two-dimensional tables called **relations.** Because these relations have the appearance of flat files, they are familiar to most users. This model is an alternative to the other two models, since any tree or network structure can be transformed into relations. Conceptually, however, the relational model differs significantly. When carefully designed, each relation is an independent structure called a **normal form.** This normal form centers around a single type of entity (or event or relationship) and contains attributes that depend solely on the entity. New relations may be formed as users enter requests for information. These relations are formed by means of powerful data manipulating operators.

Example An example may clarify these key features of a relational model. Assume that a construction firm has a human resource data base consisting of files pertaining to employees, skills, jobs, and departments. The firm acquires relational data base software and establishes suitable relations. Three of the resulting normalized relations appear in Figure 11-12. Notice that the employee and skill relations contain rows (called tuples) and columns (called domains) that pertain solely to the attributes of employees and skills. The third relation is a connection-type relation that cross-references employees and skills.

Assume that answers are needed to the following inquiries:

1. Which employees, by number, possess skill number 30?

2. Which employees, by name and social security number, possess skill number 20?

3. Which skills, by name, are possessed by employee Kimble?

First, the requester, perhaps a personnel manager, enters the inquiries in accordance with the query language specified by the relational data base management system. These inquiries will likely include operators such as SELECT, JOIN, and PROJECT. Upon interpreting these inquiries, the system will create new relations as necessary and display these for the manager.

Let us apply these steps to the listed inquiries.

1. The answer is obtained from the employee/skill relation by using the SELECT operator. The request might be worded as "SELECT EMPLOYEE-NO. FROM EMPLOYEE/SKILL WHERE SKILL-NO. EQUALS 30." A new relation would then appear in the following form:

1000	30
7000	30

2. The answer requires that the employee and employee/skill relations be combined by a JOIN operator. From this new relation, a PROJECT operator extracts the employee name, social security number, and skill-no. columns. Finally, a SELECT operator focuses on employees White and Black as those who possess skill-no. 20.

Skill

Skill no.	Skill description	No. of vacancies
10	Lathe operator	0
20	Carpenter	1
30	Arc welder	0
40	Lab technician	0
50	Truck driver	2
60	Mechanic	0

Employee

Employee no.	Employee name	SSN	Age
1000	Brown	xxx–xx–xxxx	23
2000	Smith	"	26
3000	Kimble	"	30
4000	Jones	"	32
5000	White	"	45
6000	Green	"	39
7000	Black	"	37

Employee/skill

Employee no.	Skill no.
1000	30
2000	40
3000	50
3000	60
4000	10
5000	20
6000	60
7000	20
7000	30

FIGURE 11-12 Relations of a human-resource relation data base. Based on an example in Dan C. Kneer and Joseph W. Wilkinson, "DBMS: Do You Know Enough to Choose?" *Management Accounting,* September 1984, pp. 34–38. Copyright © 1984 by National Association of Accountants, Montvale, N.J. All rights reserved. Reprinted by permission.

3. The answer requires that all three relations be combined by a JOIN operator. From this new relation, a PROJECT operator extracts the employee name and skill name columns. Finally, a SELECT operator identifies the two skills possessed by Kimble.

Advantages and Drawbacks The relational model is gaining favor in the business world. Relations are easy for managers, accountants, and others to use and understand. The model is extremely flexible, since relationships among the relations are not predetermined and any of the independent relations can serve as entry points. Thus, a larger variety of information requests are likely to be answerable than by tree or network structures. Even requests that were unanticipated by data base designers are often satisfied. Also, it is not necessary to rebuild portions of the structure to include new relationships, as is the case with tree and network structures.

The main drawback of the relational model is that current versions are inefficient. Because of cumbersome underlying physical structures, such as inverted files, they consume more storage space and are slower in responding to inquiries. Also, the relational model is subject to certain restrictions. For instance, two relations cannot be joined unless they possess a common column (e.g., the employee-no. column in the employee and employee/skill relations, the skill-no. column in the skill and employee/skill relations).

DATA BASE MANAGEMENT SYSTEMS

A **data base management system (DBMS)** is a set of software (i.e., a package) having the overall purpose of managing the data in a computer-based data base. Numerous commercial DBMS packages are available. Each package implements one or more of the logical data models. For instance, IDMS (from Cullinet Corporation) features the network model, System 2000 and IMS (from Intel and IBM Corporations respectively) the tree model, and SQL/DS (from IBM Corporation) the relational model. The environment and key functional components of a DBMS appear in Figure 11-13.

Environment of a DBMS

The DBMS interfaces with the users and application software on one side and the data base and operating system on the other side. It is the only software within the system that "knows" both the logical data structures and the physical storage arrangements. The users range from those who perform batch processing (e.g., the payroll department) to those who perform online processing (e.g., the sales order department) and those who enter inquiries via terminals and microcomputers (e.g., cost accountants). Upon receiving a request for data from any of these applications, the DBMS refers to the subschema of the requesting program in order to determine the needed data. Then together with the operat-

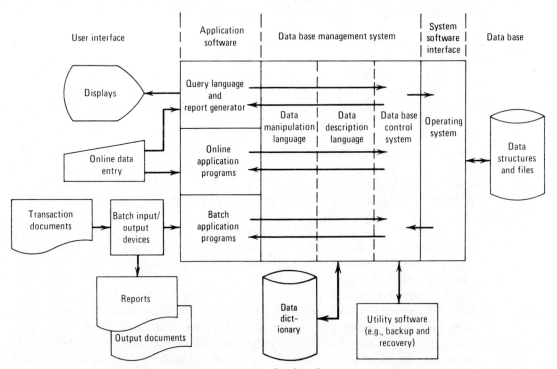

FIGURE 11-13 Environment of a data base management system.

ing system, the DBMS acquires and moves the data to the working area and back again.

Functional Components

Although the specific set of functional components varies from package to package, a reasonably complete set includes a

1. **Data base control system,** or data base manager, which controls the other components of the DBMS and communicates with the operating system.

2. **Data definition language (DDL),** which is employed to describe the logical structure of the data base. These descriptions include the schema, subschemas, and individual data items and fields. They are physically maintained in a data dictionary, which is described in the following section.

3. **Data manipulation language (DML),** which provides the means of expressing commands and inquiries that lead to data manipulations. Included in the typical DML are powerful verbs (e.g., READ, UPDATE, SORT, DISPLAY) and operands (e.g., record names, fields, key values).

4. **Query language,** which provides a variety of special commands and/or menus by which users can interactively search the data base.

5. **Report generator,** which formats special demand or ad hoc reports in accordance with specifications of users.

6. Other components, such as **security packages,** utilities that load data sets into the data base, and utilities that interface with a data communications network.

Data Dictionary

The major purpose of a data dictionary, as described in Chapter 6, is to provide details concerning data items stored in a data base. In the context of the data base approach, a **data dictionary** is a special file of data items maintained by the DBMS. Each entry in a typical data dictionary might contain the following concerning a data item: its standardized name, a description, the length of its field, the various sources from which it is entered into the data base, the records in which it appears, its mode (e.g., numeric, alphabetic), the programs in which it is used, and the reports for which it is intended. In addition, all links to other data items and records in the data base are included, as well as passwords and other security restrictions. An example of a data dictionary was shown in Figure 6-10.

DATA BASE CONTROLS AND SECURITY MEASURES

Because of its importance to a firm's operations and decision-making, and also its vulnerability, a data base requires stringent controls and security measures. All those that are suitable for online processing systems, as described in Chapter

5, also pertain to data base systems. The most relevant and critical of these controls and security measures are

1. **Sound systems development procedures.** All changes to the data base, such as the addition of new data items and the modification of the DBMS, should be carefully controlled. Otherwise, the standardization and security of the data may be threatened, and data management procedures may become flawed.

2. **Thorough documentation.** In particular the data dictionary should be comprehensive and up to date.

3. **Secure data accessing procedures.** The system of user codes and passwords should be sufficiently layered to provide precise protection over individual data sets and data items. For instance, certain sensitive data items could require as many as three passwords to access. Also, a lockout feature should prevent more than one user from accessing the same data simultaneously, causing possible loss of the data. A thorough data backup plan should be developed, including appropriate backup procedures for the data sets.

4. **Organizational addition of a data base administrator (DBA) and perhaps a security administrator.** The **DBA** should be responsible for the design and control of the data base. A primary function, therefore, is to establish and define the schema. This includes assigning standardized names to data items and sets, specifying data relationships, and compiling the data dictionary. Another function is to assign user codes and passwords and maintain other aspects of security (unless a security administrator is appointed). A third function is to control all changes made to data, as well as to software that operates the data base and programs that use the data therein. A final function is to administer the DBMS by preparing budgets, proposing policies, and communicating with programmers and users. To perform these functions effectively, the DBA should be organizationally separated from computer operations and the users.

DATA BASE DESIGN

Creating the data base was stated at the beginning of this chapter as being a key data management function. After our survey of data management fundamentals, we are ready to consider the phases in designing an effective data base.

Design Phases

The first phase consists of defining the requirements of users. This task may be achieved by studying all the current applications and compiling the total set of requirements. Another approach is by building a conceptual model of the data needs. One type of model is the **entity-relationship diagram,** which portrays all entities (e.g., customers, employees, products, general ledger accounts, sales transactions) and the relationships among them.

The second phase consists of developing an overall schema for each data base to be employed, plus the subschemas needed by the various users. All data sets, file structures, data items, relationships among the data, keys (primary and secondary), and codes should be devised.

The third phase consists of selecting the DBMS and physical storage devices. One of the most important considerations in selecting the DBMS is the desired type of logical data model. The relative advantages of each data model must therefore be weighed. Then the various commercial DBMS packages that emphasize the selected model can be evaluated.

The final phase is to implement the preferable DBMS on the physical storage media, train the personnel, and so on. These steps are discussed in Chapter 16.

These phases lead to the creation of an initial data base. A data base, however, should continually evolve to meet the changing information needs of the diverse users.

Example of Data Base Design

Manufacturers Hanover Trust Company developed a data base to support its wholesale banking systems function, which in turn maintains a number of online processing applications. The first two design phases (called conceptual and detailed conceptual design) identified entities such as bank customers, relationships such as those between customers and their accounts and lockbox deposits, data items such as customer addresses and account balances, and logical transactions such as "update account balance." The third phase (called the logical design phase) selected the IMS data base management system, the IBM DB/DC data dictionary, and specified the record keys, the IMS segments, and the hierarchical data structures. The final phase (called the physical design phase) established the pointers, magnetic disk blocks, and other physical features. It also involved implementing the data structures, preparing documentation, and testing access of data via the logical structures.[1]

SUMMARY

The data management activity has the objectives of providing sufficient, accessible, up to date, and accurate data to all users on a timely basis; of handling the data efficiently; of securing the data from loss; and of achieving all this as economically as possible. The three primary functions in data management are (1) creating a data base, including the logical and physical structures; (2) maintaining the stored data to keep them up to date and complete; and (3) retrieving needed data by appropriate search methods. Three file structures are known as sequential files, indexed sequential files, and random files. Two other structures related to these file structures are inverted files and linked lists. In choosing among these structures, designers may employ such measures as file size, activity ratio, currency of stored data, response time, and file volatility.

The data base approach is an alternative to the file-oriented approach. Features of the data base approach are data independence, data standardization, one-time data entry, shared data ownership, data security, and data integration

---

[1] Marian Herman, "A Database Design Methodology for an Integrated Database Environment," *Data Base* (Fall 1983), 12–27.

and association. Benefits of the data base approach are reduced redundancies and inconsistencies, increased flexibility, and improved accessibility of data. Its drawbacks are costly hardware and software, development and implementation complexities, and data vulnerability. Logical data models by which data may be structured within an integrated data base are the tree, network, and relational models. All have advantages and drawbacks.

A data base management system (DBMS) manages the data under the data base approach. Its functional components include the data base control system, data definition language (DDL), and data manipulation language (DML); other possible components are a query language, report generator, security package, and utilities. Controls and security measures for data bases include sound procedures for making changes, a data dictionary, a system of user codes and passwords, a lockout feature, thorough backup procedures, and a data base administrator (DBA).

Data base design includes four phases: requirements definition, conceptual (schema) design, DBMS and physical storage selection, and implementation.

REFERENCES

Burch, John, and Grudnitski, Gary. *Information Systems: Theory and Practice,* 4th ed., New York: Wiley, 1986.

Date, C. J. *An Introduction to Data Base Systems,* 4th ed., Reading, Mass.: Addison-Wesley, 1986.

Kroenke, David M. *Database Processing: Fundamentals, Design, Implementation,* 2d ed., Chicago: Science Research Associates, 1983.

Merrett, T. H. *Relational Information Systems,* Reston, Va.: Reston Publishing, 1984.

Nusbaum, Edward E.; Bailey, Andrew D., Jr.; and Whinston, Andrew B. "Data-Base Management, Accounting, and Accountants." *Management Accounting* (May 1978), 35–38.

Smith, James F., and Mufti, Amer. "Using the Relational Database." *Management Accounting* (Oct. 1985), 43–54.

QUESTIONS

1. What is the meaning of each of the following terms?

Data base	Tree (hierarchical)
Logical data structure	model
Physical storage	Parent
structure	Children
Primary key	Root node
Secondary key	Set
Sequential search	One-to-many
method	relationship
Binary search method	Network model
Index search method	Many-to-many
Sequential file	relationship
Indexed sequential file	Relational model
Bucket	Relation
Random file	Normal form
Hashing scheme	Data base
Inverted file	management system
Multiple-key inquiry	(DBMS)
Linked list	Data base control
Pointer	system
Attribute list	Data definition
Ring list	language (DDL)
Activity ratio	Data manipulation
Response time	language (DML)
Volatility	Query language
File-oriented approach	Report generator
Data base approach	Security package
Data set	Data dictionary
Data independence	Data base
Schema	administrator (DBA)
Subschema	Entity-relationship
Logical data model	diagram

2. Why do accountants need to understand data management fundamentals?

3. What are the objectives of data management?

4. What are the three primary data management functions?

5. Contrast logical and physical structures.

6. Identify the four actions that constitute file maintenance.

7. Identify five methods of searching for records in a file.

8. Identify three basic types of file structures,

and list the organization and access (search) methods employed by each.

9. Why are sequential files normally stored on magnetic tapes?

10. Describe the procedure for accessing an individual record in an ISAM file.

11. Describe the procedure for accessing an individual record by means of a hashing scheme.

12. Contrast the advantages of sequential, ISAM, and random files.

13. Describe the procedure for answering a multiple-key inquiry by use of inverted files.

14. Describe the means by which related records are associated using linked lists.

15. Identify five file-related measures.

16. What are the shortcomings of the file-oriented approach?

17. What are the features of the data base approach?

18. What are the benefits and drawbacks of the data base approach?

19. Contrast the features and advantages of the tree, network, and relational data models.

20. How does a simple network differ from a complex network?

21. Explain how new relations are formed during the use of a relational data base system.

22. Describe the operation of a DBMS in responding to requests from application programs.

23. What are the functional components that may be encompassed within a DBMS?

24. Which controls and security measures are particularly important and relevant with respect to integrated data bases?

25. What are the duties of a typical data base administrator?

26. Identify the four phases of designing an integrated data base.

27. In what situations might a firm find the file-oriented approach to be preferable to the data base approach?

28. Discuss the tradeoffs between file mainte-nance efficiency and the speedy retrieval of individual records.

29. It has been suggested that the data base is the heart of an AIS. Discuss.

30. Which of the three data management functions appears to be the most important. Why?

31. What are the benefits and drawbacks to the development of a single overall data base that includes all of a firm's data? What are the feasible alternatives to this overall data base?

32. Very few firms develop their own data base management software. Instead, they buy or lease commercial DBMS packages. Discuss the advantages and disadvantages of doing so.

REVIEW PROBLEM

Phoenix Board of Realtors

Statement

The Phoenix Board of Realtors' Multiple Listing Service (MLS) publishes a weekly listing of houses for sale in the Phoenix metropolitan area. Each listing is based on a listing contract signed by the listing realtor and the owner. In the contract are specified all the details concerning the residence: the address, asking price, number of bedrooms, number of baths, type of garage, mortgages pending, and special features. Upon being prepared, a copy of this contract is forwarded by the realtor to the MLS.

In the early years of the MLS, copies of the listing contract were distributed to member firms. However, around 1970 the data were transferred to computer-readable media; then, each Friday the listings were printed, bound into multiple-listing books, and distributed to the member firms.

The multiple-listing book actually consisted of two parts: (1) detailed descriptive data concerning each residence, arranged by MLS number; and (2) an index that referred to each detailed listing. Each index listing contained key summary data, such as the address, asking price, number of bedrooms, size of building, style and date of construction, nearest schools, and geographical area. With this summary data, realty associates could scan the index for those houses that met a potential buyer's needs. If more data were needed or if a sale were consummated, the realty associate would use the MLS number in the index to locate the detailed description.

In the late 1970s, however, the book had grown to be a bulky 700-page volume containing an average of 9000 listings. Many of the listings were inaccurate, because of sales since the preceding Friday, and the new listings were not available until the next Friday. Searches for suitable listings sometimes required an hour or more. Furthermore, continued rapid growth in real estate transactions was expected in the Phoenix area.

Consequently, the MLS contracted with a computer consultant to develop a data base and retrieval system that would rectify these problems. After careful study the consultant proposed a system having the following features.

1. *Hardware* should include a visual display terminal and impact printer in the office of each of the 400 members. At the MLS office would be a central processor containing a one megabyte primary storage unit, plus 400 megabytes of magnetic disk storage, magnetic tape backup, and a communication processor to interface with the terminals.[2]

2. *Software* should include a data base management system that allows lists and inverted lists to be created, plus a command language that enables users at realtors' offices to enter new listings and to make inquiries. Other software should consist of an elaborate operating system for coordinating the various components, as well as utility routines for calculating such real estate factors as amortization amounts.

Required

Design suitable data structures comprising a schema for this proposed system, and describe the steps involved in storing and retrieving data from the system.

Solution

The schema is depicted by the data structures shown on page 419.

The procedure for using the system is as follows: After a listing contract has been completed, a clerk in the realty firm enters the data via the office terminal. The data are stored in the two records, marked as the summary listing record and detailed data record. Pointers are established by the software as indicated, and the disk address of the summary record is added to each of the inverted lists as applicable.

When a potential buyer enters the picture, a realty associate first determines the essential parameters, such as the top price that he or she would be willing to pay, the desired number of bedrooms, and the area. Next the realty associate keys these specifications into the terminal. The DBMS then employs the inverted lists to locate those houses meeting all the specifications (if any) and displays the address and several other key facts concerning each.

For instance, assume that Ms. Betty Rowan, a realty associate with Mesa Realty, enters an inquiry concerning which homes are listed in Tempe having 1800 square feet or more, three bedrooms, an asking price of not more than $100,000, and a fireplace. The DBMS searches all the relevant inverted lists and determines that houses at disk addresses 3810 and 6530 meet these specifications; it then moves to these disk addresses and displays the following data.

MLS 0721	1705 So. Beaver Dr.	$95,000
MLS 3782	2817 E. Coolidge Ave.	$98,500

If the potential buyer shows interest, the realty associate can request a hard copy printout of the detailed descriptions of the two houses. Later, if one of the houses is sold, the realty associate enters that fact via the terminal; the house is then deleted from the file.

At any time a realtor can make a request for a printout of all houses listed with his or her firm. The DBMS will then follow the pointers that lead from the realtor record to each of the summary listing records in the realtor's list or chain.

---

[2] These facts are based on a description of a computer system actually acquired by the Phoenix MLS and reported by Joe Cole in "Homes-for-Sale List Going Electronic," *The Arizona Republic* (April 23, 1978), 13–14; and by Neal Savage in "Terminal Aid," *The Arizona Republic* (Jan. 30, 1983), SL2.

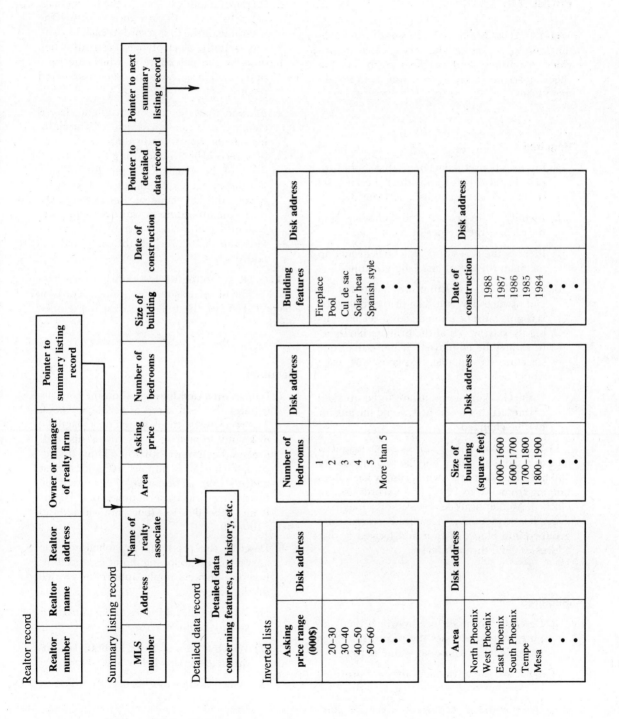

Realtor record

Realtor number	Realtor name	Realtor address	Owner or manager of realty firm	Pointer to summary listing record

Summary listing record

MLS number	Address	Name of realty associate	Area	Asking price	Number of bedrooms	Size of building	Date of construction	Pointer to detailed data record	Pointer to next summary listing record

Detailed data record

Detailed data concerning features, tax history, etc.

Inverted lists

Asking price range (000$)	Disk address
20–30	
30–40	
40–50	
50–60	
• • •	

Number of bedrooms	Disk address
1	
2	
3	
4	
5	
More than 5	

Building features	Disk address
Fireplace	
Pool	
Cul de sac	
Solar heat	
Spanish style	
• • •	

Area	Disk address
North Phoenix	
West Phoenix	
East Phoenix	
South Phoenix	
Tempe	
Mesa	
• • •	

Size of building (square feet)	Disk address
1000–1600	
1600–1700	
1700–1800	
1800–1900	
• • •	

Date of construction	Disk address
1988	
1987	
1986	
1985	
1984	
• • •	

PROBLEMS

11-1. Cactus National Bank serves a state in the southwest. Among the services that it provides to business and personal customers are checking accounts, savings accounts, and installment loans.

Required

a. List several useful data items that should appear in records for individual checking accounts, savings accounts, and loans.

b. Identify likely primary and secondary keys for each of these types of records.

c. Identify the types of transactions needed to maintain the file of checking accounts.

d. If the checking accounts are updated at the end of each day, but data in the individual accounts must be immediately available during the day, which of the primary file structures may be employed? If more than one structure is suitable, explain how each would be used by tellers.

e. If the checking accounts are to be updated as transactions occur, how would the answer to **d** be changed?

11-2. A master file is stored on a magnetic tape as a sequential file. The file is composed of 100 fixed-length records with primary key values ranging from 100 to 199. These records are not blocked. An identical file is stored on a magnetic disk. Its sequentially organized records are grouped into blocks of four and located at disk addresses 0820 through 0844.

Required

a. Describe the procedure by which the computer system accesses the record stored on magnetic tape whose key value is 163.

b. What are the advantages that are provided by the file stored on the magnetic disk?

c. Describe the procedure by which the computer system accesses the same numbered record (163) stored on magnetic disk, using the binary search method.

d. Prepare an index to convert the file on magnetic disk to an ISAM structure, using the key value of the first record in each block to represent the block of logical records. Then describe the procedure by which the computer system accesses the same numbered record.

e. Assume that the file on magnetic disk is changed to a random structure. The hashing scheme consists of dividing the key value of a record by 13 and using the first four digits of the remainder as the disk address. For instance, the disk address for the record having the key value of 100 is 6923. Describe the procedure by which the computer system would access the record having the key value of 163. Include the computed disk address.

11-3. Refer to the Review Problem for Chapter 11. The file of 10 summary listing records on page 421 shows the following data for selected fields.

Required

a. Prepare inverted files based on the four attributes that can serve as secondary keys. The records shown are stored on a magnetic disk and located at consecutive disk addresses, beginning with 250. (Thus, the record having MLS number 10 is located at address 259). In preparing the inverted file for asking price, use a range that begins from $95,000 to (but not including) $100,000.

b. Describe the procedure for obtaining the answers to the following inquiries, and show how the answers might appear on a video display screen.[3]

(1) What are the addresses of the houses for sale in Tempe?

(2) Which houses in Mesa, identified by address, are priced below $100,000?

(3) Which houses in Phoenix, identified by

---

[3] The questions in **b** of this problem can alternatively be solved by using a microcomputer-based relational data base management software package.

MLS Number	Address	Area	Asking Price (000$)	Number of Bedrooms	Date of Construction
1	2340 Cricket Dr.	Tempe	101	4	1973
2	1504 Indian St.	Phoenix	119	4	1977
3	4328 Sunset Rd.	Mesa	104	4	1976
4	2264 Robson Dr.	Mesa	98	3	1981
5	1720 Terrace Ave.	Tempe	110	5	1970
6	116 Mountain Dr.	Phoenix	130	5	1978
7	3101 Gilbert Rd.	Mesa	106	3	1980
8	1730 Brown St.	Phoenix	132	4	1983
9	2525 College Ave.	Tempe	115	5	1968
10	5150 Vista Dr.	Mesa	127	4	1985

address, have four bedrooms and were constructed in the 1980s?

c. List three more inquiries, involving at least two inverted files, that can be answered by the set of inverted files.

11-4. In the supplier record at the bottom of this page, insert the appropriate pointer values in the following pointer field, if the purpose of the resulting simple-linked list is to enable the preparation of a report arranged by date of most recent purchase, with the latest date listed first.

11-5. In each of the following situations, select the file structure (sequential, ISAM, or random) that seems to be most suitable. Justify your selections.

a. A large life insurance company with approximately 2 million policyholders maintains a single policyholder master file, which is updated twice weekly to reflect premium payments, add new policyholders, delete canceled policyholders, reflect changes to

permanent data, and to print overdue premium notices. Approximately 1 million records are affected during each processing run.

b. An automotive and truck parts supplier maintains a 10,000-record inventory master file. An average of 2500 records are updated daily to reflect sales and receipts, and approximately 30 parts are either added or deleted daily. An inventory reorder list is printed daily to notify buyers when parts on hand have declined to their reorder points; however, parts clerks need to be able to check the status of parts on hand at any time during the day, since customers often want to know how many units of particular parts are available when they call to place orders.

c. A manufacturing firm produces goods on orders received from customers. Approximately 100 orders are in production on any given day, and these orders are maintained as records in a work-in-process master file.

	SUPPLIER RECORDS			
Disk Address	Supplier Number	Date of Most Recent Purchase	Remainder of Record Content	Pointer Field
010	1000	10/3		
020	1001	9/6		
030	1002	9/17		
040	1003	8/30		
050	1004	10/7		
060	1005	9/21		
070	1006	9/14		
080	1007	10/2		
090	1008	9/11		
100	1009	9/28		
110	1010	9/5		

Each record must be accessed frequently in order to post data concerning production steps completed and to enable managers and planners to discover current order status. A five-second response time is considered tolerable. On the average, about 10 orders are begun and 10 completed daily.

d. The water department in a city with approximately 75,000 residents maintains a resident account master file. Once a month all the records in the file are updated to reflect water usage; bills are also prepared at that time, as well as a listing of residents and amounts billed.

e. A motel chain employs a room reservation system for which all rooms of each member motel represent the available inventory. Each time a room is reserved, a new record is created in the name of the person making the reservation. This record is then changed to reflect occupancy on specific dates, to add food and phone charges, to prepare the bills, and then to delete the records when the occupants leave. On the average, travelers occupy a room for one and a half nights.

11-6. The Elk Construction Co., Ltd. intends to computerize its payroll system. The company produces paychecks every two weeks for its average employee force of 2000. This work force varies in size from 1750 in the winter months to more than 3000 during the peak summer months. In addition to preparing paychecks, the payroll system must also prepare, in employee number sequence, the payroll and deduction registers. It must also post pay data to the earnings records and prepare quarterly reports.

The configuration acquired by Elk consists of a central processor with a 500,000-byte storage capacity, eight tape drives, five disk drives, one printer, and one video display terminal.

Required

a. Identify two alternative file structures that would be suitable for Elk. List the advantages of each identified file structure and the physical storage devices it would use.

b. Assume that the firm is aware of two impending changes: (1) a likely increase in the turnover rate of employees during a season, and (2) regulations that will require each terminating employee to be paid immediately and so recorded in his or her records. Which of the alternative file structures identified in **a** thereby becomes the preferable choice? Why?

(SMAC adapted)

11-7. The Bunting Construction Co. of Dayton, Ohio, is a building contractor and building materials supplier. Its annual sales for last year were $105 million. For a number of years the firm has used computers to process transactions and prepare reports and documents. It currently employs a large mainframe computer to perform both batch and online processing. For instance, it processes most of the accounting applications, such as payroll, by the batch method and maintains the relevant files on magnetic tape. On the other hand, it employs online processing, via terminals, to dispatch loads of materials to customers and to keep track of the status of construction projects.

Over the years the firm has developed and acquired over 150 application programs, and it maintains approximately 200 files. These programs and files are documented in a variety of styles; some documentation was prepared by programmers no longer with the firm, and some was acquired from software suppliers when packages were purchased. Many of the programs have not been changed significantly in several years. According to the information systems manager, the time required to make changes is very lengthy; she has not been able to spare programmers to spend this needed time in program maintenance, since she has been "pushed" to provide new programs. For instance, she has recently supervised the writing of several new engineering and bidding programs. As a consequence, the programs tend to be inefficient and unintegrated. Also, many of the data items appear in several files and are used in a variety of programs. Often these data items (e.g., raw-materials item numbers) are assigned a different name in each program.

The operations manager of Bunting recently raised a disturbing problem at a meeting of top managers. He complained that although he could make inquiries concerning individual projects via his terminal, he could not obtain certain reports—such as lists of overdue projects, cost overruns, and expected receipts of materials—in a timely manner. Other managers agreed that they likewise had difficulty in obtaining ad hoc demand reports from the information system. As a consequence of these comments, the president directed the controller to investigate the feasibility of moving to the data base approach.

Required

a. What benefits would Bunting gain by moving to the data base approach?

b. What steps should be taken in the process of converting to the data base approach?

c. How would a DBMS be selected, and what are several desirable components that it should contain?

d. Should the firm initially incorporate all files and programs within the newly established data base? If not, suggest likely areas of activity for inclusion.

11-8. Mariposa Products, a textile and apparel manufacturer, acquired its own computer in 1980. The first application to be developed and implemented was production and inventory control. Other applications that were added in succession were payroll, accounts receivable, and accounts payable.

The applications were not integrated as a result of the piecemeal manner in which they were developed and implemented. Nevertheless, the system proved satisfactory for several years. Generally, reports were prepared on time, and information was readily accessible.

Mariposa operates in a very competitive industry. A combination of increased operating costs and the competitive nature of the industry have had an adverse effect on profit margins and operating profits. Ed Wilde, Mariposa's president, suggested that some special analyses be prepared in an attempt to provide information that would help management improve operations. Unfortunately, some of the data were not consistent among the reports. In addition, there were no data by product line or by department. These problems were attributable to the fact that Mariposa's applications were developed piecemeal and, as a consequence, duplicate data that were not necessarily consistent existed on Mariposa's computer system.

Wilde was concerned that Mariposa's computer system was not able to generate the information his managers needed to make decisions. He called a meeting of his top management and certain data processing personnel to discuss potential solutions to Mariposa's problems. The concensus of the meeting was that a new information system that would integrate Mariposa's applications was needed.

Mariposa's controller suggested that the company consider a data base system that all departments would use. As a first step, the controller proposed hiring a data base administrator on a consulting basis to determine the feasibility of converting to a data base system.

Required

a. Identify the features that constitute a system under the data base approach.

b. List the benefits and drawbacks to Mariposa Products of converting to the data base approach.

c. What steps should be taken in converting to the new system?

d. What should be the duties of the data base administrator?

(CMA adapted)

11-9. Cactus National Bank (see Problem 11-1) converts to the data base approach. It desires to integrate the data pertaining to individual business and personal customers. Each customer may have one or more checking accounts, savings accounts, and installment loans. The checking and savings accounts have deposit, withdrawal, and adjusting (e.g., NSF check) transactions; the installment loans have loan and repayment transactions.

Required

a. Draw a data structure diagram (similar to Figure 11-8) that represents a data base schema for these areas. The schema should integrate all the data pertaining to an individual customer. The root node should be a record that contains the customer number, name, address, and other relevant background data. All the data pertaining to the accounts and loans should appear in separate records as children to this root parent record. The transactions, in turn, should be children of the accounts and loan records.

b. Bank tellers, who handle the checking and savings accounts, and loan officers, who administer the installment loans, are the most frequent users of the schema. Draw separate subschemas for the tellers and the loan officers. These two subschemas should, in effect, split the schema into two parts, except that each should include the root node.

11-10. Draw a data structure diagram that models each of the following situations. Then illustrate the physical implementation of a specific occurrence by means of pointers in a linked list. An example, based on Figure 11-7, is shown at the bottom of this page. Note that individual data items need not be shown, except for the pointers in the linked lists.

a. Supplier records in the accounts payable file point to their purchase orders in the open purchase order file.

b. Customer records within the accounts receivable master file point to their sales invoice records *and* to their remittance advice records maintained in separate transaction history files. (Use *two* pointer fields in the customer record.)

c. Employee records within the employee master file point to their skills records in the skills inventory file.

d. Skills records within the skills inventory file point to the employee records in the employee master file possessing such skills. (Note that the skills records are now the par-

ent records and the employee master records are now the children records.)

e. Skills records within the skills inventory file point to the employee records in the employee master file possessing such skills; department records within the department master file (containing such data items as the department number, department name, department manager, and responsibility center code) *also* point to the employees assigned to the departments. (Use *two* pointer fields in the employee record, one for the skill list and one for the department list.)

11-11. Draw a data structure diagram that models each of the following situations.

a. Supplier records (the root node) have as children the records in the open purchase order file, which in turn have as children the line items on order in each purchase order.

b. Convert the tree structure in **a** to a network structure by adding inventory records that also have the ordered items in purchase orders as children.

c. Product records (the root node) have as children the parts inventory records (since parts are used in manufacturing the products). The product records also have as children the production order records that pertain to the products being manufactured.

d. Convert the tree structure in **c** to a network structure by adding work center records that have as children both (1) the production orders in process at the respective work centers, and (2) the machine loading records.

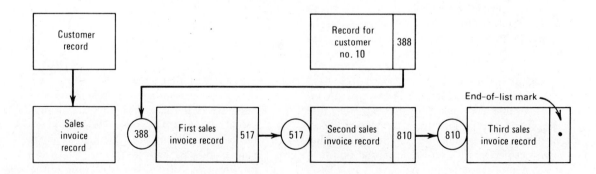

11-12. These three relations are maintained in a purchasing data base.[4]

PARTS

PARTNO	PNAME
P107	BOLT
P113	NUT
P125	SCREW
P132	GEAR

SUPPLIERS

SUPPNO	SNAME
S51	ABC Co.
S57	XYZ Co.
S63	LMN Co.

PRICES

PARTNO	SUPPNO	PRICE
P107	S51	0.59
P107	S57	0.65
P113	S51	0.25
P113	S63	0.21
P125	S63	0.15
P132	S57	5.25
P132	S63	7.50

Required

Draw the new relations created by the following inquiries.

a. Which suppliers, by name, provide part 113?

b. Which suppliers, by name, provide gears?

c. Which suppliers, by name, provide more than three parts?

d. Which parts, by name, are provided by only one supplier?

e. Which suppliers, by name, have which parts (by name and number) that are priced below $0.50?

(Courtesy of International Business Machines Corporation)

11-13. Refer to Figure 11-12. Use a microcomputer-based relational data base software package to set up the tables shown. Fill in the incomplete columns with data that you make up. Then write several queries, such as those listed in the chapter, that can be answered by means of

one or more of the tables. Use the software package to obtain and print the answers to these queries.[5]

11-14. Southeastern State University employs a DBMS based on the network model to integrate its data concerning students, classes, registration, and related matters. Among the reports and documents that the data base facilitates are class schedules for each student, class rosters (showing the list of students, by social security number, name, and major, for each class, plus the classroom number and professor), semester class schedules (showing the classes, plus times, rooms, and professors), and classroom schedules (showing the times each room is occupied and by which classes).

Required

Show, by means of a data structure diagram, the portion of the overall schema that enables these reports to be generated. The result should be a network structure that contains several many-to-many relationships, such as portrayed in Figure 11-9b. Three root nodes are needed, including the class and student records illustrated in Figure 11-10.

11-15. The Bluegrass Plumbing Supply Co. of Lexington, Kentucky, wholesales a variety of plumbing supplies to plumbing contractors throughout several states.[6] To increase sales and improve profits, it feels that it needs to improve service in processing orders, to sharpen purchasing and receiving operations, and to reduce inventory investment. Thus, the firm designs a new system pertaining to purchasing and inventory control. To implement this new system it acquires computer hardware, including terminals and magnetic disk storage. It also purchases a DBMS.

The newly designed system employs three key files: a product (finished-goods inventory) master file, a supplier master file, and an outstanding

---

[4] This problem can be solved by using a microcomputer-based relational data base management software package.

[5] This problem can be solved by using any microcomputer-based relational data base management software package.

[6] Adapted from *Information Systems in Management* by James A. Senn. © 1978 by the Wadsworth Publishing Co., Inc. Reprinted by permission of Wadsworth Publishing Co., Inc., Belmont, Cal. 94002.

purchase orders file. These files are accessed via terminals by employees concerned with sales order processing, purchasing, and receiving.

When an order from a customer is received, a sales order clerk checks via a terminal to see if the quantity shown in the inventory record is adequate to fill the order. If so, the quantity on hand is reduced to reflect the order; if not, the clerk checks to see if a purchase order is outstanding and when goods are due.

Each day, buyers in the purchasing department place purchase orders by entering (via terminals) the transaction code, the numbers of products being ordered, the order quantities, the anticipated unit prices, the supplier numbers, and the anticipated due dates. The computer system then prepares the purchase orders.

When ordered goods arrive at the receiving dock and have been counted, a receiving clerk enters the transaction code, the purchase order number, the product numbers, and the quantities received. The computer system then verifies that the purchase order is valid and that the quantities agree with those on the order. If the clerk enters an acceptance code, the system prepares a receiving report and also increases the quantity-on-hand balance in the inventory record to reflect the received goods.

Upon request of the purchasing manager, the system prepares a list of products that have fallen below their reorder points, together with their optimal reorder quantities. This list is used as the basis for making purchase order assignments to the buyers.

Required

a. List the data items that should appear in records of each of the three files, including needed pointers. For instance, the supplier master file should include the supplier number, name and address, and terms. It also should contain the lead time, so that the buyer can determine the anticipated date of arrival, and a pointer to purchase orders.

b. Prepare a data structure diagram that reflects a schema for the data base that is based on the network model.

c. Prepare and discuss separate data structure diagrams that reflect the subschemas for (1)

an order processing clerk, (2) a buyer, (3) a receiving clerk, and (4) the purchasing manager. The results should contain the portions of the schema that can satisfy the needs of each of these four users. Each subschema should include only those specific data items from the records that are necessary, however.

11-16. A preliminary survey of a firm's data base system and EDP (information system) department reveals the following.

a. There are no restrictions regarding type of transaction or access to the online terminals.

b. All users and EDP personnel have access to the extensive system documentation.

c. Before being entered in the user authorization table, user passwords and access codes are established by user management and approved by the manager of computer programming.

d. The manager of computer programming establishes and controls the data base directory. Users approve any changes to data definitions.

e. User requests for data are validated by the system against a transactions-conflict matrix to ensure data is transmitted only to authorized users.

f. System access requires the users to input their passwords, and terminal activity logs are maintained.

g. Input data is edited for reasonableness and completeness, transaction control totals are generated, and transaction logs are maintained.

h. Processing control totals are generated and reconciled to changes in the data base.

i. Output is reconciled to transaction and input control totals. The resulting reports are printed and placed in a bin outside the EDP room for pickup by the users at their convenience.

j. Backup copies of the data base are generated daily and stored in the file library area, access to which is restricted to EDP personnel.

Required

    a. List all effective controls and security measures that are currently installed.

    b. Evaluate the relative adequacies of the general and application (transaction) controls, and indicate significant omissions.

(CIA adapted)

11-17. A systems analysis has just been completed for the Southwest Paper Co. of Tucson, Arizona, which manufactures and markets various types of paper for the printing industry.[7] This analysis initially was intended to identify the informational requirements related to the purchasing function, but has been subsequently expanded to include the accounts payable function as well. The justification for expanding the investigation was based on the similarity of the data required in the data base to support both functions.

Analysis has identified the need for the purchasing department to maintain three files: (1) a supplier master file containing names, addresses, purchasing terms, and miscellaneous descriptive data; (2) an open purchase order file containing all the data related to purchase orders placed but not yet completed; and (3) a history file of purchases made in a two-year period, by product and suppliers. When purchase orders are closed upon receipt of invoices from suppliers, their data are transferred to the history file.

The accounts payable department, on the other hand, requires the following files: (1) a supplier master file containing all descriptive data necessary to produce and mail checks for purchases received, (2) a file of invoices received from suppliers but not yet paid, and (3) a one-year history file of paid suppliers' invoices. Invoices are always paid nine days after receipt and transferred in a batch to the paid-invoice-history file.

Currently, these files are maintained on magnetic tape and processed by a tape-oriented computer system. However, after their analysis the firm decides to design an integrated purchasing

and accounts payable system. This system is to be implemented on a medium-sized computer that has both magnetic tape and disk storage and can perform both batch and online processing.

Approximately 20 percent of all purchases are considered rebuys from an existing supplier. At any point in time there are 3000 active suppliers, 5000 open purchase orders, and 1500 open invoices. Annually the firm places 40,000 purchase orders.

Required

    a. What files are needed in the integrated application system?

    b. Prepare a matrix that shows the listed files across the top and that lists the data items in the respective files down the side.

    c. How should each of the logical files be structured? Explain.

    d. Assuming that a DBMS is acquired and all files are converted to magnetic disk storage, draw a data structure diagram that relates the records of files listed in **a** within a suitable purchasing/accounts payable schema. The DBMS can accommodate either the tree or network data model.

    e. Expand the schema in **d** by linking other related record types, such as inventory records.

    f. Develop a partial data dictionary for the purchasing/accounts payable schema of **d**. List 10 of the data items shown in the matrix of **b**. Assign item codes from 01 to 10 for the data items, and use reasonable values for field lengths. Use Figure 6-10 as a guide, replacing the last two columns with columns headed "Application program names" and "Record(s) to which linked." For instance, the supplier number item could be named SUPNO, and the linked record could be the open supplier invoice record.

    g. Identify specific information requests that can be answered and reports that can be generated via the schema in **d**.

11-18. A small public accounting firm provides audit, tax, and management advisory services to a variety of clients. It decides to acquire a

---

[7] Adapted from John G. Burch, Jr., and Felix R. Strater, Jr., *Information Systems: Theory and Practice,* 2d ed. (New York: John Wiley, 1979). Used with permission.

DBMS and convert to the data base approach. The areas to be included in the data base, at least initially, are its engagements with clients, time management of its professional and clerical staff, and billing.

Required

Describe the phases and steps in designing the data base system. Be specific in describing the conceptual model and schema. Assume that the logical data model chosen is the relational model.

11-19. The XYZ Company of Seattle, Washington, is a large West Coast distributor that sells a variety of merchandise on credit. Sales orders are phoned in by salespersons and recorded on special coding forms by sales clerks. Data preparation clerks then key the data onto a magnetic medium for entry into the firm's computer-based processing system.

Each sales order contains the following data items.

   a. Customer number.

   b. Customer name and address.

   c. Shipping address, if different.

   d. Date ordered.

   e. Date to be shipped.

   f. Salesperson number.

   g. Sales territory number.

   h. Products ordered, by number.

   i. Quantities of those products ordered.

Assume that C. James (customer number 1158) ordered 12 units of product number 2001 from salesperson number 315, sales territory 20, on August 11, 1989 for shipment on August 14. The coded sales transaction is portrayed at the bottom of the this page. Preceding the transaction data is the code for credit sales, CRS, which identifies the type of transaction and thus speci-

fies the application program that is to process the transaction data.

Entered sales orders are edited and stored on an open sales order disk file. As ordered goods are shipped, shipping records are prepared. (On the average, 6000 orders are shipped daily.) After conversion to magnetic tape, a batch of these records is sorted in customer-account-number order. (For convenience, an average of 40 change records pertaining to new or deleted customers are included with the shipping records.) Then all the records in the batch are processed by a file updating program.

The updating program

   a. Updates the 20,000-record accounts receivable master file stored on magnetic tape. Each record in this file is variable length and contains data as follows: customer account number, name, address, credit limit, balance at the beginning of the year, current account balance, and data for each transaction this year (transaction code, date, document number, and amount).

   b. Updates the 400-record inventory master file stored on magnetic disk. Records are organized sequentially and accessed directly via an index.

   c. Updates a sales history file stored on magnetic disk, in order to provide a historical record of sales and shipments.

   d. Updates the open sales order file by deleting the sales order if the order is completely filled, or by noting the quantity shipped if the order is partially filled.

   e. Adds a record to a back-order file on magnetic tape for each order in which shipped quantities were less than ordered quantities.

   f. Creates a sales invoice tape based on data drawn from several of the files.

The record layouts for these six files are shown on page 429. All data items shown are based on the following sources: (1) inputs from

CRS	1158	C. James	113 Main St.	Portland, Ore.	97132	800 Front St.	}

{	Portland, Ore.	97131	81189	81489	315	20	2000	12

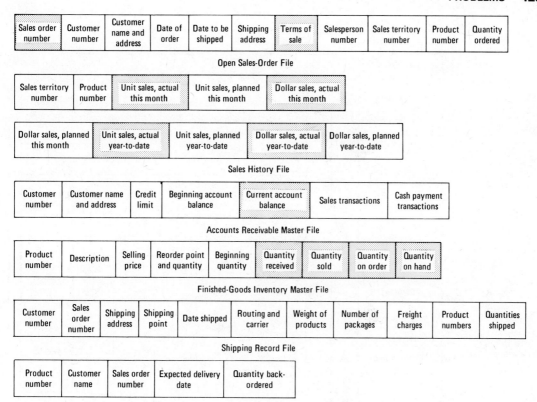

Sales order number	Customer number	Customer name and address	Date of order	Date to be shipped	Shipping address	Terms of sale	Salesperson number	Sales territory number	Product number	Quantity ordered

Open Sales-Order File

Sales territory number	Product number	Unit sales, actual this month	Unit sales, planned this month	Dollar sales, actual this month

Dollar sales, planned this month	Unit sales, actual year-to-date	Unit sales, planned year-to-date	Dollar sales, actual year-to-date	Dollar sales, planned year-to-date

Sales History File

Customer number	Customer name and address	Credit limit	Beginning account balance	Current account balance	Sales transactions	Cash payment transactions

Accounts Receivable Master File

Product number	Description	Selling price	Reorder point and quantity	Beginning quantity	Quantity received	Quantity sold	Quantity on order	Quantity on hand

Finished-Goods Inventory Master File

Customer number	Sales order number	Shipping address	Shipping point	Date shipped	Routing and carrier	Weight of products	Number of packages	Freight charges	Product numbers	Quantities shipped

Shipping Record File

Product number	Customer name	Sales order number	Expected delivery date	Quantity back-ordered

Back-Order File

Note: Data items in shaded fields are computed or generated from tables by the computer program, either at the time the record is created or at the time the record is updated.

transaction records (e.g., sales orders and shipping records), (2) tables accessed by the updating program (e.g., sales order number table and sales terms table), (3) transfers from other files (e.g., the sales order number in the shipping record file from the open sales order file), and (4) results of processing steps performed by the updating program (e.g., current account balance).

Among the outputs generated from the data in the aforementioned files are the following.

a. Sales invoices and a sales journal. The diagram on page 430 details the preparation of these outputs from the sales invoice tape, which in turn consists of data extracted from the open sales order, accounts receivable, inventory, and shipping transaction files.

b. Monthly statements and an aging analysis. The diagram on the top of page 431 shows the formats of these outputs, which are based on data drawn from the accounts receivable master file.

c. Sales analyses, such as the analysis of sales by sales territory and product line shown on the bottom of page 431.

Required

a. Complete the layout of an accounts receivable record for C. James as of August 15, based on the data in the sales order record layout and the monthly statement. Assume that this customer has a credit limit of $10,000 and that this is the first transaction by the customer.

b. Prepare a computer system flowchart to reflect the generation of the sales invoices and sales journal, beginning just after the shipping records and change records have been sorted. Also, state the number of tape drives and disk drives and printers that are needed by XYZ Company's computer installation to accommodate this sales application, assum-

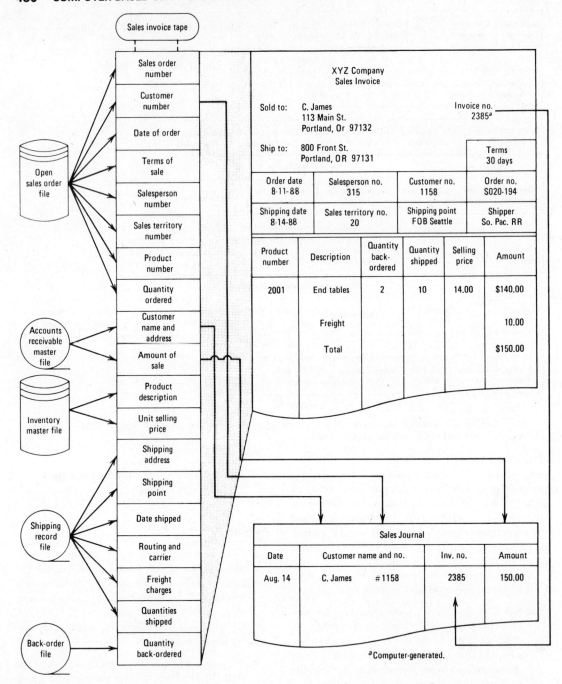

ing that each direct access file requires its own disk drive.

c. Justify the use of magnetic tape as the storage medium for the accounts receivable master file, as well as the use of magnetic disk as the storage medium for the inventory master file.

d. Suggest changes to the accounts receivable

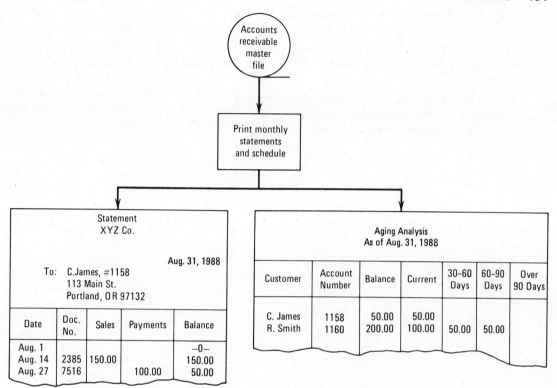

master file that should improve processing efficiency.

e. Describe the steps by which the actual dollar sales amounts are computed by the program. Include in your answer the sources of the data items used in the computations.

f. Explain, with the aid of a computer system flowchart, the computer runs needed to prepare the illustrated sales analysis from data in the sales history file.

g. XYZ converts all files in this application to magnetic disk storage. It then acquires a DBMS that can accommodate tree and network data models. Draw a data structure di-

Sales Analysis by Sales Territory and Product Line For month ending August 31, 1988 (000's of units and dollars)							
Sales territory number	**Product**	**Actual sales for month**		**Variance from budget— month**	**Actual sales year-to-date**		**Variance from budget— year-to-date**
		Units	**Dollars**		**Units**	**Dollars**	
01	1000	315	$5,985	($155)	2560	$48,640	$250
	2000	105	1,470	20	912	12,768	176
	3000	726	7,986	382	5685	62,535	425
	4000	227	4,540	(117)	1704	34,080	(310)
	Total	1373	$19,981	$130	10861	$158,023	$541
02	1000	520	$9,880	$360	4654	$88,426	$1,340
	2000	316	4,424				

agram that portrays a schema for facilitating the preparation of all the described outputs.

h. Identify specific information requests and other reports that can be generated via the schema in **g**.

i. Assume that XYZ trades in its first DBMS for another DBMS that is based on the relational model. Identify the relations that are needed to implement the schema in **g**, including the columns in each relation (except the sales history relation).

j. Give examples of information requests that can be satisfied by single SELECT, PROJECT, and JOIN commands to this relational data model when the schema described in **g** is implemented.

12

Information

Processing and

User-Focused

Systems

Discuss the concepts related to information processing.

Describe various financial reporting systems for management.

Distinguish among various types of user-support systems.

Describe several emerging tools and techniques that enable users to develop their own systems.

INTRODUCTION

One major purpose of an accounting information system (AIS) is to aid the making of decisions. Although a wide variety of users are provided decision-making information, the most important users are the managers of a firm. **Information processing** consists of the activities involved in providing this decision-making information to managers and others. The activities include collecting and storing relevant data, processing the data through decision models, and providing useful information outputs in varied forms. This chapter emphasizes decision-making, managerial reporting systems, user-support systems, and emerging means of encouraging user-developed systems.

INFORMATION PROCESSING CONCEPTS

We can better understand information processing if we are aware of information theory, decision-making, information flows, and information needs.

Information Theory

According to **information theory** (also called communication theory), communication consists of conveying information from a source via a channel to a receiver (user). On the technical level, the objective is to transmit the information accurately and completely. On the semantic level, the objective is to convey information that the user can clearly understand. On the effectiveness level, the objective is to stimulate desired results, such as sound decisions. Achieving perfect communication on all levels is difficult because of **noise** (undesired effects). A well-designed information system, however, can overcome much, if not all, of the noise.

Value of Information The value, or usefulness, of information to a user cannot be easily quantified. It can be expressed in relative terms, however. A piece of information that reduces a user's *uncertainty* concerning a particular decision situation has potentially high value. Likewise, a piece that provides little or no new intelligence to a user has little if any value *to that user*.

   Information value varies not only among different pieces of information, but also among users. A manager with a technical background may understand a machine specification and find it very useful, whereas another manager may find the information incomprehensible and hence of no value.

Information Content Content denotes substance, such as the number of units sold this week. With respect to information processing, content is valued relative to its usefulness in making a decision. For instance, the forecast of sales next month has value in making a decision concerning the purchase of more inventory. A very important example of information with valuable content is a **key success factor.** For instance, the share of the market is a key success factor to most business firms.

Information Properties In addition to content, information exhibits properties that affect the quality of decision-making. Specific information properties include

   1. **Relevance,** the degree to which the information directly affects a decision or a firm's objectives. Any key success factor, such as total return on assets, has a high degree of relevance.

   2. **Quantifiability,** the degree to which numeric values can be assigned to the information.

   3. **Accuracy,** the reliability and precision of the information.

   4. **Conciseness,** the degree to which the information has been aggregated (and hence details have been reduced).

   5. **Timeliness,** the currency of the information. Timeliness has two aspects: up-to-dateness and response time.

   6. **Scope,** the span encompassed by the information. For instance, a budgeted expense may pertain to a department, a division, or to an entire firm.

Decision-making

   Pieces of information having specific content and properties are used in making decisions. A variety of decisions are made pertaining to a firm. Most of these decisions follow, at least roughly, a rational process.

Types of Decisions Decisions may be classified by a number of dimensions, such as resource (e.g., facilities decision) and operational function'(e.g., accounting decision). One useful classification is according to degree of problem structure. Thus, a programmed or **structured decision** is one that concerns a problem situation whose factors and relationships are very clear to the decision maker. At the opposite end of the spectrum is the nonprogrammed or **unstructured decision,** which concerns a problem situation whose factors and relationships are poorly understood. Many decisions fall into the semistructured category, which ranges between these two extremes.

Perhaps the most useful way to classify decisions is in accordance with the key management activities of planning and control. Four types of decisions under this classification plan are strategic planning decisions, tactical planning decisions, management control decisions, and operational control decisions.

Strategic planning decisions, also called strategic decisions, select the policies and resources needed to achieve a firm's objectives. These decisions have long-range impacts and thus are generally made by managers at the highest level. Whether or not to develop new markets and to build new production plants are examples of problems requiring strategic decisions.

Tactical planning decisions translate strategic decisions into operational programs, plans, and instructions. For example, broad policies and strategic decisions concerning advertising are converted by tactical decisions into detailed advertising programs and budgets. One typical effect of tactical decisions is the allocation of resources among the various departments and activities of a firm. Tactical decisions have a shorter-range impact than strategic decisions, and they are also narrower in scope. Middle-level managers make most of the tactical decisions in a firm.

Management control and operational control decisions are made within the overall administrative control process of the firm. This process, as well as the constituent management control and operational control systems, was discussed in Chapter 4.

Decision Process

Although decision makers and problems requiring decisions differ greatly, the process for making effective decisions is fairly standardized. Figure 12-1 shows the steps in this **decision process.** Although the process appears to be formal, some or all of the steps can be performed informally and quickly in the case of many decisions. Also, certain steps tend to blend together.

1. **Recognize and define the problem.** The problem may be an adverse change, as when the profits of a product are declining. Or, it may be an opportunity, such as the opportunity to acquire a smaller firm with a complementary product line. Defining the problem can be difficult and involve much data gathering. It consists of expressing the desired results or criteria, the key factors in the problem situation, constraints, assumptions, time horizons, and so on.

2. **Determine alternative courses of action.** Every feasible solution to the problem or course of action should be considered, including the alternatives to "do nothing" and "keep doing as we are now."

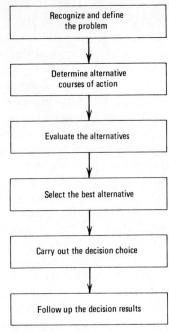

FIGURE 12-1 Steps in a decision process.

3. **Evaluate the alternatives.** To perform this step the decision maker must develop a decision model, which may be formally written or expressed implicitly in the decision maker's mind. A **decision model** (a) describes the relationships and behaviors of all significant factors, and (b) provides a means of evaluating the alternatives in terms of the criteria.

4. **Select the preferred alternative.** This step consists of "making the decision." Generally the choice is based mainly on the decision model. If the decision model is sound and all feasible alternatives have been evaluated, the selected alternative should be a good choice and perhaps even the optimal decision choice. However, in the environment of an organization, qualitative considerations may enter the picture. Thus, managerial judgment that weighs all considerations is needed for many complex and significant decisions.

5. **Carry out the decision choice.** This step consists of all the activities necessary to physically implement the decision choice.

6. **Follow up the results.** If the results achieved by an implemented decision choice are monitored and compared to expected results, the decision choice is within a control process. Thus, corrective actions can be taken if actual results are found to be differing significantly.

Information Flows

Data involved in processing transactions and performing operations flow horizontally within the operational system and the organizational units of a firm.

Information resulting from transaction processing and operations flows into the processing centers of the AIS. Then, this information, plus the processed results of other nontransactional data, becomes potential decision-making information. As needed, this information is retrieved and flows to the responsibility centers within the organization where decisions are made. These flows are generally upward through the various managerial levels, as shown in Figure 12-2. Other information often flows to managerial decision makers through the informal system.

After decisions are made by managers, the choices must be implemented. Consequently, the implemented decision results—in the form of detailed plans and instructions—generally flow downward through the managerial levels to the departments and other operational areas where they are to be carried out.

Information Needs

Information needs, with respect to properties as well as content, vary widely from decision to decision. They also vary greatly from manager to manager. For instance, the vice president of finance has far different information needs from a production department supervisor. The information system, however, should be capable of serving both equally well and distinctively. In this section we contrast information needs among differing managerial levels and organizational functions.

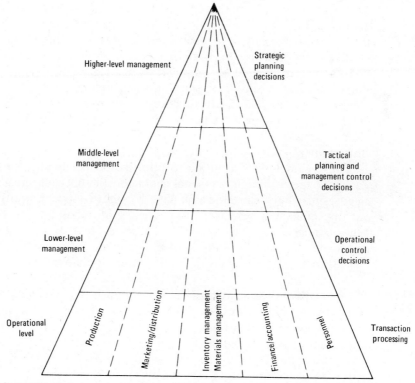

FIGURE 12-2 Levels of managerial decision-making and operation functions.

Needs at Managerial Levels Although information content is specific to decisions, information properties can be distinguished among the various managerial levels. The reason we can do so is that managers at a particular level tend to make one type of decision, and those at a different level make another type. As Figure 12-2 shows, higher-level managers make strategic decisions, lower-level managers make operational control decisions, and middle-level managers make tactical planning and management control decisions. By identifying the properties of information needed in making a particular type of decision, we can then relate the properties to a managerial level.

Information needed for strategic decisions, and hence by higher-level managers, tends to be (1) broad in scope, (2) relatively summarized, (3) qualitative as well as quantitative, and (4) drawn mainly from external sources. As with any planning decision, to be relevant the information must pertain to the future (i.e., represent estimates) and aid in choosing among the alternative courses of action. Because the future impact of strategic decisions has a long-range time frame, the estimates are not likely to be highly accurate or precise. Also, timeliness in making the decisions is not normally critical; making a sound decision is more important than a quick decision.

In contrast, information needed for operational control decisions, and hence for lower-level managers, tends to be (1) narrow in scope, (2) relatively detailed, (3) mainly quantitative, and (4) derived mainly from internal sources. As with any control decision, to be relevant the information must pertain to the recent past or present and be compared against benchmarks (e.g., reorder points). Because the time frame of operational control decisions is short-range, the information should be very accurate and precise. Decisions must generally be made in a very timely manner so that corrective actions can be promptly taken. Figure 12-3 contrasts the information properties pertaining to the two managerial levels.

Information needed by middle-level managers in making tactical planning decisions tends to exhibit properties that fall between the extremes. Management control decisions, which are made by all managers except those at the lowest level, require information having properties similar to those for operational control decisions. However, timeliness is less important and conciseness is more important.

These guidelines pertaining to information needs must be tempered, since each manager is unique. Personal characteristics have an impact on information needs, since they determine a manager's cognitive style. **Cognitive style** refers to the way a manager perceives and processes information in arriving at a decision. One manager may have an analytical style; another may prefer an intuitive approach. An area of study known as **human information processing (HIP)** reveals that cognitive styles vary widely among managers.

Needs within Organizational Functions Each organizational function needs a distinctive set of information that accords with its assigned responsibilities. However, two or more functions often share information needs. For instance, the sales forecast is information needed by the marketing, inventory management, and production functions for making decisions. Examples of information content needed by three key functions are as follows.

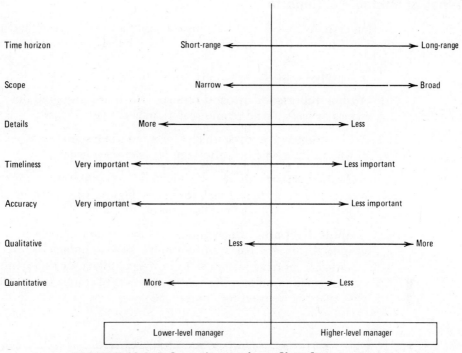

FIGURE 12-3 Information-needs profiles of two managers.

1. **Marketing:** competitors' products, prices, and plans; customers' income levels, attitudes, and desires; economic trends; sales forecasts; current volumes and profits on all products; results of advertising efforts; and customer complaints.

2. **Inventory management:** inventory quantities on hand; reorder points; carrying costs and reorder costs; forecasts of demands (sales), suppliers' products, prices, and lead times; quantities on order.

3. **Finance:** cash receipts and disbursements; interest rates; available investments and returns; bad debts and collection rates; capital expenditures; and budgeted revenues and expenses.

MANAGERIAL REPORTING SYSTEMS

Information needs are most often translated into hard copy reports and soft copy displays. Chapter 6 described various reports for managers and for users outside the firm. It also discussed the features of effective reports and displays. In this section we survey more types of managerial reports, including formal integrated systems for reporting to managers.

Types of Managerial Reports

Managerial reports were classified as operational, control, and planning reports in Chapter 6. They may also be classified according to such types as

1. **Scheduled reports,** which are issued on a periodic schedule.

2. **Ad hoc reports,** or demand reports, which are prepared on a one-time or irregular basis at the requests of managers.

3. **Event-triggered reports,** which are issued when some event, such as a breakdown of a machine or a shortage of inventory, occurs.

4. **Exception reports,** which are control reports that reflect only those circumstances needing managerial attention. Figure 12-4 portrays an exception report relating to machine downtimes.

5. **Graphical reports,** which translate tabular quantitative information into graphical formats that are often more understandable to users. Graphical reports can portray historical and projected data, or they can provide control information. Figure 12-5 shows a report of comparative plant utilization data that can be used for control purposes.

	Allan Products Co.		
	Machine Downtime Control Report		
Machining Department		Week of June 18–22	
Machine identification	Down-hours over (under) standard	Percent of production time down	Cause
123B	2.0	5.0%	Operator injured; no immediate replacement
268D	(1.5)	0.6%	
477C	1.5	4.4%	Extra maintenance required
491B	8.0	12.5%	Broken clutch; slow delivery from supplier
602F	(1.2)	1.0%	
753A	5.8	9.7%	Worn pin; trouble difficult to locate
928G	(2.0)	0%	

Notes: 1. Production time per week = 80 hours.
   2. Standard downtime per week = 2 hours or 2.5 percent.
   3. Significant deviation from standard = ±1 hour.
   4. Of the 95 machines in above department, 56 had a favorable deviation (under standard); 39 had an unfavorable deviation (over standard) during reported week.

FIGURE 12-4 An exception report.

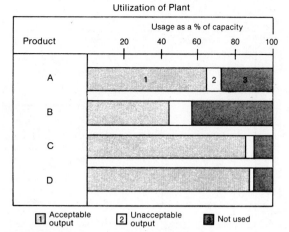

Financial Reporting System The basic reporting system utilized by almost every organization is the **financial reporting system.** It draws heavily on transactions for input data and is organized around the chart of accounts. Some of the reports generated by the system span all the activities of a firm and are intended for users outside the firm. However, most are narrower in scope and are intended for managers. Typical reports may provide information regarding the income for a division or the total expenses for a department. Certain reports may be the result of significant computations, such as reports that present financial ratios based on analyses of key values in the balance sheet and income statement.

Often reports in the financial reporting system reflect variances between actual and budgeted values. Underlying such reports are a variety of component budgets that the firm develops on an annual or other periodic basis. Figure 12-6 describes the development of component budgets and their relationships to each other. These budgets are generally the result of a painstaking process and require ranges of inputs.

Cost Accounting System The **cost accounting system** is a specialized data collection, processing, and reporting system that is embedded within the more comprehensive financial reporting system. As noted in Chapter 10, a cost accounting system is employed by those firms that convert raw materials into some type of finished good or service. It summarizes costs according to some object, such as job, process, or project. When standard costs are used, the resulting cost variance reports can pinpoint inefficiencies in the purchasing or conversion process. Cost variances typically computed include the materials price variance, materials usage variance, labor rate variance, labor efficiency variance, and overhead spending variance. Cost variance reports are provided to the responsible managers periodically—usually monthly or weekly, but sometimes daily. On the basis of these reports, the managers can decide when corrective actions are necessary.

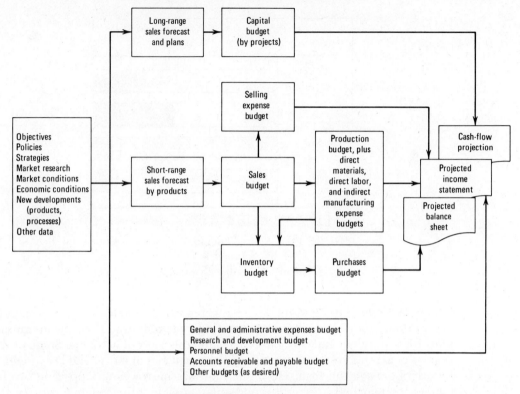

FIGURE 12-6 Development of budget reports.

Responsibility Reporting System The **responsibility reporting system** provides information that is useful for management control decisions. This system, also called a responsibility accounting system, consists of a set of correlated reports. Each report focuses on a particular responsibility center within the firm. Reports for each managerial level summarize the results of lower levels. From an overall point of view, the reports feed accountability information upward through the managerial levels of the organization. Thus, the entire set links together all managerial levels and all organizational units. Figure 12-7 illustrates this linkage among managerial levels.

Each report for a responsibility center contains budgeted amounts, which represent performance standards. If the center is cost oriented, the amounts are costs. If the center is profit oriented, the amounts are revenues and profits as well as costs.

Figure 12-8 displays a set of linked responsibility reports for the centers that are shaded in Figure 12-7. For simplicity the reports show only costs, even though the president's center is profit oriented. Also, the costs shown in each report are only those costs that are controllable by the center being reported on. The amounts shown consist of budgeted costs and variances. Although actual costs are often shown in such reports, they are not as important as the variances. Each report links to the one above by means of "rolled up" total controllable costs. Arrows trace these "roll-ups." Because each report at a higher level is a

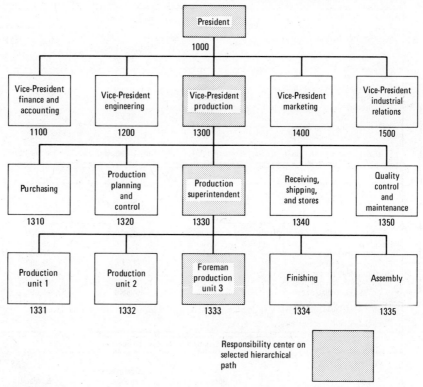

FIGURE 12-7 A portion of an organization chart used to illustrate responsibility accounting.

summary of "rolled-up" costs from lower-level reports, it is just as concise as those reports.

Coding is critical to the success of a responsibility reporting system. Each center in Figure 12-7 is coded with a group code having a hierarchical format. Each cost incurred by a center is coded. At the end of the reporting period all controllable costs are easily accumulated (1) center by center, (2) level by level, and (3) function by function.

Profitability Reporting System The **profitability reporting system** provides reports that parallel a firm's organization structure and span all its segments and activities. It emphasizes the planning for profits through such segments as product lines, classes of customers, and sales regions. Profitability reports show the impact of each segment on a firm's fixed costs and overall profits. Hence, they help managers to make decisions concerning the retention of a segment (e.g., product line), the pricing of products, the advertising needed for each product, and the allocation of sales resources to the respective sales regions and classes of customers.

Because profitability reports emphasize profit planning, they generally consist of budgeted values that have been recast from the traditional financial statement formats. However, they may also be used to supplement responsibility reports.

Cost Summary for President

Month: October	This Month		Year-to-Date	
Cost	Budget	(Over) Under Budget	Budget	(Over) Under Budget
President's office[a]	$ 36,600	$200	$ 366,000	$1,000
V.P.—finance and accounting	52,700	300	527,000	(600)
V.P.—engineering	25,300	(100)	253,000	(900)
V.P.—production	244,000	(3,860)	2,440,000	(45,659)
V.P.—marketing	120,000	(850)	1,200,000	(7,640)
V.P.—industrial relations	12,600	—	126,000	500
Total controllable costs	$491,200	$(4,310)	$4,912,000	$(53,299)

[a]Includes insurance, taxes, staff, salaries, depreciation (other than factory equipment), and miscellaneous items.

Cost Summary for Vice-President—Production

Month: October	This Month		Year-to-Date	
Cost	Budget	(Over) Under Budget	Budget	(Over) Under Budget
Vice-President's office[b]	$ 30,800	$(200)	$ 308,000	$500
Purchasing[c]	3,500	310	35,000	(878)
Production planning and control	3,200	(480)	32,000	(4,280)
Production superintendent	192,430	(3,855)	1,924,300	(44,161)
Receiving, shipping, and stores	3,370	(85)	33,700	(660)
Quality control and maintenance	10,700	450	107,000	3,820
Total controllable costs	$244,000	$(3,860)	$2,440,000	$(45,659)

[b]Includes employee benefits, overtime premium payroll taxes, staff salaries, and miscellaneous items.

[c]Includes material price variance.

Cost Summary for Production Superintendent

Month: October	This Month		Year-to-Date	
Cost	Budget	(Over) Under Budget	Budget	(Over) Under Budget
Superintendent's office[d]	$ 20,500	$200	$ 205,000	$(500)
Production unit 1	57,200	(1,650)	572,000	(14,855)
Production unit 2	21,760	710	217,600	(1,960)
Production unit 3	36,930	1	369,300	(696)
Finishing	15,240	(376)	152,400	(2,050)
Assembly	40,800	(2,740)	408,000	(25,100)
Total controllable costs	$192,430	$(3,855)	$1,924,300	$(45,161)

[d]Includes depreciation—factory equipment, staff salaries, and miscellaneous items.

Controllable Costs for Foreman, Production Unit 3

Month: October	This Month		Year-to-Date	
Cost	Budget	(Over) Under Budget	Budget	(Over) Under Budget
Direct materials	$16,000	$250	$160,000	$1,210
Direct labor[e]	17,500	(276)	175,000	(2,172)
Supervision and staff salaries	1,500	—	15,000	—
Supplies	300	10	3,000	100
Setup for jobs	560	(35)	5,600	(318)
Rework	420	52	4,200	490
Heat, light, and power	200	15	2,000	(55)
Maintenance	350	(20)	3,500	117
Other costs	100	5	1,000	(68)
Total controllable costs	$36,930	$1	$369,300	$(696)

[e]Labor rate variance = $18; labor efficiency variance = $(294).

FIGURE 12-8 Four levels of responsibility reports.

	Total	Products 1	Products 2	Products 3
Net sales	$1,575,000	$500,000	$850,000	$225,000
Less variable costs				
Direct materials	$525,000	$172,000	$290,000	$63,000
Direct labor	360,000	100,000	215,000	45,000
Variable indirect manufacturing expenses[a]	83,000	26,000	45,000	12,000
Variable selling expenses[b]	79,500	25,000	42,500	12,000
Variable administrative expenses[c]	5,500	2,000	2,500	1,000
Total variable costs	$1,053,000	$325,000	$595,000	$133,000
Contribution margin	$522,000	$175,000	$255,000	$92,000
Less fixed costs				
Committed costs assignable to products	$160,000	$55,000	$80,000	$25,000
Managed costs assignable to products	158,000	50,000	85,000	23,000
Total assigned fixed costs	$318,000	$105,000	$165,000	$48,000
Planned operating margin	$204,000	$70,000	$90,000	$44,000
Operating margin percentage		14.0%	10.6%	19.5%
Unallocated joint fixed costs	44,000			
Planned net income	$160,000			
Income taxes	83,200			
Planned net income after income taxes	$76,800			
Planned return on total assets[d]	5.1%			

[a]Schedule *A* details expenses (not shown).
[b]Schedule *B* details expenses (not shown).
[c]Schedule *C* details expenses (not shown).
[d]Expected average total assets = $1,500,000.

FIGURE 12-9 A report of planned profits by products for a manufacturing firm.

As such they would show variances of actual profits from planned profits, segregated for each segment that serves as a profit center (e.g., a sales region).

Figure 12-9 shows a profitability report for a manufacturing firm. The segments illustrated by this report are the three products sold by the firm. In the total column the costs are separated according to their variable and fixed natures. In turn, the fixed costs are separated into those costs that are directly traceable to individual products and those that are joint or common to all products. In accordance with sound managerial concepts, the joint fixed costs are *not* allocated to the products. Thus, the "bottom lines" for the products are planned operating margins, computed by subtracting the variable costs and directed fixed costs for a product from its planned sales amount. Planned returns on invested capital can also be computed for each product if desired.

Impacts of Reports on Managerial Behavior

Reports influence managerial behavior. Managers make decisions and take actions on the basis of information in reports. If the information is reported effectively, the managers are likely to make sound decisions and take desirable actions. If the information is not reported effectively, the managers are forced to, or inclined to, act in undesirable manners.

Consider the common reporting deficiency of **information overload**—providing more information than busy managers can reasonably digest. For instance, an inventory manager may receive a thick listing of all materials, showing the quantities on hand and on order; a personnel manager may receive a report containing numerous comparisons of personnel needs and availabilities. Managers who receive such reports may act dysfunctionally by simply tossing them in a corner. Other reactions might be to use the information casually (thus perhaps making errors), to use only selected items, or to have an assistant boil the report down to digestible size. These reactions can be avoided if such managers are provided exception reports.

USER-SUPPORT SYSTEMS

Computer-based information systems can provide various degrees and types of support to its diverse users. As Figure 12-10 suggests, the degree of system support ranges from simply maintaining stored raw input data to making and implementing decisions. The types of support range from transaction processing to strategic decision-making. In this section we survey three types of user-support systems. Each of these systems may be viewed as a major subsystem within the overall information system; together they comprise the management information system (MIS) discussed in Chapter 1. Each provides a different degree, as well as type, of support. Their relationships and types of support are shown in Figure 12-11.

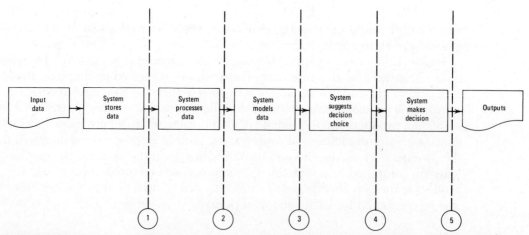

FIGURE 12-10 Levels of support provided by support systems. Adapted from Richard O. Mason, Jr., "Basic Concepts for Designing Management Information Systems." *AIS Research Paper #8* (Los Angeles: UCLA Graduate School of Administration, October 1969). Used with permission of the author.

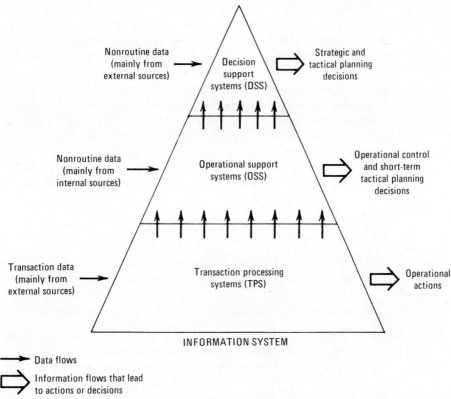

FIGURE 12-11 Types of support systems.

Transaction Processing Systems

At the lowest, or operational, layer are the familiar transaction processing systems (TPSs). Each individual TPS provides support in the form of operational actions, such as the acquiring of more merchandise for sale. Since a TPS processes data received from various sources, the degree of support is more than simple data storage but less than decision focused. A TPS does generate a variety of reports, as has been illustrated in Chapters 7 through 10. However, the reports are by-products of transaction processing and are generally of the scheduled type. Although some can aid in planning and control decisions, few are constructed around explicit decision models.

Operational Support Systems

At the middle layer are the **operational support systems (OSSs).** An OSS aids the planning and control of operations. It focuses mainly on the short-range tactical planning and operational control decisions. As noted earlier, these types of decisions, which are relatively structured, are made by middle-level and lower-level managers. The payoff from an improved OSS is increased operating efficiency, which may result in greater responsiveness and lower costs.

As Figure 12-11 shows, an OSS uses both nonroutine data from internal sources and transaction data from external sources. These data are processed and employed within decision models so that the degree of support may reach the fourth or fifth points shown in Figure 12-10. Thus, information provided by an OSS may appear in managerial reports, including those generated as by-products of transaction processing. However, certain OSSs perform their support functions automatically and generate only notices of their decisions. For example, an automatic credit-checking system may simply notify the credit manager of approvals or rejections of credit orders.

The OSSs vary in capabilities, depending on the specific decisions they are designed to support. Most effective OSSs possess the first two of the following attributes, and many possess the third and/or fourth attributes.

1. Interactive processing and inquiries by users.

2. Concurrent, or time-shared, access by a variety of users.

3. Real-time control over an ongoing process or operation. Thus, a **real-time** OSS responds in a sufficiently timely manner to incoming data to make decisions and take corrective actions necessary to control the process or operation. An example is an airline reservation system.

4. One or more embedded decision models, which are applied automatically by the system in controlling a process or operation. An example is an inventory control system that automatically signals when a purchase order is needed to replenish low stocks. Some such systems may even prepare the purchase order automatically.

In addition, some OSSs are dedicated to one particular use and type of user. An example of a dedicated OSS is an airline reservation system, which was also noted as being a real-time system.

Decision Support Systems

At the top layer are the **decision support systems (DDSs).** A DSS aids higher-level and middle-level managers in making strategic and certain tactical planning decisions. It is therefore concerned with decisions usually involving relatively unstructured problem situations that have long-range impacts. A distinctive aspect of decisions involving a DSS is that they *always* require active managerial participation and are *never* made solely by the DSS. The degree of support provided by a DSS usually reaches the third point, sometimes the fourth point, but never the fifth point (see Figure 12-10). The payoff from a DSS is improved decision-making effectiveness on the parts of participating managers.

Data for a DSS are mainly nonroutine data drawn from external sources. Information is provided in several ways. Managers receive managerial reports, such as those produced by the profitability reporting system. They can obtain ad hoc reports from the overall information system, either by having assistants compile the information or by interactively requesting the system's report generator to compile the information. Furthermore, they may interactively experi-

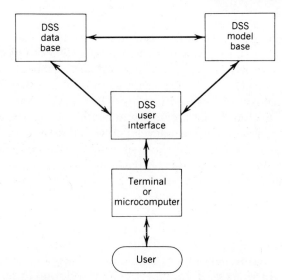

FIGURE 12-12 Key components of a decision support system.

ment with data via embedded decision models in order to gain more insight into the problem situation.

Although a DSS incorporates most of the attributes provided by an OSS, two significant differences exist. First, a DSS is never a real-time system, since timeliness is not a critical factor in the decisions with which it deals. Second, the decision models focus on more difficult problem situations. Therefore, they are designed to allow experimentation rather than provide optimal solutions.

The key components of a DSS are pictured in Figure 12-12. A data base contains the nonroutine and planning data that are relevant, including in some cases summarized transaction data. A **model base** contains the array of decision models described; it also allows managers to create new models or to combine available models. A **user interface** provides the user with a command language and other tools for interacting with the data and model bases. The user interface is examined more closely in the next section.

Examples of problem situations requiring a DSS are those involving the introduction of new products and the location of new production facilities.

Closely related to a DSS is an **executive information system (EIS)** which supports the chief executive officer of a firm. An EIS provides information needed for strategic planning, such as information concerning competitors, expected economic conditions, technological trends, and other facets of the firm's environment. For instance, an EIS may be used by a president to develop an overall strategy concerning mergers and acquisitions. In many cases the user of an EIS accesses the information stored in online data bases via desk-top terminals or microcomputers.[1]

---

[1] Jeff Moad, "The Latest Challenge for IS Is in the Executive Suite," *Datamation* (May 15, 1988), 43–52.

Expert Systems

An **expert system** is a user-support system that is designed to cope with the same type of relatively unstructured problem situations as a DSS. In a sense it is a variation of a DSS and thus has not been included in Figure 12-11.

However, an expert system functions in a very different manner from a DSS. It is a form of artificial intelligence software that enables a nonexpert user to make decisions that are as sound as those of an expert. For instance, an expert auditor system has been developed with the assistance of experienced auditors. A novice auditor can use the system to determine the best tests to perform in an audit situation. Another expert system enables an inexperienced investor to imitate experienced investment advisers in selecting sound stocks for investment.

An expert system has the data base and user interface components of a DSS. Instead of a model base, however, the expert system has a knowledge base plus an inference engine and development engine. The **knowledge base** incorporates the knowledge, rules-of-thumb, and decision rules used by experts. The **inference engine** contains the logic and reasoning mechanisms that simulate the thought process of an expert. The **development engine** consists of a program that gathers the knowledge and decision processes from the expert. To apply these components to a problem situation, the user interacts via the user interface and enters pertinent facts concerning his or her particular situation. The expert system then responds with a solution or suggestions.

Although many firms have not yet installed expert systems, an increasing number of functioning systems are being reported. An example of a control-oriented expert system is being employed by American Express. Its system interacts with the firm's data base to detect fraudulent credit card activity. Each time an authorization request is received, the expert system checks the pattern of recent expenditures. If the previous requests this week relating to a particular card, for instance, have been entered from Paris, Hong Kong, and Chicago, the system would signal that the card might be stolen.[2]

USER-DEVELOPED SYSTEMS AND RELATED TOOLS

As we have seen, user-support systems have been developed to aid managers and other users. Most user-support systems to date have been primarily built by systems analysts and other professionals. In recent years, however, users have been encouraged to develop their own user-support systems, with or without the help of professionals.

Reasons for User-developed Systems

Conventional systems development has exhibited disturbing trends and problems in recent years. One major problem is the increasing cost of systems development. An accompanying problem is the lengthy period, usually months or

---

[2] Harvey Newquist, "The Real Thing: How Artificial Intelligence Is Changing Business." *Business Software Review* (March 1988), 58.

years, between the time that a user requests a system and the time a new system has been implemented. These cost and time problems are attributable to the fact that systems analysis, design, and implementation are generally labor-intensive processes. Because of the scarcity of qualified systems analysts, their salaries have steadily risen during the past decade.

Because of the lengthy systems development period, the needs of users have often changed by the time the system is completed. Also, users cannot know in advance exactly what they need from a system; they can only determine their complete needs through experience with the actual system.

Two other trends in recent years have been (1) the declining price of computer hardware, and (2) an increasing number of computerized software system development tools. These trends, when coupled with the aforementioned problems of conventional systems development, are hastening the growth of **user-developed systems.**

Not all information systems are subject to user development, of course. Large dedicated OSSs, such as airline reservations systems, must be undertaken by professionals. Commercial software applications, such as accounting and manufacturing packages, are also likely to be prepared by professional software firms.

The types of systems that are best suited to user-development include DSSs, specialized reporting systems, and specialized transaction processing or operational support systems. These systems would normally be intended to serve only the user-builders and their immediate staffs or units.

An example of a user-developed system can be found in the purchasing department of a subsidiary of Chrysler Corporation. The administrative manager of the department needed to have a new management reporting system designed for use with the department's new minicomputer-based data base management software. With the approval of the data processing department, the purchasing administrative manager and her secretary attended a programming class for two weeks. Using the skills acquired, they programmed applications pertaining to buyers' reference files, engineering changes, and so on.[3]

Tools for User-developed Systems

Among the currently available systems development software tools are very high level programming languages, query and retrieval languages, graphics packages, model base management systems, and application generators. Collectively these software tools are known as **fourth generation languages** and packages.

Very High Level Programming Languages The very high level programming languages are the successors to FORTRAN, COBOL, and BASIC in many respects. They provide powerful, easy-to-use, concise, and versatile program instructions and features. Of particular interest to managers and accountants are the subset of languages known as financial modeling languages. These languages

---

[3] Ralph H. Sprague, Jr. and Barbara C. McNurlin, *Information Systems Management in Practice* (Englewood Cliffs, N.J.: Prentice-Hall, 1986), 281–282.

1. The **time-based simulation** technique projects the states (values) of the key factors and criteria over future time periods, given current data values and expected rates of change.
Example: A user might simulate the firm's budget over five years, with values of sales and net income being calculated each year.

2. The **"what if"** analysis technique allows the user to ask "what if" questions in order to determine how key factors will respond to assumed changes or conditions.
Example: A user might ask, "What will be the increase in my firm's labor costs next year if we grant a $2.00 per hour average increase in wage rates on January 1?"

3. The **sensitivity analysis** technique, a special version of the "what if" analysis technique, reveals the sensitivity of the decision model criteria to changes in the values of key factors.
Example: A user might ask, "What will be the effect on my firm's net income (the model criterion) if unit sales decrease by 10 percent next year?"

4. The **goal seeking analysis** technique allows the user to determine the levels of key factors needed in order to achieve a desired level in a model criterion.
Example: A user might ask, "What volume (level) of sales units must my firm generate next year in order to achieve a 25 percent share of the market?"

FIGURE 12-13 Four model manipulation or analysis techniques that may be used with a financial model.

are particularly useful in developing a DSS. They include such features as a nonprocedural approach that enables users to enter program statements without regard for sequence, statistical routines, and several manipulation techniques. Figure 12-13 lists typical model manipulative techniques. Examples of financial modeling languages include CUFFS, IFPS, PLANR, and EXPRESS.[4]

An example of a user-developed **financial model** may be found at Tanner Companies, a Phoenix-based construction firm. The model is employed in preparing the firm's budget. One of its main benefits is the aid it offers to managers for major key operating and strategic decisions. For instance, by means of "what if" analysis, the treasurer is able to evaluate the effects of refinancing a loan on the firm's net income and cash balance. He is confident that the model has led to improved cash management and reduced borrowing rates.

Constructing financial models by means of such languages as IFPS is quite straightforward. Essentially these models consist of statements that have the appearance of equations. For example, if the contribution margin percentage can be expected to remain at 30 percent of sales, this relationship is expressed as

$$\text{Contribution margin} = 0.30 \times \text{expected sales}$$

After all needed statements have been compiled into an income statement model, the user specifies the key estimates, such as the sales forecast. The model then computes the expected value of net profit.

---

[4] CUFFS is available from Cuffs Planning and Models, Ltd.; IFPS is available from Execucom Systems Corporation; PLANR is available from Coopers & Lybrand; EXPRESS is available from Management Decision Systems.

Query and Retrieval Languages **Query and retrieval languages** enable users to express requests for information in a user-friendly manner. They were introduced in Chapter 11, since they access the stored data through the data base management system (DBMS). Two of the most common approaches by which query and retrieval languages facilitate requests are the command language approach and the menu approach.

The command language approach allows the user to communicate by means of Englishlike commands. Simple but descriptive words in the language can initiate reasonably complex processing sequences. Consider the command

DISPLAY SALES FOR EACH BRANCH, PLUS TOTAL SALES

The verb *DISPLAY* tells the system to retrieve and exhibit several values on the video display screen. (*PRINT* would cause the output to appear on hard copy.) The word *TOTAL* asks for a computation.

The menu approach displays listings of items on the screen. To select the desired item (e.g., record, report) the user simply enters the number beside the described item. Although this approach is the more user-friendly of the two, it does not allow the user as much flexibility in requesting data as does the command approach.

Examples of packaged commercial query and retrieval languages are SQL (from IBM Corporation), EASYTRIEVE (from Pansophic), and INTELLECT (from Artificial Intelligence Corporation). Some of these software packages incorporate report generators and file management features.

Graphics Packages Information in graphic form has become increasingly popular. Graphs aid managers in understanding quantitative data and in spotting trends. They are especially useful in helping nonaccounting managers to interpret accounting information. When in color, and perhaps also three dimensions, graphs can be very impressive and persuasive. Graphics output are available via terminals and microcomputers; graphs may then be printed in color or black and white on plotters or laser printers. Although much of the recent growth in graphics output results from the added availability of microcomputer graphics software (as discussed in the Appendix), high-end graphics are also quite important to many firms. High-end graphics from mainframe computers or minicomputers are necessary when graphs must be of very high quality and/or in large volumes. An example of a popular high-end graphics package is SAS/GRAPH (from the SAS Institute, Inc.).

Model Base Management Systems A **model base management system (MBMS)** is the modeling counterpart to a DBMS. It is used with a model base, which forms a part of a DSS. The functions of a MBMS generally consist of providing (1) links among models in a model base, (2) a model definition language, (3) a mechanism for modifying models, and (4) a means of executing and manipulating models.

Application Generators **Application generators** are powerful software packages that allow users to develop complete applications, such as TPSs. The user specifies what he or she needs, and the package generates suitable program instructions. This resultant program can accept inputs interactively, validate the inputs, update data sets, perform other required processing steps, and generate requested reports.

An application generator can achieve all this because it contains a number of generalized programmed modules or routines. Each module can perform a certain function, such as file maintenance or report generation. It is sufficiently flexible, however, to allow the user to insert customized program instructions.

Application generators illustrate the trend to integrate several capabilities into a single software package. Examples of commercial application generators are FOCUS (from Information Builders) and RAMIS II (from Mathematica, Inc.).

Information Centers

As users have become involved in developing their own systems, firms have searched for ways to aid them. Information centers have consequently come into being. An **information center** is a physical location within a firm where users can receive computer system-oriented services. Among the services that may be offered are training in the use of computers (including microcomputers) and in system development tools, selecting computers and software, consulting on system development problems, and assisting in user-development projects. Assigned to the information center may be systems analysts, model builders, software specialists, and application specialists. These centers are likely to expand, both in numbers and in services offered, in coming years.

Hughes Aircraft Company is an example of a firm that has had an information center for several years. In one service activity, systems analysts assigned to the center wrote 12,000 lines of FOCUS code in order to help the controller's department develop an outline financial reporting system. They included sufficient documentation to enable the controller's personnel to maintain the system thereafter.[5]

Exxon Corporation has a multigroup information center in its New York corporate headquarters. The Client Support Center is the largest group; it provides consulting, training, and technical assistance in the application of end-user computing tools. Three other groups, which serve users through the Client Support Center, provide assistance with decision support system development, office systems development, and technical evaluation of new hardware and software.[6]

SUMMARY

Information processing consists of providing decision-making information to users. Information theory consists of conveying information from a source via a channel to a user. Information has value to the extent that it reduces a user's uncertainty concerning a decision situation. Information has content and such properties as relevance, accuracy, and conciseness. Decisions may

---

[5] Ralph H. Sprague, Jr. and Barbara C. McNurlin, *Information Systems Management in Practice* (Englewood Cliffs, N.J.: Prentice-Hall, 1986), 374–375.
[6] Richard T. Johnson, "The Infocenter Experience." *Datamation* (Jan. 1984), 137.

be classified as structured, unstructured, strategic planning, tactical planning, operational control, and management control. The decision process involves problem definition, determination of alternative courses of action, evaluation of alternatives, selection of the best alternative, implementation, and follow-up.

Information and data flows are horizontal for transaction processing and operations, upward to aid decision-making, and downward to implement decisions. Information needs vary among managerial levels, since managers at different levels make different kinds of decisions. Information needs also vary among organizational functions, since each function has a distinctive set of responsibilities.

Types of managerial reports include scheduled, ad hoc, event-triggered, exception, and graphical reports. Several managerial reporting systems exist in the typical firm, including the financial reporting system, the cost accounting system, the responsibility reporting system, and the profitability system. Reports can influence managerial behavior, both positively and negatively.

User-support systems include transaction processing systems (TPSs), operational support systems (OSSs), decision support systems (DSSs), and expert systems. The last two support the making of unstructured decisions and are relatively new. Users are increasingly becoming involved in developing their own systems, including DSSs. By doing so they reduce the large costs and lengthy periods required by conventional systems development. Also, powerful system development tools have become available, including very high level programming languages, query and retrieval languages, graphics packages, model base management systems, and application generators. Information centers are becoming increasingly available to aid users in undertaking their own system development efforts.

REFERENCES

Andersen, Anker V. *Graphing Financial Information: How Accountants Can Use Graphs to Communicate.* New York: National Association of Accountants, 1983.

Benson, Beth A. "Computer Graphics for Financial Management." *Management Accounting* (Jan. 1984), 46–49.

Blanning, Robert W. "Model-based and Data-based Planning Systems." *Omega* (1981), 2:163–167.

Carr, Arthur. "Accounting Information for Managerial Decisions." *Financial Executive* (Aug. 1977), 40–44.

Davis, Gordon B., and Olsen, Margrethe H. *Management Information Systems: Conceptual Foundations, Structure, and Development,* 2d ed. New York: McGraw-Hill, 1985.

Davis, Michael W. "Anatomy of Decision Support." *Datamation* (June 15, 1984), 201–208.

Head, Robert V. "Information Resource Center: A New Force in End User Computing." *Journal of Systems Management* (Feb. 1985), 24–29.

Hicks, James O., and Leininger, Wayne E. *Accounting Information Systems,* 2d ed. New York: West Publishing, 1986.

Kleim, Richard. "Computer-Based Financial Modeling." *Journal of Systems Management* (May 1982), 6–13.

Lin, W. Thomas, and Harper, William K. "A Decision-Oriented Management Accounting Information System." *Cost and Management* (Nov.–Dec. 1981), 32–36.

Martin, James. *Application Development Without Programmers.* Englewood Cliffs, N.J.: Prentice-Hall, 1982.

Martin, Merle P. "Making the Management Report Useful." *Journal of Systems Management* (May 1977), 30–37.

Murry, John P. "How an Information Center Improved Productivity." *Management Accounting* (Mar. 1984), 38–44.

Nauman, Seev, and Hadass, Michael. "DSS and Strategic Decisions." *California Management Review* (Spring 1980), 77–84.

Sprague, Ralph H., and Carlson, Eric D. *Building Effective Decision Support Systems.* Englewood Cliffs, N.J.: Prentice-Hall, 1982.

Walker, Charles W. "Profitability and Responsibility Accounting." *Management Accounting* (Dec. 1971), 23–30.

QUESTIONS

1. What is the meaning of each of the following terms?

Information processing	Cost accounting system
Information theory	Responsibility reporting system
Noise	Profitability reporting system
Information value	Information overload
Key success factor	Operational support system (OSS)
Relevance	Real-time
Quantifiability	Decision support system (DSS)
Accuracy	Model base
Conciseness	User interface
Timeliness	Executive information system (EIS)
Scope	Expert system
Structured decision	Knowledge base
Unstructured decision	Inference engine
Strategic planning decision	Development engine
Tactical planning decision	User-developed system
Managment control decision	Fourth generation language
Operational control decision	Financial model
Decision process	Query and retrieval languages
Decision model	Graphics package
Cognitive style	Model base management system (MBMS)
Human information processing (HIP)	Application generator
Scheduled report	Information center
Ad hoc report	
Event-triggered report	
Exception report	
Graphical report	
Financial reporting system	

2. What are the three levels of communication?

3. Contrast information content and properties.

4. What are several properties of information?

5. Describe the decision process, with emphasis on the decision model.

6. Contrast strategic and tactical planning decisions.

7. Give examples of strategic and tactical planning decisions.

8. What are two types of information needed for making all planning decisions?

9. Contrast management control and operational control decisions.

10. What types of information are carried by horizontal and vertical flows?

11. Contrast the properties of information needed by higher-level managers with the properties of information needed by lower-level managers.

12. Identify several types of managerial reports.

13. Describe and contrast the financial reporting and cost accounting systems.

14. What are the key features of responsibility reporting systems? Of profitability reporting systems?

15. In what ways are managers likely to react to information overload?

16. Contrast transaction processing, operational support, and decision support systems.

17. Identify the five degrees of support provided by user-support systems.

18. Identify several attributes that may be possessed by operational support systems.

19. What are examples of decisions supported by decision support systems?

20. What are the components of expert systems, and how do they differ from decision support systems?

21. Why are users increasingly developing their own systems?

22. Identify several software tools for user-development.

23. What features are included in the typical financial modeling language?

24. What types of services are provided by information centers?

25. How do information needs and reporting systems for not-for-profit organizations differ, if at all, from those for business firms?

26. In what ways are accountants best equipped to help improve information processing systems?

27. How do flows of informal information differ from flows of formal information in a firm?

28. Discuss the trade-offs between the accuracy and timeliness of an item of information.

29. How do the information needs of external users differ from the information needs of managers?

30. In what respects can reports be said to determine the design of an information system?

31. Managerial accountants generally are responsible for designing responsibility and profitability reporting systems. However, the technical accounting aspects underlying such reporting systems are only a part of the broader fabric, which includes organizational relationships, behavioral patterns, and corporate philosophies. Discuss the implications of this situation on the design approaches to be taken by accountants.

32. Can the accounting information system be viewed as a collection of integrated models?

33. Can a small firm justify the use of a decision support system?

34. What problems are likely to be encountered in the development of a decision support system?

35. What are the objections, if any, to providing "real-time" (say, hourly) financial reports to higher-level managers?

REVIEW PROBLEM

Oregon Paper Company

Statement

The Oregon Paper Company of Eugene, Oregon, was recently incorporated.[7] Although the company was founded by sawmill operators in western Oregon, its stock is publicly owned and traded on the major stock exchanges. Its main facility consists of a paper mill and adjoining offices and warehouse.

The purpose of the firm is to transform wood chips into pulp and then into kraft paper by a process consisting of more than 80 steps. Excess

---

[7] This case is roughly based on Karl Patrick's "The Concept and Development of a Total Business Information System, Part 2: The Delta Pulp and paper Company Limited," *Cost and Management* (Jan. 1969), 10–16. Reprinted with permission of the Society of Management Accountants of Canada.

pulp is sold separately as an unfinished by-product.

Resources used in the production of these products include wood, cooking and bleaching chemicals, paper additives, machine wires, and other direct materials; supplies, boiler feedwater chemicals, fuel oil, and other indirect materials; direct and indirect labor; purchased electric power, specialized equipment, and other overhead items.

One of the first concerns of the new managers was the need for a sound reporting structure. Accordingly, they established the firm's objectives, policies, organizational structure, lists of responsibilities, and lists of needed decisions. Then they employed a consulting firm to develop the details of a reporting structure geared to the foregoing.

Required

Outline the reporting structure that you, as the consultant, would design for the Oregon Paper Company.

Solution

The overall framework for the reporting structure will consist of four reporting systems: an operational control reporting system, a management control reporting system, a tactical reporting system, and a strategic reporting system.

The operational control reporting system focuses on the processes at the operational level. Its cycle ranges from an hour to a week. Reports in the system will be expressed in nonfinancial as well as financial terms. Among the key reports will be

Weekly production summaries, actual versus scheduled.

Hourly quality control reports.

Daily labor productivity reports.

Weekly machine utilization reports.

Weekly labor distribution reports.

Weekly cost accounting summaries.

Most of the reports pertain to such objects of concern as individual processes, employees, machines, and orders.

The management control reporting system focuses on departmental performances and has a monthly cycle. The key reports will be responsibility reports for all departments; each report will show variances for the respective controllable costs, with the materials variances separated into price and usage variances and the labor variances separated into rate and efficiency variances.

The tactical reporting system focuses on plantwide activities. Its cycle ranges from a month to a year. As in the case of the operational control reporting system, reports will be expressed in nonfinancial as well as financial terms. Among the key reports will be

Monthly production schedules (revised weekly or as necessary).

Monthly inventory status reports.

Monthly plant efficiency reports.

Monthly product shipment reports.

Monthly maintenance schedules.

Monthly sales analyses.

Monthly accounts receivable aging schedules.

Monthly purchase analyses.

Monthly idle-time and productivity analyses.

Monthly production cost analyses.

Annual profit plan, by product.

Annual cash budget.

The strategic reporting system focuses on long-range corporate plans. Although it is not cyclic in nature, its time horizon extends five or more years into the future. The key reports will be a capital or strategic budget, plus annual reports on competitors and markets. Other reports will be prepared on an ad hoc basis to aid managers in making specific long-range resource al-location decisions. Most reports will be expressed in financial terms.

PROBLEMS

12-1. The communication process is depicted in contemporary literature by the model shown at the bottom of this page. To be successful, the message must arrive at the intended destination in a form that depicts the true nature and impact of the event or incident that caused the message to be sent.

Management accountants are an important part of the communication process. Their responsibilities require reports in both oral and written form.

Required

a. Discuss the types of assistance a management accountant can provide at every step in the communication process.

b. Describe how managerial reports can be useful at both ends of the communication process.

(CMA adapted)

12-2. Identify alternative courses of action that should be considered and several key items of information needed in making decisions involving each of the problem situations.

a. How to expand plant capacity.

b. How to promote products.

c. How to generate a firm's growth.

d. How to reduce costs in production operations.

12-3. Describe the steps in the decision process pertaining to each of the following problem situations.

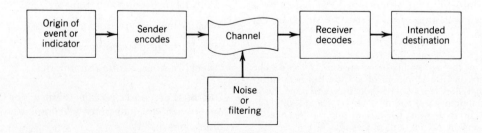

a. Whether to buy or make a part used in a final product.

b. Whether or not to replace a delivery truck.

c. Whether to introduce new product A or new product B.

12-4. Contrast the properties of information needed to make the following pairs of decisions.

a. A decision to locate a new warehouse versus a decision concerning which machine to assign a production employee tomorrow.

b. A decision concerning the possible elimination of a product line versus a decision concerning the possible promotion or reprimand of a department manager who has cost responsibilities.

12-5. Marval Products of the Bronx, New York, manufactures and wholesales several lines of luggage in two basic types: soft-side and molded. Each luggage line consists of several different pieces, each of which is available in a variety of sizes. At least one line is a complete set of luggage designed to be used by both men and women; however, most of the lines are designed specifically for either men or women. Certain of the lines also include matching attaché cases. Luggage lines are discontinued and introduced as tastes change or as product improvements are developed.

The firm also manufactures luggage for large retail firms, in accordance with each firm's unique specifications. Luggage in this category is marketed under the retail firms' private labels, rather than under the Marvel label.

Marval has been in business for 10 years, and has increased its annual sales volume manyfold.

Required

a. Identify strategic decisions that must be made periodically by Marval with respect to new and/or existing products.

b. Identify in detail the information that Marval needs during its annual review of long-term product strategy.

c. Identify in detail the information that Marval needs to prepare its sales forecast for the annual budget.

d. Describe in detail the process involved in the decision concerning whether or not to discontinue a particular luggage line.

(CMA adapted)

12-6. Brite-Snapshots, Inc., provides photographic services.[8] In planning its operations for 1989, the owner estimates the total revenues will amount to $70,000, broken down according to the major services as follows.

Photo posters	60%
Photofinishing	30%
Copywork	10%

The owner also estimates the major costs and cost groupings will be as follows.

	Photo Posters	Photofinishing	Copywork
Labor	$10,500	$7,000	$2,100
Supplies	7,000	4,000	1,300
Outside services	5,000	3,000	1,500
Other variable costs	1,500	1,000	400
Direct fixed costs	1,100	800	200

Joint fixed costs should amount to $17,400. The income tax rate may be assumed to be 34 percent.

Required

Prepare a profit planning report.

12-7. The Mecom Company of Las Cruces, New Mexico, produces sports equipment.[9] Each manager in charge of a department or higher responsibility center receives a monthly performance report. Last month (June) the costs pertaining to the fabricating department within the production function were as follows.

---

[8] This problem can be solved by using a microcomputer-based spreadsheet software package.

[9] This problem can be solved by using a microcomputer-based spreadsheet software package.

	Actual	Budgeted
Raw materials	$ 5,600	$ 6,000
Direct labor	12,800	12,000
Supplies	650	700
Utilities	1,680	1,500
Depreciation of departmental equipment	1,000	1,000
Depreciation of plant—allocated	6,000	6,000
Production administration cost—allocated	5,200	4,000
Indirect labor	4,400	4,000
Salary—department head	3,000	3,000

Each department manager is responsible for decisions concerning equipment needed in his or her department.

Required

Using the data provided, prepare June's report for the fabricating department in good form and in accordance with the concepts of responsibility reporting.

12-8. Wright Company of Princeton, New Jersey, employs a computer-based data processing system for maintaining all company records. The present system was developed in stages over the past five years and has been fully operational for the last 24 months.

When the system was being designed, all department heads were asked to specify the types of information and reports they would need for planning and controlling operations. The systems department attempted to meet the specifications of each department head. Company management specified that certain other reports be prepared for department heads. During the five years of systems development and operation there have been several changes in the department head positions, because of attrition and promotions. The new department heads often made requests for additional reports according to their specifications. The systems department complied with all these requests. Reports were discontinued only on request by a department head, and then only if it was not a standard report required by top management. As a result,

few reports were in fact discontinued. Consequently, the data processing system was generating a large quantity of reports each reporting period.

Company management became concerned about the quantity of information that was being produced by the system. The internal audit department was asked to evaluate the effectiveness of the reports generated by the system. The audit staff determined early in the study that more information was being generated by the data processing system than could be used effectively. They noted the following reactions to this information overload.

a. Many department heads would not act on certain reports during periods of peak activity. The department head would let these reports accumulate, with the hope of catching up during a subsequent lull.

b. Some department heads had so many reports that they did not act at all on the information or they made incorrect decisions because of misuse of the information.

c. Frequently, action required by the nature of the report data was not taken until the department head was reminded by someone who needed the decision. These department heads did not appear to have developed a priority system for acting on the information produced by the data processing system.

d. Department heads often would develop the information they needed from alternative independent sources, rather than utilizing the reports generated by the data processing system. This was often easier than trying to search among the reports for the needed data.

Required

a. Indicate, for each of the observed reactions, whether they are functional or dysfunctional behavioral responses. Explain your answer in each case.

b. Assuming one or more of the foregoing were dysfunctional, recommend procedures the company could employ to eliminate the dysfunctional behavior and to prevent its recurrence.

(CMA adapted)

12-9. Music Teachers Inc. is an educational association for music teachers that had 20,000 members during 1988. The association operates from a central headquarters but has local membership chapters throughout the United States. Monthly meetings are held by the local chapters to discuss recent developments on topics of interest to music teachers. The association's journal, *Teachers' Forum,* is issued monthly with features about recent developments in the field. The association publishes books and reports and sponsors professional courses that qualify for continuing professional education credit. The Statement of Revenues and Expenses for the current year follows

---

Music Teachers Inc.
Statement of Revenues and Expenses
For the Year Ended November 30, 1988
($000 omitted)

Revenues	$3,275
Expenses	
Salaries	$ 920
Personnel costs	230
Occupancy costs	280
Reimbursement to local chapters	600
Other membership services	500
Printing and paper	320
Postage and shipping	176
Instructors fees	80
General and administrative	38
Total expenses	$3,144
Excess of revenues over expenses	$ 131

The Board of Directors of Music Teachers, Inc., has requested that a segmented statement of operations be prepared showing the contribution of each revenue center (i.e., membership, magazine subscriptions, books and reports, continuing education). Mike Doyle has been assigned this responsibility and has gathered the following data prior to statement preparation.

• Membership dues are $100 per year, of which $20 is considered to cover a one-year subscription to the association's journal. Other benefits include membership in the association and chapter affiliation. The portion of the dues covering the magazine subscription ($20) should be assigned to the magazine subscriptions revenue center.

• One-year subscriptions to *Teachers' Forum* were sold to nonmembers and libraries at $30 each. A total of 2500 of these subscriptions were sold. In addition to subscriptions, the magazine generated $100,000 in advertising revenue. The costs per magazine subscription were $7 for printing and paper and $4 for postage and shipping.

• A total of 28,000 technical reports and professional texts were sold by the books and reports department at an average unit selling price of $25. Average costs per publication were as follows.

Printing and paper	$4
Postage and shipping	$2

• The association offers a variety of continuing education courses to both members and nonmembers. The one-day courses cost $75 each and were attended by 2400 students in 1988. A total of 1760 students took two-day courses at a cost of $125 for each course. Outside instructors were paid to teach some courses.

• Salary and occupancy data are as follows.

	Salaries	Square Footage
Membership	$210,000	2,000
Magazine subscriptions	150,000	2,000
Books and reports	300,000	3,000
Continuing education	180,000	2,000
Corporate staff	80,000	1,000
	$920,000	10,000

The books and reports department also rents warehouse space at an annual cost of $50,000. Personnel costs are 25 percent of salaries.

• Printing and paper costs other than for magazine subscriptions and books and reports relate to the continuing education department.

• General and administrative expenses include all other costs incurred by the corporate staff to operate the association.

Doyle has decided he will assign all revenues and expenses to the revenue centers that can be

• Traced directly to a revenue center.

- Allocated on a reasonable and logical basis to a revenue center.

The expenses that can be traced or assigned to corporate staff as well as any other expenses that cannot be assigned to revenue centers will be grouped with the general and administrative expenses and not allocated to the revenue centers. Doyle believes that allocations often tend to be arbitrary and are not useful for management reporting and analysis. He believes that any further allocation of the general and administrative expenses associated with the operation and administration of the association would be arbitrary.

Required

a. Prepare a profitability report that is segmented according to the respective sources of revenue (i.e., revenue centers).

b. In what ways can this profitability report be used by the association?

(CMA adapted)

12-10. Specify for each of the following situations whether an operational control system or decision support system is more appropriate, and what degree of support can be reasonably expected.

a. Making reservations by an airline.

b. Checking credit by a discount store.

c. Maintaining control over accounts receivable by a home appliance retailer.

d. Maintaining close control over sales and inventory by a department store.

e. Maintaining controls over the physical flows of job orders by a manufacturer that has a complex production process involving numerous parts and materials, labor inputs, machining operations, and inspections.

f. Maintaining controls over its freight cars by a railroad that carries cargo across the country.

g. Maintaining controls over the times and costs incurred on construction projects currently in progress by a contractor.

h. Providing nationwide after-sales service by a manufacturer of computer-related equipment.

i. Providing electronic transfer of funds service by a statewide bank whose depositors can have bills debited directly from their accounts into the accounts of creditors such as utilities.

j. Providing assistance to a manufacturer in making plant location decisions.

k. Providing assistance to an architect in designing a new special-purpose building.

l. Helping a manufacturer that has alternative uses for its available production space to decide whether to make or to buy parts.

m. Providing assistance to a hospital in selecting the most suitable capital expenditure projects to undertake during the next five years.

n. Providing assistance to a drug chain in establishing pricing policies.

o. Assisting an investment counselor in managing a securities portfolio.

p. Assisting a consumer goods firm in evaluating proposals for new products.

12-11. You are the sales manager of the recently formed Vega Corporation, which sells two products in three sales territories. The characteristics of two products having keen interest to you contain the up-to-date information shown at the bottom of this page.

Vega has installed an interactive DSS for use by you and the other managers. The system includes a command language, a relational data base, and a report generator.

PRODUCT FILE

Product Name	Description	Unit Cost	Unit Price	Supplier Name	Quantity on Hand
Alpha	Whirl	7.00	10.00	Cody	150
Omega	Swirl	16.00	20.00	Barker	80

Required

Show the report that the system would provide in response to each of the following command statements that you may enter.

a. REFER TO SALES FILE
   PRINT DATE AND NAME AND AMOUNT
   BY TERRITORY

b. REFER TO SALES FILE
   PRINT AMOUNT AND NAME BY
   TERRITORY
   RANKED BY AMOUNT
   IF AMOUNT LESS THAN $100, OMIT

c. JOIN SALES AND PRODUCT FILES
   PRINT CENTERED HEADING "SALES
   SUMMARY"
   SUM UNIT SALES AND AMOUNTS BY
   PRODUCT
   PRINT TOTALS AFTER NAME AND
   DESCRIPTION AND SUPPLIER
   PRINT GRAND TOTALS, UNIT SALES,
   AND AMOUNT

12-12. For several years the Programme Corporation of Urbana, Illinois, has encountered difficulties estimating its cash flows.[10] The result has been a rather strained relationship with its banker.

Programme's controller would like to develop a means by which she can forecast and plan the firm's monthly operating cash flows. The following data was gathered to facilitate cash forecasting and planning.

a. Sales have been and are expected to increase at 0.5 percent each month.

b. Of each month's sales, 30 percent are for cash; the other 70 percent are on open account.

c. Of the credit sales, 90 percent are collected in the first month following the sale and the remaining 10 percent are collected in the second month. There are no bad debts.

d. Gross margin (profit) on sales averages 25 percent.

e. Sufficient inventory purchases are made each month to cover the following month's sales.

f. All inventory purchases are paid for in the month of purchase at a 2 percent cash discount.

g. Monthly expenses are payroll, $1500; rent, $400; depreciation, $120; other cash expenses, 2 percent of that month's sales. There are no accruals.

h. Ignore the effects of corporate income taxes, dividends, and equipment acquisitions.

Required

a. Construct a financial planning model that generates the monthly operating cash inflows and outflows for any specified month.

b. If sales for the current month are $10,000, compute the cash inflows and outflows for the next two months.

(CMA adapted)

12-13. The Fast Track Racing Association of Tallahassee, Florida, intends to establish an information service.[11] Subscribers to the service will be able to obtain information about racehorses, jockeys, and trainers. Data will be collected concerning the breeding and age of a horse, plus its form, starting price, jockey, and trainer in each previous race and the upcoming races in which it has been entered. Other data to be collected will include the training, experience, and track history for each jockey and trainer, as well as the track conditions for the major tracks throughout the country during the racing days of the past two years. Up-to-the-minute data will also be provided concerning the latest official bookmaking prices and odds on each horse in upcoming races. Several thousand horses, several hundred jockeys and trainers, and several dozen tracks will be involved.

---

[10] This problem can be solved by using a microcomputer-based financial modeling software package.

[11] Based on a problem given in a Master of Science examination by the University of London and published in R. I. Tricker, *Management Information and Control Systems* (New York: Wiley, 1976), 290. Used with permission.

Required

a. Identify the key decision to be supported by this service, and design outputs that contain information useful to the subscribers.

b. Describe and justify a suitable DSS for this information service, including the degree of support that it should provide and design features that it should incorporate.

Computer

System

Networks and

Management

13

THIS CHAPTER'S OBJECTIVES ARE TO ENABLE YOU TO:

Identify the components of data communications.

Describe the features and advantages of several types of computer-based communications networks, as well as the added controls and security measures that are needed.

Survey the organization of the information systems function, including its location within the overall organizational structure.

Describe management concerns and techniques during the planning and operational phases of an accounting information system.

INTRODUCTION

As accounting information systems (AISs) have grown and computer technology has blossomed, new developments and opportunities have unfolded. One area of explosive development has been data communications. Numerous computer system networks have sprung into being within the past few years, and they are changing and expanding rapidly. Significant opportunities also exist for improving the management of the information and systems resources. Among the areas where improved resource management can be realized are in long-range system planning, development, and operation. Sound organization of the information systems function can also enhance systems development and management.

DATA COMMUNICATIONS COMPONENTS

Many modern firms have facilities—plants, warehouses, sales offices—at more than one location. Communications among these remote locations have traditionally been conducted by letters and telephone calls. Currently, however, a geographically dispersed firm may electronically link its various locations via a **wide-area data communications network.** Employees in remote locations thereby gain the same access to data, computing power, and managerial guidance as if they are physically in the home office.

Data communications networks are composed of such hardware components as terminals, modems, communication control units, central processing units, and communications channels. Figure 13-1 shows a simple data communications network, where the connecting lines between the devices represent channels. Accountants need to be aware of these data communications components and their capabilities. They may be called on to help select suitable communications options and to evaluate the adequacy of security measures in data communications networks.

Terminals

Since terminals are vital components of all online computer-based systems, they were surveyed in Chapter 3. They represent the primary interface between any online system, including a network, and the users. Terminals vary significantly in capabilities. At the low end of the range are "dumb" terminals, which essentially send and receive data. At the higher end are the very intelligent terminals, which can communicate with other units in the network, edit and format data for transmission, process data against files, and so on. Intelligent terminals obtain their versatility from their programmability.

A variety of devices can serve as terminals. For instance, microcomputers that are attached to communications channels can emulate terminals, as can minicomputers and large-size computers. **Remote job entry (RJE) stations** that allow the entry of batched data may serve as terminals. Other usable devices include those that capture data at the sources of transactions, such as optical character recognition devices, point-of-sale terminals, and automated teller machines.

Modems

Modulator-demodulator coupler units, known as **modems,** are devices that interface between a sending point and receiving point in a communications

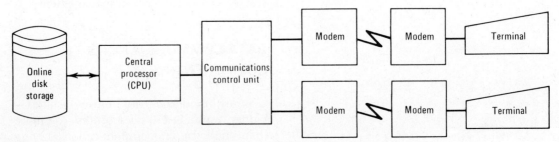

FIGURE 13-1 Components of a data communication network.

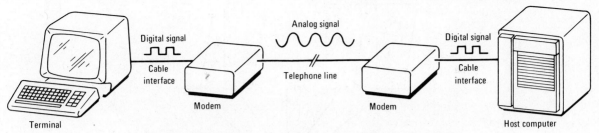

FIGURE 13-2 Use of modems in a data communication linkup.

system. As Figure 13-2 portrays, a pair of modems convert signals from the digital (discrete) form to the analog (continuous-wave) form and back again. They are necessary because voice telephone lines, the major type of communication channel, can handle only analog signals.

Modems vary in several respects. First, they differ in the ways they connect to the communications lines. Acoustical coupler modems, used with dial-up terminals, connect through touch-tone telephones that are placed into couplers. Hard-wired modems, and the terminals to which they are attached, are connected through permanent wiring. Second, they differ with respect to baud rates, the speeds at which they transmit data. Common baud rates are 300, 1200, 2400, 4800, and 9600 bits per second (bps). Third, they differ by mode of transmission. Asynchronous modems transmit on a character-by-character basis, whereas synchronous modems transmit blocks of characters. The latter mode allows faster transmission, but requires more expensive equipment.

Certain communications lines allow digital transmission and hence do not require modems. However, digital transmission is a very recent development and still has serious shortcomings.

Communications Control Units

As more and more terminals are added to a communications network, control mechanisms are needed. Three types of control mechanisms are communications processors, multiplexers, and concentrators. Although each is costly and adds to the system complexity, each serves very useful functions.

A communications processor, also known as a **front-end processor,** is a small specialized computer. It relieves the central processor of such functions as editing data, detecting and correcting errors in transmitted data, and routing messages among the terminals and central processor. Consequently, the central processor can perform more efficiently and effectively.

A **multiplexer** combines the data signals from multiple terminals into a composite signal for transmission to a single point. Figure 13-3 shows the effect of multiplexing. Without a multiplexer, 10 modems and five transmission lines would be needed in the pictured network. Consequently, the costs of eight modems and four transmission lines are saved. Another benefit of a multiplexer is increased overall transmission speed, since it may transmit at 9600 bps versus the typical terminal rate of 1200 bps.

A **concentrator** performs multiplexing, plus certain functions performed by a

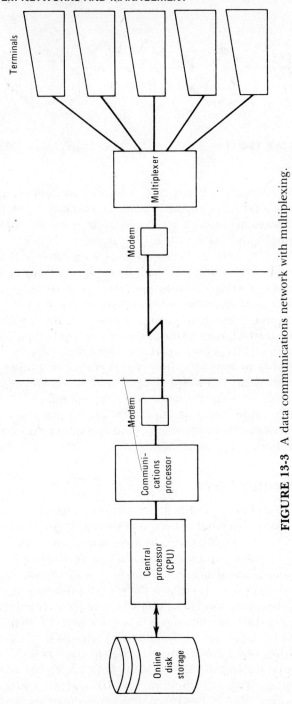

FIGURE 13-3 A data communications network with multiplexing.

communications processor. Moreover, it can more effectively utilize a shared communication line; thus, it is able to control more terminals.

The Central Processor

The central, or host, processor in a network is the recipient of messages from the remote terminals. It generally retains certain communications functions, although these functions are shared when a communications processor is employed. Special communications control programs, which operate under the broad control of the operating system, are executed by either the central processor or the communications processor. In brief, these programs move data and programs throughout the network as efficiently and speedily as possible, maintain security and data accuracy, and keep useful records of system activity.

Communications Channels

The various points in a communications network may be linked by differing types of channels. Among the commonly used media at present are copper telephone lines, coaxial cables, fiber optics cables, and microwave data transmission (both ground-hugging and ground-to-satellite-to-ground). The last two channels have particularly grown in popularity in recent years because of their advantages. For instance, fiber optics cable has an incredible capacity and is also extremely reliable. Channels of the future are likely to include modulated laser light beams.

In addition to these media, the factors affecting the movement of data include the grade of line, type of transmission, type of line service, and protocol.

Grade of Line Communication lines are graded according to their speed of transmission. **Narrow-band lines** transmit at low rates (up to 300 bps) and are mainly used by terminals. **Voice-band lines** (e.g., telephone lines) transmit in the middle range, from 300 to 9600 bps. **Wide-band lines** transmit at very high rates (up to 50 million bps) and are used by the more recently developed communications media.

Type of Transmission **Simplex transmission** involves transmission in one direction only. **Half-duplex transmission** allows transmission in both directions, but not at the same time. **Full-duplex transmission** allows transmission in both directions at the same time. Real-time processing requires full duplex; less demanding applications may be able to use half duplex or simplex.

Type of Line Service The three basic types of available service for voice-grade communications lines are **private** (leased) **lines, public** (switched, dial-up) **lines,** and **wide area telephone service (WATS) lines.** Distinguishing features of the three types are listed in Figure 13-4.

Protocol A **protocol** prescribes the manner by which data are transmitted from one computer to another. In effect, a protocol is the set of rules applied by the communications software to move data throughout one or more data communi-

	Private line	Public switched line	WATS line
Use	Available only for use by paying customer	Employs public telephone lines; requires dialing for connection and service	Employs public telephone lines; requires dialing for connection and service
Rate	Fixed with respect to time used; variable with respect to distance	Variable with respect to time used	Fixed for a minimum number of hours per month; variable above the minimum
Advantages	Least expensive at high volumes and short distances	Least expensive at low volumes and relatively long distances	Tends to be least expensive at certain intermediate volumes and distances
	No waiting for service, hence generally faster transmissions	Flexible; can access system from any telephone	Flexible; can access system from any telephone
	Lower error rate		

FIGURE 13-4 Types of services in communication lines.

cations networks. One rule concerns the way in which each message is packaged in an "envelope," so that it does not become intermixed with other messages and arrives safely at its destination. Included in a typical envelope (besides the message) might be a message number, to and from addresses, end-of-message mark, and error check. For instance, an envelope could contain a message consisting of a sales order transaction and be identified by 5621 (a sequential message number), 07216 (the disk address to which the message is directed), 27 (the number of the terminal from which the message is being transmitted), and characters that represent the end-of-message mark and allow the message to be checked for transmission errors.

VARIETIES OF DATA COMMUNICATIONS NETWORKS

Data communications networks differ in so many respects that each specific network tends to be unique. Nevertheless, they can be classified in terms of basic hardware/software architectures and services rendered. The two major architectures are centralized networks and distributed networks. Two types of networks that are characterized by the services they render are local area networks and public data networks.

Centralized Networks

A **centralized network** consists essentially of a single central processor and one or more linked terminals that are physically remote from the processor, plus the necessary communications devices and channels.

Configurations A centralized network may be arranged, or configured, in various ways. Assume that a network consists essentially of a central computer system (processor) and four terminals. By altering the arrangement of the communications channels, the three configurations in Figure 13-5 can be formed.

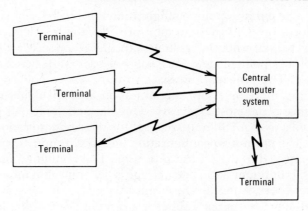

a. Point-to-point configuration.

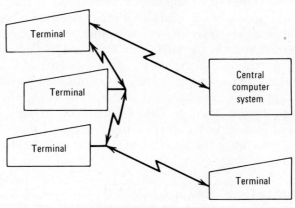

b. Multidrop configuration

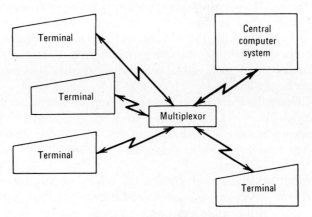

c. Multiplexed configuration.

FIGURE 13-5 Centralized network configurations.

The **point-to-point configuration** links each terminal separately to the central processor. This configuration provides the best service, since no terminal user has to wait when interacting with the processor. It also is very reliable from a network point of view, since only one user is affected if a communication channel fails. The principal drawback to the point-to-point configuration is that it requires more miles of communication lines than alternative configurations, and hence is the most expensive. This is especially true if private lines (rather than public or WATS lines) are used for the communication channels.

The **multidrop configuration** links the terminals, via "drops," to a single line connected to the central processor. This configuration is economical, since the total communication line mileage is generally minimized. However, it has several drawbacks. A terminal user must typically wait for service, since only one terminal may transmit at a time. If a communication line fails, all terminals beyond that point will be out of service. Also, only private lines may normally be used.

A **multiplexed,** or line-shared, **configuration** links a cluster of terminals to the central processor by means of a multiplexer or other line-sharing device. This configuration tends to be a compromise between the other two configurations. It generally reduces the total communication line mileage below that of the point-to-point configuration, but not as low as that of the multidrop configuration. However, the savings in overall communication line costs are offset somewhat by the cost of the line-sharing device and the single private communication line to the processor. Because of the simultaneous transmission of messages over the shared line, it reduces the waiting time below that of the multidrop configuration. Also, public or WATS lines may be used to link each terminal to the line-sharing device.

Benefits Centralized networks offer the concentrated computing power of a large processor, which can handle large volumes of transactions and the processing needs of financial planning models. Also, since large processors can accomplish such processing at low operating costs per transaction, they offer economies of scale. Because they can accommodate integrated data bases, centralized networks can provide the benefits of the data base approach. Because the facilities are centralized, they can be provided better security. Furthermore, more standardized and professional planning and control of information-related activities can be achieved.

Centralized networks are best suited for firms that have centralized organizational structures, homogeneous operations, and low processing activity at numerous remote sites. Examples are savings and loans institutions, banks with large numbers of branches, merchandising chains, motels, and airlines.

Drawbacks Although centralized networks provide several benefits, the single central processor of a centralized network creates drawbacks. It causes the network to be inflexible. Also, very complicated and costly system software is needed to move application programs in and out of their online library, to assign priorities to messages, to move data throughout the network, and so on. The network is vulnerable to disaster, since it is dependent on the functioning of a single processor. (To offset this drawback, a second central processor is sometimes linked into the network. In such networks, called duplex systems or duplex networks, the second processor automatically takes over when the main processor fails or is down for maintenance. Of course, this arrangement increases the overall cost of the network.) Finally, a centralized network may not be responsive to the needs of users at the various remote points.

Distributed Networks

The concerns and varying needs of users throughout a network have become increasingly important in many firms. In earlier days, all systems were decentralized; that is, each remote site had its own computer system. Although the users of decentralized systems had control over their own processing, they did not have easy access to centralized data nor could they transmit data and information rapidly. Thus, user-oriented distributed networks have come into being. These networks share the overall processing load of a firm among two or more processors. However, the processors are linked together into relatively unified network structures. The processors are likely to be minicomputers and microcomputers as well as mainframe computers. In fact, the advent of microcomputers has accelerated the growth of distributed networks.

Distributed networks allow a range of data entry and processing options. As in centralized networks, transactions may be entered in batches or individually at remote sites and transmitted in detail to the host computer system for processing. Alternatively, transactions may be processed by either the batch or online methods at the remote sites by **satellite systems.** Then summary results from this processing may be transmitted to the host computer. Also, summary data may be obtained from the data base located at the host computer site.

Configurations The two basic distributed network configurations are the star and ring. Figure 13-6 contrasts these configurations (with the communications devices omitted). In addition, a variety of hybrid configurations are found in practice.

The **star configuration** consists of a host computer system plus computer systems that radiate from the center of the network like spokes from a hub. It corresponds to the point-to-point configuration of centralized networks. Each distributed computer system must route all messages through the host computer. This configuration has simplicity and flexibility, although it does not allow direct communication between remote locations.

The **ring configuration** consists of a closed loop of linked computer systems. No single computer system dominates the network like the host computer system of a star configuration. Each computer system can directly communicate with its neighbors, although communication with other computer systems is relatively difficult.

If the star and ring configurations are combined, numerous hybrid configurations can be formed. Each hybrid configuration can improve communications among the various computer systems, but at an added overall cost. Perhaps the most popular hybrid is the hierarchical configuration, an example of which is pictured in Figure 13-7. The **hierarchical configuration** consists of several levels of distributed computer systems, all headed by a mainframe host computer system. Computer systems at each level download part of their processing tasks to

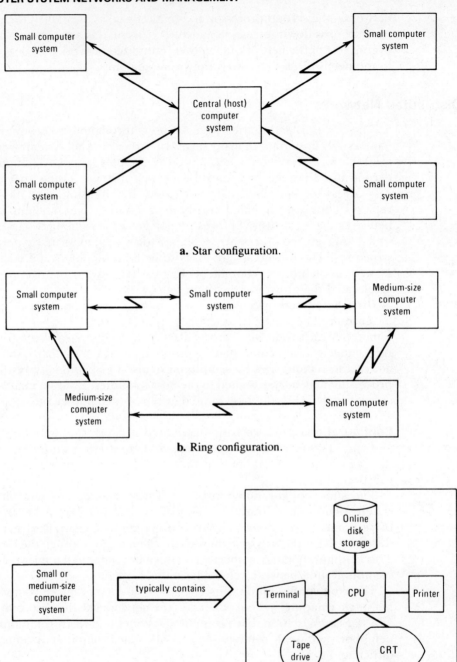

a. Star configuration.

b. Ring configuration.

FIGURE 13-6 Two basic distributed network configurations.

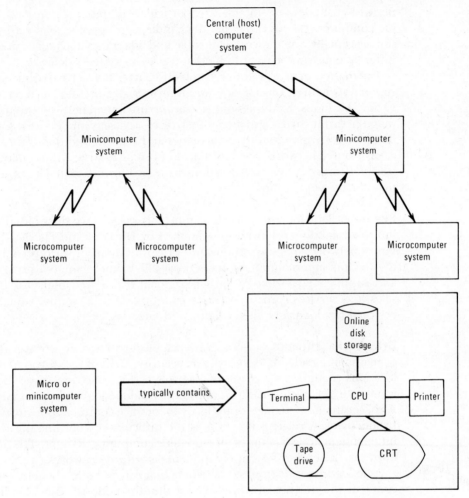

FIGURE 13-7 A distributed network having a hierarchical configuration.

lower levels and upload summary data to higher levels. This configuration is well suited to diversified firms, such as a manufacturing firm having a home office and remote plants, warehouses, and sales offices.

The term distributed networks has normally pertained to the distribution of data processing. Hence, they are sometimes called *distributed data processing* (DDP) networks. However, the data base is also subject to distribution throughout a network. For instance, files needed in processing transactions at remote sites are typically distributed to those sites, although the main data base remains with the host computer. Efforts are currently underway to develop a distributed network in which the entire data base is partitioned and distributed throughout the network.

Benefits A distributed network can be very responsive to the diverse needs of users. It also enables the facilities of the network to be used efficiently, since processing jobs can be routed to those unoccupied computer systems in the network that are most suitable. If a particular computer system fails, the remaining computer systems can generally handle its processing load with slight loss in service. Finally, the network is flexible and adaptable to change, since new computer systems can be easily added and present systems deleted.

Distributed networks are best suited for firms that have decentralized organizational structures, diverse operations or user groups, and clustered functions at various locations. Examples of firms using distributed networks are multiproduct manufacturing firms and firms that offer a variety of services. On the other hand, many firms with diverse activities and services find that centralized as well as distributed networks are desirable. For instance, large airlines may use centralized networks for their reservations systems but distributed networks for their maintenance operations.

Examples Distributed networks can be very large. Two distributed networks of international dimensions are maintained by Du Pont and Hewlett-Packard. Du Pont's network consists of thousands of workstations in various countries linked to two Cray supercomputers. Its network allows interchanges with key customers and suppliers.[1] Hewlett-Packard has global distributed networks that support sales and services, procurement, accounting, and personnel functions among regional headquarters, field offices, and factories.[2]

Drawbacks The most serious drawback of distributed networks is the difficulty of maintaining adequate control and security. Each of the distributed processing locations requires its own set of controls and security measures. Because each location is relatively small, organizational independence is not easily achieved. Also, certain local managers are likely to sacrifice control and security for greater productivity. A related drawback is the difficulty of coordinating the relatively independent and sometimes incompatible computing systems. The added cost of hardware and other system components is a third drawback.

One feature of distributed networks that can be both a benefit and drawback concerns the transfer of stored data within the network. **Downloading** involves the transfer of data sets and programs from the data base of the host computer system to one or more of the satellite systems. Downloading can be very useful, as it augments the resources of the satellite systems and allows the data base to be distributed. **Uploading** involves the transfer of data from satellite systems to the host computer. This practice can be harmful unless carefully controlled, since unedited data can contaminate the main data base.

Local Area Networks

A **local area network (LAN)** is a distributed network of hardware and software that functions within a single limited geographical area. The hardware consists of a variety of computer system devices—terminals, microcomputers, printers, disk files—linked together by coaxial or fiber optics cables and communications de-

---

[1] "Du Pont Seeks Global Communications Reach." *Datamation* (Jan. 15, 1988), 72.

[2] Cort Van Rensselaer, "Global, Shared, Local." *Datamation* (Mar. 15, 1985), 108–109.

vices. The software includes a communications protocol that functions under the overall control of the operating system.

Local area networks are most frequently used to implement automated offices. They are also used on many university campuses to form networks of instructional microcomputers. The hardware components relating to LANs are grouped into multifunction workstations that can perform data processing, word processing, data analysis, and other tasks. These workstations can also communicate with each other and even with remote sites in a wide-area network that links to the LAN. Since they are proving to be highly reliable and efficient, LANs can be expected to multiply in the future.

An example of a LAN can be found at a southern medical center. Two mainframe computers host this hospital LAN, which links the several buildings composing the center. Tied to the host computers are a minicomputer plus approximately 400 terminals, printers, and laboratory devices. The terminals are formed in a star configuration, with 150 additional terminals being linked to the minicomputer. The LAN supports such functions as patient admissions, billing, laboratory testing, patient care, and administration.[3]

Public Data Networks

A **public data network** is a privately owned network that provides to subscribers on a fee basis a variety of communications-based services. In addition to the timely and efficient transmission of data and graphics over great distances, a public data network provides such services as error detection and correction, electronic mail, electronic funds transfer, teleconferencing, and access to electronic libraries or data banks.

NETWORK CONTROLS AND SECURITY MEASURES

A communications network exposes a firm's data to serious threats of loss, unauthorized access, and errors. It requires all the accounting controls and security measures that are suitable to any online computer-based system. Because a network generally encompasses most or all of a firm's activities and organizational units, a network security policy and plan is a definite necessity.

Particular attention should be given to the communications channels and devices as well as to remote sites. Among the controls and security measures to be considered are

1. Encrypting messages that contain confidential data, or using special cables or high-speed transmissions so that the data cannot be easily intercepted and read by unauthorized persons. Plain text is typically transformed into encoded text (called ciphertext) by transposition or substitution techniques or a combination of those techniques.

---

[3] Lyle D. Ginsburg and David M. Rappaport, "Half Empty or Half Full?" *Datamation* (April 1987), 98.

2. Employing highly reliable and compatible channels and devices, as well as error detecting devices and backup transmission methods, so that errors and malfunctions are minimized.

3. Placing communications devices in protected and restricted locations so that they are not likely to be damaged.

4. Using system software that is write-protected and that performs parity checks, echo checks, and other verification checks to ensure that the software are not altered and that data are transmitted accurately.

5. Using passwords to prevent unauthorized access via terminals.

6. Validating input data, using programs that are developed centrally and downloaded from the host computer system, to detect and correct errors from being transmitted.

7. Maintaining standardized documentation and procedures throughout the network, including all remote sites.

8. Providing thorough training, preferably by a centralized systems group, to users throughout the network.

9. Performing periodic audits of all remote sites.

ORGANIZATION OF THE INFORMATION SYSTEMS FUNCTION

The information systems function has become increasingly important to a firm's well-being. Its responsibilities include operating and maintaining the accounting and other information systems, plus developing and installing new systems.

When organizing the information systems function of a typical firm, two questions arise: Where should the function be located within the overall organization structure, and how should the responsibilities be assigned within the function? If the firm is rather large and diverse, there is a third question: To what extent should the organizational structure of the function be centralized or decentralized?

Location of the Systems Function

Before the computer era, systems responsibilities were traditionally assigned to the accounting function. Often they were handled by a department whose head reported to the controller. With the advent of computers and the emergence of new functional information systems, the systems function has been relocated in many firms. Instead of being a department within the controller's area, it has been placed under the jurisdiction of a nonaccounting manager.

Figure 13-8 indicates three of the more likely locations to which the systems function has been moved. At each of these three locations it is positioned higher in the organization than when it reported to the controller. Thus, the function has generally gained status and hence "clout."

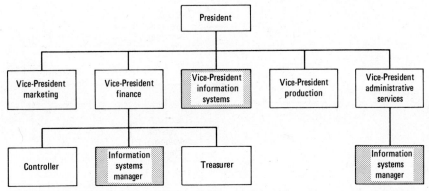

FIGURE 13-8 Three possible overseers of the information systems function and its managers.

The most conservative move has been to place the function under the vice president of finance and on the same managerial level as the controller. This move can be defended on the basis that many reports generated by the information system are financial in nature and that the function maintains a close association with its former accounting roots. On the other hand, the location under the finance function may be viewed with concern by such functions as marketing and production. Managers of those functions may perceive that financial and accounting reports receive favored treatment under such an arrangement.

Another move has relocated the systems function under a vice president of administrative services. This move allows the systems function to be truly independent, and to be perceived as such. As a consequence, the systems function has greater freedom to cross organizational boundaries and to develop integrated information systems. It also can resist pressure tactics by any function.

Some firms, however, have not established an administrative services function. Other firms may feel that the systems function deserves full recognition as a major function within the organization. In such firms the systems function may report directly to the president (or an executive vice president).

Internal Organization of the Systems Function

As discussed in Chapter 5, the responsibilities of the systems function must be segregated in a manner to effect sound internal accounting control. Figure 5-3 presented an organization chart that provided effective segregation between data processing operations and systems development responsibilities. Figure 13-9 focuses on the responsibilities that pertain to systems development and to user and staff support. The figure is suggestive only, since innumerable variations are found in practice.

Each manager or group shown in the organization chart has the following assigned responsibilities:

1. The **information systems manager** (or director) recommends objectives for the function, takes part in long-range systems planning, and directs both the systems development and operations activities of the function.

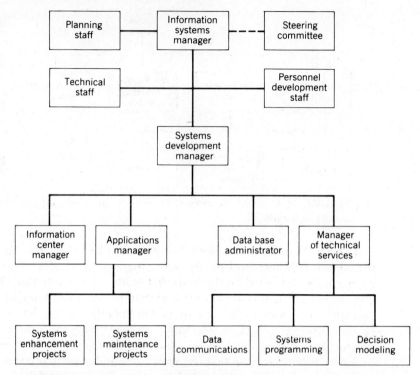

FIGURE 13-9 A partial organizational structure of the information systems function, with emphasis on systems development.

2. The systems **staff groups** aid in developing long-range plans and budgets, in evaluating the technical proficiency of hardware and software, and in recruiting and training systems professionals.

3. The **steering committee,** which is generally composed of the major users of the information system, provides overall guidance in systems development. It reviews and approves the long-range systems plans and hardware/software acquisitions, establishes priorities concerning systems development projects, controls the progress of systems projects, and monitors the performance of the function.

4. The **systems development manager** (who is on the same level as the data processing manager, not shown) directs all the systems development and maintenance activities, the user support activities, and the administration of the data base.

5. The **information center manager** directs the activities of the information center, which aids users in developing applications and in acquiring and using microcomputer hardware and software.

6. The **data base administrator** directs the design and use of the firm's data base and performs other duties as described in Chapter 11.

7. The **applications manager** supervises all new systems development projects,

other than user-developed applications, and all maintenance activities pertaining to current applications. Under this manager are the respective project managers, plus systems analysts and programmers. The applications mainly relate to transaction processing and information retrieval.

8. The **technical services manager** supervises activities related to maintaining the operating system and other system software, the data communications network, and the model base. Specialists in these areas are often available to support the specialists assigned to the information center.

Centralization Versus Decentralization

Centralization consists of grouping all systems-related activities in one central location under the line authority of an information systems manager. Figure 13-9 by implication portrays a centralized organizational structure. Decentralization consists of dispersing the systems personnel and activities throughout the organization. For instance, systems analysts, programmers, and technical specialists may be attached to each division and production plant of a large manufacturing firm, and some may be assigned to various departments and functions throughout the home office and regional offices. Decentralized personnel are generally under the line authority of the local managers, and the information systems managers maintain only functional authority.

Each type of structure has benefits. A centralized structure requires fewer systems personnel overall, can usually attract highly qualified personnel more easily, and can provide better overall control and standardization. A decentralized structure allows the dispersed systems personnel to provide faster service that is more attuned to the localized needs of the users, thereby fostering a greater spirit of harmony.

Decentralization is a matter of degree, of course. Even firms with highly decentralized systems functions retain central groups of managers and specialists. Normally the decision concerning the degree of decentralization is related to the type of computer network employed. Those firms with highly distributed networks tend to decentralize systems personnel to a significant degree.

MANAGEMENT OF INFORMATION SYSTEMS

An AIS represents a valuable set of resources to its firm. These resources—consisting of facilities, personnel, supplies, and data—must be managed. Furthermore, they should be managed throughout the life of the system, from its inception through its years of operational service. Consequently, important management concerns include the following:

1. Planning the future development of the AIS.

2. Directing future development activities relating to the AIS.

3. Accounting for the costs related to systems operations.

4. Controlling the utilization of system-related resources.

5. Auditing the adequacy of system components, such as internal controls, and the reliability of the information outputs.

In the remaining sections of this chapter we briefly introduce major issues involved in systems planning, accounting for systems-related costs, and controlling of systems-related resources. Chapter 14 explores the activity of auditing an AIS and its outputs, and Chapters 15 and 16 examine the systems development life cycle.

Because the system resources are used to produce information, a concept known as **information resource management (IRM)** has emerged. This concept emphasizes that information cuts across all organizational boundaries to knit together a firm's objectives and activities. It provides the comprehensive and focused viewpoint that guides our discussion of the management issues.

Long-range Systems Planning and Development

Assume that a newly established firm hires consultants to design and install the information system that exactly meets its needs, and that the consultants do so. Can this firm's management then ignore further systems planning and development? The answer is a resounding NO. An information system should undergo continuous planning and development throughout the life of the firm that it supports. Three major factors dictate the need for such planning and development:

1. A firm changes, and its environment changes. It may grow and/or market new products and services. New competitors may come into being, or new government regulations may be promulgated.

2. Shortcomings arise or become apparent. New managers who perceive the need for new reports may be hired. Customers may begin pressing for speedier answers to inquiries. Certain key factors, such as the bad debts ratio, develop adverse trends.

3. Information technology improves, thereby outdating currently installed hardware and software. Examples of recent technology developments include more powerful multitasking microcomputers and optical scanners.

Planning and Development Principles Management has the responsibility for both **systems planning** (defining the future direction of the information system) and **systems development** (realizing the plan through actual undertakings). These activities are becoming quite important because systems-related costs are absorbing ever-larger shares of the typical firm's available resources. They are increasingly difficult to achieve fully because changes are occurring more rapidly and lead times for systems development are growing ever longer. Although each firm's situation is unique, certain planning and development principles can be applied that generally produce successful systems.

Systems planning should

1. Extend several years (e.g., three to five) into the future.

2. Span all the activities of a firm.

3. Integrate with the firm's overall capital budgeting processes.

4. Incorporate changed priorities and new conditions.

Systems development is guided by systems planning. Sound systems planning can facilitate useful development approaches such as the modular approach, sequenced approach, tailored approach, and evolutionary approach.

The **modular approach** involves the development of an information system as a set of interconnected modules or building blocks. Each module in turn is opened like a black box, analyzed, redesigned, installed within its niche in the system, and linked to the adjoining modules. This approach, which is suitable to all but the smallest firms, has two benefits. First, it reduces the scope of a development project to manageable proportions. Second, it provides more flexibility when maintenance is necessary during the operational phase.

The **sequenced approach** involves the development of a system module according to pre-established sequence of steps. This sequence can be closely scheduled and budgeted so that project controls can be installed.

The **tailored approach** consists of developing a design that fits the characteristics of the module. If a module is mainly intended to provide information for decision support, such as a production planning or financial planning module, a decision-oriented design should be developed. If a module is mainly intended to perform transaction processing or other operations, then a design that emphasizes efficiency should be considered.

The **evolutionary approach** consists of developing a new system module that is workable and cost-effective. It is not desirable to develop a design that is too sophisticated for the intended users or too costly to justify.

Steps in Systems Planning Figure 13-10 lists several steps that comprise sound strategic systems planning. The first critical step is to obtain vocal and enthusiastic support of top management, beginning with the president. Managers at the middle and lower levels take their cues from the top. This support is becoming easier to obtain, since computer knowledge and skills have steadily moved up the management ladder in recent years.

The next step is to form a steering committee, if one is not already in existence. This committee might consist of major users, such as the vice presidents of the various organizational functions. It might be headed by the president or information systems manager.

A third planning step is to clarify the objectives of the information system and to align these objectives with the firm's objectives. To be operationally useful, they should be stated in specific terms. For instance, one objective might be to increase the capacity for processing transactions by 10 percent next year. Systems policies should also be reviewed and developed where necessary. For example, an objective of reducing processing costs might be translated into a policy that requires all purchases of new computer equipment to be approved in advance. Furthermore, constraints on systems planning should be identified. Examples are ceilings on systems expenditures and limitations on changes to the organizational structure.

The final steps are to prepare the strategic systems plan and to obtain its approval by top management. A **strategic systems plan** is essentially a blueprint

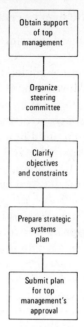

FIGURE 13-10 Steps in strategic systems planning.

for systems development in the coming years. It provides a means for coordinating systems planning with other strategic plans. In addition, it serves as a standard against which performance of the information systems function is measured.

Often the plan is divided into two parts: a one-year operational plan and a multiyear plan. The short-range plan provides adequate details for budgetary control; the long-range plan provides the broad perspective. Both parts of the plan include data concerning the planned projects that are to lead to developed system modules.

Example of Systems Planning

Weyerhaeuser, a timber products firm, introduced an information systems planning methodology in 1981.[4] This methodology, which was devised by the advanced systems planning group in the information systems department, results in the preparation of a plan of action for the current year and a long-range systems plan for the next five years. These plans are based on a decision-oriented approach, which begins with the statement of companywide and information systems objectives. One stated objective, for instance, is to "increase profitability through improved access to information for trade-off decisions related to raw materials, products and customers in manufacturing, marketing and

---

[4] Pran N. Wahi, Kenneth A. Popp, and Susan Stier, "Applications Systems Planning at Weyerhaeuser." *Journal of Systems Management* (Mar. 1983), 12–21.

logistical operations." Then the plan focuses on specific application systems. For each application system area, the plan defines the information strategies, scope, operational flows, functional responsibilities, critical success factors, planning team, and schedule. Based on this planning activity, the planning team then defines information system requirements and proposes plans of action for developing new systems.

Accounting for Systems-related Costs

Services provided by an operational information system can be very expensive. Often they include not only complex computer hardware and software, but also numerous professional systems personnel. Costs for these services may simply be absorbed into the general overhead. This accounting practice avoids sticky allocation problems. It also encourages excessive use of the computer facilities by the various departments and functions, since the facilities are in effect treated as a "free good."

Managements have recognized that accounting controls should be established in order to prevent excessive usage and runaway costs. One approach is to impose controls arbitrarily through budget ceilings. However, many managements have discovered a more flexible approach. They employ a **chargeout procedure,** whereby system-related costs are charged to users on the basis of carefully devised rates.

A soundly established chargeout procedure can provide several benefits: (1) Users are encouraged to request system services only when the benefits of such services exceed the costs. In addition, users are motivated to participate actively in the development of efficient systems. (2) Information systems management is motivated to render useful services in an efficient manner, since the procedure provides a means for evaluating the information systems activity. (3) Planning and budgeting of future systems expansions can be conducted on the basis of more objective data.

Perhaps the most critical element of a chargeout procedure is the rate. To be acceptable to users, it should be fair and easy to understand. It should also produce comparable costs for similar applications. From management's point of view, it should stimulate the systems function to perform efficiently. Figure 13-11 compares the three basic types of chargeout rates.

An actual cost rate results in the total actual costs being prorated to the users. Although it is easily understood, an actual cost rate changes from period to period. These changes occur because the actual rate is computed periodically (e.g., monthly), with the actual total costs being divided by the actual number of hours required for processing. Thus, a payroll department may be charged a relatively low cost in January, when processing volume is high. In February, however, it may be charged a much higher cost for the same services because the volume is low. It is very likely that the payroll manager will be unhappy with such fluctuations.

A standard cost rate is predetermined in much the same manner as a standard manufacturing overhead rate. That is, the cost and activity levels are estimated on the basis of reasonably efficient operations. Once the rate is computed, it is

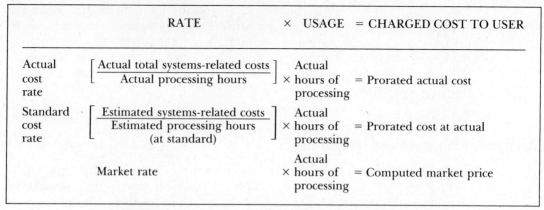

	RATE	× USAGE = CHARGED COST TO USER
Actual cost rate	$\left[\dfrac{\text{Actual total systems-related costs}}{\text{Actual processing hours}}\right]$	Actual × hours of = Prorated actual cost processing
Standard cost rate	$\left[\dfrac{\text{Estimated systems-related costs}}{\substack{\text{Estimated processing hours}\\ \text{(at standard)}}}\right]$	Actual × hours of = Prorated cost at actual processing
	Market rate	Actual × hours of = Computed market price processing

FIGURE 13-11 Three methods of computing chargeout costs.

generally held constant for at least a year. Consequently, a standard cost rate is more consistent and fairer to all the users. Moreover, it may be used to compute a standard total systems-related cost for the actual volume attained during a given month. This standard total cost may be compared to the actual total cost, in order to measure the performance of the systems function.

A market rate is based on the average prices charged in the marketplace by firms offering commercial systems-related services. This type of rate is understandable and fair. It can also motivate the systems function to perform efficiently, especially if the users are allowed to employ outside services if they choose. On the other hand, a market rate is difficult to compute in some situations, since commercial firms often vary with respect to rates. Using the market approach can be risky, too. If key users decide to employ outside services, the firm's computer facilities might stand idle and incur losses.

As firms gain experience in using chargeout procedures, they can modify their basic rates to gain flexibility. Consider the case of a firm that employs a single standard cost rate in which the activity level is based solely on processing (CPU) hours. This firm may decide to broaden the base to include usage of disk storage units, input/output devices, and data communications lines. These modifications may likely produce a rate that is fairer to the entire range of users. Since accounting applications tend to employ input/output devices and disk storage units more heavily than central processing units, for instance, accounting users would be ratably charged for the resources used. Another modification could pertain to the time of usage. High rates could be charged for usage during peak demand hours, whereas low rates could be charged for usage during offpeak demand hours.

Control of Systems-related Resources

Accounting for systems-related costs is part of a larger performance and cost-control framework. The mission of this larger framework is to assure that all systems-related resources are employed efficiently and effectively.

The first step in the control process is to develop the various standards for comparison. Performance standards are generally established through engineering studies, and cost standards are derived during the budgeting process. Then usage of the resources is measured. Finally, the actual usages are compared to the standards and reported. Several examples will illustrate these last two steps in the control framework.

Measurements of Resource Usage Computer facilities and personnel compose the major resources in a typical information system. A variety of techniques, automated as well as manual, are needed in measuring the extent to which they are used.

Manual techniques include the preparation of time reports and computer logs. **Time reporting systems** consist of time sheets which reflect the hours worked on various tasks and projects. Each task and code is generally coded. For instance, a programmer may complete a time sheet this week that includes such entries as 20 hours for programming an inventory system (coded 10-6) and 15 hours for documenting a previously programmed general ledger system (coded 12-4). **Computer logs** are records of the productive and nonproductive uses of computer facilities. A log may be prepared by a computer operator during each shift. Each processed job would be listed, together with the beginning and ending times; also, the times required for preventive maintenance, program testing, and so on would be listed.

Automated techniques include hardware and software monitors. **Hardware monitors** are electronic or electromechanical devices having probes that attach to various components of computer systems. They count the signals emitted by these devices and record the counts on a magnetic medium. **Software monitors** are software packages that reside within computer systems. They may perform the same types of counts as hardware monitors. In addition, they might perform such monitoring actions as taking "snapshots" of internal conditions and indicators at designated times.

Reports of Performance and Costs A variety of reports can be generated by combining measurements and standards. One important report with respect to computer facilities is the **equipment utilization report.** As illustrated in Figure 13-12, this report reflects the variances of actual hours from standard hours for all productive (i.e., chargeable) and nonproductive (i.e., nonchargeable) uses. It provides the basis for controlling computer usage; it also aids management in scheduling next month's processing operations and estimating future needs.

Reports that reflect the performances of systems-related personnel include

1. A report that compares the performances of data entry clerks, measured by keystrokes per hour, to standard output rates.

2. A report that compares the actual processing times of jobs handled by computer operators to scheduled processing times.

3. A report that compares performances of programmers, measured by number of instructions written per day, to standard daily quotas.

4. A report that compares the actual progress of systems analysts, who are assigned to systems projects, to milestones established for those projects.

Equipment Utilization Report					
Month: March					
Usage code	Use	Actual		Standard		Variance in hours
		Hours	%	Hours	%	Favorable (Unfavorable)
01	Production runs, regular	260	43.1	255	43.3	(5)
02	Production runs, special	4	0.7	5	0.8	1
03	Reruns	10	1.7	15	2.5	5
04	Compilations	42	7.0	40	6.8	(2)
05	Tests	80	13.3	85	14.4	5
	Total chargeable hours	396	65.8	400	67.8	4
10	Set ups	120	20.0	100	17.0	(20)
11	Equipment failure	10	1.7	15	2.5	5
12	Preventive maintenance	40	6.7	40	6.8	—
13	Idle time	12	2.0	10	1.7	(2)
14	Training	15	2.5	15	2.5	—
15	Other	8	1.3	10	1.7	2
	Total noncharge- able hours	205	34.2	190	32.2	(15)
	Total hours	601	100	590	100	(11)

FIGURE 13-12 An equipment utilization report.

Other reports may compare performance to different measurements. Also, reports may be prepared to compare actual costs to budgeted costs on the various systems projects and for the various systems departments. Still other reports may be used to analyze trends in such service-related factors as response times and error rates.

SUMMARY

A data communications network requires such components as terminals, modems, multiplexers, concentrators, front-end processors, central processors, and communications channels. The available communications channels range from copper telephone lines to microwave data transmission via satellites. Communications channels are also distinguished by grades of lines (narrowband, voice-band, wide-band), type of transmission (simplex, half duplex, full duplex), type of line service (private, public, WATS), and protocol.

The two major types of networks are centralized and distributed. Centralized networks offer economies of scale through large processors, plus all the advantages of centralized management and security. Distributed networks are responsive to user needs, less vulnerable to total failure, and flexible. The basic centralized network configurations are point-to-point, multidrop, and multiplexed. Distributed networks have two basic configurations, star and ring, but many hybrid configurations (including the hierarchical configuration) are built from these two basic configurations. Other networks include local area networks (LANs) and public data networks. Among the controls and security measures suited to networks are encrypted transmissions, reliable communications channels and devices, protected communications devices, varied systems software checks, passwords, documentation, training, and audits.

The manager of information systems often reports to the vice president of finance, the vice president of administration, or the president. Organizationally the systems function is segregated between data processing operations and systems development. Functions involved in systems development include data base administration, information center services, applications, and technical services. The systems function may be centralized or decentralized.

All firms should plan and develop their information systems carefully and with a long-range point of view. Changes occur, shortcomings arise, and information technology improves. Systems development should follow a strategic plan, be modular in nature, be tailored to each module's characteristics, and take place in a sequenced and evolutionary manner. Steps in systems planning and development consist of obtaining top management support, forming a steering committee, clarifying the objectives of the system, preparing the strategic systems plan, and obtaining approval from management. Operational systems also require management. The system-related costs can be charged to users. Chargeout rates may be based on actual costs, standard costs, or market prices. Performances can be evaluated also. First, standards are established. Then usages of resources are measured and reported.

REFERENCES

Ahituv, Niv, Neumann, Seev, and Hadass, Michael. "A Flexible Approach to Information Systems Development." *MIS Quarterly* (June 1984), 69–78.

Allen, Brandt. "An Unmanaged Computer System Can Stop You Dead." *Harvard Business Review* (Nov.–Dec. 1982), 76–87.

Buchanan, Jack R., and Linowes, Richard G. "Understanding Distributed Data Processing." *Harvard Business Review* (July–Aug. 1980), 65–75.

Cerullo, Michael J. "Data Communications: Opportunity for Accountants." *CPA Journal* (Apr. 1984), 40–47.

Holmes, Kenneth E. "Office Automation—Five Years Old and Growing." *Journal of Systems Management* (Sept. 1984), 8–11.

Kneer, Dan C., and Lampe, James C. "Distributed Data Processing: Internal Control Issues and Safeguards." *EDPACS* (June 1983), 1–14.

Lin, Chien-Hua M. "System for Charging Computer Services." *Journal of Systems Management* (Nov. 1983), 6–10.

Moulton, Rolf T. "Network Security." *Datamation* (July 1983), 121–124.

Rushinek, Avi, and Rushinek, Sara. "Distributed Processing: Implications and Applications for Business." *Journal of Systems Management* (July 1984), 21–27.

Selig, Gad J. "Approaches to Strategic Planning for Information Resource Management (IRM) in Multinational Corporations." *MIS Quarterly* (June 1982), 33–45.

Sobol, Michael L. "Data Communications Primer for Auditors." *EDPACS* (Mar. 1984), 1–5.

Vanecek, Michael T., Zant, Robert F., and Guynes, Carl S. "Distributed Data Processing: A New 'Tool' for Accountants." *The Journal of Accountancy* (Oct. 1980), 75–83.

QUESTIONS

1. What is the meaning of each of the following terms?

Wide-area data communications network	Narrow-band line
	Voice-band line
	Wide-band line
Remote job entry (RJE) station	Simplex transmission
	Half-duplex transmission
Modem	
Front-end processor	Full-duplex transmission
Multiplexer	
Concentrator	Private line

Public line
Wide area telephone
  service (WATS) line
Protocol
Centralized network
Point-to-point
  configuration
Multidrop
  configuration
Multiplexed
  configuration
Distributed network
Satellite system
Star configuration
Ring configuration
Hierarchical
  configuration
Downloading
Uploading
Local area network
  (LAN)
Public data network
Information systems
  manager
Systems staff group
Steering committee

Systems development
  manager
Information center
  manager
Data base
  administrator
Applications manager
Technical services
  manager
Information resources
  management (IRM)
Systems planning
Systems development
Modular approach
Sequenced approach
Tailored approach
Evolutionary approach
Strategic systems
  planning
Chargeout procedure
Time reporting system
Computer log
Hardware monitor
Software monitor
Equipment utilization
  report

2. What components compose a data communications network?

3. Identify the range of terminals and several devices that can serve as terminals.

4. Identify the various types of modems.

5. At what baud rates do modems transmit data?

6. Contrast front-end processors, multiplexers, and concentrators.

7. What type of software is needed for data communications networks?

8. Identify several media which can serve as communications channels.

9. Contrast the three grades of communications lines.

10. Contrast the three types of transmission.

11. Contrast the three types of line service: private, public, and WATS.

12. Contrast the three configurations that are suited to centralized networks.

13. What are the benefits and drawbacks of centralized networks?

14. Contrast the ring, star, and hierarchical configurations of distributed networks.

15. What are the benefits and drawbacks of distributed networks?

16. For what types of firms are centralized and distributed networks best suited?

17. Identify several controls and security measures that are particularly suited to communications networks.

18. What are three likely locations of the information systems function in a modern firm having a computer-based system?

19. Describe a feasible organizational structure for the systems development portion of the information systems function.

20. What are the features of a decentralized information systems function, and in what circumstances is it likely to be found?

21. Why should a firm continue to conduct systems planning and development throughout its existence?

22. Identify several principles of systems planning and development.

23. List the steps that are necessary for effective systems planning.

24. Why should system-related costs be charged to users?

25. Contrast three basic types of chargeout rates.

26. Describe the steps in a typical chargeout procedure.

27. What are the steps in controlling the performance of system-related resources?

28. Identify several manual and computer-based measurement techniques.

29. Briefly describe several reports that can serve as the means of controlling the performance of system-related resources.

30. Discuss the likely impacts of a communication network on a firm's data inputs, data base, reports, decision-making, and organizational structure.

REVIEW PROBLEM

Mertz Wholesaling Company

Statement

The Mertz Wholesaling Company maintains a home office and two warehouses (A and B). It has decided to install a computer-based network that links the home office to the warehouses. The distances from the home office to warehouses A and B are 300 and 500 miles respectively, and the distance between the two warehouses is 400 miles. The following cost data are available.

1. The monthly cost of leasing a suitable multiplexer is $500.

2. The monthly cost of leasing switching hardware for multidrops is $300.

3. The costs per minute for phone calls from the home office to warehouses A and B are $0.40 and $0.50 respectively.

4. The hours of message traffic between the home office and warehouses A and B are expected to be 40 and 30 hours respectively.

5. The monthly rates for private lines of a suitable grade are $5 per mile through the first 100 miles, $4 per mile for the next 100 miles, $3 per mile for the next 100 miles, and $2 per mile for all distances above 300 miles.

Required

If each of the two warehouses is provided a video display terminal,

a. Describe four alternatives, involving various network configurations and types of service, that may be employed in the network.

b. Compute the total monthly cost for each alternative in **a**.

c. Comment on the results obtained in **b**.

Solution

a. and b.
Alternative 1. A point-to-point configuration that links the home office to each warehouse by separate private lines.

Monthly cost from home office to A:

$$(100 \text{ miles} \times \$5) + (100 \text{ miles} \times \$4) + (100 \text{ miles} \times \$3) = \$1200$$

Monthly cost from home office to B:

$$\$1200 + (200 \text{ miles} \times \$2) = \$1600$$

Total monthly cost = $1200 + $1600 = $2800

Alternative 2. A point-to-point configuration that links the home office to each warehouse by separate public switched lines.
Monthly cost from home office to A:

$$\$0.40 \text{ per minute} \times 40 \text{ hours} \times 60 \text{ minutes per hour} = \$960$$

Monthly cost from home office to B:

$$\$0.50 \text{ per minute} \times 30 \text{ hours} \times 60 \text{ minutes per hour} = \$900$$

Total monthly cost = $960 + $900 = $1860

Alternative 3. A multidrop configuration that links the home office to warehouse B through warehouse A by private lines, as follows.

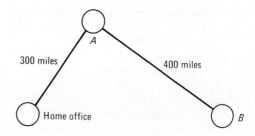

Total monthly cost:

$$\$1200 + (400 \text{ miles} \times \$2) + \$300 \text{ for hardware} = \$2300$$

Alternative 4. A multiplexed configuration that links the home office to each warehouse via private lines and a multiplexer located at the midpoint between warehouses A and B, as follows.

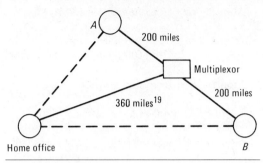

* Since the distances among the home office, warehouse A, and warehouse B form a 300-400-500 right triangle, the distance to the midpoint of A and B is $\sqrt{300^2 + 200^2} = \sqrt{130,000} = 360$.

Monthly cost from home office to multiplexer:

(100 miles × \$5) + (100 miles × \$4)
    + (100 miles × \$3) + (60 miles × \$2)
    = \$1320

Monthly cost from multiplexer to A and B:

2(200 miles × \$2) = \$800

Total monthly cost = \$1320 + \$800
                  + \$500 for multiplexer = \$2620

c. The computations show that the point-to-point configuration using private lines is the most costly alternative, followed by the multiplexed and multidrop configurations. The point-to-point configuration using public-switched lines is the least costly. However, since a configuration employing public switched lines suffers the disadvantages of longer waiting times and less accurate transmissions than private lines, this least costly alternative may not be the best choice. Furthermore, if the hours of usage increase significantly in the future, public switched lines may become more costly. In other words, there is a break-even volume above which private lines become less costly than public switched lines.

PROBLEMS

13-1. A group of three small hospitals within a large metropolitan area decide to establish an on-line computer system to serve their data processing and retrieval needs. A central processor and online disk storage devices are located in a building in the downtown section of the central city. The hospitals are in the surrounding suburbs. Each is 15 miles from the computer site. The middle hospital is five miles apart from its neighbors.

Required

a. List the data communications components needed to connect the central processor to the middle hospital, assuming that the other two hospitals are not included.

b. Identify all the options available when selecting the communications channel in **a.**

c. Describe three possible configurations by which the three hospitals may be linked to the central processor.

13-2. A firm maintains a home office and six remote locations, geographically situated as follows.

A mainframe computer is installed in the home office; each remote location houses a single terminal. The firm intends to establish a computer-based network.

Required

a. Connect the locations to form a centralized network having each of the following configurations.

(1) Point-to-point.

(2) Multidrop.

(3) Multiplexed, with the multiplexer located at ④.

(4) Point-to-point for three locations; multidrop for the remaining three locations.

(5) Point-to-point for one location; multidrop for two locations; multiplexed for the remaining three locations. Select the points for each configuration, with an eye toward designing the most suitable combinations.

b. Assuming that microcomputers are placed in the remote locations, connect the locations to form a distributed network having each of the following configurations.

(1) Star.

(2) Ring, including the home office.

(3) Combined star and ring.

13-3. The directors of Colorgraph Printing of Buffalo are reviewing a proposal to acquire Puball Publishers. Puball's operations are located in an urban area about 300 miles from Buffalo. Colorgraph's success in recent years, according to its management, is attributed in large part to its computerized information system. Puball, however, has used a computer only for financial accounting applications, such as payroll and general ledger records.

In considering the acquisitions, Colorgraph's board of directors focuses on the possibilities of two options for expanding its information system to include Puball: (1) a centralized network, or (2) a distributed network.

Required

a. Can terminals having only the capabilities of collecting, editing, transmitting, and receiving data be employed with both types of networks, or are they restricted to one of the types?

b. Compare the degree of detail likely to be transmitted from a remote location to headquarters by each of the two types of networks.

c. Explain briefly why Puball's management would be more likely involved in and concerned with data processing if a distributed network were installed. Assume that Puball would be organized as an independent profit center if acquired.

d. Explain why a distributed network would be less subject to a complete system breakdown.

(CIA adapted)

13-4. Which type of network—centralized, distributed, local—would likely be most suitable in each of the following situations?

a. An airline reservation system with local offices in most larger cities.

b. An integrated consumer-goods manufacturer that maintains close coordination among its plants, distribution centers, warehouses, and home office.

c. A savings and loan institution with numerous branch offices throughout the cities of a state.

d. A public utility that establishes automated offices throughout its headquarters facility.

e. A New York stock exchange that maintains communications with brokers on the exchange floor and brokerage offices in several northeastern cities.

f. A department store chain that allows individual stores to handle credit sales and inventory, but that distributes paychecks from the home store.

13-5. The Wunder Company maintains a central computer system at its home office in Detroit. Its six sales offices are located in Milwaukee, Cleveland, Chicago, Minneapolis, Indianapolis, and Pittsburgh. Recently the firm decided to link these six sales offices together into a distributed network. Before it selects a particular configuration, however, the management would like comparative costs for two basic configurations: (1) a star configuration, with separate leased lines from the central computer to microcomputers at each of the sales offices; and (2) a ring configuration, with leased lines connecting Detroit to Milwaukee to Minneapolis to Chicago to Indianapolis to Pittsburgh to Cleveland and back to Detroit.

The two types of costs that differ between the alternatives are for modems and data communications line charges. Each modem of the type needed rents for $50 per month. (Two modems are needed for each link.) Monthly rates to lease the needed wide-band communication lines are $10 per mile for the first 250 miles, $7 per mile for the second 250 miles, and $5 per mile for all miles over 500 miles. (These charges apply separately to each link.)

The mileages between affected cities are as follows.

From	To					
	Milwaukee	Cleveland	Chicago	Mpls.	Indianap.	Pitts.
Detroit	353	170	266	671	278	287
Milwaukee		422	87	332	268	539
Cleveland			335	740	294	129
Chicago				405	181	452
Minneapolis					586	857
Indianapolis						353

Required

Calculate the total monthly communications cost for each of the configurations, based on the figures given.

13-6. Imtex Corporation is a multinational company with approximately 100 subsidiaries and divisions, referred to as reporting units. Each reporting unit operates autonomously and maintains its own AIS. Each month, the reporting units prepare the basic financial statements and other key financial data on prescribed forms. These statements and related data are either mailed or telexed to corporate headquarters in New York City for entry into the corporate data base. Top and middle management at corporate headquarters utilize the data base to plan and direct corporate operations and objectives.

Under the current system, the statements and data are to be received at corporate headquarters by the twelfth working day following the end of the month. The reports are logged, batched, and taken to the data processing department for coding and entry into the data base. Approximately 15 percent of the reporting units are delinquent in submitting their data, and three to four days are required to receive all of the data. After the data are loaded into the system, data verification programs are run to check footings, cross-statement consistency, and dollar-range limits. Any errors in the data are traced and corrected, and reporting units are notified of all errors by form letters.

Imtex Corporation has decided to upgrade its computer communication network. The new system would allow data to be received on a more timely basis at corporate headquarters and provide numerous benefits to each of the reporting units.

The systems department at corporate headquarters is responsible for the overall design and implementation of the new system. The systems department will utilize current computer communications technology by installing "smart" computer terminals at all reporting units. These terminals will provide two-way computer communications, and also serve as microcomputers that can utilize spreadsheet and other applications software. As part of the initial use of the system, the data collection for the corporate data base would be performed by using these terminals.

The financial statements and other financial data currently mailed or telexed would be entered by terminals. The required forms would initially be transmitted (downloaded) from the headquarters computer to the terminals of each reporting unit and stored permanently on disk. Data would be entered on the forms appearing on the reporting unit's terminal and stored under a separate file for transmission after the data are checked.

The data edit program would also be downloaded to the reporting units so that the data could be verified at the unit location. All corrections would be made before transmitting the data to headquarters. The data would be stored on disk in proper format to maintain a unit file. Data would either be transmitted to corporate headquarters immediately or retrieved by the computer at corporate headquarters as needed. Therefore, data arriving at corporate headquarters would be free from errors and ready to be used in reports.

Charles Edwards, Imtex's controller, is very pleased with the prospects of the new system. He believes data will be received from the reporting units two to three days faster, and that the accuracy of the data will be much improved. However, Edwards is concerned about data security and integrity during the transmission of data between the reporting units and corporate headquarters. He has scheduled a meeting with key personnel from the systems department to discuss these concerns.

Required

Imtex could experience data security and integrity problems when transmitting data between the reporting units and corporate headquarters.

a. Identify and explain the data security and integrity problems that could occur.

b. For each problem identified, list and explain a control procedure that could be employed to minimize or eliminate the problem.

Use the following format to present your answer.

Problem Identification   Control Procedure
and Explanation   and Explanation

(CMA adapted)

13-7. Pinta Company is a regional discount chain headquartered in Montgomery, Alabama. Its stores, scattered throughout the southeast, sell general merchandise. The firm is considering the acquisition of a point-of-sale (POS) system for use in all its stores. Of the various models available, the president believes that the type using a light pen to scan the universal product code on merchandise is the most suitable. However, it is quite expensive, so Caroline Brenski, the president, asks the systems staff to prepare a report answering several questions.

Required

Prepare a report to the president that

a. Explains the functions and operation of a POS system, including its extension into credit checking and electronic transfers of funds.

b. Identifies the advantages and disadvantages of the extended POS system described in **a.**

c. Identifies the special control and security problems that the extended POS system could present, together with suitable controls and security measures that should effectively counteract these problems.

Hint: Look in the Accountant's Index for a recent article describing POS systems.

(CMA adapted)

13-8. The Greenleaf Company of Shreveport, Louisiana, has three plants for processing and canning fresh vegetables.[5] The three plants are located in Louisiana, Mississippi, and Alabama. Each plant has a warehouse where finished goods are stored and later shipped to food brokers and distributors throughout the nation. The home office performs most of the accounting and data processing tasks, including the maintainance of the "official" inventory files for the firm.

Under the owner-manager are three plant managers, one for each plant. Each plant manager has several dozen clerks, who maintain informal inventory records, perform various clerical duties, and periodically prepare sales and production performance reports. Also, the plant manager has responsibility for purchasing raw produce for expected processing within the plant. Raw produce is supplied by a variety of local growers.

Since the firm has experienced problems related to production scheduling, quality control, inventory management, purchasing, and general reporting of performance information, the owner-manager ponders the installation of a computer-based information system. An outside consultant is hired to study the situation. After several days of analysis the consultant reports that a computer-based network does appear to be feasible.

Required

Assuming that you are the consultant, prepare a recommendation—complete with narrative description, diagram, and justification—concerning the particular communications-based configuration that appears to be the most suitable for the Greenleaf Company.

13-9. The Bryan Trucking Company of Newark, Delaware, has four major functions: operations, sales, finance, and administration. Each function is headed by a vice president. Three managers report to the vice president of finance: the controller, the treasurer, and the budget di-

---

[5] Adapted from John G. Burch, Jr., Felix R. Strater, and Gary Grudnitski, *Information Systems: Theory and Practice.* 2d ed. (New York: Wiley, 1979), 118. Used with permission.

rector. In turn, four managers report to the controller: the chief financial accountant, the tax manager, the cost analysis and reports manager, and the EDP (electronic data processing) manager.

Recently the president has received several complaints. The operations and sales vice presidents have complained that they do not receive adequate reports to help them in planning trucking operations or in analyzing sales trends; they also say that the reports they do receive are often a week or so late. In fact, they say, the financial statements and accounting reports always seem to take precedence over other reports. They feel that this situation is not only unfair; it is also hazardous to the firm's financial health, since sales and operations are the primary contributions to the firm's profits. The EDP manager complains (less vocally and indirectly) that he is short of staff and hardware, since the systems budget is too restrictive. He must contest with the other accounting managers for budget resources; after all, he has been told by the controller that there are only so many dollars available for finance and accounting activities. Currently the dollars available to him are being used to maintain generally sound transaction processing systems and financial reporting; as a result, few dollars are available to provide other key management information.

The president is concerned by these complaints and feels that relevant, adequate, and timely information is vital to the firm's well-being. Therefore, a consultant from a local management consulting firm is called in to aid in resolving this problem.

Required

Prepare a report from the consultant to the president of the Bryan Trucking Company. The report should identify and weigh the alternative courses of action available and suggest a preferable course of action.

13-10. The Chem Products Corporation of Lafayette, Indiana, has employed automated data processing for a number of years. Furthermore, the manager of EDP, Mike O'Dell, has headed the data processing activities since the days when punched-card equipment was in use. Now he supervises an information system that incorporates the latest-model Burgen computer.

As in the punched-card equipment days, he reports to the controller (who in turn reports to the vice president of finance).

Mike O'Dell has organized his department so that three managers report directly to him: the manager of data preparation, the manager of systems analysis and design, and the manager of operations and programming.

Susan Hazelbaker, the manager of data preparation, supervises the data entry clerks. In addition, she maintains the data library and documentation books.

Donna White, the manager of systems analysis and design, supervises five systems analysts. They are each assigned systems design tasks, pertaining either to new systems or to systems maintenance, that they are expected to undertake on their own. In the case of most assignments, their outputs consist of flowcharts and forms layouts, from which the programmers are expected to develop new or modified programs. Often, however, the systems analysts must coordinate their efforts with the procedures and reports section, which has the responsibility of developing procedures, forms, reports, the chart of accounts, and documentation pertaining to noncomputerized operations. This procedures and reports section is headed by Doug Hines, who reports to the chief accountant, a manager on the same level as Mike O'Dell.

Bill Ferrell, the manager of operations and programming, has responsibility for three activities: computer operations, computer programming, and data control. However, the computer operators and programmers in effect form one group, since they assist each other in their respective duties and even substitute for each other when an employee is sick or on vacation. Also, of course, the computer programmers work closely with the systems analysts, since the latter provide the specifications from which the former must prepare programs. The data control clerks and the computer operators also assist each other; for instance, a computer operator may check the control totals to the batch input control sheet or may distribute the outputs to the user departments.

Required

Critique the organizational structure of the Chem Products Corporation.

13-11. State one or more quantitative objectives that might pertain to each of the following systems projects undertaken by a manufacturing firm.

a. Payroll processing system.

b. Accounts payable—cash disbursements processing system.

c. Cash receipts—accounts receivable processing system.

d. Cash management system.

e. Production management system.

f. Personnel management system.

g. General ledger—financial reporting system.

13-12. Marvin Grey is the president of the Grey Manufacturing Company, a firm located in St. Paul, Minnesota. After returning from a business equipment convention, he calls in Denise Ballard, the director of information systems, and expresses his enthusiasm for what he has just seen. He further states that he has decided that Grey Manufacturing Company should have the most advanced equipment and systems concepts available. All the warehouses, plants, and sales offices are to be tied by a communications network to the home office and to each other. Each remote site will maintain its own miniprocessors and terminals that can perform remote processing and also transmit data to the home office and to all other remote sites. A sophisticated data base with a companywide schema, plus distributed data bases at the remote sites, will store all active data.

Denise Ballard mentions in response that she has not been associated with systems development programs involving the features Marvin Grey mentioned. In fact, the present system at Grey is a basic, uncomplicated batch-oriented computer-based system that focuses on the more routine accounting transactions.

Marvin Grey responds that the system he described is essentially simple and straightforward. Thus, it should not be unduly difficult to design and implement. Denise can learn whatever else she needs to know on the job. He, for one, wants to "get the jump" on his competitors. Denise Ballard is therefore asked to present a systems development plan in three weeks.

Required

Discuss the pros and cons of Mr. Grey's approach to systems development.

13-13. Wagstaff Pharmaceuticals of Milwaukee is a drug manufacturer. Its several divisions are served by a corporate headquarters and staff functions that are centralized and located at the home office. Information system services (ISS) is one of these staff functions. Its services range from the data processing of routine transactions to the development (i.e., analysis, design, implementation) of information systems at the department, division, or functional level.

The ISS provides its services on request to the various departments and functions within the several divisions, as well as to other corporate staff functions. The systems manager assigns priorities to the various requests, usually on a first-come, first-served basis.

However, he tries to give due consideration to rush requests. The users are not charged for these services; instead, all costs related to the system are absorbed as corporate overhead.

In spite of this approach's simplicity, many managers within the firm have complained about it. They say, for instance, that often they must wait for quite a while before their requests are filled. Also, they complain, other managers seem to receive service before they do, even though they (the complaining managers) had entered their requests earlier.

Because such complaints have been increasing, the president of the firm has decided to change the approach. Henceforth, he states, the recipients of services from ISS will be charged for services they receive. At the end of each month the systems manager will compute a chargeout rate, based on actual costs for the past month and the actual number of hours the central processor was in use. This chargeout rate will then be multiplied by the number of hours required by each user's job; the resulting amounts will then be charged against each user's budget. If the services requested by a user are quite sizable or are expected to be of long duration, however, the systems manager will have authority to negotiate a lower chargeout rate for that user. On the other hand, if any user is dissatisfied with the services provided by ISS or with the rates, that user has permission to utilize outside commercial processing services.

The systems manager's performance will be evaluated according to the extent that the charges to users "cover" his budgeted costs. Thus, he is expected to be energetic in stimulating usage for the services provided by ISS. (Currently, the systems manager is evaluated according to the extent that actual costs compare with budgeted costs. He prepares his budget semiannually on the basis of his estimate of user demand; this budgetary procedure will remain unchanged under the new approach.)

Required

a. Discuss the weaknesses of the current approach for accounting for systems-related costs.

b. Discuss the advantages of the proposed accounting approach over the current approach.

c. Discuss problems that the proposed approach will likely create, and describe means of overcoming these problems.

13-14. The Lagoon Company of Gainesville, Florida, utilizes a centralized computer installation to provide data processing and information services to its various operational functions.[6] It treats the computer installation and all systems-related activities as a single cost center. Once each year a budget is prepared and a single chargeout rate is computed. This chargeout rate is then used to allocate systems-related costs to users for services provided.

At the beginning of this year the systems-related costs for the coming year were budgeted as follows.

Payroll (including salaries, benefits, and taxes)	$210,000
Equipment rental (including maintenance)	350,000
Supplies (variable)	24,000
Utilities (includes a variable component of $10 per hour)	70,000
Miscellaneous (including insurance and security)	30,000

[6] This problem can be solved by using a microcomputer-based spreadsheet software package.

The time of computer operations during the current year was expected to total 3000 hours.

During the year, four functions utilized systems-related services for the following time periods.

Accounting-finance	1000 hours
Marketing	800 hours
Adminstrative services	600 hours
Purchasing	500 hours

Required

a. Compute the chargeout rate for the year, if all the systems-related costs are fixed in behavior except for those explicitly designated to be variable.

b. Determine the amounts to be charged to each of the four functions during the year.

c. If actual systems-related costs during the year are $700,000, compute a cost variance that can help higher-level management evaluate the performance of the systems manager.

Hint: Apply flexible budgeting concepts in computing the cost variance.

13-15. The Malone Corporation of Corvallis, Oregon, installed a computer-based information system several years ago. The quality of information has improved and growth in transaction volumes has been handled with ease, but systems-related costs have also risen in an alarming fashion. Consequently, the president recently asked the firm's public accounting firm for assistance in pinpointing the problems. In response to this request, a specialist in management advisory services (MAS) from the public accounting firm visited the Malone Corporation and observed the activities within the systems department.

In her report, submitted today, the MAS specialist offers these observations.

a. No written policies or procedures concerning information systems development or operations can be found.

b. Systems projects are assigned verbally, with target completion dates being suggested casually. Projects are undertaken only upon requests of users and the concurrence of the systems manager.

c. Jobs from users are processed as received. Turnaround time for an average job is three days; however, jobs marked "rush" are given top priority and processed within one day, even if overtime is required.

d. Systems personnel are evaluated casually. Personnel turnover is high, partly because the job market is excellent but also because many employees feel that the systems manager plays favorites.

e. Reports concerning equipment utilization and personnel performance are nonexistent.

f. Documentation is scant, consisting primarily of manufacturers' publications.

Required

a. Describe the relationships between the observations by the MAS specialist and the problem of high systems-related costs.

b. Discuss the likely state of relationships between the systems manager and (1) systems personnel, and (2) users.

14

Systems

Auditing

Describe the various types of audits and their purposes.

Identify the major audit standards.

Discuss the audit process, especially with respect to financial audits and evaluation of the internal accounting control structure.

Describe the three major approaches to audits of computer-based information systems, as well as audit techniques that are applied within each of the approaches.

Discuss changes in the auditing environment and emerging auditing techniques and tools to meet these changes.

INTRODUCTION

Audits are examinations performed in order to evaluate such matters as (1) the reliability of information, and (2) the efficiency and effectiveness of information systems. Auditing has become highly refined in America, largely as a result of the efforts of the American Institute of Certified Public Accountants (AICPA), the Institute of Internal Auditors (IIA), the EDP Auditors' Association, and the multitude of public accounting firms. Another influence on auditing has been the federal Foreign Corrupt Practices Act of 1977.

Students majoring in both accounting and systems analysis have roles to play with respect to auditing. A percentage of accounting majors will accept positions as auditors, and as such will be deeply involved in audit programs and processes. Those who become industrial or governmental accountants will need to rely on the information received from accounting information systems (AISs). Thus, they will be interested in helping auditors to evaluate generated information and to detect control weaknesses in the systems. Those who become systems analysts (which could include some accounting majors) will be expected to design systems that provide reliable information. They will discover that they need to anticipate the problems and weaknesses that auditors frequently detect during their audits. In fact, systems analysts generally recognize the desirability of working closely with auditors during the analysis and design of an AIS. Doing so tends to ensure that adequate controls are built into the design, thereby minimizing costly revisions at later dates.

TYPES OF AUDITS

Audits that may be performed within a typical firm are classified as follows.

1. A management audit of the organization's structure, plans, policies, employee attitudes, and so forth.

2. An operational audit of the efficiency and effectiveness with which all resources are being used and the extent to which practices and procedures accord with established policies.

3. A compliance audit of the extent of compliance with laws, governmental regulations, contracts, and other obligations to external bodies.

4. A systems development audit of the efficiency and effectiveness with which the various phases in a systems development project are being conducted.

5. An **internal control audit** of the adequacy of the internal controls and security measures.

6. A **financial audit** of the fairness with which financial statements present the firm's financial position and results of operations.

These audits are generally performed by **internal auditors,** who are employees of the firms being audited, or **external auditors,** who are independent public accountants. Either type of auditor may be technically qualified to perform any of the audits listed. However, external auditors are usually appointed to perform financial audits because of their independent status.

Those audits that involve the information system, and especially accounting applications, are affected by the method of processing. In particular, extensive and complex computer-based processing can influence "the nature, timing, and extent of audit procedures," according to the AICPA's Statement on Auditing Standards No. 48. For instance, computer-based systems do not provide a visible or always a complete audit trail. Audits of such systems may therefore require frequent printouts of journals and ledgers and other file records. Because of the complexity of computer-based processing, a special type of auditor—the EDP auditor—has been created. An EDP auditor should have thorough knowledge of computer hardware and software, data bases, and computer-oriented controls and audit techniques.

Our focus in the following sections is on the financial audit, which is the most widely performed type. We assume the presence of both manual and computer-based processing.

AUDIT STANDARDS

Being professionals, auditors are guided by standards. Internal auditors follow the Standards for the Professional Practice of Internal Auditing, whereas external auditors observe the Statements on Auditing Standards. These two sets of standards have many more similarities than differences.

Content of Standards

Audit standards can be divided into two groups. One group specifies such professional characteristics as adequate technique training and proficiency, independent attitude, and due care during audits. Exhibiting due care involves planning the work adequately, supervising assistants properly, and gathering sufficient evidence. The other group pertains to the scope of the audits. Although each type of audit has its own scope, the financial audit must include (1) a study and evaluation of the existing structure of internal control, as well as (2) a review of all pertinent documents and records. Thus, the financial audit encompasses the internal control audit.

Effect of Computerization on Standards

As noted earlier, computerization does affect the audit procedures to be applied. On the other hand, computerization has *no* effect on the generally accepted standards of auditing. Auditors are expected to exhibit proper professionalism, which includes having adequate technical training and proficiency. They also are expected to follow the same thorough auditing process. This process must include the evaluation of all existing internal controls, including those that are computer-oriented.

AUDITING PROCESS

Figure 14-1 portrays the steps that form the necessary **auditing process** for performing a financial audit. It is based on a description issued by the AICPA.[1]

Initiate Audit Planning

The first step to planning an audit is to understand the relevant aspects concerning the firm being audited. A sound **audit plan** should be grounded in a knowledge of such aspects as management's philosophy and operating style, the organizational structure, the personnel policies and practices, the accounting information system (AIS), and various external influences. An audit plan should also be based on a clear understanding of the objectives of the audit and its scope. For instance, the objectives of an audit involving the sales transaction processing

---

[1] AICPA, *Statement on Auditing Standards No. 55*, "Consideration of the Internal Control Structure in a Financial Statement Audit" (New York: 1988).

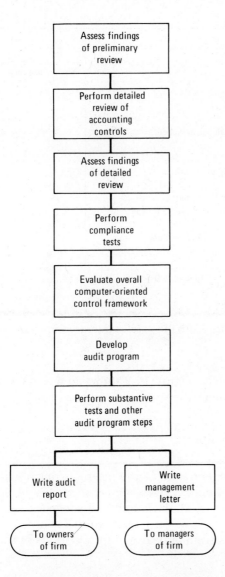

FIGURE 14-1 Steps composing the process of conducting a financial audit.

system may consist of determining that all sales are recorded and processed properly, and so forth, as listed in Chapter 8.

Review the Internal Control Structure

Next the auditor gains an understanding of the current state of the internal control structure. He or she reviews those general controls, transaction controls, clerical controls, and computer-oriented controls that are in operation. Both strengths and weaknesses are noted. Various data-gathering techniques may be used, including observation of activities, inspection of documents and records, and inquiries of key personnel. Then the understanding of the internal control structure should be documented by means of such techniques as flowcharts,

Question	Answer			
	Yes	**No**	**Not Applicable**	**Remarks**
1. Are customers' orders reviewed for accuracy and completeness before preparing sales invoices?				
2. Are customers' orders subject to approval by the credit department before being processed?				
3. Are sales invoices, shipping notices, and bills of lading prenumbered?				
4. Are employees in the sales order, inventory control, billing, and accounts receivable departments prevented from physical access to merchandise for sale?				
5. Are back orders prepared when sufficient merchandise is not on hand to fill orders?				
6. Are sales invoices compared with customers' orders and shipping notices?				
7. Are sales invoices checked for accuracy with respect to:				

FIGURE 14-2 Internal control questionnaire (partial) for sales transaction processing system.

questionnaires, and decision tables. Figure 14-2 shows an internal control questionnaire that is used to document the presence or absence of significant controls.

Assess the Control Risk

After understanding the current state of the internal control structure, the auditor is ready to form a preliminary assessment concerning its adequacy or inadequacy. From the perspective of the auditor, inadequacy is reflected by **control risk**—the risk that the currently installed internal controls will not prevent or detect significant errors from appearing in the outputs of the AIS (e.g., the financial statements).

Perform Tests of Controls

If the control risk is assessed to be so great that the installed controls cannot be relied upon (i.e., to be at the maximum level), then the auditor must expand the tests to be performed within the audit program. However, if the control risk is below the maximum level, the auditor should perform suitable tests of controls. **Tests of controls** (formerly called compliance tests) gather direct evidence concerning how well and consistently the installed controls actually function within the internal control structure. These tests may consist of observing the processing operations, of reprocessing transactions, and so on. Various specific techniques for applying tests of controls within computer-based systems are discussed in later sections.

Evaluate the Findings of the Tests of Controls

After performing the tests of controls, the auditor should be capable of fully evaluating the effectiveness level of the procedures within the internal control structure. In other words, he or she will have determined how serious the various control weaknesses appear to be. This evaluation should in turn indicate the likelihood that the auditor will detect any material errors that appear in the outputs of the system. Based on this knowledge, the auditor can construct a detailed audit program.

Develop the Audit Program

An **audit program** is a list of specific tests and procedures needed to achieve the audit objectives. In addition to stating the nature of the tests and procedures, it also clarifies their extent and timing. The auditor refers to the evaluation of the level of control risk in establishing the tests and procedures. If the level of control risk is relatively low, for example, the tests may involve smaller samples of evidence and may be performed less frequently.

Perform Substantive Tests

Substantive tests constitute the bulk of the audit program. The purpose of substantive testing in a financial audit is to obtain evidence that transactions and account balances are valid and processed in accordance with generally accepted accounting principles. Typical tests confirm the existence of various assets (e.g., inventory) and analyze the trends of key factors (e.g., inventory turnover).

Communicate Audit Results

The final step is for the auditor to report the results of the audit to the proper parties. In the case of a financial audit performed by external auditors, the owners of the firm would receive the auditor's report. If serious control weaknesses are found in the present internal control structure, the auditor will also prepare a letter to management that details suggested improvements.

AUDITING APPROACHES AND TECHNIQUES

Among the techniques applied by auditors are counting cash on hand, tracing transactions through the accounting cycle, observing the taking of physical inventories, and confirming the existence of assets. These techniques are suitable for financial audits of either manual or computer-based information systems. Additional techniques are applicable only to those information systems which employ computer-based processing of transactions. Although no single audit would employ all these computer-oriented techniques, because of the excessive costs entailed, each of the techniques can aid in tests of controls and/or substantive testing. On the other hand, they do not replace the use of system flowcharts and questionnaires in reviewing the internal control structure.

Most of these computer-oriented techniques will be discussed in the following sections. They are organized according to three key approaches to computer-based auditing: auditing around the computer, auditing through the computer, and auditing with the computer.

Auditing around the Computer

The **auditing-around-the-computer** approach treats the computer as a "black box." Instead of looking inside the "black box," the approach focuses on its inputs and outputs. Underlying this approach is the following assumption: If the auditor can show that the actual outputs are the correct results to be expected from a set of inputs to the processing system, then the processing must be reliable.

Because the computer is ignored, an auditor using the around-the-computer approach does not need to understand computer processing concepts. He or she performs an audit as if a manual processing system were involved. Thus, the techniques can be easily and economically applied.

The key technique under this approach involves tracing selected transactions from source documents to summary accounts and records, and vice versa. As Figure 14-3a shows, an auditor compares the actual results obtained by computer processing against those previously computed by hand. Any differences are likely to reflect control weaknesses. Because the controls are being tested, this technique is employed during the step involving tests of controls.

The auditing-around-the-computer approach is suitable only when three conditions are fulfilled:

1. The audit trail is complete and visible. That is, source documents are used for all transactions, detailed journals are printed out, and transaction references are carried forward from the journal to the ledgers and summary reports.

2. The processing operations are relatively straightforward and uncomplicated.

3. Complete documentation, such as systems flowcharts, must be available to the auditor.

These conditions are most likely found in independent batch processing applications, such as typical cash disbursements and payroll processing. Other types of applications, such as sales order processing systems, often fail one or another of the conditions. They may dispense with source documents, accept individual transactions at random times, or involve complicated processing. Tracing transactions in such systems can be a very difficult task for auditors.

Even when the three conditions are met, this approach may not be viewed as sufficient. Its main shortcoming is that it does not allow the auditor to determine exactly how all transactions will be handled by the computer processing programs, especially those transactions containing errors or omissions. For instance, it does not reveal how a transaction from a fictitious supplier would be processed.

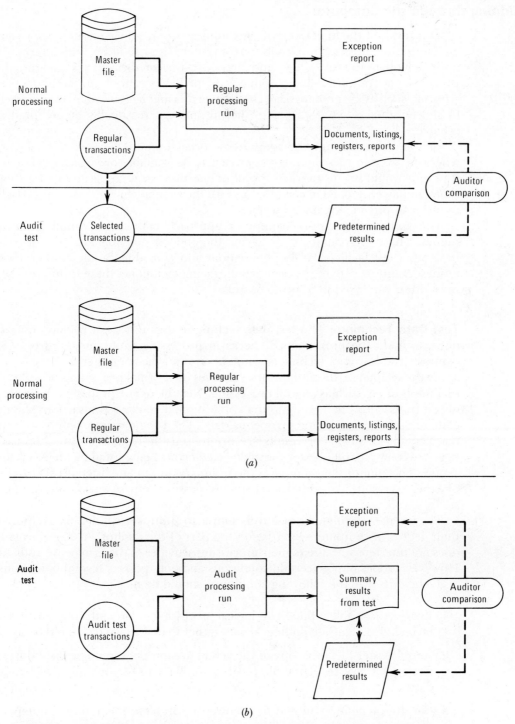

FIGURE 14-3 Auditing-around-the-computer versus auditing-through-the-computer approaches. (*a*) Auditing around the computer. (*b*) Auditing through the computer.

Auditing through the Computer

As a result of the limitations of the auditing-around-the-computer approach, an alternative approach is needed for computer-based auditing. This alternative approach opens the "black box" and directly focuses on the controls built into the processing operations. It assumes that if the processing programs have adequate controls, such as programmed checks, then errors and irregularities are not likely to slip by undetected. As a result, the outputs can reasonably be accepted as reliable.

This **auditing-through-the-computer** approach should be applied in all cases when the around-the-computer approach is not suitable or sufficient. For instance, it would be appropriate for all online processing applications. Furthermore, it may be applied in conjunction with the around-the-computer approach, in order to provide greater assurance.

The auditing-through-the-computer approach embraces a family of techniques. Those in greatest use or having the greatest potential are the test data, integrated test facility, parallel simulation, and embedded audit module techniques. As in the case of the transaction tracing technique, these techniques are most often employed in tests of controls.

Test Data Technique The **test data technique** uses test data, usually transactions, to audit the programmed checks in processing programs. Figure 14-3*b* contrasts the test data technique with the around-the-computer approach. To apply the technique, the auditor first observes the normal processing of a particular application, such as payroll processing. Next he or she prepares a collection of test transactions pertaining to the application. These test transactions should contain both valid data and erroneous data. Then the test transactions are entered for processing. The results are printed on the routine output summary (e.g., a weekly payroll register), with detected errors being listed on an exception report. The auditor then compares the summary output and listed errors to a list of expected results. Any differences suggest possible control weaknesses or omissions.

The test data technique is relatively simple to apply, since it does not require a high degree of computer expertise on the part of the auditor. Also, it normally does not interfere with the regular processing activities of the firm being audited. However, it does impose certain conditions and does possess several limitations.

To be effective, the following conditions should be met.

1. Every conceivable input error, logical processing error, and irregularity is to be included. Thus, hypothetical data rather than actual data should be used.

2. A test master file, or a copy of the actual master file, should be used during testing. Otherwise, actual file records are likely to be contaminated by test data.

3. Careful procedures should be followed to preserve the auditor's independence. The auditor should observe the processing of the test transactions and acquire the printed outputs immediately after processing. Also, the auditor should ascertain that the program used during testing is the actual

"production" program used during normal processing. A convenient means of obtaining this assurance is to arrive unannounced at the processing site during the scheduled time for processing. When the processing is completed, the auditor then requests the operator to process the test transactions before removing the program.

The limitations of the test data technique are as follows.

1. Test data can be very expensive and time-consuming to develop, since the error possibilities are numerous in even relatively simple applications. As a consequence, auditors sometimes use the test data developed by programmers during the implementation phase. A sounder alternative, however, is to employ a test data generator, a utility software package available from the computer manufacturer or software firms.

2. The technique is static; it focuses on single points in time. When programs are changed frequently, the results quickly become obsolete.

3. The technique focuses on individual applications, rather than the overall set of transaction processing systems or the data base.

4. The technique is mainly applicable to batch processing systems; it is much less suited to online processing systems.

Integrated Test Facility Technique An extended version of the test data technique is known as the **integrated test facility (ITF) technique.** It enables test data to be employed when transactions are processed by online systems.

Figure 14-4 portrays the ITF technique. Test transactions are entered into the computer system concurrently with actual (live) transactions. The test transactions consequently undergo the same processing steps and programmed checks as the actual transactions. Each test transaction, however, is identified to the

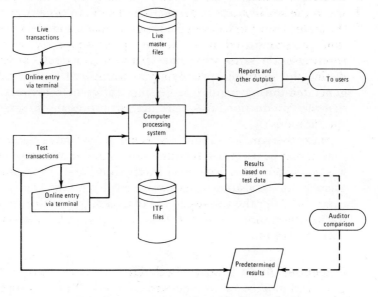

FIGURE 14-4 Integrated test facility technique.

processing programs by means of a code. This code causes the test transaction to be shunted into a special test facility (i.e., a collection of miniature files relating to the various applications being tested). In the case of a sales transaction, for example, the transaction will be deposited in special ITF files for customers and sales orders. Since the test transactions are hypothetical, the ITF files also pertain to fictitious customers, orders, and so on.

As in the test data technique, the auditor obtains printouts of the summary records and the error reports. By comparing these printouts with predetermined results, he or she determines how effectively the programmed checks detect errors. Thus, the auditor has a sound basis for evaluating the adequacy of built-in controls.

The ITF technique is more widely used than the test data technique, because of several distinct advantages.

1. It allows test transactions to simulate live transaction processing more closely, since the test transactions are entered randomly and continuously throughout the year.

2. Since the test and live transactions are entered together, the auditor is assured that the "production" programs are processing both in the same ways.

3. It enables online processing programs to be tested, while avoiding the contamination of live files.

4. It enables all online applications within a computer system to be tested in an integrated manner. Thus, the technique allows a more comprehensive evaluation of input and processing controls.

Parallel Simulation Technique As the term implies, the **parallel simulation technique** simulates the actual processing that a firm performs. Figure 14-5 shows the key features of parallel simulation. In order to employ this technique, the auditor must first develop a program that is a model of one or more "production" programs used by the firm for processing applications. Then the auditor reprocesses the same actual data that were processed earlier. Reports generated during the simulated processing are compared by the auditor to the reports generated during regular processing. Differences between the reports suggest that the "production" programs are not processing in accordance with desired specifications.

Since the parallel simulation technique validates the actual processing outputs, it may be used in substantive testing as well as in tests of controls. However, it is not widely used because of severe drawbacks. Developing a simulation program is time-consuming, expensive, and requires considerable programming expertise. After the test results are obtained, difficulties are often experienced in tracing differences between the two sets of outputs back to faults in the "production" programs.

Embedded Audit Module Technique An embedded audit module is a programmed module or segment that is inserted into an application program. Its purpose is to monitor and collect data based on transactions, particularly those

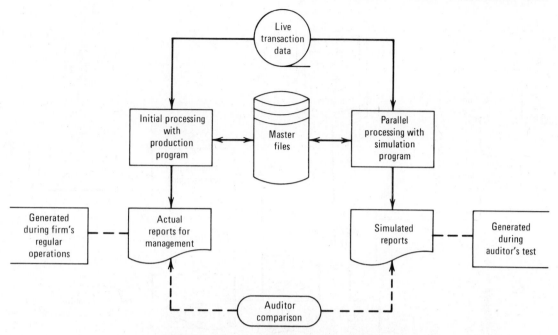

FIGURE 14-5 Parallel simulation technique.

processed by online computer-based systems. The data are then used by the auditor in the tests of controls.

Figure 14-6 depicts the features of the **embedded audit module technique.** As actual (live) transactions enter the computer system, they are edited and processed by appropriate application programs. In addition, they are checked by the audit modules that are embedded in the programs. When a transaction meets certain pre-established conditions, it is selected by the module and copied onto an audit log. Periodically the contents of the log (usually called a **system control audit review file, or SCARF**) are printed out for review by the auditor. The SCARF can reveal key aspects of programming logic, including errors and omissions.

Several features are available, some of which are optional. *Tagging* consists of placing identifying "tags" on the selected transactions. *Snapshotting* consists of capturing the contents of primary storage areas at specific points in the execution of the selected transactions. (This feature is also called extended records.) *Tracing* consists of capturing the complete trail of instructions executed during the processing of the selected transactions. *Real-time notification* involves the display of selected transactions on the auditor's terminal as they are captured by the audit module.

This technique has several advantages.

1. It enables data concerning transactions of audit interest to be easily captured, even when the audit trail is obscure.

2. It enables all processing to be monitored. For instance, intermediate and final processing results can be captured on the audit log.

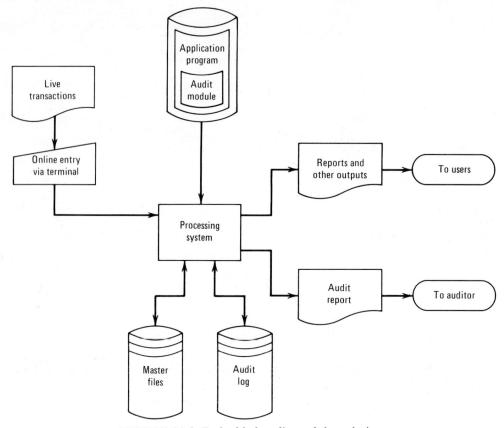

FIGURE 14-6 Embedded audit module technique.

3. It detects breaches of security as well as programming errors. For example, it can spot unauthorized attempts to access master files, enter spurious transaction data, or override processing parameters such as prices in a billing program.

Although this technique is gaining in popularity, it has certain drawbacks.

1. The times required to process transactions is increased, since the instructions contained in the audit module must also be executed.

2. Incorporating an audit module is expensive, especially if the module is added after the related application program is functioning.

3. The security requirements are heightened, since the audit module and log must be kept secure from all users of the computer system.

Auditing with the Computer

A third approach involves using the computer itself to aid in performing the steps in detailed audit programs. This **auditing-with-the-computer** approach is therefore primarily useful during substantive testing of a firm's records and files.

Audit Software The auditing-with-the-computer approach requires the availability of audit software. Audit software generally consists of a collection of program routines. Each program routine in effect serves as a "robot." It performs a mechanistic audit function such as that which traditionally would be assigned to junior auditors or clerical personnel. Because it is powered by a computer, however, an audit program routine can perform this function very quickly and accurately.

Audit software may be classified as specialized and generalized. **Specialized audit software** consists of one or more program routines that are customized to suit a particular audit situation. Because this type of software is quite expensive and time-consuming to develop, it is seldom used. **Generalized audit software (GAS)** consists of a set of program routines that are applicable to a wide variety of audit situations in most types of organizations. A GAS is typically developed by a public accounting firm, software firm, or computer manufacturer as a package. Most GAS packages are designed for easy use by auditors who are knowledgeable in programming.

Functions of a GAS Typical audit functions available in a GAS package are listed in Figure 14-7 and described as follows.

1. **Extracting or retrieving data from the files of the firm being audited.** A GAS package must have the ability to extract data from a variety of file structures, file media, and record layouts. After being extracted, the data are edited and then transferred to an audit work file. The stored data are available for use by other routines in the package.

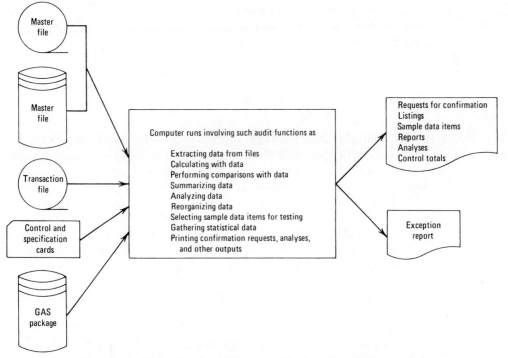

FIGURE 14-7 Applications of a generalized audit software package.

2. **Calculating with data by performing addition, subtraction, multiplication, and division operations.** For example, correctness of footings in journals may be verified by repeating the additions.

3. **Performing comparisons of data by using logical operators such as EQUAL, LESS THAN, and GREATER THAN.** Comparisons may be performed in order to select data items for testing, to ascertain consistency between items, and to verify that certain conditions are met. For instance, all 30,000 items in an inventory file might be searched in order to select for review those items having on-hand balances that exceed 1000 units. Also, all customers' records might be searched, with those accounts having balances that exceed their credit limits being listed for investigation.

4. **Summarizing data in order to provide a basis for comparison.** For example, detailed listings of salaries may be summarized for comparison with payroll reports.

5. **Analyzing data in order to provide a basis for reviewing trends or judging likelihoods.** For instance, individual accounts receivable might be aged to provide a basis for judging the likelihood of their collection.

6. **Reorganizing data by such operations as sorting and merging.** For example, the various products sold by the firm might be re-sorted in ascending order of total sales quantities in order to aid the analysis of sales.

7. **Selecting samples from an array of data.** For instance, a sample of customers might be selected randomly from the accounts receivable records, with the intention of confirming their account balances.

8. **Gathering statistical data from an array of data.** For example, the mean and median amounts of individual sales last month might be computed to aid analysis.

9. **Printing or displaying outputs, such as reports, analyses, and forms.** For instance, the confirmation request forms and envelopes might be printed for those customers mentioned in item 7.

Steps for Using a GAS Package The procedure for applying a typical GAS package to a particular application begins with the auditor planning the audit objectives and work program. Next the auditor records specifications concerning the application onto a computer-readable medium (e.g., optically scannable forms, magnetic diskette). Specifications inform the computer system of the characteristics of the firm's files to be extracted, the various functions to be performed, and the content and formats of the outputs. Then the auditor obtains copies of the application files and verifies their authenticity. Verification might consist of computing control totals of key data fields and reconciling these totals to corresponding totals in general ledger accounts.

At a prearranged time the auditor submits the specifications for processing by the firm's computer system. He or she also provides the GAS package, which may be physically stored on magnetic tape, magnetic disk, or magnetic diskette. In order to maintain effective control, the auditor closely observes all processing operations. These operations essentially consist of a series of computer runs (e.g., an extract run), followed by a calculation run, an analysis run, and a print run. When the processing is completed, the auditor then takes immediate possession of all outputs, plus the GAS package and specifications.

At this point the auditor applies his or her experience and judgment in handling the outputs. The auditor might review samples of items selected from key files, study summaries and analyses, verify extended amounts against account records, and so on.

Evaluation of GAS Packages The advantages of a GAS package are that it

1. Allows an auditor to access computer-readable records for a wide variety of applications and organizations.

2. Enables an auditor to examine much more data than could be examined through manual means. In some situations 100 percent of the records can be examined.

3. Rapidly and accurately performs a variety of routine audit functions, including the statistical selection of samples.

4. Reduces dependence on nonauditing personnel for performing routine functions, such as summarizing data, thereby enabling the auditor to maintain better control over the audit.

5. Requires only minimal computer knowledge on the part of the auditor.

The limitations of current GAS packages are as follows.

1. They do not directly examine the application programs and programmed checks. Thus, they *cannot* replace the techniques, such as the ITF technique, that audit through the computer.

2. Most cannot retrieve data from complex data structures, such as those often maintained in online data bases.

3. Most are compatible with computer systems manufactured by one or two of the largest suppliers, such as IBM. Hence, they cannot retrieve data from computer systems of other manufacturers. Although this limitation can be overcome by translating data with the aid of standard software utilities, the additional steps required can increase the cost and time of audits.

AUDITING IN A CHANGING ENVIRONMENT

Auditors are facing rapid changes in computer-based systems. Several of the most significant changes affecting audits are

1. Integrated data bases that utilize data base management systems (DBMSs) and contain complex data structures.

2. Online interactive processing systems that dispense with source documents, blur the audit trails, and utilize fourth generation user-oriented software.

3. Computer networks that connect multiple computers and terminals at various geographic locations by means of data communications lines.

Each of these advanced systems presents difficulties with respect to adequate controls, security measures, and audits. Specific controls and security measures for these systems were listed in Chapters 5, 11, and 13. Suggested auditing procedures for online data base systems and computer networks are described in the following sections. Then newly emerging audit tools and techniques are briefly discussed.

Procedures for Online Data Base Systems

During the review step, the auditor should examine the DBMS, data dictionary, and all controls and security measures. During tests of controls, the following might be performed.

1. Tracing selected transactions through the system, using a system software utility.

2. Reviewing the console log and investigating selected entries.

3. Entering test transactions for processing, using an integrated test facility.

4. Monitoring transactions with an embedded audit module, and entering selected transactions on an audit log.

Substantive testing should begin by retrieving data from the data base for review. As noted, this step may be difficult to perform if complex data structures are employed. If the available GAS package cannot achieve the retrieval, then the auditor might attempt to use the DBMS itself to perform the task. After the data are transferred to the audit work file, the auditor may apply such tests as (1) reconciling batch totals to processed results, and (2) verifying changes in account balances between successive closing dates.

An emerging development with respect to data base system audits concerns GAS packages. Current packages are being revised. Within a few years most GAS packages should have the ability to retrieve data from complex data structures in data bases.

Computer Networks

During the review steps, the auditor estimates the exposures to risk that are posed by the communications lines and dispersed processing points. Exposures may exist because of unauthorized accesses to data, lack of audit trails, transmission and processing errors, and line distortions. Then the auditor reviews all installed controls and security measures. For instance, in the case of networks involving electronic transfers of funds, he or she might note controls relating to plastic debit cards and PIN numbers.

Tests of controls might include (1) tracing a sample of transactions along the audit trail, and (2) examining selected software changes for proper authorization, testing, and final approvals. Substantive testing could include surprise visits to remote processing sites, where a GAS package could be used to retrieve data from local files and to perform a variety of detailed tests.

Emerging developments with respect to computer network audits are focusing on more thorough and integrated planning and on more sophisticated embedded audit modules. Within a few years auditors should be able to view the results of transaction processing throughout such networks. They will even be capable of retrieving the results from audit logs on command via terminals located in their own accounting offices.

Emerging Audit Tools

One new audit tool is **microcomputer audit-assist software.** The purpose of this tool is to approach a paperless and even a pencilless audit through the use of microcomputers. To apply this technique, the auditor carries a portable microcomputer into the office where the audit is being conducted. He or she then inserts a diskette containing a **template** (e.g., a prewritten spreadsheet program). The template aids the auditor in performing a tedious audit task. Examples of tasks for which templates are useful include (1) preparing trial balances, (2) listing adjusted journal entries, (3) evaluating sample results, (4) summarizing confirmation responses, (5) estimating interest and other expenses, and (6) scheduling and managing field audit times.

Another promising audit tool is the **expert auditor system.** This tool consists of a computer model that simulates the audit procedures of experienced auditors. For instance, an expert auditor system developed by Arthur Young, a Big-Eight CPA firm, is used to help inexperienced auditors devise sound audit program steps. This package, called AY/Decision Support, is one module in the firm's larger set of computerized audit tools.

SUMMARY

Audits of information systems examine such matters as the reliability of information generated and the efficiency and effectiveness of the systems. Among the types performed are management, operational, compliance, internal control, systems development, and financial audits. Audits are performed by both external and internal auditors and involve both manual and computer-based systems. Auditors are guided by standards concerning professional characteristics and the scope of audits. Standards are not affected by computerization.

The auditing process includes such steps as developing an audit plan, reviewing the internal control structure, assessing the control risk based on this review, performing tests of controls, evaluating the findings of the tests of controls, developing an audit program, performing substantive tests, and communicating the audit results. The three major approaches to audits of computer-based systems are auditing around the computer, auditing through the computer, and auditing with the computer. The first two of these approaches are mainly used for tests of controls and involve such techniques as traces of selected transactions, test data, integrated test facilities, parallel simulations, and embedded audit modules. The auditing with the computer approach uses the GAS technique.

A GAS package is a collection of programmed routines that performs audit functions such as extracting or retrieving data, calculating with data, performing comparisons with data, summarizing data, analyzing data, reorganizing data, selecting samples, gathering statistical data, and printing outputs.

Audits are being performed in a changing environment that includes online systems, data base systems, and computer networks. Several of the listed audit techniques are becoming more refined, and new audit tools are emerging to aid in performing audits in this changing environment.

REFERENCES

American Institute of Certified Public Accountants. *Codification of Statements on Auditing Standards, Numbers 1–26.* New York: AICPA, 1980.

————. *Computer-assisted Audit Techniques.* New York: AICPA, 1979.

————. *Statement on Auditing Standards No. 48: The Effects of Computer Processing on the Examination of Financial Statements.* New York: AICPA, 1984.

Borthick, A. Faye. "Audit Implications of Information Systems." *The CPA Journal* (Apr. 1986), 40–46.

Davis, Gordon B., Adams, Donald L., and Schaller, Carol A. *Auditing and EDP,* 2d ed. New York: AICPA, 1983.

Garsombke, H. Perrin, and Cerullo, Michael. "Auditing Advanced Computerized Systems in the Future." *The EDP Auditor* (1984), 1–11.

Halper, Stanley D., et al. *Handbook of EDP Auditing.* New York: Warren Gorham & Lamont, 1986.

Holly, Charles L., and Reynolds, Keith. "Audit Concerns in an On-Line Distributed Computer Network." *Journal of Systems Management* (June 1984), 32–36.

Jancura, Elise G., and Boos, Robert V. *Establishing Controls and Auditing the Computerized Accounting System.* New York: Van Nostrand Reinhold, 1981.

Lampe, James C., and Kneer, Dan C. "Audit Implications of Distributed Data Processing." *The EDP Auditor* (1984), 39–50.

Loebbecke, James K., Mullarkey, John F., and

Zuber, George R. "Auditing in a Computer Environment." *The Journal of Accountancy* (Jan. 1983), 68–78.

Nadel, Robert B. "Computer Auditing—Has Its Time Come?" *The CPA Journal* (March 1987), 24–29.

Porter, W. Thomas, and Perry, William E. *EDP Controls and Auditing,* 5th ed. Boston: Kent, 1987.

Vallabhaneni, S. Rao. "Auditing Vendor-Developed Applications Software." *The Internal Auditor* (Oct. 1986), 34–36.

Watne, Donald A., and Turney, Peter B. *Auditing EDP Systems.* Englewood Cliffs, N.J.: Prentice-Hall, 1984.

QUESTIONS

1. What is the meaning of each of the following terms?

Audit	Parallel simulation
Internal control audit	technique
Financial audit	Embedded audit
Internal auditor	module technique
External auditor	System control audit
Audit standard	review file (SCARF)
Audit plan	Auditing with the
Auditing process	computer
Control risk	Specialized audit
Test of controls	software
Audit program	Generalized audit
Substantive test	software (GAS)
Auditing around the	Microcomputer
computer	audit-assist software
Auditing through the	Template
computer	Expert auditor system
Test data technique	
Integrated test facility	
(ITF) technique	

2. What roles do accountants play with respect to auditing?

3. What types of audits may be performed in a firm?

4. Contrast an external and internal auditor.

5. What effects does computer-based processing have on audit procedures?

6. What are the key contents of audit standards?

7. What effect does computer-based processing have on audit standards?

8. List and briefly describe the steps in the auditing process.

9. Contrast tests of controls and substantive testing.

10. Contrast the around-, through-, and with-the-computer approaches.

11. Describe techniques that fall under each of the audit approaches listed in question 10.

12. Under what conditions is the around-the-computer approach suitable and sufficient in performing computer-based audits?

13. What are the conditions that should be met when using the test data technique, and what are its limitations?

14. What are the advantages of the integrated test facility technique?

15. Describe several features that are available with the embedded audit module technique.

16. What are the advantages and drawbacks of the embedded audit module technique?

17. List and briefly describe typical audit functions provided by a GAS package.

18. Describe the steps performed in using a GAS package.

19. What are the advantages and limitations of current GAS packages?

20. What significant changes in computer-based systems are affecting audits, and what emerging techniques and tools are useful in this changing environment?

21. Contrast the levels and types of computer-related knowledge needed by a general auditor and an EDP auditor.

22. Why should an external auditor, whose primary responsibility is to express an opinion concerning the representations in financial statements, suggest improvements to the information system?

23. Why do audit techniques always seem to lag behind the developments in computer technology? Can this lag be overcome in the future?

REVIEW PROBLEM

Zumbart Products

Statement

Oliver West, CPA, is performing an audit of Zumbart Products' payroll transaction system. As a part of the tests of controls, he develops test transactions and records them on a magnetic diskette. He gives the diskette to the firm's computer operator, who enters the transactions into the firm's computer and processes them while Oliver watches. After the test transactions have been processed by the firm's payroll processing program, Oliver retrieves the diskette and the exception report for the processing run. Then he compares the results, as shown on the exception report, with a sheet containing predetermined results. This latter sheet appears on page 520.

Required

a. Describe the contents of the exception report, assuming that sufficient programmed checks have been incorporated into the payroll processing program to detect all hypothetical errors that appear on the sheet of predetermined results.

b. Assume that a needed programmed check is missing. How would Oliver detect this omission, and what actions might he take as a consequence?

Solution

a. The exception report would contain such messages as listed on page 520. Brief explanations are included with the exception report.

b. If a needed programmed check is missing, a difference would arise between the sheet of predetermined results and the exception report. For instance, if a limit check is not incorporated into the program, the fifth message on the exception report would be omitted. In such a case, Oliver would include a test of hours worked in his audit program. He might review the payroll registers for selected pay periods to determine the extent of overtime hours. If they appear to be significant, he would likely audit the calculations for overtime pay in order to determine that the amounts are correct.

Test Code	Condition Being Tested	Employee Number (1)	Employee Name (2)	Department No. (3)	Hours Worked (4)	Expected Result	Actual Result
			Transaction Data				
1	Valid transaction	13251	SMITH, JOHN	1	40.0	$200 gross pay, $7800 earnings year-to-date	
2	Invalid check digit in field (1)	13629	BLACK, CHARLES	1	40.0	Exception	
3	Out of sequence in field (1)	13543	ADAMS, STEVE	1	40.0	Exception	
4	Invalid composition in field (2)	13658	BR67N, RODNEY	1	40.0	Exception	
5	Invalid relationship between fields (1) and (3)	13752	JONES, PAUL	2	40.0	Exception	
6	Out of limit in field (4)	24313	KRAUSE, KEN	2	60.0	Exception	
7	No matchup with master in field (1)	25000	TINGEY, SHERMAN	2	40.0	Exception	

Exception Report Messages

(1) EMPLOYEE 13629 HAS AN INVALID CHECK DIGIT
(2) EMPLOYEE 13543 IS OUT OF SEQUENCE
(3) EMPLOYEE 13658 HAS INVALID CHARACTERS IN NAME FIELD
(4) EMPLOYEE 13752 DOES NOT CORRESPOND WITH DEPARTMENT
(5) EMPLOYEE 24313 EXCEEDS ALLOWABLE HOURS WORKED
(6) EMPLOYEE 25000 HAS AN INVALID EMPLOYEE NUMBER

Explanation

(1) Check figure is computed by computer to be a 7.
(2) Employee number should be arranged in sequence.
(3) Only alphabetic characters should appear in the name field.
(4) The left-most digit of the employee number should correspond with the department number.
(5) A maximum limit of 56 hours worked has been established.
(6) No master record is found with number 25000 in the master file.

PROBLEMS

14-1. A large state agency maintains its own internal auditing staff. On occasion it also engages the services of auditors from a national public accounting firm. Currently the agency is involved in planning for the development and implementation of a new computer-based system.

Required

a. What types of audits might the internal auditors be assigned to perform?

b. What type of audit will the external auditors likely perform, and what role (if any) would the internal auditors likely have in this type of audit?

c. Assume that the head of the agency requests

that (1) the internal auditors vouch invoices received from suppliers and approve them for payment, and (2) the external auditors design and implement needed internal accounting controls into the new computer-based system. How should the internal and external auditors respond to these requests?

14-2. Glazer Enterprises is a holding company that has acquired many companies in different industries in order to diversify. Glazer's most recent acquisition was Tanner Stores, a regional chain of department stores.

The audit committee of Glazer's board of directors has established a policy of having the internal audit department conduct a review of the operations of all new acquisitions. The primary purpose of this review is to determine the strength of each company's internal accounting controls.

Such a review was conducted for Tanner Stores. The internal audit department reported to Glazer's senior management and audit committee that it believed there were serious weaknesses in the controls over cash receipts. As a consequence of the suspected poor controls over cash receipts, and the fact that cash receipts are part of the revenue cycle, the audit committee directed the internal audit department to conduct an audit of the revenue cycle of Tanner Stores.

Required

a. What audit standards should be followed in performing the audit of the revenue cycle?

b. Discuss the means by which the internal auditors likely determined that serious weaknesses probably exist regarding cash receipts.

c. What are the audit objectives with respect to cash receipts?

d. The audit committee decided to expand the scope of the audit as a consequence of the suspected poor controls over cash. What other course of action could have been taken?

(CMA adapted)

14-3. AndreCo is a growing manufacturer of subassembled components used in a variety of home appliances. Because sales have doubled in the past three years, management has decided to convert its manual system of information gathering and processing that has evolved during the company's first 10 years in business to a more efficient and effective system based on a planned integrated approach. AndreCo's chief financial officer, Robert Ganning, has been asked to present a plan for the development and implementation of the new system. Peter Martin, an internal auditor for AndreCo, has been asked to review the plan to assure its validity. Ganning indicated to Martin that as soon as the plan was ready, Martin would be given a copy to review and approve from the audit perspective.

"I think it would be better if we worked together throughout the process," said Martin. "I see three distinct review phases that should be handled as consecutive elements in the process of developing the new system: specification review, design review, and system review. Each phase should be completed and reviewed before the next phase is begun."

In the discussions that followed, Martin defined the three phases as follows.

a. *Specification review.* A review of the system definition to determine if the system provides for the internal control objectives of authorization, recording, safeguarding assets, and substantiation.

b. *Design review.* A review of the detailed design to ensure that the system procedures and controls will accomplish the requirements established and approved in the specification review.

c. *System review.* A trial run of the actual system during implementation to ascertain the presence of the original objective. Errors or omissions in translation of the designed system to an actual, implemented system would be detected.

Ganning and Martin agreed that a three-phase review approach would be both effective and efficient, and they proceeded on that basis.

Required

Describe specific steps to be performed under each of the listed reviews, as well as the matters being reviewed.

(CMA adapted)

14-4. ToysGalore Inc., a privately owned retail chain of toy stores operating in the Midwest, is having its financial statements audited for the first time by an external auditor. Management believes that the audited financial statements will help it to obtain the financing that will be needed for an expansion of operations.

The partner-in-charge of the audit engagement has suggested that the review and testing of the firm's internal control structure be performed at an interim date. Tom Kodd, president, replied to this suggestion by asking, "What is the purpose of reviewing and testing internal accounting controls? Won't that take a lot of time and add significantly to the cost of the audit? What criteria would you use for evaluating our internal accounting controls, and what kind of evidence would you require?"

Required

a. Explain the purpose of the external auditor's study and evaluation of internal accounting control in connection with an audit of financial statements.

b. Identify the four criteria that would be used by the external auditor to determine if the firm's internal accounting controls are adequate. *Hint:* See Chapter 5.

c. (1) Describe the review and evaluation steps or phases in the audit process.

(2) Explain what the external auditor reviews to gather evidence during each of these steps or phases of an internal accounting control study, assuming that the firm's information system is computerized.

(CMA adapted)

14-5. An internal auditor is preparing an audit program for a portion of her firm's computerized payroll application. She designates the scope of the audit to include *only* the following: payroll computation, labor cost distribution, and paycheck distribution.

Required

Indicate whether each of the following proposed audit procedures should or should not be included in the audit program. Justify any exclusions (e.g., this procedure is beyond the scope of the audit, this procedure does not provide useful audit evidence, etc.).

a. Review the computer programming related to payroll computations.

b. Determine whether checks are delivered to departmental timekeepers for distribution.

c. Perform a review of workers' compensation claims.

d. Perform a reconciliation of time card hours to hours recorded on production time cards.

e. Distribute checks to employees on a sample basis.

f. Obtain a certificate from the timekeeper pertaining to employees who were absent when the auditor distributed paychecks and who are to be paid later in the usual manner.

g. Review personnel files to verify documents in payroll files.

h. Review procedures related to the signing of paychecks.

(CIA adapted)

14-6. Linder Company of Fresno, California, is completing the implementation of its new, computerized inventory control and purchase order system. Linder's controller wants the controls incorporated into the programs of the new system to be reviewed and evaluated. This is to ensure that all necessary computer controls are included and functioning properly. She respects and has confidence in the system department's work and evaluation procedures, but she would like a separate appraisal of the control procedures by the internal audit department. It is hoped that such a review would reveal any weaknesses or omissions in control procedures and lead to their immediate correction before the system becomes operational.

The internal audit department carefully reviews the input, processing, and output controls when evaluating a new system. When assessing the processing controls incorporated into the programs of new systems applications, the internal auditors regularly employ the approach commonly referred to as auditing through the computer.

Required

a. Identify specific application controls and programmed checks that should be incorporated in the programs of the new system.

b. Describe at least two techniques that can verify the proper functioning of controls by means of the through-the-computer approach.

(CMA adapted)

14-7. The Weimer Co. of Ames, Iowa, processes its payment transactions on a computer system. Batches of payment transactions are keyed onto magnetic tape from check vouchers, sorted by supplier number, and then checked by an edit run. Each payment transaction record contains the following data field.

Data Item	Number of Characters
Supplier number	4
Voucher number	5
Voucher date	6
Invoice date	6
Invoice number	5
Purchase order number	5
Due date	6
Check number	6
Check date	6
Amount	8

Required

Prepare test data that can be used to check for the presence of the following types of programmed checks in the edit program: field check, completeness test, sign check, sequence check, check digit verification, and relationship check. State the purpose of each test and show how an exception and summary report might reflect an error detected by the test.

14-8. The Weimer Co. also processes its sales transactions on a computer system. Each sales order is entered via a terminal at a sales branch and stored on a magnetic disk at the home office to await further processing. As each sales order is entered, it is checked by an edit program. Each

transaction involving a sales order should include the following data: user code, transaction code, customer number, sales branch number, salesperson number, expected shipping data, product number(s), and quantity (or quantities).

Required

a. Prepare test data that are to be used to check for the presence of needed programmed checks in the edit program. State the purpose of each test and show how an error detected by the test might be displayed on the screen of the auditor's terminal.

b. If the integrated test facility technique is employed in conjunction with the test of sales transactions, describe the likely contents of the test facility and the report based on the contents.

14-9. Talbert Corporation hired an independent computer programmer to develop a simplified payroll application for its newly purchased computer. The programmer developed an on-line, data base microcomputer system that minimized the level of knowledge required by the operator. It was based on typing answers to input cues that appeared on the terminal's viewing screen, examples of which follow.

a. Access routine.

  (1) Operator access number to payroll file?

  (2) Are there new employees?

b. New employees routine.

  (1) Employee name?

  (2) Employee number?

  (3) Social security number?

  (4) Rate per hour?

  (5) Single or married?

  (6) Number of dependents?

  (7) Account distribution?

c. Current payroll routine.

  (1) Employee number?

  (2) Regular hours worked?

  (3) Overtime hours worked?

  (4) Total employees this payroll period?

The independent auditor is attempting to verify that certain input validation (edit) checks exist to ensure that errors resulting from omissions, invalid entries, or other inaccuracies will be detected during the typing of answers to the input cues.

Required

Identify the various types of input validation (edit) checks the independent auditor would expect to find in the EDP system. Describe the assurances provided by each identified validation check. Do not discuss the review and evaluation of these controls.

(CPA adapted)

14-10. Recently, the Central Savings and Loan Association of Jefferson City, Missouri, installed an online computer system. Each teller in the association's main office and seven branch offices has an online terminal. Customers' mortgage payments and savings account deposits and withdrawals are recorded in the accounts by the computer from data input by the teller at the time of the transaction. The teller keys the proper account by account number and enters the information in the terminal keyboard to record the transaction. The accounting department at the main office also has terminals. The computer is housed at the main office.

In addition to servicing its own mortgage loans, the association acts as a mortgage servicing agency for three life insurance companies. In this latter activity the association maintains mortgage records and serves as the collection and escrow agent for the mortgagees (the insurance companies), who pay a fee to the association for these services.

Required

Describe the way that an embedded audit module within the deposit/withdrawal processing program might be used to aid in performing tests of controls pertaining to Central's internal accounting controls.

(CPA adapted)

14-11. Boos & Baumkirchner, Inc., of Montgomery, Alabama, is a medium-sized manufacturer of products for the leisure-time activities market (camping equipment, scuba gear, bows and arrows, etc.). During the past year a computer system was installed, and inventory records of finished goods and parts were converted to computer processing. Each record of the inventory master file, which is stored on a magnetic disk, contains the following data items.

Item or part number.
Description.
Size.
Unit of measure code.
Quantity on hand.
Cost per unit.
Total value of inventory on hand at cost.
Date of last sale or usage.
Quantity used or sold this year.
Economic order quantity.
Code number of major supplier.

In preparation for the year-end physical inventory, the firm prepares two identical sets of preprinted inventory-count cards. One set is for the inventory counts and the other is for use in making audit test counts. Each card contains the following punched and interpreted data: the item or part number, the description, the size, and the unit of measure code.

In taking the year-end inventory, the firm's personnel will write the actual counted quantity on the face of each card. When all counts are complete, the counted quantity will be keypunched into the cards. The cards will be processed against the master file, and quantity-on-hand figures will be adjusted to reflect the actual count. A listing will be prepared to show any missing inventory-count cards and all quantity adjustments of more than $100 in value. These items will be investigated, and all required adjustments will be made. When adjustments have been completed, the final year-end balances will be computed and posted to the general ledger.

The auditor who will supervise the physical inventory and conduct an audit of inventory has available a general-purpose audit software package that will run on the firm's computer and can process both card and disk files.

Required

Describe several ways a general-purpose computer audit software package can be used to assist in all aspects of the audit of the inventory of Boos

& Baumkirchner, Inc. (For example, the package can be used to read the inventory master file and list items and parts with a high unit cost or total value. Such items can be included in the test counts to increase the dollar coverage of the audit verification.)

(CPA adapted)

14-12. After determining that computer controls are valid, Robert Hastings is reviewing the sales system of Rosco Corporation in order to determine how a computerized audit program may be used to assist in performing tests of Rosco's sale records.

Rosco sells crude oil from one central location. All orders are received by mail and indicate the preassigned customer identification number, desired quantity, proposed delivery date, method of payment, and shipping terms. Since price fluctuates daily, orders do not indicate a price. Price sheets are printed daily and details are stored in a permanent disk file. The details of orders are also maintained in a permanent disk file.

Each morning the shipping clerk receives a computer printout that indicates details of customers' orders to be shipped that day. After the

orders have been shipped, the shipping details are input to the computer, which simultaneously updates the sales journal, perpetual inventory records, accounts receivable, and sales accounts.

The details of all transactions, as well as daily updates, are maintained on disks that are available for use by Hastings in the performance of the audit.

Required

How may a GAS package be used by Hastings to perform substantive tests of Rosco's sales records? (Ignore accounts receivable and inventory records.)

(CPA adapted)

14-13. Solt Manufacturing Company of Honolulu, Hawaii, is undergoing an audit for the year ended June 30, 1989. During the course of the audit, Jim Peters, the auditor, plans to use a generalized computer audit software package. Solt's information systems manager has agreed to prepare special tapes of data from the pertinent magnetic tapes. Their record formats appear at the bottom of this page.

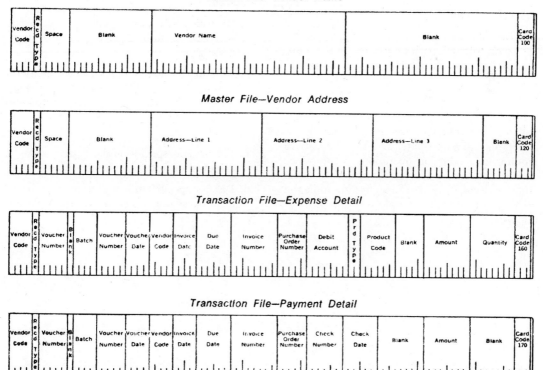

In his review of the accounts payable and related procedures, Jim learns that the following monthly outputs are prepared.

a. Cash disbursements by check number.

b. Outstanding payables.

c. Purchase journals arranged by account charged and by vendor (supplier).

He also notes that vouchers and supporting invoices, receiving reports, and purchase order copies are filed by vendor code, whereas purchase orders and checks are filed numerically.

Required

a. Describe the controls that Jim Peters should maintain over (1) preparing the special tape, and (2) processing the special tape with the generalized computer audit software.

b. Prepare for the information systems manager a schedule outlining the data that should be included on the special tape for examination of accounts payable and related procedures. This schedule should show (1) the client tape from which the item should be extracted, and (2) the name of the item of data.

c. Describe several ways that the generalized audit software package can aid in the audit of the accounts payable and related procedures.

(CPA adapted)

14-14. The Desmond Manufacturing Company of South Orange, New Jersey, recently installed an online computer system, primarily to monitor its production operations. Your public accounting firm performs the annual financial audit, and you have been assigned to audit the direct labor and materials collection and processing system.

Upon meeting with the production manager during your visit, you learn that the computer hardware used in this production system consists of a mainframe processor, terminals at the various production floor workstations and in the materials storeroom, magnetic disk drives, and a high-speed printer. The data collection and processing procedure is as follows: Data concerning labor hours worked on production jobs are entered via the production floor terminals by the production employees themselves. Data concerning direct materials charged into production are entered via the storeroom terminal by the storeskeeper. Labor and materials data are edited when entered and then stored temporarily. Late each afternoon the data are processed by a job costing program, and the relevant files (i.e., materials inventory, labor expense, and work-in-process) are updated. Outputs from this processing include job cost reports, labor distribution reports, materials usage reports, cost variance reports, and exception and summary reports. Standard costs maintained in an online file are used to convert the labor times and material quantities to dollar values and to apply overhead costs.

Required

a. Describe the review of internal accounting controls, including data-gathering techniques.

b. Describe audit techniques that will be useful in tests of controls. Assume that special audit instructions have been incorporated into the job costing program during its development.

c. List several specific audit objectives to be achieved during substantive testing.

d. Discuss specific functions that your firm's GAS package can perform during substantive testing.

PART IV

SYSTEMS

DEVELOPMENT

LIFE

CYCLE

THIS CHAPTER'S OBJECTIVES ARE
TO ENABLE YOU TO:

Describe the phases in systems development.

Identify the steps in the systems analysis and design phases.

Describe several approaches and considerations when designing information systems.

Discuss the techniques for gathering facts during systems analysis and design.

Discuss the techniques for organizing facts during systems analysis and design.

Systems

Analysis

and Design

15

INTRODUCTION

An information system undergoes **system life cycles.** Each life cycle begins with planning, progresses through several developmental phases, and leads to an operational period. The life cycle ends when the system becomes so obsolete and problem-ridden that it must be replaced. Then the next life cycle begins. Two critical developmental phases are systems analysis and systems design. This chapter examines the steps in these two phases, as well as the approaches, techniques, and tools by which they can be conducted most efficiently and effectively. The implementation phase, which follows systems analysis and design, is the subject of the next chapter.

As we noted in Chapter 13, an entire information system is usually too large and complex to tackle in a single systems development project. Thus, in the context of this chapter the term *information system* really refers to single modules of the system. Often these modules encompass individual transaction processing systems or decision support systems. However, certain modules may require very ambitious systems projects. Examples of ambitious undertakings are the conversion of the accounting information system (AIS) from manual to computer-based processing and the development of an integrated data base.

The topics in Chapters 15 and 16 are critical to the study of information systems. However, because they integrate many of the concepts and techniques discussed in earlier chapters, these system life cycle topics have been deferred until this point. Their presentation should reinforce your understanding of the structure and dynamics of an information system.

Accountants can play important roles in the analysis and design phases of any of the types of system projects listed. On the one hand they are able to help analyze the needs of transaction and decision-oriented systems modules. On the other hand they can provide expertise in the design of reports, source documents, files, processing procedures, and controls.

PRELIMINARY STEPS

Several planning steps precede the systems analysis and design phases. As Figure 15-1 shows, these steps focus on the **system project** that is to undergo development.

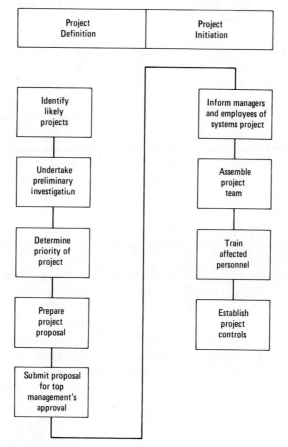

FIGURE 15-1 Preliminary steps in systems development.

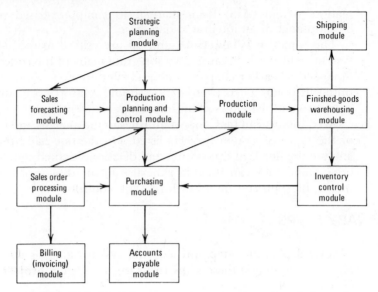

FIGURE 15-2 Modules composing a portion of an information system.

The first step is to identify likely projects within the strategic systems plan (which was described in Chapter 13). Figure 15-2 presents a diagram of eleven identified modules that can serve as project areas within a manufacturing firm. One benefit of such a diagram is to portray the linking interfaces among the modules. The next step is to explore these likely projects through a **feasibility study** or other type of preliminary investigation. Armed with facts from the investigation, the steering committee can then assign priorities to the respective projects. For instance, the inventory control project may be ranked number one because it appears that it will have the largest payoff. This step is extremely important, since it determines the order in which the projects are undertaken.

Each system project is next defined in a proposal, which includes the objectives of the project, plus the expected costs, benefits, and needed work hours. By approving this document, the steering committee bestows life to a new system project.

Before rushing to work, however, other preliminary steps are desirable. All those who will be affected by the project should be informed immediately so that they have an opportunity to adjust mentally to the impending changes. Also, these employees and managers should be oriented and trained as early as possible regarding the new skills they are expected to need. Otherwise, they are likely to resist the expected disruption to their work and social relationships. Another important step is to select the project team. Ideally it should include experts in systems development (i.e., systems analysts, programmers) plus personnel who understand the project area and represent the users' interests. For instance, a managerial accountant would be suitable if the project involved a cost accounting module. In addition, project controls such as PERT diagrams should be prepared.

STEPS IN SYSTEMS ANALYSIS

Systems analysis follows systems planning. The phase begins on the basis of an approved project proposal, which contains a description of the project and its objectives. A preliminary analysis has been performed to provide the content of the proposal. If the project is a part of a large system development, perhaps involving the acquisition of an expensive new computer system, this preliminary analysis may have been called a feasibility study. The expected benefits have been compared to the expected costs, to see if the development is likely to pay off.

After having performed the preliminary analysis, is it necessary to spend more time and money in further analysis? Yes, for these reasons:

1. The systems analysts and others composing the project team are generally not familiar with the detailed data and information flows and operations within the system module.

2. The current problems are not likely to be fully or clearly defined in the project proposal; also, other undetected problems and weaknesses may exist.

3. Detailed cost data for the present system are needed, against which estimated costs for an improved system can be compared.

4. Ideas for improving the system are often generated by studying the present system operations.

5. Users of the system are more likely to accept a changed system if their cooperation is solicited, that is, if they are asked about the present system and its problems and the changes that are needed.

Figure 15-3 shows the steps in the systems analysis phase. These steps result in a set of requirements for a new, improved system. Each step is separately considered, beginning with the **system survey.**

Survey of Present System

Scope In a system survey the project team first determines the scope of its project. If the purchases transaction processing system is the focus of the project, the survey clarifies the boundaries of this module. For instance, does the scope include the accounts payable activity? Also, does it include just the operational level, or does it extend upward to include managerial reporting? Normally the scope should encompass not only data and information flows, but also the physical operations and resource flows and organizational structures. Moreover, it may range outward to the interfaces with adjoining modules. Thus, even if the module does not include the accounts payable activity, the survey should examine the links between accounts payable and purchasing.

Data Types and Sources After determining the scope, the systems analysts must consider what types of data to gather. Certain data will usually involve key

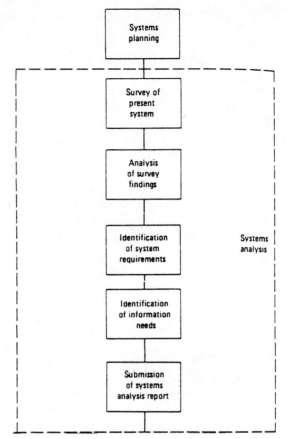

FIGURE 15-3 The steps in the systems analysis
phase.

measurements: volumes of transactions processed, times of key processing operations, costs of resources, and numbers of errors made in processing transactions. Other data are found in documents and records, such as policy statements, corporate minutes, charts of accounts, job descriptions, organization charts, manuals, budgets, source documents, and managerial reports. Still other data may pertain to historical developments, procedural sequences, and informal relationships.

The sources for such data are found both inside and outside the firm. Internal sources include file drawers and magnetic media, paperwork and physical operations, and managers and employees. External sources include customers, industry trade associations, government agencies, and trade journals such as *Moody's*. Often another useful source is a firm that has an information system similar to the one being surveyed.

In-depth studies are necessary. For instance, with respect to the external operations, the systems analysts should typically trace source documents, observe operational activities, locate control points, spot problem areas, and talk with all affected employees as well as managers.

Behavioral Approaches The project team should employ sound principles of human relations in conducting the survey. By doing so, the systems analysts express concern for the welfare of those employees and managers who will be affected by the system project. As a consequence, the affected employees and managers are less likely to resist the changes that a new system will inevitably bring. If the principles are applied skillfully, they are more likely to accept the new system, thereby helping to ensure its success.

The following concrete actions, taken by the project team, are applications of these human relations principles.

1. Communicate openly with the persons to be affected by the system project. They should be told of the project's purpose, scope, and expected duration.

2. Encourage participation by the affected persons throughout the survey. Good suggestions should be incorporated into the systems design, with full credit given to the suggesters.

3. Emphasize the positive aspects of the project. Thus, the purpose could be described as "helping employees to be more effective in their jobs" or "providing a more user-friendly system." (Such expected benefits as "cutting clerical costs" should not be stressed.) Also, those personnel policies that benefit the employees should be publicized. An example is the policy that no employee will lose his or her position as a result of a change in the system; instead, he or she will receive adequate training to handle the new system or will be transferred to a new position at no loss in pay or status.

   Aetna Life & Casualty, a large investor-owned insurance and financial services institution, employed an innovative approach with respect to its new automated office.[1] It created a unit called People Technology Programs, which has the responsibility of handling issues that overlap personnel and data processing systems. This unit focuses on four areas of concern: (1) the ease of using automated office hardware and software, (2) the impact of the automated office environment (e.g., lighting, furniture) on the health and comfort of the affected employees, (3) the involvement of managers in systems development, and (4) the considerations by the project team of human factors when designing the automated office systems. During the implementation of the automated office this unit realized that people must be handled differently than computers. Employees prefer challenging and interesting tasks, variations in duties, participation in decisions affecting them, and freedom to adopt individual working styles. Employees also want ample assistance in learning their new duties and the accompanying jargon, as well as assurances that they will not be replaced by the computer.

Analysis of Survey Findings

A survey consists essentially of asking such questions as: What is done? How is it done? Where is it done? An analysis attempts to answer such searching ques-

---

[1] Richard J. Telesca, "Aetna Plans for 'No-Fault' OA," *Datamation* (Apr. 15, 1984), 93–98.

1. Are tasks and responsibilities clearly defined and assigned?
2. Are tasks and responsibilities distributed effectively among employees and organizational units?
3. Are the policies and procedures understood and followed?
4. Does the productivity of clerical employees appear to be satisfactorily high?
5. Do the various organizational units cooperate and coordinate well in maintaining smooth flows of data?
6. Does each procedure achieve its intended objective?
7. Are redundant processing operations being performed?
8. How necessary is the result accomplished by each operation?
9. Do unnecessary delays occur in obtaining and/or processing data?
10. Do any operations cause bottlenecks in the flow of data?
11. Are the number of errors that occur in each operation minimized?
12. Are physical operations adequately planned and controlled?
13. Is the capacity of the information system (in terms of personnel and equipment and other facilities) sufficient to handle the average volumes of data without large backlogs?
14. Are the peak volumes of data handled adequately?
15. How easily does the system adapt to exceptional occurrences and growth in use?
16. How necessary is each document?
17. Is each document suitably designed for efficient use?
18. Are all of the copies of documents necessary?
19. Can reports be prepared easily from the files and documents?
20. Do unnecessary duplications occur in files, records, and reports?
21. Are files easily accessible and kept up to date?
22. Are sound performance standards developed and kept up to date?
23. Is data processing equipment being used effectively?
24. Is the system of internal control adequate?
25. Do the informal flows of data and information harmonize with the formal flows?

FIGURE 15-4 A checklist for analyzing information systems.

tions as: Why is it done? How well is it done? Should it be done at all? If so, is there a better way of doing it?

Figure 15-4 lists a number of specific questions that are analytical in nature. Numerous questions could be added to the list. In fact, separate lists could be prepared to analyze such system components as internal control systems and data bases.

Upon obtaining answers to a variety of such questions, the systems analysts should discover the severity of the underlying problems, deficiencies, and weaknesses in the system module. Having thereby fully defined the problems, they are better able to visualize what needs to be done.

Identification of System Requirements

The tangible product from the systems analysis phase is a set of **system requirements** for a new, improved system. These requirements are determined in part by reference (1) to the analysis of the present system and its problems, and (2) to expected future conditions. They also are strongly affected by the objectives stated in the strategic systems plan and project proposal.

System Objectives The objectives in the strategic systems plan are broad in nature and related to the objectives of the firm. Examples of such objectives are as follows.

1. To foster continued growth in sales by providing information regarding product demand, market trends, competitors' actions, technological developments, and so on.

2. To develop and maintain a high level of customer service by providing appropriate information that enables shipments to be delivered when promised and in good condition.

3. To incorporate new information technology on a cost-effective basis.

The objectives in a systems project proposal are more specific and quantitative. Objectives for a sales order project may include the following.

1. To shorten the average time between the receipt of a sales order and the shipping of the ordered products, so that at least 99 percent of promised delivery dates are met within two years.

2. To reduce the average time of responding to customer inquiries to less than one minute.

3. To reduce the costs of processing sales orders and of billing by 25 percent within one year.

Among the attributes that system objectives attempt to instill in an information system are

1. Efficient and hence economical operations.

2. Adequate capacity for expected growth.

3. Timeliness in responding to inquiries and providing reports.

4. Reliability of the hardware and software.

5. Accurate, up-to-date, and relevant information.

6. Simplicity and hence user-friendliness.

7. Security of the data and system facilities.

8. Flexibility and adaptability to changes and new demands.

Requirements A list of system requirements might include the following.

1. Required capacity, expressed in terms of transactions per time period.

2. Required response time in number of seconds or minutes.

3. Maximum allowable number of errors per 1000 transactions.

4. Required number of file accesses per time period.

5. Maximum allowable delay in preparing reports after an event, such as the end of an accounting period.

6. Required frequency of reports, such as weekly or daily.

7. Required processor features, such as multiprogramming and interactive processing.

8. Security through passwords at several levels of protection.

Identification of Information Needs

Most system modules generate reports for managers and key employees. Thus, an added part of the requirements often consists of needed information. Determining the information needs involves a special analysis.

An **information needs analysis** consists of several steps. Each manager's and key employee's responsibilities are clarified. In the case of managers, the responsibilities mainly relate to specific decisions that must be made. For instance, the personnel manager has responsibility for hiring decisions. After the decisions are pinpointed, the decision processes and models are analyzed (see Chapter 12). From these analyses the information needed to make the decisions can be derived.

Each information needs analysis should include both a member of the project team and an affected manager or employee. Questions that each manager should attempt to answer include: What are the key decisions that I must make, and how often do they arise? What areas do I have control over, and what factors do I need to investigate to see if they are under control? What other information would be useful to me in carrying out all my responsibilities?

Submission of a System Analysis Report

The requirements, relating both to the system and the needed information, are incorporated in a **system analysis report.** Also included in the report is a statement of the objectives and scope of the project, a summary of the problems in the present system, a list of constraints and assumptions, and a revised (but still tentative) time schedule and cost budget. Appendices may contain detailed flowcharts and other presentation materials.

This report provides the basis for review by higher management, such as members of a steering committee. If the report is approved, the project team has the "green light" to move into the systems design phase.

TECHNIQUES FOR GATHERING FACTS

Techniques for gathering facts include reviews of documents and records, observations, interviews, and questionnaires. All these techniques may be employed during systems surveys and analyses.

Reviews of Documents and Records

Documents and records, such as journal vouchers and charts of accounts, provide considerable insights for systems analysts. For instance, a chart of accounts shows how the present AIS is structured.

Reviews of documents and records should normally precede most of the other data-gathering techniques. In addition to affording an overview of the firm and its system, they provide a basis for comparison. Procedures manuals, for example, show how the system is designed to work. The procedures described therein can be compared to the facts gathered concerning how the system actually is working at present. Any differences point to possible problems.

Observations

Through observations a systems analyst can become familiar with the setting, relationships, and constraints of a system. Often an experienced analyst can spot weaknesses, especially if the visit is unannounced. For instance, a walk through the production area may reveal that employees tend to be unproductive and careless. The act of observing also provides verification. For example, assertions made through documents or questionnaires may be checked firsthand.

Interviews

Interviewing is perhaps the single most popular and important data-gathering technique. Interviews with managers enable information needs to be discovered. Interviews with employees as well as managers can clarify problems found through document reviews and observations. Equally important, interviews provide a natural means of involving managers and employees in systems development.

Good interviewing is an art that can be learned. The guidelines listed in Figure 15-5 provide the basis for learning.

Although critical to systems development, interviews do have two potential shortcomings. On the one hand, interviewees may be biased or too anxious to please. Thus, they may provide false or misleading information. On the other hand, interviewees may be antagonistic or too busy. In such cases they are likely not to cooperate.

Questionnaires

A **questionnaire** is a standard list of questions. It is an efficient means of surveying when brief answers are desired. For instance, an internal control questionnaire is used to determine which specific controls are absent in an AIS. A personnel questionnaire can be used to ascertain the opinions of employees and managers concerning a policy, procedure, or other matter relating to the firm.

Questionnaires have one major fault. They do not enable respondents to provide in-depth answers in an easy manner. Thus, it may be necessary to follow up questionnaires with interviews that explore the reasons for certain answers.

1. Ascertain the interests, background, and responsibilities of the person to be interviewed *before* the interview.

2. Gather facts concerning the matters to be discussed *beforehand.*

3. Prepare a list of the questions to be asked during the interview.

4. Obtain approval from the interviewee's superior for the interview.

5. Make an appointment that is convenient with the interviewee and be on time.

6. Notify the interviewee beforehand of the purpose of the interview and of the matters that it will cover.

7. Open the interview by explaining the interviewer's role in the study, then draw out information by pertinent questions, especially concerning the interviewee's knowledge of the situation, needs for information, and ideas for improvements.

8. Listen carefully to the interviewee's answers without interruption.

9. When conversing do not resort to jargon, broad generalizations, personal opinions, or irrelevant comments.

10. Be natural, but businesslike, so that the interview flows easily.

11. Maintain a courteous, respectful, tactful, and friendly manner throughout the interview.

12. Ask permission to take notes or use a tape recorder during the interview.

13. End the interview with a summary of the discussion, a thank you, and a prompt exit.

14. Shortly after the interview, review and complete the notes taken or conversation recorded; send a copy of the notes to the interviewee for review and correction.

FIGURE 15-5 A list of interviewing guidelines.

STEPS IN SYSTEMS DESIGN

Systems design is the creative phase of systems development. It consists of synthesizing the requirements into a cohesive and focused information framework. To be practical, the systems design must take into account such constraints as available resources and technology.

The systems design process involves two levels: conceptual design and detailed design. A **conceptual design** provides the overall system structure or architecture, plus a relatively broad view of the combined system components. It is user-oriented and logical in nature, and it is expressed as a set of specifications. A **detailed design** provides the details of each system component, such as reports and data and controls. Usually the detailed design includes such software as the application programs.

The conceptual design is developed during the systems design phase, whereas the detailed design is completed during the implementation phase. The systems design phase begins with an evaluation of two or more design alternatives, leads to the preparation of the conceptual design, and concludes with its submission for approval. Figure 15-6 shows these steps.

Evaluation of Design Alternatives

Range of Alternatives Design alternatives may range from slight modifications of the present system to radically new structures. Assume that the present system involves manual processing. One design alternative could simply add a new

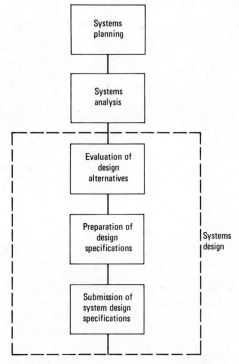

FIGURE 15-6 The steps in the systems design phase.

control or revised source document without affecting the manual processing. Another design alternative could employ a real-time computer-based system with decision support capabilities.

Because a system design incorporates a combination of features, such as input/output devices and files, the number of possible alternatives is immense. To appreciate the vastness of the design alternative universe, recall the number of decisions needed in selecting a data communications network (see Chapter 13). For example, a system design might include a star network or a ring network, it might use private or public lines, and so on.

Examples of Design Alternatives Two illustrative design alternatives are broadly portrayed in Figures 15-7 and 15-8. Although they do not reflect all necessary design choices, these broad-view diagrams suggest key differences between the two alternatives.

The first alternative employs a centralized stand-alone computer at the home office. Each sales order is received by a salesperson from a customer and delivered to the appropriate sales branch. The branch mails the order to the home office, where clerks process the order and deliver a copy to the warehouse. After the goods are picked, they are shipped to the customer. Then the shipping copy is batched with other notices of shipped orders and processed daily on the centralized computer. The resulting sales invoices are mailed to the affected customers.

The second alternative employs a data communications network. Upon receiving a sales order, the salesperson transmits the order to the sales branch via

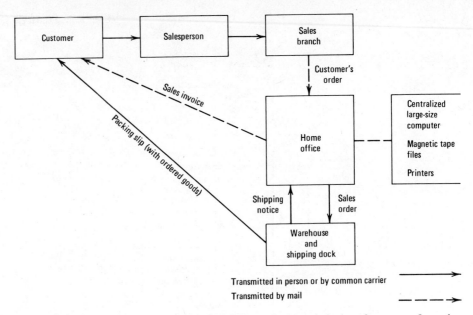

FIGURE 15-7 A broad-view diagram of the conceptual design features of a sales order processing system: centralized computer alternative.

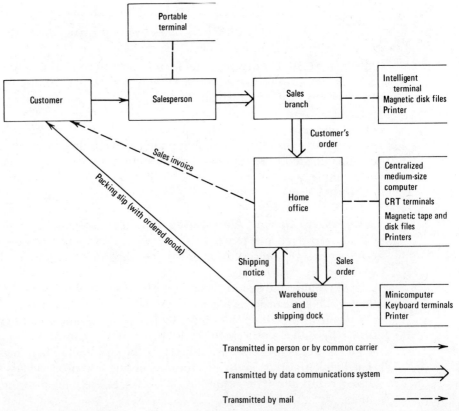

FIGURE 15-8 A broad-view diagram of the conceptual design features of a sales order processing system: distributed communications network alternative.

his or her microcomputer. At the sales branch the order is checked for completeness and accuracy. Then it is transmitted to the home office on a microcomputer that can emulate a terminal. The computer system automatically prints a copy of the sales order on a terminal at the warehouse. After the goods have been picked and shipped, the shipping department clerk transmits shipping data back to the home office via a terminal. By reference to online customer accounts receivable files, the centralized computer prepares a sales invoice and stores it on the disk. The stored invoices are printed hourly and then mailed to customers.

Narrowing of Alternatives Selecting the single best design consists essentially of eliminating all the second-best design alternatives. In order to minimize duplicative design efforts, the project team should narrow the varied alternatives as early as possible. Certain alternatives can be quickly discarded because they do not meet the systems requirements specified during the analysis phase. Others may be discarded because they would not provide all needed information. Still others may be unsatisfactory because they would consume disproportionate quantities of resources. The remaining design alternatives must be evaluated on the basis of feasibility.

Three questions should reveal the extent to which each design alternative is feasible or infeasible.

1. Is the existing state of technology adequate for the system to be achievable at the end of the project; that is, is it **technically feasible?**

2. Can and will the new system be used by the personnel for whom it is designed; that is, is it **operationally feasible?**

3. Are the expected economic benefits likely to exceed the economic costs of the new system; that is, is it **economically feasible?**

Most of the design alternatives should be eliminated by means of this screening process. However, two or more design alternatives may very likely remain. The final selection is then in the hands of higher-level management.

Preparation of Design Specifications

As mentioned earlier, the conceptual design for the selected alternative is expressed in terms of user-oriented **conceptual design specifications.** These specifications are generally grouped around the components of the information system (i.e., the data inputs, data processing procedures, the data base, the data controls and security measures, and the information outputs).

Presumably the final selection of the best design alternative will have been made prior to the preparation of these specifications. If two or more alternatives survive all screening efforts throughout this phase, however, it will be necessary to prepare two or more sets of specifications.

Design specifications will typically include such features and capabilities as listed in Figure 15-9. Other specifications, such as coding systems, data base schema, and decision models, may be added as needed.

System Components	Features
Output	Name
	Purpose
	Distribution to users
	Contents (information items)
	General format
	Frequency (or trigger)
	Timeliness (response time or delay after an event occurs)
	Output medium
Data base	File name (or data structure name)
	File type
	File size (number of records)
	Content of record (data items)
	Record size and layout
	File organization method
	Storage medium
	Data characteristic (e.g., numeric)
	Updating frequency
	Data structures
Data processing	Sequence of steps or runs
	Processing modes, cycles, volumes
	Modes of data communication
	Processing capabilities at each physical location
	Name
Data input	Purpose
	Source
	Method of collecting data
	Volume (peak and average)
	Contents (data items)
	General format
	Data entry method
	Type
Control	Purpose
and security	Specific system component affected
	Method of correcting error specific data items affected

FIGURE 15-9 Typical features included within design specifications.

Submission of System Design Specifications

System design specifications should be incorporated in a formal **system design proposal.** Higher-level management should review this proposal thoroughly. If it receives final approval, the relatively expensive systems implementation phase will begin.

A system design proposal should begin with a cover letter. This letter summarizes the findings of the design phase. Figure 15-10 presents the likely contents of a cover letter. The body of the proposal would contain the design specifications, together with system flowcharts and other presentation materials. In addi-

```
(Date)

Dear Mr. (President or other top manager)

Summary of recommended design(s)
Objectives to be achieved by design(s)
Expected benefits to be attained
Summarized needs in hardware and software
Summarized cost estimates
Expected impacts of design(s) on information
system
Expected impacts of design(s) on organization


(Signed)
```

FIGURE 15-10 Suggested contents of a cover letter for a design proposal.

tion, the proposal might contain a plan for implementing the selected design, a benefits-cost analysis, and a list of underlying assumptions. In essence, it should contain all information needed by management to make a sound decision.

SYSTEM DESIGN CONSIDERATIONS

Because the design phase is so crucial, we should pause to search for clues to a successful design. Even though much depends on creativity, several sound guidelines are available.

Design Sequence

As the final products of an information system, the outputs are the key determinant of the remaining system components. Thus, as shown in Figure 15-11, the output design specifications should be considered first.[2] The remaining specifications could be prepared in the sequence shown. Alternatively, they could be prepared concurrently with the control and security specifications.

Design Principles

A conceptual system design should reflect certain principles. Although most of these have been mentioned in earlier sections and chapters, the following list deserves added attention.

1. **Foster system objectives.** The objectives that appear in the systems plan and project proposal should be achieved to the greatest feasible extent.

---

[2] Reprinted with permission from Joseph W. Wilkinson, "Guidelines for Design Systems," *Journal of Systems Management* (Dec. 1974) 38.

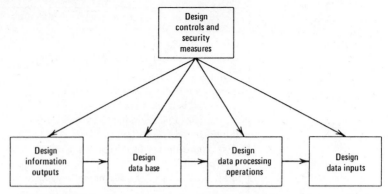

FIGURE 15-11 The sequence in designing system components. Reprinted with permission from the *Journal of Systems Management.*

2. **Incorporate reasonable trade-offs.** Since certain objectives conflict with each other, trade-offs are necessary. For instance, it may be desirable to gain a faster response time at the expense of economy. If the added benefits realized from enhancing one objective exceed the losses from sacrificing another objective, the trade-off is viewed as reasonable.

3. **Focus on functional requirements.** Design specifications should be expressed in terms of capabilities and needs. That is, they should be functional rather than hardware- and software-specific. One might specify that the primary storage should have a designated level of capacity, rather than that the MAXI 460 computer is needed.

4. **Serve multiple purposes.** Most designs should be multidimensional, thereby enabling the system to serve more than a single purpose or type of user. Generally a system module should aid in processing transactions as well as providing decision or control information; it should serve employees as well as managers (and also perhaps outside parties).

5. **Relate to users' concerns.** A system design should be as simple as possible so that the resulting system is easily usable by employees and managers. It should provide all information that the employees and managers need to fulfill their responsibilities. For instance, as many of the informal information flows as feasible should be converted to formal information flows.

6. **Provide a tailored product.** A system design should fit the particular circumstances of a firm. Thus, a general ledger system for a steel manufacturer should be quite different from a general ledger system for a university.

7. **Integrate system modules.** A system design for a single module should link the module to other modules within the overall information system. Also, the design should be relatively standardized so that the system will perform consistently throughout and maintenance is simplified.

8. **Avoid design excesses.** Although a system design should allow for anticipated growth and change, it should not be too high-powered. For instance, a

design should not specify complete automation if a mix of machines and people can achieve the same result at lower cost.

9. **Apply sound methodologies.** Although the methodologies or approaches used in creating a system design are not a part of the specifications, they are useful in producing sound results. Methodologies are discussed in the next section.

Design Methodologies

Among the design methodologies or approaches are top-down, bottom-up, prototyping, and designer's workbench.

Top-Down Approach The **top-down approach** begins with the firm's objectives and moves to the decisions needed to achieve the objectives. Then the top-down approach considers the processes for making the decisions and the specific information needs. Thus, it is equivalent to the information needs analysis. This approach is particularly useful when developing planning modules and decision support systems.

Bottom-Up Approach The **bottom-up approach** emphasizes efficiency at the operational level. Modules consist of transaction processing systems, which are built individually and then integrated at the functional and higher levels. Information generated as a by-product of transaction processing is summarized and made available for decision-making.

Prototyping Like the evolutionary approach, **prototyping** incorporates a learning process into systems development. However, the learning takes place over a shorter period (e.g., several months). Prototyping consists of devising a preliminary design initially. This prototype, which is a relatively crude version of the final design, is put to use. As experience is gained in its use, and as additional information needs become apparent, the design is refined. This fine-tuning may continue through several iterations. Although relatively expensive, this approach often produces a more satisfactory final system design.

Designer's Workbench The **designer's workbench** is a computerized version of prototyping. It allows the design to be developed and tested via online computer workstations before being put into actual use. The testing often leads to modifications that create immediate design improvements. Hence, the final system design is likely to be reached in a shorter period of time.

TECHNIQUES FOR ORGANIZING FACTS

Analyzing and designing an information system involves numerous details and complex relationships. Thus, a variety of techniques have been devised to organize these facts. Most of the techniques employ the use of diagrams or graphic representations. Generally these techniques can be applied both to analyze a present system and to design an improved system.

Fact-organizing techniques may be categorized in various ways. Certain techniques present broad or conceptual views; others provide very detailed views. Our focus in this chapter is on techniques that provide conceptual views; those that provide detailed views are discussed in the next chapter. Another division of fact-organizing techniques is between those that have been used in classical systems development and those that are an integral part of structured systems development. Although certain techniques fall into both categories, this division provides a useful basis for discussion.

Classical Systems Development Techniques

During the past 50 years, a number of techniques have been devised to meet the needs of specific analysis and design situations. These techniques have been loosely associated with the approach known as **classical systems development.** Perhaps the most widely used technique is the system flowchart. As noted in Chapter 6, the system flowchart appears in a variety of forms, such as the process flowchart, document flowchart, computer-oriented flowchart, and control-oriented flowchart.

Useful fact-organizing materials include work distribution charts, work measurement analyses, input/output matrixes, space layout diagrams, and decision flow diagrams. Each will be briefly described. Other techniques, such as forms analyses, were illustrated in Chapter 6.

Work Distribution Charts Work distribution concerns the distribution of times spent on various tasks within an activity or organizational unit. A **work distribution chart** portrays in matrix format the times worked by each employee on each task. Figure 15-12 shows a work distribution chart for a shipping department. Upon analyzing the data in such a chart, a systems analyst can more easily spot inequities and inefficiencies. After determining improvements, the analyst can then reflect the revised allocation of tasks in a new chart.

Work Measurement Analyses Numerous measurements are necessary to trace and analyze the flows related to an information system. A typical data flow is the number of sales orders received this week; an analysis of this flow may be in terms of the numbers of sales orders by various size ranges.

Work measurement consists of measuring work flows (e.g., rates of output or levels of productivity). Thus, if a clerical employee spends 20 hours processing 400 purchase orders, then his or her rate of output is 20 purchase orders per hour.

Work measurement analysis provides a means of evaluating work performances. First, work performance standards are established, usually by means of time and motion studies. Then, the actual work measurements are compared to the established standards and variances are computed.

A popular modification of work measurement is known as work sampling. Although it cannot be used to set standards and evaluate individual performances, work sampling does enable the productivity of departments to be evaluated. It is a much less expensive technique than work measurement.

No.	Activity	Hours per week	Task (M. T. Sullivan — supervisor)	Hours per week	Task (Terry Frank & Jim Williams — shipping clerks)	Hours per week	Task (Ralph Johnson — traffic clerk)	Hours per week	Task (Paul Emerson — expeditor)	Hours per week	Task (Linda Dent & Sandra Pyle — typists)	Hours per week
1	Controlling sales orders	35	Spot-checking shipping order file against outstanding order report from sales order department	2	Date-stamping and checking packing slip copies from warehouse to shipping copies; noting unshipped items on shipping copies	33						
2	Preparing shipping forms and reports	102	Reviewing summary report of shipments	1	Proofreading typed bills of lading for accuracy and completeness; preparing summary report of shipments from bills of lading copies	30 / 3					Typing bills of lading from packing slip copies; typing summary report of shipments	60 / 8
3	Scheduling, routing, and dispatching shipments	60	Preparing work assignments for shipping handlers	2	Collecting packing slips and spot-checking weights of packed shipments against weights noted on packing slip copies by handlers	8	Maintaining file of shipping rates; entering shipper, schedule, route, and charges for shipments on packing slip copies	1 / 37	Delivering bills of lading to shipper's representatives for signature	12		
4	Supervising shipping activities	25	Training employees and observing their performances; checking employees' attendance; answering employees' questions	12 / 2 / 2					Helping speed shipments and eliminating bottlenecks.	9		
5	Following status of sales orders and shipments	25	Handling customers' inquiries regarding shipments	8	Handling customers' inquiries regarding shipments	2	Answering inquiries of shippers regarding routes and charges	1	Following progress of special orders through production and into shipping area	14		
6	Performing miscellaneous activities	33	Preparing letters and memos; conferring with vice-president of marketing and other department heads	3 / 8	Collating bills of lading and shipping orders to be sent to billing department	4	Preparing special instructions for shippers	1	Picking up and delivering papers dealing with rush orders; filing	2 / 3	Typing correspondence and packing labels; filing	4 / 8
	Totals	280		40		80		40		40		80

FIGURE 15-12 A work distribution chart for a shipping department.

Input/Output Matrixes An **input/output matrix** shows the relationships between data items (inputs) and the reports (outputs) in which they appear. Figure 15-13 shows an input/output matrix pertaining to the purchases transaction system. It highlights reports that are redundant or that can be combined with other reports. For instance, the receiving register in effect duplicates the receiving report; it may therefore be replaced by a copy of the receiving report.

Other useful matrixes show relationships between (1) users and the reports they receive, (2) data items and files in which they are stored, and (3) organizational units and related responsibilities.

Space Layout Diagrams Floor plan-like drawings, called **space layout diagrams,** can aid in arranging the physical and paperwork flows. For purposes of analysis, the current flows can be superimposed onto the space layout. Then

Data Item and Source (Output →)	Sales order—invoice	Bill of lading	Back order	Shipment record	Delayed order report	Inventory flash report	Sales flash report	Sales analysis by salesperson	Sales analysis by product
Date of event or output	X	X	X	X	X	X	X	X	X
Customer order number (sales branch)	X								
Name of customer (customer's order)	X	X							
Address of customer (customer's order)	X								
Place to be shipped (customer's order)	X	X							
Quantities ordered (customer's order)	X				X		X		
Product numbers (customer's order)	X	X	X	X		X	X	X	X
Product descriptions (product file)	X	X	X						
Unit prices (pricing file)	X		X						
Scheduled delivery date (production control department)	X								
Priority (sales order dept.)	X								
Sales order—invoice no. (sales order dept.)	X		X	X	X				
Credit terms (credit dept.)	X								
Salesperson number (customer's order)	X							X	
Sales branch number (customer's order)	X						X		
Channel of distribution code (sales branch)	X								
Special delivery instructions (customer's order)	X	X							
Freight charges (shipping data file)	X	X							
Bill of lading number (shipping data file)		X		X					
Where shipped from (shipping data file)		X							
Products shipped (shipping dept.)		X							
Quantities shipped (shipping dept.)		X		X					
Routing (shipping data file)	X	X							
Method of shipment (shipping data file)	X	X							
Carrier (shipping data file)	X	X							
Weight of shipment (shipping dept.)		X							
Packaging data (shipping dept.)		X							
Back order number (finished-goods whse.)			X						
Quantities backordered (finished-goods whse.)			X						
Availability date (production control department)			X						
Dates of shipments (shipping dept.)			X		X				
Cost of order (cost acctg. dept.)	X								
Total sales amount (billing dept.)	X						X	X	X
Status of orders (production control department or finished-goods whse.)					X				
Units forecasted to be sold (sales forecasting dept.)							X		
Number of days delayed (production control department)					X				
Percent of orders delayed (production control department)					X				
Units below reorder points (inventory control department)						X			
Units forecasted to be ordered (inventory control department)						X			
Units actually sold (sales analysis department)							X		
Salesperson's quotas (sales branch)								X	
Contribution margins (sales analysis department)									X
Percent of total market (sales analysis department)									X

FIGURE 15-13 An input/output matrix.

proposed flows can be drawn onto another copy of the space layout. Scaled cutouts of desks, machines, and other fixtures are helpful in trying different arrangements.

Decision Flow Diagrams In order to determine information needs, managerial decisions must be identified. A **decision flow diagram** shows the relationships between chains of decisions and key items of needed information. For instance, the decisions required in production (e.g., when to begin production) can be related to needed information (e.g., production schedules).

Structured Systems Development Techniques

During the 1970s a new body of techniques was devised. These techniques, known collectively as **structured systems development,** represent a disciplined approach to systems analysis and design. Structured systems development increases the quality and efficiency of systems analysis and design. It also aids communication between systems analysts and users. Key features of structured systems development include

1. A clear integrated view of the overall systems project area.
2. A partitioning of the overall project area (i.e., a systematic division of the project area into smaller modules).
3. An emphasis on the logical, rather than the physical, data and information flows.
4. An emphasis on easy-to-understand diagrams.

Structured techniques include hierarchy charts, data flow diagrams, data dictionaries, and data structure diagrams.

Hierarchy Charts A **hierarchy chart,** also known as a structure chart and business model, describes the overall logical structure of a system or system module. Figure 15-14 shows a hierarchy chart of the sales transaction processing system. It contains three levels of a system hierarchy. More levels could be added below the third level, with each level reflecting a higher degree of detail.

Data Flow Diagrams Flow-type diagrams have become increasingly popular in recent years. In Chapter 6 data flow diagrams were described as a means of documenting transaction processing systems. They are more important, however, as an integral part of structured development. In contrast to system flowcharts, **data flow diagrams** present logical views of system activities. Thus, they do not include such physical features as computer processing, online disk files, and paper outputs. As a consequence, they allow systems analysts to visualize system activities in their essential aspects and free of physical constraints.

Data flow diagrams should relate to hierarchy charts. For instance, a data flow diagram that parallels all the activities shown at the third level in Figure 15-14 can be prepared. Alternatively, data flow diagrams that depict the activities of

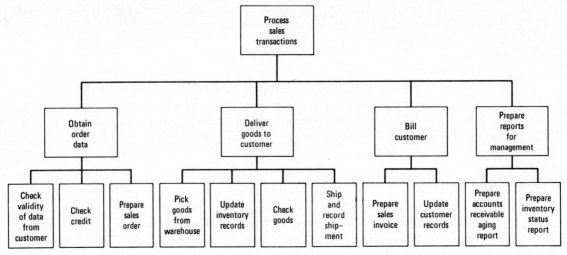

FIGURE 15-14 A hierarchy chart of the sales transaction processing system.

any module within the hierarchy chart could be prepared. Figure 15-15 shows data flow diagrams that pertain to the "deliver goods to customer" module and the "ship and record shipment" module. Note that the latter diagram reveals more details than the former, since it relates to a module at a lower level.

Data Dictionaries In the context of structured development, a **data dictionary** provides a definition for all data mentioned in the data flow diagrams. As Figure 6-10 shows, a definition for a data item may include the primary key, description, and mode. When data items represent combinations of other data items, the relationships should be stated. For instance, a data item labeled CUSTOMER-ADDRESS may appear as

CUSTOMER-ADDRESS = STREET-ADDRESS + CITY + STATE + ZIP-CODE

Data Structure Diagrams As described in Chapter 11, a **data structure diagram** presents the logical relationship between data items. The relationship may involve the records in two or more files, as shown in Figure 11-7. Alternatively, the relationship may involve individual data items. For instance, CUSTOMER-ADDRESS would be shown in a box at the upper level of a data structure diagram, with its constituent data items being shown in separate boxes on a lower level. Each data item, such as CITY, would be connected to the box at the upper level.

Example of a Structured Systems Analysis Methodology

A number of methodologies have been devised to aid systems analysts in applying systems analysis and design techniques. Specific methodologies or packages include Business Information System Analysis and Design (BISAD) from Honeywell Information Systems, Structured Analysis and Design Techniques

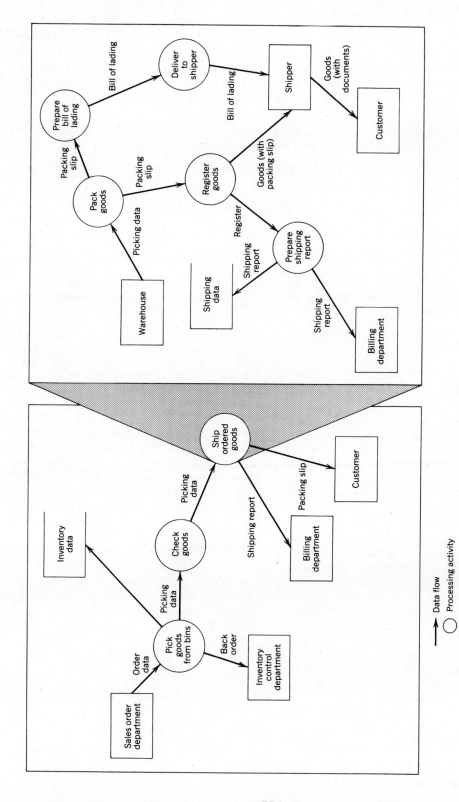

FIGURE 15-15 Two levels of data flow diagrams, based on a hierarchy diagram.

(SADT) from Softech, Inc., and Business Systems Planning (BSP) from IBM Corporation.

Certain business firms have refined their own methodologies. An example is Structured Systems Analysis (SSA), an integrated set of techniques assembled by Exxon;[3] SSA applies diagrams and techniques in the following order.

1. Global business model, which shows the overall relationships among the functions of the business firm under study.

2. Function matrix, which relates the responsibilities for each function identified in the global model.

3. Data flow diagrams, such as that shown in Figure 15-15.

4. Detailed activity models, similar to the diagram shown in Figure 15-14.

5. Data structure diagram, which shows the logical structure (e.g., a hierarchy) of data items listed in the data dictionary.

6. Glossary, which lists the various business terms used in the various operations.

SUMMARY

A system life cycle involves planning, systems analysis, systems design, systems implementation, and systems operational phases. Preliminary planning steps lead to an approved system project. Systems analysis is necessary to familiarize the systems analysts with the system module to be developed, define fully the current problems, gather detailed cost data, generate ideas for improvement, and gain the acceptance of the users. The systems analysis begins with a survey of the present system, leads to an analysis of the survey findings, moves to an identification of system requirements and information needs, and concludes with the submission of a system analysis report. If the report is approved, the systems design phase begins. It consists of identifying design alternatives, narrowing these alternatives, preparing specifications for a conceptual design, and submitting the specifications for approval. The conceptual design specifications should be based on sound design principles and involve appropriate design methodologies.

Systems analysis and design involve the use of fact-gathering and organizing techniques. Fact-gathering techniques include reviews of documents and records, observations, interviews, and questionnaires. Fact-organizing techniques may be roughly divided between classical and structured systems development techniques. Classical techniques include system flowcharts, work distribution charts, work measurement analyses, input/output matrices, space layout diagrams, and decision flow diagrams. Structured techniques include hierarchy charts, data flow diagrams, data dictionaries, and data structure diagrams.

REFERENCES

Ahituv, Niv; Hadass, Michael; and Neumann, Seev. "A Flexible Approach to Information System Development." *MIS Quarterly* (June 1984), 69–78.

Burch, John G. Jr., and Grudnitski, Gary. *Information Systems: Theory and Practice,* 4th ed. New York: Wiley, 1986.

Davis, William S. *Systems Analysis and Design: A Structured Approach.* Reading, Mass.: Addison-Wesley, 1983.

---

[3] Kathleen S. Mendes, "Structured Systems Analysis: A Technique to Define Business Requirements," *Sloan Management Review* (Summer, 1980), 51–63.

Giovinazzo, Vincent J. "Designing Focused Information Systems." *Management Accounting* (Nov. 1984), 34–41.

Highsmith, Jim. "Structured Systems Planning." *MIS Quarterly* (Sept. 1981), 35–54.

Mendes, Kathleen S. "Structured Systems Analysis: A Technique to Define Business Requirements." *Sloan Management Review* (Summer 1980), 51–63.

Wetherbe, James C. *Systems Analysis for Computer-based Information Systems.* New York: West Publishing, 1979.

Whitten, Jeffrey L.; Bentley, Lonnie D.; and Ho, Thomas I. M. *Systems Analysis and Design Methods.* St. Louis: Mosby, 1986.

QUESTIONS

1. What is the meaning of each of the following terms?

System life cycle	Designer's workbench
System project	Interviewing
Feasibility study	Questionnaire
System survey	Classical systems
System requirements	development
Information needs	Work distribution
analysis	chart
System analysis report	Work measurement
Conceptual design	analysis
Detailed design	Input/output matrix
Technical feasibility	Space layout diagram
Operational feasibility	Decision flow diagram
Economic feasibility	Structured systems
Conceptual design	development
specifications	Hierarchy chart
System design	Data flow diagram
proposal	Data dictionary
Top-down approach	Data structure
Bottom-up approach	diagram
Prototyping	

2. What are the major phases in the system life cycle?

3. What preliminary planning steps should be undertaken?

4. Why is a systems analysis phase necessary?

5. Identify several aspects of the scope of a system project.

6. Identify several internal and external sources of data.

7. Describe several behavioral actions, which a system project team may take, that represent applications of human relations principles.

8. What questions does an analysis of survey findings attempt to answer?

9. List several possible objectives of (a) an information system, and (b) a system project.

10. What are several attributes of an information system?

11. List several desirable system requirements.

12. Identify several information needs for a firm's president.

13. What is likely to be contained in a systems analysis report?

14. Briefly describe several techniques for gathering facts.

15. What are the steps in the systems design phase?

16. Identify several system design alternatives.

17. On what bases are system design alternatives evaluated?

18. What types of specifications are included in a conceptual design of an information system?

19. What are the likely contents of the cover letter to a system design proposal?

20. Identify several principles of systems design.

21. Contrast the top-down, bottom-up, prototyping, and designer's workbench approaches to systems design.

22. Contrast the classical and structured systems development approaches.

23. Briefly describe several classical fact-organizing techniques.

24. Briefly describe several structured fact-organizing techniques, and indicate how they are related to each other.

25. Should a small business firm adopt a top-down, bottom-up, or compromise approach to systems design?

26. Discuss the reasons for *not* analyzing the present information system.

27. Discuss the advantages and disadvantages of (a) stopping all reports, and (b) requiring each manager to explicitly request the continuation of any report that he or she feels is really needed.

28. If a systems manager attempts to be concerned with both the users and the technical aspects of the information system, will not one or the other be slighted?

29. If designing an information system is essentially a creative process, why attempt to teach systems design in a formal course?

30. Discuss the following statement: "The physical operations should drive the AIS."

31. What added difficulties, if any, are likely to be encountered when designing an information system for a not-for-profit organization instead of a profit-oriented firm?

REVIEW PROBLEM

Precise Manufacturing Company

Statement

The following cover letter has been prepared to accompany the conceptual design specifications for the sales order processing system module.

(Date)

Mr. John Curtis, President
Precise Manufacturing Company
Chicago, Illinois

Dear Mr. Curtis:

Enclosed is a proposal pertaining to a redesigned sales order and management system. This design proposal is based on a thorough survey and analysis of the present system, together with a careful consideration of the objectives to be achieved.

Summary of Recommended Design. We propose that the sales order and management system be redesigned to employ on-line input and processing, and reconfigured to be a computer network. A mainframe computer would be installed in the home office, a microcomputer in the warehouse, and intelligent terminals in the sales branches. These distributed processors would be linked by a data communications network consisting of leased lines. In addition, "dumb" terminals would be located in the key departments (i.e., sales order, credit, billing, shipping, warehouse) and linked to the computers. Each salesperson would transmit orders to the appropriate sales branch via a portable terminal. Sales and inventory files would be stored on magnetic disks and backed up on magnetic tapes. Sales orders, sales invoices, plus managerial reports and other documents, would be generated on printers located in the home office, warehouse, and sales branches. In addition, key managers would be provided with portable microcomputers for use in accessing the data base and retrieving desired sales information.

Objectives to be Achieved. This redesigned system should achieve the following objectives stated in the initial project proposal.

1. To improve the processing of sales orders so that needed information is available to managers and interfacing systems.

2. To enhance sales processing efficiency, especially with respect to times, and the benefit-cost ratio.

3. To reduce sales processing and billing errors.

Summarized Resource Needs. Hardware needs consist of one medium-sized current-model computer with one megabyte primary storage capacity, and one microcomputer with 768K primary storage capacity, 10 intelligent terminals, three portable microcomputers, 12 "dumb" terminals, approximately 80 portable terminals, 24 impact and nonimpact printers, 22 modems, and one front-end processor. Software needs consist of an operating system, a data communications software system, a network data base management system, a sales application software package (including a credit-checking model), an inventory control package, a report generator, a sales forecast package, and a financial modeling package. Additional personnel needs include a data base administrator, a systems programmer, and an applications programmer. Costs are expected to be approximately $2 million for systems development, hardware, software, plus the following for annual recurring operations.

Computer operations	$ 7,500
Maintenance contract	120,000
Communications lines	160,000
Information system maintenance	30,000
Data and information control	20,000
Information system administration	20,000
Total recurring costs	$357,500

These costs, however, should be offset by roughly $900,000 in annual benefits as a result of clerical savings, inventory carrying cost savings, savings in stock-out costs, savings in interest charges on working capital and other funds, savings from reduced errors, and increased contribution margins from greater sales arising from better customer service and managerial decisions. Also, certain costs (including all one-time costs) are to be allocated to the inventory and financial management projects, since the hardware and part of the software should benefit those areas.

Expected Impacts. With respect to the information system, the mode of data input and processing will change from batch to online. More editing and processing and routine decision-making steps will be performed by the computer system. With respect to the organization, fewer clerks will be needed. On the other hand, the remaining clerks and managers will need intensive training in the use of the newly implemented system. This training should help to offset expected resistance from those affected.

We will be pleased to discuss this recommendation with you at your convenience.

Sincerely,

Tod Stuart
Information Systems Manager

Required

The benefits to be expected from the new system have been omitted from the cover letter. Prepare a list of benefits that should have been inserted after "Objectives to Be Achieved."

Solution

Expected Benefits to Be Attained. The recommended system design can easily meet all system requirements. Since the requirements have been derived by reference to observed weaknesses in the present system, the redesigned system is expected to overcome all such weaknesses. In specific terms, the redesigned system is expected to

1. Provide adequate capacity to meet sales volumes during the next five years.

2. Reduce the time needed to process sales order transactions so that almost all promised delivery dates are met and backlogs are minimized.

3. Provide greater efficiency and effectiveness in processing and maintaining fin-

ished-goods inventories so that sufficient goods are available to fill most orders and back orders are minimized.

4. Establish adequate controls over sales order transactions so that transaction data are not lost, and input and processing errors are almost completely eliminated.

5. Maintain up-to-date records pertaining to the status of open sales orders and finished-goods inventory, as well as sufficient backup records and audit trails.

6. Render greater accessibility to stored data so that inquiries by clerks, managers, and customers can be quickly answered.

7. Provide more timely, accurate, and relevant information (e.g., sales forecasts, sales analyses, profitability reports) for managerial decision-making. (Although all information needed by the vice president of marketing cannot be satisfied by this system, a large proportion can be.)

8. Provide tangible and intangible benefit values that exceed the relatively high level of one-time and recurring costs. (Although savings in operating costs—as listed in the project proposal—are not likely to be realized, the larger-than-expected benefits should more than offset the added costs.)

PROBLEMS

15-1. List the questions that should be asked in analyzing each of the following problem situations, which have occurred within a manufacturing firm.

a. Production costs have risen significantly because of increased overtime, idle time waiting for materials, and reworking of products.

b. Credit losses have increased because of a heightened delinquency rate.

c. Late shipment of orders has increased because of bottlenecks in production and the warehouse.

d. Customer complaints have increased because of the poor quality of products.

e. Finished-goods inventory levels have fluctu-

ated widely because of large errors in forecasting sales.

15-2. Assume that you have been assigned the responsibility of designing for a bank the portion of the information system pertaining to depositor transactions and depositor-oriented management reports. The bank, which has a main office and a dozen branches, currently employs an information system that essentially involves manual processing of transactions. It generates very few reports that focus on depositor activity. Your first task is to specify alternative system designs (say, six) that consist of various combinations of system components and capabilities. Include in each alternative such aspects as data processing, input modes, data base features, output characteristics, and decision support levels.

15-3. Refer to Problem 3-10, which states that Auto Barn is considering the acquisition of a computer system. Its current manual system can no longer handle the increasing sales and inventory transactions. Also, the managers are not receiving the information they need to make planning and control decisions. To foster the change, the president has just hired Lynn Barton, an accountant who has several years of experience as a systems consultant with one of the larger local public accounting firms. She has been appointed as manager of information systems, with the responsibility of directing the development of a new computer-based system.

Required

Describe the major steps that should be taken in the planning, analysis, and design phases of this systems development.

15-4. Rose Publishing Company devotes the bulk of its work to the development of high school and college texts. The Printing Division has several production departments and employs 400 persons of which 95 percent are hourly rated production workers. Production workers may work on several projects in one day. They are paid weekly based on total hours worked.

A manual time card system is used to collect data on time worked. Each employee punches in and out when entering or leaving the plant. The Timekeeping Department audits the time cards daily and prepares input sheets for the computerized functions of the payroll system.

Currently, a daily report of the previous day's time card information by department is sent to each departmental supervisor in the Printing Division for verification and approval. Any changes are made directly on the report, signed by the supervisor and returned to the Timekeeping Department. The altered report serves as the input authorization for changes to the system. Because of the volume and frequency of reports, this report changing procedure is the most expensive process in the system.

Timekeeping submits the corrected hourly data to General Accounting and Cost Accounting for further processing. General Accounting maintains the payroll system that determines weekly payroll, prepares weekly checks, summarizes data for monthly, quarterly, and annual reports, and generates W-2 forms. A weekly and monthly payroll distribution report is prepared by the Cost-Accounting Department that shows the labor costs by department.

Competition in college textbook publishing has increased steadily in the last three years. While Rose has maintained its sales volume, profits have declined. Direct labor cost is believed to be the basic cause of this decline in profits, but insufficient detail on labor utilization is available to pinpoint the suspected inefficiencies. Chuck Hutchins, a systems consultant, was engaged to analyze the current system and to make recommendations for improving data collection and processing procedures. Excerpts from the report that Hutchins prepared follow.

. . . An integrated Time and Attendance Labor Cost (TALC) system should be developed. Features of this system would include direct data entry; labor cost distribution by project as well as department; online access to time and attendance data for verification, correction, and update; and creation and maintenance of individual employee work history files for long-term analysis.

. . . The TALC system should incorporate uniquely encoded employee badges that would be used to electronically record entry to and exit from the plant directly into the data system.

. . . Labor cost records should be maintained at the employee level, showing the time worked in the department by project.

Thus, labor cost can be fully analyzed. Responsibility for correct and timely entry must reside with the departmental supervisors and must be verified by project managers on a daily basis because projects involve several departments.

. . . Online terminals should be available in each department for direct data entry. Access to the system will be limited to authorized users through a coded entry (password) system. Departmental supervisors will be allowed to inspect, correct, verify, and update only time and attendance information for employees in their respective departments. Project managers may access information recorded for their projects only and exceptions to such data must be certified outside the system and entered by the affected supervisor.

. . . Appropriate data should be maintained at the employee level to allow verification of employee personnel files and individual work-history by department and project. Access to employee master file data should be limited to the Personnel Department. Work-history data will be made available for analysis only at the project or departmental level, and only to departmental supervisors and project managers for whom an employee works.

Required

a. List sources of the facts that were gathered during the analysis of the current payroll system.

b. Briefly describe techniques that were likely used to gather facts; specify at least one fact that was likely gathered by each technique.

c. List questions that were likely asked during an analysis of the facts uncovered during the survey of the current system.

d. List the benefits of the proposed system that should appear in the system design proposal.

e. The items listed in the box represent many of the system and information requirements for a new payroll system. List other requirements, both system and informational, that are desirable in a new system. (Some of these requirements, such as timeliness, may be implied in the statements in the box.)

f. The departmental supervisors and project managers are both allowed in the proposed system to have access to labor distribution data on a limited basis. Discuss the reasons for allowing each of the parties to have access to the data specified. The limitations on data may cause conflicts between the parties. Discuss behavioral actions that could be taken by the systems consultant to reduce or eliminate these possible conflicts.

(CMA adapted)

15-5. Rasher's Grocery Stores is a local chain of 10 stores in Tampa, Florida. Each store has an average of four cash registers and serves 600 customers daily. However, growth trends indicate that 800–900 customers likely will be served daily at each store within three years.

For several years the management of Rasher's has been watching developments in computerized POS systems. It has become convinced that the benefits of such systems—increased productivity, more effective use of checkout stations, improved control over inventories, and automatic verification of customer credit—will have a healthy effect on the firm's slim profits.

Recently, therefore, management requested the information systems manager to undertake an analysis and feasibility study. After several weeks of investigation, the information systems manager concludes that a centralized computer with disk files and POS terminals in each store is the most likely configuration, based on a rough comparison of benefits and costs. However, this determination depends on the ability of the POS system to accomplish certain feats.

Thus, the system should reduce the average checkout time from 4 minutes to 2.5 minutes. It should enable a credit check to be performed in 10 seconds or less, and the response to each keyed-in grocery sale should not exceed 2 seconds. No more than one error in 1000 transactions should be caused by the system, and the system should reduce human checkout errors by 25 percent.

In addition to aiding the checkout procedure, the POS system should provide inventory reorder reports and other daily management information within one hour after the stores close at 9:00 p.m. It should also have the capacity of storing all the price data, plus inventory records and sales history data; all these data might require as much as 100 million bytes of storage.

Required

a. List several objectives of the POS systems project.

b. Describe the fact-gathering techniques that were likely employed during the analysis and feasibility study, and associate at least one fact with each technique.

c. List questions that should have been asked during the analysis of the survey findings.

d. List the system requirements and information needs for the proposed POS system. Be as specific as possible.

15-6. George Morrill is the purchasing manager for Tolliver Electronics, Inc., an Amherst, Massachusetts, manufacturer of high-quality electronics products. Before becoming purchasing manager, he was an electronics technician and quality control supervisor.

George will be making decisions with regard to

a. Selecting the suppliers from whom to buy parts and subassemblies (tactical planning decisions).

b. Establishing purchasing policies (strategic planning decisions; to be made together with higher-level managers within the firm).

c. Hiring and evaluating supervisors, buyers, and other purchasing department personnel (management control decisions).

d. Negotiating purchase contracts (tactical planning decisions).

Required

a. Describe the analysis that should be performed to determine George's information needs.

b. List several information items needed for making each of these decisions.

c. List the properties of information needed for the second and fourth decisions.

15-7. For each of the following described systems, propose an alternative system design and sketch broad-view diagrams of both the present and proposed systems.

a. A department store employs a POS system to process its sales transactions. The cash registers on each floor are in effect stand-alone intelligent terminals. Transactions are processed by each register and then captured on optical scannable paper tape. At the end of each day, the tapes are carried to the accounting department, read into the store's computer, and processed to update magnetic-tape files and print sales and cash summaries.

b. A distributor employs a centralized data preparation section to key data concerning shipped orders onto magnetic tape. Then the transactions are processed to update magnetic-tape files and to produce sales invoices.

c. A retail chain with 10 outlets employs a centralized order-filling system. Each store prepares replenishment orders when stocks run low. These orders are mailed to the warehouse, which fills the orders and ships the merchandise to the ordering store. When warehouse stocks need to be replenished, the warehouse sends a purchase requisition to the purchasing department. Purchase orders are then prepared and mailed to suppliers. Copies of the orders filled by the warehouse and their corresponding purchase orders are sent to the computer data processing department, where they are keyed to magnetic tape and processed against files stored on magnetic disks.

d. A manufacturer with a factory and local warehouses employs a decentralized order-processing system. Minicomputers are located at each warehouse, whereas larger computers are located at the factory and the home office. All these computers utilize magnetic-tape files. Orders are received from customers at the home office. Formal sales orders are prepared and mailed to the warehouse, which maintains an inventory file on magnetic tape. Next, the home office prepares sales invoices, which are mailed to customers. Periodically the home office initiates production orders to the factory. The

factory maintains production records via its computer. It ships the finished goods directly to the warehouses according to pre-established proportions and provides information to the home office.

15-8. Which data-gathering technique(s) appear to be most appropriate in each of the following cases; why?

a. Determining the procedure that should be followed by the cashier in preparing the bank deposit.

b. Determining the information needs of the personnel manager.

c. Determining the average number of work orders processed during a typical day.

d. Determining how the sales order processing procedure is actually performed.

e. Investigating the general level of productivity in the finished-goods warehouse.

f. Surveying the general adequacy of internal accounting controls in the cash disbursements procedure.

g. Surveying the opinions of all employees concerning the possible change to flextime.

h. Investigating the complaint that ordered products are frequently out of stock.

i. Determining the extent to which transaction documents are miscoded.

15-9. Jack Ladd has recently joined the Wexler Home Products Company of Long Beach, California. His title is Systems Analyst I, a position for which he is qualified by virtue of receiving a degree in business systems analysis from the local university. He has performed exceedingly well in his first several assignments. Thus, his supervisor feels confident in assigning Jack to perform an interview. He gives Jack the assignment late Thursday afternoon.

The interview is to take place with the manager of inventory, Colin Blunt. Jack's task is two-fold: (1) to uncover facts that can aid in correcting problems that have been traced to the inventory management function, and (2) to gain Blunt's cooperation in an analysis and redesign of the inventory management system.

Jack resolves to deal with these tasks in an expeditious manner. Therefore, he appears bright and early Friday morning at Blunt's office. He explains that his business is urgent, so Blunt cancels his scheduled staff meeting to talk with Jack.

Jack opens the interview by telling Blunt that top management is "concerned about serious problems in the inventory management function." He continues by explaining that he is there to help correct these problems. "In fact," he says, "our systems group can completely redesign your inventory procedures without bothering you at all. All we need is your story concerning the problems, and we can get started. We'll even keep mum during our study so that the employees won't know what is going on. That way, they can keep on with their work and won't be worried about possible layoffs when the new system is installed."

Jack continues by offering suggestions concerning several small problems pertaining to inventories that he had noted while walking through the area that morning. He also explains the workings of scientific inventory order models, including their ability to "minimize the array of inventory expenditures and optimize return on investment." Jack feels that this will show Blunt that he "knows his stuff."

After Jack has completed this exposition, he asks Blunt if he is willing to cooperate. "After all," as Jack added, "it's to your benefit to clear up these problems before more are uncovered." Blunt replies (as Jack clicks on his tape recorder) that he will have to discuss the matter with his superior, the production manager.

Jack feels that this reply is a rebuff to his efforts. Therefore he states that he has another meeting to attend, gets up, and leaves. When he sees his supervisor later that morning, Jack repeats what Blunt had said and ends by exclaiming, "I don't think that Mr. Blunt wants to cooperate. He certainly didn't offer any facts, and he seemed to be stalling when I put the question to him."

Required

Critique the interviewing approach of Jack Ladd.

15-10. Six employees compose the accounts payable department of the Hubbard Sales Company, a Stillwater, Oklahoma, firm. They per-

form the following sets of tasks for the designated number of hours daily.

Supervisor (Alice Whitespan)

Supervise employees	4 hours
Aid in verifying invoices	2 hours
Approve disbursement vouchers	½ hour
Aid in preparing checks	½ hour
Other activities, such as correspondence	1 hour

Accounts Payable Documentation Clerks (John Culver and Susan Lynch)

Handle purchase order copies	2 hours
Handle receiving report copies	2 hours
Process suppliers' invoices	10½ hours
Assemble disbursement voucher packets	1½ hours
Other activities, such as filing	1 hour

Freight Bill Clerk (Joyce Itel)

Prepare, verify, and post freight bills	4½ hours
Assemble and review disbursement vouchers	1½ hours
Other activities	1 hour

Disbursement Control Clerk (Pat Chase)

Assemble, review, and approve disbursement vouchers	4 hours
Prepare and review checks	3 hours
Other activities	1 hour

Typist-clerk (Brian Bush)

Type checks (and accompanying voucher stubs)	5 hours
Other activities, such as typing correspondence and filing	2 hours

Required

a. Prepare a work distribution chart, using such tasks as supervision, purchase order processing, voucher processing, and so on.

b. Identify weaknesses in the distribution of tasks, such as illogical assignments of tasks and assignments that appear to violate internal control concepts.

15-11. Refer to Problem 9-14. Masters Merchandising, Inc. decides to employ structured design techniques in developing a new information system for inventory management. It determines that the major activities under inventory management are (1) storing and recording additions to merchandise, (2) replenishing inventory, (3) preparing inventory-related reports for management, (4) monitoring inventory usage, and (5) receiving ordered merchandise. It reaffirms the subactivities listed in the referenced problem.

Required

a. Prepare a hierarchy chart for inventory management.

b. Prepare a data flow diagram for the activity "replenish inventory."

c. Prepare a lower level data flow diagram for the subactivity "prepare purchase order."

15-12. The Auto Rite Corp. of St. Paul replaces mufflers, transmissions, brakes, and other key automobile parts. Its dozen shops throughout the city service a total of about 200 car owners on an average day and 300 car owners on a busy day. Each shop maintains a standard inventory of 1000 different types and sizes of mufflers and other parts. A manager and an average of four mechanics staff each shop. All shop managers report to a shop operations superintendent.

After a thorough analysis by the firm's controller, the president decides that a minicomputer system is needed to handle the various transactions at the shops and to prepare such outputs as shop orders for the mechanics, itemized receipts of work done for customers, and daily analyses of jobs performed for managers. The minicomputer system will have terminals at the respective shops, with the processor and disk files and printer being located at the main office. The selected system should provide features that aid data entry, foster data control and security, and enable users to access specific shop orders. It should be capable of operating 12 hours per day, processing 60 transactions per hour, and re-

sponding to 90 percent of all data requests within 10 seconds. It should also accommodate a data base management system which the president plans to acquire next year.

Required

Prepare specific conceptual design specifications for the shop order processing system, based on the foregoing description, and an analysis of the needed inputs, files, and outputs. Make assumptions concerning quantitative values (e.g., the average data record consists of 300 characters).

15-13. Harold Seymour is a management accountant with XLB Company. He is serving on a project team that is responsible for recommending a new regional sales distribution system. Although the project team has approved the draft for the final report of the project team, which is to be submitted to top management, Seymour is not pleased with the approved report.

Jane Bier of the marketing department was appointed the leader of the team because she had experience with sales distribution systems. Seymour was assigned to the team for his expertise in budgets and cost analysis and because of his involvement in a similar project with a previous employer.

The project team worked well together identifying the positive and negative factors of the various alternatives. These factors were considered as the proposed regional distribution system was molded and designed. Seymour used his prior experience to explain the impact some of the negative factors could have on the volume and cost estimates for the proposed system.

The sales volume, costs, and cost savings estimates are very optimistic. The major negative factors and their impact have been discussed in the meetings, but are not mentioned in the report or in the supporting financial data. Seymour knows from his previous experience that some of the negative factors could easily occur and could have a significant influence on the estimated financial benefits of the system to the company.

In other words, Seymour believes that the final report lacks a proper balance. He argues that the potential negative factors and their financial impact should be identified and discussed in the report for top management. The project team as a whole does not think the report needs to be revised because the system as designed is good, and the final conclusions will be the same.

The draft of the final report was composed by Bier. Seymour agrees with the proposed system and the overall conclusions of the report, but he does not believe the report is complete. Bier strongly favors the proposed system even though she has not developed the basic design. Bier's strong positive attitude for the proposed system is reflected throughout the report.

Required

a. Discuss the need to include negative factors in the system design report.

b. Discuss the bases, other than financial, on which the proposed system alternative should be evaluated.

c. Assuming that the proposed system alternative is approved by management, what behavioral actions should be taken by the project team to help ensure its successful implementation and use?

(CMA adapted)

15-14. Kids Incorporated is a medium-sized toy manufacturer headquartered in Oakland, California. The firm manufactures three lines of toys: plastic toys, metal toys, and electric toys. Each line consists of approximately 30 individual toy products. Although the toys are manufactured in the same plant, each line is separated organizationally from the others. However, all three lines are sold by all members of the sales force, who are assigned to the five regional sales territories covering the continental United States.

The president of Kids Incorporated, May Uno, has become increasingly dissatisfied with the firm's information system. She and her fellow managers can only obtain information from the system at the end of the month. Because of the present highly competitive conditions in the toy-making industry, such infrequent reports put the firm at a disadvantage. Upon questioning the controller, the president learns that the information system also has serious weaknesses at the operational level.

Thus, May Uno informs Jim Moni, the controller, that he is to study and develop a redesigned information system. She states that the

only constraint is "to leave the organizational structure untouched. Otherwise, you have free rein." However, she insists that the study be completed within four months, as conditions have become intolerable.

Jim realizes that he does not have the time or expertise to undertake such a systems study. Therefore, he hires Jerry Low, a recent MBA graduate, as a special staff assistant. Jerry is assigned the system study as his first project; he is to report to Jim Moni when the study is completed and again when the revised system design is prepared.

Jerry Low goes to work. He researches what other firms are doing and talks to computer manufacturers. He follows their ideas and approaches as closely as possible. He designs forms to aid in maintaining better control over production and marketing operations. He designs reports to provide more timely sales and competitive information to managers. He chooses a computer that is the most modern version available. In fact, it will not be on the market for another two months, although he is assured that it can be delivered within the four-month deadline.

At the end of four months Jim Moni, together with Jerry Low, attends a meeting of the president and top managers of the firm. Jerry presents the design for the new system. All the managers are impressed. They enthusiastically approve the acquisition of the computer system and the entire system design.

One month later the new computer-based information system is in place, thanks to the efforts of Jerry Low and several sales engineers from the computer manufacturer. The employees, operating managers, and supervisors then see the system for the first time. They had not been told about it earlier, so that they would not become upset. Some respond to this surprise with grumbles and mumbles; some are even overheard to say that they had guessed something like this was in the works. The grumbles, mumbles, and comments are suppressed, however, when May Uno announces that no one will be fired because of the new system.

Three months pass. To the surprise of the managers, as well as May Uno and Jerry Low, the complaints come rolling in. More time goes by, and the complaints become a crescendo. Finally, when it is evident that the system is not working, but instead is causing dissatisfaction, the computer and system are scrapped. The firm returns to the old way of doing things. The only feature retained is the more timely preparation of managerial reports.

Required

List the weaknesses and strengths of the approach to systems development followed by Kids Incorporated.

16

Systems

Justification,

Selection, and

Implementation

Discuss the factors affecting the determination of a system's economic feasibility.

Describe the options and steps in the selection of computer hardware and software for a new system.

Identify the steps in the implementation of a new system.

Identify various techniques employed in a detailed system design.

Contrast two major control techniques pertaining to a system project.

INTRODUCTION

Most system designs require firms to acquire resources before the designs can be transformed into reality. These resources often include new personnel to operate and maintain the systems. Increasingly, the needed resources include computer hardware and/or software. In some cases firms are acquiring their first computer systems. In other cases they are replacing currently owned computer systems with more up-to-date computer systems. In still other cases they are adding new hardware, such as data communications facilities or terminals, to existing computer systems. Alternatively, they might simply be adding new applications software to an existing computer system.

In all systems projects involving new resources, the system designs must be justified. That is, they must be shown to be feasible—technically, operationally, and economically. Accountants are often asked to aid in determining economic feasibility, since it is based on financial concepts. Thus, economic feasibility is emphasized in this chapter.

Feasibility computations underlying the justifications may be included in the system design proposals. Alternatively, they may be included in separate feasibility study reports. As suggested in the previous chapters, feasibility studies are likely to be commenced at the inception of systems projects. Regardless of when and in what vehicles the feasibility computations appear, they should be approved by management before the resources are actually acquired.

Upon management's approval of a design's feasibility, the most suitable resources can be selected. The selection process often involves the evaluation of proposals from several computer hardware and software suppliers.

Systems implementation takes place concurrently with the selection of hardware and software. This lengthy phase usually consists of numerous and varied activities.

In addition to examining all these topics, this chapter surveys key project control and detailed design techniques.

DETERMINATION OF ECONOMIC FEASIBILITY

Economic Feasibility Concepts

In Chapter 11 we noted that data can be viewed as an economic resource. This view also pertains to information. Both values and costs are attached to items of information. A typical value is the "surprise value" of new relevant information concerning an impending decision. Typical costs are those involved in collecting and processing the information.

Information economics is the area of study concerning values and costs of information and their trade-offs. A principle of information economics is that added information should be gathered and provided for any purpose, such as making a decision, as long as the value of the added information exceeds the costs of obtaining the information.

Consider the information pertaining to units of product scrapped during a production process. Each scrapped unit results in a lost sale. To combat these lost sales, we could prepare a daily report showing the scrap rate and causes of scrappage. This report will have value if it provides the production manager with information that helps him or her to make decisions leading to reduced scrappage. If the value exceeds the costs of providing the information, the report is economically feasible. However, added information concerning the exact time each unit is scrapped will likely not be worth its added cost of collection.

Since information systems collect and process information, they are affected by the principles of information economics. Consequently, design decisions concerning any aspect of an information system should be likewise governed. Assume, for example, that we are concerned about the number of internal accounting controls to design into a particular system. Our design decision should be based on a trade-off between (1) the value of the added accuracy gained from each additional control, and (2) the direct cost of each control plus the indirect cost resulting from a loss in processing efficiency.

At the level of a system project, the information economics principle can be restated as follows: A proposed investment in information system resources is economically feasible if the benefits (values) derived from the use of the acquired resources exceed the added costs related to the investment. Thus, the costs and benefits pertaining to investments in information systems should be explored.

Costs Related to Information System Resources

Relevant costs for determining economic feasibility consist of those involved in (1) the acquisition of system resources, (2) the development of a new or improved information system, and (3) the operation and maintenance of the new or improved information system during the lives of the resources. Most of these costs will be future cash outflows and hence must be estimated.

One-time Costs Costs in the first two categories together represent the amount of the initial investment in a new or improved system. Since they normally are incurred only once during a life cycle of a system module, they are called **one-time costs.**

Figure 16-1 lists typical one-time costs. Many of the costs are for the salaries of the project team and a variety of other personnel, such as training specialists and construction workers. Other costs pertain to computer hardware and software, although all such items listed in the figure would not likely be included in a single project. Almost all the costs are to be actually incurred during the implementation phase of a project. The activities for which they will be incurred are discussed in a later section.

Recurring Costs Figure 16-2 lists typical **recurring costs,** which can be broadly defined as all system-related costs other than one-time costs. Recurring costs may be categorized by system functions, as in the figure. Alternatively, they may be grouped by object classes such as labor, supplies, equipment, and overhead.

Nonfinancial factors such as transaction volumes and response times significantly affect cost levels. For feasibility calculations to be sound, these factors must be carefully estimated.

Benefits Related to Information System Resources

Information systems can provide a variety of benefits or added values. These benefits may consist of savings in collecting or processing information. For instance, a computer-based system may replace a number of clerks and hence reduce labor costs. Benefits may consist of added revenues for the firm. For example, a new system may process and fill customers' orders more speedily, thereby creating satisfied customers. Greater numbers of such customers may then give the firm their repeat business, hence leading to higher sales. Other benefits may include better information, which in turn leads to better decision-making.

Tangible Benefits A **tangible benefit** is a cost saving or revenue increase that can be estimated in dollars. Displaced personnel cost savings can be measured by the reduced salaries, for example. Reduced inventory levels result in cost savings that can be measured by expected savings in carrying costs. In some cases the benefits are not as easily estimated as in these examples. Estimates should be developed

System Design Costs

Detailed design
Programming

System Installation and Conversion Costs

System and program testing
File conversion
Retraining of displaced employees
Training of newly hired analysts, programmers, and operators
Inefficiencies caused by learning new equipment and procedures

System Site Preparation Costs

Construction of wiring and piping systems
Construction of electrical power supply
Construction of air conditioning system
Construction of sprinkler system
Construction of other miscellaneous facilities, such as false floor-
ing, file storage vault, and special lighting

System Hardware Costs

Central processing unit
Additional processors
Secondary storage devices
Input/output devices
Data communications equipment
Terminals
Peripheral equipment, such as key-to-tape devices
Transportation of equipment

System Software Costs

Operating system, utility routines, compilers
Data communications software
Application program packages
Data management software packages
Decision model software packages
Outside computer time-sharing rentals

FIGURE 16-1 One-time costs for a new or improved computer-based information system.

when possible, however, in order to provide a sound basis for calculating economic feasibility.

Intangible Benefits An **intangible benefit** is one whose value cannot be measured with reasonable accuracy. Examples of intangible benefits that information systems may provide are

Data Preparation and Handling Costs

(Wages and salaries for data preparation clerks, tape librarian, and others; supplies; peripheral equipment rentals or obsolescence)

Computer Operations and Maintenance Costs

(Wages and salaries for computer operators, custodians, technicians, and supervisors; supplies; repair parts; utilities; equipment service contracts; space rentals; freight; data transmission fees; computer-related equipment rentals or obsolescence; taxes; insurance; building occupancy)

Information System Maintenance Costs

(Salaries for programmers and system analysts)

Data and Information Control Costs

(Wages and salaries for internal auditors, control clerks, and others; printing fees applying to programming manuals and other documentation; security systems)

Information System Administration Costs

(Salaries of system managers, data base administrator, secretaries, and others)

FIGURE 16-2 Recurring costs for a new or improved computer-based information system.

1. Better and more selective information for decision-making.

2. More timely reporting to managers, both at the home office and at remote locations.

3. Improved control over operations, leading to increased labor productivity, better utilization of equipment, fewer materials shortages, fewer errors, higher product quality, and so on.

As may be apparent, the line between tangible and intangible benefits is rather blurred. For instance, a higher level of customer service might be either type of benefit. If better customer service arises from faster deliveries, and the consequent impact of added repeat sales can be measured, it is a tangible benefit. If better customer service is based on faster responses to customer inquiries, the impact is probably not measureable and thus the benefit is intangible.

Example of Benefits

Benefits pertaining to complex information systems projects are not easy to assemble. However, they have been fruitfully gathered with respect to such complex systems as decision support systems, data base systems, and logistics systems. For example, Yamazaki Machinery Company of Japan installed an $18 million computer-integrated manufacturing (CIM) system several years ago. Among the reported benefits of this CIM system have been reductions in needed production machines, factory employees, floor space, and in average processing time. Other likely benefits include savings in inventory investment, higher product quality, and greater flexibility in changing products.[1]

Economic Feasibility Computations

Several criteria are available to evaluate the economic feasibility of a proposed system design. Perhaps the most suitable criterion in the majority of cases is the net present value of an investment. Other criteria also employed include the payback period and the benefit-cost ratio. All these criteria incorporate the same considerations as any capital budgeting situation. That is, an investment in information systems resources is no different, economically speaking, than investments in a delivery truck or a headquarters building.

Net Present Value A discounted cash flow model is used to find the **net present value** of an investment. Future cash inflows and outflows are discounted to the present time and compared. If the total present value of cash inflows exceeds the total present value of cash outflows, the net present value is positive. The investment is then evaluated as being economically feasible. If the net present value is negative, however, the investment is considered to be economically infeasible.

Estimates or measures of the following factors are needed in order to compute the net present value of an investment.

1. The cash outflows, such as the acquisition cost of the system (e.g., computer hardware and software), plus the operating and maintenance costs of the system during its economic life.

2. The cash inflows, such as the cost savings or other benefits to be derived from the acquired system during its economic life.

3. The economic (as opposed to the physical) life of the system.

4. The salvage value of the system at the end of its economic life.

5. The salvage value (if any) of the system being replaced.

6. The tax considerations, such as the tax rate and depreciation.

7. The required rate of return on invested capital, also called the opportunity cost of capital.

To illustrate the net present value method, assume that a small firm has designed a new system requiring the acquisition of a microcomputer system. The relevant data are as follows.

---

[1] Robert S. Kaplan, "Must CIM Be Justified by Faith Alone?" *Harvard Business Review* (Mar.–Apr. 1986), 87–92.

Purchase price of the hardware and software, as well as the costs of systems development	$ 45,000
Annual recurring operating and maintenance costs of the present accounting information system	240,000
Expected annual recurring operating and maintenance costs of the proposed computer system	220,000
Salvage value of the present data processing equipment (equal to its book value)	5,000
Expected salvage value of the computer system at the end of its economic life (four years)	10,000
Depreciation method	Straight-line
Required after-tax rate of return	14 percent

Figure 16-3 displays the computation of the net present value, assuming that the tax rate is zero. The present value (PV) factors have been taken from the table that appears on page 592. The net present value is a positive $24,200. However, this amount is suspect, since the tax rate has in effect been ignored.

Figure 16-4 displays the computation of the net present value if the tax rate is assumed to be 34 percent. Note that the net present value has dropped from $24,200 to $13,054, as a result of the smaller annual cash inflows. Thus, the effect of taxes is generally to reduce the extent to which a proposed investment is economically feasible. Unless taxes are considered, however, the computations cannot be viewed as realistic.

One-time costs	($45,000)	
Less: salvage value of present equipment	5,000	
Net investment (cash outflow)		($40,000)
Annual operating costs, present system	$240,000	
Annual operating costs, proposed system	220,000	
Annual savings in operating costs	$ 20,000	
Total cost savings, at present value (PV): (PV of $20,000 for 4 years at 14% = $20,000 × 2.914)		58,280
Salvage value of proposed computer system at PV: (PV of $10,000 to be received in 4 years = $10,000 × 0.592)		5,920
Total cash inflows, at PV		$64,200
Excess of returns at PV		$24,200

Note: Outflows are shown in parentheses.

FIGURE 16-3 Computations using the net present value model, ignoring the effects of income taxes.

Net investment (cash outflow)	($40,000)
Before-tax annual cost savings = $20,000	
After-tax annual cost savings: $20,000 × (1 − 0.34) = $13,200	
Depreciation tax shield^a = 2,975	
After-tax annual cash inflows $16,175	
Total cost savings at present value (PV): (PV of $16,175 for 4 years at 14% = $16,175 × 2.914)	47,134
Salvage value of proposed computer system at PV: (PV of $10,000 to be received in 4 years = $10,000 × 0.592)	5,920
Total cash inflows, at PV	$53,054
Excess of returns at PV	$13,054

^{a} Depreciation expense per year $= \dfrac{\$45,000 - \$10,000}{4} = \$8,750$

Depreciation tax shield per year = depreciation expense × tax rate = $8,750 × 0.34 = $2,975

Note: Outflows are shown in parentheses.

FIGURE 16-4 Computations using the net present value method, including the effects of income taxes.

Payback Period The **payback period** criterion reflects the number of years required to recover the net investment. Although it does not measure the return on investment, the payback period can be used as a useful screening device.

In the previous example, the payback period is computed as

$$\frac{\text{Net investment}}{\text{After-tax annual cash inflow}} = \frac{\$40,000}{\$16,175} = 2.47 \text{ years}$$

Benefit-Cost Ratio The **benefit-cost ratio** measures the effectiveness gained from each invested dollar. Thus, it enables competing investment opportunities to be compared in a sound manner. For the previous example the benefit-cost ratio is

$$\frac{\text{Total present value of cash inflows}}{\text{Present value of net investment}} = \frac{\$53,054}{\$40,000} = 1.33$$

Since the ratio exceeds 1.00, the investment is economically feasible.

SELECTION OF SYSTEM HARDWARE AND SOFTWARE

Figure 16-5 shows the steps following the design of a new system and the determination that it is feasible. These steps consist of soliciting proposals from suppliers for needed computer hardware and software, evaluating these proposals, and selecting the specific hardware and software on the basis of the evaluations. After these steps are completed, the implementation phase begins.

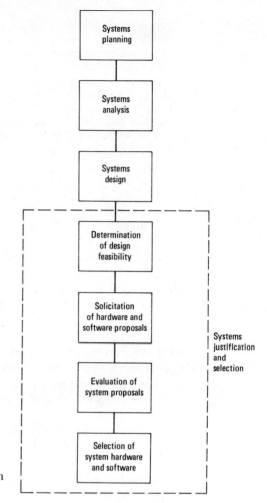

FIGURE 16-5 Systems justification and selection in the systems development process.

Acquisition Options

Before examining the selection steps, we might consider the various options that are available when acquiring a new system.

Purchasing Versus Leasing Computer hardware and software can be purchased, as was tacitly assumed in the economic feasibility example. Alternatively, however, the hardware and software may be leased on a long-term financing contract. Each option has advantages. Purchasing generally requires a smaller cash outlay in the long run. On the other hand, leasing involves a smaller initial cash outlay, provides greater flexibility, lessens the risks of obsolescence, and in some cases yields greater tax benefits.

Single Suppliers Versus Multiple Suppliers A computer system consists of hardware, software, input/output devices, storage devices, communications devices, and business forms and supplies. Most if not all of these items may be acquired from a single supplier, such as one of the large computer manufacturers. Using a single supplier tends to simplify the acquisition process. Also, this option assures that the various items will be compatible.

Alternatively, a firm may acquire the needed items from a variety of suppliers. Among the types of suppliers that may be used as sources are

1. Large computer manufacturers, such as IBM and NCR.

2. Peripheral equipment manufacturers.

3. Software product firms.

4. Computer-leasing firms.

5. Sellers and brokers of used-computer equipment.

6. Business forms and supplies firms.

This alternative option generally results in lower initial costs, since the firm can shop for the best buys. However, it may lead to greater inconveniences and problems if not handled carefully. For example, the information systems director of a firm buys several microcomputers of a brand that has been urgently requested by departmental managers; after the purchase the director discovers that the microcomputers are incompatible with the mainframe and hence cannot be tied into the firm's network.

In-house System Versus Outside Computing Service Most firms that use computer services operate and maintain their own computer hardware and software. It is not necessary that information system resources physically reside on a firm's premises, however. A firm may instead acquire commercial computer services from outside.

Outside computing services are mainly provided by two types of firms: service bureaus and time-sharing utilities. A **service bureau** is a firm that provides batch data processing services at a remote location. A subscribing firm prepares the source data records, such as time cards and sales orders. It then transports these records to the site of the service bureau. When the desired outputs are prepared, they are returned to the subscriber.

A **time-sharing service center** is a firm that provides batch or online data processing service through one or more online terminals located on a subscriber's premises. The subscribing firm prepares the source data records and enters them via the terminals. After processing takes place within the center's computer system, the outputs are produced on the subscriber's terminals or connected printers. Some of the subscriber's files are usually stored online within the center's computer system.

Perhaps the most important benefit gained from using an outside computing service is economy. Since the fees are related to usage, a subscriber pays only for what is used. Another benefit is that outside computer services generally make available professional assistance, specialized software, and specialized data bases. For instance, a small insurance firm may subscribe to a service that provides assistance in devising needed reports, that employs insurance-oriented processing programs, and that enables the firm to receive current economic and industry statistics from an online commercial data base. A third benefit is that outside computing services provide added capacity or backup. This benefit is particularly useful to a large firm that has fluctuating data processing loads.

Using outside computing services can create problems, however. Data security and accessibility may be weakened, since data records are turned over to an outside party. Outputs can be delayed, since outside services tend to require longer turnaround times. Also, processing costs can become excessive if transaction volumes continue to grow. Subscribing firms should therefore carefully monitor the use of outside services.

A hybrid type of outside service is provided by a **facilities management** firm, which manages the in-house computer facilities of a subscribing firm for a fee. This service can be helpful to a firm that desires to keep data processing operations under its roof, but that does not have the time or expertise to operate the information system.

Electronic Data Systems (EDS) Corporation, the largest information processing services firm in the United States, serves more than 4000 client firms. Its services include designing information systems, managing systems facilities, and providing data processing and bookkeeping services. General Motors Corporation, which owns EDS and is also its largest client, receives data processing and employee benefits services from EDS.[2]

Other Options When selecting a computer system, a firm should also consider the following options.

1. Should software packages be purchased from software products suppliers, or should the software be written by the firm's programmers?

2. Should a single mainframe computer be acquired, or should a variety of smaller computers be acquired?

3. Should the hardware and software be selected by the firm, or should the firm employ consultants to select and install the hardware and software? (If the latter option is chosen, the resulting system is called a **turnkey system.** All the acquiring firm needs to do is "turn the key" to start the system operating.)

Solicitation of Proposals

Most of the options listed involve suppliers of computer resources. In order to acquire the needed computer resources, a firm must inform suppliers of its needs and obtain responses from the suppliers. Since the needs can be rather involved and sometimes complex, a careful solicitation procedure should be employed.

The most important step in this procedure is to prepare a **request for proposal (RFP).** The purpose of an RFP is to portray to the suppliers the system that has been conceptually designed. A key portion of an RFP is a set of system (e.g.,

---

[2] "Up from Payroll: New Age for the Service Bureau," *Business Software Review* (Mar. 1988), 60.

hardware, software) specifications. These specifications are evolved from the design specifications, which in turn are based on the system requirements and information needs. Supplementing these specifications might be specimen source documents, report formats, record layouts, flowcharts, internal control matrices, transaction volumes, and so on. In addition, the RFP states the system support requirements that suppliers should meet. Support requirements might pertain to programming assistance, training programs, test facilities, and maintenance assistance.

A cover letter summarizes the contents of the RFP, lists critical constraints, and states the data to be provided by each supplier. Constraints might include the deadline date for the response and the ceiling on planned system expenditures. The data requested from each supplier should focus on how the supplier's hardware and/or software will satisfy the design specifications. Other data might consist of prices, existing users, expected delivery dates, electric power and other technical requirements, maintenance agreements, and so on.

With the RFP in hand, the requesting firm must decide which suppliers are to receive it. Since the available suppliers are numerous, some means of screening are necessary. Consultants can be engaged to aid in the screening process, or the firm can turn to catalogs or computer industry publications such as *Auerbach's Infotech Reports* or *Datapro Reports*. The objective is to locate those reputable suppliers whose products and/or services appear most capable of satisfying all the specifications in the RFP.

After narrowing the available suppliers to a manageable number—perhaps three to six—the requesting firm then mails the RFP. When the deadline date has passed, it begins the evaluation process.

Evaluation of Proposals

Each proposal from a supplier is first reviewed, in order to see that it responds directly to all specifications and requests. If a proposal is seriously deficient, it should be eliminated from further consideration.

The key evaluation step consists of applying proven techniques. Three such techniques are the benchmark problem, simulation model, and weighted-rating analysis.

Benchmark Problem Technique The **benchmark problem technique** is useful for showing how well proposed hardware or software can be expected to perform in typical circumstances. In evaluating hardware, a typical application program, such as an inventory updating program, is chosen as the benchmark problem. This program is run on the hardware of each supplier whose proposal is being evaluated. Times required to process a given test data set are compared. The specific hardware having the lowest time "wins" the benchmark test. If competing software packages are being evaluated, they are run on the same computer hardware.

Simulation Model Technique Although the benchmark problem technique deals with an important aspect of performance, it ignores many equally important considerations. A broader-based technique involves the use of a mathematical model that simulates the computer system. When "stepped through" simulated processing activities, the **simulation model technique** provides data concerning access times, response times, run times, throughputs, cost levels, and equipment utilization. It is particularly useful in evaluating real-time computer systems.

Weighted-Rating Analysis Technique Because the simulation model technique is expensive and overlooks key qualitative factors, a third technique has become dominant. The **weighted-rating analysis technique,** also known as point scoring, provides an inexpensive means of evaluating all factors relevant to computer resource selection.

Figure 16-6 shows a table of the type used in the weighted-rating analysis technique. Included in this table are factors pertaining to hardware, software, and support. Proposals from suppliers A and B are being compared. Weights have been assigned by the evaluators, based on their judgment concerning the relative importance of each factor. Raw scores are based on information gathered from the proposals and other sources. Weighted scores are computed by multiplying weights and raw scores. The weighted scores are totaled and compared.

		A's Proposal		B's Proposal	
Factor	Weight	Raw score	Weighted score	Raw score	Weighted score
Hardware					
Performance, e.g., response time	10	5	50	3	30
Compatibility with existing hardware and software	10	4	40	3	30
Modularity	5	3	15	4	20
Reliability	5	4	20	5	25
Ability to deliver on schedule	5	2	10	5	25
Special features, e.g., control features, security packages	5	5	25	3	15
Hardware subtotals	40		160		145
Software					
Range of capabilities	10	3	30	4	40
Efficiency in use	8	5	40	3	24
Ease in making changes	7	4	28	3	21
Advanced features, e.g., firmware	5	5	25	2	10
Software subtotals	30		123		95
Support					
Assistance, training, and documentation	5	2	10	5	25
Test arrangements	5	3	15	4	20
Backup facilities	5	3	15	5	25
Maintenance and service	7	3	21	5	35
Reputation, experience, and financial condition	8	3	24	5	40
Support subtotals	30		85		145
Totals	100		368		385

FIGURE 16-6 A weighted rating table for hardware and software selection.

The weighted-rating table can be modified to evaluate hardware alone or software alone. It may be used to compare as many proposals as desired. Its main drawback is that the evaluations are essentially subjective, since the weights and raw scores are assigned on the basis of judgment.

SYSTEMS IMPLEMENTATION

After the needed system resources are selected by the evaluation team, a report is prepared and presented to management. If approval is given to acquire the selected resources, the project then enters the implementation phase. Implementing a new information system design consists of three major steps: (1) performing preliminary actions, (2) executing activities leading to an operational system, and (3) conducting follow-up activities and evaluations.

Preliminary Actions

The implementation phase generally engages the efforts of many persons over a period that is much longer than the preceding phases combined. Frequently it entails considerable costs. Therefore, actions such as the following should be taken before beginning the actual implementation activities.

1. Establish plans and controls regarding the implementation activities. Plans should include cost budgets, time schedules, and work plans. Certain controls can be based on these plans. For instance, Gantt charts and network diagrams are often prepared to control the time dimension. They are described in a later section. Other controls might include progress review meetings and periodic exception reports.

2. Inform the managers and employees of the implementation project, including the expected impact on work units within the organization.

3. Reorganize the project team if desirable. Since the implementation phase requires managerial rather than technical skills, a new project leader may be appointed. A likely source from which to draw a new leader is the area being redesigned.

4. Negotiate contracts with the suppliers whose hardware and software have been selected. In order to avoid undesirable terms, an attorney should review the contracts before signing.

5. Carefully consider the impact of the project on the users, since human factors are at least as important as the mechanistic activities. The behavioral approaches described in Chapter 15 can and should be carried over into the implementation period.

Implementation Activities

The activities that take place during implementation vary widely from project to project. Also, the sequences in which the activities are executed cannot be

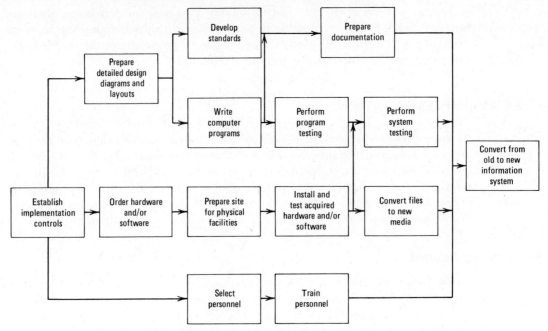

FIGURE 16-7 A network diagram of systems implementation activities.

standardized. Figure 16-7 presents a network diagram of typical activities and their sequences. It is the basis for the following discussion.

Personnel Selection and Training Often newly installed systems require added personnel. Preferably new personnel should be drawn from the present employee force. Current employees already understand the firm's objectives and operations, and the morale of all employees is enhanced by a fill-from-within policy. Also, the costs are less than hiring a person from outside the firm. However, in some cases no current employees have the required skills or expertise. For this reason, needed systems analysts are generally acquired from outside the firm.

Regardless of their sources, employees in new positions almost always require training. This training will relate to aspects of the new positions, including procedures, needed information, and computer devices. In the cases of persons acquired from outside, the training also will pertain to the firm's operations.

Physical Preparation Often the sites of the new system must be constructed or modified. Computer workstations may need to be installed, humidity control may need to be added, and so on. If possible, these physical preparations should be completed before the delivery dates of ordered computer hardware and other facilities.

Detailed System Design The conceptual system design is made operational by filling in a variety of details. If the new design is to be computer-based, these details will include precise record layouts, spacing-charted report formats, and computer programming instructions. Even when the software is acquired in packaged form, detailed changes are often necessary to tailor the packages to the firm's specific circumstances. The documentation employed in completing the detailed design, including logic diagrams, are discussed in a later section.

Program and System Testing All newly acquired software and hardware must be thoroughly tested so that errors and malfunctions can be spotted and eliminated. Computer programs that the firm writes require multiple tests. Programmers should first manually **"desk check"** each program by tracing through its logic. Then they should develop test data and execute the programs using these data. Results obtained with the test data should be compared to manually computed results. Computer hardware such as processors and terminals should be tested, usually in accordance with the manufacturers' procedures.

System testing consists of determining that the software are fully compatible with the hardware. Test programs and data may be used in this testing activity. Every system attribute, such as processing speeds and storage capacities, should be fully tested and compared to design specifications. Application programs should be linked together, as they would be expected to function in real operations, and **string tested.**

Standards Development Major system changes generally call for new standards. These standards may pertain to

1. System components, such as standardized data items and codes.

2. Performance, such as standardized employee productivity rates.

3. Documentation, such as standardized flowcharting techniques.

Documentation Although sometimes slighted, adequate documentation is an important implementation activity. It provides the basis for later system changes and aids new employees in performing their duties and responsibilities. Needed documentation includes narrative descriptions, program listings, test data, operating instructions, sample documents, report and file layouts, flowcharts, and other descriptive materials pertaining to the features and operations of the information system.

File Conversion Most system changes affect the files and data bases. Files are to be converted either from manual forms to computer-based forms, or from one computer medium to another. **File conversions** often involve such steps as (1) "cleaning up" the data items in the present files, (2) writing special programs to perform the actual data transfer, (3) physically transferring the data from the present files to the new storage medium, (4) reconciling the new files with the control totals of the old files, and (5) storing the old files as backup.

Final System Conversion The time when a newly designed system replaces a current system and becomes fully operational is known as the cutover point. Several approaches to cutover are available.

1. Under the **direct cutover approach,** cutover takes place as soon as all prior implementation activities are completed. This approach is quite risky and should only be used when a change is urgent.

2. Under the **parallel operation approach,** the new and present systems are operated side-by-side, and the resulting outputs (e.g., reports, account balances) are compared. If the results agree over a reasonable period (e.g., two or more operating cycles), the present system is abandoned. This approach is suitable when the outputs are not drastically changed in the new system (e.g., in a basic transaction processing system).

3. Under the **modular approach,** the new system is tested and converted in a modular or phased manner. For instance, a bank that has developed a new processing system may convert one branch at a time. A manufacturing firm that has developed a new data base may convert one data area (e.g., labor data, materials data) at a time. This approach is most suitable when the new system is significantly different from the present system and can reasonably be segmented.

Follow-up and Evaluation

Even though a new system is ready for operations, it should not be viewed as being in its final form. Typically it must undergo a "shakedown" period. Hidden quirks must be uncovered and ironed out. System components must be fine-tuned. Users must learn how to operate the system, even when unusual conditions occur. To assure that these results are achieved, certain members of the project team should be assigned as troubleshooters. They can observe operations, provide assistance, and make necessary adjustments.

Any necessary changes in programs, however, should be carefully controlled, since programs perform the processing steps in computer-based systems. Thus, they should follow the same authorization and review procedure as noted in the discussion regarding system development controls in Chapter 5.

After the new system has stabilized, the project should be evaluated. This **postimplementation evaluation** enables the information systems manager (1) to assess the degree to which the project objectives have been met, (2) to spot any additional modifications that might be needed, (3) to evaluate the project team's performance, and (4) to improve future systems developments.

PROJECT CONTROL TECHNIQUES

Two of the most widely used techniques for scheduling and controlling systems projects are Gantt charts and network diagrams.

Gantt Charts

A **Gantt chart** is a bar chart with a calendar scale. Figure 16-8 presents a Gantt chart that schedules seven major implementation activities. Each planned activity appears as a bar that marks the scheduled starting date, ending date, and dura-

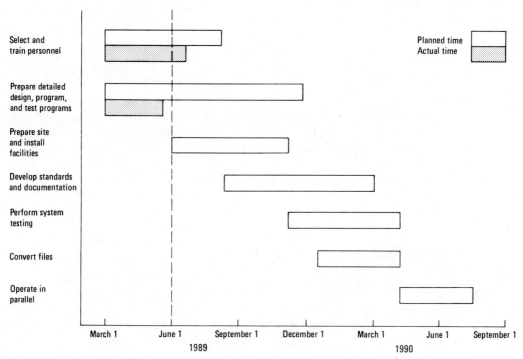

FIGURE 16-8 A Gantt chart of systems implementation activities.

tion. Below each planned activity bar appears a bar representing actual progress to date.

The appeal of a Gantt chart is that it clearly reflects the current status at a glance. For instance, if this is June 1 we can see that the activity labeled "select and train personnel" is ahead of schedule, whereas the activity labeled "test programs" is behind schedule. The major drawback of the chart is that it does not show relationships among the various activities. To overcome this deficiency, we must turn to network diagrams.

Network Diagrams

A **network diagram** reflects the relationships among the various activities encompassed by a project. It is constructed by a planner who has knowledge of the situation, since the durations of the activities and their relationships must be realistically estimated. Network diagrams are particularly useful for planning and controlling a large project which has hundreds of activities. Two analysis techniques that employ network diagrams are (1) Program Evaluation and Review Technique (PERT), and (2) Critical Path Method (CPM). Our discussion follows the terminology of PERT and the single-estimate approach of CPM.

Network Features Figure 16-9 presents a network diagram for a simple project. This example project is composed of nine activities, labeled A through J. If the project pertains to system implementation, the activities would be similar to those shown in the Gantt chart of Figure 16-8. The number of weeks appearing with

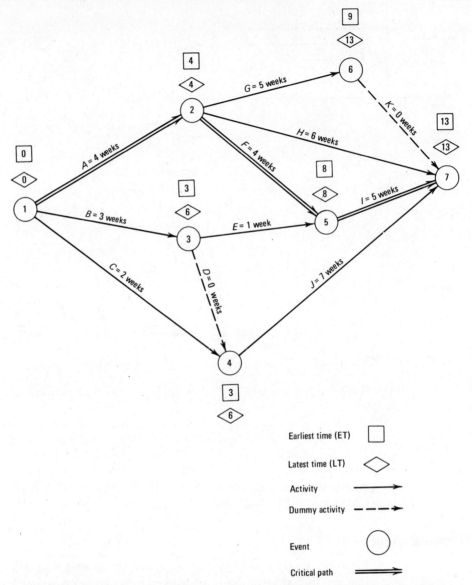

FIGURE 16-9 A network diagram of a simple project, with key values added.

each activity is the activity time. Activities D and K have zero weeks, since they are "dummy" activities. The circles containing numbers from 1 through 7 are events or milestones in time. Four paths can be traversed from event 1 to event 7: A–G–K, A–H, A–F–I, B–E–I, B–D–J, and C–J.

Three key resultants from a network diagram are

1. The overall project time (i.e., the time required to complete all activities within the project).

2. The critical path (i.e., the path which corresponds to the overall project time).

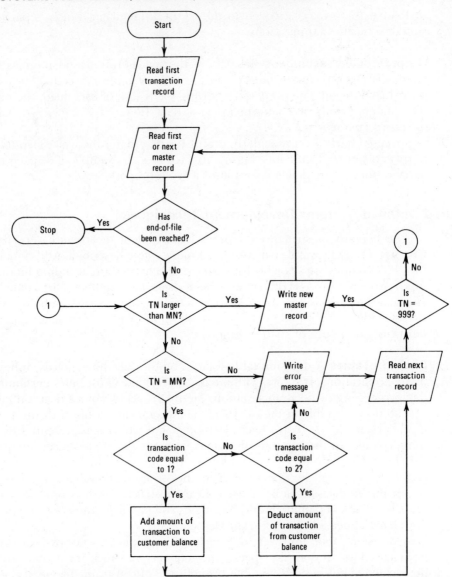

NOTE: TN refers to the customer number on a transaction record. MN refers to the customer number on a master record.

Processing step   Input or output step   Decision point   Terminal point

FIGURE 16-10 A program flowchart.

3. The slack times [i.e., the differences between the earliest time (ET) and latest time (LT)]. Slack times measure the extent of allowable delay for noncritical paths, since slack times along critical paths are zero.

Computations First the ETs are determined. They may be based either on events or activities; we choose the former. In our example most of the ETs are easily computed. However, when more than one path leads to an event, we need a rule for deciding which ET is correct. The rule is that the ET should always be the largest of the times required along the various paths. For instance, at event 5 the competing times are 8 weeks (along path A–F) and 4 weeks (along path B–E). Thus, 8 weeks is the correct ET.

After all ETs are computed, the overall project time can be determined. In the example it is 13 weeks.

The next step is to determine each LT. An LT for a particular event is the latest time that an event can take place without delaying the completion of the overall project. When more than one path leads from a particular event toward the terminal event (number 7 in our example), the proper LT is the smallest of the LT values for the respective paths. We begin by assigning the LT at the terminal event to be the overall project time (e.g., 13 weeks). Then we work backward to each event. For event 5, the LT is 13 weeks minus 5 weeks, or 8 weeks. For event 2, the LT is the smallest of 4 weeks (13 weeks minus 5 weeks minus 4 weeks along path F–I), 8 weeks (13 weeks minus 0 weeks minus 5 weeks along path G–K), and 7 weeks (13 weeks minus 6 weeks along path H).

After all ETs have been computed, the critical path becomes known. In the example, it is path A–F–I. Note that the ET and LT are equal (and hence the slack time is zero) for each event along this critical path.

The slack times now can be easily computed. For instance, the slack time along path B–E is 3 weeks, since the slack time at event 3 is 6 weeks minus 3 weeks.

Throughout the course of a project, the network diagram can provide effective control. It points to those activities that are behind schedule. By showing the paths where the slack times are the greatest, it suggests how resources may be shifted to hasten the project's completion. Packaged computer programs are available to assist in using network diagrams and keeping track of progress.

DETAILED SYSTEMS DESIGN

One of the more time-consuming and important system implementation activities consists of preparing the detailed design. Various data organization techniques are available to aid this activity. As in Chapter 15, we will divide our discussion of selected techniques between classical system development techniques and structured systems development techniques.

Most of the detailed design techniques are applied manually by systems analysts. However, certain techniques are being automated. For instance, software is available to aid in preparing flowcharts and developing data structures. Although automated systems development has lagged the development of hardware and applications software, we can expect to see great strides in this area during the next few years.

Classical Detailed Systems Development Techniques

Program Flowcharts A widely used classical technique is the **program flow-chart.** Figure 6-11 shows that program flowcharts are detailed "blowups" of system flowcharts. That is, a program flowchart provides details of the steps involved within a computer processing symbol of a system flowchart. It portrays the logical operations, arranged sequentially, to be performed by a computer when carrying out the instructions of a computer program. For instance, a program flowchart may show the details of the rectangular box in a system flowchart labeled "sort sales transaction records by customer number."

Program flowcharts may be prepared by means of only four standard symbols, which are connected by flowlines. Figure 16-10 shows a program flowchart and identifies the four symbols. The purpose of the depicted flowchart is essentially to specify the steps involved in updating an accounts receivable master file. If desired, more detail could be provided in a separate flowchart. For instance, the steps required to "write new master record" might be detailed. The more detailed flowchart would then be called a microprogram flowchart, whereas the flowchart in the figure would be called a macroprogram flowchart.

To understand the program flowchart in Figure 16-10, we need to know that the transaction file consists of a batch of records pertaining to sales transactions and cash receipts transactions. A record contains three data items: a transaction code (e.g., SL for a sale and CR for a cash receipt), a three-digit customer number, and the dollar amount of a transaction. The transaction records have been transcribed from source documents onto magnetic tape prior to the start of the flowcharted procedure. They have also been sorted in customer number order. The last record in the transaction file is a "dummy" record containing customer number 999. No record in the master file, which is considerably larger than a typical transaction file, is as large as 999.

The major steps in updating the master file are as follows.

1. Read transaction and master records.

2. Compare the customer numbers of the records.

3. If the customer numbers are equal, update the balance in the master record by adding (for a sale) or subtracting (for a cash receipt) the transaction amount.

4. When a master record has been updated by all the transactions having its customer number, then write the updated master record onto a new magnetic tape.

5. If the customer numbers for a transaction and master record are not equal, read new records until a match is found.

The flowchart also contains tests to determine when the files have been completely read and when an error has been made in recording data on the records.

Coding, or writing instructions composing a program, can be done by reference to the program flowcharts. For instance, a program based on the flowchart in Figure 16-10 may be coded in the COBOL language, which is particularly suited to business applications.

Other Detailed Techniques Records for the needed transaction and master files are described by record layouts. In the previous example a three-field transaction record layout would be prepared, showing the length of each field, the name of the data item contained, and the mode of data. (Figure 6-8 shows two examples of record layouts.)

Spacing charts are particularly useful for describing the exact layouts of reports and source documents. Figure 16-11 shows an example of a spacing chart used to portray the detailed format of a typical report.

Structured Detailed Systems Development Techniques

The benefits of structured systems development techniques were listed in Chapter 15, and several structured techniques were described. Additional structured techniques are available for detailed systems design, including hierarchical input process output (HIPO) diagrams, decision trees, bubble charts, data hierarchy diagrams, decision tables, Warnier-Orr diagrams, structured English, and pseudocode. Brief views of decision tables and Warnier-Orr diagrams should illustrate the nature of such techniques.

Decision Tables A **decision table** focuses on the "decision choices" inherent in many applications. It shows, within a matrix format, all the rules pertaining to a data processing or decision situation. Figure 16-12 presents a decision table.

The decision table in Figure 16-12 has several similarities with the program flowchart in Figure 16-10. Each decision point, which is represented by a diamond symbol in the program flowchart, appears as a separate condition in the decision table. Each processing and input/output step, which is represented by a rectangle or parallelogram symbol in the program flowchart, appears as an action in the decision table. Each logical construct, which is represented by a branch—a link of diamonds and rectangles and parallelograms—in the program flowchart, appears as a rule in the decision table.

A decision table, however, differs in two significant ways from a program flowchart. First, it does not specify the sequence in which the actions are to be performed. Thus, a decision table presents the unconstrained logic of the situation being portrayed. Second, its construction is based on mathematical principles. Thus, a "full" decision table consists of two rules, where R^2 is the number of independent conditions. A "collapsed" table (such as shown in Figure 16-12) is then developed by eliminating all redundant rules.

Consequently, a decision table can be described as a systematically constructed logic diagram of a decision-oriented situation. A decision table can easily be linked to other decision tables covering related situations; also it can be partitioned into a set of decision tables that provide more detail. Because of these features, a decision table qualifies as a structured technique.

Detailed decision tables are useful aids in designing structured computer programs. They are particularly helpful when the situation being programmed involves numerous conditional branches.

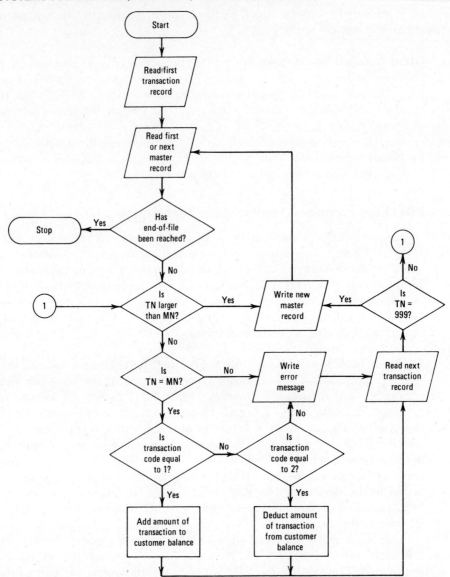

NOTE: TN refers to the customer number on a transaction record. MN refers to the customer number on a master record.

FIGURE 16-10 A program flowchart.

SHARE PRINT CHART   PROG. ID. _____   PAGE _____

(SPACING: 6 LINES PER INCH. DEPTH: 51 LINES)   DATE _____

PROGRAM TITLE _____

PROGRAMMER OR DOCUMENTALIST: _____

CHART TITLE _____

→ Fold back or dotted line

JOURNAL VOUCHER LISTING

FOR XX/XX/XX

J-V. NO.	ACCOUNT NUMBER	DR/CR	DESCRIPTION	DATE	AMOUNT
XXXX	XXX.X	XX	XXXXXXXXXXXXXXXXXXXXXX	XX/XX/XX	XXX,XXX,XXX.XX
XXXX	XXX.X	XX	XXXXXXXXXXXXXXXXXXXXXX	XX/XX/XX	XXX,XXX,XXX.XX
XXXX	XXX.X	XX	XXXXXXXXXXXXXXXXXXXXXX	XX/XX/XX	XXX,XXX,XXX.XX

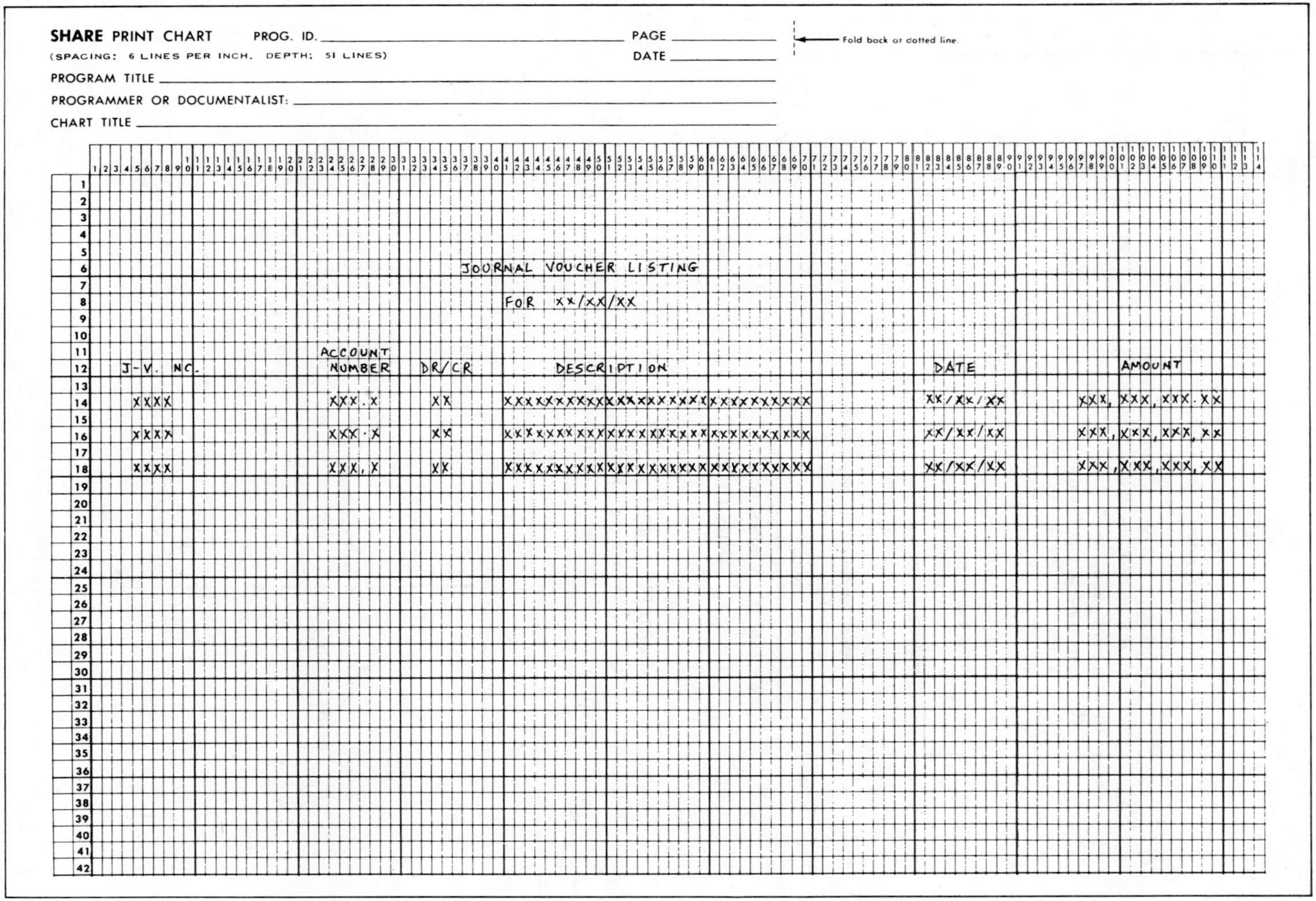

FIGURE 16-11 A report layout on a spacing chart.

		Rule					
	Condition	1	2	3	4	5	6
C1.	Has end-of-file indicator been reached?	N	N	N	N		Y
C2.	Is customer number on transaction record larger than number on master record?	Y	N	N	N		
C3.	Is customer number on transaction record equal to number on master record?		N	Y	Y		
C4.	Is transaction a sale?			Y			
C5.	Is transaction a payment?				Y		
C6.	Is customer number the dummy 999?		N	N	N	Y	
	Action						
A1.	Read transaction record.		X	X	X		
A2.	Read master record.	X				X	
A3.	Write new master record.	X				X	
A4.	Write error message.		X				
A5.	Add amount of transaction to customer balance.			X			
A6.	Deduct amount of transaction from customer balance.				X		
A7.	Stop processing.						X

NOTE: Y means yes, N means no.

FIGURE 16-12 A decision table.

Warnier-Orr Diagrams Jean-Dominique Warnier and Ken Orr developed a technique employing **Warnier-Orr diagrams**. These diagrams are used to represent in graphical format a processing sequence, a file structure, or the structure

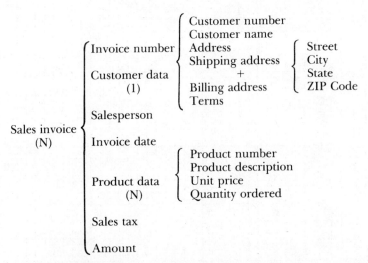

Note: (a) Number or letter in parentheses indicates the number of times the item occurs.
  (b) The + means that either or both of the items may appear.

FIGURE 16-13 A Warnier-Orr diagram of the data hierarchy within a sales invoice.

of a document or report. Hence, a Warnier-Orr diagram provides an alternative to a detailed hierarchy chart, a data hierarchy diagram, a HIPO diagram, and structured English.

Figure 16-13 displays the structure of a sales invoice. Each bracket indicates a grouping of data; as the brackets move to the right in the diagram, the data items become more detailed (i.e., at lower levels in the hierarchy).

Warnier-Orr diagrams provide easy-to-read data and processing documentation. They can be decomposed to very detailed levels. Hence, they are widely used to aid in writing structured computer programs. Their main drawback is that they are not well-suited for large-scale and data base oriented systems.

SUMMARY

Information is an economic resource. Information economics, the study of values and costs of information, states that added information should be gathered for any purpose as long as its value exceeds its costs. Relevant costs for determining economic feasibility include acquisition costs of new information system resources, costs of developing the system, and costs of operating and maintaining the new system. Benefits of a new system include tangible benefits, such as cost savings and revenue increases, and intangible benefits, such as better and more timely information. Computations for economic feasibility are based on methods involving net present value, payback period, and the benefit-cost ratio.

In selecting system hardware and software, options to be considered include purchasing versus leasing, single suppliers versus multiple suppliers, in-house systems versus outside computing services, packaged software versus software written inside the firm, and single mainframe computers versus multiple small computers. Proposals should be solicited from relevant suppliers of computer resources. Then these proposals should be evaluated, using such techniques as the benchmark problem, simulation model, and weighted-rating analysis.

Systems implementation begins with plans and controls being established, managers and employees being informed, and the project team being reorganized. Major activities include personnel selection and training, physical site preparation, detailed system design, program and system testing, standards development, documentation, file conversion, and final system conversion. An implemented system should be followed up and evaluated. Two project control techniques are Gantt charts and network diagrams. Detailed systems design may involve both (1) classical development techniques, such as program flowcharts, record layouts, and spacing charts, and (2) structured development techniques, such as decision tables and Warnier-Orr diagrams.

REFERENCES

Benjamin, Robert I. *Control of the Information System Development Cycle.* New York: Wiley, 1971.

Carroll, Archie B. "Behavioral Aspects of Developing Computer-based Information Systems." *Business Horizons* (Jan.–Feb. 1982), 42–51.

Egyhazy, Csaba J. "Technical Software Development Tools." *Journal of Systems Management* (Jan. 1985), 8–13.

Issacs, P. Brian. "Warnier-Orr Diagrams in Applying Structured Concepts." *Journal of Systems Management* (Oct. 1982), 28–32.

Kaplan, Robert S. "Must CIM Be Justified by Faith Alone?" *Harvard Business Review* (Mar.–Apr. 1986), 87–95.

Kiem, Robert T., and Janaro, Ralph. "Cost/Benefit Analysis of Management Information Systems." *Journal of Systems Management* (Sept. 1982), 20–25.

Ladd, Eldon. "How to Evaluate Financial Software." *Management Accounting* (Jan. 1985), 39–43.

London, Keith R. *Decision Tables.* Princeton, N.J.: Auerbach Publishers, 1972.

Martin, James, and McClure, Carma. *Structured Techniques for Computing.* Englewood Cliffs, N.J.: Prentice-Hall, 1985.

McFadden, Fred R., and Seever, James D. "Costs and Benefits of a Data Base System." *Harvard Business Review* (Jan.–Feb. 1978), 131–139.

Multinovich, J. S., and Vlahovich, Vladimir. "A Strategy for a Successful MIS/DSS Implementation." *Journal of Systems Management* (Aug. 1984), 8–15.

Sussman, Philip N. "Evaluating Decision Support Software." *Datamation* (Oct. 15, 1984), 171–172.

Vanecek, Michael. "Computer System Acquisition Planning." *Journal of Systems Management* (May 1984), 8–13.

QUESTIONS

1. What is the meaning of each of the following terms?

Information economics	Weighted-rating analysis technique
One-time cost	Desk check
Recurring cost	System testing
Tangible benefit	String testing
Intangible benefit	File conversion
Net present value	Direct cutover approach
Payback period	Parallel operation approach
Benefit-cost ratio	
Service bureau	Modular approach
Time-sharing service center	Postimplementation evaluation
Facilities management	Gantt chart
Turnkey system	Network diagram
Request for proposal (RFP)	Program flowchart
	Coding
Benchmark problem technique	Decision table
Simulation model technique	Warnier-Orr diagram

2. What are several alternative information system changes that involve the acquisition of computer resources?

3. Describe the information economics concepts that concern information and information system resources.

4. List several one-time and recurring costs in system development projects.

5. Contrast and identify tangible and intangible benefits in system developments.

6. What are the relevant factors in the net present value method?

7. Construct the computations under the net present value, payback period, and benefit-cost ratio methods.

8. What acquisition options are available to designers of information systems?

9. What are the benefits and drawbacks of outside computing services?

10. Describe the procedure for selecting computer hardware and software.

11. What should be included in an RFP?

12. Contrast the benchmark problem, simulation model, and weighted-rating analysis methods.

13. What are several preliminary actions that should be taken prior to the beginning of implementation activities?

14. Briefly describe several typical implementation activities.

15. Contrast the direct, parallel operation, and modular approaches to final system conversion.

16. What are the benefits of a postimplementation evaluation?

17. Contrast a Gantt chart and a project network diagram.

18. What are three resultants gained from a network diagram?

19. What are the similarities and differences between a program flowchart and decision table?

20. What are the uses of a Warnier-Orr diagram?

21. Discuss the respective contributions that a systems analyst and accountant can make in the procedure that determines whether or not an information system is feasible, as well as the desirability of having them closely coordinate their efforts during the procedure.

22. Contrast the benefits that can be expected from an improved purchases transaction processing system with those to be expected from an improved budgetary control system.

23. What criteria should apply in the selection of decision support software?

24. Does a firm ever complete the design and implementation of a new information system?

25. Discuss the hidden costs traceable to employee fears and uncertainties concerning a new information system.

26. A systems analyst has just developed a design for a new production information system. She is justly proud of the design, since it is innovative and well-structured. However, the production manager and his employees are very critical of the new system and refuse to use it properly. Discuss.

REVIEW PROBLEM

Precise Manufacturing Company, Second Installment

Statement

On April 30 the steering committee of the Precise Manufacturing Company approves the final feasibility report of the sales order processing and management project. The information systems manager then establishes the implementation period, which is to extend for a full 52 weeks. He divides the overall phase into such major activities as detailed design, training, and so

on. These activities are reflected in the network diagram shown at the bottom of this page. Activity times appear in parentheses after the activity labels and are stated in weeks. Events appear at the beginning and end of each activity, starting with event 1 and finishing with event 11. Event 11 marks the cutover point. By means of this network diagram, the project leader guides and controls the activities of her project team during the next year. The work of the project generally progresses in a smooth manner. Only one significant delay is encountered: the ordered hardware and software arrive a month late. Consequently, the equipment installation activity is not completed until October 25, approximately a month behind schedule. However, since adequate slack time is available, the overall project time is not lengthened.

Required

Verify the critical path shown in the network diagram and compute the slack times for the various events.

Solution

The critical path shown in the diagram is equal to the project time of 52 weeks, or the cumulative times of the activities along the path (3 + 16 +

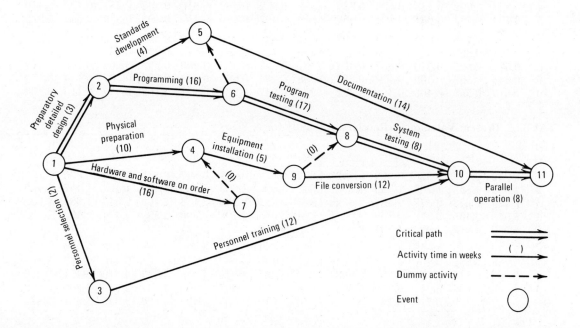

$17 + 8 + 8 = 52$). This total time is greater than the time along any other path from event 1 to event 11. For instance, the total time along path 1–2–5–11 is computed as $3 + 4 + 14 = 21$ weeks.

The "slack" times are as follows.

Event	ET (weeks)	LT (weeks)	Slack Time (weeks)
1	0	0	0
2	3	3	0
3	2	32	30
4	16	27	11
5	19	38	19
6	19	19	0
7	16	27	11
8	36	36	0
9	21	32	11
10	44	44	0
11	52	52	0

PROBLEMS

Note: When necessary for solving the following problems, refer to present value tables at the bottom of this page.

16-1. The Pence Company of Ellensburg, Washington, a local grower and distributor of produce, is investigating the economic feasibility of acquiring a small computer system to aid in processing transactions and providing information for managers.[3] It has gathered the following data.

Purchase price of hardware and software	$85,000

---

[3] This problem can be solved by using a microcomputer-based spreadsheet software package.

PRESENT VALUE TABLES

TABLE 1 Present Value of $1

Years	5%	6%	8%	10%	12%	14%	15%	16%	18%	20%	22%	24%	25%
1	0.952	0.943	0.926	0.909	0.893	0.877	0.870	0.862	0.847	0.833	0.820	0.806	0.800
2	0.907	0.890	0.857	0.826	0.797	0.769	0.756	0.743	0.718	0.694	0.672	0.650	0.640
3	0.864	0.840	0.794	0.751	0.712	0.675	0.658	0.641	0.609	0.579	0.551	0.524	0.512
4	0.823	0.792	0.735	0.683	0.636	0.592	0.572	0.552	0.516	0.482	0.451	0.423	0.410
5	0.784	0.747	0.681	0.621	0.567	0.519	0.497	0.476	0.437	0.402	0.370	0.341	0.328
6	0.746	0.705	0.630	0.564	0.507	0.456	0.432	0.410	0.370	0.335	0.303	0.275	0.262
7	0.711	0.665	0.583	0.513	0.452	0.400	0.376	0.354	0.314	0.279	0.249	0.222	0.210
8	0.677	0.627	0.540	0.467	0.404	0.351	0.327	0.305	0.266	0.233	0.204	0.179	0.168
9	0.645	0.592	0.500	0.424	0.361	0.308	0.284	0.263	0.225	0.194	0.167	0.144	0.134
10	0.614	0.558	0.463	0.386	0.322	0.270	0.247	0.227	0.191	0.162	0.137	0.116	0.107

TABLE 2 Present Value of $1 Received Annually for N Years

Years (N)	5%	6%	8%	10%	12%	14%	15%	16%	18%	20%	22%	24%	25%
1	0.952	0.943	0.926	0.909	0.893	0.877	0.870	0.862	0.847	0.833	0.820	0.806	0.800
2	1.859	1.833	1.783	1.736	1.690	1.647	1.626	1.605	1.566	1.528	1.492	1.457	1.440
3	2.723	2.673	2.577	2.487	2.402	2.322	2.283	2.246	2.174	2.106	2.042	1.981	1.952
4	3.546	3.465	3.312	3.169	3.037	2.914	2.855	2.798	2.690	2.589	2.494	2.404	2.362
5	4.330	4.212	3.993	3.791	3.605	3.433	3.352	3.274	3.127	2.991	2.864	2.745	2.689
6	5.076	4.917	4.623	4.355	4.111	3.889	3.784	3.685	3.498	3.326	3.167	3.020	2.951
7	5.786	5.582	5.206	4.868	4.564	4.288	4.160	4.039	3.812	3.605	3.416	3.242	3.161
8	6.463	6.210	5.747	5.335	4.968	4.639	4.487	4.344	4.078	3.837	3.619	3.421	3.329
9	7.108	6.802	6.247	5.759	5.328	4.946	4.772	4.607	4.303	4.031	3.786	3.566	3.463
10	7.722	7.360	6.710	6.145	5.650	5.216	5.019	4.833	4.494	4.192	3.923	3.682	3.571

Other one-time costs, such as
costs pertaining to design
and implementation $40,000

Annual savings in operating costs $38,000

Salvage value of the computer system
in five years $22,000

Salvage value of presently owned
processing devices $0

Expected economic life of the
computer system   5 years

Required after-tax rate of return   18 percent

Required

   a. Compute the net present value of the returns from the proposed investment in the
   computer system, ignoring the effects of
   taxes.

   b. Compute the payback period, ignoring the
   effects of taxes.

   c. Compute the benefit-cost ratio, ignoring the
   effects of taxes.

   d. Compute the net present value of the after-
   tax returns, assuming that (1) the marginal
   income tax rate is 34 percent, (2) all one-
   time costs are depreciated over the economic life according to the straight-line
   method, and (3) the book value of the presently owned processing devices is zero. Ignore the investment tax credit.

   e. Compute the payback period under the assumptions stated in **d.**

   f. Compute the benefit-cost ratio under the assumptions stated in **d.**

   g. Evaluate the economic feasibility of the proposed investment in the computer system,
   based on the results obtained in the preceding parts.

16-2. Newton Enterprises of Morgantown,
West Virginia, is considering the installation of a
new-model computer-based processing system to
replace the various accounting machines and ear-
lier-model computer equipment presently used
for processing.[4] The purchase price of the com-

_____
[4] This problem can be solved by using a microcomputer-based spreadsheet software package.

puter hardware and software is expected to total
$420,000, with an additional $100,000 required
for the analysis, design, and implementation of
the new system. The new system is expected to
have a six-year economic life, at the end of which
the resale value of the computer hardware is estimated to be $50,000.

   Annual operating and maintenance costs for
the present manual information system have av-
eraged $370,000 over the past two years and are
not expected to change in the foreseeable future.
By contrast, the operating costs of the proposed
computer-based system, if installed, would not be
expected to exceed $170,000 in each of the first
two years and $120,000 in each of the last four
years. In addition, maintenance expenses are expected to average $30,000 per year over the life
of the system.

   Management has specified that at least a 22
percent rate of return (after income taxes) must
be earned on all investments. The presently
owned processing equipment can be sold for
$25,000, its book value.

Required

   a. Compute the net present value of the returns from the proposed investment in the
   computer-based processing system, ignoring the effects of taxes.

   b. Compute the payback period, ignoring the
   effects of taxes.

   c. Compute the benefit-cost ratio, ignoring the
   effects of taxes.

   d. Compute the net present value of the after-
   tax returns, assuming that (1) the marginal
   income tax rate is 34 percent, and (2) all
   one-time costs are depreciated over the economic life according to the sum-of-years'-
   digits method. Ignore the investment tax
   credit.

   e. Compute the payback period under the assumptions stated in **d.**

   f. Compute the benefit-cost ratio under the assumptions stated in **d.**

   g. Evaluate the economic feasibility of the proposed investment in the computer-based
   processing system, based on the results obtained in the foregoing parts.

16-3. The I. M. Reliable Company of Hamilton, Ontario, sells bicycles through various retail outlets and handles its own parts inventory in one large warehouse.[5] Annual company sales exceed $3 million, with daily savings averaging more than $15,000. The company has experienced a recent overall growth of 5 percent and is projecting an annual growth of 10 percent.

The existing computer system for handling inventory is tape-oriented. It is being taxed to the limit of its capacity. Management believes that conversion to a modernized computer-based inventory control system will provide greater flexibility, speed, and continued growth potential. As a result, management authorizes a feasibility study.

As the analyst doing the study, you obtain data concerning the costs of the present system and projected costs for two new alternative systems, called A and B. (See the tables on this page and on page 595.)

Additional gathered data indicate that alternative A will provide for an eventual growth

greater than the 10 percent projection and would take 21 months to implement. Moreover, this alternative will provide updated status reports, automatic invoicing, and preprinted customer statements.

Alternative B will provide for the projected 10 percent growth only and requires redesigning if further growth is to be accommodated. Although this alternative will meet the basic requirements of the company, it will not allow interrelation of the various programs; that is, the output of one program cannot be used as input to another program.

Required

a. Compute the annual savings and the net cumulative annual savings of each alternative as compared to the costs of the current system.

b. Which alternative would you recommend to management? Discuss the intangible benefits; also describe other data that could aid you in developing your recommendation.

(SMAC adapted)

---

[5] This problem can be solved by using a microcomputer-based spreadsheet software package.

Current Costs

Type of Cost	Year 1	Year 2	Year 3	Year 4	Year 5
Personnel	$42,000	$55,000	$68,000	$80,000	$100,000
Equipment rentals	30,000	34,000	38,000	42,000	45,000
Supplies	20,000	22,000	24,000	26,000	28,000
Overhead	18,000	20,000	22,000	24,000	28,000
	$110,000	$131,000	$152,000	$172,000	$201,000

Alternative A

Type of Cost	Year 1	Year 2	Year 3	Year 4	Year 5
Systems development costs					
Systems design	$80,000	$10,000			
Programming	65,000	10,000			
Training	6,000				
Physical planning	4,000				
Conversion and test	5,000	8,000			
Recurring costs					
Personnel		30,000	$35,000	$40,000	$45,000
Rentals		30,000	33,000	36,000	39,000
Supplies		25,000	27,000	29,000	31,000
Overhead		20,000	25,000	30,000	35,000
	$160,000	$133,000	$120,000	$135,000	$150,000

Alternative B

Type of Cost	Year 1	Year 2	Year 3	Year 4	Year 5
Systems development costs					
Systems design	$30,000				
Programming	25,000				
Training	3,000				
Conversion and test	5,000				
Recurring costs					
Personnel	7,000	$30,000	$35,000	$40,000	$45,000
Rentals	5,000	22,000	25,000	28,000	31,000
Supplies	4,000	20,000	22,000	24,000	26,000
Overhead	3,000	12,000	17,000	22,000	27,000
	$82,000	$84,000	$99,000	$114,000	$129,000

16-4. The following are results of benchmark problems run on configurations A, B, and C.[6] The benchmark problems run on each configuration are representative sample workloads, which test for both input/output and internal processing capabilities of each configuration. The monthly rental, based on projected usage of at least 176 hours per month, is $30,000 for configuration A, $34,000 for configuration B, and $32,000 for configuration C.

BENCHMARK RESULTS: CPU TIMES (IN SECONDS) FOR COMPILATION AND EXECUTION OF DIFFERENT PROGRAMS

	Type of Problem		
Vendor	Process-Bound Problem	Input/Output–Bound Problem	Hybrid Problem
A	400.5	640	247.5
B	104.9	320	260.3
C	175.4	325	296.8

Required

a. Based on the three benchmark problems, which vendor's (supplier's) configuration is preferable?

b. Compute cost-effectiveness indices by dividing the total benchmark time of each configuration by that vendor's monthly payments. How do these computations affect the results?

----

[6] Adapted from John G. Burch and Gary Grudnitski, *Information Systems: Theory and Practice,* 4th ed. (New York: Wiley, 1986). Used with permission.

16-5. The Kenmore Company has determined that a new interactive computer system is economically feasible with respect to its accounting transaction processing applications.[7] It has requested and received proposals from three suppliers of hardware and software. The system evaluation team assigns the following weights and ratings to the relevant factors.

		Supplier		
Factor	Weight	X	Y	Z
Hardware performance	20	8	7	9
Software suitability	15	9	6	7
Hardware features	10	7	8	7
Software features	10	8	6	5
Overall price	15	7	9	8
Support by supplier	20	8	10	8
System reliability	10	10	9	10

Required

a. Compute the total evaluations of the suppliers, using the weighted-rating analysis technique, and explain the results.

b. Describe the uncertainties involved in using the data provided.

c. What other techniques might aid in making the final selection?

16-6. The Tootle Corporation of Newark, New Jersey, has decided to acquire a data base

----

[7] This problem can be solved by using a microcomputer-based spreadsheet software package.

Factor	Weight	Supplier		
		Able	Baker	Charlene
Ease of use	(12)	10	8	10
Compatibility to variety of hardware	(10)	7	9	8
Software support by supplier	(10)	7	10	8
Price of package	(9)	8	10	6
Reliability	(8)	9	6	10
Query language facility	(8)	8	9	8
Training provided by supplier	(6)	6	8	8
Performance	(6)	10	8	10
Documentation	(5)	5	9	7
Data definition facility	(5)	10	7	8
Reputation of supplier	(5)	8	8	10
Enhancements	(4)	7	5	9
Ease of installation	(4)	7	5	9
CODASYL compatibility	(4)	10	8	10
Flexibility to accommodate changes	(4)	5	6	8

management system.[8] After receiving proposals from three suppliers, the feasibility study team employs a weighted-rating analysis as its chief means of evaluation. In preparing to apply this evaluation technique, it assigns weights to the relevant factors to be considered and then rates each supplier on each of the factors on a scale from 1 to 10. The results are listed on the top of this page with the numbers in parentheses being the weights.

Required

Complete the weighted-rating analysis and explain the results.

16-7. Artists' Delights, Inc., of Lawrence, Kansas, is a manufacturer of paints, brushes, and other art supplies. Although the firm has prospered for a number of years because of its quality products, it currently is experiencing several problems. For instance, it is having difficulty in keeping its catalog up to date, in conducting low-cost and efficient production operations, in maintaining adequate inventories, and in making prompt deliveries of ordered goods. Since the president recognizes that most, if not all, of these problems are related to the firm's information system, he has authorized the director of infor-

mation systems to undertake a systems development investigation.

The director forms a steering committee, which in turn establishes several project areas. It assigns the highest priority to the inventory area and approves the organization of a project team. After analyzing inventory operations and management, the team recommends that a computer-based system be considered as a replacement for the present manual information and processing system. Upon the concurrence of the steering committee, a feasibility study then is undertaken. Based on costs and benefits developed during this study, a computer-based information system is found to be feasible.

At this point the steering committee asks the director to prepare plans that reflect the activities necessary to acquire a computer-based system and to put it into operation. If the plans appear reasonable, the steering committee likely will give its approval to proceed.

The director thus sits down and ponders. He is aware that the present information system has many deficiencies, including weak standards and documentation. He also recognizes that no one in the firm has experience with computers. Because of these deficiencies he intends to acquire well-documented software packages for the first applications to be implemented on the anticipated computer system. However, he does want to develop the programs for the other applications, which he hopes can be in process later this year.

---

[8] This problem can be solved by using a microcomputer-based spreadsheet software package.

Required

Prepare an appropriate list of implementation activities for the director to submit to the steering committee. Arrange the activities in approximate chronological order.

16-8. A savings and loan association has decided to undertake the development of an in-house computer system to replace the processing it currently purchases from a time-sharing service. The internal auditors have suggested that the systems development process be planned in accordance with the systems development life cycle concept.

The following nine items have been identified as major systems development activities that will have to be undertaken.

  a. System test.

  b. User specifications.

  c. Conversion.

  d. System planning study.

  e. Technical specifications.

  f. Postimplementation review.

  g. Implementation planning.

  h. User procedures and training.

  i. Programming.

Required

  a. Rearrange these nine items to reflect the sequence in which they should logically occur. If certain items would likely occur roughly at the same time, bracket those items.

  b. An item not included in the list is file conversion. List the key steps involved in this activity.

  c. Describe the results that the postimplementation review should achieve.

  d. Describe the ways that the three final system conversion approaches would be applied in this situation.

(CIA adapted)

16-9. Dorothy Sadfoss is a systems analyst for the Brookside Manufacturing Company of Boulder, Colorado. Since Dorothy is a hard-working and intelligent graduate of a nearby university, she was recently given a challenging assignment:

developing a new purchase-ordering system for the firm.

Having been exposed to the latest forecasting techniques (in a senior-level course she took two years ago), she decided that they should provide the foundation for her design of the purchasing system. Consequently, she developed a sophisticated ordering model that incorporated exponential smoothing forecasts, economic order quantities, quantity discount analysis, and supplier evaluation features. As a result, the system would automatically produce a purchase order that needed only to be approved by a buyer and the purchasing manager before being mailed to the supplier.

Upon presenting her new design to her superior and then to higher management, Dorothy was accorded a puzzled reception. However, after she pointed out such benefits as reduced inventory costs and fewer stock-outs, the reception became quite warm and approval was granted.

She then turned to the implementation of her new purchase ordering system. After writing the necessary programs and conducting extensive tests, she presented the system to the buyers at a special meeting. (The purchasing manager could not attend, since he was out of town. However, he had been informed the previous week by the president that the new system had the approval of top management and that he was to allow Dorothy complete freedom in putting the new system into effect.) At the meeting, several buyers were impressed, especially since the new system involved the use of computer terminals. A few buyers seemed a bit dubious, but Dorothy assured them of the benefits.

When the new system was completely installed, Dorothy met again with the buyers to explain the use of new forms and the sequence of steps necessary to operate the installed terminals. She also left some operating instructions, which she had written the previous weekend, consisting of about 20 typed pages. (She had meant to develop some diagrams and other instructional aids to show at the meeting, but the implementation schedule was rather tight and she did not have time.) At the end of the same day the president issued a bulletin in which he stated that the new system would require the services of one-half the current number of buyers. For the present all buyers would be kept; however, at the end of the month only those buyers who appeared to have adjusted most easily and enthusiastically to the new system would be kept in their positions. Others would be transferred to new positions (if available) and completely retrained in their duties or would be helped to find employment outside the firm.

Required

Discuss people-related problems caused by actions taken and not taken by Dorothy and the president during the development and implementation of the new purchase ordering system. Suggest specific steps which, if taken during this period, would have rendered the new system more operationally feasible.

16-10. Thrift-Mart, Inc., is a chain of convenience grocery stores in Washington, D.C. Elvira Jones, the development manager for the chain, has been assigned the project of finding a suitable building and establishing a new store. Her first step is to enumerate the specific activities to be completed and to estimate the time required for each activity.

Activity Designation	Description of Activity	Expected Activity Time (weeks)
1 to 2	Find building	4
2 to 3	Negotiate rental terms	2
3 to 4	Draft lease	5
2 to 5	Prepare store plans	4
5 to 6	Select and order fixtures	1
6 to 4	Accept delivery of fixtures	6
4 to 8	Install fixtures	3
5 to 7	Hire staff	5
7 to 8	Train staff	4
8 to 9	Receive inventory	3
9 to 10	Stock shelves	1

She then asks you to develop suitable planning and control mechanisms, based on the listed data. She tells you that the activity designations refer to the bounding events for each activity. For instance, event 1 refers to the beginning of the search for a building and event 2 refers to the completion of the search.

Required

a. Prepare a network diagram to aid in coordinating the activities.

b. Determine the overall project time and the critical path of the project.

c. Prepare a Gantt (bar) chart to monitor and control the progress of the 11 activities listed, assuming that the project will begin on March 1. Use the diagram prepared in **a** as a guide.

d. Verify that the ending date on the Gantt chart reconciles with the overall project time determined in **b.**

e. Elvira would like to finish the project two weeks earlier than the schedule indicates. She believes that she can persuade the fixture manufacturer to deliver the fixtures in four weeks instead of six weeks. Would this step achieve the objective of reducing the overall project time by two weeks?

f. The project cannot be implemented successfully unless the required resources are available as needed. What information does Elvira need to administer the project in addition to that shown by the diagrams prepared in the previous requirements?

(CMA adapted)

16-11. Whitson Company, of Vancouver, B.C., has just ordered a new computer for its financial information system. The present computer is fully utilized and no longer adequate for all the financial applications Whitson would like to implement. The present financial system applications must be modified before they can be run on the new computer. Additionally, new applications which Whitson would like to have developed and implemented have been identified and ranked according to priority.

Sam Rose, manager of data processing, is responsible for implementing the new computer system. Sam listed the specific activities which had to be completed and determined the estimated time to complete each activity. In addition, he prepared a network diagram to aid in the coordination of the activities. The activity list and the network diagram are presented on page 599.

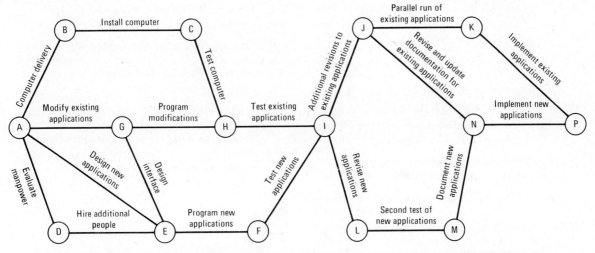

Activity	Description of Activity	Expected Time Required to Complete (in weeks)
AB	Wait for delivery of computer from manufacturer	8
BC	Install computer	2
CH	General test of computer	2
AD	Complete an evaluation of manpower requirements	2
DE	Hire additional programmers and operators	2
AG	Design modifications to existing applications	3
GH	Program modifications to existing applications	4
HI	Test modified applications on new computer	2
IJ	Revise existing applications as needed	2
JN	Revise and update documentation for existing applications as modified	2
JK	Run existing applications in parallel on new and old computers	2
KP	Implement existing applications as modified on the new computer	1
AE	Design new applications	8
GE	Design interface between existing and new applications	3
EF	Program new applications	6
FI	Test new applications on new computer	2
IL	Revise new applications as needed	3
LM	Conduct second test of new applications on new computer	2
MN	Prepare documentation for the new applications	3
NP	Implement new applications on the new computer	2

Required

a. Determine the number of weeks that will be required to implement fully Whitson Company's financial information system (i.e., both existing and new applications) on its new computer, and identify the activities that are critical to completing the project.

b. The term *slack time* is often used in conjunction with network analysis.

(1) Explain what is meant by slack time.

(2) Identify an activity which has slack time, and indicate the amount of slack time available for that activity.

c. Whitson Company's top management would like to reduce the time necessary to begin operation of the entire system.

(1) Which activities should Sam Rose attempt to reduce in order to implement the system sooner? Explain your answer.

(2) Discuss how Sam Rose might proceed to reduce the time of these activities.

d. The general accounting manager would like the existing financial information system applications to be modified and operational in 22 weeks. Determine the number of weeks that will be required to modify the existing financial information system applications and make them operational.

(CMA adapted)

16-12. The Greenspray Company of St. Johns, Newfoundland, is a retailer of fishing supplies. Recently it acquired a minicomputer system. One of the high-priority applications is to have a program that evaluates wholesalers from whom Greenspray might purchase supplies for resale. The criteria that the program is to apply are as follows.

a. A quality rating from 1 to 3 for each wholesaler; 1 represents the highest rating.

b. Percentage of times in the past each wholesaler has been late in delivering orders.

c. Whether each wholesaler's prices have been stable or unstable.

d. Whether each wholesaler is in an economically undepressed ("well-off") area or a depressed area.

e. Whether or not each wholesaler has suggested new products from time to time.

The decision rules according to which actions are to be applied by the program are as follows.

a. If the quality rating is 1, award the wholesaler 20 percent of the business.

b. If the quality rating is 2, and the wholesaler is not more than 10 percent late, award him 15 percent of the business.

c. If the quality rating is 2 and the wholesaler is more than 25 percent late, reject him.

d. If the quality rating is 2 and the wholesaler is between 10 and 25 percent late, award him 10 percent of the business, but only if prices have been stable.

e. If the quality rating is 3 and the wholesaler is not more than 5 percent late, award him 10 percent of the business, but only if he is in a depressed area and if he has been good at suggesting new products.

Required

a. Compute the total number of possible rules that would be listed within a "full" decision table of the limited entry form.

b. Prepare a "collapsed" decision table that shows the logic needed to write a program for the selection of wholesalers by the Greenspray Company.

(SMAC adapted)

16-13. The Snyder Company of Bethlehem, Pennsylvania, processes its payroll weekly by means of a computer-based processing system. Payroll transaction records are keyed from time cards to magnetic tape. Then they are processed to prepare paychecks, update the payroll master file, and print a payroll register.

The data items appearing in each transaction record consist of the transaction code, employee number, employee name, department number, pay category (hourly or salaried), and the hours worked (if an hourly employee).

The data items appearing in each record of the payroll master file consist of the employee number, employee name, social security number, department number, regular hourly wage (if an hourly employee), number of exemptions, other deduction factors, total gross earnings year-to-date, total deductions year-to-date (various), and total net pay year-to-date.

In addition to preparing the various outputs noted, the update processing program performs the following checks.

a. A field check on each numeric and alphabetic field on the transaction record.

b. A relationship check to see that the first digit

of the employee number agrees with the department number on the transaction record.

c. A relationship check to see that if the pay category code specifies a salary employee, there is no number appearing in the hours-worked field on the transaction record.

d. A limit check to see that the number of hours worked does not exceed 80.

e. A sequence check to see that the employee number on each succeeding transaction record is larger than the number on the previous record.

f. A sign check to see that the computed net pay is not negative.

g. A cross-footing balance check to see that gross pay less deductions equals net pay.

The processing program also

a. Prints all errors on an exception report (including multiple errors found in a single transaction record), together with identifying data for the erroneous transactions; then bypasses the erroneous transactions.

b. Accumulates a hash total on employee numbers, a quantity total on hours worked, and a record count of the transaction records (including erroneous transactions); prints the control totals on the exception report at the end of the processing run.

c. Lists erroneous transactions on a suspense tape.

d. Writes a new payroll master file on magnetic tape.

Required

a. Prepare a macroprogram flowchart of the update and paycheck preparation run using "Edit," "Pay Computation," "Net Pay Programmed Checks," and "Output" processing modules or subroutines. Assume that both transaction and master records have presumably been sorted in employee number sequence.

b. Prepare a microprogram flowchart of the "Edit" module.

PART V

ASSIGNMENT

CASES

CASE A

Wekender

Corporation

Wekender Corporation of San Diego owns and operates 15 large departmentalized retail hardware stores in major metropolitan areas of the southwestern United States. The stores carry a wide variety of merchandise, but the major thrust is toward the weekend "do-it-yourselfer." The company has been successful in this field, and the number of stores in the chain has almost doubled since 1983.

Each retail store acquires its merchandise from the company's centrally located warehouse. Consequently, the warehouse must maintain an up-to-date and well-stocked inventory to meet the demands of the individual stores.

The company wishes to hold its competitive position with similar-type stores of other companies in its marketing area. Therefore, Wekender Corporation must improve its purchasing and inventory procedures. The company's stores must have the proper goods to meet customer demand, and the warehouse, in turn, must have the goods available. The number of company stores, the number of inventory items carried, and the volume of business are all providing pressures to change from basically manual processing to computer-based processing procedures.

Top management has determined that the following items should have high priority in the new system.

a. Rapid ordering to replenish warehouse inventory stocks with as little delay as possible. (Approximately 2500 vendors are in the active list.)

b. Quick filling and shipping of merchandise to the stores. (This involves determining if sufficient stock exists.)

c. Some indication of inventory activity. (Approximately 1000 purchase orders are placed weekly.)

d. Perpetual records in order to determine quickly inventory level by item number. (Approximately 10,000 separate items of merchandise are active.)

Current warehousing and purchasing procedures are as follows. Stock is stored in bins and is located by an inventory number. The numbers generally are listed sequentially on the bins to facilitate locating items for shipment. However, this system frequently is not followed and, as a result, some items are difficult to locate.

Whenever a retail store needs merchandise, a three-part merchandise request form is completed. One copy is kept by the store and two copies are mailed to the warehouse the next day. If the merchandise requested is on hand, the goods are delivered to the store, accompanied by the third copy of the request. The second copy is filed at the warehouse.

If the quantity of goods on hand is not sufficient to fill the order, the warehouse sends the quantity available and notes the quantity shipped on the request form. Then a purchase memorandum for the shortage is prepared by the warehouse. At the end of each day, all the memos are sent to the purchasing department.

When the purchase memoranda are received from the warehouse, purchase orders are prepared. Vendor catalogs are used to select the best source for the requested goods, and the purchase order is prepared and mailed. Copies of the order are sent to the accounts payable department and the receiving area; one copy is retained in the purchasing department.

When ordered goods are received, they are checked at the receiving area, and a receiving report is prepared. One copy of the receiving report is retained at the receiving area, one is forwarded to the accounts payable department, and one is filed at the warehouse with the purchase memorandum (if a purchase memorandum had been prepared).

When the receiving report arrives in the accounts payable department, it is compared with the purchase order on file. Both documents are also compared with the vendor's invoice before payment is authorized.

The purchasing department strives periodically to evaluate the vendors for financial soundness, reliability, and trade relationships. However, because the volume of requests received from the warehouse is so great, this activity currently does not have a high priority.

Each week a report of the open purchase orders is prepared to determine if any action should be taken on overdue deliveries. This report is prepared manually by scanning the file of outstanding purchase orders.

REQUIRED

a. Describe a computer-based system that best suits the stated needs of Wekender's warehousing and purchasing procedures. Justify your choice.

b. Draw a hardware configuration diagram of the components needed in the described computer-based system. If a computer network has been selected, include needed data communications devices.

c. Draw system flowchart(s) that portray the processing procedures.

d. Draw the format of a merchandise request form.

e. Identify the needed files and data items within the records of the files.

f. Draw a record layout related to one of the master files.

g. Draw the formats of three useful managerial reports pertaining to warehousing and purchasing activities, and indicate the purpose of each report.

h. Devise a code for identifying inventory items.

i. List the general and application controls that would be appropriate for the described computer-based system.

j. Assume that Wekender Corporation decides to convert to the data base approach. (1) Specify the methods by which each of the identified files should be organized and accessed. (2) Describe and diagram useful data structures that might be formed from certain data fields and/or records within these files. (3) Specify several information-retrieval needs that could be aided by means of the noted data structures, such as the preparation of reports designed in **g**.

k. Prepare a cover letter for a system design proposal that includes the preceding required items as specifications. Assume any facts and values that would normally be contained in such a letter.

(CMA adapted)

CASE B

Microcomputer

Merchandise

Mart

STATEMENT

Background

Microcomputer Merchandise Mart (MMM) is a St. Louis merchandiser of microcomputers and related equipment. Among the products that it sells are video display terminals, printers, modems, hard disk drives, diskettes, and business software packages. The firm sells these products through retail stores that are located in shopping centers within the St. Louis metropolitan area. It also provides limited product service to customers, who consist primarily of small businesses, professionals, and other individuals.

Bill Princeton and Jill Harvard, two members of the sales force of a large microcomputer manufacturer, established MMM in 1980. They still own a significant portion of the outstanding stock of the firm. During its several years of existence MMM has done very well. Not only have sales grown fairly rapidly, but the product lines have been expanded and the employees have increased in number. This growth has occurred in spite of the fact that several new competitors have started operations in every year since 1980.

Currently, the firm handles five brands of microcomputers, as well as several brands of terminals, printers, and other peripherals. To sell these products, it maintains three retail stores, plus one warehouse attached to a main office. It employs 70 persons, ranging from the president to a janitor.

Organization and Functions

The president of MMM is Bill Princeton. Reporting to him are seven managers: Tod Dartmouth, Betsy Stanford, Bob Brown, Jack Yale, Paul Cornell, Jill Harvard, and Tom Carnegie. Tod is in charge of purchasing activities and supervises several buyers who specialize in the various product lines. Betsy oversees clerks and bookkeepers who process transactions and maintain the accounting records. Bob directs the operations of the several retail stores. Each store, together with its salespersons and clerks, is under the day-to-day control of a store manager. An assistant to Bob handles the advertising. Jack serves as administrative manager, with responsibilities for personnel, insurance, budgeting, cost analysis, and systems and procedures. Paul is in charge of servicing activities and the crew of servicepeople. Jill performs the duties of treasurer. Reporting to her is a credit manager, cashier, and finance clerks. Tom maintains the warehousing operations, which include receiving, storing, shipping, and customer delivery.

Operational and Financial Aspects

The company sells its products for cash or on credit. It has about 2000 credit customers. The firm acquires products for sale from 100 suppliers. In most cases, MMM receives a purchase discount from a supplier, if paid within 10 days, although in certain cases full payment is due in 30 days. Usually freight and sales tax are added to the invoices by suppliers. Most suppliers allow returns.

MMM maintains its cash in two bank accounts. There is one account for general funds and one for payrolls. The company also has petty cash and change drawer funds. Among the resources that it owns are the office building, warehouse, and retail stores; the land on which these buildings are located; the furniture and fixtures in each of the buildings; cash registers and other office equipment; and vehicles in the warehouse and vehicles for delivering ordered merchandise. All the buildings currently have mortgages that are being paid off, and certain vehicles are being financed by short-term notes.

MMM is capitalized as a corporation, solely by means of $100 par common stock. The stock was sold at a premium. It earns revenues by sales of microcomputers and other computer equipment, and by servicing the equipment. Most products are sold at established prices, but trade discounts are allowed on occasion to small businesses and professional firms. The firm allows returns and allowances within a specified period from the dates of sales. It does not finance any sales; instead, it refers customers to banks and consumer finance companies. It allows cash discounts on sales if paid in full within 10 days; otherwise, it expects full payment within 30 days.

The perpetual inventory method for recording purchases is employed by MMM. The firm prefers to record managerial salaries separate from clerical salaries and wages. Commissions are paid to the salespersons in the various retail stores. Other expenses include utilities, supplies, donations, dues and subscriptions, advertising, insurance, repairs and maintenance, in addition to those arising from credit sales and fixed assets and loan transactions. It prefers to provide separate expense accounts for major operating activities, although it groups all office-related expenses (e.g., accounting, credit) under the category of office expenses. It also records all purchase discounts lost as an expense.

Accounting Records

The following journals and ledgers are employed by MMM for processing transactions through the accounting cycle:

General journal.

Sales journal.

Purchases journal.

Cash receipts journal.

Cash disbursements journal.

Payroll register.

General ledger.

Accounts receivable subsidiary ledger.

Accounts payable subsidiary ledger.

All credit sales are entered in the sales journal. All purchases of merchandise, supplies, and fixed assets, plus all related expenses, are entered into the purchases journal. All checks, excluding paychecks, are entered in the cash disbursements journal. Paychecks, written on a payroll bank account, are entered in the payroll register. Amounts equal to the total payroll are written on the general bank account.

The accounting records are entered and posted manually. Betsy supervises the posting to the general ledger; she prepares and posts the adjusting journal entries herself. Then she prepares a trial balance and financial statements with the aid of an electronic spreadsheet package to compute key financial ratios and to print hard copy financial reports for the other managers.

Sales-related Procedures[1]

Sales orders are received by salespersons either in person or by phone. Customers may come into a retail store, see demonstrations, and select the preferred microcomputers and related equipment. Or they may visit several competing stores and call the salespersons when they have made their decisions. In some cases salespersons go to the premises of prospective customers and demonstrate the use of computers in their businesses or professions.

Regardless of how received, sales orders are recorded by salespersons on order forms. Three copies of each order are prepared—the original for the customer, the second copy for the salesperson, and the third copy for posting. If cash in full is paid by the customer at the time of the sale, his or her copy is marked paid, and the sale is rung up on a cash register. (The customer also receives the cash receipt tape.) If no cash or if only a partial payment (i.e., a deposit) is received at the time of the sale, the sale is treated as a credit sale.

Credit sales must be approved prior to processing by the salespersons, who initial the posting copy. After approval is granted for a sale, the posting copy is sent to the warehouse. There the ordered items are assembled and checked off the posting copy. Any out-of-stock items are noted on the copy. Then the assem-

---

[1] *Note:* Service procedures are excluded in this description.

bled goods are forwarded to the shipping department, together with the posting copy. The shipping department prepares the goods for shipment, completes a bill of lading, and ships the order. It also returns to the accounting department the posting copy, which has been marked to reflect the quantities actually shipped. In addition to the original bill of lading given to the carrier, one copy accompanies the goods and another is filed.

A billing clerk in the accounting department prepares a sales invoice from the posting copy. He or she refers to a pricing sheet in the preparation of the sales invoice. Then the clerk enters the sale in the sales journal. The original of the sales invoice is mailed to the customer, the second copy is sent to the credit manager, the third copy is sent to the warehouse to post the disposition of goods to the inventory ledger cards, and the fourth copy is given to a bookkeeper (together with the posting copy of the order) to post to the accounts receivable ledger records. After the accounts receivable ledger record is posted, the fourth copy is used by the bookkeeper to post to the general ledger; then each fourth copy of the invoice and the posting copy of the order are filed together by customer name.

If an order cannot be completely filled because there is an insufficient quantity of an item on hand, the warehouse clerk uses the copy of the sales invoice to prepare a back order and sends it to the purchasing manager.

The mail received each day is opened by the cashier. Each letter containing a cash remittance is set aside. After all mail is opened, the cashier verifies that each cash remittance is accompanied by the top portion of the sales invoice or by a letter stating the amount mailed. If a cash amount is unaccompanied, the cashier prepares a cash remittance advice. She then sends the pile of remittance notifications and advices to a bookkeeper for entry into the cash receipts journal, posting to the accounts receivable and general ledgers, and filing. Next she prepares a bank deposit slip, combining the cash received in the mail with the cash from the three cash registers of the retail stores for the previous day. She takes the deposit to the bank and returns with a bank-stamped duplicate deposit slip, which she files chronologically.

The cash received each day via the cash registers is checked at the end of the day by each store manager. He or she balances the amount received against the total shown on the cash register tape, using a cash sales summary sheet; he or she files the tape for possible future reference. Then the manager delivers the cash and summary sheet to the cashier at the main office by 9 A.M. the following morning. The cashier verifies that the total amount of cash agrees with the total shown on the summary sheet; then she adds the cash to the amount received by mail that day (as already noted). She files the summary sheets with the returned deposit slip.

Plans for Systems Development

During the past year MMM has become increasingly aware that it needs to modernize its information system. Not only are its clerks and bookkeepers having difficulty in processing the growing volume of transactions, but its physical operations and management are becoming less efficient and effective. For instance, it processes numerous back orders, thereby signifying that merchandise levels are not being adequately controlled. It often ships ordered products later than promised. Its budgets are often wildly unrealistic and its profit margins are shrinking.

Thus, MMM decides to develop a computer-based information system. Preliminary investigation indicates that the benefits from such a system will significantly exceed the expected costs. The first area that it decides to computerize is the revenue cycle and related decision support activities. Although the managers agree that they should not select the specific computer models until further development, they strongly believe that the system should employ microcomputers. An added advantage from developing such a system is that it can serve as the basis for demonstrations to potential customers who are also considering the computerization of their information systems.

Design Features for the New Computer-based Revenue System

In order to ensure that the new computer-based system is soundly designed, the president hires Mark Anders, an experienced information systems consultant from the St. Louis office of a large public accounting firm. After a careful analysis of the present revenue system and its problems, Mark proposes the following conceptual design.

Processing Steps The computer-based system is to utilize online entry and processing of sales-related transactions. Cash sales (in full or partial) will be entered via point-of-sale terminals, whereas credit sales will be entered by data entry clerks (in the sales department) based on sales order forms prepared by the salespersons. As in the present system, customers will receive receipts for cash, sales orders to acknowledge orders placed, and the ordered goods (together with packing slips). Salespersons also receive copies of system-generated sales orders. When the orders have been entered and edited, they are stored in an online sales order file and then processed to update the relevant files (i.e., sales file, merchandise inventory file, accounts receivable file, general ledger file). A picking order is generated for the warehouse, which assembles the ordered items and transmits to the shipping department. (Any items not available are placed on a back order, which is automatically generated when the merchandise inventory file shows the on-hand quantities to be less than the ordered quantities.) When the goods for an order are shipped, the shipping clerk enters the data, and a bill of lading and packing slip are generated; a shipping file is updated. Also, the computer system prepares a sales invoice for the customer and stores a copy in an online sales invoice file. At the end of each day, a program prints replenishment reports from the merchandise inventory file. These reports show the items (and related quantities) whose on-hand balances have fallen below pre-established minimum points for each of the retail stores. These reports are used by the warehouse to pick the needed items and to forward the items to the shipping department for delivery to the stores.

With respect to cash received through the mail in payment of accounts, the mailroom clerk daily endorses the checks received with restrictive endorsements and prepares a remittance listing of amounts received. These remittances, together with related batch totals, are entered by the clerk into a terminal. The receipts data are edited by the computer system and then posted to the accounts receivable master file. The mail clerk then forwards the cash to the cashier and the remittance advices to the accounts receivable bookkeeper. (Cash from the stores is delivered, together with the cash register receipt tapes, to the cashier at the end of each day.) The computer system prepares a deposit slip in duplicate, plus listings of customer account activity and the cash receipts journal. The cashier compares the checks and deposit slip and takes them to the bank. The bookkeeper compares the remittance advices, the activity listing, and the cash receipts journal; if they agree, the hard copies are filed chronologically and a copy of the journal is sent to the cashier. The computer system automatically updates the general ledger to reflect the total cash received and the reduction in the accounts receivable balance.

Data Entry The computer system will be programmed to provide assistance to clerks during data entry. When a clerk first accesses the system, a master menu appears. The clerk enters the appropriate number for the desired item from the menu. Then a preformatted screen display appears. The clerk enters data items onto the screen display, usually working from a previously completed form (e.g., a sales order form prepared by the salesperson or a remittance advice generated earlier by the system as a part of the sales invoice.) The entered data are edited by a program. If the clerk indicates that the data are acceptable (by responding with a YES when the system asks, "Are all entered data correct?" the system accepts the data for further processing and storage.

Data Base The files needed by MMM with respect to the revenue cycle include a sales transaction file, cash receipts transaction file, shipping file, accounts receivable master file, pricing file, general ledger file, open sales orders file, sales invoice file, deposit slip file, cash remittance file, merchandise inventory master file, and back order file.

These files will be included in a data base under the control of a data base management system (DBMS) of the network type. Records in the following files are to be linked because of associations that are relevant to the needs for operational and decision-making information: accounts receivable, merchandise inventory, cash receipts, sales, back order, general ledger, and sales invoice.

Controls and Security Measures Emphasis will be placed on controls and security measures. The procedures, for instance, include a sounder segregation of duties. A number of programmed checks will be employed. Clerks will be aided in the entry of data via the use of menus and preformatted screens. Security measures will be sufficiently comprehensive to assure the privacy and integrity of data and the protection of facilities and assets. Documentation will be thorough. A variety of application controls, in addition to programmed checks, will be incorporated into each of the transaction processing systems.

Auditing of the new computer-based system will involve approaches that trace transactions "around the computer," that examine the way edit programs handle a variety of input errors that are intentionally introduced via test transactions, and that aid the auditors in performing substantive tests of MMM's data inputs, outputs, and files.

Networking Features Because MMM has several retail stores, the design encompasses the use of a data communications network. This computer network will be relatively simple, but it requires a number of design choices (e.g., the type of network, type of configuration, and so on).

REQUIRED

    a. Prepare a description of the small computer industry, including the competition, markets, needed resource inputs, technological developments, and legal obligations.

    b. Prepare a diagram of the operational functions.

    c. Draw an organization chart.

    d. Design or obtain a source document pertaining to one of the basic transactions handled by the firm.

    e. Devise a coded chart of accounts that would be suitable for MMM. List all expense accounts under the categories "Operating Expenses" and "Nonoperating Expenses."

    f. Devise group coding structures that will accommodate revenue and expense transactions for MMM.

    g. Draw suitable formats for the purchases journal and the accounts payable subsidiary ledger.

    h. Prepare a segment of an internal control questionnaire for the revenue cycle.

    i. List the control weaknesses in the current procedure and recommend improvements.

    j. Complete the document system flowchart of the current sales and cash receipts procedure whose beginning appears on page 614.

    k. Draw a hardware configuration diagram that portrays the key components of the new computer system; ignore the data communications network devices.

    l. Prepare a system flowchart of the procedure for the proposed computer-based revenue cycle.

    m. Draw data entry screens that illustrate the use of (1) a menu for the revenue cycle, and (2) a preformatted screen display relating to the cash receipts transaction.

    n. Draw record layouts for the accounts receivable and the open sales order files, indicating the sequence of the data items, the length of each field, and the mode of data.

    o. Prepare a table that lists the storage medium, primary key, and organiza-

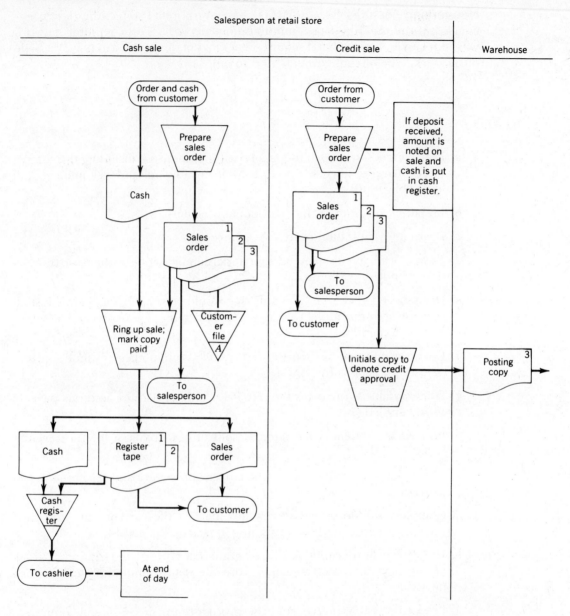

tion/access method for each file, assuming that the files are not physically linked.

p. Prepare a data structure diagram showing a network-type schema for the data and records needed in the revenue cycle of MMM; also, identify the subschemas needed for sales and cash receipts processing and reporting preparation. (Note that *all* identified files do not need to be included in the schema and subschemas.)

q. Prepare the logical views of several key relations needed in revenue cycle processing, assuming that a relational data base model is selected.

r. List several key decisions that must be made by MMM relative to product sales. Identify in each example the type of decision and the responsible manager.

s. Select a strategic decision and operational control decision from the list of key decisions. For each of these two decisions, identify the needed information and key properties.

t. List several reports that can aid managers in planning and controlling revenue-generating activities; describe the purpose of each.

u. Design the formats of two reports that will aid MMM in profit planning and control of key profit centers, respectively.

v. List the security measures needed with respect to MMM's revenue cycle.

w. List the application controls that are suitable for cash receipts transaction processing; also prepare a list of programmed edit checks that should be employed by an edit program for sales order entry, and indicate the fields of data being verified by each check.

x. Prepare a list of test transactions that may be performed during compliance testing of the sales transaction processing system.

y. Describe the uses of a GAS package in performing substantive tests of the sales transaction processing system.

z. Describe a suitable computer network for MMM, including type, configuration, communications line service, and grade of lines. Also draw a configuration diagram that portrays the described network.

CASE C

Grind

and Cast

Corporation

STATEMENT

The Grind and Cast Corporation of Las Vegas, Nevada, produces grinding balls and castings for use by mining and other heavy industries in the western United States. Although both products are manufactured in the same plant, the production process is quite different. Grinding balls are manufactured in a continuous high-volume process with a high degree of mechanization. Castings are manufactured in small numbers according to job orders and with a considerable amount of labor.

Although the firm is firmly established in the sales of grinding balls, it is still struggling with respect to the production and sales of castings. Production is inefficient and costly, cost estimates are quite inaccurate, and a high percentage of casting orders are shipped late.

It has become quite clear to the management of Grind and Cast that the production information system requires an extensive redesign. Better information is needed to aid in estimating costs, planning production, tracking castings as they flow through the production process, and controlling direct materials and labor costs.

After a thorough analysis of operations, as well as of benefits and costs, the management decides to install an online production information system that supports both operations and decision-making. Although the system will improve the production of grinding balls as well as castings, its principal focus will be on the latter.

Accordingly, a system is designed that begins with the online entry of each sales order as received. As each sales order is entered, it updates the customer's master file and adds a record to the castings job order file. At the end of each day, an open casting job order register is printed. At the beginning of each week the production planning department reviews the production schedule prepared the previous week and the five open casting job order registers for the previous week.

It then makes up a new production schedule and enters the schedule data into the system via its visual display terminal. The system then automatically prints a release-to-moulding work center report and a multipart job card. The multipart job card has a perforated section to show all needed information concerning the job.

Job cards are issued to the moulding work center on the date that production is to begin. The cards accompany the job as it moves through the various work centers. At the end of each day the work center supervisor writes onto the perforated section the quantity of good castings completed, the number scrapped, and the work center number; then he or she returns the section to the production planning department. At the beginning of the next day the production planning department enters the progress of each job via its terminal. Daily reports, showing production in each work center broken down by job number, are produced from these data.

The major files consist of

1. A *work center file*, showing for each work center the work center number and all jobs in progress, including quantities on hand and completed each day.

2. A castings *open job order file*, showing for each job the job order number, casting number, ordered quantity, order date, promised date, on-hand quantity, quantity scrapped, and priority code.

3. An *engineering file*, showing the details concerning each type of casting.

4. A *master schedule file*, showing for each job the job order number, casting number, ordered quantity, scheduled production date, estimated shipping date, quantities currently in all of the work centers (i.e., moulding, pouring, shake out, heat treat, finishing, and shipping), quantity scrapped, actual starting date, actual date moved to shipping, quantity shipped, actual shipping date, and price.

REQUIRED

a. Prepare system flowcharts to portray the online entry and processing of job orders through production, including the updating of all the previously listed files except the engineering file.

b. Design a data entry screen for the input of data concerning progress of production jobs at each work center.

c. Design the formats for the daily open order register and the daily production report by work center. Note that the former simply reflects the new job orders created during a particular day, whereas the content of the latter is described in the problem statement.

d. Assume that the designed system allows online inquiries. Design two screens that display information of interest concerning casting jobs.

e. Draw a record layout of the open job order file.

f. From the description of the files, it is apparent that certain files are closely related to others and that there are data redundancies. Sketch a diagram that shows a useful schema (i.e., a plan of data structures, or linkages among related types of records) for the casting production data base.

g. Devise a code for identifying raw materials.

h. List the general and application controls that would be appropriate for the new computer-based system, including programmed edit checks and fields of data verified by the checks.

CASE D

Delmo Inc.

Delmo Inc. of Harrisburg, Pennsylvania, is a wholesale distributor of automotive parts that serves customers in the states east of the Mississippi River. The company has grown during the last 25 years from a small regional distributorship to its present size.

The states are divided into eight separate territories in order to service Delmo customers adequately. Delmo salespersons regularly call on current and prospective customers in each of the territories. Delmo customers are of four general types.

a. Automotive parts stores.

b. Hardware stores with an automotive parts section.

c. Independent garage owners.

d. Buying groups for garages and service stations.

Because Delmo Inc. must stock such a large variety and quantity of automotive parts to accommodate its customers, the company acquired its own computer system very early and implemented an inventory control system first. Other applications, such as cash receipts and disbursements, sales analysis, accounts receivable, payroll, and accounts payable, have since been added.

Delmo's inventory control system comprises an integrated purchase ordering and perpetual inventory system. Each item of inventory is identified by an inventory code number; the code number identifies both the product line and the item itself. When the quantity on hand for an item falls below the specified stock level, a purchase order is automatically generated by the computer. The purchase order is sent to the vendor after approval by the purchasing manager. All receipts, issues, and returns are entered into the computer daily. A printout for all inventory items within product lines, showing receipts, issues, and current balances, is prepared weekly. Current status for a particular item carried in the inventory can be obtained daily if desired, however.

Sales orders are filled within 48 hours of receipt. Sales invoices are prepared by the computer the same day that the merchandise is shipped. At the end of each month, several reports are produced that summarize the monthly sales. The current month's and year-to-date sales by product line, territory, and customer class are compared to the same figures from the previous year. In addition, reports showing only the monthly figures for product line within territory and customer class within territory are prepared. In all cases the reports provide summarized data. In other words, detailed data such as sales by individual customers or products are not listed. Terms of 2/10, net 30 are standard for all of Delmo's customers.

Customers' accounts receivable are updated daily for sales, sales returns and allowances, and payments on account. Monthly statements are computer prepared and mailed following completion of entries for the last day of the month. Each Friday a schedule is prepared showing the total amount of accounts receivable outstanding by age—current accounts (0–30 days), slightly past-due accounts (31–90 days), and long-overdue accounts (over 90 days).

Delmo Inc. recently acquired Wenrock Company, a wholesale distributor of tools and light equipment. In addition to servicing the same type of customers as Delmo, Wenrock also sells to equipment rental shops. Wenrock's sales region is not so extensive as Delmo's, but the Delmo management has encouraged Wenrock to expand the distribution of its products to all of Delmo's sales territories.

Wenrock Company uses a computer service bureau to aid its accounting functions. For example, certain inventory activities are recorded by the service bureau. Each item carried by Wenrock is assigned a product code number that identifies the product and the product line. Data regarding shipments received from manufacturers, shipments to customers (sales), and any other physical inventory changes are delivered to the service bureau daily, and the service bureau updates Wenrock's inventory records. A weekly inventory listing showing beginning balance, receipts, issues, and ending balance for each item in the inventory is provided to Wenrock on Monday morning.

Wenrock furnishes the service bureau with information about each sale of merchandise to a customer. The service bureau prepares a five-part invoice and records the sale in its records. This processing is done at night, and all copies of each invoice are delivered to Wenrock the next morning. At the end of the month, the service bureau provides Wenrock with a sales report classified by product line showing the sales in units and dollars for each item sold. Wenrock's sales terms are 2/10, net 30.

The accounts receivable function is still handled by Wenrock's bookkeeper. Two copies of the invoice are mailed to the customer. Two of the remaining copies are filed—one numerically and the other alphabetically by customer. The alphabetic file represents the accounts receivable file. When a customer's payment is received, the invoice is marked "paid" and placed in a paid invoice file in alphabetic order. The bookkeeper mails monthly statements according to the following schedule:

10th of the month A–G

20th of the month H–O

30th of the month P–Z

The final copy of the invoice is included with the merchandise when it is shipped.

Wenrock has continued to use its present accounting system and supplies Delmo management with monthly financial information developed from this system. However, Delmo management is anxious to have Wenrock use Delmo's computer and information system because that would reduce accounting and computer costs, make the financial reports of Wenrock more useful to Delmo management, and provide Wenrock personnel with better information to manage the company.

At the time Delmo acquired Wenrock, it also hired a new marketing manager with experience in both product areas. The new manager wants Wenrock to organize its sales force using the same territorial distribution as Delmo, to facilitate the management of the two sales forces.

The new manager also believes that more useful sales information should be provided to individual salespersons and to the department. Although the monthly sales reports currently prepared provide adequate summary data, the manager would like additional details to aid the sales personnel.

REQUIRED

a. Identify and briefly describe the additional data Wenrock Company must collect and furnish in order to use the Delmo information system. Also identify the data, if any, currently accumulated by Wenrock that no longer will be needed because of the conversion to the Delmo system.

b. Devise codes for identifying inventory items and customers.

c. Design data entry screens for capturing data pertaining to the sales and cash receipts transactions, assuming that data are entered by the online method.

d. Draw suggested layouts of Delmo's inventory and accounts receivable master records, based on the descriptions of their uses in processing.

e. Based on the data currently available from the Delmo information system, what additional reports could be prepared that would be useful to the marketing manager and the individual salespersons? Briefly explain how each report would be useful to the sales personnel.

f. List the general and application controls that would be appropriate for the combined system, assuming that online processing is performed.

g. Largely because of the acquisition of Wenrock and the expansion of the overall sales territory, cash management has become an important concern to Delmo. The treasurer therefore needs a weekly report that estimates cash receipts for the following week. To develop the data for the report, he suggests that the timing of payments by credit customers against their accounts be monitored week by week. Other reporting needs have been recognized, such as sales analyses and the reports described in **e**. Thus, the president of Delmo is considering the desirability of implementing the data base approach. Describe, with the aid of a data structure diagram, a schema that spans the sales and cash management activities of Delmo. Identify three related reports whose preparation can be aided by the use of data structures in this schema, and illustrate their preparation by means of an example.

(CMA adapted)

CASE E

Browning

Companies

Browning Companies of El Paso, Texas, is a construction-oriented firm that provides a variety of products and services. The products include sand, gravel, aggregates, regular concrete, and ready-mix concrete. The services consist of constructing pavements, earthworks such as parks, concrete structures, and other projects.

Browning's organization is headed by a president. Reporting to him are a sales manager, treasurer, controller, chief engineer, administrative services manager, products manager, and construction manager. The products manager is responsible for manufacturing the various products, storing the products until ordered, and then transporting them to the points where needed. The construction manager is responsible for initiating and completing all construction projects. Lower-level managers and employees number about 1800.

Facilities consist of an office building, an adjacent crushing and sand plant, concrete batching plant, storage silos, maintenance shop, warehouse, processing equipment and devices (such as drag lines, wheel loaders, and conveyors), delivery trucks, construction vehicles, and other vehicles and equipment. In addition, the firm leases 18 offices for supervising construction activities in nearby Texas and New Mexico towns.

Processing and Dispatching

The raw materials are dredged from the Rio Grande River bottom, conveyed to the nearby plant, crushed, screened, mixed, and otherwise processed. Finished products are checked for quality and then stored until orders are received. Ordered products are then dispatched by trucks to the points where needed, which may be the locations of customers' facilities or the sites of construction projects. Most of the trucks are ready-mix concrete trucks which pour at the dispatched locations or sites. The diagram on the bottom of this page shows these operational functions, as well as the functions needed to support them.

Dispatching is performed by three dispatchers who prepare delivery tickets based on telephone calls received from customers, on sales orders taken by salespersons, or on requisitions received from construction supervisors. The next available truck is assigned to fill an order. If more than one truck is available in the dispatching area, the one that has been waiting the longest is assigned. Upon receiving his or her assignment, the driver is given two copies of the delivery ticket, which show the person to whom sold, the date, the truck number, and the quantity sold. The driver then loads at the warehouse or silo and gives the copies to a warehouse worker, who records the weight loaded on the tickets and returns a copy to the driver. After the load has been delivered, the driver initials the delivery ticket and returns the ticket to the dispatcher. The dispatcher then stamps the time of return on the delivery ticket. At the end of each week the tickets are delivered to the cost accounting department.

Certain problems in this dispatching procedure have been noted. Delivery tickets are sometimes lost. Customers on occasion dispute bills received for concrete and other products. Truck drivers tend to have excessive idle time on some days and to work overtime hours (with time-and-a-half pay) on other days. The times required to deliver loads to the same location tend to vary appreciably between truck drivers.

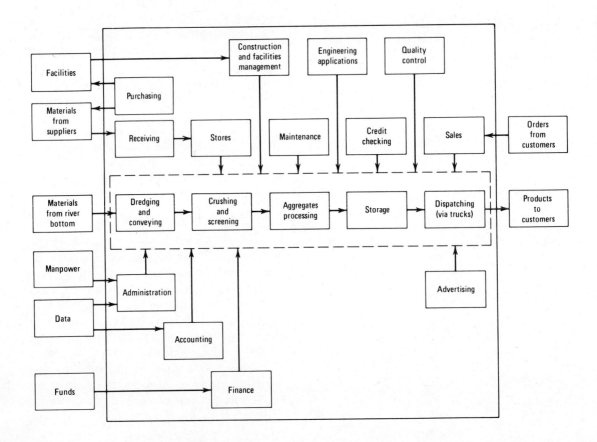

Timekeeping and Payroll

The timekeeping and payroll procedures relating to construction employees also exhibit significant weaknesses. One reason is that the firm acquired a couple of small contractors in recent years. It was forced to hurriedly blend their procedures with its own in order to pacify the employees. Another reason is that the firm converted the payroll procedure to a newly acquired computer system at about the same time. As a result, the timekeeping and payroll procedures are inefficient. During peak construction periods, the processing becomes such a bottleneck that other processing tasks are delayed for several days. Job costing is also delayed (as described in the next section), as are managerial reports pertaining to payroll and labor distribution.

The current timekeeping and payroll procedures pertaining to construction employees are as follows.

a. Time cards are forwarded from the various construction sites to the home office. Each card contains the employee number, hours worked, location code, and job order charge code. The time cards are batched by the payroll department according to location, and totals are computed on straight-time hours and overtime hours.

b. Batches are sent to the data processing department for keying to magnetic tape and for verifying.

c. After each batch of time transactions has been balanced against the predetermined batch totals, the tape is stored until the day for paycheck preparation.

d. On the day that paychecks are to be prepared, all magnetic tapes containing employee time data are merged by the computer operator and new batch totals are computed. Next the time transactions are sorted by employee number. Then they are processed against the payroll master file (consisting of earnings data), which is also maintained on magnetic tape. The first step in this processing is to check for invalid employee numbers. Transactions for which no master records can be matched are listed on an exception report and transferred to a suspense tape. After errors in transactions are corrected or needed records for new employees are added to the master file, the transactions are reprocessed against the payroll master file to confirm that all employee numbers in transactions match with those in master records.

e. After all employee numbers have been validated, the transactions are re-sorted by construction sites. Then they are processed against the employee master file (containing deductions data and pay rates, and likewise maintained on magnetic tape) to determine the gross pay, deduction amounts, and net pay for each employee. These amounts are printed on a payroll register.

f. The payroll register is returned to the payroll department, where its sheets are manually scanned by payroll clerks for unusual occurrences. The clerks look, for instance, for an employee who has worked more than 40 hours but whose pay line shows no overtime amount. They also verify that all new employees appear and terminated employees do not.

g. Necessary corrections are made to the payroll register, which is then returned to the data processing department. After correcting the erroneous transactions, the data processing department again processes the transaction data against the employee master file, this time to prepare the paychecks as well as to print the check register. Finally the paychecks are distributed.

h. Several days are allowed to elapse in order to allow time for errors in pay amounts and job charge codes to be reported by the construction offices. Then the data processing department makes necessary corrections, sorts copies of the paychecks by employee numbers, updates the payroll master file, and prints the year-to-date payroll report. Finally, it re-sorts the transaction data on the transaction file by job order charge codes and prepares labor distribution reports.

Job Costing

The purpose of the job costing procedure is to assign all appropriate costs to each construction job or project and to prepare desirable reports to management. Since one of the major categories of cost is labor cost, the job costing procedure suffers from the delays and inefficiencies of the time and payroll procedures. These delays in turn delay the billings for the respective jobs, since billings are based on costs incurred to date. In addition, the procedure does not provide suitable reports for managerial planning and control of construction activities.

As previously mentioned, the labor costs pertaining to job costing are obtained from labor distribution reports. The materials costs pertaining to Browning products are obtained from the dispatch tickets. Outside purchases of materials are obtained from disbursement vouchers, as are direct and purchased overhead items, such as supplies and utilities. Allocated costs, such as depreciation of construction vehicles and salaries of construction managers, are obtained from journal vouchers.

Disbursement vouchers and journal vouchers are processed in a manner akin to time records and payrolls. Thus, they are batched, stored on magnetic tape, and posted to the accounts payable and general ledger master files, respectively.

Reports relating to job costing are limited to periodic summaries of accumulated costs for the open jobs, final summaries of completed jobs, and listings of completed jobs for the current year.

Planning Prospects

Browning has been growing steadily in spite of the limitations of its accounting information system (AIS). In fact, it expects to expand its operations significantly during the next several years. It will very likely need to increase the capacity of its aggregate processing operations or to build a new plant. It also intends to bid on construction jobs in more distant locations, which will likely lead to the need for a larger truck fleet. Furthermore, it is considering the possibility of branching into new types of construction, such as shopping centers and motels.

In order to be successful in such new endeavors, Browning's management realizes that it needs to improve its planning, control, and data processing activities. Thus, the top managers meet to decide upon specific actions that should be taken.

REQUIRED

a. Specify various steps that are desirable for establishing sound planning and information systems development.

b. Describe the features of various financial planning models that could aid Browning in performing overall planning and in making specific decisions such as the manner in which to expand physical facilities.

c. Describe the architectures of two alternative computer networks that might be considered by Browning for improving the dispatching, payroll, and job costing procedures. Specify as many features of the architectures as feasible from the given facts.

d. Design a new timekeeping and payroll system, including (1) inputs, (2) outputs, (3) files, (4) processing steps and modes, and (5) key controls.

e. Design a new job costing system, including (1) inputs, (2) outputs, (3) files, (4) processing steps and modes, and (5) key controls.

f. Describe the main features of a new dispatching system.

g. Discuss the differences between the methods of costing construction jobs and the likely method of costing the products during the production process at the plant.

h. Specify the structures and features of a data base that integrates the three systems designed in **d**, **e**, and **f**. Assume that the data base employs the network model.

CASE F

Representative

Distributing

Company (RDC)[1]

[1] This case is designed for use in "hands-on" microcomputer assigned projects involving electronic spreadsheet and data base management system packages.

STATEMENT

The Representative Distributing Company (RDC) is a Phoenix wholesaler of office equipment. Among the 16 products that it distributes are desks, chairs, bookcases, tables, filing cabinets, sofas, and safes. The firm sells on credit to 30 Arizona customers, mainly retail office furniture and/or supply stores. It purchases the products on credit from 12 office furniture manufacturers. Terms of both sales and purchases are net invoice amount if paid within 30 days, or 2 percent discount if paid within 10 days of the invoice date.

The firm was founded in 1982 as a corporation by Jack Pollard, who serves as president and chairperson of the board. Other officers of the firm include a vice president, controller–treasurer, sales manager, purchasing manager, and distribution manager. All these managers, plus three outside directors, comprise the board of directors. All stock is owned by the directors. During its several years of operation the firm has grown steadily in sales volume. Although this growth has been funded in part by bond issues, it has mainly been supported by yearly net earnings. As the financial statements for the most recent year indicate, the firm's net earnings and current financial condition are generally satisfactory.

RDC operates from a single office building and adjacent warehouse, which are leased. Roughly a dozen employees (other than the managers listed) comprise the work force. All the employees are salaried. These employees use an accounting information system (AIS) which was computerized two years ago. At the heart of the system is a multitasking microcomputer. Attached online to this computer are four terminals, two printers, a 60-megabyte hard disk, and a tape cartridge backup storage unit. Among the available applications software are integrated accounting packages (e.g., general ledger, accounts receivable, accounts payable modules), an electronic spreadsheet package with graphics capabilities, and a relational data base management system (DBMS) package.

REQUIREMENTS PERTAINING TO A SPREADSHEET PACKAGE

a. Enter on a spreadsheet the financial statements listed on this page and on page 630; omit the dollar signs and commas within amounts, but include

Representative Distributing Company
Statement of Financial Position
As of December 31, 1988

ASSETS

Current Assets	
Cash	$ 2,960,000.00
Accounts Receivable	1,100,000.00
Merchandise Inventory	6,270,000.00
Supplies	150,000.00
Prepaid Expenses	820,000.00
Total Current Assets	$11,300,000.00
Fixed Assets	
Furniture and Fixtures (net of depreciation)	$ 2,720,000.00
Equipment (net of depreciation)	3,030,000.00
Delivery Vehicles (net of depreciation)	580,000.00
Total Fixed Assets	$ 6,330,000.00
Other Assets	$ 1,810,000.00
Total Assets	$19,440,000.00

LIABILITIES

Current Liabilities	
Accounts Payable	$ 1,620,000.00
Salaries and Wages Payable	380,000.00
Income Taxes Payable	1,570,000.00
Sales Taxes Payable	290,000.00
Other Accrued Payables	310,000.00
Total Current Liabilities	$ 4,170,000.00
Bonds Payable (2,000 bonds of $1,000 each @ 10%, due on December 31, 1998)	$ 2,000,000.00
Total Liabilities	$ 6,170,000.00

OWNERS' EQUITY

Capital Stock ($10 stated value, 800,000 shares authorized, issued, and outstanding)	$ 8,000,000.00
Additional Paid in Capital	400,000.00
Retained Earnings	4,870,000.00
Total Owner's Equity	$13,270,000.00
Total Equities	$19,440,000.00

Representative Distributing Company
Income Statement
For the Year Ended December 31, 1988

Net Sales	$27,400,000.00
Cost of Sales	14,200,000.00
Gross Margin	$13,200,000.00
Expenses	
Selling Expenses	$ 560,000.00
Warehousing and Shipping Expenses	2,800,000.00
Other Operating Expenses	1,340,000.00
Administrative Expenses	4,140,000.00
Nonoperating Expenses, including Interest	250,000.00
Total Expenses	$ 9,090,000.00
Net Income before Taxes	$ 4,110,000.00
Income Taxes	1,315,200.00
Net Income after Taxes	$ 2,794,800.00

the decimal points and cents. Print the entered financial statements, and then save them in a file (e.g., FIN).

b. Enter the heading "SELECTED FINANCIAL RATIOS" on the spreadsheet just below the financial statements. Then set up labels for the following ratios and enter on the spreadsheet appropriate formulas into cells within the G column.

(1) Current ratio.

(2) Return on net sales (where return is net income before taxes).

(3) Return on owners' equity (where return is net income after taxes).

(4) Return on total assets (where return is net income after taxes, plus bond interest times the complement of the tax rate).

(5) Average accounts receivable collection period.

(6) Debt/equity ratio (where debt is total liabilities, and equity is total owners' equity).

Print only the section of the spreadsheet showing the calculated results of the financial ratios. *Hint:* The formulas for the ratios should refer to the cells where the appropriate financial statement values reside. Also, expand column G on the spreadsheet to a width that can easily accommodate the formulas.

c. Print a display of the underlying formulas, including the spreadsheet border in the printout (if the spreadsheet package in use allows the border to be printed).

d. Develop a template for the income budget for the firm using the formula mode. The template should have the following heading:

REPRESENTATIVE DISTRIBUTING COMPANY
INCOME BUDGET
FOR THE NEXT TWO YEARS
(Thousands of Dollars)

ITEM   ESTIMATES

[   ] [   ]

Follow these procedures in developing the template:

(1) Use side headings that parallel the income statement already entered in **a.**

(2) Add this statement after the Net Sales item: Based on current sales of $____ . The ruled space following the dollar sign should occupy a specific cell, e.g., E14.

(3) Enter formulas to compute the value of each line item in the income statement for two years, and place these formulas in cells in two adjoining columns below the heading "Estimates" (e.g., columns G and H). In setting up formulas use cell references, such as the cell where the current sales value is located (e.g., E14).

(4) Derive the formulas from the assumptions listed in the Budget Assumption on this page.

(5) Save the template in a new file (e.g., BUDTEMP).

Hint: To save time in preparing the template, load the financial statements and copy the portion pertaining to the income statement side headings onto a new space on the worksheet.

Representative Distributing Company
Budget Assumptions

1. Net sales are expected to increase 10 percent each year over the sales of the previous year.

2. Cost of sales averages 55 percent of net sales.

3. Selling expenses average 3 percent of net sales.

4. Warehousing and shipping expenses average 8 percent of net sales, plus a fixed portion of $1 million.

5. Other operating expenses average 2 percent of net sales, plus a fixed portion of $800,000.

6. Administrative expenses are expected to average 13 percent of net sales, plus a fixed portion of $2 million.

7. Nonoperating expenses are expected to remain fixed at $250,000 per year for the foreseeable future.

8. Income taxes average 32 percent of net income before taxes.

e. Load the budget template and switch to the values mode. Then enter the two budget years (e.g., 1989 and 1990) in the brackets below the heading "ESTIMATES" and the current net sales value in the cell on the Net Sales line. If formulas have been correctly entered on the template, the two years of estimated values should promptly appear for all the income statement items through the Net Income After Taxes. Save the resulting budget in a new file (e.g., BUDG), with the values appearing in the integer display format or mode.

f. Reload the budget template. Assume that the value of current net sales is expected to increase by $3 million. Make this change on the budget template (i.e., perform this "what if") and observe the results. Save these results in a new file (e.g., BUDG2).

g. Reload the budget template. Switch to the formula mode. Then make changes in the formulas based on these revised assumptions.

(1) Net sales are expected to increase by only 3 percent each year over the sales of the previous year.

(2) The cost of sales is expected to average 60 percent of net sales for the next two years.

(3) The selling expenses are expected to rise to 5 percent of net sales for the next two years.

(4) The nonoperating expenses are expected to rise to a fixed level of $500,000 for the next two years.

After these changes are made, save the template in a new file (e.g., BUDREV). Then reload the file and enter the current net sales and two budget years (e.g., 1989 and 1990). Save the results as *integer* values in a new file (e.g., BUDG3).

h. Reload the revised template just saved in **g.** Now consider a "worst case"— an increase of cost of sales to 70 percent of net sales for the next two years. Make this change and recalculate the expected net incomes after taxes for the next two years. Do the values of net incomes and income taxes appear to be correct? If not, revise the template by modifying the formula for income taxes. This formula should include a logical function that has the IF–THEN format. Each statement in the function should be set off by commas (e.g., A,B,C, where A is an IF, B is a THEN, C is an ELSE). The statement for the first budget year should begin as: IF (G30 > 0 . . .), where G30 is assumed to be the cell on the Income Taxes line. For convenience, the logical function can be placed in another cell below the income budget (e.g., A38) and referenced by the cells on the Income Taxes line. After modifying the template by means of this logical function and saving the template in a new file (e.g., BUDWST), enter the current net sales and observe the results. Save the results as integer values in a new file (e.g., BUDG4).

i. Reload the original template (e.g., BUDTEMP). Change the side label pertaining to Net Sales to read Break-even Sales. Calculate on a separate sheet of paper the level of break-even sales for the first budget year, using the formula

Break-even sales = fixed expenses + variable expenses

where variable expenses equal the variable expense percentage times the break-even sales amount. Enter the calculated amount of break-even sales in the sales cell for the first budget year, and verify that the amount of net income is zero. Repeat the process for the second budget year. Save the results for the second year in a new file (e.g., BESALES).

j. Print each of the saved files. In the case of templates, include the border (if the spreadsheet package in use allows the border to be printed).

(1) Budget template named BUDTEMP in **d** (formula display format).

(2) Budget estimates named BUDG in **e** (integer display format).

(3) Budget estimates based on "what ifs" and named BUDG2 in **f** (integer display format).

(4) Revised budget template named BUDREV in **g** (formula display format).

(5) Budget estimates based on revised budget template and named BUDG3 in **g** (integer display format).

(6) "Worst case" budget template named BUDWST in **h** (formula display format).

(7) Budget estimates based on "worst case" budget template and named BUDG4 in **h** (integer display format).

(8) Break-even sales for the second budget year and named BESALES in **i** (integer display format).

k. Reload the file containing the original budget results (see **e**). View a simple bar graph of net sales for the two budget years. Use "Net Sales" as the main heading. Add labels for the time axis, but ignore labels for the y axis. Plot the graph.

l. Assign number 2 to the next graph, a stacked-bar graph of cost of sales, total expenses, and net income before taxes for the two budget years. Use a main heading of "MAJOR COMPONENTS OF SALES," which should be typed in a cell below the budget template before beginning the graph. Add time labels, but ignore labels for the y axis. Then plot the graph.

m. Assign number 3 to the next graph, an X–Y graph of NET SALES versus NET INCOME AFTER TAXES for the two budget years. Use a subheading that states, "In Thousands of Dollars." Use "Net Sales" as the x axis label and "Net Income after Taxes" as the y axis label. Use the actual years (e.g., 1989 and 1990) as point values. Plot the graph.

REQUIREMENTS PERTAINING TO A DATA BASE MANAGER PACKAGE

a. Review the background facts concerning RDC. Then examine the tables within the relational data base maintained by the firm on pages 635 and 636. Draw a data model that shows the relationships among these tables, based on the key data items shown for the tables.

b. Open a new data base called CUSTDB in the data base package that is available to you. Then establish the five tables described in **a** and enter the data they contain. Note that the table names and column names listed in the legend should be used for identification when storing the data.

c. Obtain printed outputs of the complete Sale table and Product table.

d. Obtain a printed output of these columns from the Customer table: CUSTNO, NAME, CITY, ZIP, CUSBAL. Sort the output by ZIP Codes.

e. Search the appropriate tables for the specified characteristics, and obtain printed outputs of the indicated columnar data.

(1) All customers who are located in Tempe, printing customer number, city, and current balance.

(2) All products for which the quantity on hand is less than 40 units, printing product number, description, and quantity.

(3) All sales made to customer number 1140, printing customer name and sales amount.

(4) All amounts received between July 1 and July 20 that were larger than $2000, printing the receipt number, date of receipt, and amount.

(5) All customers having a current balance in excess of $1000, printing customer name, Zip Code, and current balance (and sorted by Zip Code in ascending order).

f. Design a form, entitled PRODFORM, to be used in entering product-related data. Then enter the following data for a new product.

No. 72   SAFE, WALL

Cost: $310.00   Price: $428.00

Quantity on hand: 3 units

Obtain a printed copy of the product data entry form by entering a command that is provided by the software package you are using.

g. Design a report that is entitled "Inventory Valuation Report as of July 31" and that has a data base name of PRODRPT. This report has the following column headings:

Number   *Description*   *Unit Cost*   *Quantity on Hand*   *Valuation*

Legend

CUSTNO: customer number	CRELMT: credit limit
NAME: name of customer	CUSBAL: account balance
ADDRESS: address of customer	PRODNO: product number
CITY: city	DESCR: description of product
ZIP: Zip Code	SUPNO: supplier number
PHONE: telephone number	COST: unit cost of product

PRICE: unit price of product
QOH: quantity on hand
REGNO: cash receipt number
DATE: date of transaction
RECAMT: amount of cash receipt
SALENO: sale number
SALAMT: amount of sale

TABLE: CUST

CUSTNO	NAME	ADDRESS	CITY	STATE	ZIP	PHONE	CRELMT	CUSBAL
1010	BROWN'S OFFICE MART	109 W. YALE ST.	TEMPE	AZ	85282	967-0012	$5,000.00	$2,240.00
1015	SILVERFIELD FURNITURE	56 E. ARKWAY DR.	FLAGSTAFF	AZ	80071	921-5917	$7,000.00	$6,810.00
1020	THE FURNITURE SUPERSTORE	303 N. ROBSON AVE.	MESA	AZ	85201	969-1565	$3,000.00	$1,780.00
1025	MORTON'S FURNITURE	10 SPENCE RD.	TEMPE	AZ	85282	945-4888	$5,000.00	$800.00
1030	CROWN'S CASUAL FURNITURE	101 N. MCTELLIPS ST.	PHOENIX	AZ	85602	934-0114	$8,000.00	$1,500.00
1035	THE FURNITURE PLACE	1028 E. CAPTAIN DR.	GLENDALE	AZ	88001	991-8810	$6,500.00	$1,360.00
1050	THE FURNITURE WAREHOUSE	13 N. EXTENSION RD.	MESA	AZ	85202	834-8181	$7,000.00	$1,412.00
1055	DRIGHTON'S SECURITY SERVICES	89 E. TELLA DR.	SCOTTSDALE	AZ	85612	945-9601	$8,000.00	$2,370.00
1060	COSTLESS FURNITURES, INC.	1861 E. KELLA ST.	GLENDALE	AZ	87212	922-1867	$7,000.00	$2,300.00
1070	BUDGET FURNITURE STORE	161 N. 61ST ST.	MESA	AZ	85606	892-6001	$8,000.00	$0.00
1080	FURNITURE AND ETC., INC.	333 S. EVEN AVE.	CHANDLER	AZ	85230	963-2077	$8,000.00	$0.00
1085	THE FURNITURE GALLERIES	2200 N. GOODY DR.	SUN CITY	AZ	86621	861-6610	$9,000.00	$0.00
1090	THE CHAIR EXPERTS	593 E. BECK ST.	FLAGSTAFF	AZ	87321	952-3210	$5,000.00	$2,407.00
1095	THE SOFA CONNECTIONS	9321 HAITS ST.	PHOENIX	AZ	82891	933-6391	$7,000.00	$0.00
1105	THE BOOKCASE, INC.	1886 N. COLUMBUS ST.	MESA	AZ	85821	899-5122	$7,000.00	$0.00
1110	MITCHELL'S HOUSE OF LAMPS	1095 E. ELAY DR.	GLENDALE	AZ	85202	867-6243	$8,000.00	$0.00
1115	P & P FURNITURES	63 E. MEDIA ST.	PHOENIX	AZ	85321	956-7771	$6,000.00	$0.00
1120	A-1 FURNITURES, INC.	115 S. LOYD ST.	TEMPE	AZ	85281	967-7791	$5,000.00	$3,600.00
1130	REGESTER HOME FURNISHINGS	283 E. DADY ST.	TEMPE	AZ	85283	968-4425	$6,000.00	$0.00
1135	KIPPER'S BUSINESS INTERIORS	77 W. TOY DR.	PHOENIX	AZ	82503	861-6774	$5,000.00	$1,905.00
1140	THE SHOWROOM	1111 W. SHEILA DR.	SCOTTSDALE	AZ	86634	890-3335	$6,000.00	$2,335.00
1150	MESA FURNITURE SHOPPE	838 N. CONNELL WAY	MESA	AZ	83201	834-1551	$4,000.00	$0.00
1155	THE AFFORDABLE FURNITURES	1000 W. WARREN RD.	CHANDLER	AZ	85224	963-6161	$9,000.00	$2,800.00
1160	THE WOODWORK, INC.	2021 S. STELLAR PKWY.	CHANDLER	AZ	85224	963-2000	$7,000.00	$550.00
1165	RICHIE'S FURNITURE MART	5106 E. FALCON DR.	MESA	AZ	85205	981-3838	$5,000.00	$0.00
1170	RELIABLE OFFICE FURNISHINGS	40 E. BASELINE AVE.	MESA	AZ	85204	934-7799	$4,000.00	$3,310.00
1175	VALUE FURNITURE CO.	20 WILLIAMS RD.	MESA	AZ	85207	891-0001	$8,000.00	$560.00
1185	PST FURNITURE SHOWCASE	2107 E. FRYE RD.	SCOTTSDALE	AZ	86651	977-4321	$7,000.00	$850.00

TABLE: PRODUCT

PRODNO	DESCR	SUPNO	COST	PRICE	QOH
10	DESK, STANDARD	352	$170.00	$240.00	114
11	DESK, EXECUTIVE	366	$210.00	$295.00	30
20	CHAIR, STANDARD	354	$80.00	$113.00	140
21	CHAIR, EXECUTIVE	354	$156.00	$218.00	50
22	CHAIR, FOLDING	364	$40.00	$56.00	310
25	SOFA	362	$370.00	$520.00	25
30	TABLE, COMPUTER	370	$80.00	$112.00	47
31	TABLE, CONFERENCE	372	$350.00	$490.00	10
32	TABLE, FOLDING	364	$80.00	$114.00	169
40	LAMP, TABLE	360	$60.00	$84.00	90
41	LAMP, FLOOR	360	$80.00	$116.00	78
50	BOOK CASE	368	$98.00	$138.00	30
60	FILE CABINET, 4 DRAWER	356	$134.00	$188.00	60
61	FILE CABINET, 2 DRAWER	356	$65.00	$91.00	28
62	STORAGE CABINET	350	$120.00	$170.00	120
70	SAFE, FLOOR	358	$280.00	$395.00	12

TABLE: RECPT

RECNO	CUSTNO	DATE	RECAMT
3285	1160	07/04/89	$1,000.00
3286	1105	07/04/89	$4,200.00
3287	1025	07/10/89	$2,400.00
3288	1165	07/10/89	$1,780.00
3289	1150	07/12/89	$1,800.00
3290	1130	07/14/89	$2,000.00
3291	1095	07/17/89	$4,160.00
3292	1115	07/21/89	$2,360.00
3293	1070	07/24/89	$5,120.00
3294	1080	07/25/89	$1,000.00
3295	1110	07/28/89	$900.00
3296	1085	07/31/89	$4,200.00

TABLE: SALE

SALENO	CUSTNO	DATE	SALAMT
5109	1120	07/03/89	$3,600.00
5110	1035	07/04/89	$1,360.00
5111	1130	07/05/89	$2,000.00
5112	1095	07/07/89	$4,160.00
5113	1170	07/09/89	$3,310.00
5114	1115	07/11/89	$2,360.00
5115	1010	07/14/89	$2,240.00
5116	1140	07/17/89	$2,335.00
5117	1085	07/20/89	$7,200.00
5118	1055	07/24/89	$2,370.00
5119	1015	07/28/89	$6,810.00
5120	1155	07/31/89	$8,500.00

TABLE: PROD/SL

PRODNO	SALENO	QUAN
10	5109	15
62	5110	8
40	5111	10
41	5111	10
25	5112	8
20	5113	10
21	5113	10
11	5114	8
30	5115	20
60	5116	10
61	5116	5
10	5117	30
70	5118	6
50	5119	5
25	5119	8
31	5119	4
22	5120	50
32	5120	50

The valuation column is to be computed (by the software package) as the product of unit cost times quantity on hand. Also, include a footing section that shows the total valuation. Obtain a printed output of the report.

h. Use suitable commands to form new tables that can answer the following inquiries, and obtain a printed output of each table.

  (1) To which customers (by numbers and names) were sales made in July, and what were the dates and amounts of the sales?

  (2) Which products (by numbers and descriptions) were sold to which customers (by numbers and names) in July, and in what quantities?

  (3) To which Mesa customers (by names) were sales made in July, which products (by descriptions) did these customers buy, and what were the sales dates?

Appendix

Microcomputers

in Small

Businesses

INTRODUCTION

Microcomputers have invaded the business world. Millions are being acquired each year. In fact, microcomputers represent the fastest growing segment of the computer market. They have moved en masse into large and medium-sized firms, even though such firms may already have installed mainframe computers and/or minicomputers. In these firms the microcomputers may function either as stand-alone computers or as linked members of a computer network. Furthermore, microcomputers are extending the computer revolution to numerous small businesses, professional organizations, and homesteads.

Accountants, among others in the business world, are feeling the tremendous impact of microcomputers. These efficient and powerful machines expand the capacity of accountants and other professionals to handle complex undertakings. They reduce the necessity for time-consuming, repetitive, and mind-numbing operations. Thus, it is not surprising that new applications for microcomputers are being discovered every day.

Benefits and Drawbacks

Microcomputers provide four major benefits, especially in comparison with the mainframe and minicomputers used by larger firms:

1. Low cost of acquisition and maintenance.

2. Control by individual users, such as managers and key employees.

3. Versatility that enables a wide range of information processing needs to be met.

4. Ease of use by nonprogrammers and others new to computer technology.

As might be expected, microcomputers also have disadvantages. From the point of view of users, their technology is changing so rapidly that by the time one model has been mastered, another has taken its place. From the point of view of larger firms, microcomputers are difficult to control and to incorporate into networks effectively. For instance, unauthorized persons have often been able to gain access to corporate data bases via networked microcomputers.

Types of Microcomputers

Microcomputers may be classified according to size, use, and method of handling inputs. However, we should note that these classification schemes overlap, and the types within each scheme tend to blur.

With respect to size, microcomputers range in both directions from the standard model. At the small end are the **portable computers,** which vary from suitcase models weighing 20 lbs to handheld models weighing less than 2 lbs. Portable computers generally have a **liquid crystal display (LCD)** instead of the more common cathode ray tube (CRT) screen. At the other end are the supermicrocomputers, which in effect are small minicomputers. They provide greater primary storage capacity, word size, and processing speed than the standard microcomputer models.

With respect to use, microcomputers can be employed in a wide variety of applications and situations. They may be assigned to business applications such as general ledger accounting or to engineering applications such as product design. They may be employed as the sole computer within a small business firm or as a member of a network of computers within a large government agency. Most microcomputers currently in use are **dedicated** to a single task at a time. For instance, a particular microcomputer in a small firm may be used to handle sales orders during the morning and then to prepare the payroll that afternoon. Some microcomputers being installed in firms, however, enable more than one task to be performed at a time. In other words, they function in a multitasking mode. Figure A-1 shows a **multi-tasking microcomputer** system to which 10 video display terminals and two printers are connected.

A third classification plan is according to the way inputs are handled. In **operator-oriented microcomputer systems** the transactions are en-

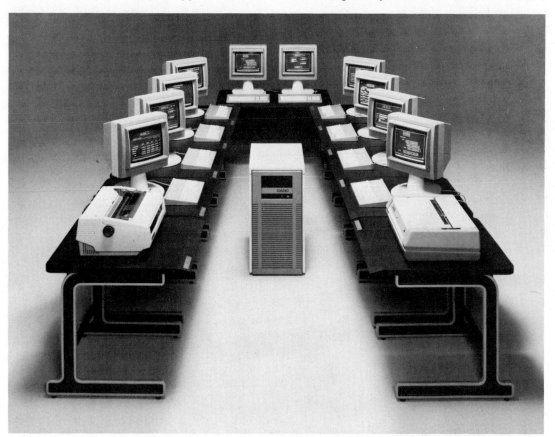

FIGURE A-1 A multitasking microcomputer system. Copyright © 1987 by Contel Business Systems.

tered manually by clerks through the keyboards or other devices. Each transaction is edited and processed completely before the next transaction is entered. Many operator-oriented microcomputer systems employ video display terminals for data entry. These terminals may be specialized to accommodate certain types of tasks, such as the small accounting computer system (portrayed in Figure A-2) which handles postings to accounts receivable ledger cards. A **file-oriented microcomputer system,** in contrast, feeds batches of data into the system via devices such as optical scanners or magnetic tapes. Thus, data entry is essentially under the control of the system itself.

The remainder of this appendix surveys microcomputer hardware, software, and application packages, plus the selection and installation of microcomputer systems. Although the survey pertains to microcomputers in large as well as small firms, most of the examples pertain to small business firms and professional organizations.

HARDWARE

The most commonly encountered components in current microcomputer systems are pictured in Figure A-3. A keyboard is the input device, a printer is the output device for hard copy, and a CRT screen is the output device for soft copy. The unit to the left of the user contains the microprocessor. Although you have probably used these hardware components in previous courses, we should review their functions and key features. We will also explore varied types of input/output devices, secondary storage media, and communications units.

Microprocessor

To paraphrase a comment in Chapter 3, the **microprocessor** is the heart of a microcomputer. Like the processor for a mainframe computer or minicomputer, a microprocessor incorporates three units. Certain features, however, are unique to a microprocessor. Physically it resembles a single chip, which may measure less than an inch wide and several inches long. This chip, usually made of silicon, contains several hundred thousand logic gates that perform the control and arithmetic-logic functions. It also contains registers that store small quantities of data for very fast access. Accompanying the chip are primary or main memory chips containing both random access memory (RAM) and read-only memory (ROM).

FIGURE A-2 A small accounting computer system. Courtesy of © Monroe Systems of Business, Inc.

FIGURE A-3 Components of a microcomputer system in action. Courtesy of International Business Machine Corporation.

The microprocessor chip and memory modules are mounted on a main circuit board, often called a **motherboard.** Attached to this motherboard via a bus bar will likely be a disk controller, a **serial interface** (i.e., a communications link), a **parallel interface** (i.e., a printer and plotter link), an expansion slot for **add-in memory boards,** and other assorted devices such as terminal keyboards, timers, and oscillators. Furthermore, various enhancement devices can be plugged into provided slots, such as an accelerator card, a clock/calendar, a graphics board, and a voice synthesizer. The **accelerator card** increases the processing speed, the **clock/calendar** keeps track of the time and day, the **graphics board** allows the presentation of graphical displays on the screen, and the **voice synthesizer** enables the microcomputer to provide oral responses.

Being smaller and less sophisticated than their larger cousins, microcomputers process at slower speeds, handle smaller words of data, and store smaller quantities of data in their primary memo-ries. As of 1988 the typical microcomputer processed about a million instruction cycles per second, employed a word size of 16 bits, and provided at least 640 K (thousands of bytes, or kilobytes) of RAM. By 1990 microcomputers should process tens of millions of instruction cycles per second, employ word sizes of 32 bits, and maintain 10 M (millions of bytes, or megabytes) bytes of RAM.

Input/Output Devices

Data are typically entered into microcomputers by means of keyboards. Although key entry is slow, it has the advantage of allowing human users to interact directly with the microcomputer and the software that it executes. Also, current keyboard models include such features as 10-key numeric pads and special-function keys.

In addition to the keyboard, a variety of specialized input devices are now available for microcomputers. A hand-operated **mouse** allows users to point to and manipulate objects on the CRT screen. For instance, they can be used to open documents and files and to edit them easily and quickly. A **joystick** performs similar functions. A **light pen** allows users to draw lines and shapes on the screen. An **optical scanner** allows users to enter data by scanning bar and other character codes. A **voice input device** allows users to enter data in the form of speech. A **touch input device** allows users to enter data (or instructions) by touching the CRT screen. Figure A-4 shows a terminal that allows inputs from a mouse as well as a keyboard.

Outputs from microcomputer systems are most often provided on CRT screens and by means of printers. The CRT screens display soft copy outputs, such as the graph shown in Figure A-4. If color display and graphics adapter cards have been added to the motherboard, the graphs would appear in color. Printers provide hard copy outputs on paper. Although printers are relatively expensive components in microcomputer systems, they are indispensible in today's paper-trail business world.

Three major types of printers used with the microcomputer systems are dot-matrix, daisy-wheel, and laser printers. The **dot-matrix printer** provides relatively high-speed printing (e.g., 100 to 900 characters per second) at the most reasonable cost. Printer characters from dot-matrix printers are lower in quality than those from the other types of printers, since the characters are formed of closely spaced tiny dots. However, the quality has been improving, since manufacturers have generally moved to the 24-pin printheads. The **daisy-wheel printer** produces letter-quality printing that is as sharp as that provided by the more expensive typewriters. It derives its name from print wheels that resemble daisies with petals radiating from a central hub. These print wheels may be changed very quickly to provide different typefaces as desired. The drawback of the daisy-wheel printer is the relatively slow rate (i.e., 30 to 60 characters per second) at which it types. The **laser printer** is a nonimpact printer that incorporates a laser device, a photosensitive drum, and a paper-handling mechanism. The printer operates by shining short bursts from a laser beam onto the drum, which thereby becomes sensitized. Next the drum is rotated through a toner bath to pick up the ink (toner) on the sensitized areas. This ink is

FIGURE A-4 A CRT terminal that allows data or commands to be entered via a mouse. Courtesy of Hewlett-Packard.

then transferred to paper moving under the drum. A laser printer produces high-quality printing at relatively high rates of speed (e.g., 8 pages per minute). However, it is considerably more expensive than the other types of printers.

Secondary Storage Media

The magnetic disk is the most widely used secondary storage medium. A disk controller allows a microcomputer to employ one or more disk drives, on which magnetic disks rotate. Two types of rotating magnetic disks are diskettes and hard disks.

The **diskette,** or floppy disk, consists of a circular piece of material coated with magnetic oxide and covered with a protective jacket. Diskettes are available in three sizes—8 in., 5¼ in., and 3½ in.—as shown in Figure A-5. Some diskettes are able to store data on both sides. Diskettes are inserted into the disk drives of microcomputers via slots in the microprocessors. (In Figure A-3, for instance, a horizontal slot appears in the front of the microprocessor, just above the keyboard.) Although most microcomputers provide single disk drives for diskettes, some have twin disk drives for added convenience. Twin disk drives are labeled as either drives 1 and 2 or as A and B.

Diskettes offer several advantages. First, they allow direct access of data records. Second, they are convenient to store and transport. Third, they are quite inexpensive.

A magnetic **hard disk** for a microcomputer typically consists of a single platter, either 5¼ in. or 3½ in. in diameter. It may be mounted on three types of drives:

1. A **Winchester drive** that is mounted within the microprocessor housing, usually next to a diskette drive.

2. A **hard disk card** or board that is inserted into an expansion slot within the microprocessor.

3. A **Bernoulli box** that is attached externally to the microprocessor. In this arrangement the disk is in the form of a removable cartridge.

One advantage of a hard disk is that it rotates more rapidly than a diskette, thus allowing faster access to the data it stores. Another advantage is that its storage capacity is many times greater than that of a diskette. Common capacities for marketed hard disks are 10, 20, 40, 60, and 80 megabytes. Diskettes can store from ½ megabyte to 1½ megabytes of data characters.

Magnetic tape is also used as a storage medium with microcomputer systems. Magnetic disks are used to store files and software while actively employed in processing, but magnetic tape is principally used as a backup medium. That is, periodically data on magnetic disks are (or should be) "dumped" onto magnetic tapes to provide security for file data. Two forms of magnetic tape are **tape cassettes** and **tape cartridges.** These tape forms can hold very large quantities of data and be loaded very quickly. For instance, a standard tape cartridge holds 60 megabytes of data and can be loaded in 12 minutes.

Optical disks represent the third medium for secondary storage. These disks, known as **CD ROM** (compact disk read-only memory), are inserted into externally attached optical disk drives. Available in 8 in. and 5¼ in. sizes, optical disks are generally used to store data bases of such reference matter as financial results and market analyses. Typical capacities of each side of optical disks are 400 and 600 megabytes.

Communications Devices

When microcomputers are linked to a mainframe computer or to each other, communications devices are needed. The main device of concern to a microcomputer user is the modem, which may be mounted internally (within the microprocessor casing) or attached externally. **Modems** transmit data at speeds (baud rates) up to

FIGURE A-5 Three sizes of diskettes. Reprinted with permission from Stephen A. Moscove and Mark G. Simpkin, *Accounting Information Systems,* 3d ed., New York: Wiley, 1987.

19,200 characters per second. Other devices that may be needed when microcomputers are linked into networks include front-end processors, channel controllers, and emulation products.

SOFTWARE

The advent of microcomputers has led to an explosion of software packages, for two major reasons: (1) microcomputers are being sold in huge volumes, and (2) most of the purchasers and users of microcomputers are not professional programmers and do not care to learn to program. Although game programs and personal-use programs receive much of the attention, many of the software packages are designed for business use. In order to provide this torrent of packages, a number of software vendors have come into existence. Among the more familiar names are Management Sciences of America, Microsoft, Cullinet, Lotus Development, and Digital Research.

Our survey of microcomputer software begins with operating systems and continues to accounting applications, spreadsheets, data base management systems, and word processing systems.

Operating Systems

The **operating system** is the key system software that guides the operation of a microcomputer and all its components. Generally the operating system is provided on a diskette by the microcomputer manufacturer. In some cases the operating system is proprietary and unique to an individual manufacturer. An example is APPLE-DOS, which is used exclusively with Apple microcomputers.

More often it is common to a variety of microcomputer models and makes. Examples of two operating systems for 16-bit microprocessors are UNIX (developed by American Telephone & Telegraph Company) and MS-DOS (developed by Microsoft Corporation). Any application software package written to comply with the MS-DOS operating system, for instance, will function on all IBM microcomputers and IBM-compatible microcomputers (e.g., Zenith, Compaq). In the future a single standard operating system may evolve, although one is not yet in sight. At present, new operating systems are constantly under development. For instance, OS/2 has been developed by Microsoft Corporation for use with the PS/2 line of IBM microcomputers.

The first step for a purchaser of a microcomputer is to "customize" the provided operating system to accommodate the particular hardware configuration of the microcomputer system. This customized operating system is either retained on the diskette or loaded onto the microcomputer's hard disk. Then, before each use the operating system is initiated or "booted" with the aid of its "bootstrap" program stored in ROM. The user is informed that a successful "boot" has occurred by means of a prompt or a message notifying him or her to take some action. For instance, a C> is a prompt that appears when the operating system has been booted from the hard disk.

Among the actions that may be taken by a microcomputer user when such a prompt appears are

1. Enter or "call up" an application package.

2. Enter or "call up" a programming language suitable to microcomputers, such as BASIC.

3. Specify a utility program.

Before discussing various application packages in following sections, let us survey some of the **utility programs** available via the MS-DOS operating system and the related commands.

Command	Function of the Utility Program
COPY	Copies individual files from one disk to another
DIR	Provides a directory of all files on a specified disk
DEL	Deletes individual files from a disk
FORMAT	Prepares a disk to accept data or program files
DISKCOPY	Makes an exact copy of a disk
MD	Makes a new directory on a hard disk
CLS	Clears the monitor screen and moves the cursor back to the upper left corner of the screen

Accounting Application Packages

Most **accounting application packages** focus on common transactions. For instance, a typical set of packages covers transactions affecting the general ledger, accounts receivable, accounts payable, inventory, and payroll. Each of these packages verify and edit entered transaction data, process the data, update established master files, and produce various documents and reports. They normally include subsidiary ledgers for customers, suppliers, and employees. Designers of such packaged sets normally use a modular approach, with the various transaction modules (e.g., accounts receivable) being integrated into the general ledger module. This design allows the subsidiary ledgers related to the various modules to be updated concurrently with the general ledger.

Primary customers for such accounting packages are small business firms and firms having branch operations. Since these types of users are generally new to computers, the designers attempt to render the accounting packages as user-friendly as possible. Thus, they extensively employ menus, account prompts, forced balancing of transaction amounts, simplified report and financial statement formats, thorough audit trails, and easy-to-understand documentation. Figure A-6 displays menus provided by a popular accounting package. These menus aid users in commanding the system to enter transaction data, post the data to files, print trial balances and financial statements, and perform various editing and diskette maintenance functions.

An enormous number of accounting application packages are currently available from a variety of software vendors. Generally they are designed with flexibility in mind; that is, they allow a using firm to tailor the packages to the particular characteristics and needs of the firm. Also, an increasing number of packages are being specifically designed for individuals working in specialized types of organizations, such as doctors, lawyers, certified public accountants, contractors, bankers, manufacturers, and so forth. Furthermore, accounting packages are incorporating additional features, such as budgets and forecasts.

Electronic Spreadsheets

The software package known as an **electronic spreadsheet** has become the most popular ac-counting and business application since the first version, VisiCalc, burst on the scene in 1978. Since that date versions known as Lotus 1-2-3, SuperCalc, and Multiplan have appeared. (These names, and others to be mentioned in later sections, are registered trademarks.) An electronic spreadsheet is a multicolumn worksheet projected onto the CRT screen of a computer system. It allows accountants and others to work with a huge number of rows and columns, to perform powerful computer-aided functions, and to store the results in computer-readable files.

The electronic spreadsheet has four attributes that enable it to be an effective business planning tool.

1. It displays data in a form (i.e., columnar worksheet) that is familiar to accountants and other financially oriented persons.

2. It eliminates the onerous chore of manual calculating, since it performs calculations such as footing, cross-footing, and extensions. At the same time, it does not require users such as accountants to act as programmers in order to gain desired results.

3. It allows accountants and other users to ask "what-if" questions and to obtain complete recalculations very quickly. Thus, an accountant who is preparing a forecast may change a sales estimate from an increase of 1 percent per month to 3 percent per month. The spreadsheet formulas will then automatically recalculate the expected sales levels. If the sales forecast is a part of a budgeted income statement, the spreadsheet formulas will also recalculate the expected net income amounts and all intervening expense amounts.

4. It enables templates to be constructed and repeatedly used in solving various problems. Figure A-7 shows a template for use in computing and presenting budgeted income statements and variances. This template provides the format for a budget report, showing the user where to insert the estimated and actual amounts. Then underlying formulas, which were specified by the designer of the template, compute the net income and variances.

Menu 1—Data Entry

```
                        BPI SYSTEMS, INC.
                  General Accounting—Version 1.10
                      Menu 1—Data Entry

   1   Run Queue                     2   Erase Queue
   3   Change/Exit BPI System        4   Enter Company Code and Dates
   5   Change Menu                   6   Print on Screen/Printer

  11   Enter Cash Disbursements     21   Print Cash Disbursements
  12   Enter Cash Receipts          22   Print Cash Receipts
  13   Enter Invoice Register       23   Print Invoice Register
  14   Enter Merchandise Purchased  24   Print Merchandise Purchased
  15   Enter Cash Register          25   Print Cash Register
  16   Enter General Journal        26   Print General Journal
  17   Enter Standard Entries       27   Print Mdse Purchased (Due Date)
  18   Enter External Entries

  Data Drive    : B                 As-Of   Date: MM/DD/YY
  Company Code: XXXXXX              Today's Date: MM/DD/YY
  Password     : XXXXXX

  Command Queue: Empty

  Enter Command Number ⇒
```

Menu 2—Posting

```
                        BPI SYSTEMS, INC.
                  General Accounting—Version 1.10
                      Menu 2—Posting

   1   Run Queue                     2   Erase Queue
   3   Change/Exit BPI System        4   Enter Company Code and Dates
   5   Change Menu                   6   Print on Screen/Printer

  31   Post Ledgers                 41   Process End-of-Month
  32   Print Income Statement       42   Process End-of-Quarter
  33   Print Trial Balance          43   Process End-of-Fiscal-Year
  34   Print Balance Sheet          44   Process End-of-Fourth-Quarter

  Data Drive    : B                 As-Of   Date: MM/DD/YY
  Company Code: XXXXXX              Today's Date: MM/DD/YY
  Password     : XXXXXX

  Command Queue: Empty

  Enter Command Number ⇒
```

FIGURE A-6 Three major menus used by an accounting application package. Reprinted with permission of Computer Associates.

Menu 3—Maintenance

```
                    BPI SYSTEMS, INC.
               General Accounting—Version 1.10
                    Menu 3—Maintenance

    1   Run Queue                  2   Erase Queue
    3   Change/Exit BPI System     4   Enter Company Code and Dates
    5   Change Menu                6   Print on Screen/Printer

   71   Create Company            73   Print Schedules
   72   Edit Accounts             74   Change Company Code

   Data Drive    : B              As-Of   Date: MM/DD/YY
   Company Code: XXXXXX           Today's Date: MM/DD/YY
   Password      : XXXXXX

   Command Queue: Empty

   Enter Command Number ⇒
```

FIGURE A-6 (*Continued*)

Electronic spreadsheets are widely used by accountants, both in public accounting firms and in industrial firms. They are employed in such uses as preparing analyses for tax planning, preparing consolidated financial statements, performing financial analyses, performing sensitivity analyses to determine the impacts of changes in key factors (e.g., interest rates) on profitability, preparing depreciation schedules, and preparing cash and operational budgets.

	A	B	C	D	E	F
1	Account		Budget	Actual	Variance	Variance
2	Name		Amount	Amount	(Dollars)	(Percent)
3						
4	Sales		....	....	0	0
5	Cost of sales		....	....	0	0
6	Gross margin		0	0	0	0
7	Operating exp.		....	....	0	0
8	Nonoper. exp.		....	....	0	0
9	Total expenses		0	0	0	0
10	Net income		0	0	0	0
11						
12						
13						
14						

Notes: 1. Letters mark columns; numbers mark rows.
2. The spaces denoted by ..... indicate amounts to be entered, whereas the spaces marked by 0 indicate amounts to be computed by the spreadsheet software.

FIGURE A-7 A template of a budgeted income statement.

Data Base Management Systems

A software package that enables users to manage data and files is known as a **data base management system (DBMS).** Although DBMS packages have been used with mainframe computer systems since the early 1970s, they have also become important to microcomputer users. Among the currently available packages are dBase III, R:Base, Condor, Oracle, and Knowledge Man. All employ the relational model and require 128 K or more of primary storage capacity.

The DBMS packages for microcomputers vary widely in capabilities. A simple, file-oriented package allows users to develop mailing lists and keep track of stored records. A more sophisticated data-oriented package allows users to build multiple files to desired specifications, keep the files up to date, sort records on desired keys, retrieve desired data items quickly from one or more files, summarize values of data items, and construct special reports according to requested formats. None of these uses requires the DBMS users to write involved program instructions.

Small businesses and professionals are becoming avid DBMS users. For instance, merchandising firms such as VCR movie rental companies maintain inventories by means of DBMS's. Doctors maintain patients' medical history records; lawyers prepare legal briefs and perform searches for case precedents; accountants maintain client records and prepare bills.

Word Processing Systems

Word processing software provides the ability to draft text directly on a video screen and to make changes easily and quickly. Typically included features allow users to move blocks of text to different locations, to insert words, to reblock paragraphs, and to check misspellings. A word processing package stores the results either on a diskette or hard disk, from which the text may be printed as many times as desired. Popular word processing packages include WordStar and Word Perfect.

Other Software Available for Microcomputers

As firms, especially those without larger computers, attempt to utilize their microcomputers

more effectively, they are likely to encounter software such as

1. **Financial modeling packages,** which aid the budgeting process by allowing users to estimate the financial impacts of alternative courses of action. Examples of financial modeling packages are Javelin and IFPS-Personal.

2. **Graphics packages,** which enable users to display financial and other information in easy-to-understand graphical and pictorial forms. Presentation graphics include pie charts, bar graphs, and line graphs. Freehand graphics allow pictures to be drawn or "painted." Both types of graphics are often shown in color and may appear in two or three dimensions. Examples of graphics packages are Chart-Master and Telepaint.

3. **Desk-top publishing packages,** which enable users to format and print professional-quality newsletters and other textual products. The published materials often include pictures as well as text. Examples of desk-top publishing packages are Ventura Publisher and PC Page Maker.

4. **Office automation packages,** which enable users to perform housekeeping functions that improve overall clerical productivity. For instance, accounting firms use timekeeping packages that allow them to record the hours worked by staff members and the clients for whom they worked. Many firms use electronic calendars to help their employees keep track of appointments, meetings, and so on.

5. **Message-oriented packages,** which enable users to transmit various forms of information to geographically dispersed locations. **Electronic mail** software transmits written messages via data communication networks to recipients who have electronic storage "mailboxes." **Voice mail** software transmits spoken messages to the telephones of recipients, assuming that the telephones serve as terminals of a data communications network. **Facsimile (fax)** software transmits images (e.g., documents, pictures, graphics) in the form of signals to receiving points, where machines convert the signals back

into the images. These types of message-oriented software can be extensions of automated offices.

6. **Integrated packages,** which combine two or more software packages and provide interfaces among them. For instance, packages such as Symphony and Framework combine an electronic spreadsheet, a DBMS, a graphics package, and a word processing package.

7. **Data bank services,** which enable subscribers to have access to specialized external data bases. For instance, the Dow Jones Retrieval Service allows subscribers to obtain a variety of data concerning listed stocks, bonds, and other securities.

SELECTION AND INSTALLATION OF MICROCOMPUTERS

Selecting the proper microcomputer is not an easy task, particularly for small business firms that have never owned computers. Hundreds of microcomputer models are available from scores of manufacturers. Consequently, such firms are clearly in need of help and advice. Among others, many accountants offer professional and experienced assistance in selecting and installing microcomputer systems. Assistance is also available from a rapidly growing number of microcomputer-oriented books and articles in professional journals.

Selection Criteria

The first step is to define in specific terms the computing problems of the firm. Is the firm having difficulty in processing the increasing volumes of transactions? Are managers making decisions based on inadequate information and analysis? Is information needed to answer customers' questions hard to keep up to date and to locate quickly?

The second step is to analyze and specify the particular computing needs and requirements of the firm. What volumes of transactions are expected during the coming years? How important are complete audit trails? How timely should information in the master files be provided to inquirers? What user-friendly features are necessary to enable the clerks to operate the microcomputer system easily and successfully?

The third step is to design the key features of a desirable system, including the outputs, inputs, data base, controls, and processing procedures. Included in this step, or in a related step, should be a comparison of the expected benefits and costs of the needed system. Unless the benefits exceed the costs, the system should be deferred.

The fourth step is to evaluate the available software packages needed to achieve the design. Only after the software packages have been selected should the microcomputer hardware be evaluated. This sequence is based on the maxim that "the software drives the hardware," i.e., the hardware only serves as the vehicle within which the software functions.

In evaluating both the software and hardware, all specified needs must be satisfied. Other matters should also be considered, such as

1. The assistance provided by the manufacturers with respect to training, testing, and documentation.

2. The availability of maintenance service.

3. The ease in expanding the system by means of added storage modules, enhancement boards, and upgrades.

4. The proven performance of the system and its manufacturers.

Installation

Several steps are also necessary to install a new microcomputer system satisfactorily. First, the hardware and software should be fully tested, in accordance with the directions provided by the manufacturers. Next, the designed applications should be incorporated. For instance, a developed chart of accounts might be included in a purchased general ledger software package. Documentation concerning the designed system should be prepared, including flowcharts, error correction procedures, audit trails, and so forth. Files should be converted from the present system to the new system. All users should then be adequately trained in the use of the microcomputer system.

For more details concerning the steps in selecting and installing computer systems, refer to Chapter 16.

EXAMPLES OF MICROCOMPUTER-BASED SYSTEMS

Continental Motor Inn[1]

Continental Motor Inn, a relatively small Cumberland, Maryland, firm, installed a microcomputer-based system several years ago to replace a manual system. The hardware configuration essentially consists of three Victor microcomputers, plus two dot-matrix printers and one daisy-wheel printer.

Bob King, the president, did all the programming himself. His programs, which are menu-driven, pertain to the following applications.

1. General ledger processing, with daily balance sheets and income statements.

2. Payroll preparation, including quarterly payroll tax reports.

3. Liquor inventory recordkeeping.

4. Accounts receivable processing.

5. Accounts payable processing and check preparation.

6. Employee (e.g., waiters) scheduling.

As a result of these computerized accounting system applications, the inn has increased gross income by 50 percent, tripled the number of employees, and expanded to a second location.

This increased business has kept Bob so busy that he has not had time to write new programs. Thus, he is considering the acquisition of two programs to control the food inventories and room reservations. Since these programs operate only on IBM and IBM-compatible microcomputers, and because the current microcomputers are being used to their capacities, he is also considering the acquisition of an IBM PC.

Radio Corporation of America (RCA)[2]

During the early 1980s the controller's function of RCA collected financial information from the firm's operating units by means of the postal service, facsimile mail, telephone, and "dumb" terminals. Reliance on such diverse collection systems resulted in financial reporting that was unwieldly, prone to error, and incapable of timely responses to rapidly changing needs. Consequently, the controller commissioned the development of a new firmwide financial reporting system.

A project team was appointed that included a manager, four full-time systems analysts, and three part-time systems analysts. After investigation and analysis, the team recommended that common hardware and software units be linked to the mainframe computer by means of public telephone lines. Data would be entered via menus that were identical for all reporting units. Entered data would be uploaded to the mainframe computer; consolidated results would then be downloaded to microcomputers located in the offices of key managers.

The hardware configuration selected for each remote location consisted of an IBM PC XT, a Hayes modem, and an Epson printer. The software used to develop the input forms and output reports was Lotus 1-2-3. Upon being ordered and shipped, these hardware and software components were duly installed at the various locations. Previously designed menus, input forms, and output reports and graphs were tested. Field personnel were trained in the use of the new input systems. Documentation was also prepared and delivered to all locations. Conferences were held three times each year thereafter to evaluate the new systems and to discuss possible improvements.

REFERENCES

Chew, Robert L. and Goel, Rajoo. "Transaction Processing Using Lotus 1-2-3." *Journal of Systems Management* (Jan. 1987), 30–37.

Cooper, Michael S. "Micro-based Business Graphics." *Datamation* (May 1, 1984), 99–105.

Edwards, Chris. "Developing Microcomputer-based Business Systems." *Journal of Systems Management* (Apr. 1983), 36–38.

Flores, Ivan, and Terry, Christopher. *Microcomputer Systems.* New York: Van Nostrand-Reinhold, 1982.

---

[1] Carolyn Allen, "PC's Make It Better Inn-Side," *Modern Office Technology* (June 1985), 129–34.

[2] Bill Tomaskovic, "RCA Implements a Micro-based Corporate Financial Reporting Network," *Journal of Accounting and EDP* (Spring 1987), 11–17.

Heintz, Carl. "Seeking Solutions with Spreadsheets." *Interface Age* (Sept. 1983), 52–54.

Himrod, Bruce W. "Microcomputers for Small Business." *The Journal of Accountancy* (Dec. 1979), 44–50.

Karon, Paul. "Deloitte Haskins & Sells: New York Firm's Accountants Take PCs along for On-the-Spot Client Service." *PC Week* (June 24, 1986), 75–79.

Konkel, Gilbert J. "Word Processing and the Office of the Future." *The Arthur Young Quarterly* (Winter 1982), 2–9.

Lees, John D., and Lees, Donna D. "Realities of Small Business Information System Implementation." *Journal of Systems Management* (Jan. 1987), 6–13.

MacNichols, Charles, and Clark, Thomas. *Microcomputer-based Information and Decision Support Systems for Small Businesses.* Reston, Va.: Reston Publishing, 1983.

Needleman, Theodore. *Microcomputers for Accountants.* Englewood Cliffs, N.J.: Prentice-Hall, 1983.

Page, John, and Hooper, Paul. *Microcomputer Accounting and Business Applications.* Reston, Va.: Reston Publishing Co., 1985.

Person, Stanley. "A Microcomputer in a Small CPA Firm." *The CPA Journal* (Mar. 1984), 20–25.

Rohm, Wendy Goldman. "The Overused, Underused, Betterused Micro." *Infosystems* (Apr. 1987), 60–63.

Rose, Tawn A. "Microcomputers For Financial Consulting." *Management Accounting* (Feb. 1984), 42–45.

Schwartz, Donald A. "Microcomputers Take Aim on Small Business Clients." *The Journal of Accountancy* (Dec. 1979), 57–62.

Shuster, Harvey L., and Warner, Paul D. "Micros for Small Business: The Time Is Now." *Management Accounting* (Mar. 1984), 45–48.

Smith, L. Murphy, and Bain, Craig E. "Computer Graphics for Today's Accountant." *CPA Journal* (Feb. 1987), 18–35.

Wayune, Robert C., and Frotman, Alan. "Microcomputer: Helping Make Practice Perfect." *The Journal of Accountancy* (Dec. 1981), 34–39.

Wolfe, Christopher, and Wiggins, Casper E. "Internal Control in the Microcomputer Environment." *The Internal Auditor* (Dec. 1986), 54–60.

Yoder, Steven E., and Knight, Sherry D. *Microaccounting.* Englewood Cliffs, N.J.: Prentice-Hall, 1985.

Zarley, Craig. "Corporate Users Turn to CD ROM for Business Applications." *PC Week* (Dec. 2, 1986), 41, 49.

QUESTIONS

1. What is the meaning of each of the following terms?

Portable computer	Hard disk
Liquid crystal display (LCD)	Winchester drive
Dedicated microcomputer	Hard disk card
Multitasking microcomputer	Bernoulli box
Operator-oriented microcomputer system	Tape cassette
File-oriented microcomputer system	Tape cartridge
Microprocessor	CD ROM
Motherboard	Modem
Serial interface	Operating system
Parallel interface	Utility program
Add-in memory board	Accounting application package
Accelerator card	Electronic spreadsheet
Clock/calendar	Data base management system (DBMS)
Graphics board	Word processing software
Voice synthesizer	Financial modeling package
Mouse	Graphics package
Joystick	Desk-top publishing package
Light pen	Office automation package
Optical scanner	Message-oriented package
Voice input device	Electronic mail
Touch input device	Voice mail
Dot-matrix printer	Facsimile (fax)
Daisy-wheel printer	Integrated package
Laser printer	Data bank service
Diskette	

2. What are the benefits provided by microcomputers, relative to mainframe and minicomputers?

3. How may microcomputers be classified?

4. Describe the construction of a microprocessor.

5. What devices may be attached to the motherboard?

6. Identify several devices by which data may be entered into a microcomputer system.

7. Contrast the three types of printers used with microcomputers.

8. Describe the various types of secondary storage media for microcomputers.

9. Why have microcomputers led to a dramatic increase in software packages?

10. What are the major functions of the operating system of a microcompuer?

11. Identify several utility programs provided by the MS-DOS operating system.

12. Describe desirable features of an accounting application package.

13. Describe several attributes of electronic spreadsheet packages.

14. Describe several typical capabilities of data base management system software packages for microcomputers.

15. Describe several typical features of word processing systems.

16. Identify several other types of software packages that are available for microcomputers.

17. Identify the criteria by which to select microcomputers for small business firms.

18. List the steps for installing a new microcomputer system.

REVIEW PROBLEM

Computers Aplenty, Inc.

Statement

Computers Aplenty, Inc. (CAI), is a recently established computer retail store. It merchandises and services four makes of microcomputers and related components such as terminals, printers, magnetic tape casettes, diskettes, and so forth. It also carries a variety of business application software packages. Currently the store is managed by its owner, Jay Sparks, and employs 12 sales and service personnel.

Jay has high hopes that the store will grow rapidly in revenues and that more stores will be established. He recognizes the importance of an efficient and effective accounting information system (AIS) in achieving these hopes. Thus, he decides to utilize a microcomputer from his stock as the heart of the system. With the aid of a microcomputer he believes that the various transactions will be processed promptly, the files can be kept up to date, and needed information may be easily and quickly retrieved.

Required

a. Draw and label a hardware configuration diagram that reflects a suitable microcomputer system for CAI.

b. List several applications that would be suitable for CAI's microcomputer system.

c. Briefly describe software that would be suitable for use by CAI's microcomputer system.

d. Assume that CAI does grow rapidly so that two additional stores are established and a total of 50 employees comprise the work force. Discuss alternative ways that the microcomputer system described in **a** might feasibly be augmented or replaced to accommodate this growth.

Solution

a. A suitable microcomputer system hardware configuration would likely consist of a microcomputer, plus a nonremovable hard disk drive, one diskette drive, a cassette tape drive, one video display terminal, and one printer. A labeled configuration diagram appears as follows.[3]

---

[3] The symbols employed in the diagram are based on the computer system flowchart symbols appearing in Figure 3-11.

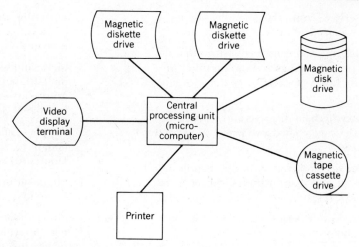

b. Applications that would be suitable for the microcomputer system include

(1) General ledger accounting.

(2) Accounts payable processing.

(3) Accounts receivable processing.

(4) Cash disbursements processing.

(5) Cash receipts processing.

(6) Payroll processing.

(7) Service order processing.

(8) Inventory recordkeeping and control.

(9) Sales analysis and forecasting.

(10) Cash forecasting and management.

(11) Budgetary planning and control.

(12) Capital investment analysis.

c. Software that would be suitable for the microcomputer system includes

(1) An operating system.

(2) Utility programs, such as text editors and directories.

(3) Compilers for BASIC and COBOL.

(4) An integrated package that includes an electronic spreadsheet, data manager, and word processor.

(5) Application packages for general ledger accounting and the remaining applications listed under **b.**

d. When CAI consists of three stores and 50 employees, a single microcomputer system is not sufficient. Alternative systems that might be considered include

(1) Separate microcomputer systems for each store.

(2) A minicomputer system located at the main store, with terminals located at the other stores and tied by communications lines to the minicomputer.

(3) A multitasking microcomputer system located at the main store, with terminals located at the other stores and tied by communications lines to the supermicrocomputer.

(4) A microcomputer at the main store, accompanied by the utilization of a commercial computer service bureau or time-sharing service.

PROBLEMS

A-1. Microcomputers are widely used by a variety of firms. Identify several uses of microcomputers by the following types of firms. Be as specific as possible.

a. Full-service bank that handles deposits, makes loans, and manages trusts.

b. Engineering and construction firm that designs office buildings and various other projects for businesses and government organizations.

c. Motorcycle chain that sells and services motorcycles and related two-wheel motorized vehicles.

d. Full-service brokerage firm that handles investment and margin trades, performs investment research, and manages portfolios.

e. University that performs teaching, research, and administration.

A-2 Microcomputers are widely used in public accounting firms. For instance, tax specialists use them to assist in preparing tax returns and in tax planning. Describe several specific problems encountered by management advisory services (MAS) consultants in which microcomputers may be of assistance.

A-3. Co-op Sales of Dayton, Ohio, was established on June 1. Merchandise will be sold on credit, with payment due in 15 days. Inventory will be recorded by the periodic inventory method. The accounting records will consist of a general journal, sales journal, purchases journal, cash receipts journal, check register, general ledger, accounts receivable subsidiary ledger, and accounts payable subsidiary ledger. Within the general ledger will be the following accounts: Cash, Accounts Receivable, Merchandise Inventory, Supplies, Prepaid Expenses, Furniture and Fixtures, Accumulated Depreciation—Furniture and Fixtures, Accounts Payable, Notes Payable, Accrued Expenses Payable, FICA Taxes Payable, Income Taxes Payable, Capital Stock, Retained Earnings, Sales, Purchases, Purchase Discounts, Cost of Goods Sold, Salaries Expense, Depreciation Expense, Utilities Expense, Supplies Used, Rent Expense, Taxes Expense, Interest Expense, and Miscellaneous Expense.

Co-op's June transactions are as follows.

June 1 Capital stock is issued and sold for $50,000.

1 Rent on a building for a year is paid in advance to the Monoco Realty Co., $2400. (Check number 1 is issued.)

1 Furniture and fixtures are acquired in exchange for a 60-day, 15 percent note in the amount of $16,000.

2 Merchandise inventory is acquired on 2/10, net/30 terms from Tenny's Wares; invoice 283 shows an amount payable of $8000.

3 Supplies amounting to $800 are bought for cash from Vicor's Supply House. (Check number 2.)

4 Merchandise is sold to Loman's Outlet on invoice number S1, $1200.

5 Merchandise is purchased on 2/10, net 30 terms from Simon Manufacturing; invoice 101 shows an amount payable of $4500.

8 Bill is received from the city for building inspection, $50.

9 Merchandise is sold to Rustic Retailer, $2800. (Invoice number S2.)

10 Bill is received from the Bugle News for advertising, $220.

11 Check number 3 is mailed to Tenny's Wares for amount due.

12 Merchandise is sold to Sam's Stores, $4200. (Invoice number S3.)

15 Salaries are paid for the first half of June, $1600, less income taxes withheld of $240 and FICA taxes withheld of $110. (The payroll transaction is entered in the general journal, since special checks are issued to the employees. Normally a payroll register would support a payroll transaction, but it is omitted in this problem to avoid excessive details.)

18 Remittance is received from Loman's Outlet for amount owed. (Remittance advice number R1 is prepared.)

19 Checks numbers 4 and 5 are mailed to the city and the newspaper for bills owed.

22 Merchandise is sold to Loman's Outlet, $3600. (Invoice number S4.)

24 Remittance is received from Rustic

Retailer in the amount of $1000. (Remittance number R2.)

26 Merchandise is sold to Polly's Parlors, $1900. (Invoice number S5.)

29 Bill is received for utilities, $300.

30 Salaries are paid for the second half of June, $1600, less income taxes withheld of $240 and FICA taxes withheld of $110.

30 Adjustments are made based on the following:

    a. The ending merchandise inventory amounts to $3800. (The adjusting entry should involve debits to the Merchandise Inventory, Cost of Goods Sold, and Purchase Discounts accounts, with an offsetting credit to the Purchases account.)

    b. The interest on the note payable has accrued for one month.

    c. One month's prepaid rent has expired.

    d. The depreciation rate on furniture and fixtures is 12 percent per year, and the depreciation method to be used is straight-line.

    e. The amount of unused supplies at the end of the month is $200.

    f. The employer's contribution to payroll taxes must match the amount of the employees' contribution to FICA taxes.

    g. The losses resulting from bad debts are estimated to be 2 percent of the balance of Accounts Receivable at the end of the month.

Required

Access the general ledger program (general accounting system package) via your school's microcomputer system, in accordance with directions provided by your instructor. Then perform the following.

a. Enter the listed accounts into the chart of accounts and assign numeric codes to the accounts.

b. Set up accounts receivable and accounts payable subsidiary ledgers.

c. Set up, or verify the availability of, a general journal, sales journal, invoice register (or purchases journal), and check register (or cash disbursements journal).

d. Enter all transactions listed, including the adjusting journal entries, into the appropriate journals and post the entries. Remember that all transactions that cannot be fitted into a special journal may be entered into the general journal.

e. Print an adjusted trial balance, income statement, and balance sheet.

f. Print all journals, ledgers, and schedules that the available general accounting system package will allow.

A-4. The firm of Wu & Wright, CPAs, has just acquired an electronic spreadsheet package for use on its microcomputer.[4] As their first application the partners decide to prepare an income statement template, to enter data of a client firm into the income statement, and to determine the effects on net income resulting from changes in certain factors.

They begin by inserting the diskette containing the spreadsheet package into disk drive A and turning on the computer. After obtaining the logo of the package, they stroke the indicated key and obtain the control panel. This panel displays the rows and columns of the worksheet. (To be more precise, it displays a "window"—the first few rows and columns of the complete worksheet—plus a menu of commands.)

Then with the aid of the electronic spreadsheet manual and the menu, they develop a template for an income statement as follows.

---

[4] Problems A-4 and A-5 are adapted from an application in Frederick H. Wu, "Teaching Managerial (Cost) Accounting with Electronic Spreadsheet Software," published in *Issues in Accounting Education, 1984* (Sarasota, Fla.: American Accounting Association, 1984). Used with permission.

Template No. 1: Income Statement

. . . .

Income Statement
For the Year Ended Dec. 31, ...

Sales		$...........
Less Cost of Goods Sold:		
Finished Goods, Jan. 1	$...........	
Cost of Goods Manufactured	....	
Cost of Goods Available for sale	$ 0	
Finished Goods, Dec. 31	....	
Cost of Goods Sold		0
Gross Margin		$ 0
Less Selling and Admin. Expenses:		
Sales Commissions	$ 0	
Sales Salaries	....	
Shipping Expenses	0	
Administrative Expenses	....	0
Net Income		$ 0

Documentation for Template

a. Amounts indicated by .... are to be entered by user.

b. Amounts indicated by 0 are to be calculated by formulas that have been stored in the memory of the spreadsheet software package.

c. The stored formulas are

(1) Cost of goods available for sale = beginning finished goods + cost of goods manufactured. (The formulas for this and following relationships are expressed by the software in terms of cells; e.g., C12 is C9 + C10.)

(2) Cost of goods sold = cost of goods available for sale − ending finished goods.

(3) Gross margin = sales − cost of goods sold.

(4) Selling and administrative expenses = sales commissions + sales salaries + shipping expenses + administrative expenses.

(5) Net income = gross margin − selling and administrative expenses.

(6) Sales commissions = 0.05 × sales.

(7) Shipping expenses = 1/30 × sales.

Required

Access the electronic spreadsheet package available on your school's microcomputer system, in accordance with your instructor's directions. Then perform the following.

a. Prepare the template, including the underlying formulas.

b. Enter these data into the template: ABC Company; 1988; 1,200,000 (for sales); 100,000 (for beginning finished goods); 900,000 (for cost of goods manufactured); 150,000 (for ending finished goods); 100,000 (for sales salaries); and 100,000 (for administrative expenses).

c. Print the income statement based on this data.

d. Change the sales amount in the template to 2,000,000, and print the resulting income statement.

A-5. Refer to Problem A-4. The partners of Wu & Wright, CPAs, decide to add supporting detail to their first spreadsheet application. A schedule of cost of goods manufactured is a logical choice, since it provides supporting details to a key line in the income statement. In the process of developing this schedule they list the following formulas:

a. Cost of direct materials available = beginning inventory + cost of purchases.

b. Direct materials used = cost of direct materials available for use − ending inventory.

c. Total indirect manufacturing costs = SUM (i.e., the sum of costs beginning with sandpaper and ending with fire insurance on equipment).

d. Manufacturing costs during the year = direct materials + direct labor + indirect manufacturing costs.

e. Manufacturing costs to account for = manufacturing costs during the year + beginning work-in-process.

f. Cost of goods manufactured = manufacturing costs to account for − ending work in process.

Required

a. Prepare a template for the schedule of cost of goods manufactured. Use the same conventions used in Problem A-4 to indicate amounts to be entered and calculated.

b. Enter the following data into the template: ABC Company; 1988; 40,000 (beginning inventory); 400,000 (purchases); 50,000 (ending inventory); 300,000 (direct labor costs); 2000 (cost of sandpaper); 5000 (cost of lubricants and coolants); 40,000 (cost of materials handling); 20,000 (cost of overtime premium); 10,000 (cost of idle time); 40,000 (cost of indirect labor); 50,000 (cost of factory rent); 40,000 (cost of depreciation on equipment); 4000 (cost of property taxes); 3000 (cost of fire insurance on equipment); 10,000 (beginning work in process); and 14,000 (ending work in process). Print the schedule of cost of goods manufactured based on this data.

c. Change the amount of purchases from $400,000 to $600,000 and the amount of idle time from $10,000 to $30,000; print the resulting schedule of cost of goods manufactured and the income statement.

d. Change the beginning work-in-process from $10,000 to $0 and the ending work in process from $14,000 to $50,000; return all other amounts to those shown in **b**; print the resulting schedule of cost of goods manufactured and the income statement.

Note: In designing the template for this problem, be sure it is linked to the income statement in the same file. Otherwise, the changes in the cost of goods manufactured schedule will not be reflected in the income statement.

A-6. The Wonderful Widget Co. has just completed its budget process for the coming year. On page 658 appears the resulting projection of operations and cash flow, accompanied by a list of assumptions on which the projection was prepared.

Required

Access the electronic spreadsheet package available on your school's microcomputer system, in accordance with your instructor's directions. Then perform the following.

a. Set up the format for the projection shown on page 658, enter the relevant formulas based on the assumptions, then enter the estimated sales amount for January of 1000 (i.e., $1,000,000), and specify that the CALCULATE function be performed. If all your formulas are correct, the display on your screen should appear exactly as the projection on page 658.

b. Print the projection of operations and cash flow.

c. Increase the estimated sales amount for January by 20 percent and calculate the remainder of the projected amounts; print the projection.

d. Reflect the following changes in assumptions: Materials cost 20 percent of sales, income taxes average 38 percent of net income from operations, the increase in accounts receivable equals the increase in sales for the month, the inventories remain the same from month to month, and the increase in accounts payable equals twice the increase in materials and marketing and administration expenses for the month.

e. Re-enter an estimated sales amount for January of 1000, recalculate all amounts based

WONDERFUL WIDGET CO.
PROJECTION OF OPERATIONS AND CASH FLOW
FOR THE YEAR 198X
(THOUSANDS OF DOLLARS)

	JAN.	FEB.	MAR.	APR.	MAY	JUNE	JUL.	AUG.	SEP.	OCT.	NOV.	DEC.	TOTAL FOR YEAR
SALES, NET	1000	1020	1040	1061	1082	1104	1126	1149	1172	1195	1219	1243	13412
COST OF SALES													
MATERIALS	250	255	260	265	271	276	282	287	293	299	305	311	3353
DIRECT LABOR	250	255	260	265	271	276	282	287	293	299	305	311	3353
FACTORY OVERHEAD	200	204	208	212	216	221	225	230	234	239	244	249	2682
TOTAL	700	714	728	743	758	773	788	804	820	837	853	870	9388
GROSS PROFIT	300	306	312	318	325	331	338	345	351	359	366	373	4024
EXPENSES													
MARKETING	100	102	104	106	108	110	113	115	117	120	122	124	1341
ADMINISTRATION	80	82	83	85	87	88	90	92	94	96	98	99	1073
INTEREST	20	20	21	21	22	22	23	23	23	24	24	25	268
TOTAL	200	204	208	212	216	221	225	230	234	239	244	249	2682
NET INCOME FROM OPERATIONS	100	102	104	106	108	110	113	115	117	120	122	124	1341
INCOME TAXES	50	51	52	53	54	55	56	57	59	60	61	62	671
NET INCOME	50	51	52	53	54	55	56	57	59	60	61	62	671
ADJUSTMENTS FOR CASH FLOW													
ACCOUNTS RECEIVABLE	0	-40	-41	-42	-42	-43	-44	-45	-46	-47	-48	-49	-487
INVENTORIES	0	-42	-43	-44	-45	-45	-46	-47	-48	-49	-50	-51	-511
ACCOUNTS PAYABLE	0	4	4	4	5	5	5	5	5	5	5	5	52
INCOME TAXES	0	0	0	0	0	0	0	0	0	0	0	0	0
NET ADJUSTMENTS	0	-78	-79	-81	-82	-84	-86	-88	-89	-91	-93	-95	-946
CASH FLOW FOR MONTH	50	-27	-27	-28	-28	-29	-29	-30	-31	-31	-32	-33	N/A
CUMULATIVE CASH FLOW	50	23	-4	-32	-60	-89	-118	-148	-179	-210	-242	-275	-275

on these changed assumptions, and print the projection.

f. Based on the changed assumptions in **d**, view a pie chart that shows the proportions of cost of sales, total expenses, and income taxes for the year; prepare a hard copy of the chart on a plotter.

g. View a bar chart of the sales amounts for the 12 months of the year; prepare a hard copy of the chart on a plotter.

h. View a stacked bar chart of the net income after taxes and the gross profit for the 12 months of the year; prepare a hard copy of the chart on a plotter.

i. View a line graph of three types of operating expenses for the 12 months of the year; prepare a hard copy of the graph on a plotter.

j. View an *X-Y* graph of net sales versus gross profit; prepare a hard copy of the graph on a plotter.

Assumptions for Projection of Operations and Cash Flow

(a) Net sales the first month are $1,000,000 and increase at the compound rate of 2 percent per month.

(b) Materials cost 25 percent of sales.

(c) Direct labor costs 25 percent of sales.

(d) Factory overhead is 80 percent of direct labor.

(e) Marketing expenses are 10 percent of sales.

(f) Administration expenses total 8 percent of sales.

(g) Interest averages 2 percent of sales.

(h) Income taxes average 50 percent of net income from operations.

(i) Cash flow is reduced by the increases in accounts receivable which equals two times the increase in sales for the month.

(j) Cash flow is reduced by the increase in inventories which equals three times the increase in cost of sales for the month.

(k) Cash flow is increased by the increase in accounts payable, which equals one-half the increase in materials and marketing and administration expenses for the month.

(l) Income tax payments will not differ significantly from the accrual, so no adjustment is necessary.

(m) No adjustments have been made for depreciation (a noncash expense) or equipment purchase (a cash requirement but not an expense) because it is assumed that they will be approximately equal during the year.

(n) Amounts having decimal remainders are rounded up.

A-7. The Gripper Brake Company is a small New Orleans manufacturer of brakes, brake linings, and other parts of braking systems. It sells approximately 100 different sizes and varieties of brake products to garages and retail outlets of motor vehicle products in 10 states. With a work force of 30 employees and three managers, Gripper generated sales revenues last year of $8 million. Moreover, John Hartley, the owner and top manager of Gripper, foresees rapid growth in sales during the coming years.

Mr. Hartley, however, has become aware that the firm is already suffering growing pains. For instance, it is having difficulty in processing the increasing number of sales orders and in delivering orders to customers by promised dates. When customers inquire about the status of their orders, clerks often must spend hours tracking down the answers. Critical parts and materials needed in manufacturing ordered products are frequently out of stock. Losses from bad debts have been increasing at an alarming rate.

These problems lead Mr. Hartley to seek help from Jeff Harris, the firm's public accountant. After a careful investigation Jeff recommends that the firm acquire its own computer system. Upon agreement from Mr. Hartley, he investigates further and proposes three alternatives: (a) a minicomputer system, (b) a multitasking microcomputer system, and (c) three separate dedicated microcomputers.

Required

a. Describe the hardware components that appear to be suitable for each of the foregoing alternative computer systems and draw a hardware configuration diagram for each.

b. Contrast the benefits to Gripper of the three alternative computer systems.

c. List the types of software that should be acquired by Gripper, regardless of the alternative selected.

d. After installing the selected computer system, Gripper acquires software applications packages that perform general ledger accounting and that process sales orders. Briefly describe other software application packages that would aid Gripper in solving its current and future problems.

e. Assume that dedicated microcomputers having hard disks and single diskette drives are selected. Describe specific uses of diskettes and a hard disk with respect to data entry and storage for the inventory application. If a tape cartridge is included, what specific use would it have?

A-8. Prepare an evaluation table that lists the key considerations pertaining to the acquisition of microcomputers. Next visit a microcomputer store and note all the computer models available for sale. Then rank each of the models with respect to the considerations in the evaluation table. Assume that a microcomputer is to be acquired for a small business with which you are familiar.

A-9. The Campus Bookstore (described in the Review Problem at the end of Chapter 1) decides to install stand-alone microcomputers for use in applications other than those pertaining to general ledger and accounting transactions. Describe various types of software packages and applications that would be helpful, especially with respect to information processing. *Hint:* Refer to microcomputer journals such as *Byte Magazine* and *PC Week.*

A-10. Prepare a comparative listing of several specific spreadsheet software packages and data base management system software packages that are currently available. Include for each package its major capabilities and features, as well as its current list price. *Hint:* Refer to microcomputer journals such as *Byte Magazine* and *PC Week* and to such reports as those provided by *Datapro Research Corporation.*

Glossary

Accelerator card An add-in board or card that is connected to the motherboard of a microcomputer via a bus bar for the purpose of increasing the processing speed of the microprocessor.

Access log A record that shows all attempts to access an online data base of a computer system; the device is generally an integral component of the security software.

Access time The time required for a computer processor to retrieve data from primary storage for processing, or to transfer data from primary storage to another storage device.

Accounting An information system (AIS) that consists of recording, classifying, and summarizing transactions that are economic in nature and presenting the resulting information in financial terms.

Accounting application package A software package that has the purpose of processing accounting transactions, storing the results, and preparing financial reports such as sales journals and income statements.

Accounting control A control, such as organizational independence and well-designed source document, that comprises a key part of the accounting control system of a firm.

Accounting control system The component internal control structure that is designed to safeguard the assets of a firm and to ensure the accuracy and reliability of the firm's data and information.

Accounting cycle The sequence of steps that processes such typical accounting transactions as sales, purchases, cash receipts, cash disbursements, and payroll; it generally employs a double-entry accounting process that maintains an equality of debits and credits in each transaction.

Accounts receivable aging schedule A scheduled report that lists the amounts owed by customers and analyzes these amounts according to their ages (i.e., length of times outstanding).

Accuracy The degree to which information is free from errors.

Acknowledgment procedure An accounting control that consists of requiring employees or others to acknowledge their accountability for assets; usually the acknowledgment process involves placing a signature or initials on a copy of a source document.

Acoustical coupler modem A modem that employs a device to enable a touch-tone telephone to be connected to a dial-up terminal so that digital data can be transmitted over telephone lines to another point in a computer system.

Activity log A record of images or "snapshots" of items in a file that are changed by transactions; this record is maintained as part of a procedure to back up files kept on magnetic disks in a computer-based system so that the files can be reconstructed if necessary.

Activity ratio A measure of the percentage of records of a master file that are to be accessed during a processing run.

Add-in memory board A board or card that is connected to the motherboard of a microcomputer via a bus bar; it provides an expansion of secondary magnetic disk storage.

Ad hoc report A nonrecurring demand report that is requested by a user to provide needed information, usually pertaining to an upcoming decision; increasingly the user obtains the report via direct interaction with the computer system.

Address The precise specification of a location in the primary or secondary storage of a computer system.

Administrative control An internal control that has the objective(s) of promoting operational efficiency and/or encouraging adherence to management's policies and procedures.

Analog form The waveform assumed by data that are transmitted via telephone lines.

Application A significant task to which a computer-based information system is applied.

Application control A transaction-oriented internal control that pertains to the input, processing, or output stages of a transaction processing system.

Application generator A powerful software package that allows users to develop their own complete computer-based applications.

Application program The instructions (software) developed to perform the data or information processing steps required by a particular application.

Applications manager The manager within the information systems organization who supervises all new systems development projects, other than user-developed applications, and all maintenance activities related to current applications.

Arithmetic-logic unit The component of the central processing unit that executes arithmetic calculations and logical operations.

Asset accountability control An internal control that helps to safeguard a firm's assets by permitting access to assets only in accordance with management's authorization or by comparing recorded accountability with the existing assets.

Asynchronous modem A modem that involves the character-by-character transmission of messages, with each character being encompassed by start and stop bits.

Attribute A characteristic pertaining to an entity, activity, or event.

Attribute list A list or chain that is established within a file with respect to an attribute (characteristic) of interest; this type of list enables data concerning the attribute to be retrieved rapidly.

Audit An examination by an auditor of evidence pertaining to the representations and actions of an object firm.

Audit plan A plan that describes the scope, objectives, and internal control structure encompassed in a particular audit.

Audit program A list of the specific tests and steps needed to achieve the audit objectives that are stated in the audit plan.

Audit standard A criterion or standard of performance that should be observed by auditors; standards may be divided between those that specify professional characteristics and those that specify the scope of audits.

Audit trail A set of references that enable source items to be traced to outputs in which they appear, and vice versa.

Auditing A careful procedure by which objective evidence is collected in order to evaluate representations concerning actions and events.

Auditing process The systematic procedure by which an audit is planned, the steps are objectively performed, and the results are evaluated.

Auditing around the computer An audit approach that focuses on the inputs and outputs of a computer-based system, rather than on the computer processing activity.

Auditing through the computer An audit approach that directly focuses on controls built into the processing programs.

Auditing with the computer An audit approach that involves the use of the power of the computer to aid in performing the substantive tests required by audit programs.

Authorization control An internal control that ensures that management's policies are enforced through the approval of transactions.

Automated office   An office served by a computer system that is linked together by a local area network, thereby allowing users to share resources and to communicate electronically.

Automated teller machine (ATM)   A type of computer terminal that has the purpose of processing transactions of bank customers automatically.

Back order   A form or source document prepared to acquire goods needed to fill a customer's order when sufficient goods are not on hand.

Backup file   A copy of a data or program file that is created and maintained for reconstruction if the original is destroyed.

Backup system   Computer hardware or related equipment that is available on a stand-by basis for use when the normally used hardware or equipment fails in service.

Balance forward method   The method for reflecting payments from customers that applies the payments against an outstanding account balance rather than against specific invoices.

Batch control log   A record of each batch of transactions received by the data control section of the data processing function.

Batch processing   A mode of processing whereby groups or batches of transactions are accumulated, batch totals are computed, and the batches are entered into processing.

Batch total   A sum of numerical items appearing on a batch of source documents; the total is precomputed and then compared with totals computed during batch processing operations.

Baud rate   The speed, usually measured in bits per second, by which data are transmitted from one location to another.

Benchmark problem technique   An evaluation technique whereby an identical data processing activity or task is executed on two or more computer systems and results (usually in terms of processing times) are compared.

Benefit-cost ratio method   A method of evaluating the economic feasibility of an investment, using a ratio of benefits to the net investment cost (both expressed at present values).

Bernoulli box   An add-on magnetic disk storage device that is attached externally to a microprocessor.

Bill of lading   A document that represents a contract between a shipping firm and the common carrier and that provides proof that the shipped goods have been transferred to the carrier.

Bill of material   A document that lists the materials required in a particular product.

Binary search method   A search in which the set of items (e.g., the records in a file) is divided into two equal segments during a series of steps until the desired item is located.

Bit   A binary digit, the smallest unit of measure pertaining to data stored in a computer system; a combination of bits composes a single character of data.

Block   A group of logical records that are stored and handled as a unit or physical record; a block is generally separated from adjoining blocks by interblock gaps.

Block code   A coding scheme in which blocks of sequential numbers are reserved for specified categories of items.

Bottom-up approach   An approach for developing an information system whereby the lowest or operational level in a firm is initially developed and then the development process proceeds upward through successively higher levels of the organization.

Boundary   The demarcation between a system and its environment.

Bubble memory   A type of primary computer storage that consists of a thin magnetic film, on which bubbles representing data are formed when a magnetic force is applied.

Budget master file   A file that consists of the account values composing the budget of a firm.

Bucket   A block of records to which the index in an ISAM file points when a desired record is to be accessed directly.

Byte   A group of bits that represents a character of data.

Callback procedure   A security procedure whereby the connection is automatically broken after a caller enters a password from a terminal; the security software then dials the authorized phone number of the terminal from which the call was apparently made to ascertain that the authorized terminal was indeed used.

Capital investment proposal   A form employed to request, review, and approve the acquisition of a fixed asset.

Card punch machine   A device used to produce punched cards as output.

Cash management cycle   A transaction-oriented cycle that is concerned with the acquisition and disbursement of the cash resource.

Cash requirements report   A managerial report that shows the needs for cash during a specified future period.

CD ROM (Compact disk, random access memory)   An optical disk storage device attached externally to a microcomputer.

Central processing unit (CPU)   The central hardware of a computer that contains the arithmetic-logic, primary storage, and control components.

Centralized network   A computer-based network that consists of a mainframe computer and a number of geographically dispersed terminals that serve as input/output devices for the computer.

Chain   A linked list of records, such as an attribute list, that are connected by means of embedded pointers.

Chargeout procedure   A procedure for assigning or charging system-related costs to the users on the basis of chargeout rates.

Chart of accounts   A listing of all accounts composing the general ledger of a firm.

Check digit   A digit that is added to the remaining digits of a data item (e.g., the digits of a customer number), in order to provide the means of performing a verification of the accuracy of the remaining digits.

Check register   A journal for recording the cash disbursements of a firm.

Check voucher   A check, together with such details as account distribution and invoice numbers.

Child record   A type of record within a hierarchical or network data model that is subordinate to one or more parent records.

Chip   A tiny piece of silicon upon which logic or memory circuits are etched.

Classical systems development   The traditional approach to information systems development that involves the use of such techniques as systems flowcharts, work measurements, and so on.

Classification   The act of grouping items into classes according to a systematic plan.

Clock/calendar   An enhancement in microcomputer systems, usually in the form of an add-on board, that automatically maintains the time and date for users.

Coding   The assignment of symbols, such as letters and numbers, in accordance with a classification plan.

Cognative style   The approach by which a person employs mental facilities in solving a problem, such as making a decision; two examples of cognative styles are analytical and intuitive.

Collusion   A conspiracy by two or more persons to commit fraud.

Compiler language   A high-level procedural programming language that requires a compiler to convert the source commands written by a programmer into the object code that can be understood by the particular computer on which the program is to be executed.

Compliance test   A procedure by which an auditor determines if observed internal controls are functioning as prescribed.

Completeness check   A programmed check that verifies that all required data have been entered concerning a transaction.

Computer crime   An illegal act, such as embezzlement, performed with respect to a computer-based information system, either by an employee of the firm owning the system or by an outside party.

Computer hardware   The physical equipment and devices composing a computer system.

Computer log   A record of the productive and nonproductive uses of computer facilities.

Computer output microfilm (COM)   A hardware output device that generates highly compressed output on microfilm by means of a photographic process.

Computer software   The instructions that guide the operation of computer hardware and enable users to perform a variety of applications.

Computer system flowchart   A system flowchart that portrays the flows of data and information through a computer-based information system, showing such features as input methods, internal controls, storage media, and output reports.

Concentrator   A data communications device that enables messages from several points in a computer network to be edited and transmitted simultaneously over a single communications line.

Conceptual design   A design process that provides the overall system architecture, plus a relatively broad view of the combined system components.

Conceptual design specifications The "blueprints" that describe the conceptual design.

Conciseness *See* information conciseness.

Console log A record, maintained by the operating system, that reflects the actions of the computer system and the requests and responses of the computer operators during processing activities.

Constraint A restriction pertaining to a system, such as a limitation on available resources.

Control objectives The purposes of the internal control structure of a firm and its component systems.

Control point A point in the processing of a transaction where an internal control is needed to ensure the accuracy and reliability of the data.

Control process A regulatory process that has the overall purpose of aiding an entity (e.g., a firm, a system) to achieve its objectives and plans.

Control report A managerial report that aids the operational or management control processes.

Control risk The risk that currently installed internal controls will not prevent or detect significant errors in outputs of an AIS.

Control unit The component in the CPU that interprets program instructions and coordinates the various devices attached to the CPU.

Control-oriented flowchart A system flowchart that emphasizes the points where internal accounting controls are present.

Corrective control An internal control that is self-correcting.

Cost accounting system An information system that collects, processes, and reports data concerning the conversion of raw materials into finished goods.

Cost-benefit analysis A comparison of the costs and benefits involved in an information system development project; the analysis may consist of matching costs and benefits or of computing a benefit/cost ratio.

Credit memo A source document that records the approval of the return of merchandise by a customer.

Customer order A source document that reflects the order of merchandise by a customer and that normally leads to a sale.

Cylinder Vertically aligned tracks on the multiple surfaces of a magnetic disk pack.

Daisy-wheel printer A printer that employs a daisy-shaped print element and that produces outputs with the quality of typed letters.

Data Raw facts and figures and symbols that together form the inputs to an information system.

Data bank services A public service, such as an electronic library, to which an individual or firm can subscribe and retrieve useful data via its computer system.

Data base An integrated collection of stored data files and sets that are available for retrieval by an information system.

Data base administrator The individual who has responsibility for creating, managing, and controlling the data that are stored in a data base.

Data base approach An approach to designing data bases that focuses on the integration of data needed by a variety of computer-based applications.

Data base control system The software that controls the various components of a data base management system and that communicates with the operating system.

Data base management system (DBMS) A software package that has the overall purpose of managing the data in a computer-based data base.

Data collection The major activity of an information system that encompasses such steps as capturing, recording, validating, and editing data that are entered into an information system for processing.

Data collection terminal A specialized on-line terminal device that captures and enters data into an information system.

Data communications network A computer-based network that consists of terminals, modems, CPUs, and other hardware components that are linked by communications channels.

Data control The major activity in an information system that has the purpose of safeguarding assets and ensuring the reliability of data.

Data control section An organizational unit within the information systems function that monitors and controls the inflows of data to, and outflows of data from, the data processing unit.

Data definition language (DDL) The language component of a DBMS that describes the logical structure of the data base.

Data dictionary A listing of the data items

composing a data base, together with descriptive details such as field sizes and relationships.

Data documentation The documentation, such as the data dictionary, that includes the descriptions of the data within a data base.

Data entry screen A preformatted form or sequence that appears on a video display screen for the purpose of guiding the entry of data.

Data flow diagram A diagram that documents the logical flows of data through a transaction processing system.

Data independence The feature of the data base approach that involves the decoupling of the data base from the various application programs that utilize the data base.

Data library The organizational unit within the information systems function that maintains custody of files needed in data processing operations.

Data management The major activity of an information system that has the purpose of storing, maintaining, and retrieving data.

Data manipulation language (DML) The language component of a DBMS that provides the means of expressing requests and inquiries.

Data processing The major activity of an information system that involves such processing steps as transcribing, sorting, merging, and performing calculations with data.

Data set A structured arrangement of data that are stored under the data base approach.

Debit memorandum A source document that is prepared when a purchase return or allowance is granted.

Decision model A representation or model that describes the factors and relationships in a situation that requires a decision.

Decision process A rational and systematic process for making a decision.

Decision support system (DSS) A computer-based interactive information system that has the purpose of assisting managers in making high-level planning decisions in which the problem situations are relatively unstructured.

Decision table A matrix technique by which the logic of a problem situation is portrayed in terms of conditions and actions.

Decision flow diagram A flow technique by which chains of decisions and needed items of data are related.

Dedicated microcomputer A microcomputer that is used to serve one function, such as word processing, at any given period of time.

Deposit slip A document that lists the amounts of received funds that are being deposited into a bank account.

Designer's workbench A computerized version of the prototyping approach to information systems development.

Desk check A testing procedure whereby programmers manually trace the logic of newly written programs.

Desk-top publishing package A software package that enables microcomputers to produce professional-quality publications.

Detailed design A level of information system design that provides the details of each system component and often includes the application software.

Detective control A type of internal control that detects errors and irregularities in an information system.

Development engine The software component of an expert system that gathers the knowledge and decision processes from the human expert.

Dialogue prompt The method of aiding data entry by means of conversational suggestions and inquiries provided by the application program.

Dial-up terminal A terminal that is connected to a computer system by dialing via a touch-tone telephone.

Digital form Data that are stored in a computer system in a discrete form.

Direct access storage device (DASD) A secondary storage device, such as a magnetic disk, that allows direct access of data at specified addresses.

Direct cutover approach An approach to final systems conversion in which the newly implemented system is put into operation and the current system is abandoned without parallel testing.

Disaster contingency plan A detailed document that identifies all potential threats to a computer system of a firm and specifies needed preventive and corrective security measures.

Disbursement voucher A source document that reflects the obligations incurred for purchases of goods or services from a supplier.

Diskette A flexible or "floppy" disk that can be inserted into a diskette drive of a microcomputer in order to accept or transfer data.

Distributed network A computer-based network that incorporates a variety of processors at geographically disbursed locations so that local users can perform certain processing functions.

Distribution log A listing of persons authorized to receive the various outputs from application programs.

Document flowchart A diagram that depicts the flows of source documents and generated documents through the various steps of a procedure; one of its prominent features is that it highlights the organizational units in which the processing takes place.

Documentation The various procedure manuals and other means of describing the components of an information system and its operations.

Dot-matrix printer A printer, usually employed in microcomputer systems, that forms characters by means of a series of dots.

"Dumb" terminal A computer terminal device that can only accept data and produce outputs (i.e., that cannot process data).

Earnings register An output from the payroll procedure that shows amounts earned by employees.

Echo check A programmed edit check that "echoes" back descriptive data relating to the data items entered for processing.

Economic feasibility The condition whereby the expected benefits are likely to exceed the expected costs of developing a new or improved information system.

Edit check A programmed internal control employed in computer-based systems to detect erroneous or incomplete data during the entry or processing stages.

Electronic mail A software system that transmits written messages via data communications networks to recipients.

Electronic spreadsheet A software package that provides a multicolumn worksheet for use in analytical and modeling applications.

Embedded audit module technique A through-the-computer auditing technique that involves the embedding of audit modules in application programs for the purpose of testing data processed by the programs.

Employee services management cycle A transaction processing cycle whose purpose is to facilitate the exchange of cash with employees for needed services.

Encryption A procedure whereby data are

encoded in order to prevent unauthorized persons from understanding the content.

Entity-relationship diagram A means of building a conceptual model of a data base by portraying the relevant entities and the relationships among them.

Environment The conditions and elements that lay beyond the boundary of a system.

Equipment utilization report A managerial control report that shows the uses of computers and other equipment and the percentage of time during which the equipment is not in use.

Error correction procedure A procedure by which detected errors in data are corrected.

Event-triggered report A managerial control report that is generated (triggered) by a condition requiring attention.

Evolutionary approach An approach to systems development that involves a series of changes over time, with each change incorporating a somewhat more advanced system.

Expenditure cycle A transaction processing cycle that spans the requisitioning and purchasing of needed goods and services and the payment for the goods and services.

Exception and summary report A control report that lists detected errors and exceptional conditions and includes such summary values as batch control totals.

Exception report A managerial control report that contains only those items or conditions that have been predefined as exceptional and that thus warrant special attention.

Execution time The time that a processor requires to perform a single computation.

Executive information system A type of DSS that supports strategic planning.

Expert auditor system An audit tool that consists of a computer model that simulates the audit procedures of experienced auditors and thus aids relatively inexperienced auditors in making necessary decisions concerning audit programs.

Expert system A computer-based user-support system that is built with the assistance of a human expert and that suggests the best decisions or actions to take in relatively unstructured situations.

External auditor An independent auditor who conducts examinations of client firms and expresses opinions on the basis of such examinations.

External file label A physical label that is attached to the outside of a magnetic tape or disk container to identify the contents of the files stored thereon.

Facilities management firm A vendor organization that manages the information systems facilities of client firms for fees.

Facilities management cycle A transaction processing cycle that encompasses the acquisition, maintenance, and disposition of fixed assets.

Facsimile (Fax) The transmission of images in the form of signals to receiving points where the signals are converted back into the images; facsimile requires special software and hardware devices.

Feasibility study A preliminary investigation that explores the feasibility of undertaking a systems development project, such as the conversion to a computer-based system.

Feedback A process whereby information output from an operation returns ("feeds back") to the operation or its regulator as an input.

Feedforward A process whereby information is generated by a control system in order to anticipate potential problem areas so that corrective actions can be taken in advance.

Fidelity bond A contractual arrangement with an insurance firm to provide indemification to the insuring firm in case the dishonesty of a specified employee causes loss to the firm.

Field A portion of a record that contains the value of a data item.

Field check A programmed edit check that determines if each field in an input record contains data of a desired mode (e.g., numeric).

File A collection of logically related records.

File conversion An implementation activity that consists of converting the data in one or more files from the current medium to the medium specified for a new information system.

File maintenance The processing of master files to update balances, to make changes in permanent data items as necessary, to add new records, and to delete expired records.

File volatility The frequency with which records are added to, or deleted from, a file over a period of time.

File-oriented approach The data management approach that focuses on the files needed in individual applications.

File-oriented microcomputer system A microcomputer system in which the system controls

data entry through such devices as optical scanners or magnetic disks.

Financial accounting The branch of accounting that has the purpose of generating such scorekeeping information as balance sheets and income statements for a firm.

Financial audit An examination of the fairness with which financial statements present a business entity's financial position and results of operations.

Financial modeling package A software package that enables financial aspects of a firm or situation to be represented in a symbolic manner.

Financial reporting system A reporting system that draws upon accounting transactions for input data and prepares such outputs as financial statements.

Finished goods status report An operational report that lists the current status of each finished good or product maintained for sale by a manufacturing firm.

Fixed asset change form A source document that serves as the basis for transferring, retiring, selling, or otherwise disposing of fixed assets.

Fixed asset register An operational report that lists all fixed assets for use by a firm.

Flat file A file structure in which each record is identical with respect to data items and no repeating fields appear.

Foreign Corrupt Practices Act An act passed in 1977 that includes the requirement that publicly held corporations maintain sound systems of internal accounting control.

Form analysis sheet A worksheet that is designed to reflect the analysis of a particular source document or other form.

Fourth generation language A high-level problem-oriented computer language that is user-friendly and often suited to specialized applications, such as financial modeling.

Front-end processor A small communications computer processor that relieves the central or mainframe computer of functions related to data editing and transmission.

Full-duplex transmission A type of transmission that allows data to be transmitted in both directions over a communication line at the same time.

Gantt chart A bar chart that shows the scheduled time periods for the various activities of a project, together with the extent of completion of each activity.

General authorization An internal control procedure that establishes standard conditions under which transactions are approved and executed.

General control A class of internal controls that includes organization, documentation, security, and other nontransactional controls.

General journal An accounting book of original entry that can accommodate any type of accounting transaction.

General ledger A master file that contains records pertaining to all the accounts in the chart of accounts of an entity.

General ledger and financial reporting cycle The transaction processing cycle that accepts all the financial transactions deriving from the remaining cycles and generates financial reports on a cyclical basis.

General ledger analysis A type of control report that aids in verifying the accuracy of postings to the general ledger.

Generalized audit software (GAS) package A software package that is used by auditors to perform audit program steps under the auditing with the computer approach.

Grandfather-father-son procedure A procedure for providing two or more generations of backup copies of data files, usually when the magnetic tape medium is used.

Graphics board An add-in board for microcomputers that allows the presentation of graphical displays on video screens.

Graphics package A software package that enables users to display information in graphical forms.

Group code A coding system that incorporates two or more subcodes, each of which reveals a facet pertaining to the object being coded.

Half-duplex transmission A type of transmission that allows data to be transmitted over a communications line in both directions, but not at the same time.

Hard disk A magnetic disk that is made of a rigid material and sealed within a disk unit to provide protection against damage.

Hardware check A control built into a computer processor or other hardware devices, such as input and output devices, for the purpose of detecting malfunctions that may cause errors or loss of data.

Hardware configuration An arrangement of the hardware components composing a computer system; hardware configurations may be described by means of diagrams.

Hardware monitor A device that is connected to a computer processor to gather data concerning the degree of utilization of the various components such as the processor, secondary storage units, and so on.

Hard-wired modem A modem that is attached to a terminal, either internally or externally, by means of permanent wiring.

Hashing scheme A randomizing procedure that transforms the primary key of a record into a randomized address of a magnetic disk or other direct access storage device.

Header label The initial record of a sequentially organized file that identifies the file and provides other relevant characteristics.

Hierarchical configuration A configuration of a distributed computer network that consists of a hierarchy of several levels of computers which is headed by a mainframe or host computer.

Hierarchical model A data model that represents a tree structure, with a root node to which parent and child records attach.

Hierarchy chart A business model that describes the overall logical structure of a system or system module.

History file A type of file that contains data reflecting the history of past transactions concerning an entity, such as sales.

Human information processing (HIP) An area of study that is concerned with the manner by which humans process information in order to make decisions.

Image reader An input device that involves the use of either a microfilm recorder or a facsimile scanner.

Impact printer A category of printer that prints one line or character at a time.

Imprest basis A method of controlling resources, such as petty cash, whereby a fund is maintained at a fixed level in the general ledger and is reimbursed periodically on the basis of paid vouchers.

Incomplete prebilling A procedure whereby a sales order-invoice is prepared at the time the order is approved and is then completed as the sales invoice when the goods are shipped.

Index search method A method of retrieving data from a data base by means of an index that cross-references data keys against the addresses where the records are stored.

Indexed sequential (ISAM) file A file structure that employs a sequential method for organizing the records and an index search method for accessing individual records.

Inference engine The component of an expert system that contains the logic and reasoning mechanisms that simulate the thought process of the human expert.

Information Data made useful and meaningful through processing.

Information accuracy The property of information relating to reliability and precision.

Information center A physical location and/or organizational unit within a firm where users can receive computer systems services; a center is normally headed by an information center manager, who may report to the information systems manager.

Information conciseness The property of information relating to the degree of aggregation.

Information economics An area of study concerning values and costs of information and their trade-offs.

Information generation A major activity of an information system that concerns the preparation of reports for users.

Information needs analysis A procedure employed in the top-down approach to systems development whereby the information needs of users are analyzed by reference to the decisions that they make.

Information overload The result of providing more information to managers and other users than they can reasonably digest and apply.

Information processing The activities involved in providing useful decision-making information to managers and other users.

Information quantifiability The property of information concerned with the degree to which numeric values can be assigned.

Information relevance The property of information concerned with the degree to which an item of information affects a decision.

Information resources management (IRM) The concept that information is a vital resource that requires careful management.

Information scope The property of information concerned with the span encompassed by the information.

Information systems manager The top manager within the information systems function of a firm.

Information theory The concepts related to the communication of information from a source via a channel to a receiver.

Information timeliness The property of information concerned with the currency of the information.

Information value The usefulness of information, measured by the extent to which a given piece of information reduces a user's uncertainty concerning a particular decision situation.

Input control A type of transaction control that is concerned with the accuracy and completeness of data during the input stage.

Input/output matrix A systems analysis technique that depicts the relationships between input data items and the reports in which they appear.

Intangible benefit A type of benefit pertaining to an information system whose value cannot be measured with reasonable accuracy.

Integrated package A software package that combines two or more major functions, such as data base management and word processing.

Integrated test facility (ITF) technique A computer-based audit technique that uses hypothetical transactions to test the edit programs in online applications.

Interblock gap (IBG) A space or gap that separates physical blocks of data stored on a magnetic tape or disk.

Interface A common boundary between subsystems within a system.

Interleaved storage access A technique by which partitions in the primary storage unit are controlled separately so that data may be retrieved in one partition while being entered in another.

Internal auditor An auditor who is an employee of the firm in which he or she performs audits.

Internal control audit A type of audit that involves the review and evaluation of the internal control structure of a firm.

Internal control structure A framework that composes all the internal controls and security measures of a firm.

Interviewing technique A data-gathering technique often employed by analysts to obtain information from managers and employees concerning system needs, operations, and so on.

Inventory status report An operational report that lists the status of each inventory item maintained by a firm.

Inverted file An index that is arranged by a secondary file key and is thereby inverted from the primary key of the sequential file on which is it based.

Job-time ticket A source document that records the time spent by an employee on a particular job.

Journal voucher A source document that contains a single transaction and that replaces the general journal.

Joystick An input stick device that is tilted in any direction to move a cursor on a video display screen of a microcomputer.

Just-in-time (JIT) system A specialized information system that virtually eliminates the need for manufacturing inventories, since it schedules deliveries to coincide with the production process.

Key success factor A piece of information that is vital to the success of a firm.

Key verification A process whereby the keying of data is verified by means of rekeying the same data and noting differences; its purpose is to ensure that correct data are entered for processing.

Keyboard/printer terminal A type of computer terminal that consists of a keyboard for data entry and a printer for output; it does not incorporate a video display screen.

Key-to-disk system An input system that consists of a number of keyboard stations at which clerks prepare data for entry; the typical system performs validating and editing steps before recording the data onto magnetic tapes or disks.

Key-to-tape encoder An input device that transcribes data onto a magnetic tape; an encoder may be a stand-alone device or grouped into a key-to-tape system.

Kilobyte A measure of storage that represents 1024 characters or bytes.

Kiting A form of embezzlement that involves covering cash shortages by transferring checks among two or more bank accounts.

Knowledge base The component of an expert system that incorporates the knowledge, rules-of-thumb, and decision rules used by experts.

Labor distribution summary An operational report that arrays the hours worked by employees according to jobs or accounts.

Lapping A form of embezzlement that consists of concealing a cash shortage by means of delaying postings of collections to the proper customers' accounts.

Laser printer A nonimpact page printer that uses laser beams to form images.

Legal compliance report A type of report that is prepared to satisfy a legal requirement; often the recipient of this type of report is a governmental agency.

Light pen A stylus input device that enters data when a user "draws" on the face of a light-sensitive display screen.

Limit check A programmed edit check that compares entered data values against predetermined limits and indicates when the limits are exceeded.

Linked list A collection of logically related data that are linked by means of embedded pointers.

Liquid crystal display (LCD) A display screen of a portable microcomputer that is composed of a liquid crystal substance.

Local area network (LAN) A distributed network of computer processors and software, usually formed into workstations and servers, that functions within a single limited geographical area.

Lockout A software security feature that prevents two programs from accessing the same record in a file concurrently.

Logical data model A means of modeling the logical relationships among files and data sets within a data base; three data models are known as the tree, network, and relational models.

Logical data structure A data-related structure within a data base that can reflect a logical view of the relationships among the files and data sets.

Logistics management The activities within a firm that span the acquisition of needed resources through the distribution of merchandise or products to customers.

Mainframe computer A large-scale processor that often serves as the center of a firm's computer system.

Machine language A type of computer programming language that employs a binary code and that pertains to one specific computer.

Magnetic disk A secondary storage medium that consists of rotating disk surfaces that can store data in magnetized form; it is the most popular direct access storage device.

Magnetic ink character recognition (MICR) device An input device that recognizes characters printed with a special magnetic ink; MICR devices are mainly used to handle bank checks.

Magnetic tape A secondary storage medium that consists of a reel of tape that can contain data in magnetized form; it is the most commonly employed sequential access storage medium.

Management control A control process that focuses on managerial performance and has the objective of promoting the efficient and effective acquisition and use of a firm's resources.

Management control decision A managerial decision that is based on information provided by the management control process.

Management information system (MIS) The type of information system that provides needed information to the managers of a firm for use in decision-making.

Managerial accounting The branch of accounting that has the purpose of providing attention-direction and decision-making information to the internal users of a firm.

Managerial report An output of an information system that has the purpose of aiding the managers in planning, controlling, and directing the operations of their firm.

Many-to-many relationship A relationship within a data structure in which parent records can have many child records and child records can also have many parent records.

Master file A type of file that contains records pertaining to the current status of entities such as customers or inventory items.

Material issue slip A source document that reflects the quantities of specific raw materials that are issued into the production process, often for use on a particular job order.

Materials requirements planning (MRP) A procedure that controls the materials aspect of the production process by ensuring that proper quantities of raw materials, parts, and subassemblies are available when needed for scheduled production orders.

Megabyte A million bytes or characters of data.

Menu screen A list of options that is displayed on a video screen for choice by the user of the terminal or microcomputer.

Microcomputer A type of computer, smaller than a minicomputer or mainframe computer, that is usually operated by a single user at any point in time.

Microcomputer audit-assist software Packaged software that enables an auditor to gain assistance via a microcomputer in performing an audit.

Microfilm A storage medium that enables data to be stored in microscopic form at a relatively low cost.

Microprocessor An integrated circuit stored on a silicon chip; the processor unit of a microcomputer.

Microprogram Instructions that are permanently fixed on read-only memory by the computer manufacturer; microprograms are also called microcodes or firmware.

Millisecond One-thousandth of a second.

Minicomputer A middle-sized computer that is larger than a microcomputer but smaller than a mainframe computer.

Mnemonic code A coding system in which the codes provide visible clues concerning the objects they represent.

Model base A collection of models, in the form of software, that are available in a decision support system to be accessed by users.

Model base management system (MBMS) A software system, analogous to a data base management system, that maintains the model base by providing links among the models and means of defining, manipulating, and modifying the models.

Modem A communications device that modulates and demodulates signals so that data in digital form may be transmitted over lines that only accept data in analog form.

Modular approach An approach to systems development by which the information system is treated as a group of interdependent modules so that development and maintenance may be performed more easily.

Monthly statement An output that shows the transactions for the past month and the current balance owed by a customer.

Motherboard The main circuit board of a microcomputer, to which the various components are attached by means of a bus bar.

Mouse An input device that enables a user

to move the cursor on the video screen of a monitor, thereby pointing to command options or performing other desired functions.

Move ticket A source document, also called a traveler, that authorizes the physical movement of production orders from one work center or process to another.

Multidrop configuration A centralized network arrangement that links the remote terminals to the central computer by means of "drops" from a single communications line.

Multiple-key inquiry A type of information inquiry from a user than requires the access of two or more inverted files, each of which is organized according to a particular secondary key.

Multiplexed configuration A centralized network arrangement that links a cluster of remote terminals to the central computer by means of a multiplexer or other line-sharing device.

Multiplexer A line-sharing device, essentially a small specialized computer, that combines the data signals from multiple terminals into a composite signal for transmission to a single point, such as a central computer.

Multiprocessing A mode of operation in which two or more processors composing a single computer system perform separate processing tasks simultaneously.

Multiprogramming A mode of operation in which two or more programs can be executed concurrently within the same central processing unit.

Multitasking microcomputer A type of super microcomputer that allows two or more terminals to be attached to the central processor so that multiple tasks can be performed concurrently.

Nanosecond One billionth of a second.

Narrow-band line A communication line that transmits data at low baud rates and is mainly used by dial-up terminals.

Net present value method A method for determining economic feasibility that involves the discounting of future cash flows to compute the net present value of a systems investment.

Network diagram A diagram, such as a PERT diagram, that reflects the relationships among the various activities encompassed by a project in order to provide the means for planning and controlling the project.

Network model A data structure, also called a plex structure, that allows more than one root node and many-to-many as well as one-to-many relationships.

Noise A term that refers to effects that inhibit the perfect communication of information.

Nondestructive readout The process of reading or transferring data from a computer-based storage medium that does not erase the data from the source being read.

Nonimpact printer A type of printer that involves a nonimpact process and that typically prints an entire page at a time.

Nonrecurring adjusting journal entry An ad hoc type of adjusting journal entry, such as an adjustment for a change in inventory methods, that is not expected to recur on a period-by-period basis.

Normalization A process, necessary when relational data base management systems are employed, that transforms tree or network models into relations.

Office automation An application that results in the installation of networks of automated workstations within business offices, in order to improve productivity and decision-making.

Offline The condition in which a device is not connected directly to a central processing unit, even though it can be viewed broadly as being involved in the functioning of the computer system.

One-time cost A cost of acquiring and/or developing the resources in an information system.

One-to-many relationship A relationship within a data structure in which a parent record may have one or more child records, but a child record may have only one parent record.

One-write processing A mode of processing in which the data entry and posting steps are performed simultaneously with the preparation of source documents.

Online The condition in which a device is connected directly to the central processing unit.

Online processing approach A processing approach in which each transaction is processed as soon as it is captured and entered into the computer system.

Open invoice method A method of maintaining accounts receivable in which each payment from a customer is matched against a specific invoice.

Open orders report An operational report that lists the outstanding sales or purchase orders as of the report date.

Open payables report An operational report that lists the unpaid invoices or vouchers concerning amounts due to suppliers.

Operating documentation Documentation that includes the operating instructions for various computer programs of a firm, together with related information of interest to computer operators.

Operating system System software that controls and coordinates the overall operation of a computer system.

Operational control A process that promotes efficiency in the operational tasks performed by a firm.

Operational control decision A decision that has the purpose of effecting operational control.

Operational feasibility The type of feasibility that relates to the extent to which an information system can and will be used by the personnel for which it has been designed.

Operational report A type of managerial report that details the current status of an entity, such as inventory, or that summarizes the results of operations in a particular area of activity.

Operational support system A type of user-support system that aids tactical planning and operational support within a firm.

Operational system The work system of a firm that encompasses its physical and operational processes.

Operations list A document that specifies the sequence of operations that must be performed in fashioning and assembling the parts and materials used in manufactured products.

Operator-oriented microcomputer system A microcomputer system in which the transactions are entered manually by clerks and operators through keyboards or other input devices.

Optical character recognition (OCR) device An input device that employs an optical process to recognize characters that are written or printed in an acceptable font.

Optical disk A secondary storage medium that employs lasers to write onto, or read from, a disk surface.

Order acknowledgment An output document, often a copy of a sales order, that is sent to a customer to acknowledge the order.

Organization chart A hierarchical diagram that portrays the organizational units of a firm and their relationships.

Organizational control A type of control that embodies the principle of organizational independence.

Organizational independence A clear and logical division of assigned duties and responsibilities within an organizational structure.

Organizational structure The arrangement of duties and responsibilities by which the managers of a firm direct and coordinate the operations.

Overdue deliveries report A managerial control report that highlights the orders that have not been shipped by the scheduled shipping date.

Output control The type of transaction control that pertains to the output stage of a transaction processing system.

Overlapping A mode of operation that enables a computer system to perform processing, input, and output functions simultaneously.

Packing list An output document that lists the items being shipped on an order and their quantities.

Page A segment of a computer program that can be transferred into the primary storage unit of a computer and executed; the use of pages facilitates the execution of very lengthy programs.

Parallel interface The link to a microcomputer motherboard that accommodates a printer or plotter.

Parallel operation approach An approach to the final conversion of a new information system in which the new and old systems are operated side-by-side for a reasonable period, and the resulting outputs are compared.

Parallel processing The simultaneous execution of two or more programs within a single computer processor.

Parallel simulation technique An auditing-through-the-computer technique that involves the simulation of actual processing performed earlier by a firm and the comparison of the resulting outputs.

Parent record A type of record in a tree or

network structure that "owns" one or more child records.

Parity bit A bit added to a character (byte) or word for the purpose of enabling the accuracy of the character or word to be checked.

Password A user code that must be entered into a computer system before the user is allowed to access data or execute programs.

Payback period method A method for determining the economic feasibility of an investment (e.g., a new computer system) in which the period required to recover the investment is computed.

Paycheck An output document that represents a cash disbursement to an employee for services rendered.

Periodic dump and restruction procedure A data backup procedure in which the contents of master files are periodically copied and transaction logs are accumulated.

Personnel action form A source document that authorizes a particular action (e.g., an increase in salary) with respect to an employee.

Physical storage structure The arrangement of data stored on a physical storage medium, such as a magnetic disk.

Picking list A source document, often a copy of a sales order, that authorizes the picking of ordered merchandise or products from the warehouse.

Planning report A type of managerial report that aids in making planning decisions; this type of report usually contains future-directed information that reveals the differences among alternative courses of action.

Plotter An output device that makes hard copies of graphical presentations.

Pointer A data item whose value consists of a storage address where data of interest are stored.

Point-of-sale terminal A type of online input device that accepts data concerning a sale; often an optical scanner is used to capture the data.

Point-to-point configuration A centralized network configuration in which each remote terminal is linked by a separate communication line to a central processor.

Portable computer A type of small computer that can be carried by a user from place to place.

Postimplementation evaluation An evalua-

tion performed after a new information system has been implemented and put into operation, in order to determine that the objectives have been met and performance is satisfactory.

Prebilling A billing procedure in which the sales invoice for a sale is completely filled in as soon as the order is approved.

Preformatted screen The display of a form on a video screen in order to aid the entry of transaction data by a clerk.

Preventive control A type of internal control whose purpose is to prevent errors or loss of data.

Primary key The coded data item by which the records of a file are most likely to be sequenced.

Primary storage unit The component of a central processing unit in which data processing takes place.

Printer An output device that provides hard copy.

Private line A telephone communications line that provides exclusive service to a lessee for a fixed service charge that is dependent on the length of line.

Problem-oriented language A high-level computer programming language that enables programs to be developed by specifying the key aspects of a problem; this type of language is often described as a fourth generation language.

Procedure A specific sequence of steps that involves the processing of data.

Procedure-oriented language A high-level computer programming language that requires the programmer to write instructions that follow a logical sequence in solving problems; this type of language is often described as a third generation language.

Processing control A type of transaction control that pertains to the processing stage of a transaction processing system.

Processing cycle The period of time between successive processings of batched data.

Processor The central processing unit of a computer.

Product conversion cycle The transaction cycle that involves the conversion of raw materials into finished goods by means of a manufacturing or construction process.

Production order A source document that incorporates data pertaining to a single order that is routed through the product conversion cycle.

Profitability reporting system A managerial reporting system that emphasizes the planning of profits for a firm and its segments.

Program documentation Documentation that includes program flowcharts, source program lists, and other items pertaining to computer programs.

Program flowchart A flowchart that portrays the logic of a computer program.

Protocol A set of rules that prescribes the manner by which data are transmitted from one point to another throughout a data communications network.

Prototyping A systems development approach that incorporates a learning process, since it consists of devising a preliminary system design and then refining the design as experience is gained in the use of the system.

Public data network A communications network, owned by a firm such as IBM, that provides a variety of services to subscribers on a fee basis.

Public line A telephone communications line, also called a dial-up line or switched line, that provides service based mainly on the amount of time used.

Punched card A storage medium that consists of a card containing a number of columns (e.g., 80) into which holes are punched; the holes represent numeric or alphabetic characters.

Purchase analysis A managerial report that presents an analysis of purchases made by the firm.

Purchase order A source document that is used to order quantities of raw materials or merchandise from a supplier.

Purchase requisition A source document that is used to request the ordering of needed raw materials or merchandise.

Query language A computer language that enables users to express requests for information from computer systems in a "user-friendly" manner; a query language is often a component of a DBMS or a DSS.

Questionnaire technique A data-gathering technique that involves the distribution of questionnaires to persons who have knowledge desired by analysts or auditors.

Random file A type of file in which records are stored throughout a direct access storage medium in a random manner.

Random access memory (RAM) A type of storage location that allows data and instructions to be written to as well as read from.

Range check A programmed edit check that determines whether an entered data value is within a prescribed range.

Raw materials management cycle See product conversion cycle.

Raw materials status report An operational report that reflects the current status of each raw material item in inventory.

Read-only memory (ROM) A type of storage location from which data or instructions can be read but to which new data or instructions may not normally be written.

Real-time A response time that is sufficiently brief to enable a system to control a process or satisfy an urgent need of a user.

Reassessment An internal control that consists of a reevaluation of an asset value, such as the reassessment of a recorded inventory value on the basis of a physical count.

Receiving report A source document that records the quantities of merchandise or materials items received in a delivery.

Reconciliation An internal control that consists of comparing values computed independently, such as the comparison of the balance in a control account with the total of balances in a subsidiary ledger.

Record A collection of logically related data items.

Record layout A diagram that depicts the arrangement and sizes of fields in a record.

Recurring cost A type of information system cost that is incurred on a period-by-period basis.

Reference file A type of file that contains data to be referenced during data processing steps.

Register A record of receipts, shipments, or other events; a type of accounting journal.

Relation A two-dimensional table that serves as the logical data store in a relational data base.

Relational model A type of data model that stores data in relations and enables relationships to be implicitly established among the relations.

Relationship check A programmed edit check that involves the comparison of two or more data items to determine if they are logically related.

Relevance See information relevance.

Reliability The consistency in results from processing like data.

Remittance advice A source document that reflects the receipt of a payment from a customer.

Remote job entry station A terminal, geographically separated from a central computer, that feeds data (e.g., batches of transactions) to the computer for processing.

Report format The arrangement of information on a report.

Report generator A software package that enables a user to specify the characteristics of a desired report and to obtain the report on demand; a report generator is often a component of a DBMS or a DSS.

Request for proposal (RFP) A document that is prepared for distribution to suppliers of computer hardware or software or other system components; it solicits responses from the suppliers that meet the requirements of a new system being developed.

Reservation terminal A type of terminal used by such firms as airlines to handle reservations.

Resource management cycle A transaction processing cycle that manages a resource such as materials, employee services, facilities, and cash.

Response time The length of time required for a computer system to provide information after a request or inquiry has been entered.

Responsibility center An organizational unit within a firm where specified responsibilities are centered.

Responsibility reporting system A managerial reporting system that provides a set of correlated control reports concerning the responsibility centers of a firm.

Revenue cycle The transaction processing cycle that spans the sales of merchandise or products and the receipts of cash for the sales.

Review An internal control involving an independent verification of asset values or other matters concerning a firm's operations.

Ring configuration A type of distributed network configuration in which the remote computer processing sites are linked in a closed loop.

Ring list A type of linked list in which a pointer connects the last record in the list to the first record or root record.

Risk exposure The exposure of a firm's data or resources to errors or loss or damage because of the inadequacy of controls.

Rollback and recovery A security procedure that is employed when data files are lost; in the rollback phase the backup files are loaded, and in the recovery phase the transactions are entered from an activity log and processed against the backup files.

Root node The top or entry node (record) of a tree or network structure.

Sales invoice A source document that reflects the amount of a sale; if the sale is for credit the sales invoice is the posting medium.

Sales order A source document that reflects the merchandise or products ordered by a customer and the quantities of each item.

Satellite system A remote site in a distributed network at which local processing takes place.

Scheduled report A report that is generated and distributed on a regularly scheduled basis.

Schema The logical view of all the associations among the data sets composing a data base.

Scope *See* information scope.

Screen display A soft copy display of information on the screen of a video display monitor.

Secondary key A code of an attribute within the record of a file, usually a master file.

Security measure A type of internal control that has the purpose of protecting assets (including data) from unauthorized access or use or theft.

Self-checking digit A programmed edit check that is based on a digit attached to a code for an entity, in order that the computer system can perform an algorithm to verify that the code has been entered correctly.

Separate order and billing A procedure in which a sales order is initially prepared and later a sales invoice is prepared as a separate document after the goods have been shipped.

Sequence code A coding system in which numbers are assigned in sequential order.

Sequenced approach An approach to systems development which involves the application of a pre-established sequence of steps.

Sequential access file A file access method in which the records are accessed sequentially.

Sequential file A file in which the records are organized sequentially, usually in ascending order.

Serial interface The link in a microcomputer that connects the communications component (e.g., the modem) to the motherboard.

Service bureau An outside computing service firm that provides batch data processing services to subscribers.

Set A data structure which consists of a parent record and a child record.

Sign check A programmed edit check that determines if entered data are correct by examining the sign of a particular value, such as an account balance.

Simplex transmission A type of transmission that allows data to be transmitted in only one direction over a communication line.

Simulation model technique A computer selection and evaluation technique that involves the use of a mathematical model to simulate the operation of the computer system.

Shipping notice A source document that reflects the merchandise items or products that have been shipped against an order and the quantities of each.

Software check A check performed by system software, such as an operating system, to detect malfunctions and/or to alert operators.

Software monitor A software routine that resides within a computer system to gather data concerning the utilization of components or the status of internal conditions.

Source data automation (SDA) An approach to data collection in which transaction data are captured in computer-readable form at their source and entered for processing; an optical scanner is an example of an SDA device.

Source document A form used to record the details of a transaction; often a source document is used as the source of posting to a master file and may be used to reflect accountability for actions taken.

Space layout diagram A data organization technique that portrays the arrangement and use of space within an office or other area.

Special journal A type of journal that provides a specialized format tailored to a commonly recurring type of transaction.

Specialized audit software A set of audit routines that are customized to suit a particular audit situation.

Specific authorization An internal control procedure that establishes the conditions under which a specific type of transaction is to be approved and executed.

Spooling A procedure whereby information is stored temporarily on a secondary storage medium and then later printed offline onto hard copy.

Standard adjusting journal entry A journal entry that records the same adjustment (e.g., for depreciation expense) at the end of each accounting period on a recurring basis.

Star configuration A type of distributed network configuration in which each of the remote computer processing sites is linked directly to a central point.

Steering committee A group of major information system users in a firm which has the overall responsibility for planning and guiding systems development.

Stewardship report A type of report (e.g., the annual report to stockholders), that relates to the stewardship responsibilities of a firm.

Strategic planning decision A managerial decision that is based on information provided by the strategic planning process.

Strategic systems plan A blueprint for future systems development in a firm.

String testing A testing procedure in which several application programs are linked together and tested as they would function in real operations.

Structured decision A decision situation whose factors and relationships are sufficiently well understood that it could be programmed for the computer.

Structured systems development A body of techniques that allows a disciplined approach to the analysis and design of information systems.

Subschema The portion of the schema of a data base (i.e., the logical view) that is of interest to a particular user.

Subsidiary ledger A master file that contains the records concerning entities such as customers.

Substantive test A test, performed as a part of an audit program, that has the purpose of gathering evidence concerning financial transactions and statements.

Subsystem An interdependent part of a system.

Supplier's invoice A source document provided by a supplier to a firm that has purchased goods or services.

Suspense file A file onto which transactions containing detected errors are entered until investigated and corrected.

Symbolic language A computer programming language, also called an assembly language or a second generation language, that employs symbols and is relatively efficient.

Synchronous modem A modem that allows blocks of characters to be transmitted as units.

System A unity composed of two or more subsystems that have a common objective.

System application documentation Documentation that pertains to a particular computer system application.

System control audit review file (SCARF) The key output from an embedded audit module.

System flowchart A diagram that portrays the sequential flow of data and/or operations pertaining to a transaction processing system or other system.

System life cycle The cycle spanning the life of an information system and including such phases as planning, analysis, design, implementation, and operation.

System project An organized undertaking that has the purpose of developing a new information system module.

System requirements The set of requirements for a new information system that is based on a survey and analysis.

System standard An established feature of an information system, which may pertain to components, performance, documentation, and so on.

System survey An investigation of the present information system and the need for a new information system.

System testing A testing procedure that has the purpose of ascertaining that the software are compatible with the hardware.

Systems analysis report The report prepared at the end of the systems analysis phase that contains the system requirements.

Systems design proposal The report prepared at the end of the systems design phase that contains the conceptual system specifications.

Systems development manager The manager who has overall responsibility within the information systems function for the development of new information systems.

Systems development procedure The procedure followed in developing a new information system.

Systems hierarchy A framework that consists of levels of systems and subsystems.

Tactical planning decision A managerial decision that is based on information provided by a tactical planning process.

Tailored approach An approach to systems development that consists of developing designs to fit the specific characteristics of the system modules.

Tangible benefit A type of benefit pertaining to an information system whose value can be measured with reasonable accuracy.

Tape cartridge A secondary storage device that loads magnetic tape and is often used in a data backup procedure.

Tape cassette A secondary storage device similar to a tape cartridge.

Tape file protection ring A plastic ring that prevents data from being accidentally written onto a magnetic tape.

Tax accounting The branch of accounting that has the purposes of preparing tax returns and aiding the making of decisions having tax implications.

Technical feasibility The type of feasibility that is concerned that the existing state of technology is adequate to accommodate a new system design.

Technical services manager A manager within the information systems function who supervises activities relating to the system software and communications network and other technologies.

Template A prewritten spreadsheet program that aids an auditor in performing an audit task.

Terminal An online input/output device.

Test data technique An auditing-through-the-computer technique that involves the use of test transactions to audit the programmed checks in an application program.

Test of control *See* compliance test.

Time and/or attendance form A source document used to record the time that an employee worked on assigned tasks or was in attendance.

Time reporting system A data recording procedure in which time sheets are prepared to reflect hours worked on various tasks and projects.

Timeliness *See* information timeliness.

Timesharing The concurrent servicing of two or more users by a single computer processor.

Timesharing service center A type of outside computing service in which terminals are located in the offices of subscribing firms so that data may be transmitted directly to the center for processing and/or storage and outputs can be generated on output devices in the subscribers' offices.

Top-down approach An approach for developing an information system whereby the objectives are first established and then the information needs for managerial decision-making are determined.

Touch input device An input device in which the person enters data by touching the screen of the CRT monitor.

Trailer label The last record of a sequentially organized file that contains control totals concerning the data in the records.

Transaction control A class of internal accounting controls that relates to the various transactions being processed by an information system.

Transaction file A type of file that contains the individual transactions of a like nature (e.g., sales).

Transaction log A record of all transactions entered for processing by a system; it is generally maintained as a backup file.

Transaction processing The procedures by which data concerning various types of transactions are processed by the accounting information system.

Transaction processing cycle The sequence of steps performed in order to process one or more related transactions.

Tree model *See* hierarchical model.

Trial balance A listing of all account balances in the general ledger of a firm so that the total of the credit balances may be compared with the total of the debit balances.

Turnaround document A source document that is printed by the computer system as an output document, and then is later returned to be used as computer-readable input to the computer system.

Turnkey system A computer system that is completely installed in a firm by an outside supplier so that it is ready to operate as soon as the "key is turned on."

Unstructured decision A decision situation whose factors and relationships are not well understood and thus cannot be fully modeled and programmed for solution by a computer system.

Uploading Transferring data from a small processor or terminal within a network to the data base of a central computer.

User documentation Documentation pertaining to procedures for entering data and other concerns of a user of an information system.

User interface The component of a DSS by which a user interacts with the model base and data base.

User-developed system An information system or application that is developed primarily by the person who is to use it.

Utility program A software routine that is necessary to the functioning of a computer system and/or the applications it executes.

Validity check A programmed edit check that compares entered numbers and codes against authorized lists to determine if they are valid.

Vendor performance report A managerial control report that analyzes the performance of suppliers (vendors) from which a firm purchases goods and services.

Video display terminal A type of terminal input device that includes a CRT display monitor.

Virtual storage A technique of program swapping that allows users to view primary storage as being virtually unlimited.

Voice band line A communication line that transmits data in the middle band of baud rates.

Voice input device An audio input terminal that allows the entry of data or commands by verbal means.

Voice mail A software package that transmits spoken messages to the telephones of recipients.

Voice synthesizer A device that allows a microcomputer to provide oral responses.

Voucher register A special journal that lists the disbursements vouchers prepared with respect to invoices to be paid.

Voucher system A procedure in which vouchers are prepared on the basis of suppliers' invoices and entered into a voucher register.

Vouching The process in which invoices received from suppliers are checked against supporting documents and the extensions and totals are recalculated.

Warnier-Orr diagram A structured analysis and design technique that can be used to graphically represent a processing sequence, file structure, or document/report structure.

Wide area telephone service (WATS) line A telephone communications line that provides service for a fixed amount per month plus a variable amount over a minimum number of hours used.

Weighted-rating analysis technique An evaluation technique in which all relevant factors concerning the systems resource being considered are listed and then weighted based on the judgment of the evaluators.

Wide-band line A communications line that transmits data at very high baud rates.

Winchester drive A hard disk drive that is mounted within the housing of a microcomputer.

Word processing system A software package that provides the ability to draft text directly on a video screen and to make changes easily.

Word size The number of bits that can be addressed by a computer processor and handled in a single operation.

Work distribution chart A data organization technique that employs a matrix to show the distribution of times spent on various tasks within an activity or organization.

Work measurement analysis A classical analytical technique that involves the measurement of flows related to an information system or operational system.

Work-in-process ledger sheet A record that summarizes the materials, parts, labor, and overhead pertaining to an open production order.

WORM The characteristic of an optical disk in which data can be Written only Once but Read Many times.

Index